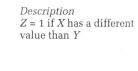

Control

In — Out

Control

(a) Switch view

Control

In — Out

Control

(b) Transistor view

Control

In — Out

Control

(c) Schematic symbol

Figure 4.14 CMOS transmission gate.

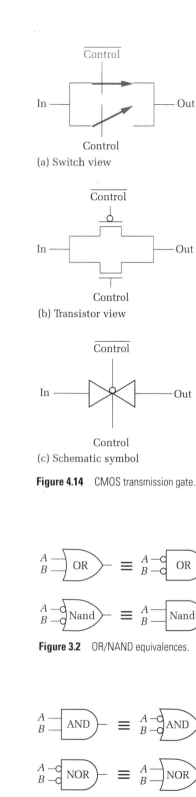

$$A \atop B$$ OR ≡ $$A \atop B$$ OR

Figure 3.2 OR/NAND equivalences.

$$A \atop B$$ AND ≡ $$A \atop B$$ AND

$$A \atop B$$ NOR ≡ $$A \atop B$$ NOR

Figure 3.3 AND/NOR equivalence.

Description
Z = 1 if X has a different value than Y

Description
Z = 1 if X has the same value as Y

Gates

X
Y
Z

Gates

X
Y
Z

Truth Table

X
0
0
1
1

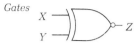

0
1
0
1

(a) XOR

Figure 2.8 Representations of the XOR and XNOR operations.

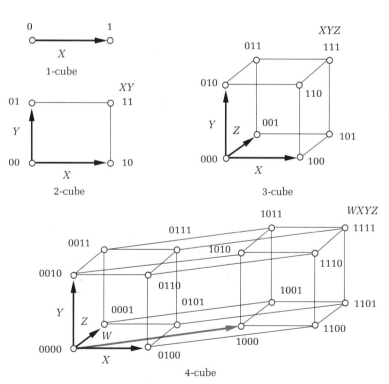

0 —→ 1
X
1-cube

XY
01 — 11
Y
00 —→ 10
X
2-cube

XYZ
011 111
010 110
Y Z 001
000 100
X
3-cube

WXYZ
0011 0111 1011 1111
0010 1010 1110
0110 1001 1101
0001 0101 1110
Y Z 1000 1100
W
0000 0100
X
4-cube

Figure 2.25 *N*-dimensional cubes.

Contemporary Logic Design

Contemporary Logic Design

Randy H. Katz
University of California, Berkeley

The Benjamin/Cummings Publishing Company, Inc.

Redwood City, California ■ Menlo Park, California ■ Reading, Massachusetts
New York ■ Don Mills, Ontario ■ Wokingham, U.K. ■ Amsterdam ■ Bonn
Sydney ■ Singapore ■ Tokyo ■ Madrid ■ San Juan

Executive Editor: Dan Joraanstad
Sponsoring Editor: Jennifer Young
Developmental Editor: Jamie Spencer
Editorial Assistant: Laura Cheu
Marketing Manager: Mary Tudor
Production Editors: Megan Rundel, Brian Jones
Text and Cover Design: Rob Hugel, XXX Design
Copyeditor: Mary Prescott
Proofreader: Elizabeth Wiltsee
Illustrations: Rolin Graphics Inc.
Indexer: Ira Kleinberg
Composition: Rad Proctor, Proctor-Willenbacher
Film: The Courier Connection
Cover Printer: New England Book Components, Inc.
Text Printer and Binder: Courier/Westford
Senior Manufacturing Coordinator: Merry Free Osborn

The cover illustration is a reproduction of "Décalcomanie" by the twentieth-century Belgian surrealist painter René Magritte. We chose this particular painting by the author's favorite painter to reflect the duality of computer design. "Décalcomanie" © 1992 C. Herscovici/ARS, New York.

Library of Congress Cataloging-in-Publication Data

Katz, Randy H., 1955–
    Contemporary logic design / Randy H. Katz.
        p.   cm.
    Includes bibliographical references and index.
    ISBN 0-8053-2703-7
    1. Electronic digital computers—Circuits—Design. 2. Integrated circuits—Very large scale integration—Design—Data processing. 3. Logic design—Data processing. 4. Computer-aided design. I. Title.
    TK7888.4.K36 1994
    621.39′5—dc20   93-9013
                                            CIP
ISBN 0-8053-2703-7

    4 5 6 7 8 9 10–CRW–999897969594

The Benjamin/Cummings Publishing Company, Inc.
390 Bridge Parkway
Redwood City, California 94065

For the long nights, and even longer weekends,
of solicitude while I worked on this book,
I dedicate it to my loving wife, Jennifer.

Preface

Rationale and Audience

Visit your favorite technical bookstore and you will find shelf upon shelf of books that introduce hardware design. This comes as no surprise; the topic has fascinated computer scientists and engineers for four decades. Much of the earliest computer research focused on the methods and algorithms now commonly taught in an introductory sophomore/junior course on hardware design.

Despite its roots as the oldest of computer science disciplines, hardware design is still undergoing rapid change as it responds to the evolution in the underlying electronics technologies, such as the emergence of very large scale integrated (VLSI) circuits. The 1980s saw a revolution in the way hardware design was actually being practiced in industry. This revolution was driven by (1) the pervasive use of software tools to assist in the process of hardware design and (2) the emergence of rapid implementation technology, so-called *programmable logic*, that allows the designer to implement his or her system more quickly. Necessity is the mother of invention, and as an instructor of hardware and VLSI design courses, I felt that none of the existing texts used an approach that reflects my vision of how hardware design should be taught to undergraduates. The result is this book, *Contemporary Logic Design*.

This text reflects my view that the use of computer-aided design software integrated into the course is as important as the use of a conventional, hands-on hardware laboratory. *Contemporary Logic Design* introduces students to a wide range of software tools, including schematic capture, logic simulation, Boolean minimization (*espresso*), multi-level minimization (*mis*), and state assignment tools (*nova, mustang, jedi*). This software is available on IBM PCs (*LogicWorks,* ViewLogic, FutureNet-DASH, Xilinx Design Suite); Apple Macintoshes (*LogicWorks,* MacABEL); and UNIX workstations (ViewLogic, Xilinx Design Suite, Berkeley OCT Tools) and is attractively priced for university use. The goal is decidedly not to train students in specific software packages, but to give them an appreciation for where the tools fit into the hardware design process, as well as their strengths and weaknesses. Further information about ordering *LogicWorks* and the Berkeley OCT tools is given later in the Preface.

One of the difficult things about developing a book on introductory hardware design is to identify the intended audience. Is it mathematically oriented computer science students, or more electrically oriented computer and electrical engineering students? I strongly believe that all students in the computer science and electrical engineering curriculum should take such a course, and I have tried to appeal to both sets of students. In the main body of the text, I have attempted to be relatively abstract about the details of the underlying circuit technology. At the same time, most chapters contain a *Practical Matters* section where I present more of the technology details, such as how to compute fan-outs of TTL logic families or how to read a timing diagram or data sheet. Through this approach, the instructor can make the choice about the level of hardware detail to provide.

Topic Selection and Organization

The book is organized into twelve chapters and two appendices. Chapters 1 through 5 cover combinational logic design, the design of digital circuits without feedback. Chapter 1 lays the groundwork by presenting a broad overview of the hardware design process, digital hardware technologies, and design representations. Many of the topics introduced here will be revisited and expanded in later chapters. Chapter 1 does assume some knowledge of binary number systems and a rudimentary knowledge of electronics (such as a freshman physics course in electronics). For students unfamiliar with these topics, the appendices should prove useful. Appendix A covers number systems, including the binary, octal, decimal, and hexadecimal representations, and the various methods for converting between them. Appendix B introduces, in a gentle way, the basic concepts of electronics, such as voltage, current, resistance, capacitance, power, RC delay, and so on.

Chapter 2 covers two-level logic minimization, including pencil-and-paper methods as well as those that depend on computer-based tools. Since not every instructor will have access to a software laboratory, you may have to skip these sections. The *Practical Matters* section covers TTL Packaged Logic and Schematic Documentation Standards.

Chapter 3 covers multilevel logic minimization. This includes conversions to NAND and NOR gate forms, signal delay, and glitches/hazards. Traditional design methods have focused on two-level logic, but these are largely unsuitable for sophisticated implementation technologies, such as gate arrays. A definitive study of multilevel logic techniques requires more mathematical maturity than that possessed by the typical sophomore or junior computer science or electrical engineering student. Nevertheless, we introduce the concepts by example. In a course pressed for time, you may skip Section 3.2, *CAD Tools for Multilevel Logic Synthesis*, returning to it later as an advanced concept. The *Practical Matters* section covers reading a data sheet, simple calculations such as power consumption and fan-out, and use of switches and LEDs.

Chapter 4 covers programmable and steering logic, such as programmable logic arrays (PLAs), open-collector gates, tri-state gates, multiplexers, decoders, and read-only memories (ROMs). Section 4.2.1, *Switch and Steering Logic*, covers transistor switches and how they can be used to implement conventional gates, multiplexers, and decoders. Once again, you may choose to skip this section, returning to it later.

Chapter 5 presents arithmetic circuits as a long case study of combinational design techniques. Appendix A should be reviewed before the material in this chapter is presented. An instructor may skip this chapter if he or she wishes to move on to sequential logic design more quickly, inserting it again after Chapter 10 (see below).

Chapters 6 through 10 cover sequential logic design, that is, logic circuits with feedback or state. Chapter 6 introduces the most primitive sequential circuit, the flip-flop, and various aspects of circuit timing, such as clock skew and metastability. Section 6.5, *Self-Timed and Speed-Independent Circuits,* is an advanced topic that can be skipped for later coverage. The *Practical Matters* section in this chapter covers switch debouncing and using a timing generator integrated circuit.

Chapter 7 presents a variety of sequential logic case studies, such as registers, RAMs, shift registers, and counters. The chapter uses counters as a long case study for the sequential logic design method. The *Practical Matters* section covers the timing of a static RAM component and includes the design of a simple memory controller.

Chapter 8 concentrates on a more general approach to finite state machine design. It introduces Moore and Mealy state machines and covers finite state machine word problems.

Chapter 9 covers finite state machine optimization. The standard pencil-and-paper methods for state reduction (row matching, implication chart), state assignment, and state machine partitioning are presented.

Section 9.3.4, *Computer Tools:* Nova, Mustang, Jedi, describes representative computer-based approaches to state assignment. If you do not have the Berkeley OCT Tools, this section should be skipped.

Chapter 10 covers a variety of implementation strategies for finite state machines, such as programmable logic, TTL MSI components (counters, multiplexers, and decoders), and advanced programmable logic devices (PLDs). The latter, covered in Section 10.3, *FSM Design with More Sophisticated Programmable Logic Devices,* is an advanced topic. A quarter-long course may skip this chapter at the instructor's discretion.

Chapters 11 and 12 use the design of a simple processor as a long case study for the combinational and sequential design methods presented in the first ten chapters. A quarter-length course is likely to skip these chapters. Chapter 11 introduces the concept of partitioned control and datapath and the use of register transfer operations to describe their interaction. It also focuses on datapath design issues, such as busing strategies and their implications for control complexity.

Chapter 12 covers several alternative controller implementation strategies, such as random logic, time state, jump counter, branch sequencers, and microprogramming. The goal is not to present a definitive treatment of these topics, but rather to provide a way of tying together many concepts of finite state machine design and implementation introduced in Chapters 6 through 10.

Some of the topics we specifically do not cover include general design of asynchronous state machines (we concentrate on synchronous design methods instead) and digital-to-analog or analog-to-digital conversion logic (our emphasis is on digital hardware systems). I would have liked to include more material on designing board-level digital systems, such as printed circuit board design, noise, grounding, shielding, and transmission lines, but the book is already too long!

A typical quarter-length course will cover the following chapters (this assumes a bare-bones coverage of the material):

Chapter 1

Chapter 2, possibly skipping Section 2.4.2, Espresso *Method*

Chapter 3, possibly skipping Section 3.2, *CAD Tools for Multilevel Logic Synthesis*

Chapter 4, possibly skipping Section 4.2.1, *Switch and Steering Logic*

Chapter 5, possibly delayed until after Chapter 9

Chapter 6, skipping Section 6.5, *Self-Timed and Speed-Independent Circuits*

Chapter 7

Chapter 8

Chapter 9, possibly skipping Section 9.3.4, *Computer Tools:* Nova, Mustang, Jedi

I have successfully covered all twelve chapters of this book in a single semester, but not in strict chapter order. This rapid coverage was made possible through my use of an extensive collection of course transparencies, which I also made available to the students. Instructors can obtain these from the publisher (see below). I covered Chapters 1 through 4, then 6 through 12, returning to Chapter 5 only at the end of the semester. In addition, such topics as switch logic and self-timed circuits were covered as advanced subjects toward the end of the semester.

The Complete Teaching Package

The teaching package available for *Contemporary Logic Design* contains a wealth of supporting materials, which we describe here.

Logic Design Software

LogicWorks: Interactive Circuit Design Software, by Capilano Computing Systems, Ltd. This integrated schematic entry and simulation package designed for educational use is reasonably priced. *LogicWorks* allows students to experiment with simple to complex logic circuits using elements ranging from gates to TTL parts to microprocessors.

- Macintosh version: 31312-5.

- IBM 3.5″ version: 31310-9.

- A *LogicWorks Laboratory Manual* consisting of twelve exercises and two final projects is available free to adopters of *LogicWorks:* 31313-3.

- *LogicWorks* is available at a discount when packaged with *Contemporary Logic Design.*

Instructional Support Materials

In developing our course at Berkeley, I have prepared an extensive set of class-tested laboratory and instructional materials. Please note that, with the exception of the *Instructor's Guide,* these items are all available via anonymous FTP from bc.aw.com. Once you have accessed the FTP, type cd ~ftp/bc/digitaldesign.

1. *Lecture Transparencies* A set of approximately 600 transparencies, including worked-out examples, figures, and more detailed explanations of various topics. Transparency text can be edited and the illustrations themselves modified using Microsoft's PowerPoint 3.0 software.

   - Macintosh version: 32707-X.

   - IBM 3.5″ version: 32705-3.

   - Also available via anonymous FTP from bc.aw.com.

2. *Instructor's Guide*   Includes fully worked-out solutions to most problems, midterms and final exams, and course syllabi: 32704-5.

3. *Circuit Diagrams*   One hundred fifty figures from *Contemporary Logic Design* were generated using *LogicWorks.* These are available for use by instructors via anonymous FTP from bc.aw.com.

4. *Hardware Labs*   Eight laboratory exercises designed to give students hands-on experience with the basic building blocks of TTL design. Available only via anonymous FTP from bc.aw.com.

5. *Software Labs*   Three tutorials using the Berkeley tools for logic synthesis (*espresso, mis*) and state assignment (*nova, mustang, jedi*), keyed to design examples in the text. Available only via anonymous FTP from bc.aw.com.

6. *Berkeley Tools*   To obtain ordering information for the Berkeley tools discussed in the text and used in the software labs, contact anonymous ftp:ilpsoft.berkeley.edu. Detailed instructions for copying can be found in a <readme> file on the server, or write to:

> Software Distribution Office
> Industrial Liaison Program
> 105 Cory Hall
> University of California, Berkeley
> Berkeley, California 94720
> Phone: (510) 643-6687
> Fax: (510) 643-6694

Errors

A book of this length is certain to contain errors and omissions. If you find any errors or have constructive suggestions, we would appreciate hearing from you. We also welcome your ideas for new examples and problems (along with their solutions) to include in the next edition. You can send your comments and bug reports electronically via Internet to dd@bc.aw.com, or you can mail this information to:

> Computer Engineering Editor
> The Benjamin/Cummings Publishing Company, Inc.
> 390 Bridge Parkway
> Redwood City, California 94065
> Fax: (415) 594-4488

Acknowledgments

Many people have helped me in completing this project. My relationship with Benjamin/Cummings began with Alan Apt as my sponsoring editor; Jake Ward and Lisa Moller continued the project; and Jennifer Young brought it to its completion. These sponsoring editors have played a critical role in obtaining feedback on the manuscript and helping to shape it into a more effective text. Input from the Benjamin/Cummings marketing department, especially Mary Tudor, has also enhanced the appeal of this text to instructors at all types of schools.

Professors John Beetem of the University of Wisconsin-Madison, Barry Fagin of Dartmouth University, John Lindenlaub of Purdue University, Christos Papachristou of Case Western Reserve University, James Pugsley of the University of Maryland, Rob Rutenbar of Carnegie-Mellon University, and Mike Smith of the University of Hawaii reviewed several drafts of this book and provided many useful comments. Professor Mary Jane Irwin of Penn State University took a brave chance and used an early draft of the book in her advanced undergraduate course.

I especially wish to thank Professors Ron Fearing and Richard Newton of the University of California, Berkeley, Professors Carl Ebeling and Gaetano Borriello of the University of Washington, Professors Don Kirk and Jack Kurzweil of San Jose State University, and Professor Sharad Malik of Princeton University, who all used drafts of this text in their courses, despite the bugs. I hope it didn't hurt their teaching evaluations! Gaetano Borriello deserves an added note of thanks for performing a technical edit of the text and art. And of course, my students in the Fall 1990, 1991, and 1992 offerings of *Computer Science 150: Components and Techniques of Digital Design* suffered much as the book underwent its inevitable evolution. Suzanne Mercer and Joy Ku are to be congratulated on their champion (grammatical as well as technical) bug-finding skills.

I did not initially intend to write a book at all, but to find a way to "rapidly prototype" a new curriculum in hardware design. This got off the ground in 1989 through a curriculum development grant from the National Science Foundation Engineering Education Directorate. The National Science Foundation also supported the widespread dissemination of the course materials I developed (particularly the course transparencies, software/hardware laboratory manual, and demonstration circuits) through an additional grant administered by the MIPS Division of the CISE Directorate. The National Science Foundation continues to support further refinement of these materials through its support of the multicampus Engineering Synthesis Coalition, the goal of which is to radically improve undergraduate engineering education. That is a goal that I decidedly share, and I am grateful for their ongoing encouragement and support.

Randy H. Katz
Berkeley, California
May 1993

Brief Contents

Detailed Contents

Contemporary Logic Design

1 Introduction

Introduction

Computer hardware has experienced the most dramatic improvement in capabilities and costs ever known to humankind. In just 40 years, we have seen room-sized computers, with little more processing power than today's pocket calculators, evolve into fingernail-sized devices with near supercomputer performance. This miracle has been made possible through advances in digital hardware, which now pervades all aspects of our lives. Just think how the lowly rotary telephone has become the cordless, automated answering machine. It can digitize your greeting, remember your most frequently dialed numbers, and allow you to review, save, and erase your phone messages.

This book will teach you the fundamental techniques for designing and implementing complex systems. A *system* has inputs and outputs and exhibits explicit behavior, characterized by functions that translate the inputs into new outputs. *Design* is the process by which incomplete and inexact requirements and specifications, describing the purpose and function of an object, are made precise. *Implementation* uses this precise description to create a physical product. You can see design and implementation in everything around you—buildings, cars, telephones, furniture, and so on.

This book is about the fundamental techniques used to design and implement what we call *synchronous digital hardware systems*. What does each of these words mean? A *hardware system* is one whose physical components are constructed from electronic building blocks, rather than wood, plastic, or steel. A hardware system can be digital or analog. The inputs and outputs of a *digital system* fall within a discrete, finite set of values. In an *analog* system, the outputs span a continuous range. In this book, we concentrate on systems in the digital domain. A *synchronous system* is one whose elements change their values only at certain specified times. An *asynchronous system* has outputs that can change at any time. It is safer and more foolproof to build our systems using synchronous methods, which is the focus of this book.

To see the difference between synchronous and asynchronous systems, think of a digital alarm clock. Suppose that the alarm is set for 11:59, and the alarm sounds when the time readout exactly matches 11:59. In a synchronous system, the outputs all change at the same time. The clock advances from 10:59 to 11:00 to 11:01, and so on. In an asynchronous system, the hours and minutes are not constrained to change simultaneously. So, looking at the clock, you might see it advance from 10:59 to 11:59 (momentarily) to 11:00. And of course, this would make the alarm sound at the wrong time.

You can best understand complex hardware systems in terms of descriptions of increasing levels of detail. Moving from the abstract to the most detailed, these levels are called system, logic, and circuit. The *system level* abstractly describes the input, output, and behavior. A system-level description focuses on timing and sequencing using flowcharts or computer programs. The *logic level* deals with the composition of building blocks, called *logic gates*, which form the physical components used by system designers. At the *circuit level*, the building blocks are electrical elements, such as transistors, resistors, and capacitors, which implement the logic designer's components. Thus, abstract system descriptions are built upon logic descriptions, which in turn depend on detailed circuits.

This book is primarily for logic designers, but to learn logic design you must also know something about system and circuit design. What are the best logic building blocks to support the system designer? How are they constructed from the available electrical elements? What kinds of blocks are needed? How much does it cost to build them? We approach the material from the perspective of computer science rather than electrical engineering: the only prerequisite knowledge we assume is an understanding of binary numbers, basic electronics, and some limited familiarity with a programming language, such as C or PASCAL. You can review binary numbers in Appendix A and basic electronics in Appendix B.

New technology is making this an exciting time for hardware designers. Traditionally, they have had to build their hardware before being able to check for proper behavior. This situation is undergoing radical change because of the new technology of *rapid prototyping*. Designers use computer programs, called *computer-aided design (CAD) tools*, to help create implementations and verify their behavior before actually building them.

Even the basic logic components used in hardware implementation are undergoing change. In conventional logic design, the building blocks perform fixed, unchangeable functions. Today, they are being replaced by flexible logic building blocks whose function can be configured for the job at hand. This remarkable technology is called *programmable logic*, and you will learn how to use it in your designs.

Hardware design is the "art of the possible," creatively finding the balance between the requirements of systems on one side and the opportunities provided by electronic components on the other. But first, you need to understand the basics of the design process, so let's begin there.

1.1   The Process of Design

Design is a complex process, more of an art than a science. It is not simply a matter of following predetermined steps, as in a recipe. The only way to learn design is to do design. Let's introduce the concept with an example. Your boss has given you the job of designing and implementing a simple device to control a traffic light.

So how do you begin? Figure 1.1 portrays the three somewhat overlapping phases through which every design project must pass: *design*, *implementation*, and *debugging*. Not surprisingly, these are the same whether the object being designed is a complex software system, an engineering system like a power plant, or an electronic system like a computer. Let's look at each of these phases in more detail.

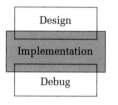

Figure 1.1   The phases of design.

1.1.1   Design as Refinement of Representations

Complex systems can be described from three independent viewpoints, which we shall call *functional*, *structural*, and *physical*. The functional view describes the behavior of the system in terms of its inputs and outputs. The structural view describes how the system is broken down into ever more primitive components that form its implementation. Finally, the physical view describes the detailed placement and interconnection of the primitive building blocks that make up the implementation. You can think of design as a process of precisely (and creatively) determining these aspects.

To illustrate these concepts, consider a simplified representation of a car. Its inputs are gasoline and the positions of the accelerator pedal, brake pedal, and steering wheel. Its output is the power that moves the vehicle in a given direction with a given speed. The detailed specification of how the inputs determine the direction and speed of the car constitutes its functional description.

The car system can be broken down into major interacting subsystems, such as the engine and the transmission. These are made up of their own more primitive components. For example, the engine consists of carburetion and cooling subsystems. This is the structural description.

At the most detailed level, the subsystems are actually primitive physical components: screws, metal sheets, pipes, and so forth. The car's cooling subsystem can be described in terms of a radiator, water reservoir, rubber tubing, and channels through the engine block. These form the physical representation of the car.

Design Specification   Let's return to our hardware example: the traffic light controller. Your design begins with understanding what you want to design and the constraints on its implementation. This is the *design specification*. Your goal is to obtain a detailed and precise functional description from the design specification.

You begin by determining the system's inputs and outputs. Then you identify the way the outputs are derived from the inputs. You would probably start by asking your boss about the traffic light's functional capabilities. Here is what your boss tells you:

- The traffic light points in four directions (call them N, S, E, W).
- It always illuminates the same lights on N as S and E as W.
- It cycles through the sequence green-yellow-red.
- N-S and E-W are never green or yellow at the same time.
- The lights are green for 45 seconds, yellow for 15, red for 60.

You can see that the inputs and outputs are not described explicitly here, but a little thought should help. Since each light must be turned on or off, there must be one output for each color (green, yellow, red) and each direction (East, West, North, South). That's 12 different outputs. Not all of these are unique. Since North and South are identical, as are East and West, the number of unique outputs is six.

But what are the inputs? Something has to tell the system when to start processing. We call this the "start" or more commonly the *reset* signal. In addition, the system must be equipped with some periodic signals to indicate that 15 or 45 seconds have elapsed. These signals are often called *clocks*. The inputs could be represented by two independent clocks or by a single 15-second clock with additional hardware to count one or three "ticks." Since your boss has not specified this in detail, it is up to you to decide. It is not unusual for the initial design specification to be ambiguous or incomplete. The designer must make critical decisions to complete the specification. This is part of the creativity demanded of the designer: filling in the details of the designs subject to the specified constraints.

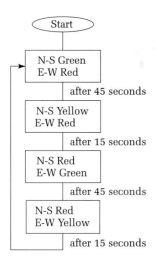

Figure 1.2   Functional behavior of a system.

How are the inputs and outputs related? There are many ways to represent the functional behavior of a system, such as the flowchart shown in Figure 1.2. The start signal causes the green N-S lights and the red E-W lights to be illuminated. When the 45-second clock tick arrives, new outputs are turned on: the N-S green lights go off, the yellow lights go on, and the E-W lights stay red. After another 15-second clock tick, N-S yellow goes off, N-S red goes on, E-W red goes off, and E-W green goes on. A similar sequence of events happens when the light configuration changes to N-S red, E-W green, and then to N-S red and E-W yellow. After this, the whole process repeats.

Design Constraints   At this point, you have a pretty good feeling about the function of the traffic light. The next set of issues deals with the system's performance characteristics. You need to consider the operational speed of the hardware, the amount of space it takes up, the amount of power it consumes, and so on. These are called the design's *performance metrics*. Constraints on performance influence the design by forcing you to reject certain design approaches that violate the constraints.

So now you must go back to ask the boss a few questions. How fast must the hardware be? How much can it cost? How small does it have to be? What is the maximum power it can consume? Answering these questions will help you identify the appropriate implementation approach.

The traffic light system changes its outputs every few seconds. Your boss tells you that a very slow, inexpensive technology can be used.

The traffic light hardware must fit in a relatively small box to be placed next to the structural support for the lights. Your boss tells you that a 6 inch by 6 inch by 1 inch space is available for the hardware. You recognize that old-fashioned, oversized vacuum tubes are out, but neither is an advanced technology needed. For the kinds of technologies we will be describing in this book, this space could hold approximately 20 components.

How much can it cost? Erecting a set of traffic lights probably costs several thousand dollars. Despite this, your boss tells you that the hardware cannot exceed $20 in total component cost. This rules out the hottest microprocessor currently available (which costs a few hundred dollars), but the constraint should be easy to meet with simple inexpensive components.

How much power can the system consume? The boss limits you to less than 20 watts, about one third of the power consumed by a typical light bulb. At this power level, you won't have to worry about fans.

If a given component consumes less than 1 watt, the power and area constraints together restrict your design to no more than 20 components. At a dollar a component, the design should also be able to meet the cost constraint.

Design as Representation   Design is a complicated business. It has been said that *to design is to represent.* Our initial representation of the traffic light controller was a rather imprecise set of constraints expressed in English. We refine this into something more detailed and precise, suitable for implementation. We start by identifying the system's inputs and outputs. Then we obtain a more formal behavioral description, such as the flowchart shown in Figure 1.2. Ultimately, we refine the design to a level of detail that can be implemented directly by the primitive building blocks of our chosen implementation technology.

In this book, we will develop methods for transforming one design representation into another. Some approaches are very well understood, while others are not. For example, nobody has yet proposed a foolproof method to transform an English statement into a flowchart. However, where such procedures are reasonably well understood, programmers have codified them into computer-aided design tools. These tools are being used, for example, to manipulate a logic design into a form that is the simplest to implement with gates and wires. It is not too far-fetched to imagine software that could translate a restricted flowchart into primitive hardware. As we learn more about the representations of a design, we will introduce the tools that can derive one representation from another.

1.1.2   Implementation as Assembly

Here we examine the different approaches for implementing a design from simpler components. Primarily, these are top-down decomposition and bottom-up assembly.

Top-Down Decomposition   It is easier to understand the operation of the whole by looking at its pieces and their interactions. The "divide and conquer" approach breaks the system down into its component subsystems. Each is easier to understand on its own.

This is a good strategy for constructing any kind of complex system. The process of *top-down decomposition* starts with the description of a whole system and replaces it with a series of smaller steps—each step is a more primitive subsystem.

For example, Figure 1.3 shows one of the possible decompositions of the traffic light system. It is broken down into timer and light sequencer subsystems. The timer counts the passing of the seconds and alerts the other components when certain time intervals have passed. The light sequencer steps through the unique combinations of the traffic lights in response to these timer alerts.

The decomposition need not stop here. The light sequencer is further decomposed into a more primitive sequencer and a decoder. The decoder generates the detailed signals to turn on the appropriate light bulbs.

The decomposition of the design into its subsystems is its structural representation. The approach can continue to any finer level of detail.

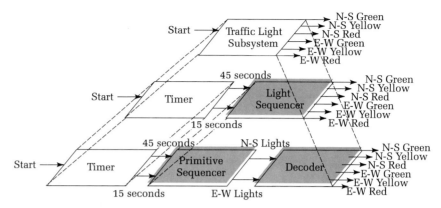

Figure 1.3 One possible functional decomposition of the traffic light controller.

Bottom-Up Assembly The alternative approach to top-down decomposition is *bottom-up assembly*. In any particular technology, there are primitive building blocks that can be clustered into more complex groupings of blocks. These are appropriately called *assemblies*.

Consider the implementation of an office building. The most primitive components are objects like walls, doors, and windows. These are composed to form assemblies called rooms. Assemblies of rooms form the floors of the building. Finally, the assembly of the individual floors forms the building itself. By determining how to construct such assemblies, you move the process from design to implementation.

Rules of Composition An important facet of design by assembly is the notion of *rules of composition*. They describe how items can be combined to form assemblies. When followed, they ensure that the design yields a functionally correct implementation. This has sometimes been called *correctness by construction*.

When it comes to hardware design, the rules of composition fall into several classes, of which the most important are electrical and timing rules. An electrical signal can become *degraded* when it is stretched out in time and reduced in amplitude by distributing it too widely within an electrical circuit. This makes it unrecognizable to the rest of the logic. Electrical rules determine the maximum number of component inputs to which a given output can be connected to make sure that all signals are well-behaved.

Timing rules constrain how the periodic clocking signals effect changes in the system's outputs. In this book, we develop a disciplined design approach that is well-behaved with respect to time. This is called a *synchronous timing methodology*. A single reference clock triggers all events in the system, such as the transition among the light configurations in the traffic light controller. Certain events come from outside the system, and are inherently independent of the internal timing of the system. For example, a pedestrian can walk up to the traffic light and push a button to get the light to change to green faster. We will also learn safe methods for handling these kinds of signals in a clocked, synchronous system.

Physical Representation   As a logic designer, you construct your design by choosing components and composing them into assemblies. The components are electrical objects, logic gates, that you compose by wiring them together. In general, there is more than one way to realize a particular hardware function. Design optimization often involves selecting among alternative components and assemblies, choosing the best for the task at hand within the speed, power, area, and cost constraints on the design. This is where the real creativity of engineering design comes into play.

1.1.3   Debugging the System

The key elements of making a hardware system work are, first, understanding what can go wrong and, second, using simulation to find problems before you even build the system.

What Can Go Wrong   As Murphy's law says, if things can go wrong in designing a hardware system, they will. For a system to work properly, the design must be flawless, the implementation must be correct, and all of the components must be operational.

Even a design that is perfect at the system level can be sabotaged by an imperfect implementation at the physical level. You may have chosen the wrong components or wired them incorrectly, or the components themselves could be faulty.

Simulation Before Construction   Designers today take advantage of a new approach that allows them to use computer programs to simulate the behavior of hardware. When you do *simulation before construction*, the only problems that should remain are either a flawed translation of the design into its component-level physical implementation or bad components. Simulation is becoming increasingly important as discrete components wired together are replaced by programmable logic, where the wiring is no longer visible for easy fixing.

1.2   Digital Hardware Systems

In this section we examine what makes digital systems different from other kinds of complex systems. We will distinguish between digital and analog electronics, briefly describe the circuit technology upon which digital hardware systems are constructed, and examine the two major kinds of digital subsystems. These are circuits <u>without memory, called</u> *combinational logic*, and circuits with memory, known as *sequential logic*.

1.2.1   Digital Systems

Digital systems are the preferred way to implement hardware. In this section we look at what makes the digital approach so important.

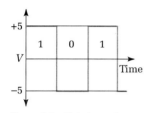

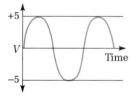

Figure 1.4   Digital waveform.

Digital Versus Analog   *Digital systems* have inputs and outputs that are represented by discrete values. Figure 1.4 shows a digital system's typical output waveform. The X axis is time and the Y axis is the measured voltage. This system has exactly two possible output values, represented by +5 volts and −5 volts, respectively. Such systems are called *binary* digital systems. If you are unfamiliar with the binary number system, you should read Appendix A before continuing. Note that there is nothing intrinsic to the digital approach that limits it to just two values. The key is that the number of possible output values is finite.

In *analog systems* the inputs and outputs take on a continuous range of values, as shown in Figure 1.5. Analog waveforms more realistically represent quantities of the real world, such as sound and temperature. Digital waveforms only approximate these with many discrete values.

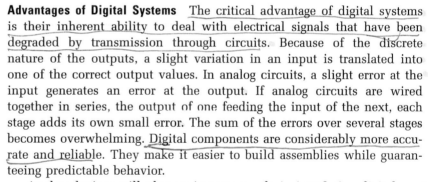

Figure 1.5   Analog waveform.

Advantages of Digital Systems   <u>The critical advantage of digital systems is their inherent ability to deal with electrical signals that have been degraded by transmission through circuits.</u> Because of the discrete nature of the outputs, a slight variation in an input is translated into one of the correct output values. In analog circuits, a slight error at the input generates an error at the output. If analog circuits are wired together in series, the output of one feeding the input of the next, each stage adds its own small error. The sum of the errors over several stages becomes overwhelming. <u>Digital components are considerably more accurate and reliable.</u> They make it easier to build assemblies while guaranteeing predictable behavior.

Analog devices still play an important role in interfacing digital systems to the real world. After all, the real world operates in an analog fashion—that is, continuously. Interface circuits, such as sensors and actuators, are analog. Often you will find the two kinds of circuits mixed in real systems. The digital logic is used for algorithmic control and data manipulation, while the analog circuits are used to sense and manipulate the surrounding environment.

Binary Digital Systems   The simplest form of digital system is binary, with exactly two distinct values for inputs and outputs. Binary digital systems form the basis of just about all hardware systems in existence today.

The main advantage of binary systems is that the two alternative values are particularly easy to encode with physical quantities. We use the symbols 1 and 0 to stand for the two values, which can be interpreted as "yes" and "no" or "on" and "off." 1 and 0 might be physically realized by different voltage values (5 volts vs. 0 volts), magnetic polarizations (North vs. South), or the flow or lack thereof of electrical current.

Mathematical Logic   Perhaps the greatest strength of digital systems is their rigorous formulation founded on mathematical logic and Boolean algebra. We will cover these topics in detail in Chapter 2, but it is useful to introduce a few basic concepts here first. *Mathematical logic* allows us to reason about the truth of a set of statements, each of which may be true or false. *Boolean algebra* is an algebraic system for manipulating logic statements.

As an example, let's look at the following logic statement:

IF the garage door is open

AND the car is running

THEN the car can be backed out of the garage

It states that the conditions—the garage is open and the car is running—must be true before the car can be backed out. If either or both are false, then the car cannot be backed out. If we determine that the conditions are valid, then mathematical logic allows us to infer that the conclusion is valid.

This example may seem remote from hardware design, but logic statements are exactly how we describe the control for a hardware system. The sequencing through the various configurations of the traffic light example of Figure 1.2 can be formulated as follows:

IF N-S is green

AND E-W is red

AND 45 seconds has expired since the last light change

THEN the N-S lights can be changed from green to yellow

The three conditions must be true before the conclusion can be valid ("change the lights from green to yellow").

It should not surprise you that statements like this are actually at the heart of digital controller design. A computer program, containing control statements like IF-THEN-ELSE, is a perfectly valid behavioral representation of a hardware system.

Boolean Algebra and Logical Operators   Boolean algebra, developed in the 19th century by the mathematician George Boole, provides a simple

X	Y	X AND Y
0	0	0
0	1	0
1	0	0
1	1	1

(a)

X	Y	X OR Y
0	0	0
0	1	1
1	0	1
1	1	1

(b)

X	NOT X
0	1
1	0

(c)

Figure 1.6 Truth tables for AND, OR, and NOT operations.

algebraic formulation of how to combine logic values. Consisting of variables, such as X, Y, and Z, and values (or symbols) 0 and 1, Boolean algebra rigorously defines a collection of primitive logical operations, such as AND, for combining the values of Boolean variables.

Figure 1.6(a) shows the definition of the AND function in terms of a truth table. A *truth table* is a listing of all possible input combinations correlated with the outputs you would see if you applied a particular set of input values to the function. Think of 0 as representing false ("no") and 1 as true ("yes"). If the variable X represents the condition of the door (0 = closed, 1 = open) and Y the running status of the car (0 = not running, 1 = running), then the truth table succinctly indicates the condition(s) under which the car can be backed out of the garage. These are exactly the input combinations that yield the value 1 for X AND Y.

OR and NOT are other Boolean operations. If either the Boolean variable X is true or the variable Y is true, then X OR Y is true (see Figure 1.6(b)). If X is true, then NOT X is false; if X is false, then NOT X is true. The truth table for this operation is shown in Figure 1.6(c).

1.2.2 The Real World: Ideal Versus Observed Behavior

So far, we have considered the ideal world of mathematical abstractions. Here we look at the real-world realities of hardware systems.

Although we find it convenient to think of digital systems as having only discrete output values, when such systems are realized by real electronic components, they exhibit aspects of continuous, analog behavior. They do so because output transitions are not instantaneous and because it is too difficult to design electronics that recognize a single voltage value as a logic 1 or 0. Digital logic must be able to deal with degraded signals. It can recognize a degraded input as a valid logic 1 or 0 and thus generate outputs at the correct voltage levels.

As an example, let's assume that "on" or logic 1 is represented by +5 volts. "Off" or logic 0 is represented by 0 volts. Figure 1.7 shows a signal waveform of an output switching from on/logic 1 to off/logic 0. You might observe a waveform like this on an oscilloscope trace. The transition in the figure is certainly not instantaneous. Other values besides +5 volts and 0 volts are visible, at least for an instant in time.

All electronic implementations of Boolean operations incur some delay. Why aren't they instantaneous? A water faucet provides a useful analogy.* Theoretically, a water faucet is either on, with water flowing, or off, with no flow. However, if you observed the action of a faucet being

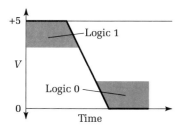

Figure 1.7 Digital transition versus time.

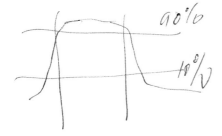

---

*This idea is not really that far-fetched, since electrical effects are ultimately due to the flow of electrons, which act in a way quite analogous to water. See Appendix B for more details about the water-electricity analogy.

shut off, you would see the stream of water change from a strong flow, to a dribbling weak flow, to a few drips, and finally to no flow at all.

The same thing happens in electrical devices. They start out by draining the output of its charge rather quickly, so that its voltage drops toward 0. But eventually the discharge slows down to a trickle and finally stops.

Voltage Ranges for Logic 1 and 0   Digital systems may seem to require a single reference voltage with which to represent logic 1 and logic 0. However, this is neither possible nor desirable. Some variation in the behavior of electrical components is unavoidable, simply because of manufacturing variations. Not every device will output a perfect +5 volts or 0 volts. Furthermore, a by-product of any interconnection of electrical components is *noise*, which causes the degradation of electrical signals as they pass through wires. Even a perfect +5 volt output signal may appear as a substantially reduced voltage farther along a wire.

The tolerance of digital devices for degraded inputs is called the *noise margin*. Voltages near the reference voltages are treated by the devices as though they were a perfect logic 1 or 0. A degraded input, as long as it is within the noise margin, will be mapped into an output voltage very close to the reference voltages. Cascaded digital circuits can correct signal degradations.

1.2.3   Digital Circuit Technologies

The two most popular integrated circuit technologies for the fundamental building blocks of digital (as well as analog) systems are *MOS (metal-oxide-silicon)* and *bipolar* electronics. Without going into the details, an integrated circuit technology is a particular choice of materials that either conduct, insulate, or sometimes conduct. The last are called *semiconductors*, and the technology usually goes by the name of *semiconductor electronics*. The three kinds of materials interact with each other to allow electrons to flow selectively. In this fashion, we can construct electrically controlled switches.

Transistors: Electrically Controlled Switches   The basic electrical switch is called a *transistor*. To get a feeling for how it behaves, let's examine the MOS transistor, which is perhaps the easiest to explain. We will describe MOS switches in more detail in Chapter 4.

A MOS transistor is a device with three terminals: *gate*, *source*, and *drain*. Figure 1.8 shows the standard symbol for what is known as an nMOS (*n*-channel MOS) transistor. When the voltage between the gate and the source exceeds a certain threshold, the source and drain terminals are connected and electrons can flow across the transistor. We say that the switch is conducting or "closed." If this voltage is removed

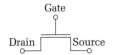

Figure 1.8   nMOS transistor.

from the gate, the switch no longer conducts electrons and is now "open." Based on this simplified analysis, a MOS transistor is a voltage-controlled switch.

Although bipolar transistors are quite different from MOS transistors in detailed behavior, their conceptual use as switching elements to implement digital functions is very similar. We discuss bipolar transistor operation in Appendix B.

Gates: Logic Building Blocks   Building upon transistor switches, we can construct logic gates that implement various logic operations, such as AND, OR, and NOT. (Logic gates are not the same as transistor gates.) Logic gates are physical devices that operate over electrical voltages rather than symbols like 1 and 0. A typical logic gate, implemented in the technologies you will study in this book, interprets voltages near 5 V as a logic 1 and those near 0 V as a logic 0.

For example, an AND gate is a circuit with two inputs and one output. It outputs a logic 1 voltage whenever it determines that both of its inputs are at a logic 1 voltage. In all other cases, it outputs a logic 0 voltage.

Some aspects of gate behavior are not strictly digital. Consider the *inverter*, implementing a function that translates 1 to 0 and 0 to 1. Figure 1.9 illustrates the inverter's output voltage as a function of input voltage. This figure is called a *transfer characteristic*.

Imagine that the gate's input starts at 0 volts (V), with voltage slowly increasing to +5 V. The output of the inverter holds at +5 V for some range of input values and then begins to change abruptly toward 0 V. As the input voltage continues to increase, the output slowly approaches 0 V without ever quite getting there.

The "stickiness" at a particular output voltage is what contributes to a good noise margin. Input voltages near the ideal values have the same effect as perfect logic 1 and logic 0 voltages. Any input voltage within the gray region near 0 V will result in an output voltage very close to +5 V. The same is true for the input voltages near +5 V: these yield values very close to 0 V at the output.

Gates like the inverter are readily available as preexisting modules, designed by transistor-level circuit designers. Designers who work with gates are called *logic designers*. By using logic gates, rather than transistors, as the most primitive modules in the design, we can hide the differences between MOS and bipolar transistors.

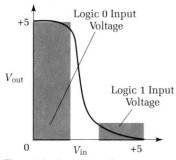

Figure 1.9 Inverter transfer characteristic.

1.2.4   Combinational Versus Sequential Switching Networks

It is often useful for digital designers to view digital systems as networks of interconnected gates and switches. These *switching networks* take one or more inputs and generate one or more outputs as a function of those inputs. Switching networks come in two primitive forms. *Combinational*

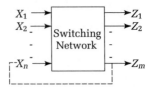

Figure 1.10 Switching networks.

switching networks have no feedback—that is, there is no wire that is both an output and input. *Sequential* switching networks have some outputs that are fed back as inputs. Figure 1.10 shows a "black box" switching network, with its inputs and outputs. If some of the outputs are also fed back as inputs (dashed line), the network is sequential.

Combinational Logic: Circuits Without a Memory Combinational switching networks are those whose outputs depend only on the current inputs. They are circuits without a memory. Simply stated, the outputs change a short time after the inputs change. We cover combinational logic circuits in depth in Chapters 2, 3, 4, and 5.

A switch-controlled house lamp is a simple example of a combinational circuit. The switch has two settings, on and off. When the switch is set to on, the light goes on, and when it is set to off, the light goes off. The effect of setting the switch does not depend on its previous configuration.

Contrast this with a "three-position" lamp that can be off, on but dim, and on but bright. Turn the switch once, and the lamp is turned on dimly. Turn it again, and the lamp becomes bright. Turn it a third time, and the lamp goes off. The behavior of this lamp clearly depends on its previous configuration: it is a sequential circuit.

Another combinational network is a two-data-input binary adder, sometimes called a *full adder*. This circuit adds together two binary digits (also called *bits*) to form a single-bit output: $0 + 0 = 0$, $0 + 1 = 1$, $1 + 0 = 1$, and $1 + 1 = 0$ (with a carry of 1).

The full adder has a third input that represents the carry-in of an adjacent addition column. We also generate a carry-out to the next addition column. The bits to be added are A and B, the sum is *Sum*, the carry-in is *Cin*, and the carry-out is *Cout*.

The values of *Sum* and *Cout* are completely determined by the inputs. For example, if $A = 1$, $B = 1$, and $Cin = 1$, then $Sum = 1$ and $Cout = 1$ (that is, one plus one plus one is three in binary numbers, or 11_2). A block diagram of the full adder is shown in Figure 1.11.

```
A  ──→ ┌───────┐ ──→ Sum
B  ──→ │ Full  │
Cin──→ │ adder │ ──→ Cout
       └───────┘
```

Figure 1.11 Full adder block diagram.

Sequential Logic: Circuits with a Memory We discuss sequential logic circuits in Chapters 6, 7, 8, 9, and 10. In this kind of network, the outputs depend on the current inputs and the history of all previous inputs. This is a potentially daunting requirement if the system must remember the entire history of input patterns. In practice, though, arbitrary inputs lead the sequential network through a small number of unique configurations, called *states*.

A sequential network is a function that takes the current configuration (state) of the circuit and the inputs, and maps these into a new state with new outputs. After a delay, the new state becomes the current state, and the process of computing a new state and outputs repeats.

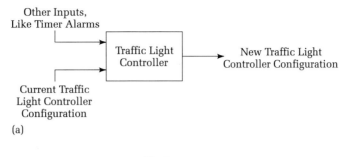

(a)

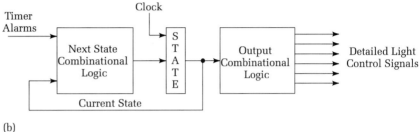

(b)

Figure 1.12   Block diagram of traffic light controller.

For our purposes, the configuration of the network changes in response to a special reference signal, the *clock*. This is what makes the system *synchronous*. There are forms of sequential circuits with no single indication of when to change state. We call these *asynchronous systems*.

The traffic light controller would be implemented by a sequential switching network. Even if it has been running for years, it can be in only one of four unique states at any point in time, one for each of the unique configurations of the lights.

Figure 1.12(a) shows a generic block diagram of the traffic light controller's switching network. The inputs are the timer alarms and the traffic light configuration, and the outputs are the network's new configuration. Figure 1.12(b) shows the controller in more detail. It consists of two blocks of combinational logic separated by clocked logic that holds the state. Let's look at these blocks in more detail:

1. The first combinational logic block, the *next state logic*, transforms the current state and the status of the timer alarms into the new state. The next state network contains logic to implement statements like this:

     IF the controller is in state N-S green/E-W red

     AND the 45-second timer alarm is sounded

     THEN the next state becomes N-S yellow/E-W red when the clock signal is next true

As you may guess, not all inputs are relevant in every state. If the controller is in state N-S yellow/E-W red, for example, then the next state function examines only the 15-second timer; the 45-second timer is ignored.

2. The state block contains *storage elements*, primitive sequential networks that can either hold their current values or allow them to be replaced. (Storage elements are described in more detail in Chapters 6 and 7.) These are loaded with a new configuration when the external clock signal ticks. You can see that the current state feeds back as input to the first combinational logic block.

3. The last logic block, or *output logic*, translates the current state into control signals for the lights and the countdown timers. For example, on entering the new state N-S yellow/E-W red, the output logic asserts control signals to change the N-S lights from green to yellow and to commence the countdown of the 15-second timers.

1.3   Multiple Representations of a Digital Design

A digital designer must confront the many alternative ways of thinking about digital logic. In this section, we examine some of the commonly encountered representations of a digital design. We examine them bottom-up, starting with the switch representation and proceeding through Boolean algebra, truth table, gate, waveform, blocks, and behaviors (see Figure 1.13).

Behaviors are the best representation for understanding a design at its highest level of abstraction, perhaps during the earliest stages of the design. On the other hand, switches may be the most appropriate representation if you are implementing the design directly as an integrated circuit. We will cover each of these representations in considerably more detail in subsequent chapters.

1.3.1   Switches

Switches are the simplest representation of a hardware system we will examine. While providing a convenient way to think about logic statements, switches also correspond directly to transistors, the simple electronic devices from which all hardware systems are constructed.

Basic Concept   A switch consists of two connection terminals and a control point. The connection terminals are denoted by small circles; the control point is represented by an arrow with a line through it.

Switches provide a rather idealized abstraction of how transistors actually behave. If you apply true (a logic 1 voltage) to the control point, the switch is closed, tying together the two connection terminals. Setting false (a logic 0 voltage) on the switch control causes the switch to open, cutting

Switch
Boolean Algebra
Truth Table
Gate
Waveform
Block
Behaviors

Figure 1.13   Some of the possible representations of a digital design.

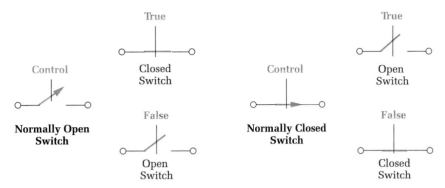

Figure 1.14   Switch building blocks.

the connection between the terminals. We call such switches *normally open:* the switch is open until the control point becomes true.

There are actually two different kinds of transistors. So just as there are normally open switches, there are also normally closed switches. The notation is shown in Figure 1.14. A *normally closed* switch is closed until its control point becomes true.

Switches can represent logic clauses by associating the logic clause with the control point of the switch. A normally open switch is closed when the clause associated with the control point is true. We say that the clause is *asserted*. The switch is open, and the connection path is broken, when the clause is false. In this case, we say that the clause is *unasserted*. Normally closed switches work in a complementary fashion.

Switch Representation of Logic Statements   Switch circuits suggest a possible implementation of the switching networks presented in the previous section. The network computes a logical function by routing "true" through the switches, controlled by logic clauses.

Let's illustrate the concept with the example of the car in the garage. Figure 1.15 gives a switching network for determining whether it is safe to back the car out. The three conditions, *car in garage, garage door open*, and *car running*, control the switching elements. The input to the network is "true"; the output is true only when all three conditions are true. In this case, a closed switch path exists from the true input to the output.

EXAMPLE:

IF car in garage
AND garage door open
AND car running
THEN back out car

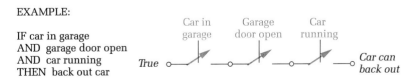

Figure 1.15   Switch representation of logic statement.

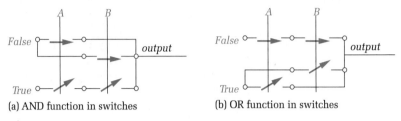

(a) AND function in switches   (b) OR function in switches

Figure 1.16   Switch representation of AND and OR operations.

But what happens if the car is not in the garage (or the garage door isn't open or the car isn't running)? Then the path between true and the output is broken. What is the output value in this case? Actually, it has no value—it is said to be *floating*.

Floating outputs are not desirable in logic networks. We really should have a way to force the output to false when the car can't be backed out. Every switch output should have a path to true and a complementary path to false.

This is shown in Figure 1.16 for the implementations of AND and OR operations. Note how placing normally open switches in series yields an AND. When A and B are true, the switches close and a path is established from true to the output. If either A or B is false, the path to true is broken, and one of the parallel normally closed switches establishes a connection from false to the output.

In the OR implementation, the parallel and series connections of the switches are reversed. If either A or B is true, one or both of the normally open switches will close, making a connection between true and the output. If both A and B are false, this path is broken, and a new path is made between false and the output.

The capabilities of switching networks go well beyond modeling such simple logic connectives. They can be used to implement many unusual digital functions, as we shall see in Chapter 4. In particular, there is a class of functions that can best be visualized in terms of directing inputs to outputs through a maze of switches. These are excellent candidates for direct implementation by transistor switches. For some examples, see Exercise 1.8.

1.3.2   Truth Tables

The switch representation is close to how logic functions are actually implemented as transistors. But this is not always the simplest way to describe a Boolean function. An alternative, more abstract representation tabulates all possible input combinations with their associated output values. We have already seen the concept of a truth table in Figure 1.6.

A	B	Sum	Carry
0	0	0	0
0	1	1	0
1	0	1	0
1	1	0	1

Figure 1.17 Half adder truth table.

A	B	Cin	Sum	Cout
0	0	0	0	0
0	0	1	1	0
0	1	0	1	0
0	1	1	0	1
1	0	0	1	0
1	0	1	0	1
1	1	0	0	1
1	1	1	1	1

Figure 1.18 Full adder truth table.

Let's consider a simple circuit with two binary inputs that generates sum and carry outputs (there is no carry-in input). This circuit is called a *half adder*. Its truth table is shown in Figure 1.17. The network has two inputs, A and B, and two outputs, *Sum* and *Carry*. Thus the table has four columns, one for each input and output, and four rows, for each of the 2^2 unique binary combinations of the inputs.

Figure 1.18 shows the truth table for the full adder, a circuit with two data inputs A and B, a carry-in input *Cin*, and the *Sum* and *Cout* outputs of the half adder. The three inputs have 2^3 unique binary combinations, leading to a truth table with eight rows.

Truth tables are fine for describing functions with a modest number of inputs. But for large numbers of inputs, the truth table grows too large. An alternative representation writes the function as an expression over logic operations and inputs. We look at this next.

1.3.3 Boolean Algebra

Boolean algebra is the mathematical foundation of digital systems. We will see that an algebraic expression provides a convenient shorthand notation for the truth table of a function.

Basic Concept The operations of a Boolean algebra must adhere to certain properties, called *laws* or *axioms*. One of these axioms is that the Boolean operations are commutative: you can reverse the order in which the variables are written without changing the meaning of the Boolean expression. For example, OR is commutative: X OR Y is identical to Y OR X, where X and Y are Boolean variables.

The axioms can be used to prove more general laws about Boolean expressions. You can use them to simplify expressions in the algebra. For example, it can be shown that X AND (Y OR NOT Y) is the same as X, since Y OR NOT Y is always true. The procedures you will learn for optimizing combinational and sequential networks are based on the principles of Boolean algebra, and thus Boolean expressions are often used as input to computer-aided design tools.

Boolean Operations Most designers find it a little cumbersome to keep writing Boolean expressions with AND, OR, and NOT operations, so they have developed a shorthand for the operators. If we use X and Y as the Boolean variables, then we write the complement (inversion, negation) of X as one of X', $\overline{X}$, !X, /X, or \X. The OR operation is written as X + Y, X # Y, X ∨ Y, or X | Y. X AND Y is written as X & Y, X • Y, X ∧ Y, or more simply X Y. Although there are certain analogies between OR and PLUS and between AND and MULTIPLY, the logic operations are not the same as the arithmetic operations.

Complement is always applied first, followed by AND, followed by OR. We say that complement has the highest priority, followed by AND

and then OR. Parentheses can be used to change the default order of evaluation. The default grouping of operations is illustrated by the following examples:

$$\overline{A} \bullet B + C = ((\overline{A}) \bullet B) + C$$

$$\overline{A} + B \bullet C = (\overline{A}) + (B \bullet C)$$

Equivalence of Boolean Expressions and Truth Tables   A Boolean expression can be readily derived from a truth table and vice versa. In fact, Boolean expressions and truth tables convey exactly the same information.

Let's consider the structure of a truth table, with one column for each input variable and a column for the expression's output. Each row in which the output column is a 1 contributes a single ANDed term of the input variables to the Boolean expression. This is called a *product term*, because of the analogy between AND and MULTIPLY. Looking at the row, we see that if the column associated with variable X has a 0 in it, the expression $\overline{X}$ is part of the ANDed term. Otherwise the expression X is part of the term. Variables in their asserted (X) or complemented ($\overline{X}$) forms are called *literals*.

There is one product term for each row with a 1 in the output column. All such product terms are ORed together to complete the expression. A Boolean expression written in this form is called a *sum of products*.

Example   Deriving Expressions from Truth Tables   Let's go back to Figure 1.17 and Figure 1.18, the truth tables for the half adder and the full adder, respectively. Each output column leads to a new Boolean expression, but defined over the same variables associated with the input columns. The Boolean expressions for the half adder's *Sum* and *Carry* outputs can be written as:

$$Sum = (A\overline{B}) + (\overline{A}B)$$

$$Carry = AB$$

The half adder *Sum* is 1 in two rows: $A = 1$, $B = 0$ and $A = 0$, $B = 1$. The half adder *Carry* is 1 in only one row: $A = 1$, $B = 1$.

The truth table for the full adder is considerably more complex. Both *Sum* and *Cout* have four rows with 1's in the output columns. The two functions are written as:

$$Sum = (A\overline{B}\,\overline{Cin}) + (\overline{A}B\,\overline{Cin}) + (\overline{A}\,\overline{B}\,Cin) + (AB\,Cin)$$

$$Cout = (\overline{A}B\,Cin) + (A\overline{B}\,Cin) + (AB\,\overline{Cin}) + (AB\,Cin)$$

As we shall see in Chapter 2, we can exploit Boolean algebra to simplify Boolean expressions. By applying some of the simplification theorems of

Boolean algebra, we can reduce the expression for the full adder's *Cout* output to the following:

$$Cout = (A\ Cin) + (B\ Cin) + (AB)$$

Such simplified forms reduce the amount of gates, transistors, wires, and so on, needed to implement the expression. Simplification is an extremely valuable tool.

You can use a truth table to verify that the simplified expression just obtained is equivalent to the original. Start with a truth table with filled-in input columns but empty output columns. Then find all rows of the truth table for which the product terms are true, and enter a 1 in the associated output column. For example, the term *A Cin* is true wherever $A = 1$ and $Cin = 1$, independent of the value of *B*. *A Cin* spans two truth table rows: $A = 1$, $B = 0$, $Cin = 1$ and $A = 1$, $B = 1$, $Cin = 1$.

Figure 1.19 shows the filled-in truth table and indicates the rows spanned by each of the terms. Since the resulting truth table is the same as that of the original expression (see Figure 1.18), the two expressions must have the same behavior.

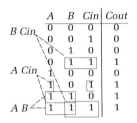

Figure 1.19 Truth table of reduced carry-out expression.

1.3.4 Gates

For logic designers, the most widely used primitive building block is the logic gate. We will see that every Boolean expression has an equivalent gate description, and vice versa.

Correspondence Between Boolean Operations and Logic Gates Each of the logic operators has a corresponding logic gate. We have already met the inverter (NOT), AND, and OR functions, whose corresponding gate-level representations are given in Figure 1.20. Logic gates are formed internally from transistor switches (see Exercise 1.12).

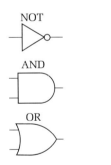

Figure 1.20 Standard logic gates.

Correspondence Between Boolean Expressions and Gate Networks Every Boolean expression has a corresponding implementation in terms of interconnected gates. This is called a *schematic*. Schematics are one of the ways that we capture the *structural view* of a design, that is, how the design is constructed from the composition of primitive components. In this case, the composition is accomplished by physically wiring the gates together.

This leads us to some new terminology. A collection of wires that always carry the same electrical signal, because they are physically connected, is called a *net*. The tabulation of gate inputs and outputs and the nets to which they are connected is called the *netlist*.

Example **Schematics for the Half and Full Adder** A schematic for the half adder is shown in Figure 1.21. The inputs are labeled at the left of

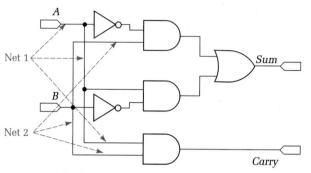

Figure 1.21 Schematic for a half adder circuit.

the figure as A and B. The outputs are at the right, labeled *Sum* and *Carry*. *Sum* is the OR of two ANDed terms, and this maps directly onto the three gates as shown in the schematic. Similarly, *Carry* is described in terms of a single AND operation and thus maps onto a single AND gate. The figure also shows two different nets, labeled Net 1 and Net 2. The former corresponds to the set of wires carrying the input signal A; the latter are the wires carrying signal B.

The full adder's schematic is given in Figure 1.22(a). Each of the outputs is the OR of four 3-variable product terms. The OR operator is mapped into a four-input OR gate, while each product term becomes a three-input AND gate. Each connection in the schematic represents a physical wire among the components. Therefore, there can be a real implementation advantage, in terms of the resources and the time it takes to implement the network, in reducing the number of gates and using gates with fewer inputs.

Figure 1.22(b) shows an alternative implementation of the *Cout* function using fewer gate and wires. The design procedures in the next chapter will help you find the simplest, easiest to implement gate-level representation of a Boolean function.

Schematics Rules of Composition The *fan-in* of a logic gate is its number of inputs. The schematics examples in Figures 1.21 and 1.22 show gates with fan-ins of 1, 2, 3, and 4. The *fan-out* of a gate is the number of inputs to which the gate's output is connected. The schematics examples have many gates with fan-outs of 1, that is, gates whose output connects to exactly one input of another gate. However, some signals have much greater fan-out. For example, signal A in the full adder schematic connects to six different gate inputs (one NOT and five AND gates).

The schematic representation places no limits on the fan-ins and fan-outs. Nevertheless, fan-in and fan-out are restricted by the underlying

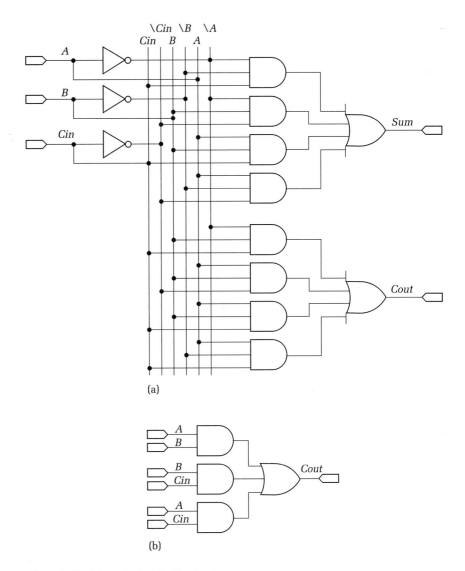

Figure 1.22 Schematics for full adder circuit.

technology from which the logic gates are constructed. It is difficult to find OR gates with greater than 8 inputs, or technologies that allow gates to fan out to more than 10 or 20 other gates. A particular technology will impose a set of *rules of composition* on fan-ins and fan-outs to ensure proper electrical behavior of gates. In Chapter 3 you will learn how to compute the maximum allowable fan-out of a gate.

1.3.5   Waveforms

Waveforms describe the time-varying behavior of hardware systems, while switches, Boolean expressions, and gates tell us only about the static or "steady-state" system behavior. We examine what waveforms can tell us in this subsection.

Static Versus Dynamic Behavior   The representations we have examined so far are static in nature. They give us no intuition about how a circuit behaves over time. For the beginning digital designer, such as yourself, understanding the dynamic behavior of digital systems is one of the hardest skills to develop. Most problems in digital implementations are related to timing.

Gates require a certain propagation time to recognize a change in their inputs and to produce a new output. While settling into this long-term state, a digital system's outputs may look quite different from their final so-called steady-state values. For example, using the truth table representation in Figure 1.17, if we knew that the inputs to the half adder circuit were 1 and 0, we would expect that the output would be 1 for the *Sum* and 0 for the *Carry*.

Waveform Representation of Dynamic Behavior   The waveform representation provides a way to capture the dynamic behavior of a circuit. It is similar to an oscilloscope trace. The X axis displays time, and the values (0 or 1) of multiple signal traces are represented by the Y axis.

Figure 1.23 shows a waveform produced for the half adder circuit. There is a trace for each of the inputs, *A* and *B*, and the outputs, *Sum* and *Carry*, arranged along the time axis. Each time division represents 10 abstract time units, and we have assumed that all gates experience a 10-time-unit delay.

From the figure, you can see that the inputs step through four possible input combinations:

Time

0–50	A is 0, B is 0
51–100	A is 0, B is 1
101–150	A is 1, B is 0
151–200	A is 1, B is 1

Let's look closely at the *Sum* and *Carry* waveforms. You can see that, in general, they follow the pattern expected from the truth table, but are offset in time. The *Sum* output changes through 0 to 1 to 1 to 0. Note that something strange happens during the second transition—we will examine this later when we discuss glitches. The *Carry* stays 0 until the last set of changes to the inputs, at which point it changes to 1. Let's look at an example signal trace through the half adder in more detail.

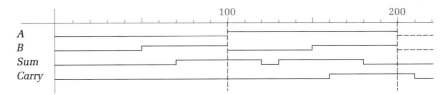

Figure 1.23 Timing waveform of half adder.

Example   Tracing Propagation Delays in the Half Adder Looking in particular at time step 51, the B input changes from 0 to 1. Twenty time units later, the *Sum* output changes from 0 to 1. Why does this happen?

Figure 1.24 shows a logic circuit instrumented with probes on every one of the circuit's nets. The probes display the current logic value on a particular net. The nets with changing values are highlighted in the figure.

Let's examine the sequence of events and the detailed propagation of signals more closely, using Figure 1.24. Figure 1.24(a) shows the initial input conditions (A and B are both 0) and the values of all internal nets.

The situation immediately after B changes from 0 to 1 is shown in Figure 1.24(b). The set of wires attached to the input switch now carry a 1. At this point, the topmost AND gate has both of its inputs set to 1. One gate delay (10 time units) later, the output of this gate will change from 0 to 1. This is shown in Figure 1.24(c).

Now one of the inputs to the OR gate is 1. After another 10-time-unit gate delay, the *Sum* output changes from 0 to 1 (see Figure 1.24(d)). Since the propagated signal passes through two gates, the logic incurs two gate delays, or a delay of 20 time units, as shown in the waveform of Figure 1.23. The propagation path that determines the delay through the circuit is called the *critical path*.

Glitches Propagation delays are highly pattern sensitive. Their duration depends on the specific input combinations and how these cause different propagation paths to become critical within the network. It takes 30 time units (three gate delays) for *Sum* to change after Y changes at time step 151. Did you notice the strange behavior in the *Sum* waveform between time steps 120 and 130? The input combination is 1 and 0, but for a short time *Sum* actually generates a zero output! This behavior is called a *glitch*, a short time during which the output goes through a logic value that is not its steady-state value. This can lead to anomalous behavior if you are not careful. You will learn how to design circuits to avoid glitches in Chapter 3.

1.3.6   Blocks

The block diagram representation helps us understand how major pieces of the hardware design are connected together. We examine it in this subsection.

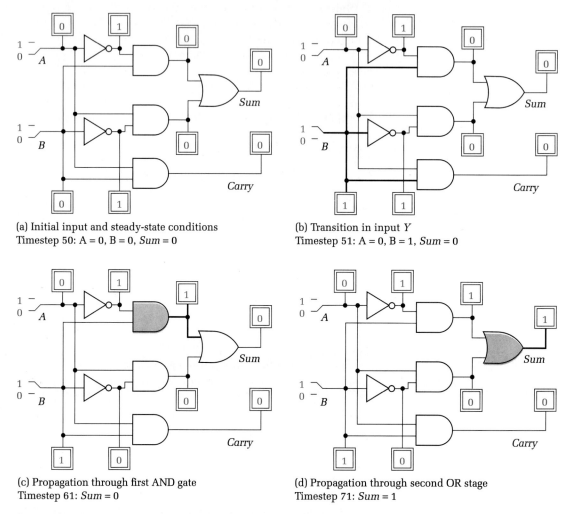

(a) Initial input and steady-state conditions
Timestep 50: A = 0, B = 0, *Sum* = 0

(b) Transition in input *Y*
Timestep 51: A = 0, B = 1, *Sum* = 0

(c) Propagation through first AND gate
Timestep 61: *Sum* = 0

(d) Propagation through second OR stage
Timestep 71: *Sum* = 1

Figure 1.24   Tracing the propagation of inputs through the half-adder schematic.

Basic Concept   A *block* represents a design component that performs some well-defined, reasonably high-level function. For example, it would not make much sense to associate a block with a single logic gate, but several interconnected logic gates could be associated with a block. The full adder is a good example of a block-sized function.

Each block clearly identifies its inputs and outputs. A block can be directly realized by some number of gates, as in Figure 1.22, or it can be constructed from a composition of gates and more primitive blocks.

Example   Full Adder Block Diagram   Figure 1.25 shows how two instances of the same building block, the half adder, can be used to implement a full adder. As you can see from the output waveforms of Figure 1.26, the composed circuit behaves like the full adder constructed directly from logic gates.

Compare the waveforms to the truth table of Figure 1.18. For the most part, the truth table is mirrored in the waveforms, with slight timing variations. The *Sum* waveform also includes some glitches, highlighted in the figure.

The block diagram representation reduces the complexity of a design to more manageable units. Rather than dealing with the full complexity of the full adder schematic and its 13 gates, you need only understand the much simpler half adder (just six gates) and its simple composition to implement the full adder.

Waveforms capture the timing relationships between input and output signals. But they are not always the best way to understand the abstract function being implemented. This is where behavioral representations play an important role. We examine them next.

1.3.7   Behaviors

The behavioral description focuses on how the block behaves. Waveforms are a primitive form of behavioral description. Other, more sophisticated behavioral representations depend on specifications written in hardware description languages.

Basic Concept   The *behavioral description* focuses on block behavior. In a way, the waveform representation provides a primitive behavioral

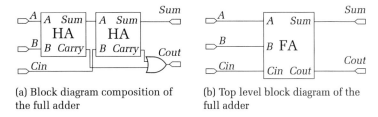

(a) Block diagram composition of the full adder

(b) Top level block diagram of the full adder

Figure 1.25   Internal and external block diagram views of the full adder.

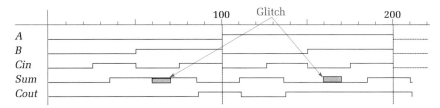

Figure 1.26   Waveform representation of the full adder.

description, but the cause-and-effect relationships between inputs and outputs are not obvious from the waveforms. Waveforms are sometimes augmented with timing relationships to place specific performance constraints on a block. For example, a timing constraint might be "the *Sum* output must change no later than 30 time units after an input changes," and this may have a significant influence on the choice of the block's implementation.

Hardware Description Languages   The most common method of specifying behavioral descriptions is through a hardware description language. These languages look much like conventional high-level computer programming languages. However, conventional programming languages force you to think of executing a single statement of the program at a time. This is unsuitable for hardware, which is inherently parallel: all gates are constantly sampling their inputs and computing new outputs. The high degree of parallelism is one of the things that makes hardware design difficult.

By way of examples, we will introduce two different hardware description languages, ABEL and VHDL. ABEL is commonly used as a specification language for programmable logic components. It is a simple language, suitable for digital systems of moderate complexity. VHDL is more complete, and it is capable of describing systems of considerable complexity.

ABEL   ABEL can specify the relationship between circuit inputs and outputs in several alternative ways, including truth tables and equations. The basic language unit is the module, which corresponds to a block in our terminology. Pins on integrated circuit packages are connections to the outside world. Part of the ABEL specification associates input and output variables with specific pins on the programmable logic component chosen to implement the function.

The truth table form of the half adder looks like this:

```
MODULE half_adder;

A, B, Sum, Carry PIN 1, 2, 3, 4;

TRUTH_TABLE ([A, B] -> [Sum, Carry])
   [0, 0] -> [0, 0];
   [0, 1] -> [1, 0];
   [1, 0] -> [1, 0];
   [1, 1] -> [0, 1];

END half_adder;
```

The specification is nothing more than a tabulation of conditions on inputs *A* and *B* and the corresponding output values that should be associated with *Sum* and *Carry*.

Another way to describe the relationship between inputs and outputs is through Boolean equations. The module definition would be written as follows:

```
MODULE half_adder;

A, B, Sum, Carry PIN 1, 2, 3, 4;

EQUATIONS
   Sum = (A & !B) # (!A & B);
   Carry = A & B;

END half_adder;
```

Here, & is the AND operator, ! is negation, and # is OR.

VHDL   VHDL is a widely used language for hardware description, based on the programming language ADA. It is used as the input description for a number of commercially available computer-aided design systems. Although we are not concerned with the details of the VHDL syntax, it is worthwhile to look at a sample description of the half adder, just to see the kinds of capabilities VHDL provides. A VHDL "model" for the half adder follows:

```
-- ***** inverter gate model *****
-- external ports
ENTITY inverter_gate;
   PORT (A: IN BIT;  Z: OUT BIT);
END inverter_gate;

-- internal behavior
ARCHITECTURE behavioral OF inverter_gate IS
BEGIN
   Z <= NOT A AFTER 10 ns;
END behavioral;

-- ***** and gate model *****
-- external ports
ENTITY and_gate;
   PORT (A, B: IN BIT;  Z: OUT BIT);
END and_gate;

-- internal behavior
ARCHITECTURE behavioral OF and_gate IS
BEGIN
   Z <= A AND B AFTER 10 ns;
END behavioral;
```

```
-- ***** or gate model *****
-- external ports
ENTITY or_gate;
   PORT (A, B: IN BIT;  Z: OUT BIT);
END or_gate;

-- internal behavior
ARCHITECTURE behavioral OF or_gate IS
BEGIN
   Z <= A OR B AFTER 10 ns;
END behavioral;

-- ***** half adder model *****
-- external ports
ENTITY half_adder;
   PORT (A, B: INPUT;  Sum, Carry: OUTPUT);
END half_adder;

-- internal structure
ARCHITECTURE structural of half_adder IS
   -- component types to use
   COMPONENT inverter_gate
      PORT (A: IN BIT;  Z: OUT BIT);
   END COMPONENT;
   COMPONENT and_gate
      PORT (A, B: IN BIT;  Z: OUT BIT);
   END COMPONENT;
   COMPONENT or_gate
      PORT (A, B: IN BIT;  Z: OUT BIT);
   END COMPONENT;

   -- internal signal wires
   SIGNAL s1, s2, s3, s4: BIT;
BEGIN
   -- one line for each gate, describing its
   -- type and its connections
   i1: inverter_gate PORT MAP (A, s1);
   i2: inverter_gate PORT MAP (B, s2);
   a1: and_gate PORT MAP (B, s1, s3);
   a2: and_gate PORT MAP (A, s2, s4);
   a3: and_gate PORT MAP (A, B, Carry);
   o1: or_gate PORT MAP (s3, s4, Sum);
END structural;
```

The *entity declarations* declare the block diagram characteristics of a component—that is, the way it looks to the outside world. The *architecture declarations* define the internal operation. Usually these are written in a form that looks much like programming statements. The inverter,

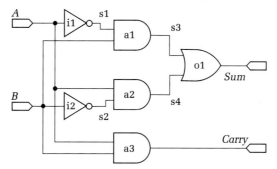

Figure 1.27 Structural definition of the half adder.

AND, and OR behaviors are so simple that they do not do justice to VHDL's capability of expressing hardware behavior. This definition of the half adder is entirely structural: it is merely a textual form of specifying the schematic, shown in Figure 1.27.

1.4 Rapid Electronic System Prototyping

Rapid prototyping is the ability to verify the behavior of digital systems and to construct working systems rapidly. Suppose you have designed a 12-hour digital clock, and now you want to redesign it as a military-style 24-hour clock. In the old style of digital system implementation, you would need to redesign your clock substantially, tearing up a bunch of wires, changing the gates, and rewiring the design. In the new style, you could simply revise your ABEL description, execute the description on a computer to check that it behaves the way you want it to, recompile the description for a programmable logic component, and simply replace that one piece of your design with a single new component.

Rapid prototyping depends critically on a set of hardware and software technologies. We review them next.

1.4.1 The Rationale for Rapid Prototyping

Rapid prototyping allows system construction to proceed much more quickly than in the past, perhaps sacrificing some performance (speed, power, or area) in return for faster implementation. The advantage is that you can test the validity of a concept more easily if you can implement it rapidly. You have the luxury of examining a number of alternatives, choosing the one that best fits the design constraints.

It is fairly straightforward to sketch the flow of states through the traffic light controller of Figure 1.2. Yet it will take most of this textbook for you to learn the detailed process by which this flowchart is mapped into a physical implementation realized by interconnected logic gates. And even when you have your schematic, you must still wire the design together correctly before it can "light the lights!"

For rapid prototyping to be effective, it is most important to capture the design intent through high-level specifications. This is why hardware description languages are becoming so important. Computer-aided design tools can take these descriptions and expeditiously map them into ever more detailed representations of the design, eventually yielding a description, such as interconnected gates, suitable for implementation. The designer's emphasis is changing from focusing on the tactics of design to managing its strategy: the specification of the design intent and constraints, the selection of the appropriate design tools to use, and the subjective evaluation of design alternatives.

1.4.2   Computer-Aided Design Tools

Computer-aided design tools play an important role in rapid prototyping. They speed up the process of mapping a high-level design specification into the physical units that implement the design, usually gates or transistors. You can modify the input description to try a new alternative, then quickly examine its detailed realization and compare it to the original.

Besides support for exploring design alternatives, design tools can improve the quality of the design by simulating the implementation before it is physically constructed. A simulation can verify that a design will operate as expected before it is built. In general, design tools fall into two broad classes, synthesis and simulation (or verification and analysis), which we describe next.

Synthesis   Synthesis tools automatically create one design representation from another. Usually the mapping is from more abstract descriptions into more detailed descriptions, closer to the final form for implementation. For example, a VHDL description could be mapped into a collection of Boolean equations that preserve the behavior of the original specification, while describing the system at a greater level of detail. A second tool might take these Boolean equations and a library of gates available in a given technology, and generate a gate-level description of the system.

Not all synthesis tools necessarily map from one representation to another. Some can improve a given representation by mapping a rough description into an optimized form. Logic minimization tools, using sophisticated forms of the algorithms of Chapter 2, can reduce the original Boolean equations to much simpler forms.

Simulation   Simulators are programs that can dynamically execute an abstract design description. Given a description of the circuit and a model for how the elements of the description behave, the simulator maps an input stimulus into an output response, often as a function of time. If the behavior is not as expected, it is almost always easier to identify and repair the problem in this description than to troubleshoot your final product. Simulators exist for all levels of design description, from the most abstract behavioral level through the detailed transistor level. For our purposes, two forms of simulation are the most relevant: logic and timing.

Logic simulation models the design as interconnected logic gates that produce the values 0 and 1 (and others that will be introduced in the next chapter). You use the simulator to determine whether the truth table behavior of the circuit meets your input/output expectations. For the simple circuits we have examined so far, we can enumerate all the possible inputs and verify that the output behavior matches the truth table. For more complex circuits, it is not feasible for you to generate all possible inputs, so only a small set of judiciously selected test cases can be used.

Timing simulation is like logic simulation, except that it introduces more realistic delay. In other words, the elements of the description not only compute outputs from inputs, they also take time. In general, timing simulation verifies that the shapes of waveforms match your expectations for the timing behavior of the system. For example, if we modeled all the gates in this chapter as having 0 time units of delay, we would not have observed the glitches of Figure 1.23.

Simulation has its limitations, and it is important that you appreciate these. First, simulators are based on abstract descriptions and models, so they provide a simplified view of the world. A simulator demonstration that a design is "correct" does not guarantee that the "wired up" implementation will work. Logic simulators contain no electrical models. You might exceed the fan-out for a given technology, which could cripple the physical circuit, and many logic simulators would not detect this problem. Second, the simulator is only as good as your choice of test cases. The circuit may not operate correctly on the one input combination you did not test!

1.4.3   Rapid Implementation Technology

The design process, with or without CAD tools, yields a selection of specific building blocks that now have to be wired up to implement the design. Stop for a moment and think about the task of wiring up the full adder, with its 13 gates and 37 wires. If this seems tedious to you, consider that this is really a very simple circuit. And imagine troubleshooting the circuit to find a burnt-out gate, tearing up the wires, replacing the gate, and reconnecting all the wires again. This is one of the most time-consuming, tedious, and error-prone steps in the entire design process.

New implementation technologies accelerate the physical implementation of the design. Making this step fast has other advantages. If a bug is discovered, it can be fixed and the implementation regenerated rapidly

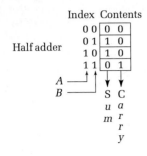

Half adder

Index	Contents
0 0	0 0
0 1	1 0
1 0	1 0
1 1	0 1

A ⎤
B ⎦ → S C
    u a
    m r
      r
      y

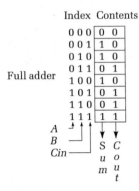

Full adder

Index	Contents
0 0 0	0 0
0 0 1	1 0
0 1 0	1 0
0 1 1	0 1
1 0 0	1 0
1 0 1	0 1
1 1 0	0 1
1 1 1	1 1

A ⎤
B ⎥ → S C
Cin ⎦   u o
     m u
       t

Figure 1.28 Realizing Boolean functions through 1's and 0's.

("rapid reworking"). Also, the design can be changed more easily in response to real performance feedback by getting the system into operation more quickly.

Programming with 1's and 0's So far, you might have the feeling that we build hardware exclusively from wired-up gates, but this is not the way all hardware is implemented. A popular technique is to store a logic function's truth table in a special electronic device called a memory (this is discussed in more detail in Chapter 6).

The inputs form an address that is used as an index into an array of storage elements. The 0's and 1's stored there represent the values of the outputs of the function. By storing multibit words at the memory locations, you can use this technique to implement multiple-output combinational networks (see Figure 1.28). Changing a function is as easy as directly changing the values in the memory.

The drawback is that the size of the memory doubles for each additional input: a one-input memory has two address locations (0 and 1), a two-input memory has four (00, 01, 10, 11), a three-input memory eight, and so on. So this technique has limited utility for functions with a large number of inputs. Also, there may be speed advantages to using discrete gates rather than memories.

User-Programmable Devices You can usually implement a function by selecting the desired components from a catalog and simply wiring them up. A new approach, based on *programmable logic devices (PLDs),* is becoming popular. Rather than use prefabricated parts, you build the design out of configurable components. You can imagine a sort of universal gate that could be configured with a truth table to yield an inverter, an AND gate, or an OR gate, depending on what is needed. Although this oversimplifies how these devices work, the basic idea is that their function can be customized to the task at hand.

Beyond functional configuration, the devices contain interconnection wires that can be configured by the designer. Based on memory elements containing truth tables that you provide, even the components can be wired together at your command.

Computer-aided design tools and user-programmable devices are radically changing the way digital design is being done. Where appropriate in this text, we will give more details of this exciting new technology.

Chapter Review

This chapter has introduced you to the basic process of design, which you can really learn only by doing, and the kinds of systems we are interested in designing, namely combinational and sequential digital systems. We have attempted to develop an appreciation for the many different ways to represent a digital design, from simple interconnected switches through programming language–like behavioral descriptions. Finally, we have reviewed the changing technological landscape, focusing on the new approaches for building digital systems more rapidly: computer-aided design tools and user-programmable devices. We are now ready to begin a more serious study of the design and implementation techniques for digital systems.

Further Reading

A very good description of the design process can be found in Chapter 3 of S. Dasgupta's book *Computer Architecture: A Modern Synthesis*, John Wiley, New York, 1989. An excellent discussion of a variety of programmable logic technologies can be found in R. C. Alford's book, *Programmable Logic Designer's Guide*, published by Howard W. Sams & Co., Indianapolis, IN, in 1989. For those not familiar with the basic background concepts of electronics, a gentle introduction can be found in T. M. Frederiksen's work, *Intuitive Digital Computer Basics*, published by McGraw-Hill, New York, in 1988 (the entire "Intuitive" series is quite good). The classic text on digital design for very large scale integrated circuits is by Carver Mead and Lynn Conway, *Introduction to VLSI Systems*, Addison-Wesley, Reading, MA, 1980. The complete spectrum of computer-aided design tools is described in Steven Rubin's text *Computer Aids for VLSI Design*, Addison-Wesley, Reading, MA, 1987. Carlo Séquin covers the issues involved in managing the complexity of large complex digital designs in his paper "Managing VLSI Complexity: An Outlook," which appeared in *Proceedings of the IEEE*, 71:1, 149–166 (January 1983).

Exercises

1.1 *(Description of Digital System Behavior)* Develop flowchart-like diagrams similar to Figure 1.2 for the following variations on the basic traffic light controller described in Section 1.1.1. Make reasonable assumptions about the duration of lights if not otherwise specified. Consider each variation independently (each is independent of the original specification represented by Figure 1.2).

a. Suppose a left-turn arrow is added, but only in the direction of drivers facing North from the South (they wish to make left turns from South to West). The green arrow should be illuminated for 15 seconds, and during this time the lights are red for East-West and red for the South-facing traffic. The drivers facing North see the sequence: green arrow (15 seconds), green (30 seconds), yellow (15 seconds), red (60 seconds), and repeat. From this specification, you should be able to determine the light timings for the other three directions.

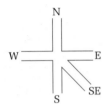

Figure Ex1.1   Intersection for Exercise 1.1(d).

b. Consider adding Walk–Don't Walk signs in all directions. These cycle through green Walk, flashing red Don't Walk, and solid red Don't Walk. The lights are green for 30 seconds, flashing red for 15 seconds, and solid red for 75 seconds.

c. In all directions, add push-buttons that have the following effect: if the light is red in the direction in which the pedestrian wishes to cross, the green time duration in the other direction is reduced from 45 to 30 seconds. Pushing the button more than once or from more than one corner has no further effect.

d. Consider the design of a traffic light for a five-way intersection. The directions are N-S, E-W, and SE (see Figure Ex1.1). No direction should be green for more than 45 seconds and yellow for more than 15. Every direction should eventually see a green light. *Warning:* Make sure you never have more than one direction green at the same time!

1.2 *(Design as Assembly)*   Think of a complex system that you know well, such as the automobile you drive or the structure in which you live.

a. Describe the decomposition of this "complex object" into ever more primitive components, stopping at a reasonable level of "most primitive" component (e.g., a brick, a nail, a piece of lumber).

b. Consider some alternative representations of your complex system. Briefly explain what they are. (*Hint*: Do the electrician and the sanitation engineer refer to the same representation of your house when they need to repair something?)

1.3 *(Logical Statements)*   Write logic statements for the traffic light variants of Exercise 1.1, using IF-THEN statements and AND, OR, and NOT connectives, as described in Section 1.2.1.

1.4 *(Logical Statements)*   Make the following assumptions about a burglar alarm system in your home: (1) you cannot set the alarm unless all windows and doors are closed; (2) the system is "preset" if (1) is true and the secret code has been entered; (3) the system is "set" if (2) is true and 45 seconds have elapsed since presetting the alarm; (4) if the alarm is set, opening any window or a door other than the front door will cause the alarm to sound immediately; (5) if the front door is opened and the alarm is set, it will sound if the system is not disarmed within 30 seconds; (6) the system is disarmed by entering the secret code. Write logic statements for:

a. Setting the alarm

b. Disarming the alarm

c. Sounding the alarm

1.5 *(Analog vs. Digital)* Consider the inverter transfer characteristic described in Section 1.2.3. Suppose two inverter circuits are placed in series so that the output of the first inverter is the input to the second inverter. Assume initially that the input to the first stage is a logic 1 represented by 5 volts. Of course, the output of the second stage will be identical, at least initially. Describe what happens to the outputs of the first and second stages as the first stage input slowly changes from 5 volts to 0 volts. Do this by drawing a graph whose X axis is time and whose Y axis is voltage, showing two curves, one each for (a) the first stage output and (b) the second stage output.

1.6 *(Combinational vs. Sequential Circuits)* Which of the following contain circuits that are likely to be combinational and which contain sequential circuits? Explain your rationale.

a. A washing machine that sequences through the soak, wash, and spin cycles for preset periods of time.

b. A three-input majority circuit that outputs a logic 1 if any two of its inputs are 1.

c. A circuit that divides two 2-bit numbers to yield a quotient and a remainder.

d. A machine that takes a dollar bill and gives three quarters, two dimes, and a nickel in change, one at a time through a single coin change slot.

e. A digital alarm clock that generates an alarm when a preset time has been reached.

1.7 *(Switching Networks)* Draw switching networks as described in Section 1.3.1 for the three conditions of Exercise 1.4.

1.8 *(Switching Networks)* Although we concentrate mostly on gate-level designs in the following chapters, switching logic as described in Section 1.3.1 is quite useful for functions that "steer" inputs to outputs, such as *shifters* and *multiplexers/ demultiplexers*. The functions of these devices are described by the following specifications. Design networks of switches for the following functions:

a. A 2-bit-wide *shifter* takes two input signals, i_0 and i_1, and shifts them to two outputs, o_0 and o_1, under the control of a shift signal. If this signal SHIFT is false, then the inputs are connected straight through to the outputs. If SHIFT is true, then i_0 is routed to o_1 and o_0 should be set to a 0.

b. A 1-bit *demultiplexer* takes an input signal IN and shifts it to one of two outputs, o_0 and o_1, under the control of a single SELECT signal. If SELECT is 0, then IN is connected through to o_0 and o_1 is connected to a 0. If SELECT is 1, then IN is connected to o_1 and o_0 should be connected to a 0.

c. A 2-bit *multiplexer* takes two input signals, i_0 and i_1, and shifts one of them to the single output OUT under the control of a 1-bit select signal. If the SELECT signal is false, then i_0 is passed to OUT. If SELECT is true, then i_1 is passed to OUT.

1.9 *(Truth Tables)* Write truth tables for the three functions of Exercise 1.8.

1.10 *(Boolean Algebra)* Write sum of products expressions for the truth tables of Exercise 1.9.

1.11 *(Gates)* Given the Boolean expressions of Exercise 1.10, draw logic schematics using AND, OR, and INVERT gates that implement those functions.

1.12 *(Design Representations)* Examine the three switching networks in Figure Ex1.12. Write a truth table for each of the networks. For each input combination, describe briefly how the network operates.

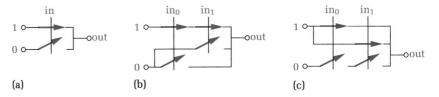

(a) (b) (c)

Figure Ex1.12 Switching networks for Exercise 1.12.

1.13 *(Waveforms)* Trace the propagation of 1's and 0's through the half adder of Section 1.3.4 to explain why the glitch occurs when the inputs switch from $A = 0$, $B = 1$ to $A = 1$, $B = 0$. Assume all gates have the same delay of 10 time units.

1.14 *(Block Diagrams)* Given the truth table for the half adder, show that the composition of two half adders and an OR gate as in Section 1.3.6 yields the same truth table as the full adder.

1.15 *(Waveform Verification)* This chapter has described two different gate-level implementations for a full adder circuit: direct implementation, as in Figure 1.22, and hierarchical implementation via cascaded half adders, as in Figure 1.25(a). Would you expect the waveform behaviors of these implementations to be identical? Justify your answer.

1.16 *(Behaviors)* Write a program in your favorite programming language that mimics the behavior of (a) the basic traffic light controller of Section 1.1.1 and the four variations (b through e) described in Exercise 1.1.

1.17 *(Synthesis)* Simplify the following Boolean expressions by examining their truth tables for simpler terms that cover multiple 1's rows of the truth table:

$$F(A, B, C) = \overline{A}BC + A\overline{B}C + A\overline{B}C + AB\overline{C} + ABC$$

$$F(A, B, C) = \overline{A}\overline{B}C + A\overline{B}C + AB\overline{C} + ABC$$

1.18 *(Programming with 1's and 0's)* Describe the contents of a memory that you would use to implement the three functions of Exercise 1.8. Identify the address inputs and signal outputs.

1.19 *(Truth Tables)* Consider a function that takes as input two 2-bit numbers and produces as output a 3-bit sum. Write the truth table for this function.

1.20 *(Truth Tables)* An increment-by-1 function takes a single-bit input and generates a *Sum* and *Carry* as follows. If the input is 0, *Sum* is 1 and *Carry* is 0. If the input is 1, *Sum* is 0 and *Carry* is 1. Using the truth table for the full adder, demonstrate that you can implement the increment-by-1 function by setting *Cin* of the full adder to 1 while the *B* input is set to 0. Can you think of any reasons why it may be advantageous to use a standard building block like the full adder rather than a special circuit?

2 Two-Level Combinational Logic

O purblind race of miserable men,
How many among us at this very hour
Do forge a lifelong trouble for ourselves,
By taking true for false, and false for true!
—Alfred, Lord Tennyson

Introduction

This chapter begins our detailed examination of the implementation of digital systems. We start with *combinational logic design*, the design and implementation of logic functions whose outputs depend solely on their inputs. The full adder introduced in Chapter 1 is just such a circuit.

We start with the representation of a function as a Boolean equation or a truth table. We will introduce a "canonical," or standard, representation of Boolean equations, called the *sum of products two-level form*. We can think of this as a unique way to represent a Boolean function, like a fingerprint. The form expresses the function as ANDed terms (first level of gates) that are then ORed together (second level of gates). An alternative canonical form, the *product of sums form*, has ORs at the first level and ANDs at the second level.

You can implement a Boolean function as logic gates in more than one way. It is highly desirable to find the simplest implementation—that is, the one with the smallest number of gates or wires. The process of reducing a Boolean function to its simplest two-level form is called *Boolean minimization* or *reduction*. We will introduce the detailed algorithm for minimization, as well as a simple method suitable for pencil and paper. We emphasize methods that will help you to visualize what is going on during reduction.

This chapter builds on the themes introduced in Chapter 1, within the framework of combinational logic design. Namely, we emphasize:

- *Multiple representations*, including Boolean equations, truth tables, waveforms, and interconnected gate descriptions of a Boolean function. In particular, we introduce the standard canonical representations that form the basis of the various simplification and implementation methods.

- *Rapid prototyping technology* involving the use of computer-based software for reducing Boolean equations and truth tables to their simplest two-level form.

2.1 Logic Functions and Switches

In Chapter 1 you saw that (at least some) Boolean expressions can be represented by logic gates and vice versa. Actually, all Boolean functions can be implemented in terms of AND, OR, and NOT gates. Because of this close relationship between the laws of Boolean algebra and the behavior of logic gates, theorems that are true for Boolean algebra can also be used to transform digital logic into simpler forms.

2.1.1 Boolean Algebra

Boolean algebra is at the heart of understanding all digital systems. You are now ready to study its fundamental structure.

Axioms of Boolean Algebra   A Boolean algebra consists of a set of elements B, together with two binary operations $\{+\}$ and $\{\bullet\}$ and a unary operation $\{'\}$, such that the following axioms hold:

1. The set B contains at least two elements a, b such that $a \neq b$.

2. *Closure*: For every a, b in B,

    a. $a + b$ is in B

    b. $a \bullet b$ is in B

3. *Commutative laws*: For every a, b in B,

    a. $a + b = b + a$

    b. $a \bullet b = b \bullet a$

4. *Associative laws*: For every a, b, c in B,

    a. $(a + b) + c = a + (b + c) = a + b + c$

    b. $(a \bullet b) \bullet c = a \bullet (b \bullet c) = a \bullet b \bullet c$

5. *Identities*:

   a. There exists an identity element with respect to {+}, designated by 0, such that $a + 0 = a$ for every a in B.

   b. There exists an identity element with respect to {•}, designated by 1, such that $a • 1 = a$ for every a in B.

6. *Distributive laws*: For every a, b, c in B,

   a. $a + (b • c) = (a + b) • (a + c)$

   b. $a • (b + c) = (a • b) + (a • c)$

7. *Complement*: For each a in B, there exists an element a' in B (the complement of a) such that

   a. $a + a' = 1$

   b. $a • a' = 0$

   Note: We use A' and $\overline{A}$ interchangeably to represent complement in this chapter.

It is easy to verify that the set $B = \{0, 1\}$ and the logical operations OR, AND, and NOT satisfy all the axioms of a Boolean algebra. Simply substitute 0 and 1 for a and b, OR for +, AND for •, and NOT for ', and show that the expressions are true. For example, to verify the commutative law for +:

$$0 + 1 = 1 + 0 \qquad 0 • 1 = 1 • 0$$
$$1 = 1 \; \surd \qquad\qquad 0 = 0 \; \surd$$

A *Boolean function* uniquely maps some number of inputs over the set $\{0, 1\}$ into the set $\{0, 1\}$. A *Boolean expression* is an algebraic statement containing Boolean variables and operators. A theorem in Boolean algebra states that any Boolean function can be expressed in terms of AND, OR, and NOT operations. For example, in Section 1.3.3 we saw one way to map a truth table into a Boolean expression in the *sum* (OR) of *products* (AND) form.

In fact, there are other ways to represent the function using new logical operations, to be introduced next. These operations are interesting because they are easier to implement with real transistor switches.

Boolean Operations Revisited   Let's review the elementary Boolean operations and how these are represented as gates, truth tables, and switches. Figure 2.1, Figure 2.2, and Figure 2.3 summarize the representations for the COMPLEMENT/NOT, AND, and OR operations, respectively.

Take the Boolean expression $Z = \overline{A} • \overline{B} • (C + D)$. A version of the expression with parentheses would be $(\overline{A} • (\overline{B} • (C + D)))$. Each pair of parentheses represents the expression generated by a single gate. Thus,

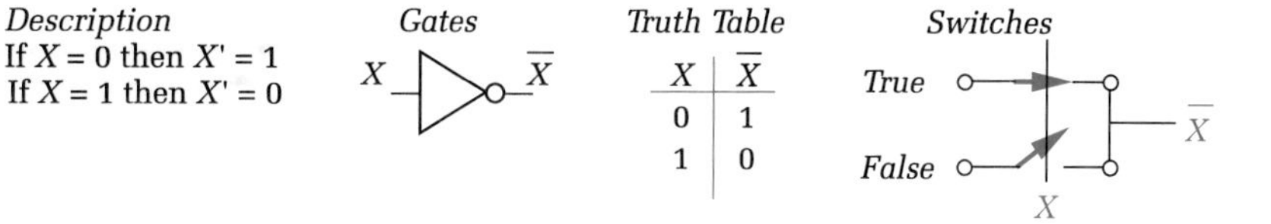
Description
If $X = 0$ then $X' = 1$
If $X = 1$ then $X' = 0$
Gates
X
$\overline{X}$
Truth Table
X | $\overline{X}$
0 | 1
1 | 0
Switches
True
False
X
$\overline{X}$

Figure 2.1 Representations of complement.

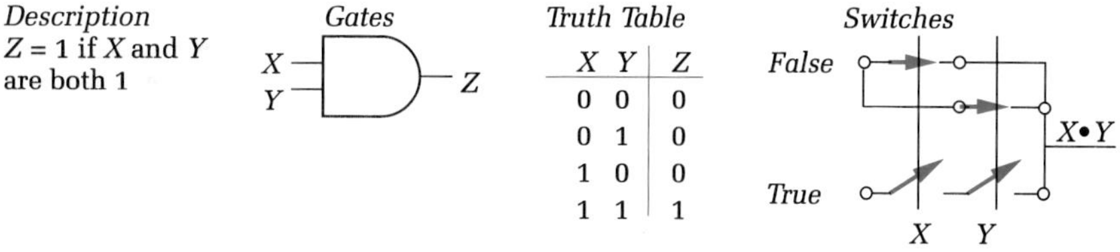
Description
$Z = 1$ if X and Y are both 1
Gates
X
Y
Z
Truth Table
X Y | Z
0 0 | 0
0 1 | 0
1 0 | 0
1 1 | 1
Switches
False
True
$X \bullet Y$
X Y

Figure 2.2 Representations of AND.

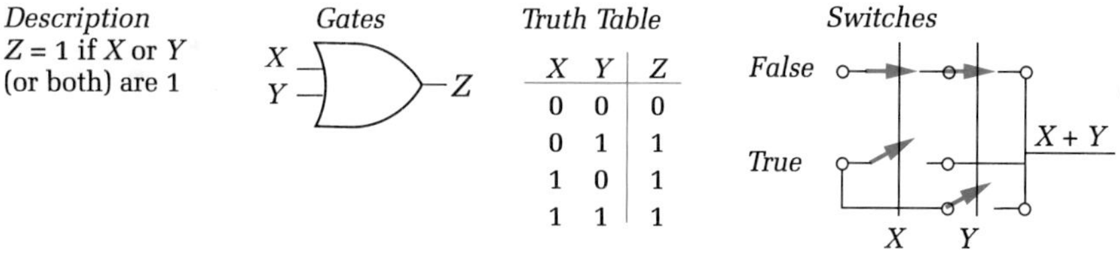
Description
$Z = 1$ if X or Y (or both) are 1
Gates
X
Y
Z
Truth Table
X Y | Z
0 0 | 0
0 1 | 1
1 0 | 1
1 1 | 1
Switches
False
True
$X + Y$
X Y

Figure 2.3 Representations of OR.

the circuit is built up through a set of intermediate results, from the inside out:

$$T_2 = (C + D)$$
$$T_1 = (\overline{B} \bullet T_2)$$
$$Z = (\overline{A} \bullet T_1)$$

The gate-level implementation is shown in Figure 2.4(a), using two input gates. The primitive gates need not be limited to two inputs, however. Figure 2.4(b) shows the same circuit implemented using a three-input AND gate. These implementations are equivalent because of the associative law of Boolean algebra.

Each appearance of a variable or its complement in an expression is called a *literal*. In the preceding expression, we can see that there are four variables and four literals. The following expression has 10 literals but only three variables (A, B, and C): $Z = A\overline{B}C + AB + \overline{A}B\overline{C} + \overline{B}C$. Each literal represents the connection of a variable or its complement to a unique gate input.

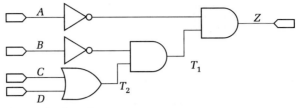

(a) Gate-level implementation

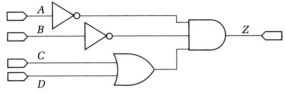

(b) Alternative realization

Figure 2.4 Two equivalent gate-level implementations.

2.1.2 Additional Kinds of Logic Gates

There are other functions of two Boolean variables besides AND, OR, and NOT. In fact, there are 16 possible functions, the number of different ways you can write down the different choices of 0 and 1 for the four possible truth table rows. A truth table representation of the 16 functions is shown in Figure 2.5. The constant functions 0 and 1 and the functions X, $\overline{X}$, Y, $\overline{Y}$, $X \bullet Y$, and $X + Y$ represent only half of the possible functions. We now introduce the remaining Boolean operators.

NAND and NOR   Two of the most frequently encountered Boolean operators are NAND (not AND) and NOR (not OR). Their gate, truth table, and logical switch representations are shown in Figure 2.6 and Figure 2.7. The NAND operation behaves as if an AND is composed with a NOT: it yields a logic 0 in the truth table rows where AND is a 1,

X	Y	F0	F1	F2	F3	F4	F5	F6	F7	F8	F9	F10	F11	F12	F13	F14	F15
0	0	0	0	0	0	0	0	0	0	1	1	1	1	1	1	1	1
0	1	0	0	0	0	1	1	1	1	0	0	0	0	1	1	1	1
1	0	0	0	1	1	0	0	1	1	0	0	1	1	0	0	1	1
1	1	0	1	0	1	0	1	0	1	0	1	0	1	0	1	0	1

$$0 \qquad X \bullet Y \quad X \qquad Y \quad X + Y \qquad \overline{Y} \qquad \overline{X} \qquad 1$$

Figure 2.5   The 16 functions of two Boolean variables.

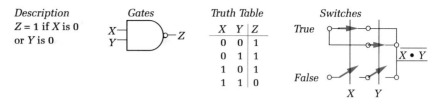

| Description | Gates | Truth Table | Switches |

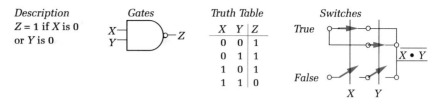

Description
$Z = 1$ if X is 0
or Y is 0

Gates

Truth Table

X	Y	Z
0	0	1
0	1	1
1	0	1
1	1	0

Switches

Figure 2.6 Representations of NAND.

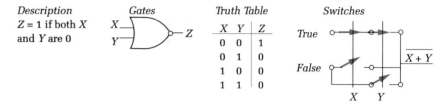

Description
$Z = 1$ if both X
and Y are 0

Gates

Truth Table

X	Y	Z
0	0	1
0	1	0
1	0	0
1	1	0

Switches

Figure 2.7 Representations of NOR.

and it yields a 1 in the rows where AND is 0. The gate representation is an AND gate with a small circle or "bubble" at its output, denoting negation.

If you take a close look at the logic switch representation in Figure 2.6 and compare it to Figure 2.2, you will see that it looks like an AND function with the true and false inputs reversed. NAND is true, and a switching path exists from true to the output, when either X is 0 (the top normally closed switch is closed) or Y is 0 (the bottom normally closed switch is closed). Alternatively, it is false when X and Y are both true, closing the path from false to the output.

NOR behaves in a similar fashion, but now with respect to OR. Once again the truth table outputs are complemented, and we draw the NOR gate as an OR gate with a bubble at the output. The switch representation in Figure 2.7 shows a topology like the OR gate of Figure 2.3, with the true and false inputs reversed. Both X and Y must be zero to close the normally closed switches and establish the path from true to the output.

NAND and NOR gates far outnumber AND and OR gates in a typical digital design, even though these functions are less intuitive. For electrical reasons, revealed in more detail in Appendix B, normally open switches are better at passing low voltages than high voltages. For example, 0 V at one side of the switch will yield close to 0 V at the other, but 5 V will yield approximately 3.5 V at the other side. The opposite behavior is true about normally closed switches. Thus, the switch configurations of Figures 2.6 and 2.7 are better behaved electrically than those of Figures 2.2 and 2.3.

Since any Boolean expression can be represented in terms of AND, OR, and NOT gates, it is hardly surprising that the same statement can be made about NAND, NOR, and NOT gates. In fact, NOT gates are superfluous: if you carefully examine the truth tables of Figures 2.6 and 2.7, you'll see that NAND and NOR act like NOT when both inputs are identically 0 or 1. We shall see an efficient method for mapping Boolean expressions into NAND and NOR logic in Section 2.2.2.

XOR/XNOR   This leaves six functions still unnamed in Figure 2.5. Two of these, frequently of use, are exclusive OR (XOR, also known as the *inequality gate* or *difference function*) and exclusive NOR (XNOR, also known as the *equality gate* or *coincidence function*). Their truth tables and gate representations are given in Figure 2.8. XOR is true when its inputs differ in value. XNOR is true when its inputs coincide in value. The Boolean operator for XOR is ⊕; XNOR is usually represented as the complement of XOR. As with any Boolean function, these can be implemented in terms of AND, OR, and NOT operations:

XOR: $X \oplus Y = X\overline{Y} + \overline{X}Y$

XNOR: $\overline{X \oplus Y} = \overline{X}\,\overline{Y} + XY$

If you examine the truth table of Figure 2.8(a), you can see that XOR is precisely the function needed to implement the half adder sum of Chapter 1!

Implication   The remaining four functions are based on a Boolean operator called *implication*. X implies Y (written $X \Rightarrow Y$) is true under two

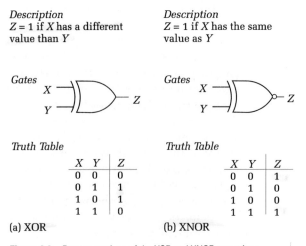

Description
$Z = 1$ if X has a different value than Y

Description
$Z = 1$ if X has the same value as Y

Gates

Gates

Truth Table

X	Y	Z
0	0	0
0	1	1
1	0	1
1	1	0

Truth Table

X	Y	Z
0	0	1
0	1	0
1	0	0
1	1	1

(a) XOR

(b) XNOR

Figure 2.8   Representations of the XOR and XNOR operations.

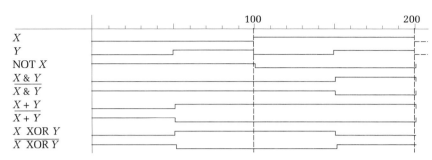

Figure 2.9 Timing waveforms for NOT, AND, NAND, OR, NOR, XOR, XNOR.

conditions: either X is false or both X and Y are true. The four remaining functions become $X \Rightarrow Y$, $Y \Rightarrow X$, NOT $(X \Rightarrow Y)$, and NOT $(Y \Rightarrow X)$. These are not commonly found as primitives readily available for realizing digital systems, so they won't be of much use to you. The timing waveforms for the common functions, AND, OR, NAND, NOR, XOR, and XNOR, are shown in Figure 2.9. The figure assumes a single-time-unit gate delay in computing new outputs from inputs.

2.1.3 Justification for Logic Minimization

Logic minimization uses a variety of techniques to obtain the simplest gate-level implementation of a Boolean function. But simplicity depends on the metric we use. We examine these metrics in this subsection.

Time and Space Trade-Offs   One way to measure the complexity of a Boolean function is to count the number of literals it contains. Literals measure the amount of wiring needed to implement a function. For electrical and packaging reasons, gates in a given technology will have a limited number of inputs. While two-, three-, and four-input gates are common, gates with more than eight or nine inputs are rare. Thus, one of the primary reasons for performing logic minimization is to reduce the number of literals in the expression of the function, thus reducing the number of gate inputs.

An alternative metric is the number of gates, which measures circuit area. There is a strong correlation between the number of gates in a design and the number of components needed for its implementation. The simplest design to manufacture is often the one with the fewest gates, not the fewest literals.

A third metric is the number of cascaded levels of gates. Reducing the number of logic levels reduces overall delay, as there are fewer gate delays on the path from inputs to outputs. However, putting a circuit in a form suitable for minimum delay rarely yields an implementation with

A	B	C	Z
0	0	0	0
0	0	1	1
0	1	0	0
0	1	1	1
1	0	0	0
1	0	1	1
1	1	0	1
1	1	1	0

(a) Function truth table

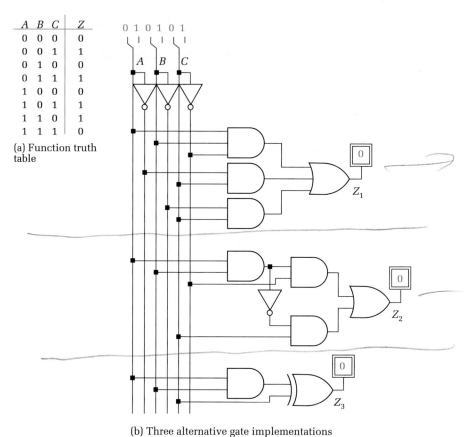

(b) Three alternative gate implementations

Figure 2.10   Alternative realizations of Z.

the fewest gates or the simplest gates. It is not possible to minimize all three metrics at the same time.

The traditional minimization techniques you will study in this chapter emphasize reducing delay at the expense of adding more gates. Newer methods, covered in the next chapter, allow a trade-off between increased circuit delay and reduced gate count.

Example   To illustrate the trade-offs just discussed, consider the following three-variable Boolean function:

$$Z = \overline{A}\overline{B}C + \overline{A}BC + A\overline{B}C + AB\overline{C}$$

The truth table for this function is shown in Figure 2.10(a). You would probably implement the function directly from the preceding equation,

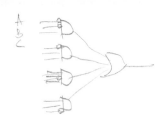

using three NOT gates, four 3-input AND gates, and a single 4-input OR gate. This is called a *two-level implementation*, with variables and their complements at the zeroth level, AND gates at the first level, and an OR gate at the second level.

You could implement the same truth table with fewer gates. An alternative two-level implementation is given in Figure 2.10(b) as function Z_1:

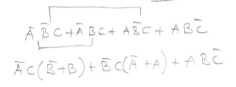

$$Z_1 = AB\overline{C} + \overline{A}C + \overline{B}C$$

It uses the same number of inverters and OR gates but only three AND gates. The original function has 12 literals. This alternative has only seven, thus reducing the wiring complexity.

The implementation of function Z_2 is called *multilevel*:

$$Z_2 = T\overline{C} + \overline{T}C$$
$$T = AB$$

The longest path from an input to an output passes through four gates. This contrasts with three gate delays in the two-level functions. In terms of gate counts, the circuit uses two rather than three inverters and only two-input AND and OR gates. Here you can see a trade-off between gate count and performance: Z_2 uses simpler gates, but it is not as fast as Z_1.

Z_3 shows a third realization that uses an XOR gate:

$$Z_3 = (AB) \oplus C$$

XOR is sometimes called a *complex gate*, because you normally implement it by combining several NAND or NOR gates (see Exercise 2.12). Although this implementation has the lowest gate count, it is also likely to have the worst signal delay. An XOR gate tends to be slow compared with the implementations for Z based on simple AND and OR gates.

Figure 2.11 shows the timing waveforms for the three circuit alternatives, assuming (somewhat unrealistically) a single time unit delay per gate. All have equivalent behavior, although they exhibit slightly different propagation delays. All three circuits show a glitch on the transition $ABC = 1\ 0\ 1$ to $ABC = 1\ 1\ 0$.

2.2 Gate Logic

You now know that there are many gate-level implementations with the same truth table behavior. In this section, you will learn the methods for deriving a reduced gate-level implementation of a Boolean function in two-level form. This usually yields circuits with minimum delay, although gate counts are typically not minimized.

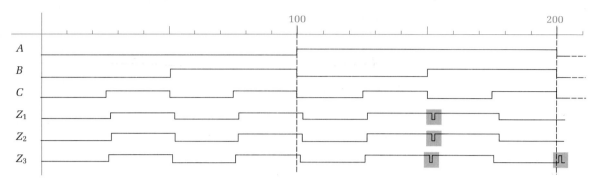

Figure 2.11   Waveform behavior of three implementations of the truth table of Figure 2.10(a).

2.2.1   Laws and Theorems of Boolean Algebra

Boolean algebra provides the foundation for all of the simplification techniques we shall discuss. Based on the Boolean laws of Section 2.1, we can prove additional theorems that can be used as tools to simplify Boolean expressions. For example, if E_1 and E_2 are two expressions for the same Boolean function, we say that E_2 is simpler than E_1 if it contains fewer literals. This usually (but not always) means that the simpler expression will also contain fewer Boolean operations.

Duality   Before we provide a tabulation of useful laws and theorems, it is important to describe the concept of *duality*. Every Boolean expression has a dual. It is derived from the original by replacing AND operations by OR operations and vice versa, and replacing constant logic 0's by logic 1's and vice versa, while leaving the literals unchanged. It is a fundamental theorem of Boolean algebra, which we do not prove here, that any statement that is true about a Boolean expression is also true for its dual. Once we discover a useful theorem for simplifying a Boolean expression, we obtain its dual as a bonus. For example, the *dual* of the Boolean theorem $X + 0 = X$, written $(X + 0)^D$, is the theorem $X \bullet 1 = X$.

The switch diagrams of Figures 2.2 and 2.3 illustrate the physical basis of the duality between AND and OR operations. The series path of normally open switches in the AND is replaced by parallel paths in the OR. A similar exchange occurs for the paths of normally closed switches. NAND and NOR exhibit the same kind of dual relationships.

Useful Laws and Theorems   The following is a list of frequently used laws and theorems of Boolean algebra. Some are generalized from Section 2.1. The second column shows the duals of the expression in the first column.

Dual form.

Operations with 0 and 1:

1. $X + 0 = X$ **1D.** $X \bullet 1 = X$

2. $X + 1 = 1$ **2D.** $X \bullet 0 = 0$

Idempotent theorem:

3. $X + X = X$ **3D.** $X \bullet X = X$

Involution theorem:

4. $(X')' = X$

Theorem of complementarity:

5. $X + X' = 1$ **5D.** $X \bullet X' = 0$

Commutative law:

6. $X + Y = Y + X$ **6D.** $X \bullet Y = Y \bullet X$

Associative law:

7. $(X + Y) + Z = X + (Y + Z)$ **7D.** $(X \bullet Y) \bullet Z = X \bullet (Y \bullet Z)$
$= X + Y + Z$ $= X \bullet Y \bullet Z$

Distributive law:

8. $X \bullet (Y + Z) = X \bullet Y + X \bullet Z$ **8D.** $X + (Y \bullet Z) = (X + Y) \bullet (X + Z)$

Simplification theorems:

9. $X \bullet Y + X \bullet Y' = X$ **9D.** $(X + Y) \bullet (X + Y') = X$

10. $X + X \bullet Y = X$ **10D.** $X \bullet (X + Y) = X$

11. $(X + Y') \bullet Y = X \bullet Y$ **11D.** $(X \bullet Y') + Y = X + Y$

DeMorgan's theorem:

12. $(X + Y + Z + ...)' = X' \bullet Y' \bullet Z' \bullet ...$ **12D.** $(X \bullet Y \bullet Z \bullet ...)' = X' + Y' + Z' + ...$

13. $\{f(X_1, X_2, ..., X_n, 0, 1, +, \bullet)\}'$
$= \{f(X_1', X_2', ..., X_n', 1, 0, \bullet, +)\}$

Duality:

14. $(X + Y + Z + ...)^D = X \bullet Y \bullet Z \bullet ...$ **14D.** $(X \bullet Y \bullet Z \bullet ...)^D = X + Y + Z + ...$

15. $\{f(X_1, X_2, ..., X_n, 0, 1, +, \bullet)\}^D$
$= f(X_1, X_2, ..., X_n, 1, 0, \bullet, +)$

Theorem for multiplying and factoring:

16. $(X + Y) \bullet (X' + Z)$ **16D.** $X \bullet Y + X' \bullet Z = (X + Z) \bullet (X' + Y)$
$= X \bullet Z + X' \bullet Y$

Consensus theorem:

17. $X \bullet Y + Y \bullet Z + X' \bullet Z = X \bullet Y + X' \bullet Z$ 17D. $(X + Y) \bullet (Y + Z) \bullet (X' + Z)$
$$= (X + Y) \bullet (X' + Z)$$

The notation $f(X_1, X_2, ..., X_n, 0, 1, +, \bullet)$ used in theorems 13 and 15 represents an expression in terms of the variables X_1, X_2, ..., X_n, the constants 0, 1, and the Boolean operations + and $\bullet$. Theorem 13 states succinctly that, in forming the complement of an expression, the variables are replaced by their complements—that is, 0 is replaced by 1 and 1 by 0, and + is replaced by $\bullet$ and $\bullet$ by +.

Since any of the listed theorems can be derived from the original laws shown in Section 2.1, there is no reason to memorize all of them. The first eight theorems are the most heavily used in simplifying Boolean expressions.

Verifying the Boolean Theorems   Each of the theorems can be derived from the axioms of Boolean algebra. We can prove the first simplification theorem, sometimes called the *uniting theorem*, as follows:

$X \bullet Y + X \bullet Y' = X?$

$X(Y + Y')$	$= X$	distributive law (8)
$X(1)$	$= X$	complementarity theorem (5)
X	$= X \checkmark$	identity (1D)

As another example, let's look at the second simplification theorem:

$X + X \bullet Y = X?$

$X \bullet 1 + X \bullet Y$	$= X$	identity (1D)
$X(1 + Y)$	$= X$	distributive law (8)
$X(1)$	$= X$	identity (2)
X	$= X \checkmark$	identity (1)

DeMorgan's Theorem   DeMorgan's theorem gives a procedure for complementing a complex function. The complemented expression is formed from the original by replacing all literals by their complements; all 1's become 0's and vice versa, and ANDs become ORs and vice versa. This theorem indicates an interesting relationship between NOR, OR, NAND, and AND:

$$\overline{X + Y} = \overline{X} \bullet \overline{Y} \qquad \overline{X \bullet Y} = \overline{X} + \overline{Y}$$

X	Y	$\overline{X}$	$\overline{Y}$	$\overline{X+Y}$	$\overline{X} \bullet \overline{Y}$
0	0	1	1	1	1
0	1	1	0	0	0
1	0	0	1	0	0
1	1	0	0	0	0

X	Y	$\overline{X}$	$\overline{Y}$	$\overline{X \bullet Y}$	$\overline{X}+\overline{Y}$
0	0	1	1	1	1
0	1	1	0	1	1
1	0	0	1	1	1
1	1	0	0	0	0

Figure 2.12   DeMorgan's law.

Note that $\overline{X+Y} \neq \overline{X}+\overline{Y}$ and $\overline{X \bullet Y} \neq \overline{X} \bullet \overline{Y}$. In other words, NOR is the same as AND with complemented inputs while NAND is equivalent to OR with complemented inputs! This is easily seen to be true from the truth tables of Figure 2.12.

Let's use DeMorgan's theorem to find the complement of the following expression:

$$Z = \overline{A}\overline{B}C + \overline{A}BC + A\overline{B}C + AB\overline{C}$$

Step by step, the complement is formed as follows:

$$\overline{Z} = \overline{\overline{A}\overline{B}C + \overline{A}BC + A\overline{B}C + AB\overline{C}}$$

$$= \overline{\overline{A}\overline{B}C} \bullet \overline{\overline{A}BC} \bullet \overline{A\overline{B}C} \bullet \overline{AB\overline{C}}$$

$$= (A + B + \overline{C}) \, (A + \overline{B} + \overline{C}) \, (\overline{A} + B + \overline{C}) \, (\overline{A} + \overline{B} + C)$$

Note that duality and DeMorgan's law are *not* the same thing. The procedure for producing the dual is similar, but the literals are not complemented during the process. Thus, the dual of NOR is NAND (and vice versa); the dual of OR is AND (and vice versa). Remember, any theorem that is true for an expression is also true for its dual.

Example   The Full Adder Carry-Out   We can use the laws and theorems just introduced to verify the simplified expression for the full adder's carry-out function. The original expression, derived from the truth table, is

$$Cout = \overline{A}B\,Cin + A\overline{B}\,Cin + AB\,\overline{Cin} + AB\,Cin$$

The first step uses theorem 3, the idempotent theorem, to introduce a copy of the term $AB\,Cin$. Then we use the commutative law to rearrange the terms:

$$= \overline{A}B\,Cin + A\overline{B}\,Cin + AB\,\overline{Cin} + AB\,Cin + AB\,Cin$$

$$= \overline{A}B\,Cin + AB\,Cin + A\overline{B}\,Cin + AB\,\overline{Cin} + AB\,Cin$$

We next use the distributive law to factor out the common literals from the first two terms:

$$= (\overline{A} + A)\,B\,Cin + A\overline{B}\,Cin + AB\,\overline{Cin} + AB\,Cin$$

We apply the complementarity law:

$$= (1)\,B\,Cin + A\overline{B}\,Cin + AB\,\overline{Cin} + AB\,Cin$$

and the identity law:

$$= B\,Cin + A\overline{B}\,Cin + AB\,\overline{Cin} + AB\,Cin$$

We can repeat the process for the second and third terms. The steps are: (1) idempotent theorem to introduce a redundant term, (2) commutative law to rearrange terms, (3) distributive law to factor out common literals, (4) complementarity theorem to replace $(X+\overline{X})$ with 1, and (5) identity law to replace $1 \bullet X$ by X:

$$= B\,Cin + A\overline{B}\,Cin + AB\,\overline{Cin} + AB\,Cin + AB\,Cin$$

$$= B\,Cin + A\overline{B}\,Cin + AB\,Cin + AB\,\overline{Cin} + AB\,Cin$$

$$= B\,Cin + A\,(\overline{B}+B)\,Cin + AB\,\overline{Cin} + AB\,Cin$$

$$= B\,Cin + A\,(1)\,Cin + AB\,\overline{Cin} + AB\,Cin$$

The final simplification, using the distributive theorem, complementarity theorem, and identity law, proceeds similarly:

$$= B\,Cin + A\,Cin + AB\,(\overline{Cin} + Cin)$$

$$= B\,Cin + A\,Cin + AB\,(1)$$

$$= B\,Cin + A\,Cin + AB$$

This is exactly the reduced form of the expression we used in Chapter 1. Although it leads to a simpler expression, applying the rules of Boolean algebra in this fashion does not guarantee you will obtain the simplest expression. A more systematic approach will be introduced in Section 2.3.

Boolean Algebra and Switches   We have already observed the close correlation between Boolean functions and switching circuits. Each of the laws and theorems we have discussed has a switching circuit analog. These provide a good way to remember the various theorems.

Some of the switch circuit equivalents are shown in Figure 2.13. To simplify the diagrams, we show only the paths from true to the output. The idempotent theorems are depicted in Figure 2.13(a). Obviously, two identically controlled switches, either in series or in parallel, behave as a single switch, since both are open or closed at the same time.

Figure 2.13(b) shows some of the identity laws. An open connection represents logic 0; a shorted connection represents logic 1. An open connection in parallel with a normally open switch has no effect on the switching function and can be eliminated. A shorted connection in parallel with a normally open switch guarantees that a connected path

$A \cdot A = A$

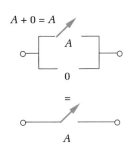

$A + A = A$

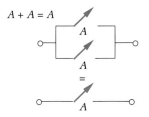

(a) Switch equivalent of idempotent laws

$A + 0 = A$

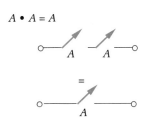

$A + 1 = 1$

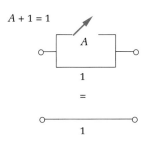

(b) Switch equivalent of identity laws

$A + \overline{A} = 1$

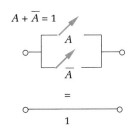

$A \cdot \overline{A} = 0$

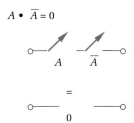

(c) Switch equivalent of complementarity laws

$X Y + X \overline{Y} = X$

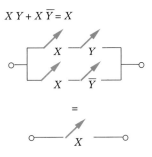

$X + X Y = X$

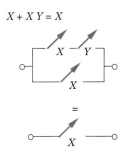

(d) Switch equivalent of simplification theorems

Figure 2.13 Switch equivalents of some laws and theorems of Boolean algebra.

always exists to the output. This leaves the function completely independent of the normally open switch.

The complementarity theorems are shown in Figure 2.13(c). Two switches in parallel, controlled by complementary signals, ensure that one is always open while the other is closed, thus guaranteeing a path to the output. Two switches in series, controlled by complementary signals, guarantee that the connection path is always broken by one of them. This is equivalent to an open connection.

Figure 2.13(d) shows the switch equivalents of some simplification theorems. In the first network, the existence of a connection between input and output depends only on X, since Y and $\overline{Y}$ are in parallel and one of the switches will be closed while the other is open. If X is true, the connection is made; if X is false, the connection is broken. In the second network, Y's effect is made redundant by the two X switches in parallel.

2.2.2   Two-Level Logic Canonical Forms

To compare Boolean functions when expressed in algebraic terms, it is useful to have a standard form with which to represent the function. This standard term is called a *canonical form*, and it is a unique algebraic signature of the function. You will frequently encounter two alternative forms: *sum of products* and *product of sums*. We introduce these next.

Sum of Products You have already met the *sum of products* form in Section 1.3.3. It is also sometimes known as a *disjunctive normal form* or *minterm expansion*. A sum of products expression is formed as follows. Each row of the truth table in which the function takes on the value 1 contributes an ANDed term, using the asserted variable if there is a 1 in its column for that row or its complement if there is a 0. These are called *minterms*. Technically, a minterm is defined as an ANDed product of literals in which each variable appears exactly once in either true or complemented form, but not both. The minterms are then ORed to form the expression for the function. The minterm expansion is unique because it is deterministically derived from the truth table.

Figure 2.14 shows a truth table for a function and its complement. The minterm expansions for F and $\overline{F}$ are

A	B	C	F	$\overline{F}$
0	0	0	0	1
0	0	1	0	1
0	1	0	0	1
0	1	1	1	0
1	0	0	1	0
1	0	1	1	0
1	1	0	1	0
1	1	1	1	0

Figure 2.14 Sample truth table.

$$F = \overline{A}BC + A\overline{B}\,\overline{C} + A\overline{B}C + AB\overline{C} + ABC$$

$$\overline{F} = \overline{A}\,\overline{B}\,\overline{C} + \overline{A}\,\overline{B}C + \overline{A}B\overline{C}$$

We can write such expressions in a shorthand notation using the binary number system to encode the minterms. Figure 2.15 shows the relationship between the truth table row and the numbering of the minterm. Note that the ordering of the Boolean variables is critical in deriving the minterm

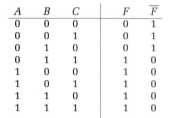

A	B	C	Minterms
0	0	0	$\overline{A}\,\overline{B}\,\overline{C} = m_0$
0	0	1	$\overline{A}\,\overline{B}\,C = m_1$
0	1	0	$\overline{A}\,B\,\overline{C} = m_2$
0	1	1	$\overline{A}\,B\,C = m_3$
1	0	0	$A\,\overline{B}\,\overline{C} = m_4$
1	0	1	$A\,\overline{B}\,C = m_5$
1	1	0	$A\,B\,\overline{C} = m_6$
1	1	1	$A\,B\,C = m_7$

Figure 2.15 Shorthand notation for minterms of three variables.

index. In this case, A determines the most significant bit and C is the least significant bit. You can write the shorthand expression for F and $\overline{F}$ as

$$F(A,B,C) = \Sigma\, m(3,4,5,6,7) = m_3 + m_4 + m_5 + m_6 + m_7$$

$$\overline{F}(A,B,C) = \Sigma\, m(0,1,2) = m_0 + m_1 + m_2$$

where m_i represents the ith minterm. The indices generalize for functions of more variables. For example, if F is defined over the variables A, B, C, then m_3 (011_2) is the minterm $\overline{A}BC$. But if F is defined over A, B, C, D, then m_3 (0011_2) is $\overline{A}\,\overline{B}CD$.

The minterm expansion is not guaranteed to be the simplest form of the function, in terms of the fewest literals or terms, nor is it likely to be. You can further reduce the expression for F by applying Boolean algebra:

$$
\begin{aligned}
F(A, B, C) &= A\overline{B}(C + \overline{C}) + \overline{A}BC + AB(\overline{C} + C) \\
&= A\overline{B} + \overline{A}BC + AB \\
&= A\overline{B} + AB + \overline{A}BC \\
&= A(\overline{B} + B) + \overline{A}BC \\
&= A(1) + \overline{A}BC \\
&= A + \overline{A}BC \\
&= A + BC
\end{aligned}
$$

The one step you may find tricky is the last one, which applies rule 11D, $(X \bullet \overline{Y}) + Y = X + Y$, substituting A for Y and BC for X.

A and BC are called *product terms*: ANDed strings of literals containing a subset of the possible Boolean variables or their complements. For F defined over the variables A, B, and C, $\overline{A}BC$ is a minterm and a product term, but BC is only a product term.

The minimized gate-level implementation of F is shown in Figure 2.16. Each product term is realized by its own AND gate. The product term A is the degenerate case of a single literal. No AND gate is needed to form this term. The product terms' implementations are then input to a second-level OR gate. The sum of products form leads directly to a two-level realization.

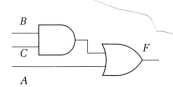

Figure 2.16 Two-level AND-OR gate-level implementation.

We can repeat the simplification process for $\overline{F}$, but DeMorgan's theorem gives us a good starting point for applying Boolean simplification:

$$\overline{F} = \overline{(A + BC)} = \overline{A}(\overline{B} + \overline{C}) = \overline{A}\,\overline{B} + \overline{A}\,\overline{C}$$

Although this procedure is not guaranteed to obtain the simplest form of the complement, it does so in this case.

Product of Sums   The involution theorem states that the complement of a Boolean expression's complement is the expression itself. By using DeMorgan's theorem twice, we can derive a second canonical form for Boolean equations. This form is called the *product of sums* and sometimes the *conjunctive normal form* or *maxterm expansion*.

The procedure for deriving a product of sums expression from a truth table is the logical dual of the sum of products case. First, find the rows of the truth table where the function is 0. A *maxterm* is defined as an ORed sum of literals in which each variable appears exactly once in either true or complemented form, but not both. We form a maxterm by ORing the uncomplemented variable if there is a 0 in its column for that row, or the complemented variable if there is a 1 there. This is exactly opposite to the way we formed minterms. There is one maxterm for each 0 row of the truth table; these are ANDed together at the second level.

The products of sums for the functions F and $\overline{F}$ of Figure 2.14 are

A	B	C	Maxterms
0	0	0	$A + B + C = M_0$
0	0	1	$A + B + \overline{C} = M_1$
0	1	0	$A + \overline{B} + C = M_2$
0	1	1	$A + \overline{B} + \overline{C} = M_3$
1	0	0	$\overline{A} + B + C = M_4$
1	0	1	$\overline{A} + B + \overline{C} = M_5$
1	1	0	$\overline{A} + \overline{B} + C = M_6$
1	1	1	$\overline{A} + \overline{B} + \overline{C} = M_7$

Figure 2.17   Maxterm shorthand for a function of three variables.

$$F = (A + \overline{B} + C)\,(A + B + \overline{C})\,(A + \overline{B} + C)$$

$$\overline{F} = (A + \overline{B} + \overline{C})\,(\overline{A} + B + C)\,(\overline{A} + B + \overline{C})\,(\overline{A} + \overline{B} + C)\,(\overline{A} + \overline{B} + \overline{C})$$

Once again, we often use a shorthand notation. Figure 2.17 shows the relationship between maxterms and their shorthand form. We can write F and $\overline{F}$ as

$$F\,(A, B, C) = \Pi M\,(0,1,2) = M_0 \bullet M_1 \bullet M_2$$

$$\overline{F}\,(A, B, C) = \Pi M\,(3,4,5,6,7) = M_3 \bullet M_4 \bullet M_5 \bullet M_6 \bullet M_7$$

where M_i is the ith maxterm.

Interestingly, the maxterm expansion of F could have been formed directly by applying DeMorgan's theorem to the minterm expansion of $\overline{F}$:

$$\overline{F} = \overline{A}\overline{B}\overline{C} + \overline{A}\overline{B}C + \overline{A}B\overline{C}$$

$$\overline{\overline{F}} = \overline{(\overline{A}\overline{B}\overline{C} + \overline{A}\overline{B}C + \overline{A}B\overline{C})}$$

$$F = (A + B + C)\,(A + B + \overline{C})\,(A + \overline{B} + C)$$

Of course, the same is true for deriving the minterm form of F from the maxterm form of $\overline{F}$:

$$\overline{F} = (A + \overline{B} + \overline{C})\,(\overline{A} + B + C)\,(\overline{A} + B + \overline{C})\,(\overline{A} + \overline{B} + C)\,(\overline{A} + \overline{B} + \overline{C})$$

$$\overline{\overline{F}} = \overline{(A + \overline{B} + \overline{C})\,(\overline{A} + B + C)\,(\overline{A} + B + \overline{C})\,(\overline{A} + \overline{B} + C)\,(\overline{A} + \overline{B} + \overline{C})}$$

$$F = \overline{A}BC + A\overline{B}C + A\overline{B}\,\overline{C} + AB\overline{C} + ABC$$

It is easy to translate a product of sums expression into a gate-level realization. The zeroth level forms the complements of the variables if they are needed to realize the function. The first level creates the individual maxterms as outputs of OR gates. The second level is an AND gate that combines the maxterms.

We can find a minimized product of sums form by starting with the minimized sum of products expression of $\overline{F}$. To complement this expression, we use DeMorgan's theorem:

$$\overline{F} = \overline{A}\overline{B} + \overline{A}\overline{C}$$
$$\overline{\overline{F}} = \overline{\overline{A}\overline{B} + \overline{A}\overline{C}}$$
$$F = (A + B)(A + C)$$

Figure 2.18 shows the four different gate-level implementations for F discussed so far: canonical sum of products (F_1), minimized sum of products (F_2), canonical product of sums (F_3), and minimized product of sums (F_4). In terms of gate counts, the product of sums canonical form is more economical than the sum of products canonical form. But the minimized sum of products form uses fewer gates than the minimized product of sums form. Depending on the function, one or the other of these forms will be better for implementing the function.

To demonstrate that the implementations are equivalent, Figure 2.19 shows the timing waveforms for the circuits' responses to the same inputs. Except for short-duration glitches in the waveforms, their shapes are identical.

Conversion Between Canonical Forms   We can place any Boolean function in one of the two canonical forms, sum of products or product of sums. It is easy to map an expression in one canonical form into the other. The procedure, using the shorthand notation we already introduced, is summarized here:

1.   To convert from the minterm expansion to the maxterm expansion, you rewrite the minterm shorthand notation to maxterm shorthand, replacing the term numbers with those not used in the minterm list. This is equivalent to applying DeMorgan's theorem to the complement of the function in minterm form.

    Example: $F(A,B,C) = \Sigma\, m(3,4,5,6,7) = \Pi\, M(0,1,2)$

2.   To convert from the maxterm expansion to the minterm expansion, you rewrite the maxterm shorthand notation to minterm shorthand, replacing term numbers with those not used in the maxterm list. This is equivalent to applying DeMorgan's theorem to the complement of the function in maxterm form.

    Example: $F(A,B,C) = \Pi\, M(0,1,2) = \Sigma\, m(3,4,5,6,7)$

3.   To obtain the minterm expansion of the complement, given the minterm expansion of the function, you simply list the minterms not in F. The

same procedure works for obtaining the maxterm complement of a function expressed in maxterm form.

Example:

$$F(A,B,C) = \Sigma\, m(3,4,5,6,7) \quad\Longleftrightarrow\quad F(A,B,C) = \Pi\, M(0,1,2)$$
$$\overline{F}(A,B,C) = \Sigma\, m(0,1,2) \quad\Longleftrightarrow\quad \overline{F}(A,B,C) = \Pi\, M(3,4,5,6,7)$$

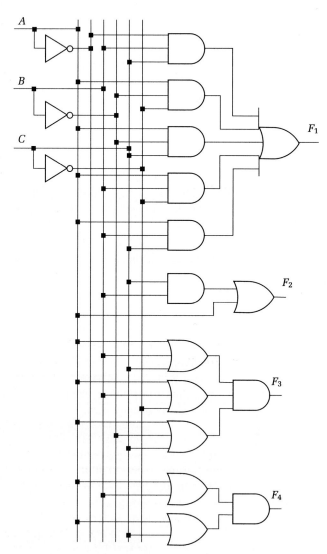

Figure 2.18   Four implementations of *F*.

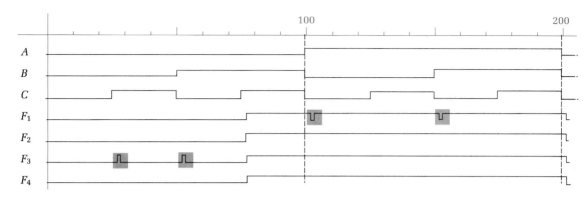

Figure 2.19 Timing waveforms for the four implementations of *F*.

4. To obtain the maxterm expansion of the complement, given the minterm expansion of the function, you simply use the same maxterm numbers as used in *F*'s minterm expansion. The same procedure applies if a minterm expansion of the complement is to be derived from the maxterm expansion of the function.

   Example:

   $$F(A,B,C) = \Sigma \, m(3,4,5,6,7) \qquad F(A,B,C) = \Pi \, M(0,1,2)$$

   $$\overline{F}(A,B,C) = \Pi \, M(3,4,5,6,7) \qquad \overline{F}(A,B,C) = \Sigma \, m(0,1,2)$$

2.2.3 Positive Versus Negative Logic

When you implement logic gates as electronic devices, they operate on voltages rather than logic levels. There are always two interpretations of any truth table describing the operation of a gate, based on positive or negative logic. It is only through a choice of one of these conventions that the voltage levels can be interpreted as logic levels. The output voltages are the same; only the logical interpretation is different.

General Concept   So far, we have assumed that logic 1 is represented by a higher voltage than logic 0. This convention is often called *active high* or *positive logic*. When you want a particular signal to be asserted (for example, "open the garage door"), you place a positive voltage on the signal and it is interpreted as a logic 1. An alternative convention is sometimes more convenient, especially when using NAND and NOR gates to implement logic that initiates an event (*enable logic*) or inhibits it from taking place (*disable logic*). It is called *active low* or *negative logic*. In this case, a low voltage is used to denote that a signal is asserted, while the high voltage is used to represent an unasserted signal.

Consider Figure 2.20, which shows a truth table expressed in terms of two relative voltages, high and low. Under the interpretation of positive logic, the truth table describes an AND function. But if we interpret the voltage levels according to negative logic, we obtain an OR function instead. This follows because an OR function and an AND function are duals, derived by replacing 0's in one truth table with 1's in the other, and vice versa.

Given a function in positive logic, we can find its equivalent negative logic function simply by applying duality. For example, the dual of the NOR function, $\overline{A + B} = \overline{A} \bullet \overline{B}$, is $\overline{A + B} = \overline{A} \bullet \overline{B}$. Of course, this is the NAND. We can verify this with the truth tables of Figure 2.21.

Example Because of the very real possibilities for confusion, designers prefer to avoid mixing positive and negative logic in their designs. However, this is not always possible. For example, a positive logic output, asserted high, might connect to a negative logic input, asserted low. To illustrate this point, let's take an example from the traffic light controller from Chapter 1.

Figure 2.20 Alternative truth table interpretation in positive and negative logic.

Voltage Truth Table			Positive Logic			Negative Logic		
A	B	F	A	B	F	A	B	F
low	low	low	0	0	0	1	1	1
low	high	low	0	1	0	1	0	1
high	low	low	1	0	0	0	1	1
high	high	high	1	1	1	0	0	0

Figure 2.21 Alternative truth table interpretation for NAND and NOR in positive and negative logic.

Voltage Truth Table			Positive Logic			Negative Logic		
A	B	F	A	B	F	A	B	F
low	low	high	0	0	1	1	1	0
low	high	low	0	1	0	1	0	1
high	low	low	1	0	0	0	1	1
high	high	low	1	1	0	0	0	1

Your task is to define three signals, *Change_Lights*, *Change_Request*, and *Timer_Expired*, such that *Change_Lights* is asserted whenever *Change_Request* and *Timer_Expired* are asserted. In positive logic/active high notation, the latter two signals should be ANDed to implement *Change_Lights*. This is shown in Figure 2.22(a).

If you use negative logic, and the signals are to be asserted active low, the AND gate is replaced by its dual, an OR gate. *Change_Lights* is asserted low only when both *Change_Request* and *Timer_Expired* are low. In all other cases, *Change_Lights* is unasserted high. This is shown in Figure 2.22(b).

It can be confusing to keep track of whether positive or negative logic conventions are being used in a circuit. As an alternative, we adopt a notation that assumes that all gates are positive logic, but we explicitly keep track of whether signals are asserted high or asserted low. A "bubble" is placed on the input or output that is to be asserted low.

To make it easier to follow signal polarity within a schematic, active low input bubbles should be matched with active low output bubbles. Continuing with the example, Figure 2.22(c) shows a case with mismatched

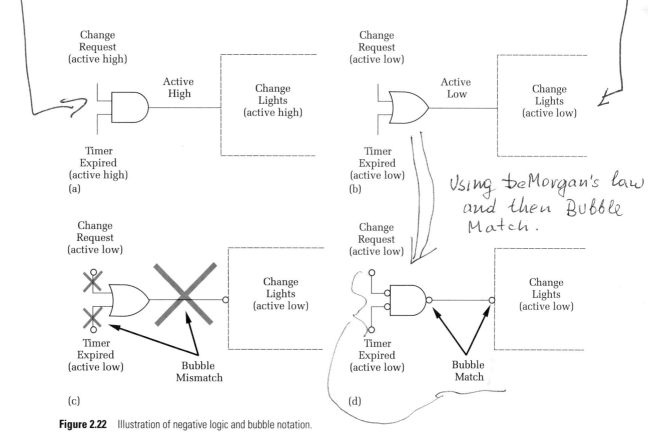

Using DeMorgan's law and then Bubble Match.

Figure 2.22 Illustration of negative logic and bubble notation.

bubbles. Starting with Figure 2.22(d), we add bubbles to indicate the active low polarity of the three signals. You can see that the inputs and the output of the OR gate do not match the polarity of signals to which they are attached.

How do we make the polarities match? By DeMorgan's theorem, the following is true:

$$A + B = \overline{\overline{A + B}} = \overline{\overline{A} \cdot \overline{B}}$$

An OR gate is equivalent to an AND gate with inverted inputs and outputs. By replacing the OR gate in Figure 2.22(c) with an AND gate of this kind, we do not change the sense of the logic but neatly match up the signal polarities. This is shown in Figure 2.22(d). The figure clearly indicates that *Change_Request* and *Timer_Expired* must both be asserted low to cause the active low *Change_Lights* signal to become asserted.

2.2.4   Incompletely Specified Functions

We have assumed that we must define an n-input function on all of its 2^n possible input combinations. This is not always the case. We study the case of incompletely specified functions in this subsection.

Examples   Incompletely Specified Functions   Let's consider a logic function that takes as input a binary-coded decimal (BCD) digit. *BCD digits* are decimal digits, in the range 0 through 9, that are represented by four-bit binary numbers, using the combinations 0000_2 (0) through 1001_2 (9). The other combinations, 1010_2 (10) through 1111_2 (15), should never be encountered. It is possible to simplify the Boolean expressions for the function if we assume that we *do not care* about its behavior in these "out of range" cases.

Figure 2.23 shows the truth table for a BCD increment by 1 circuit. Each BCD number is represented by four Boolean variables, A B C D. The output of the incrementer is represented by four 4-variable Boolean functions, W X Y Z.

The output functions have the value "X" for each of the input combinations we should never encounter. When used in a truth table, the value X is often called a *don't care*. Do not confuse this with the value X reported by many logic simulators, where it represents an undefined value or a *don't know*. Any actual implementation of the circuit will generate some output for the don't-care cases. When used in a truth table, an X simply means that we have a choice of assigning a 0 or 1 to the truth table entry. We should choose the value that will lead to the simplest implementation.

To see that don't cares eventually are replaced by some logic value, let's consider the BCD incrementer truth table. The function Z looks as

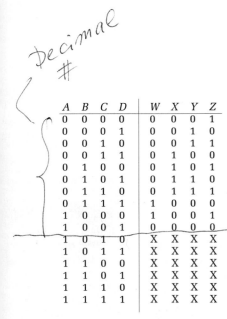

Decimal #

A	B	C	D	W	X	Y	Z
0	0	0	0	0	0	0	1
0	0	0	1	0	0	1	0
0	0	1	0	0	0	1	1
0	0	1	1	0	1	0	0
0	1	0	0	0	1	0	1
0	1	0	1	0	1	1	0
0	1	1	0	0	1	1	1
0	1	1	1	1	0	0	0
1	0	0	0	1	0	0	1
1	0	0	1	0	0	0	0
1	0	1	0	X	X	X	X
1	0	1	1	X	X	X	X
1	1	0	0	X	X	X	X
1	1	0	1	X	X	X	X
1	1	1	0	X	X	X	X
1	1	1	1	X	X	X	X

Figure 2.23   Truth table for BCD increment by 1.

if it could be realized quite simply as the function $\overline{D}$. If we choose to implement Z in this way, the X's will be replaced by real logic values. Since the inputs 1010_2 through 1111_2 will never be encountered by the operational circuit, it shouldn't matter which values we assign to those truth table rows. We choose an assignment that makes the implementation as simple as possible.

Don't Cares and the Terminology of Canonical Forms   In terms of the standard Σ and Π notations, minterms or maxterms assigned a don't care are written as d_i or D_i, respectively. Thus the canonical form for Z is written as

$$Z = m_0 + m_2 + m_4 + m_6 + m_8 + d_{10} + d_{11} + d_{12} + d_{13} + d_{14} + d_{15}$$

$$Z = M_1 \bullet M_3 \bullet M_5 \bullet M_7 \bullet M_9 \bullet D_{10} \bullet D_{11} \bullet D_{12} \bullet D_{13} \bullet D_{14} \bullet D_{15}$$

Proper specification of don't cares is critical for the successful operation of many computer-aided design tools that perform minimization of Boolean expressions. The terminology they use is slightly different from that commonly found in the logic design literature, but it is really nothing more than a reformulation of the basic truth table specification.

Let's introduce the concepts by way of the truth table of Figure 2.23. This function is *multioutput* because it is represented by four output bits defined over the same inputs. It is *incompletely specified* because it contains don't cares in its outputs. For each of the function's output columns, we can define three sets: the on-set, off-set, and don't-care set. The *on-set* contains all input combinations for which the function is 1. The *off-set* and *don't-care set* are defined analogously for 0 and X, respectively. Thus the on-set for the incrementer's W output is {[0,1,1,1], [1,0,0,0]}; its off-set is {[0,0,0,0], [0,0,0,1], [0,0,1,0], [0,0,1,1], [0,1,0,0], [0,1,0,1], [0,1,1,0], [1,0,0,1]; and its don't-care set is {[1,0,1,0], [1,0,1,1], [1,1,0,0], [1,1,0,1], [1,1,1,0], [1,1,1,1]}.

2.3   Two-Level Simplification

Now you are ready to learn the practical methods for reducing a Boolean expression to its simplest form in two levels. The result is an expression with the fewest literals and thus less wires in the final gate-level implementation.

We begin by defining the essential concept of Boolean cubes. These are truth table entries that can be combined into Boolean expressions with a reduced literal count. Then we examine the K-map method, an effective paper-and-pencil approach for identifying Boolean cubes for functions with a modest number of variables. The method rearranges the truth table rows into a special tabular structure that places candidate entries for combining next to each other.

2.3.1   Motivation

We can always use the rules of Boolean algebra from Section 2.1 to simplify an expression, but this method has a few problems. For one thing, there is no algorithm you can use to determine that you've obtained a minimum solution. When do you stop looking for a simplification theorem to apply? Another problem is that you often have to make the expression more complicated before you can simplify it. In our examples, we sometimes substituted $(X + \overline{X})$ for 1 to add more terms. Then we rearranged the terms to obtain advantageous groupings that helped to simplify the expression in a later step. It is against human nature to climb out of a "local minimum" in the hope of finding a better global solution. But this is exactly what we often have to do. And finally, it is just too cumbersome (and error prone) to manipulate Boolean expressions by hand.

Given that computer-based tools have been developed for Boolean simplification, why bother to learn any hand method, especially when these break down for problems with many variables? Certainly no hand method will be effective for equations involving more than six variables. But you still need knowledge of the basic approach. Observing the symmetries in a circuit's function helps to understand its behavior and to visualize what is going on inside the circuit. As CAD tools become ever more sophisticated, you need a deeper knowledge of algorithms they apply to use the tools effectively. And don't forget that CAD tools are written by mere mortals and do not always do the correct things! You must still be able to check the output of the tool.

A	B	F
0	0	0
0	1	0
1	0	1
1	1	1

(a)

A	B	G
0	0	1
0	1	0
1	0	1
1	1	0

(b)

Figure 2.24   Two simple truth tables.

The Essence of Boolean Simplification   Let's look at what is really going on in simplification with the simple truth table of Figure 2.24(a). The function is $F = A\overline{B} + AB$. We can simplify this equation by applying one of the Boolean simplification theorems, called the *uniting* theorem: $A(\overline{B} + B) = A$.

Notice that the two truth table rows that make up the on-set of F have A asserted, while one row has $B = 0$ and the other has $B = 1$. For a subset of the on-set (in this case, the whole on-set), *A's value stays the same while B's value changes*. This allows us to factor out B using the uniting theorem.

Now examine Figure 2.24(b). The function is $G = \overline{A}\overline{B} + A\overline{B}$. Applying the uniting theorem again, we obtain $(\overline{A} + A)\overline{B} = \overline{B}$. Once again, the on-set contains two rows in which B's value does not change (it is equal to 0) and A's does change. Thus we can factor out A, leaving $\overline{B}$.

The essence of simplification is repeatedly to find two-element subsets of the on-set in which only one variable changes its value while the other variables do not. You can eliminate the single varying variable from the term by applying the uniting theorem.

Wouldn't it be nice if there was a way to arrange the truth table rows so that the entries to which this technique could be applied are obvious? We shall present just such a representation, the Boolean cube, next.

2.3.2   Boolean Cubes

A *cube* is usually defined as a solid object bounded by six equal squares. This concept can be generalized to other than three dimensions. A two-dimensional cube is a square, a one-dimensional cube is a line, and a zero-dimensional cube is a point.

We can represent the truth table of an *n*-input Boolean function as a "cube" in an *n*-dimensional Boolean space. There is one axis for each variable, over which it can take on exactly two values: 0 or 1.

Figure 2.25 shows the form of Boolean 1-, 2-, 3-, and 4-cubes. Each node in the figure is labeled with its coordinates in the *n*-dimensional space. The axes are listed in alphabetical order, from highest to lowest order. The structure generalizes beyond four dimensions, but it is rather hard to visualize these.

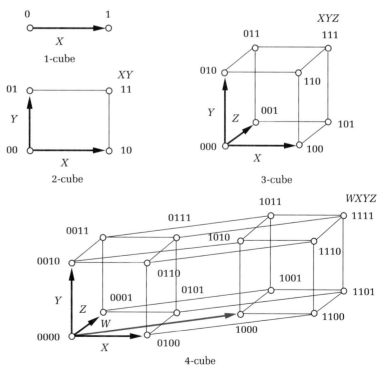

Figure 2.25   *N*-dimensional cubes.

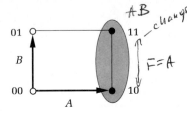

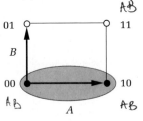

(a) Truth table of Figure
2.24(a) as a 2-cube.

(b) Truth table of Figure
2.24(b) as a 2-cube.

Figure 2.26   Examples of mapping
truth tables onto cubes.

Examples   Mapping Truth Tables onto Cubes   Now let's examine how to map a truth table onto a cube, using the simple examples of Figure 2.24. The elements of the on-set are represented by black nodes and those of the off-set by white nodes (don't cares are represented by X nodes, although we do not have any in this example).

Figure 2.26 shows the mapping. Observe that the elements of the functions' on-sets are next to each other in the truth table's Boolean cube. This tells you that the uniting theorem can be used to eliminate a variable. In the figure, we have circled elements of the on-set that are directly adjacent. We call such a circled group of nodes an *adjacency plane*. Each adjacency plane corresponds to a product term. In Figure 2.26(a), the circled nodes yield the term A; in Figure 2.26(b), the term is $\overline{B}$.

You can think about these adjacencies as distances between nodes in the Boolean cube. Two nodes are distance 1 apart if they are connected by an edge in the cube. They are distance 2 apart if they are separated by a path of two connected edges. If this is the case, the two nodes are on the same plane. Two nodes are distance 3 apart if they are separated by a path of three connected edges and no shorter path exists between the two nodes. Then the nodes are in the same three-dimensional cube.

In the on-set/adjacency plane of Figure 2.26(a), A's value stays 1 while B's varies between 0 and 1. This is an immediate clue that the uniting theorem can reduce the function to the single literal A. Similarly, in Figure 2.26(b) the adjacency plane is circled, and the nodes involved have B retaining its value while A varies. The uniting theorem reduces the expression to the term $\overline{B}$.

As an example of a three-variable function and its mapping onto a 3-cube, let's return to the full adder's carry-out function examined in Section 2.2.1. The truth table and its mapping onto a 3-cube are shown in Figure 2.27. The on-set is arranged on 3 one-dimensional adjacency planes: the edges containing the nodes 011-111, 111-101, and 110-111. In the first segment, A varies between 0 and 1 while B and Cin remain asserted and unvarying. This reduces to the term $B\ Cin$. For the second

A	B	Cin	Cout
0	0	0	0
0	0	1	0
0	1	0	0
0	1	1	1
1	0	0	0
1	0	1	1
1	1	0	1
1	1	1	1

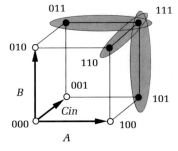

Figure 2.27   Full adder carry-out truth table in a 3-cube.

segment, B varies, yielding the term $A\, Cin$. In the final segment, Cin varies, and the resulting term is AB. The final expression becomes

$$Cout = B\, Cin + A\, Cin + AB$$

This method lets us obtain the final expression much more quickly than using Boolean algebra. Note that each adjacency plane contributes one product term to the final expression. Since each plane is an edge in a three-dimensional cube, the two 3-variable minterms in the plane are reduced to a single 2-variable product term.

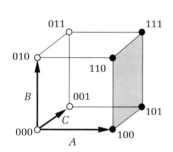

Figure 2.28 Higher dimensions of adjacency.

Adjacencies of Higher Dimensions What about adjacency planes of higher dimensionality than single edges, such as a two-dimensional plane within a 3-cube? Consider the function depicted in the 3-cube of Figure 2.28. One entire face of the cube is included in the on-set. Intuitively, we should expect this surface to reduce to the single literal A because all other variables vary between 0 and 1 within the surface.

Let's verify that this is the case. The four line segments on the surface are denoted by the nodes 110-111, 101-111, 100-101, and 100-110. Applying the uniting theorem to each segment independently yields the terms AB, AC, $A\overline{C}$, and $A\overline{B}$, respectively. We can continue to apply the uniting theorem:

$$AB + AC + A\overline{B} + A\overline{C} = A\,(B + \overline{B}) + A\,(C + \overline{C}) = A + A = A$$

In the 3-cube, if the on-set is a two-dimensional plane, it contributes a single 1-variable product term to the expression for the function.

For the 3-cube, the relationship between the dimensionality of the adjacency plane and the term it represents is the following:

- A zero-dimensional adjacency plane, a single node, yields a three-literal product term. For example, $101 = A\overline{B}C$. This is the same as a minterm.

- A one-dimensional plane, an edge, yields a two-literal product term. For example, $100\text{-}101 = A\overline{B}$.

- A two-dimensional plane yields a one-literal product term. For example, $100\text{-}101\text{-}111\text{-}110 = A$.

- A three-dimensional plane, the whole cube, yields a term with no literals in it; that is, it reduces to the constant logic 1.

This generalizes to cubes of higher dimensions. An m-dimensional adjacency plane within an n-dimensional cube will reduce to a term with $n - m$ literals.

The fewer planes needed to include all of the 1's in the truth table, the fewer the terms in the function's final expression. Planes of higher dimensionality generate terms with fewer literals in them. Thus, computer-aided design algorithms for minimization attempt to find the smallest number of the highest-dimensionality adjacency planes that contain all the nodes of the function's on-set (perhaps including elements of the don't-care set as well). This process is called finding a *minimum cover* of the function.

2.3.3   K-Map Method

The cube notation makes obvious the adjacencies among truth table rows. Adjacencies provide visual clues as to where to apply the uniting theorem to elements of the on-set that are distance 1 (a line), 2 (a square), 3 (a cube), etc. apart within the n-dimensional cube that represents the function. The problem for humans is the difficulty of visualizing adjacencies in more than three dimensions. To circumvent this problem, at least for expressions up to six variables, we introduce an alternative reformulation of the truth table called the Karnaugh map or *K-map*.

General Concept   A K-map for a Boolean function specifies values of the function for every combination of the function's variables. Just like a truth table, an n-variable K-map has 2^n entries. Rather than the linear enumeration of the truth table entries, a K-map has two and sometimes three dimensions, indexed by the values of the input variables.

Figure 2.29 shows K-map templates for two-, three-, and four-variable Boolean functions. The entries are labeled with the decimal equivalent of the binary number formed by joining the column with the row indices. For example, entry 3 in the three-variable K-map is labeled by the

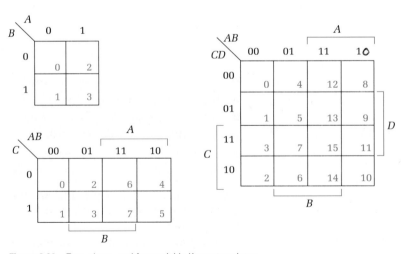

Figure 2.29   Two-, three-, and four-variable K-map templates.

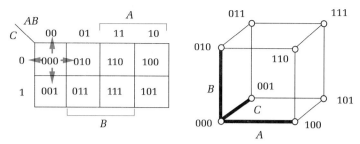

Figure 2.30 K-map adjacencies.

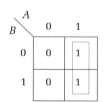

(a) K-map for truth table
of Figure 2.24(a)

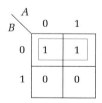

(b) K-map for truth table
of Figure 2.24(b)

Figure 2.31 Two-variable maps for
the example functions of Figure 2.24.

column $AB = 01$ and the row $C = 1$ ($ABC = 011_2 = 3$). The labels are included only for your convenience in filling in the K-map from the truth table: they correspond to the row number of the associated truth table entry.

The only surprising thing is the ordering of the indices: 00, 01, 11, 10. This is called a *Gray code*. It has the property that when advancing from one index to the next adjacent index, only a single bit changes value. This property is not true for the standard binary sequence 00, 01, 10, 11.

The structure of the K-map is chosen so that any two adjacent (horizontal or vertical, but not diagonal) elements are distance 1 apart in the equivalent cube representation (they share a common edge). This is shown in Figure 2.30 for a three-variable K-map and three-dimensional Boolean cube. Note that K-map square 0 is adjacent to squares 1, 2, and 4. The K-map actually folds back on itself. The elements in the rightmost column are adjacent to the elements in the leftmost column; the elements in the top row are adjacent to the elements in the bottom row.

Example   Two-Variable Maps Figure 2.31 shows the two-variable maps for the example functions F and G of Figure 2.24. The K-map is filled in directly from the truth table. Each truth table row corresponds to a K-map entry. The values of the variables are the indices, and the truth table's output value is placed into the K-map's square with the corresponding index.

In Figure 2.31(a), the terms of the function are $A\overline{B} + AB$, as denoted by the 1's in the $A = 1$, $B = 0$ and $A = 1$, $B = 1$ map entries. We can apply the uniting theorem to reduce this to the single literal A. The K-map shows immediately that the two entries are adjacent. The A variable value remains unchanged while the B value varies from 0 to 1. Looking at this group should tell you that the B term can be eliminated, leaving us with A.

The same analysis holds for Figure 2.31(b). The function is $\overline{A}\,\overline{B} + A\overline{B}$, and its on-set is row adjacent in the K-map. This demonstrates the

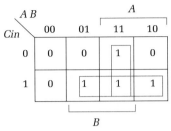

Figure 2.32   K-map for truth table of Figure 2.27.

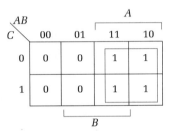

Figure 2.33   K-map for Figure 2.28.

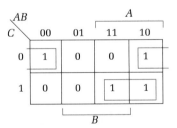

Figure 2.34   K-map for $f = \sum m(0,4,5,7)$.

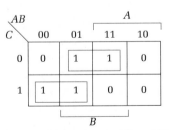

Figure 2.35   Complement of Figure 2.34.

advantage of the K-map over the truth table for recognizing adjacencies. A varies from 0 to 1 while B holds at 0 for this K-map row. We can reduce the function to the single literal $\overline{B}$.

Example   Three-Variable Maps   Figure 2.32 shows the three-variable K-map for the full adder carry-out function of Figure 2.27. You can see that three different two-element adjacencies cover the on-set (recall that adjacency is not defined for diagonal entries). The first is the column indexed by $A = 1$, $B = 1$. Since Cin varies from 0 to 1, it can be eliminated, yielding the term AB. The second is the adjacency indexed by $A = 0$, $B = 1$, $Cin = 1$ and $A = 1$, $B = 1$, $Cin = 1$. A varies while B and Cin remain unchanged, yielding the term $B\,Cin$.

Observe that the bar labeled B along the bottom of the K-map tells you that B remains unchanged within the middle two columns and $\overline{B}$ in the two outer columns. The final adjacency is indexed by $A = 1$, $B = 1$, $Cin = 1$ and $A = 1$, $B = 0$, $Cin = 1$. B varies and A and Cin remain unchanged, resulting in the term $A\,Cin$. Once again, the labeled bar at the top of the K-map reminds us that A remains unchanged within the last two columns and $\overline{A}$ in the first two columns. The final expression is $AB + B\,Cin + A\,Cin$. There is one term in the reduced expression for each circled adjacency group in the K-map.

Let's revisit the function of Figure 2.28. Its K-map is given in Figure 2.33. The four elements of the on-set are adjacent, and we can circle them all. Within this grouping, both B and C vary while A remains asserted, reducing to the single literal A.

Another case of adjacency is illustrated by Figure 2.34, which shows the K-map for the function $F(A,B,C) = m_0 + m_4 + m_5 + m_7$. Recall that the leftmost and rightmost columns of the K-map are adjacent. Thus we can combine m_0 ($\overline{A}\,\overline{B}\,\overline{C}$) and m_4 ($A\overline{B}\,\overline{C}$) to form the term $\overline{B}\,\overline{C}$. We can also combine m_5 and m_7 to form the term AC. Thus, $F = AC + \overline{B}\,\overline{C}$.

You might be tempted to circle the terms m_4 and m_5, as they are also adjacent. But you obtain the most reduced solution only by finding the smallest number of the largest possible adjacency groups that completely cover the on-set. Recall that the number of groups equals the number of product terms, and larger groupings have a smaller number of literals. The term formed from m_4 and m_5 is redundant because both entries are already covered by other terms. We will become more formal about the process of obtaining the minimum solution a bit later on in this section.

K-maps provide a good mechanism for finding the reduced form of the complement very quickly. Figure 2.35 contains the K-map for the complement of Figure 2.34. All we have done is to replace the 0's with 1's and vice versa. The complement can be read out immediately as $\overline{F} = B\overline{C} + \overline{A}C$. Contrast this method with the method using Boolean algebra:

$$F = AC + \overline{B}\,\overline{C}$$

$$\overline{F} = \overline{(AC + \overline{B}\,\overline{C})}$$

	$= \overline{(AC)}\ \overline{(\overline{B}\,\overline{C})}$	DeMorgan's theorem
	$= (\overline{A} + \overline{C})\ (B + C)$	DeMorgan's theorem
	$= \overline{A}B + \overline{A}C + B\overline{C} + C\overline{C}$	Distribution theorem
	$= \overline{A}B + \overline{A}C + B\overline{C}$	Complement and identity
	$= \overline{A}B\,(C + \overline{C}) + \overline{A}C + B\overline{C}$	Complement and identity
	$= \overline{A}BC + \overline{A}C + \overline{A}B\overline{C} + B\overline{C}$	Distribution and commutivity
	$= \overline{A}C + \overline{A}B\overline{C} + B\overline{C}$	$X + XY = X$ with $X = \overline{A}C$, $Y = B$
	$= \overline{A}C + B\overline{C}$ $\sqrt{}$	$X + XY = X$ with $X = B\overline{C}$, $Y = \overline{A}$

The K-map yields the result much more quickly!

Example   **Four-Variable Maps**   Now let's consider a four-variable function $F(A,B,C,D) = \Sigma\, m(0,2,3,5,6,7,8,10,11,14,15)$. The K-map is shown in Figure 2.36. Remember that the strategy is to cover the on-set with as few groups as possible, so we must try to find large groups of adjacency. Also, don't forget that the number of elements in an adjacency group is always a power of 2.

The elements m_2, m_3, m_6, m_7, m_{10}, m_{11}, m_{14}, m_{15} form an adjacency group of eight. This collapses to the single literal C. (Recall that a three-dimensional plane within a four-dimensional cube yields a term with $4 - 3 = 1$ literal.) The elements m_5 and m_7 result in the term $\overline{A}BD$ (a one-dimensional plane in a four-dimensional space results in a term with $4 - 1 = 3$ literals). The final grouping involves the corner terms: m_0, m_2, m_8, m_{10}. To see this adjacency, you must recognize that the map folds back on itself.

Examining Figure 2.37 should make this clearer. In the figure, look for the minterm indices 0000, 0010, 1010, and 1000. The corner elements reduce to the term $\overline{B}D$ (a two-dimensional plane within a four-dimensional space results in a term with $4 - 2 = 2$ literals). The minimized form of the function is

$$F = C + \overline{A}BD + \overline{B}\overline{D}$$

Finding the Minimum Product of Sums Form   The K-map can also be used to find a function's minimum product of sums expression. In this case we search for elements of the off-set, simply circling the maximal adjacent groups of 0's. We interpret the indices in a fashion complementary to the

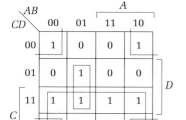

Figure 2.36   K-map of a four-variable function.

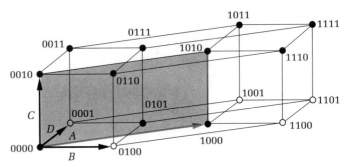

Figure 2.37 The adjacency of the four corner squares of the K-map when viewed in the 4-cube.

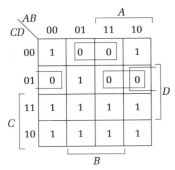

Figure 2.38 K-map of a four-variable function.

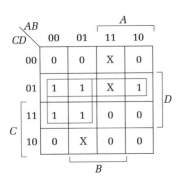

Figure 2.39 Use of don't-care entries in the K-map.

procedure for finding the minimum sum of products expression. If the variable that is left unchanged in a grouping of 0's has index 0, then that variable contributes an asserted literal to the term. If the index is 1, it contributes a complemented literal.

This method works because we begin by solving for the function's complement in sum of products form, by circling the 0's. Then we apply DeMorgan's theorem to get a product of sums expression by interpreting the indices as complements. Let's look at an example.

Let's reconsider the K-map in Figure 2.36. $\overline{F}$ in minimum sum of products form is found by circling the K-map's 0's rather than its 1's: $\overline{F} = B\overline{C}\overline{D} + A\overline{C}D + \overline{B}\overline{C}D$. By applying DeMorgan's theorem, we get F in product of sums form:

$$\overline{\overline{F}} = \overline{B\overline{C}\overline{D} + A\overline{C}D + \overline{B}\overline{C}D}$$

$$F = (\overline{B} + C + D)\,(\overline{A} + C + \overline{D})\,(B + C + \overline{D})$$

Figure 2.38 shows the same K-map as Figure 2.36, but this time with the 0's circled. You can see that three groups of two 0's each can be found. Since these are one-dimensional adjacency groups in a four-dimensional space, there are three literals in each term. The term formed from M_4 and M_{12} is $(\overline{B} + C + D)$: B, C, and D remain unchanged and B's index is 1 while C's and D's are 0. This is just shorthand for applying DeMorgan's theorem to the $B\overline{C}\overline{D}$ term of the complement. The terms formed from M_1, M_9 and M_9, M_{13} are $(B + C + \overline{D})$ and $(\overline{A} + C + \overline{D})$, respectively. Each term is ANDed to form the final expression:

$$F = (\overline{B} + C + D)\,(\overline{A} + C + \overline{D})\,(B + C + \overline{D})$$

Don't Cares in K-maps The last wrinkle we consider is the use of don't cares within the K-map. Figure 2.39 shows a K-map for the function $F(A,B,C,D) = \Sigma\, m(1,3,5,7,9) + \Sigma\, d(6,12,13)$. The group of four elements reduces to $\overline{A}D$. If we assume that the X's are all 0, we can cover the remaining member of the on-set with the term $\overline{B}\overline{C}D$. However, if we assume that the element d_{13} is 1, we can form a larger adjacency group that yields the term $\overline{C}D$. This has fewer literals. So the values of don't cares should be selected to maximize the size of the adjacency groups. The expression for F becomes $\overline{A}D + \overline{C}D$.

In product of sums form, the shorthand expression is written as $F(A,B,C,D) = \Pi\, M(0,2,4,8,10,11,14,15) \bullet \Pi\, D(6,12,13)$. Figure 2.40 shows the groupings we use to find the minimum product of sums form. We form a group of eight 0's (remember that the top and bottom rows are adjacent) and one of four 0's by judicious use of don't cares (D_6, $D_{12} = 0$). The expression for F becomes $D(\overline{A} + \overline{C})$.

Application

2.3.4 Design

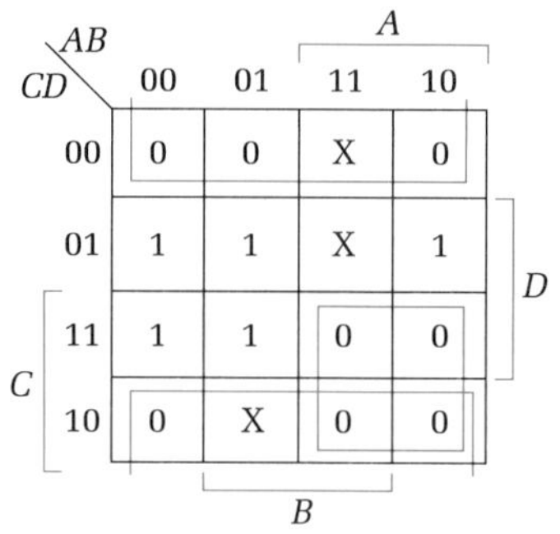

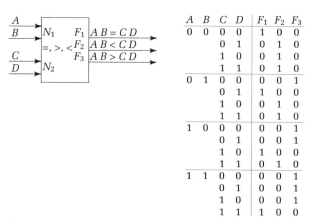

Figure 2.40 Groupings for product of sums form.

Two-Bit Comparator Now we are ready to examine a fairly substantial design example using the methods we have seen so far. The goal is to design a circuit that takes as input two 2-bit numbers for comparison, N_1 and N_2, and generates three outputs: $N_1 = N_2$, $N_1 < N_2$, and $N_1 > N_2$. We denote the numbers N_1 and N_2 by the single-bit inputs A, B and C, D, respectively.

The first step in tackling any problem like this is to understand fully the behavior of the circuit being designed. You can do this best by drawing a block diagram showing inputs and outputs and creating a truth table for each output as a function of the inputs.

These are shown in Figure 2.41. It is fairly straightforward to fill in the table. For example, the first row compares the N_1 input 00 to the N_2 input 00. The F_1 function (=) is true, while F_2 (<) and F_3 (>) are false. In the second row, 00 < 01, so F_1 and F_3 are false while F_2 is true. The rest of the table is filled in a similar way.

A	B	C	D	F_1	F_2	F_3
0	0	0	0	1	0	0
		0	1	0	1	0
		1	0	0	1	0
		1	1	0	1	0
0	1	0	0	0	0	1
		0	1	1	0	0
		1	0	0	1	0
		1	1	0	1	0
1	0	0	0	0	0	1
		0	1	0	0	1
		1	0	1	0	0
		1	1	0	1	0
1	1	0	0	0	0	1
		0	1	0	0	1
		1	0	0	0	1
		1	1	1	0	0

Figure 2.41 Block diagram and truth table of 2-bit comparator.

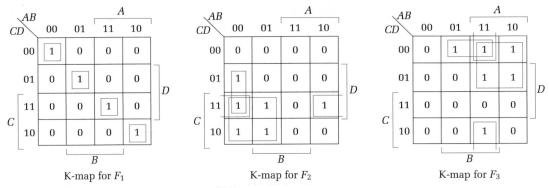

Figure 2.42 K-maps for the 2-bit comparator.

The next step is to prepare K-maps for each of the outputs. This is shown in Figure 2.42. Let's start with the K-map for F_1. There are no adjacencies in this K-map! Each of the four elements of the on-set contributes a four-variable term to the expression for F_1:

$$F_1 = \overline{A}\overline{B}\overline{C}\overline{D} + \overline{A}B\overline{C}D + A\overline{B}C\overline{D} + ABCD$$

This is the minimized sum of products form for the function. However, by using Boolean algebra, we can simplify this expression some more:

$$F_1 = \overline{A}\overline{C}\,(\overline{B}\overline{D} + BD) + AC\,(\overline{B}\overline{D} + BD)$$
$$= (\overline{A}\overline{C} + AC)\,(\overline{B}\overline{D} + BD)$$
$$= (\overline{A \oplus C})\,(\overline{B \oplus D})$$

We can get a much simpler form, $(A \text{ XNOR } C)\,(B \text{ XNOR } D)$, but it is not in sum of products form. 1's on K-map diagonals provide a good hint that the function can be expressed more economically in terms of XOR or XNOR operations.

The K-map for F_2 has three adjacency groups, two with two elements and another with four elements. The former yield product terms with three literals, $\overline{A}\overline{B}D$ and $\overline{B}CD$, the latter a term with two literals, $\overline{A}C$. The expression for F_2 becomes

$$F_2 = \overline{A}\overline{B}D + \overline{B}CD + \overline{A}C$$

The K-map for F_3 is a little more complicated. It consists of two groups of two elements each (three literals) and one group of four elements (two literals). The minimum sum of products expression for F_3 becomes

$$F_3 = A\overline{C} + AB\overline{D} + B\overline{C}\overline{D}$$

Two-Bit Binary Adder The next function we examine is a 2-bit binary adder. It takes as input two 2-bit binary numbers, N_1 and N_2, and produces a 3-bit binary number, N_3, as the result. The block diagram and truth table for these functions are shown in Figure 2.43. Once again, N_1 is represented by the inputs A and B, N_2 by C and D, and N_3 by the Boolean functions X, Y, and Z.

The K-maps for the outputs are shown in Figure 2.44. The maps for the X and Z outputs are more straightforward than for Y, and we will start with these. The function for X reduces to two 2-element groups (three literals each) and one 4-element group (two literals):

$$X = AC + BCD + ABD$$

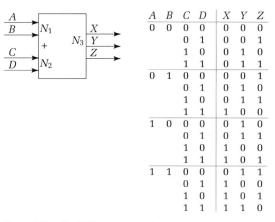

A	B	C	D	X	Y	Z
0	0	0	0	0	0	0
		0	1	0	0	1
		1	0	0	1	0
		1	1	0	1	1
0	1	0	0	0	0	1
		0	1	0	1	0
		1	0	0	1	1
		1	1	1	0	0
1	0	0	0	0	1	0
		0	1	0	1	1
		1	0	1	0	0
		1	1	1	0	1
1	1	0	0	0	1	1
		0	1	1	0	0
		1	0	1	0	1
		1	1	1	1	0

Figure 2.43 Block diagram and truth table of 2-bit binary adder.

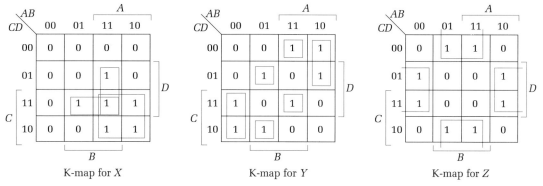

K-map for X K-map for Y K-map for Z

Figure 2.44 K-maps for the 2-bit binary adder.

Z exhibits two 4-element groups (two literals each) and reduces to the expression:

$$Z = B\overline{D} + \overline{B}D = B \oplus D$$

By careful examination of the K-map, we can often spot opportunities for reduction using XOR and XNOR operators. We will show this by reducing the literal count for the function Y by good use of XOR/XNOR.

The two straightforward terms of Y are $\overline{A}BC$ and $A\overline{B}\overline{C}$. The remaining four single-element groups yield the terms: $\overline{A}B\overline{C}D$, $\overline{A}BC\overline{D}$, $AB\overline{C}D$, and $ABCD$. We can further reduce $AB\overline{C}D$ and $\overline{A}BC\overline{D}$ (to $A\overline{C}\overline{D}$ and $\overline{A}\overline{C}D$) but for the moment we do not do this.

Factoring yields the expressions

$$\overline{A}BC + A\overline{B}\overline{C} \qquad = \overline{B}(A \oplus C)$$

$$\overline{A}B\overline{C}D + \overline{A}BC\overline{D} = \overline{A}B(\overline{C}D + C\overline{D}) = \overline{A}B(C \oplus D)$$

$$AB\overline{C}\overline{D} + ABCD = AB(\overline{C}\overline{D} + CD) = AB(\overline{C \oplus D})$$

We can factor the latter two expressions:

$$\overline{A}B(C \oplus D) + AB(\overline{C \oplus D}) = B(A \oplus C \oplus D)$$

Y becomes:

$$Y = \overline{B}(A \oplus C) + B(A \oplus C \oplus D)$$

This expression has just seven literals. Compare it to the reduced form, assuming only AND, OR, and NOT gates are allowed:

$$Y = \overline{A}BC + A\overline{B}\overline{C} + A\overline{C}\overline{D} + \overline{A}\overline{C}D + \overline{A}BC\overline{D} + ABCD$$

This expression requires two 4-input AND gates, four 3-input AND gates, and a 6-input OR gate, for a total of 7 gates and 20 literals. The revised expression requires a 2-input OR gate, two 2-input XOR gates, and two 2-input AND gates, a total of 5 simpler gates and 7 literals to implement the function. The two alternative implementations are shown in Figure 2.45.

BCD Increment by 1 Function   We introduced the BCD increment by 1 function in Section 2.2.4 as an example of a function with don't cares. The truth table of Figure 2.23 yields the four 4-variable K-maps of Figure 2.46.

We attempt to form the largest adjacency groups we can, taking advantage of don't cares to expand the group wherever possible. The

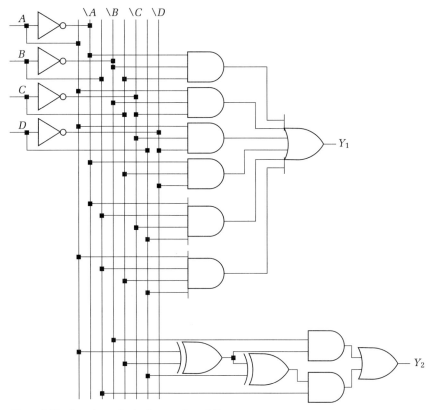

Figure 2.45 Two alternative implementations of Y.

function W can be implemented by two terms: $W = BCD + A\overline{D}$. These are formed from adjacency groups of two elements and four elements, respectively. Notice how we have taken advantage of adjacencies that wrap from the top of the K-map to the bottommost row.

The function X is implemented by three terms: $X = B\overline{D} + B\overline{C} + \overline{B}CD$. Once again, we have attempted to take advantage of adjacencies that wrap from top to bottom or left to right in the K-map.

The function Y is implemented by two terms: $Y = \overline{A}\overline{C}D + C\overline{D}$. This is derived from groups of two and four entries, respectively. The final function Z is implemented by a group of eight nodes, which reduces to the single literal $\overline{D}$.

Once again, notice that adjacency groups are always formed by groups of 1 (4 literals), 2 (3 literals), 4 (2 literals), 8 (1 literal), or 16 (0 literals, a constant 0 or 1) elements, always a power of 2. Also notice how the adjacencies are formed: above, below, to the left, to the right of an element of the on-set, including those that wrap around the edges of the K-map.

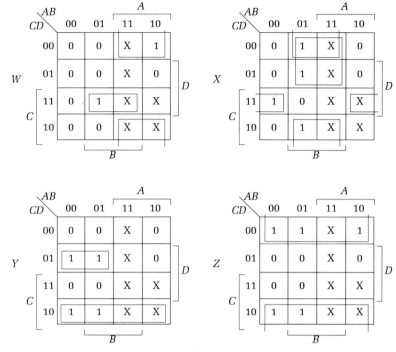

Figure 2.46 BCD increment by 1 K-maps.

2.3.5 Process of Boolean Minimization

We are now ready to be more precise about the process for obtaining a minimized expression. An *implicant* of a function F is a single element of the on-set or any group of elements that can be combined together in a K-map. We have been calling these adjacency groups or planes up to this point. A *prime implicant* is an implicant that cannot be combined with another one to eliminate a literal. In other words, you grow implicants to cover as much of the on-set as possible (each prime implicant is an implicant with as few literals as possible). Each prime implicant corresponds to a product term in the minimum sum of products expression for the function. The trick is to find the fewest prime implicants that cover the elements of the on-set. If a particular element of the on-set is covered by a single prime implicant, it is called an *essential prime implicant*. All essential primes must be part of the minimized expression.

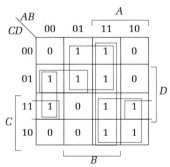

Figure 2.47 Prime implicants.

Example   Illustrating the Definitions Let's look at some examples to make these concepts more concrete. The four-variable K-map of Figure 2.47 contains six prime implicants: $\overline{A}\,\overline{B}D$, $B\overline{C}$, AC, $\overline{A}CD$, AB,

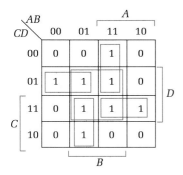

Figure 2.48 Essential primes.

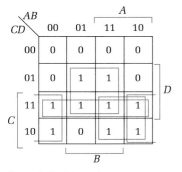

Figure 2.49 More primes.

and $\overline{B}CD$. Only AC and $B\overline{C}$ are essential. Adding the additional implicant $\overline{A}\,\overline{B}D$ covers the entire on-set. Thus the minimized expression for the function becomes:

$$F = \overline{A}\,\overline{B}D + B\overline{C} + AC$$

As another example, consider the function whose K-map is given in Figure 2.48. It contains five prime implicants: BD, $AB\overline{C}$, ACD, $\overline{A}BC$, and $\overline{A}\,\overline{C}D$. All but the first implicant are essential. The minimized form is

$$F = AB\overline{C} + ACD + \overline{A}BC + \overline{A}\,\overline{C}D$$

As a final example, consider the K-map of Figure 2.49. It contains four prime implicants: BD, CD, AC, and $\overline{B}C$. The implicant CD is inessential, since the 1's it covers are already covered by the remaining implicants, all of which are essential. The minimized function is

$$F = BD + AC + \overline{B}C$$

Deriving a Minimized Expression from a K-map A procedure for finding a minimum sum of products expression from the K-map is the following:

Step 1: Choose an element from the on-set. Find all of the "maximal" groups of 1's and X's adjacent to that element. Check for adjacency in the horizontal and vertical directions. Remember that the K-map wraps from top row to bottom and leftmost column to rightmost. The prime implicants (adjacency groups) thus formed always contain a number of elements that is a power of 2.

Repeat step 1 for each element of the on-set to find all prime implicants.

Step 2: Visit an element of the on-set elements. If it is covered by a single prime implicant, it is essential and will contribute a term to the final sum of products expression. The 1's covered by the implicant do not need to be visited again.

Repeat step 2 until all essential prime implicants have been found.

Step 3: If there remain 1's uncovered by essential prime implicants, select a minimum number of prime implicants that cover them. Try several alternative covers to find the one with the fewest possible implicants.

Example   Application of the Step-by-Step Algorithm Figure 2.50 shows the algorithm applied to a complete example. The function represented in the K-map is $F(A,B,C,D) = \sum m(4,5,6,8,9,10,13) + d(0,7,15)$.

Figure 2.50(a) gives the starting configuration. We scan down the K-map's columns, top to bottom and left to right, skipping 0's and X's,

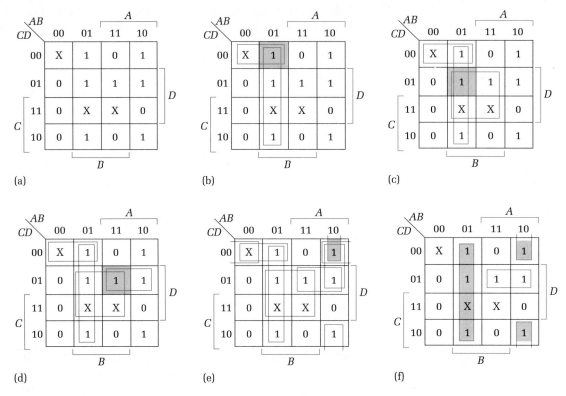

Figure 2.50 Finding prime implicants, step by step.

searching for a 1. The first 1 we encounter is term m_4. Expand in all directions, combining adjacent 1's and X's into the largest implicant groups you can find. Two such groupings are possible, represented by the terms $\overline{A}B$ and $\overline{A}\,\overline{C}\overline{D}$. These are circled in Figure 2.50(b).

Continuing down the column, we next come to m_5. At this point we should add only new implicants that are not already contained within an implicant found so far. BD is the only implicant we can add under this rule, as shown in Figure 2.50(c).

The next element of the on-set is m_6, but no new implicant can be added because the set of implicants already contains $\overline{A}B$. So we continue searching for the next element of the on-set, which is m_{13}. We can now add the implicant $A\overline{C}D$. Note that the implicant ABD is already covered by the prime implicant BD, so we do not add it to the K-map. The state of the process to this point is shown in Figure 2.50(d).

The next 1 is m_8, which contributes three additional prime implicants, $A\overline{B}\,\overline{C}$, $A\overline{B}\,\overline{D}$, and $\overline{B}\,\overline{C}\overline{D}$. This is shown in Figure 2.50(e). The process continues with m_9 and m_{10}, but these add no new prime implicants.

All the elements of the on-set are now covered, and we have obtained all prime implicants. The next step is to identify the essential prime implicants. The highlighted prime implicants of Figure 2.50(f), $\overline{A}B$ and $A\overline{B}\overline{D}$, are the essential primes because they exclusively cover m_6 and m_{10}, respectively.

The last step is to cover the remaining 1's not already covered by the essential primes. This is accomplished by the single prime implicant $A\overline{C}D$. The process of enumerating prime implicants found six of them, yet three were sufficient to cover the entire on-set. The final minimized function is

$$F(A, B, C, D) = \overline{A}B + A\overline{B}\overline{D} + A\overline{C}D$$

2.3.6 K-Maps Revisited: Five- and Six-Variable Functions

The K-map method is not limited to four variables or less, although using it to visualize functions with more than four variables becomes more challenging. It is important to remember that within an n-variable map we must check for adjacencies in n directions. Fortunately, we can handle the adjacencies for up to six variables, simply by stacking two or four 4-variable K-maps.

Five-Variable K-Maps A five-variable map is shown in Figure 2.51(a). Let's consider the following Boolean function:

$$F(A,B,C,D,E) = \sum m(2,5,7,8,10,13,15,17,19,21,23,24,29,31)$$

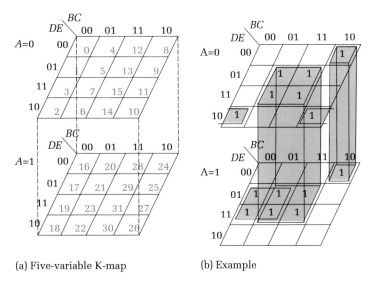

(a) Five-variable K-map   (b) Example

Figure 2.51 Five-variable K-map and example.

The filled in K-map is shown in Figure 2.51(b). We have omitted the 0 entries to reduce the clutter in the figure. When searching for adjacencies, besides looking in the four horizontal and vertical squares as we did in the four-variable K-map, we must also look either up or down. The example's on-set is covered by the four prime implicants CE (group of 8), $A\overline{B}E$ (group of 4), $B\overline{C}\overline{D}\overline{E}$ (group of 2), and $\overline{A}\overline{C}D\overline{E}$ (group of 2).

Six-Variable K-Map The six-variable K-map is to the five-variable map as the four-variable is to the three-variable: the number of four-variable planes is increased from two to four. This is shown in Figure 2.52(a).

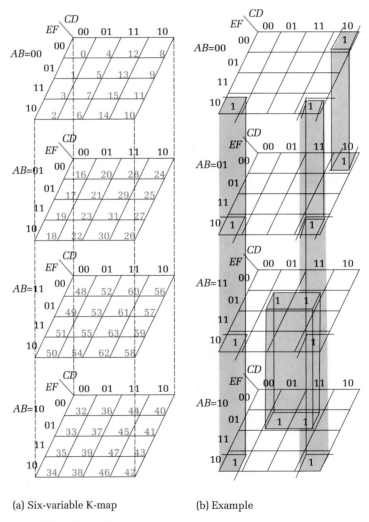

(a) Six-variable K-map   (b) Example

Figure 2.52 Six-variable K-map and example.

An example six-variable K-map is shown in Figure 2.52(b). The function is

$$F(A,B,C,D,E,F) = \Sigma\ m(2,8,10,18,24,26,34,37,42,45,50,53,58,61)$$

In addition to horizontal and vertical adjacencies, the planes immediately above and below the element being examined must be checked. The top plane also wraps around onto the bottom plane. In the figure, the on-set is covered by three prime implicants: $\overline{D}E\overline{F}$ (a group of 8), $AD\overline{E}F$ (a group of 4), and $\overline{A}C\overline{D}F$ (a group of 4).

2.4   CAD Tools for Simplification

The algorithm we presented in the previous section for extracting essential prime implicants from a K-map could form the basis for computer-based tools. In this section, we examine computer-based algorithms for two-level simplification in more detail. We begin with the Quine-McCluskey method, the first complete algorithm for simplification. We complete this section by covering the methods used in *espresso*, a popular tool for two-level minimization. While not guaranteed to find the best two-level expression, *espresso* uses several tricks to find a good solution as fast as possible.

2.4.1   Quine-McCluskey Method

Except in special cases or for particularly sparse truth tables, the K-map method simply breaks down beyond six variables. We need a more systematic algorithm. The Quine-McCluskey method, developed in the mid-1950s, finds the minimized representation of any Boolean expression. It provides a systematic procedure for generating all prime implicants and then extracting a minimum set of primes covering the on-set.

The method finds the prime implicants by repeatedly applying the uniting theorem, just as we did earlier in this section. The contribution of Quine-McCluskey is to provide a tabular method that ensures that all prime implicants are found. To understand how it works, let's use the same example as in Figure 2.50: $F = \Sigma\ m(4,5,6,8,9,10,13) + d(0,7,15)$.

Finding Prime Implicants   The first step is to list all elements of the on-set and don't-care set in terms of their minterm indices, represented as a binary number. The elements are grouped according to the number of 1's in the binary representation.

Table 2.1 shows the structure of a Quine-McCluskey implicant table. The first column contains the minterms of the on-set, that is, single points in the Boolean space. In the example, each of these represents a four-variable product term (a minterm). As a result of applying the method, the second column will contain implicants that form edges in

Table 2.1   Quine-McCluskey Implication Table

Column I	Column II	Column III
0000 √	0-00 *	01-- *
	-000 *	
0100 √		-1-1 *
1000 √	010- √	
	01-0 √	
0101 √	100- *	
0110 √	10-0 *	
1001 √		
1010 √	01-1 √	
	-101 √	
0111 √	011- √	
1101 √	1-01 *	
1111 √	-111 √	
	11-1 √	

the Boolean space: three-variable product terms. After another iteration of the method, the third column will contain larger implicants that represent planes in the Boolean space: two-variable terms. A third iteration will find implicant cubes in the space: one-variable terms.

We begin the method by filling in the first column of the table as follows. Each group of the minterm indices of the on-set and don't care set is separated by a blank line. The first group has no 1's in the indices, the second has one 1 in each index, the third has two 1's in each index, and so on.

To apply the uniting theorem systematically, compare the elements in the first group against each element in the second. If they differ by a single bit, it means that the minterms the numbers represent are adjacent in n-dimensional Boolean space. For example, $0000 = \overline{A}\,\overline{B}\,\overline{C}\,\overline{D}$ and $0100 = \overline{A}B\overline{C}\overline{D}$ can be combined into the implicant $\overline{A}\,\overline{C}\overline{D}$ according to the uniting theorem. The latter term is represented symbolically by 0-00. Every time a new implicant is formed, it is placed in the next column. Since each group differs in its 1's count by one, it is sufficient to restrict comparisons to adjacent groups to detect when the uniting theorem can be applied.

Let's apply the Quine-McCluskey algorithm to the whole first column. We begin with the first group (no 1's) against the second group (one 1's). 0000 is compared against 0100 and 1000, yielding terms for the second column of 0-00 and -000 respectively. Every time a term contributes to a new implicant, it receives a check mark. This means that the implicant is not prime: it can be combined with some other element to form a larger implicant.

We repeat for the second group against the third group. 0100 combines with 0101 and 0110, giving 010- and 01-0 in the second column. 1000 combines with 1001 and 1010, resulting in 100- and 10-0.

Now we try the third group against the fourth group. 0101 combines with 0111 and 1101 to give 01-1 and -101. 0110 combines with 0111 to yield 011-. 1001 combines with 1101 to give 1-01. 1010 does not combine with any element of the fourth group.

When we compare the fourth to the fifth group, two additional terms are added: -111 and 11-1.

The procedure is repeated for the groups in column II. For the elements to be combined, they must differ by a single bit and must have their "-" in the same bit position. The elements of the first group do not combine with any elements of the second group. We mark these with asterisks because they are prime implicants: we have expanded them as much as possible.

In the second and third groups, 010- can be combined with 011-, yielding 01-- for the third column. 01-0 and 01-1 are combined to derive the same condensed term. 100- and 10-0 cannot be combined further and are prime implicants.

Between the third and fourth groups only the additional term -1-1 is added to the third column, derived from the combinations of -101 and -111, and 01-1 and 11-1.

The elements of the third column cannot be reduced further. Both are marked as prime implicants. Since no new implicants are added, we have found all prime implicants, and the first phase of the algorithm can now terminate.

The algorithm has found the following prime implicants:

$$0\text{-}00 = \overline{A}\,C\overline{D} \qquad \text{-}000 = \overline{B}\,\overline{C}\,\overline{D}$$

$$100\text{-} = A\overline{B}\,C \qquad 10\text{-}0 = A\overline{B}\,\overline{D}$$

$$1\text{-}01 = A\,C\overline{D} \qquad 01\text{--} = \overline{A}\,B$$

$$\text{-}1\text{-}1 = BD$$

These are shown circled in the K-map of Figure 2.53. They are exactly the same as the prime implicants we found in the previous section. Note that in this portion of the procedure, the don't cares have been treated as though they are 1's.

Finding the Minimum Cover The second step of the method is to find the smallest collection of prime implicants that cover the complete on-set of the function. This is accomplished through the *prime implicant chart* (as opposed to the implication chart used in the first phase), as shown in Figure 2.54.

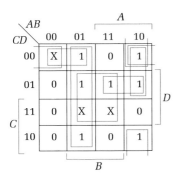

Figure 2.53 Prime implicants found by the Quine-McCluskey method.

The prime implicant chart is organized as follows. The columns are labeled with the minterm indices of the on-set. Note that don't cares are not included in this stage. The rows are labeled with the minterms covered by a given prime implicant. This is done by taking the indices of the prime implicant representation and replacing each "-" by all possible combinations of 1's and 0's. For example, -1-1 becomes 0101, 0111, 1101, 1111, which are the indices of the minterms m_5, m_7, m_{13}, and m_{15}. An X is placed in the (row, column) location if the minterm represented by the column is covered by the prime implicant associated with the row. The initial configuration is given in Figure 2.54(a).

Next, we look for essential prime implicants. These are immediately apparent whenever there is a single X in any column. This means that there is a minterm that is covered by one and only one prime implicant.

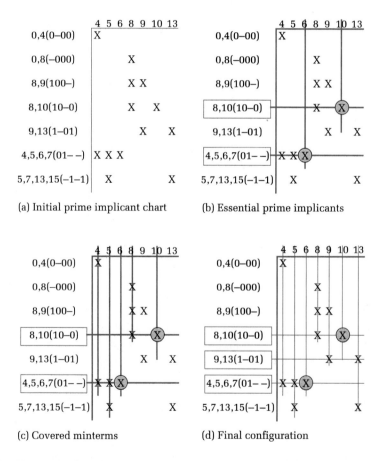

Figure 2.54   The prime implicant chart.

The essential prime implicants must participate in the final cover. We place a line through the column and row in which the essential prime implicant has been found and place a box around the prime. This is shown in Figure 2.54(b).

The essential prime implicants usually cover additional minterms. We cross out any columns that have an X in a row associated with an essential prime. These minterms are already covered by the essential primes. This is shown in Figure 2.54(c).

In the example, two minterms are still uncovered, represented by the columns 9 and 13. The final step is to find as few primes as possible that cover the remaining minterms. In our example, the single prime implicant 1-01 covers both of these. Adding it to the two essential prime implicants already found completes the cover. This is shown in Figure 2.54(d). The solution found here is identical to the one we found earlier in Figure 2.50.

2.4.2   *Espresso* Method

Unfortunately, the number of prime implicants grows very quickly as the number of inputs increases. It can be shown that the upper bound on the number of prime implicants is $3^n/n$. Finding a minimum set cover is also known to be a very difficult problem, a so-called NP-complete problem. This means that there are not likely to be any efficient algorithms for solving it.

Thus, much of the work in logic minimization has concentrated on heuristic methods to perform these two steps more quickly, finding a minimal solution rapidly rather than guaranteeing a minimum solution will be found. The primary technique avoids generating all prime implicants by judiciously computing a subset of primes that still cover the on-set. In this subsection, we will examine the algorithms and techniques used in *espresso*.

Algorithms Used in *Espresso*   *Espresso* is a program for two-level Boolean function minimization, readily available from the University of California, Berkeley. It combines many of the best heuristic techniques developed in earlier programs, such as *mini* and *presto*. Although a detailed explanation of the operation of *espresso* is beyond the scope of this book (see Brayton et al. in the chapter references), the basic ideas employed by the program are not difficult to understand. They are as follows:

1. Rather than start by generating all implicants and then finding those that are prime, *espresso* expands implicants into their maximum size. Implicants that are covered by an expanded implicant are removed from further consideration. This process is called EXPAND. How well

this works depends critically on the order and direction in which implicants are expanded. Much of the power of *espresso* lies in its methods for directing and ordering the expansion.

2. An irredundant cover (that is, one for which no proper subset is also a cover) is extracted from the expanded implicants. The method is essentially the same as the Quine-McCluskey prime implicant chart method. This step is called IRREDUNDANT COVER.

3. At this point, the solution is usually pretty good, but under certain conditions it can still be improved. There might be another cover with fewer terms or the same number of terms but fewer literals. To try to find a better cover, *espresso* first shrinks the prime implicants to the smallest size that still covers the logic function. This process is called REDUCE.

4. Since reduction yields a cover that is typically no longer prime, the sequence of steps REDUCE, EXPAND, and IRREDUNDANT COVER are repeated in such a fashion that alternative prime implicants are derived. *Espresso* will continue repeating these steps as long as it generates a cover that improves on the last solution found.

5. A number of other strategies are used to improve the result or to compute it more quickly. These include (a) early identification and extraction of essential prime implicants, so they need not be revisited during step 4; (b) using the function's complement to check efficiently whether an EXPAND step actually increases the coverage of the function (the minterms covered by an expanded implicant may already be covered by another expanded implicant, so the newly expanded implicant should not be placed in the cover); and (c) a special "last gasp" step which guarantees that no single prime implicant can be added to the cover in such a way that two primes can then be eliminated.

```
.i 4
.o 1
.ilb a b c d
.ob f
.p 10
0100    1
0101    1
0110    1
1000    1
1001    1
1010    1
1101    1
0000    -
0111    -
1111    -
.e
```

Figure 2.55 *Espresso* inputs.

```
.i 4
.o 1
.ilb a b c d
.ob f
.p 3
1-01    1
10-0    1
01--    1
.e
```

Figure 2.56 *Espresso* outputs.

Espresso's input is an encoded truth table. For the example of Figure 2.50, the input is shown in Figure 2.55. The first two lines describe the number of inputs and outputs of the function. The next two describe the input symbol names and the name of the output function. The next line gives the number of product terms used in specifying the function. In this case, there are 10 terms: seven 1's and three don't cares. Each term is listed by its minterm index, encoded in binary, followed by a 1 or a "-." The latter indicates a don't care. The last line indicates the end of the list of product terms.

The output minimized truth table is shown in Figure 2.56. The first four lines have the same meaning as before. The encoding for the minimum cover is identical to that used in the Quine-McCluskey method. 1-01 corresponds to $A\overline{C}D$, 10-0 to $A\overline{B}\overline{D}$, and 01-- to $\overline{A}B$.

To see how the iteration of REDUCE, IRREDUNDANT COVER, and EXPAND can improve the cover, consider the four-variable K-map of Figure 2.57. Figure 2.57(a) shows the primes as found by *espresso* after

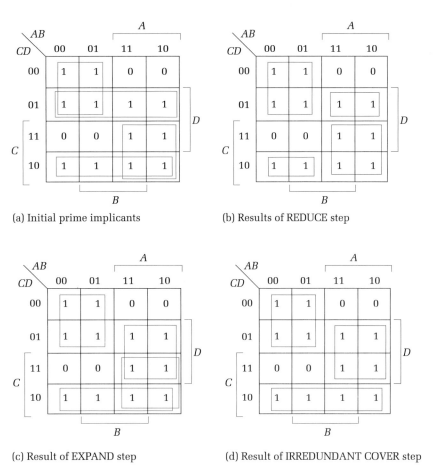

(a) Initial prime implicants

(b) Results of REDUCE step

(c) Result of EXPAND step

(d) Result of IRREDUNDANT COVER step

Figure 2.57 Four-variable K-maps.

executing steps 1 and 2 for the first time. It has four prime implicants and is an irredundant cover, but this is not the minimum cover possible.

The results of the REDUCE step are shown in Figure 2.57(b). The prime implicant $\overline{C}D$ has been reduced to the implicant (no longer prime) $A\overline{C}D$, and $C\overline{D}$ has been reduced to $\overline{A}C\overline{D}$ (also no longer prime). The particular choice of reductions depends on heuristics and *espresso*'s order of execution. The result of the second iteration of EXPAND is shown in Figure 2.57(c). *Espresso* retains the last irredundant cover, and its expansion algorithms guarantee that it never generates the same cover twice. The IRREDUNDANT COVER extracted by *espresso* is given in Figure 2.57(d). The three-product-term cover is indeed an improvement on the original result.

2.5   Practical Matters

So far, we have concentrated on the mathematical aspects of representing hardware in terms of Boolean functions and the techniques and algorithms for obtaining minimized Boolean expressions. In this section, we shift the focus to more practical considerations, such as the underlying technologies used to implement digital functions, how logic gates are combined into integrated circuit packages, and the standard techniques for documenting logic schematics.

2.5.1   Technology Metrics

When it comes to the performance aspects of the design, there are differences in the underlying technologies that may make one technology more attractive than another. Bipolar circuits come in a wide range of TTL (transistor-transistor logic) families, with different trade-offs in circuit speed and power, and the very high speed ECL (emitter-coupled logic) family. The most popular MOS family is CMOS (complementary MOS), consisting of both n-channel and p-channel devices (see Appendix B). The main technology metrics, summarized in Figure 2.58, include gate delay, degree of integration, power dissipation, noise margin, component cost, fan-out, and driving capability. In general, faster gates consume more power, generate more heat, cannot be packaged as densely, and are more sensitive to noise problems.

Metric	Bipolar	MOS
Gate delay	Low	Medium
Integration	Low	High
Power	High	Low
Noise	Good	Good
Cost	Low	Medium
Fan-out	Fair	Good
Drive	Good	Low

Figure 2.58   Comparison between bipolar and MOS technologies.

Gate delay: If an input change causes an output change, the gate delay is the time delay between the changes. It is usually measured from the input reaching 90% of its final value to the output reaching 90% of its final value. In general, bipolar technologies are faster than MOS, with ECL achieving the fastest switching times, although the gap between MOS and bipolar is narrowing.

Degree of integration: This represents the area required to implement a given function in the underlying technology. MOS circuits pack much more densely than bipolar. For small-scale integrated (SSI) circuits, a package containing up to 10 logic gates, and for medium-scale integrated (MSI) circuits, a package containing up to 100 gates, this metric is probably not very important. However, in large-scale gate arrays and very large scale integrated circuits (VLSI), containing thousands of gates, MOS has a distinct integration advantage over bipolar.

Power dissipation: Gates consume power as they perform their logic functions, generating heat that must be dissipated. Bipolar circuits typically switch faster than MOS, thus generating more heat and consuming more power. ECL circuits consume the most power. MOS circuits, especially CMOS, can be designed to consume very little power, as evidenced by the lifetime of the battery powering a digital watch's CMOS circuitry. However, in MOS circuits, power is in part a function of the frequency with which the circuit changes outputs. Surprisingly, CMOS circuits may exceed the power dissipation of bipolar circuits at the same very high switching speeds.

Noise margin: This is the maximum voltage that can be added to or subtracted from the logic voltages and still have the circuit interpret the voltage as the correct logic value. Modern TTL and CMOS technologies have good noise margins. ECL gains some of its speed from reduced voltages for representing 0 and 1, and this reduced voltage swing requires tighter noise margins.

Component cost: In general, TTL components are very inexpensive, MOS components are medium in cost, and ECL components are the most expensive.

Fan-out: We defined fan-out in Chapter 1 as the number of gate inputs to which a given gate output could be connected because of electrical limitations. Fan-out is a metric related to the ease with which gates can be composed into more complex functions. MOS circuits can be cascaded with a large number of other MOS circuits without suffering degradation in the transmitted signals. However, signal delays do increase with fan-out. The speed of bipolar circuits does not vary with fan-out, but signal quality is dramatically reduced as the fan-out increases.

Driving capability: Discrete gates, as presented in this chapter, are usually placed with other gates in ready-to-use packages. Driving capability measures the speed of communications between packaged components. In general, MOS circuits have less circuit drive than bipolar circuits, making their package-to-package delay greater. Because of differences in the internal electronics, you must be very careful when mixing bipolar and MOS within the same system. Although MOS circuits can drive many other MOS circuits, they can typically drive only a single bipolar circuit.

2.5.2   TTL Packaged Logic

TTL is a family of packaged logic components that enjoys widespread use in industry. In fact, it is so well known by designers that even libraries for VLSI components, implemented in the radically different MOS technology, provide exactly the same kinds of logic functions from NAND gates to binary adders and beyond. Knowledge of the logic functions available in TTL carries over readily to just about every technology that can be used for digital design. And most students learning hardware design for the first time will work with TTL technology in their introductory hardware laboratories.

In this chapter we've seen the various kinds of simple logic gates. A TTL *integrated circuit* package typically contains several of these. The Texas Instruments 74-series components provide the standard numbering scheme used by industry. For example, the name for a package containing four 2-input NAND gates is "7400," while a "7404" contains six (hex) inverters.

Small- and Medium-Scale Integration   Components containing a handful of primitive gates are called small-scale integration or SSI components. These components typically contain fewer than 10 logic gates in a single package. In Chapter 4 we shall meet medium-scale integration or MSI components. These implement more complex functions than simple two-input gates and typically contain between 10 and 100 logic gates.

In TTL technology, logic gates are available in rectangular dual in-line packages, also known as "dips." Pins that connect internal logic to the outside are placed along the two long edges of the package. A 14-pin package is shown in Figure 2.59, along with a diagram of its internal logic and pin connectivity. A typical 14-pin package measures approximately 0.75 inch in one dimension and 0.3 inch in the other.

TTL packages come in a variety of pin configurations, from 14-pin packages (7 pins per side) all the way up to 64-pin packages (32 pins per side). In a TTL package, the top edge is usually distinguished by an indentation. The pin immediately to the left of this is labeled #1. You will often find a small bump next to this pin.

The pins are numbered counterclockwise starting with pin #1 at the upper left-hand corner. The pin at the lower left-hand corner (pin #7 in this case) is usually connected to ground (GND), while the pin at the upper right-hand corner (pin #14) is connected to the power supply (VCC). If in doubt, you should always consult the data book for the logic components

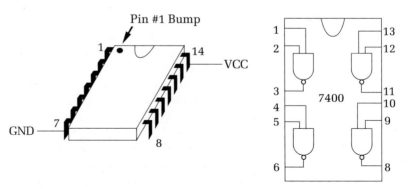

Figure 2.59   Dual in-line package.

you are using to verify the numbering scheme. Always make sure you understand which pins are to be connected to the power supply.

The figure also shows the pin connectivity for a 14-pin package containing four 2-input NAND gates. Notice how the pins are connected within the package to the gates' inputs and outputs. Usually, related input and output pins are adjacent on the package, but this is not always so. You should always consult the logic family's data book for component pin-out maps.

Subfamilies of TTL TTL is a *logic family*. This means that the components have been designed so they can be interconnected without too much concern about proper electrical operation. For example, all TTL components operate with a 5 V power supply. There are actually several subfamilies of TTL, all implementing the same logic functions but representing different trade-offs between speed of operation and the amount of power they consume. In general, the faster the component, the more power it consumes.

Standard TTL components are listed as 74XX, where XX is the component number. High-speed TTL components are denoted by 74HXX and low-power TTL components by 74LXX. H components are about one third faster than standard but use twice as much power. L components use one tenth of the power but experience four times the delay. These families were popular in the 1970s but are now considered obsolete.

A major innovation was the introduction of Schottky TTL in the mid-1970s. The internal design of the gates was changed to incorporate a faster kind of transistor structure. The 74SXX family was faster than H TTL but used about the same power as H. This led to the introduction of LS TTL, low-power Schottky TTL, which is one of the most popular families in use today. LS TTL is as fast as standard TTL but uses only 20% of its power.

Innovation did not stop there. Two additional TTL families, AS and ALS are now also available. AS TTL has twice the speed of S TTL at comparable power consumption, and ALS uses less power than LS while offering higher speed. Although the complete catalog of standard components is available in LS TTL, only a relatively small subset is available in these newer technologies.

Speed-Power Product From the preceding discussion, you may find it a little difficult to know which TTL family is best to use. It is always desirable to have a high-speed system, but usually the components are more expensive and the system consumes more power. Higher power consumption translates into a system that runs hotter and needs more expensive cooling and power supplies. An important figure of merit for the purpose of comparing the efficiency of logic families is the *speed-power product*. To obtain this metric, we multiply the delay through a gate by the power it consumes. Smaller numbers are better: reduced delay and reduced power are ideal.

A typical standard TTL gate has a delay of 9 nanoseconds (ns) and consumes 10 milliwatts (mW). Its speed-power product is 90. The same gate in LS TTL experiences the same delay but consumes only 2 mW. The speed-power product is a better 18. ALS TTL has a delay of 5 ns and consumes only 1.3 mW. Its speed-power product is an even better 6.5. This represents an extremely efficient technology. LS and ALS components are used when the goal is good speed with low power consumption.

Now let's look at higher-speed components. S TTL has a delay of 3 ns, a power consumption of 20 mW, and a speed-power product of 60. Not much faster than ALS, but it uses a lot more power! AS TTL has a delay of 1.6 ns, a power consumption of 20 mW, and a speed-power product of 32. This is the technology of choice for high-speed designs where power consumption need not be low.

So far, we have considered literal count as the primary way to determine the simplicity of a design. Integrated circuit package count is another critical design metric. In TTL technology, a single package typically contains six inverters, four 2-input gates, three 3-input gates, and two complex gates per integrated package.

Look back at the three implementations of the function Z in Figure 2.9. Implementing Z_1 in TTL requires three packages: one package of inverters, one package of three 3-input AND gates, and one package of three 3-input OR gates. Z_2 also uses three packages: one package of inverters, one package of four 2-input AND gates, one package of four 2-input OR gates. But Z_3 needs only two packages. Once again, Z_3 is the most area-efficient design.

2.5.3   Schematic Documentation Standards

Although it is frequently ignored, proper documentation is one of the most important skills of a designer. You must be able to describe your design to other designers.

This means that documentation is primarily about standard ways of doing things. It includes the following:

■ *Representing the design on paper.* This involves ways of drawing components and describing their compositions. A project team must develop and adhere to a standard convention for naming components and the signal wires that interconnect them.

■ *Representing interfaces.* An interface describes everything you need to know about a subsystem to use it without understanding all its internal workings. This is like the description of a subroutine in a computer program: the documentation describes what the subroutines do as well as the names, types, and functions of its parameters.

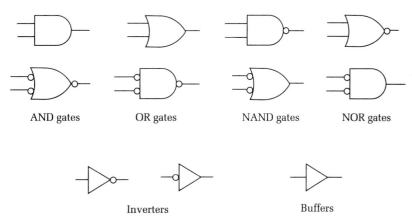

Figure 2.60 Standard SSI gate symbols.

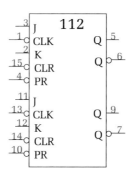

Figure 2.61 MSI component schematic.

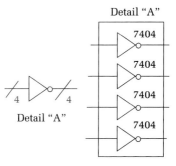

Figure 2.62 Use of a detail letter.

Hardware interfaces are similar to software interfaces, but somewhat more complicated. A hardware interface describes the behavior of the design, as well as the names of signals and how to connect to them.

Standard Schematic Symbols Throughout this chapter, we have used standard gate symbols to represent common SSI components, such as AND, OR, NAND, NOR, XOR, and inverter gates. Gates always have two representations: normal logic and dual logic. The dual representation is used to conserve inversions when using active low signals.

Some examples are shown in Figure 2.60. These are recognized by digital designers everywhere, so you should use them in your work as well. Do not use any other symbols for the same functions.

Conventions for MSI components are less rigid, but the following are typical. Functions are represented by blocks with input/output signals rather than discrete gates. Figure 2.61 contains a schematic symbol for the 74112 dual *J-K* flip-flop, a 16-pin TTL component that will be introduced in Chapter 6. Inputs are drawn on the left, outputs on the right. The general flow of data is from left to right and top to bottom. All signals are labeled with meaningful names. Bubbles on pins or names that end in a slash ("/") indicate signals that are active low. The numbers identify package pin numbers. The connections to ground (pin #8) and the power supply (pin #16) are usually not shown in schematics. Every logic symbol must, without exception, have its part number written inside it.

At times, you will use different instances of the same set of gates in several places in your schematic. The best way to handle this is to draw the gates once, then box them in with a dashed line and label them with a detail letter, as in Figure 2.62. When you use these gates in a particular place in your schematic, draw a single symbol for the function to be performed, like the single 4-bit wide inverter in the figure, labeling it with the detail letter. The idea is that you expand the detail with its definition.

Names   All signals that are not entirely local to an individual schematic drawing must be given a name. If a signal connects to many places in one drawing, it is more convenient to name the signal once and label local wires with this name where it is used, rather than draw wires to connect the uses together.

Names are an important form of documentation, so it is a good idea to name any wire whose usage is not trivial. You should use names that are understandable and describe the function performed by the signal. For example, if a signal causes the B Register to be cleared, then name the signal CLEAR BREG, not 52 or CB. More than one word in a name is fine. Many people capitalize signal names so that they are easy to distinguish from text in documentation. Each signal name must be unique within the project.

Polarization and Bubbles   To see an application of practical bubble matching, consider Figure 2.63. The designer is trying to AND together two related data bits, identified as XA_0 and XA_1. Unfortunately, the NAND gate output has the opposite sense from what the designer wants: if both bits are 1's, then the NAND output is a 0. As signals pass through levels of logic, it is quite typical for the polarity to switch back and forth.

To make it easier to deal with inverting logic, we think about signals in two separate ways, both of which are reflected in the convention for signal names. The first element of a signal name indicates its function: LOAD PC, or XA<0> AND XA<1>. The second gives the signal's polarity as either high (.H) or low (.L). An .H or .L polarity indicator is added to every signal name to indicate whether its function occurs when the signal is 1 or 0. For example, in Figure 2.63, the signal XA<0>_AND_XA<1>.L is at a low voltage ("true") when both XA<0> and XA<1> are at high voltages (also "true"). Thus, the signal is given an .L polarity. If an AND gate had been used instead of NAND, the polarity would be .H. If a signal is not marked with a polarity indicator, it defaults to positive logic. To be absolutely clear, it is a good idea to mark all signals explicitly.

A signal with positive (.H) polarity is asserted at a high voltage level, and a signal with negative (.L) polarity is asserted at a low voltage level. A

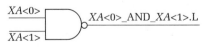

Figure 2.63   Example of polarity inversion.

bubble on a logic symbol indicates that an input or output is inverted. An input with a bubble means that the input signal is to be asserted low. A bubbled output is asserted when its voltage is low. A bubbled input should almost always match a bubbled output or another signal that is specified as being asserted active low. Inputs and outputs without bubbles match .H signals or other bubbleless inputs and outputs.

Because it makes drawings so much easier to read, you should match bubbles wherever possible. Where they match, you can simply ignore polarity. For example, although Figure 2.64 and Figure 2.65 are equivalent, in Figure 2.65 it is much easier to see that five active high input signals are being ANDed together.

In a few cases, bubbles cannot be made to match. Usually these cases involve some form of *inhibition*. That is, when the signal is asserted, something is NOT happening. Figure 2.66 shows an example where a clear pulse (ClearReg) is being controlled by another signal (Enable). The actual clear signal is active low and should be asserted

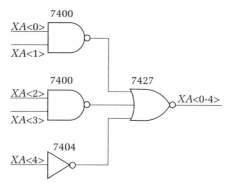

Figure 2.64   Incorrect bubble matching.

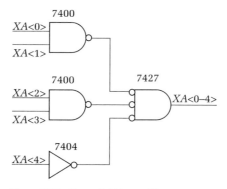

Figure 2.65   Correct bubble matching.

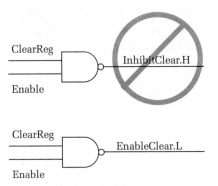

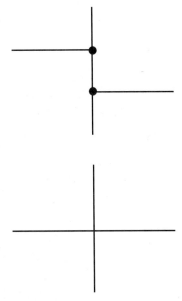

Figure 2.66 A case where polarity and bubbles don't match.

Figure 2.67 Wiring connection (top) and crossover (bottom).

only when both Enable and ClearReg are asserted. When the output of the NAND gate is high, the Clear signal is inhibited. Note the use of the positive logic form of the output signal polarity.

Since the gate's output is active low but the signal label is active high, we have a mismatch. It would be clearer if the gate output were labeled with the action that takes effect when the signal is asserted active low. Careful renaming of a signal can make the mismatch go away. In this case, you simply replace *InhibitClear.H* with *EnableClear.L*.

Crossovers and Connections All connections between wires must be marked with "blobs," as shown in Figure 2.67. Be careful to make it crystal clear when signals cross without connection and when connections are made.

Hierarchical Documentation and Cross-References Large designs cannot fit on a single sheet of paper. They must be suitably distributed over many pages, and signals will cross page boundaries. Even if everything did fit on one sheet, it probably wouldn't be practical to draw wires for every connection: the sheet would turn into a rat's nest of lines. Thus, you need to make proper use of hierarchy and abstraction in your presentation of the design.

The first pages should contain a coarse block diagram showing the main group of components. Only signals that leave or enter one of these blocks should be shown. Subsequent pages will expand these blocks hierarchically into more and more details. Thus the same signal may appear in several disconnected places. It is important to keep track of where signals are used, making it easier to scan the drawings and to verify signal fan-outs.

You are expected to observe several conventions in order to keep track of signal usage. All inputs to a sheet should enter at the top or left edge of the sheet; all outputs from the sheet should terminate at the bottom or right edge. If a signal is both an input and an output, you may take your pick.

Each page of your project should be named in some conspicuous place and should also be numbered. Signals that leave a page should carry a unique label and an indication of other pages on which they can be found entering. Correspondingly, all entering signals should carry the proper name label and an indication of the page from which they come. Ideally, if each page corresponds to some block in a previous page, then that previous page is a block diagram that shows all the interconnections between the blocks. The inputs and outputs to any block should correspond to all the entering and exiting signals on the detailed page and should carry the same signal names.

Chapter Review

In this chapter, we have introduced a variety of primitive logic building blocks: the Inverter, AND, OR, NAND, NOR, XOR, and XNOR gates, with which we can implement any Boolean function. We have also presented the two primary canonical forms for describing a Boolean function: sum of products and product of sums. A function may have many equivalent Boolean expressions but only one representation in a canonical form. The process of logic minimization seeks to find the equivalent expression with the minimum number of terms and the fewest literals per term. Don't-care conditions on the inputs can be used to simplify the expression substantially. Reduced expressions lead to realizations of circuits with the fewest gates and the fewest inputs, at least if the target is a two-level circuit realization. (Multilevel logic minimization will be discussed in the next chapter.)

The minimum expression can be obtained through judicious application of the laws and theorems of Boolean algebra, although this is a tedious and error-prone process. The K-map provides a graphical reformulation of the truth table that helps us visualize multidimensional adjacencies. These identify opportunities for successively applying the uniting theorem ($AB + A\bar{B} = A$) to reduce a function to its minimum equivalent form. Of course, the K-map method does not provide an algorithm, a detailed sequence of steps, which guarantees that the best possible solution will be obtained. Although ideally suited for pencil-and-paper solutions, for all practical purposes the method is limited to six variables.

On the other hand, the Quine-McCluskey method is a rigorous algorithm suitable for any number of variables, but it requires a large number of steps to find the minimum form. As a compromise, we presented the algorithms of *espresso*, a computer-aided design tool for logic minimization. It identifies implicants and expands them into primes in much the same way as a human designer does in the K-map, but it applies heuristic methods systematically to improve the good solution it obtains initially. However, it is not guaranteed to obtain the minimum two-level expression, only a very good solution.

In the final section of the chapter, we examined some aspects of TTL logic and documentation standards for schematics. TTL logic comes in packages with standard conventions for power supply connections and pin-outs. Documentation standards deal with ways to draw schematics, making them readable by other designers. The conventions include standard approaches for schematic shapes, signal naming, polarity conservation, data flow, and component interconnection.

Further Reading

George Boole's original work was published in the middle of the 19th century. Obviously, he did not have computer hardware in mind at the time. Instead, he attempted to develop a mathematical basis for logic. The basic axioms that we presented in Section 2.1 are called Huntington's axioms. These were published by E. V. Huntington in a paper entitled "Sets of Independent Postulates for the Algebra of Logic," in *Transactions of the American Mathematical Society* (Volume 5) in 1904. C. E. Shannon was the first to show how Boolean algebra could be applied to digital design in his landmark paper "A Symbolic Analysis of Relay and Switching Circuits," in *Transactions of the AIEE*, 57, 713–723, 1938.

The K-map method was described in an article by M. Karnaugh in 1953 ("A Map Method for Synthesis of Combinational Logic Circuits," *Transactions of the AIEE, Communications and Electronics*, 72, I, 593–599, November 1953). Interestingly, despite the fact that Karnaugh is given the credit, the original idea is from E. W. Veitch ("A Chart Method for Simplifying Boolean Functions," *Proceedings of the ACM*, May 1952, pp. 127–133). The major difference is in how the boxes of the map are labeled: Karnaugh used the familiar Gray code scheme and Veitch used an alternative "distance 1" code, which is harder to remember.

The K-map method is adequate only for relatively simple problems. The Quine-McCluskey method forms the basis of all algorithms for reducing equations of an arbitrary number of variables. The original papers that describe the method can be found in W. V. Quine, "A Way to Simplify Truth Functions," *American Mathematical Monthly*, 62, 9, 627–631, 1955, and E. J. McCluskey, "Minimization of Boolean Functions," *Bell Systems Technical Journal*, 35, 5, 1417–1444, November 1956.

A very detailed mathematical description of the algorithms at the heart of computer-aided design tools like *espresso* can be found in R. K. Brayton, G. D. Hachtel, C. T. McMullen, and A. L. Sangiovanni-Vincentelli, *Logic Minimization Algorithms for VLSI Synthesis*, Kluwer Academic Publishers, Boston, 1984.

All digital design textbooks describe Boolean simplification in one form or another. For alternative approaches, see J. F. Wakerly, *Digital Design Principles and Practices*, Prentice-Hall, Englewood Cliffs, NJ, 1990; S. H.

Unger, *The Essence of Logic Circuits*, Prentice-Hall, Englewood Cliffs, NJ, 1989; and C. H. Roth, Jr., *Fundamentals of Logic Design*, West Publishing Co., St. Paul, MN, 1985.

Exercises

Nothing should be made by man's labor which is not worth making, or which must be made by labor degrading to the makers.

—William Morris

2.1 *(Gate Logic)* Draw schematics for the following functions in terms of AND, OR, and inverter gates.

  a. $X(Y+Z)$

  b. $XY+XZ$

  c. $\overline{X(Y+Z)}$

  d. $\overline{X}+\overline{YZ}$

  e. $W(X+YZ)$

2.2 *(Gate Logic)* Draw the schematics for the following functions using NOR gates and inverters only:

  a. $[\overline{X+(\overline{Y+Z})}]$

  b. $[\overline{(\overline{X+Y})+(\overline{X+Z})}]$

2.3 *(Gate Logic)* Draw the schematics for the following functions using NAND gates and inverters only:

  a. $[\overline{X(\overline{YZ})}]$

  b. $XY+XZ$

2.4 *(Gate Logic)* Draw switch networks for the XOR and XNOR Boolean operators.

2.5 *(Gate Logic)* Design a hall light circuit to the following specification. There is a switch at either end of a hall that controls a single light. If the light is off, changing the position of either switch causes the light to turn on. Similarly, if the light is on, changing the position of either switch causes the light to turn off. Write your assumptions, derive a truth table, and describe how to implement this function in terms of logic gates or switching networks.

2.6 *(Laws and Theorems of Boolean Algebra)* Use switching diagrams to demonstrate the validity of the following simplification theorems:

  a. $X+XY=X$

  b. $(X+\overline{Y})Y=XY$

  c. $\overline{(X+Y)}=\overline{X}\bullet\overline{Y}$

2.7   *(Laws and Theorems of Boolean Algebra)*   Prove the following simplification theorems using the first eight laws of Boolean algebra:

  a. $(X + Y)(X + \overline{Y}) = X$

  b. $X(X + Y) = X$

  c. $(X + \overline{Y})Y = XY$

  d. $(X + Y)(\overline{X} + Z) = XZ + \overline{X}Y$

2.8   *(Laws and Theorems of Boolean Algebra)*   Verify that

  a. OR and AND are duals of each other.

  b. NOR and NAND are duals of each other.

  c. XNOR and XOR are duals of each other.

  d. XNOR is the complement of XOR:

$$\overline{(X\overline{Y} + \overline{X}Y)} = \overline{X}\overline{Y} + XY$$

2.9   *(Laws and Theorems of Boolean Algebra)*   Prove, using truth tables, that

$$XY + YZ + \overline{X}Z = XY + \overline{X}Z$$

2.10   *(Laws and Theorems of Boolean Algebra)*   Use DeMorgan's theorem to compute the complement of the following Boolean expressions:

  a. $A(B + CD)$

  b. $ABC + B(\overline{C} + \overline{D})$

  c. $\overline{X} + \overline{Y}$

  d. $X + Y\overline{Z}$

  e. $(X + Y)Z$

  f. $X + \overline{YZ}$

  g. $X(Y + Z\overline{W} + \overline{V}S)$

2.11   *(Laws and Theorems of Boolean Algebra)*   Form the complement of the following functions:

  a. $f(A,B,C,D) = [A + \overline{BCD}][\overline{AD} + B(\overline{C} + A)]$

  b. $f(A,B,C,D) = A\overline{B}C + (\overline{A} + B + D)(AB\overline{D} + \overline{B})$

2.12   *(Laws and Theorems of Boolean Algebra)*   Using Boolean algebra, verify that the schematic of Figure Ex2.12 implements an XOR function.

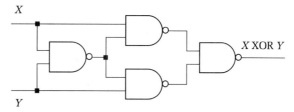

Figure Ex2.12 XOR implemented by NAND gates.

2.13 *(Boolean Simplification)* Simplify the following functions using the theorems of Boolean algebra. Write the particular law or theorem you are using in each step. For each simplified function you derive, how many literals does it have?

a. $f(X,Y) = XY + X\overline{Y}$

b. $f(X,Y) = (X + Y)(X + \overline{Y})$

c. $f(X,Y,Z) = Y\overline{Z} + \overline{X}YZ + XYZ$

d. $f(X,Y,Z) = (X + Y)(\overline{X} + Y + Z)(\overline{X} + Y + \overline{Z})$

e. $f(W,X,Y,Z) = X + XYZ + \overline{X}YZ + \overline{X}Y + WX + \overline{W}X$

2.14 *(Boolean Simplification)* Consider the function $f(A,B,C,D) = (AD + \overline{A}C)[\overline{B}(C + B\overline{D})]$.

a. Draw its schematic using AND, OR, and inverter gates.

b. Using Boolean algebra, put the function into its minimized form and draw the resulting schematic.

2.15 *(Canonical Forms)* Consider the function $f(A,B,C,D) = \Sigma\, m(0,1,2,7,8,9,10,15)$.

a. Write this as a Boolean expression in canonical minterm form.

b. Rewrite the expression in canonical maxterm form.

c. Write the complement of f in "little m" notation and as a canonical minterm expression.

d. Write the complement of f in "big M" notation and as a canonical maxterm expression.

2.16 *(Canonical Forms and Boolean Simplification)* Given the following function in product of sums form, not necessarily minimized:

$$F(W,X,Y,Z) = (W + \overline{X} + \overline{Y})(\overline{W} + \overline{Z})(W + Y)$$

a. Express the function in the canonical sum of products form. Use "little m" notation.

b. Reexpress the function in minimized sum of products form.

   c. Express $\overline{F}$ in minimized sum of products form.

   d. Reexpress $\overline{F}$ in minimized product of sums form.

2.17 *(Boolean Simplification)*   Using K-maps, find the following:

   a. Minimum sum of products form for the function and its complement given in Exercise 2.15.

   b. Minimum product of sums form for the function and its complement given in Exercise 2.15.

2.18 *(Boolean Simplification)*   Use Karnaugh maps (K-maps) to simplify the following functions in sum of products form. How many literals appear in your minimized solutions?

   a. $f(X,Y,Z) = \Pi\, M(0,1,6,7)$

   b. $f(W,X,Y,Z) = \Pi\, M(1,3,7,9,11,15)$

   c. $f(V,W,X,Y,Z) = \Pi\, M(0,4,18,19,22,23,25,29)$

   d. $f(A,B,C,D) = \Sigma\, m(0,2,4,6)$

   e. $f(A,B,C,D) = \Sigma\, m(0,1,4,5,12,13)$

   f. $f(A,B,C,D,E) = \Sigma\, m(0,4,18,19,22,23,25,29)$

   g. $f(A,B,C,D,E,F) = \Sigma\, m(3,7,12,14,15,19,23,27,\,28,29,31,35,39,44,$
      $45,46,48,49,50,52,53,55,56,57,59).$

2.19 *(Boolean Simplification)*   Determine the minimized realization of the following functions in the sum of products form:

   a. $f(W,X,Y,Z) = \Sigma\, m(0,2,8,9) + \Sigma\, d(1,3)$

   b. $f(W,X,Y,Z) = \Sigma\, m(1,7,11,13) + \Sigma\, d(0,5,10,15)$

   c. $f(V,W,X,Y,Z) = \Sigma\, m(2,8,9,10,13,15,16,18,19,23) + \Sigma\, d(3,11,17,22)$

   d. $f(V,W,X,Y,Z) = \Sigma\, m(0,1,2,9,13,16,18,24,25) + \Sigma\, d(8,10,17,19)$

2.20 *(Boolean Simplification)*   Use the K-map method to find the minimized product of sums expressions for the following Boolean functions:

   a. $f(A,B,C) = A \oplus B \oplus C$

   b. $f(A,B,C) = AB + BC + AC$

   c. $f(A,B,C,D) = \Sigma\, m(1,3,5,7,9) + \Sigma\, d(6,12,13)$

   d. $f(A,B,C,D) = \Pi\, M(0,1,6,7)$

   e. $f(A,B,C,D) = \Sigma\, m(0,2,4,6)$

2.21 *(Positive and Negative Logic)*   Show the following:

   a. A positive logic AND is equivalent to a negative logic OR.

   b. A positive logic NOR is equivalent to a negative logic NAND.

c. A positive logic XOR is equivalent to a negative logic XNOR.

d. A positive logic XNOR is equivalent to a negative logic XOR.

2.22 *(Quine-McCluskey Method)* Use the Quine-McCluskey method to find the minimum equivalent forms for the following Boolean expressions.

   a. $f(X,Y,Z) = \Sigma\, m(2,3,4,5)$

   b. $f(A,B,C,D) = \Sigma\, m(0,1,4,5,12,13)$

2.23 *(Quine-McCluskey Method)* Given the function $F(A,B,C,D) = \Sigma\, m(1,5,7,8,9,13,15) + d(4,14)$, find the minimum sum of products form using the Quine-McCluskey method. Show your process of deriving the prime implicants. Include the implication chart from which your minimum sum of products form is derived.

2.24 *(Karnaugh Map Method)* There may be more than one true minimum equivalent form for a given Boolean expression. Demonstrate this by drawing a four-variable K-map that has two different minimized forms for the same Boolean expression, each with the same number of terms and literals.

2.25 *(Karnaugh Map Method)* Using a four-variable K-map, fill it with 1's and 0's to find a function that illustrates the following points. Write the expressions for each of the requested forms and count the number of terms and literals for each one:

   a. The minimized sum of products and product of sums forms have the same number of terms and literals.

   b. The minimized sum of products form has fewer terms and literals than the minimized product of sums form.

   c. The minimized product of sums form has fewer terms and literals than the minimized sum of products form.

2.26 *(Combinational Logic Design)* Consider a five-input Boolean function that is asserted whenever exactly two of its inputs are asserted.

   a. Construct its truth table.

   b. What is the function in sum of products form, using "little m" notation?

   c. What is the function in product of sums form, using "big M" notation?

   d. Use the Karnaugh map method to simplify the function in sum of products form.

2.27 *(Combinational Logic Design)*   In this chapter, we've examined the BCD increment by 1 function. Now consider a binary increment by 1 function defined over the 4-bit binary numbers 0000 through 1111.

a. Fill in the truth table for the function.

b. Fill in the four 4-variable K-maps, and find the minimized sum of products for each output function.

c. Repeat the process for the minimized product of sums form. Which leads to the simpler implementation in terms of the number of literals?

2.28 *(Combinational Logic Design)*   In this chapter, we've examined a 2-bit binary adder circuit. Now consider a 2-bit binary subtractor, defined as follows. The inputs A, B and C, D form the two 2-bit numbers N_1 and N_2. The circuit will form the difference $N_1 - N_2$ on the output bits F (most significant) and G (least significant). Assume that the circuit never sees an input combination in which N_1 is less than N_2. The output bits are don't cares in these cases.

a. Fill in the four-variable truth table for F and G.

b. Fill in the K-map for the minimum sum of products expression for the functions F and G.

c. Repeat to find the minimum product of sums expression for F and G.

2.29 *(Combinational Logic Design)*   Consider a four-input function that outputs a 1 whenever an odd number of its inputs are 1.

a. Fill in the truth table for the function.

b. Fill in the K-map to find the minimum sum of products expression for the function. What is it? Can the function be minimized using the K-map method?

c. Can you think of a more economical way to implement this function if XOR gates are allowed? (*Warning*: It will be very tedious to try to simplify this function using Boolean algebra, so think about the question first!)

2.30 *(Combinational Logic Design)*   Design a combinational circuit with three data inputs D_2, D_1, D_0, two control inputs C_1, C_0, and two outputs R_1, R_0. R_1 and R_0 should be the remainder after dividing the binary number formed from D_2, D_1, D_0 by the number formed by C_1, C_0. For example, if D_2, D_1, $D_0 = 111$ and C_1,

$C_0 = 10$, then R_1, $R_0 = 01$ (that is, the remainder of 7 divided by 2 is 1). Note that division by zero will never be requested.

a. Fill in truth tables for the combinational logic functions R_1 and R_0.

b. Derive minimized sum of product realizations of these functions using the Karnaugh map method.

c. Draw a circuit schematic that implements R_1 and R_0 using NAND gates only. You may assume any fan-in gates that you need.

3 Multilevel Combinational Logic

It is a riddle wrapped in a mystery inside an enigma.

— *Sir Winston Churchill*

Introduction

In the previous chapter, we introduced the basic methods for describing Boolean functions as minimized two-level networks constructed from AND, OR, and NOT gates. In this chapter, we extend the discussion in three main directions:

■ *The conversion of AND/OR and OR/AND networks to NAND-NAND and NOR-NOR networks.* AND and OR gates are rarely used in digital systems; you must learn how to convert them to networks with NAND and NOR gates.

■ *Design strategies for implementing logic in more than two levels.* Just as a complex algebraic expression can be simplified by factoring out common subexpressions, you can implement a Boolean function in fewer gates if you factor it judiciously. This leads to a fundamental trade-off between time (more levels of logic to pass through) and space (fewer gates needed to implement the function).

■ *Computer-aided design tools.* Multilevel logic depends on more sophisticated methods for finding an efficient design solution. We examine *misII*, a computer-based tool for performing multilevel logic design.

■ *Time response in digital networks.* We will look more closely at the dynamic behavior of combinational logic gates. *Hazards*, which cause undesirable transitions at the outputs, can lead to improper circuit behavior. You will learn the procedures for obtaining *hazard-free* designs.

3.1 Multilevel Logic

Given a Boolean function expressed in minterm or maxterm canonical form, you now know how to reduce it into a minimal two-level form with the fewest terms and literals. Let's consider the function $f\,(A, B, C, D, E, F, G)$:

$$f = ADF + AEF + BDF + BEF + CDF + CEF + G$$

It is already in its minimal sum of products form. Its implementation as a two-level network of AND and OR gates requires six 3-input AND gates and one 7-input OR gate, a total of seven gates and 19 literals (see Figure 3.1(a)).

We can do better if we replace the two-level form with a so-called *factored form*. We express the function with common literals factored out from the product terms whenever possible.

By recursively factoring out common literals, we can express the function f as:

$$f = (AD + AE + BD + BE + CD + CE)\,F + G$$

$$f = [(A + B + C)\,D + (A + B + C)\,E]\,F + G$$

$$f = (A + B + C)(D + E)\,F + G$$

Expressed as a series of expressions, each in the two-level form, f becomes

$$f = XYF + G$$

$$X = A + B + C$$

$$Y = D + E$$

When written this way, the function requires one 3-input OR gate, two 2-input OR gates, and a 3-input AND gate, a total of four gates and nine literals. The intermediate functions X and Y count as literals in the final expression for f.

The implementation from the factored form is shown in Figure 3.1(b). You can significantly reduce the number of wires and gates needed to implement the function, but this implementation probably has worse delay

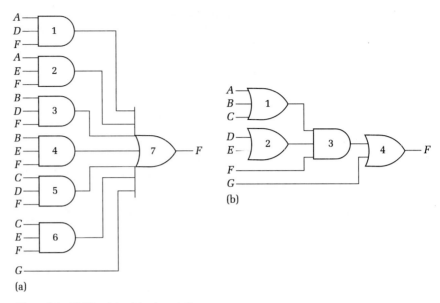

Figure 3.1   Multilevel circuit implementation.

because of the increased levels of logic. In general, multilevel implementa-tions are more gate efficient than two-level implementations but have worse propagation delay.

In this section we will be concerned with two issues: how to express logic networks solely in terms of NAND and NOR gates, and how to take advantage of multilevel logic to reduce the overall gate count.

3.1.1   Conversion to NAND/NAND and NOR/NOR Networks

The canonical forms you have studied so far are expressed in terms of AND and OR gates, but you will rarely encounter these in digital systems. The underlying technologies are more efficient at implementing NAND and NOR gates. In fact, AND and OR gates are most commonly realized by fol-lowing a NAND or NOR gate with an inverter. In addition, NAND and NOR functions are *complete*; that is, a function expressed in terms of AND, OR, and NOT operations can be implemented solely in terms of NAND or NOR operations. Frequently, you will be confronted with the task of mapping a network with an arbitrary number of levels of AND and OR gates into one that consists only of NAND or NOR gates. We will begin the discussion with two-level networks and extend it to multilevel networks.

Visualization: DeMorgan's Theorem and Pushing Bubbles   The conversion process depends critically on DeMorgan's theorem. Recall that

$$\overline{AB} = \overline{A} + \overline{B} \qquad \overline{A + B} = \overline{AB}$$

and that

$$A + B = \overline{(\overline{A}\overline{B})} \qquad AB = \overline{(\overline{A}+\overline{B})}$$

In essence, a NAND function can be implemented just as well by an OR gate with its inputs inverted. Similarly, a NOR function can be implemented by an AND gate with its inputs complemented. The conversion from one form to the other is often called "pushing the bubble." This is simply a way to remember DeMorgan's theorem. As the bubble "pushes through" an AND shape, it changes to an OR shape with bubbles on the inputs. Similarly, pushing the bubble through an OR shape transforms it to an AND shape with bubbles on the inputs.

Figure 3.2 summarizes the relationship between OR gates and NAND gates. An OR gate is logically equivalent to a NAND gate with its inputs inverted. Similarly, an AND gate is equivalent to a NOR gate with its inputs complemented. This is shown in Figure 3.3. The schematic symbols on either side of the $\equiv$ in Figures 3.2 and 3.3 can be freely exchanged without changing the function's truth table.

AND/OR Conversion to NAND/NAND Networks Consider the simple gate network in Figure 3.4(a). Let's replace the first-level AND gates by their NOR equivalents and the OR gate by its NAND equivalent. The equivalent circuit is shown in Figure 3.4(b). Note that the output inversion at the first-level gates matches the input inversion at the second level. These cancel each other out, as shown in Figure 3.4(c). Both the first- and second-level gates are NAND. Unfortunately, this does not properly conserve the bubbles at the first-level inputs and the second-level outputs. This is corrected in Figure 3.4(d), where we have replaced the NAND gates with their equivalent forms. Now the bubbles are properly matched.

A	$\overline{A}$	B	$\overline{B}$	$A+B$	$\overline{A \bullet \overline{B}}$	$\overline{A}+\overline{B}$	$\overline{A} \bullet \overline{B}$
0	1	0	1	0	0	1	1
0	1	1	0	1	1	1	1
1	0	0	1	1	1	1	1
1	0	1	0	1	1	0	0

Figure 3.2 OR/NAND equivalences.

A	$\overline{A}$	B	$\overline{B}$	$A \bullet B$	$\overline{\overline{A}+\overline{B}}$	$\overline{A} \bullet \overline{B}$	$\overline{\overline{A}+\overline{B}}$
0	1	0	1	0	0	1	1
0	1	1	0	0	0	0	0
1	0	0	1	0	0	0	0
1	0	1	0	1	1	0	0

Figure 3.3 AND/NOR equivalence.

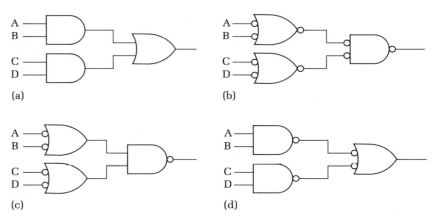

Figure 3.4 AND/OR to NAND/NAND.

As a shortcut, you can simply insert matching inversions at the first-level outputs and second-level inputs to convert an AND/OR network to a NAND/NAND network.

AND/OR Conversion to NOR/NOR Networks Suppose you are now restricted to mapping the AND/OR network into a NOR-only network. As a shortcut, you can simply replace the first-level AND gates with NOR gates (AND with inverted inputs) and the second-level OR gate with a NOR gate.

But this is not logically equivalent. Every time a new inversion is introduced, it must be balanced by a complementary inversion. To correct the problem, we introduce additional inverters at the inputs and the output (see Figure 3.5).

To keep track of the need for inverted inputs to the first-level gates, we use the notation for active low inputs: \A, \B, \C, and \D. Since it is common to have both a Boolean variable and its complement available as circuit inputs, the conversion may not lead to additional inverters. Similarly, the extra inverter at the output can be eliminated if the circuit can be transformed so that the function is computed in negative logic. In other words, the output is connected to an input expecting an active low signal.

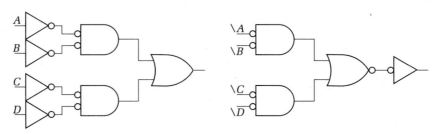

Figure 3.5 AND/OR conversion to NOR/NOR.

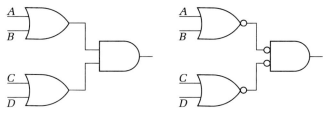

Figure 3.6 OR/AND conversion to NOR/NOR.

OR/AND Conversion to NOR/NOR Network Now let's consider a gate implementation for a simple expression in product of sums form. We can map this expression into a NOR/NOR network simply by replacing the OR gates with NOR gates and the AND gate with a NOR gate (an AND gate with inverted inputs). You can see in Figure 3.6 that the inversions we introduced cancel each other out.

OR/AND Conversion to NAND/NAND Networks Implementing the expression using NAND-only logic introduces exactly the same problems we have already seen in Figure 3.5. The correct transformation replaces the OR gates with NAND gates (OR gates with inverted inputs) and the AND gate with a NAND gate. To maintain equivalence with the original function, you need to place inverters at the inputs and at the output. This is shown in Figure 3.7.

Generalization to Multilevel Circuits We can extend the transformation techniques to multilevel networks. Consider the function

$$F = A(B + CD) + B\overline{C}$$

Its implementation in AND/OR form is shown in Figure 3.8(a). You can see how we have arranged the logic into alternating levels of AND and OR gates. This makes it easier to observe the places where the conversion to NAND/NAND gates can take place. You simply replace each AND with a NAND and each OR with a NAND in its "alternative" form (OR with inverted inputs).

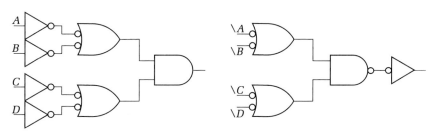

Figure 3.7 OR/AND conversion to NAND/NAND.

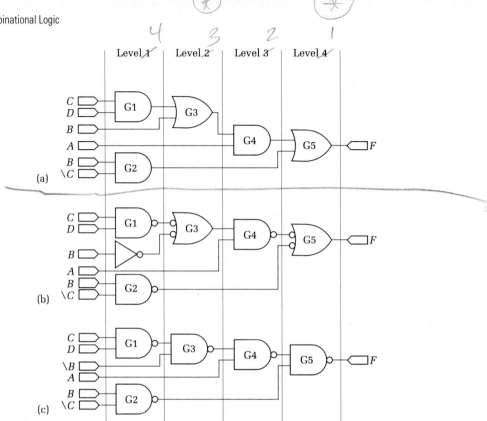

Figure 3.8   Multilevel conversion to NAND logic.

The application of this procedure is shown in Figure 3.8(b). We have grouped levels 1, 2 and 3, 4 into AND/OR circuits. These can be replaced by equivalent NAND/NAND networks directly.

Note that the literal B input to gate G3 must be inverted to preserve the original sense of the signal wire. Always remember to conserve the introduction of inversions. Any internal signal wires that undergo an odd number of inversions must have an additional inverter inserted in the path.

The final NAND-only network is shown in Figure 3.8(c). We have eliminated an inverter by replacing the B input to G3 with a connection to its complemented literal.

Suppose your target is a NOR-only network. You can take the same approach when the initial network is expressed as alternating OR and AND levels. You should place OR gates at the odd levels and AND gates at the even levels. You can immediately replace these by NOR gates. Any unmatched input bubbles should be corrected by inserting inverters or using the complemented literal where necessary.

It is a little more complicated when transforming alternating AND/OR networks (OR/AND networks) into NOR-only circuits (NAND-only circuits). Nevertheless, you can still apply the same basic techniques.

For example, suppose you want to map the AND/OR/AND/OR network of Figure 3.8(a) into NOR gates. You should invert the inputs to the odd levels while inserting an extra inversion at the output of the even levels. The extra inversions between adjacent even and odd levels can be saved if they cancel each other. This is shown in Figure 3.9(a) between levels 2 and 3, for gates G3 and G4. The final NOR-only circuit is shown in Figure 3.9(b). All but one of the literals have been inverted and an extra inversion has been inserted at the output. You can implement this last inversion by a NOR gate with both inputs tied to the same signal.

Figure 3.10 shows an example in which the circuit cannot be placed into a form that alternates between AND and OR gates. The multilevel function is

$$f = AX + X + D$$

$$X = BC$$

single input on * levels must be changed (inverted)

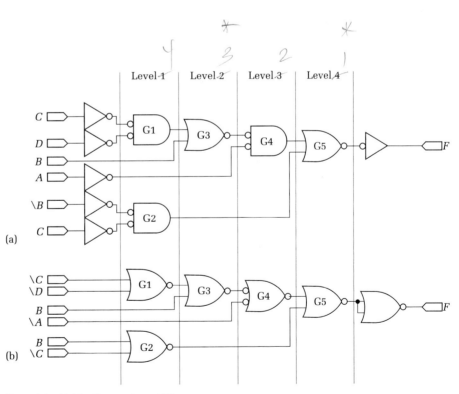

Figure 3.9 Multilevel conversion to NOR gates.

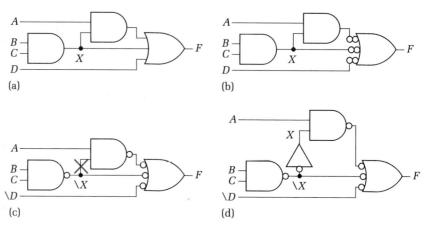

Figure 3.10 Another multilevel conversion example.

Figure 3.10(a) shows the initial AND/OR network. We begin by introducing double inversions at the inputs to the last-stage OR gate (Figure 3.10(b)). We propagate these back to the outputs of the two AND gates and the input D (Figure 3.10(c)). Note how the connection to D has been replaced by a connection to its complement to match the bubble on the OR's input.

There is still one problem with this circuit. The NAND gate computes the complement of the function X, not X. To conserve bubbles and the sense of the signals, the NAND output must be inverted before it can be input to the second-stage NAND gate. The final converted circuit is shown in Figure 3.10(d).

3.1.2 AND-OR-Invert/OR-AND-Invert Building Blocks

Up to this point, we have been thinking about multilevel logic circuits constructed from discrete gates. In some digital circuit technologies, such as TTL, primitive forms of multilevel logic are readily available as prepackaged components. Multiple-input AND-OR-Invert (AOI) and OR-AND-Invert (OAI) functions are available as single complex gates in these technologies. We examine these building blocks next.

General Concept Conceptually, an AOI logic block is a three-level logic circuit consisting of AND gates at the first level, an OR gate at the second level, and an inverter at the output. Similarly, an OAI block has OR gates at the first level, an AND gate at the second level, and an inverter at the third level. In essence, several discrete gates are subsumed by a single complex gate, with the internal wiring already done for you.

A function like an AOI may seem a bit odd at first, but remember that it is much easier to build inverting logic like NAND and NOR gates than AND and OR gates in most digital circuit technologies. Figure 3.11(a) shows the logical view of the AOI block, and Figure 3.11(b) gives a possible implementation in terms of switches. If A and B are true or C and D are true, the normally open switches establish a closed path from false to output Z.

In all other cases, true will be routed to the output through the normally closed switches. For example, if $A = 0$, $B = 1$, $C = 1$, and $D = 0$, the normally closed switches controlled by A and D will be closed, making the connection between true and the output Z. Switch implementations of OAI circuits look very similar.

The implementation in Figure 3.11(b) uses eight switches. If we had implemented the function using straightforward logic gates, we would need 14 switches: four each for the three 2-input gates and two for the inverter.

The particular circuit in Figure 3.11(a) is called a *two-input two-stack* AOI gate. This means it consists of two 2-input AND gates (each AND gate corresponds to a stack). A three-input two-stack AOI gate has two 3-input gates at the first level, a two-input three-stack AOI gate has three 2-input gates at the first level, and so on. The number of stacks is exactly the number of inputs to the second-level OR gate. Analogous concepts and terminology apply to OAI blocks.

Implementing Logic with AOI and OAI Blocks   Let's start with a simple example. We will implement the XOR function using AOI blocks. Recall that XOR's behavior is described by the equation

$$A \oplus B = A\overline{B} + \overline{A}B$$

A straightforward implementation using discrete gates requires two 2-input AND gates, one 2-input OR gate, and two inverters.

How do we implement this with AOI logic? Simply find the complement of the function in sum of products form. The final inversion in the

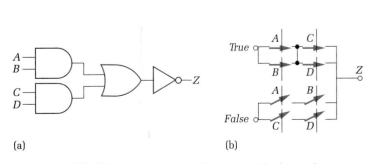

(a)   (b)

Figure 3.11   AND-OR-Invert block and a possible switch-level implementation.

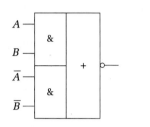

Figure 3.12 AOI implementation of XOR function.

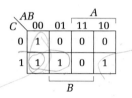

Figure 3.13 Example K-map.

AND/OR/Invert network will return the function to the sense in which we want it.

The complement of the XOR function, XNOR, is the following:

$$\overline{(A \oplus B)} = AB + \overline{A}\,\overline{B}$$

The circuit is constructed by providing A and B as inputs to the first stack and $\overline{A}$ and $\overline{B}$ as inputs to the second stack. This is shown in Figure 3.12.

The approach for OAI logic implementation is analogous. Using the K-map, we implement an OR/AND function by forming prime implicants around zeros and reading them out in product of sums form.

Example Let's consider the three-variable function $F(A, B, C) = \Sigma\, m(2, 4, 6, 7)$. Figure 3.13 gives the K-map for its complement, $\Sigma\, m(0, 1, 3, 5)$. In minimized form, the complement is expressed as

$$\overline{F} = \overline{A}\overline{B} + \overline{A}C + \overline{B}C \qquad F = (\overline{B} + C)\,(\overline{A} + C)\,(A + \overline{B})$$

Thus F can be implemented by two-input three-stack AOI or OAI gates. The inputs are wired to the literals of the complement of F. For the AOI implementation, you wire $\overline{A}\overline{B}$ to the first stack, $\overline{A}C$ to the second, and $\overline{B}C$ to the third.

Example A 4-Bit Comparator Let's say your task is to implement a 4-bit comparator. Such a circuit has eight inputs organized as two sets of four input bits, labeled A_3 through A_0 and B_3 through B_0. The circuit's single output Z is asserted when $A_3 = B_3$, $A_2 = B_2$, $A_1 = B_1$, and $A_0 = B_0$. We assume that we have only inverters, NOR gates, and AOI gates.

Consider the logic for determining the equality of each pair of bits:

$$F_0 = (A_0 = B_0) = A_0 B_0 + \overline{A}_0 \overline{B}_0$$

$$F_1 = (A_1 = B_1) = A_1 B_1 + \overline{A}_1 \overline{B}_1$$

$$F_2 = (A_2 = B_2) = A_2 B_2 + \overline{A}_2 \overline{B}_2$$

$$F_3 = (A_3 = B_3) = A_3 B_3 + \overline{A}_3 \overline{B}_3$$

The comparator function becomes $F = F_0 \bullet F_1 \bullet F_2 \bullet F_3$, which can be equivalently rewritten as the following if we use a NOR gate:

$$F = \overline{\overline{F}_0 + \overline{F}_1 + \overline{F}_2 + \overline{F}_3}$$

Now we can express the bitwise equality functions in AOI form. Each F_i is already in AND/OR form. Since the NOR gate needs the complements of the F_i at its inputs, these can implemented directly with AOI gates.

Figure 3.14 shows the implementation in terms of AOI gates at the first level and a NOR gate at the second level. Each AOI gate implements the complement of F_i—recall that the complement of equality (XNOR) is difference (XOR). The NOR function, when written as an AND gate with complemented inputs, negates the XOR functions to restore the XNORs.

Under the constraints of this particular problem, there is a real advantage to using these complex gates. Counting each AOI block as a single gate, the schematic of Figure 3.14 uses 13 gates: eight inverters, four AOI gates, and a 4-input NOR gate. An implementation using discrete AND and OR gates (or NOR and NAND gates) would require 8 more gates, since the function performed by the 4 complex gates would be replaced by 12 discrete gates. Even if the use of the AOI blocks represents no savings in circuit area, the transition away from discrete logic offers a considerable advantage in reducing wiring complexity.

TTL AOI Components   TTL packaged logic has available a number of AND-OR-Invert circuits (OR-AND-Invert gates are not readily available in TTL). See Figure 3.15 for a sample collection of schematic shapes. The 7451 package contains two 2-input 2-stack AOI gates. This particular package has 14 pins. The two gates use 10 of these (4 inputs, 1 output times 2),

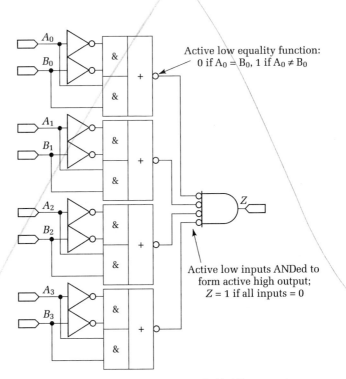

Figure 3.14   Four-bit comparator implemented with AOI gates.

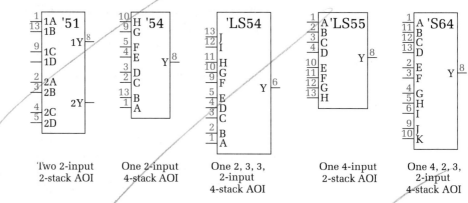

Figure 3.15   Schematic shapes of various TTL AOI components.

plus power and ground. This leaves two unconnected pins (the 74LS51, not shown in the figure, takes advantage of these previously unused connections by providing one 3-input 2-stack AOI gate and one 2 × 2 gate). Other components include the 7454 2-input 4-stack AOI gate (the 'LS version comes with two 2-input stacks and two 3-input stacks), the 74LS55 4-input 2-stack AOI gate, and the 74S64 AOI gate, constructed from a 4-input stack, two 2-input stacks, and a 3-input stack.

3.2   CAD Tools for Multilevel Logic Synthesis

We can obtain minimized two-level logic networks from the canonical sum of products or product of sums form, by applying the appropriate reduction methods (K-maps, Quine-McCluskey, a two-level logic minimizer like *espresso*, etc.). Signal propagations can be fast, because no signal has to travel through more than two gate levels (not counting zeroth-level inversions). The drawback is the potential for large gate fanins, which can reduce gate performance and increase circuit area in some technologies. In many technologies, including TTL, gates with more than four inputs are rare, if they exist at all. In a practical gate-level realization of a network, the large fan-in gates must be replaced by a multiple-level network of smaller fan-in gates. This has motivated much recent interest in multilevel logic synthesis.

3.2.1   General Concept

An optimal two-level network is one that uses the smallest number of product terms and literals to realize a given truth table. It is not so easy to define optimality for multilevel networks. Is the network optimal if it has the smallest number of gates? Or is it more critical to have the fewest literals in the resulting expression? Hence, the process with multi-level systems is called *synthesis* rather than *optimization*. The goal is to create or "synthesize" a reasonable multilevel implementation, without any pretense that the result is the best that is possible.

The synthesis process involves two steps. The first, *technology-independent* stage factors out common sublogic to reduce gate fan-ins, increasing the number of gate levels as a side effect. This step is independent of the kinds of gates that will eventually be used to implement the network. It works by exploiting basic mathematical properties of Boolean expressions.

The second, *technology-dependent* stage maps the resulting factored Boolean equations into a particular implementation using a library of available gates. For example, if only 2-input OR gates are found in a particular library, then a 4-input OR gate would have to be mapped into three 2-input OR gates (see Figure 3.16). Such reorganizations of the logic network can introduce additional levels of logic in the function's implementation, possibly affecting the delay through the circuit.

3.2.2   Factored Forms and Operations

Multilevel synthesis systems place Boolean expressions in a special "tree-structured" form and perform special operations on these forms. We introduce them in this subsection.

Factored Form   The multilevel synthesis system places an expression into a *factored form*. Simply stated, this is an expression that alternates between AND and OR operations, a kind of "sum of products of sums of products...." The following function is in factored form:

$$X = (AB + \overline{B}C) [C + D(E + A\overline{C})] + (D + E)(FG)$$

Examining the expression, we see that no further subexpressions can be factored out. For the purpose of counting literals, the factored form for X can be rewritten as a sequence of two-level expressions:

$$X = F_1 F_2 + F_3 F_4 \qquad F_3 = D + E$$
$$F_1 = (AB + \overline{B}C) \qquad F_4 = FG$$
$$F_2 = C + DF_5 \qquad F_5 = E + A\overline{C}$$

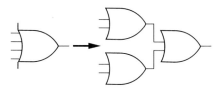

Figure 3.16   Effects of technology mapping.

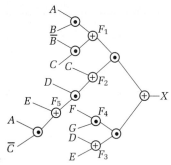

Figure 3.17 Graphical representation of a factored form.

The structure of the expression is a little clearer if it is represented in the form of a graph or tree, where the "leaves" represent literals and the internal nodes represent either an AND or OR operation. This graphical representation is shown in Figure 3.17. For the most part, the ANDs and ORs alternate between adjacent nodes of the tree.

Criterion for Multilevel Simplification In modern VLSI technologies, designers have observed that gates (internal nodes of the graph of Figure 3.17) require relatively little circuit area but connections (arcs of the graph) use significant area. Even for the modest levels of circuit integration available in TTL, the complexity of a circuit realization is strongly related to the number of wires used in its construction. Because the number of internal connections tends to scale with the number of literals, most multilevel logic synthesis systems attempt to minimize the number of literals. The literal count is based on the multilevel expression written as a sequence of two-level expressions. For the function depicted in Figure 3.17, for example, the literal count is 18. Note that when they are referenced in expressions, the functions F_1, F_2, F_3, F_4, and F_5 count as literals.

No procedure for multilevel simplification guarantees, like the Quine-McCluskey algorithm for two-level logic, that it will derive an optimal multilevel network. With a two-level minimizer like *espresso*, it is possible to specify the equations, run the program, and simply examine the result. Not so with multilevel synthesis systems. Rather than follow a precise algorithm, these systems provide a rich set of operations to manipulate the logic network. Normally you would apply the operations to the network interactively, although standard "scripts" have been developed that achieve good results. You do not need a deep understanding of the underlying operations to use these scripts.

The basic operations for manipulating a multilevel network are (1) decomposition, (2) extraction, (3) factoring, (4) substitution, and (5) collapsing. In the following sections, we will describe each of these operations and illustrate it with a simple example.

Decomposition Decomposition takes a single Boolean expression and replaces it by a collection of new expressions. Consider the function

$$F = ABC + ABD + \overline{A}\,\overline{C}\overline{D} + \overline{B}\overline{C}\overline{D}$$

This expression is in reduced sum of products form and has 12 literals. It requires nine gates, counting inverters, for implementation (see Figure 3.18(a)). However, the expression can be decomposed into two much simpler functions:

$$F = XY + \overline{X}\overline{Y} \qquad X = AB$$
$$Y = C + D$$

The resulting set of functions has eight literals and requires seven gates for implementation (see Figure 3.18(b))—nothing is free, though, and the number of gate levels has increased from two to three.

Extraction   Whereas you apply decomposition to a single function, you apply extraction to a collection of functions. This operation identifies common subexpressions in the collection of functions to which it is applied. It is perhaps the hardest multilevel operation to implement, because it must express functions in terms of their factors and then find the factors they share in common.

Let's look at an example of extraction. We start with the functions

$$F = (A + B)\,CD + E$$

$$G = (A + B)\,\overline{E}$$

$$H = CDE$$

Note that the extraction operation does not require the functions to begin in a two-level form.

In this example, the extraction operation discovers that the subexpressions $X = (A + B)$ and $Y = (CD)$ are common to F, G, and F, H, respectively. These subexpressions are called *primary divisors* or, more technically, *kernels* and *cubes*. Reexpressed in these terms, the functions can be rewritten as

$$F = XY + E$$

$$G = X\overline{E}$$

$$H = YE$$

$$X = A + B$$

$$Y = CD$$

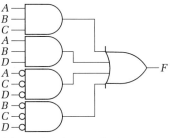

(a) Two-level circuit before decomposition

(b) Multilevel circuit after decomposition

Figure 3.18   Effects of decomposition.

The original collection of functions contains 11 literals and requires eight gates for implementation. (In Figure 3.19(a), the bubble at the input of the gate that computes G counts as one inverter gate.) The revised set of functions, after extraction, still contains 11 literals but now needs only seven gates for its implementation. You can see in Figure 3.19(b) that the single-level implementation for H has been replaced by a two-level implementation after extraction. The number of gates is reduced, but the function H now incurs worse delay.

Factoring   Factoring takes an expression in two-level form and reexpresses it as a multilevel function without introducing any intermediate subfunctions. It can be used as a preliminary step before extraction, to identify potential common subexpressions.

As an example, let's consider the following function in sum of products form. It has nine literals and can be implemented with five gates (Figure 3.20(a)):

$$F = AC + AD + BC + BD + E$$

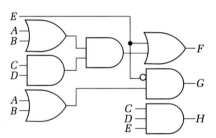

(a) Functions before extraction   (b) Functions after extraction

Figure 3.19   Effects of extraction operation.

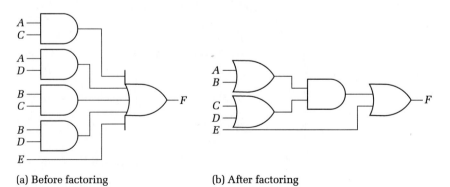

(a) Before factoring   (b) After factoring

Figure 3.20   Effects of factoring operation.

After factoring, the number of literals is reduced to seven:

$$F = (A+B)(C+D) + E = XY + E$$

$$X = A+B$$

$$Y = C+D$$

This can be implemented with four gates (Figure 3.20(b)).

Substitution   Substituting a function G into a function F reexpresses F in terms of G. For example, if $F = A + BC$, and $G = A + B$, then F can be rewritten in terms of G as follows:

$$F = A + BC$$

$$= G(A + C)$$

Once common subexpressions have been identified, substitution can be used to reexpress functions as factored forms over the subexpressions.

Collapsing   Collapsing is the reverse of substitution. It might be used to reduce the number of levels of logic to meet a timing constraint. As an example, we can collapse G back into F:

$$F = G(A + C)$$

$$= (A + B)(A + C)$$

$$= AA + AC + AB + BC$$

$$= A + BC$$

The number of literals used to express F has been reduced from five to three.

Polynomial Division and Multilevel Factoring   All of the multilevel operations have strong analogies with the multiplication and division of polynomials. The strategy is to rewrite the expression for a function F in terms of the subexpressions P, Q, and R, which represent the divisor, quotient, and remainder, respectively. In generic terms, F is written as

$$F = PQ + R$$

As a more concrete example, given the two expressions:

$$X = AC + AD + BC + BD + E$$

$$Y = A + B$$

We could write X "divided" by Y as follows:

$$X = Y(C+D) + E$$

The divisor is $Y = (A + B)$, the quotient is $(C + D)$, and the remainder is E. Expanding the expression with the distributive law would yield the original equation for X.

Finding divisors is a rather difficult problem when the laws of Boolean algebra are considered. Multiplying Boolean expressions can yield unusual results because of the variety of simplification theorems you can apply. For example, consider the functions F and G:

$$F = AD + BCD + E$$

$$G = A + B$$

Under the normal rules of algebra, G does not divide into F. The so-called *algebraic* divisors of F are D and $(A + BC)$. That is, F can be divided by D, leaving the quotient $A + BC$ with remainder E. It can also be divided by $A + BC$, leaving D as the quotient and E as the remainder.

However, if we apply the rules of Boolean algebra, then G does divide into F. We can write the quotient of F divided by G as

$$F/G = (A + C)D$$

This is because F can be rewritten as

$$
\begin{aligned}
F &= [G(A + C)D] + E \\
&= (A + B)(A + C)D + E \\
&= (AA + AC + AB + BC)D + E \\
&= (A + BC)D + E \\
&= AD + BCD + E \quad \sqrt{}
\end{aligned}
$$

The existence of Boolean divisors greatly increases the number of potential factorings of a set of expressions. Many optimization systems restrict themselves to the easier-to-find algebraic factors.

It should be clear from this discussion that the challenge in multilevel logic synthesis is to develop algorithms that can find good divisors. These lead to factored expressions with the greatest number of common subexpressions. By factoring out these subexpressions, we can minimize the number of literals needed to express a collection of functions. Extensive heuristics, beyond the scope of our discussion here, have been developed to identify good divisors.

3.2.3   A Tool for Multilevel Synthesis: *MisII*

MisII is a tool developed at the University of California at Berkeley to assist in performing multilevel synthesis. You must interact with *misII* to accomplish the synthesis. The complete range of operations it supports is beyond the scope of this text, but we will examine a useful subset that can be used to rearrange expressions into multilevel forms. Although the best results can be obtained by working with *misII* in its interactive mode, some carefully crafted standard scripts of *misII* operations, developed by experts, are available for novice designers.

Example   A Session with *MisII*   Let's look at an example session with *misII*. In the following sequence of operations, we will (1) read a file containing Boolean equations that describe the combinational network to be manipulated (it is also possible to describe the network as a truth table, using *espresso* input format), (2) initially perform a two-level simplification (*misII* actually uses *espresso* as a subroutine), (3) decompose the resulting functions into a multilevel network, and (4) map the decomposed network onto the gates of a given gate library.

The following sequence of commands reads in the equations that describe the sum and carry-out (co) functions of the full adder from a standard text file, prints out the network in two-level form, and then prints out the network in its factored form:

```
% misII
UC Berkeley, MIS Release #2.1 (compiled 3-Mar-89 at
5:32 PM)
misII> re full.adder
misII> p
 {co} = a b ci + a b ci' + a b' ci + a' b ci
 {sum} = a b ci + a b' ci' + a' b ci' + a' b' ci
misII> pf
 {co} = a b' ci + b (ci (a' + a) + a ci')
 {sum} = ci (a' b' + a b) + ci' (a b' + a' b)
```

The first line requests *misII* to read an equation file named `full.adder`. The *p* command prints out the network in two-level form. The *pf* command prints the network in a factored form.

The next sequence performs a two-level simplification. We then print out the results in two-level and factored forms:

```
misII> sim1 *
misII> p
 {co} = a b + a ci + b ci
 {sum} = a b ci + a b' ci' + a' b ci' + a' b' ci
```

```
misII> pf
{co} = ci (b + a) + a b
{sum} = ci (a' b' + a b) + ci' (a b' + a' b)
```

The command *sim1* requests *misII* to simplify the network using *espresso* as a two-level minimizer. The * tells *misII* to apply simplification to each node in the network in turn. You can see the results by typing *p* and *pf*.

Next, we ask *misII* to perform a good decomposition on all of the nodes of the network and then print out the result:

```
misII> gd *
misII> pf
{co} = a [2] + b ci
{sum} = a' [3]' + a [3]
[2] = ci + b
[3] = b' ci' + b ci
```

The *gd* command is how you request a "good decomposition." *MisII* generates potential factors and chooses those that will most reduce the number of literals. A quick decomposition, specified by *qd*, is faster, but the quality of the result is usually not as good. *MisII* comes up with a three-level network, with the subexpressions (ci + b) and (b' ci' + b ci) factored out. The simplified two-level network has 18 literals; the multilevel network has only 14 literals.

So far, the manipulations are technology independent. If we were to implement the network in terms of arbitrary input AND and OR gates, we would stop right here. However, *misII* has the ability to map the expressions onto the gates of a predefined gate library. We make use of a library of frequently used gates developed at Mississippi State University (see Figure 3.21 for a listing of some of the available gates), which is distributed with the *misII* software:

```
misII> rlib msu.genlib
misII> map
misII> pf
[361] = b' ci' + a'
[328] = b'
[329] = ci'
{co} = [328]' [329]' + [361]'
[3] = b ci' + b' ci
{sum} = [3] a' + [3]' a
```

```
misII> pg
 [361] 1890:physical 32.00
 [328] 1310:physical 16.00
 [329] 1310:physical 16.00
 {co} 1890:physical 32.00
 [3] 2310:physical 40.00
 {sum} 2310:physical 40.00
misII> pat
 ... using library delay model
 {sum} : arrival=( 2.2 2.2)
 {co} : arrival=( 2.2 2.2)
 [328] : arrival=( 1.2 1.2)
 [361] : arrival=( 1.2 1.2)
 [329] : arrival=( 1.2 1.2)
 [3] : arrival=( 1.2 1.2)
 ci : arrival=( 0.0 0.0)
 b : arrival=( 0.0 0.0)
 a : arrival=( 0.0 0.0)
misII> quit
%
```

The command *rlib msu.genlib* makes the contents of this library known to *misII*, while the *map* command maps the current network onto the gates of the specified library. If the network is now printed with *pf*, the structure has been changed to reflect the available gate primitives. This is made a little more obvious by using the print gates command, or *pg*. The internal nodes of the network are described in terms of the gates chosen for their implementation, identified by the gate number as shown in Figure 3.21.

In this case, *misII* has chosen inverters (1310), XORs (2310), and OR-AND-Invert gates (1890) to implement the functions. The numbers following the word "physical" describe the relative size of these gates, so you can see that XORs require considerably more area than inverters: 40 units versus 16.

Figure 3.22 depicts the implementation of the full adder in terms of these gate primitives. The figure shows the gate numbers and internal node numbers. Recall that $\overline{A(B+C)} = \overline{A} + \overline{BC}$ by DeMorgan's theorem, so the OR-AND-Invert gate and the Invert-AND-OR gate are really the same.

The *pat* command prints an estimate of the arrival of signals at various nodes of the network. A simple unit delay model is used. The model charges each circuit node with 1 time unit for each gate level plus 0.2 time unit for each gate fan-out. Because the sum and co outputs are two levels away from the inputs and the first-level gates fan out to only a single input, the model expects the outputs to change within 2.2 delay units of the input changes.

Number	Name	Function
1310	inv	$\overline{a}$
1120	nor2	$\overline{a+b}$
1130	nor3	$\overline{a+b+c}$
1140	nor4	$\overline{a+b+c+d}$
1220	nand2	$\overline{a \cdot b}$
1230	nand3	$\overline{a \cdot b \cdot c}$
1240	nand4	$\overline{a \cdot b \cdot c \cdot d}$
1660	and2/nand2	$(a \cdot b, \overline{a \cdot b})$
1670	and3/nand3	$(a \cdot b \cdot c, \overline{a \cdot b \cdot c})$
1680	and4/nand4	$(a \cdot b \cdot c \cdot d, \overline{a \cdot b \cdot c \cdot d})$
1760	or2/nor2	$(a+b, \overline{a+b})$
1770	or3/nor3	$(a+b+c, \overline{a+b+c})$
1780	or4	$(a+b+c+d)$
1870	aoi22	$\overline{a \cdot b + c \cdot d}$
1880	aoi21	$\overline{a + b \cdot c}$
1860	oai22	$\overline{(a + b)(c + d)}$
1890	oai21	$\overline{a\,(b + c)}$
1970	ao22	$a \cdot b + d \cdot e$
1810	ao222	$a \cdot b + c \cdot d + e \cdot f$
1910	ao2222	$a \cdot b + c \cdot d + e \cdot f + g \cdot h$
1930	ao33	$a \cdot b \cdot c + d \cdot e \cdot f$
2310	xor2	$a \cdot \overline{b} + \overline{a} \cdot b$
2350	xnor2	$\overline{a} \cdot \overline{b} + a \cdot b$

Figure 3.21 Gates supported by the MSU cell library.

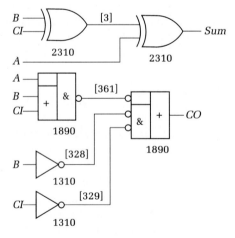

Figure 3.22 Implementation of full adder using MSU gate primitives.

Examples **More Multilevel Logic Manipulations** It takes considerable skill and experience with the logic manipulation operations we have described to achieve good multilevel designs. Fortunately, experts in multilevel logic design have developed generic scripts of operations that can be used to good effect even by novice logic designers. We will see how well *misII* does in our combinational logic circuit case studies: the full adder, the 2-bit adder, and the BCD increment by 1 circuit.

MisII is distributed with several different scripts. Throughout this section we will use a particular technology-independent script called, appropriately enough, "script." To invoke *misII* in a noninteractive mode, reading its commands from a text file, type the following:

```
misII -f script -t pla <espresso truth table file>
```

The -f parameter is followed by the name of a file containing *misII* commands. The -t pla parameter tells *misII* that the circuit description is in an *espresso* truth table format. The parameter is followed by the name of the file containing the truth table description.

Running *misII* against the full adder truth table yields the following output in BLIF (Berkeley Logic Interchange Format), a standard language for describing multilevel logic functions:

```
.model full.adder
.inputs a b ci
.outputs sum co
.names a b ci co sum
1--0 1
-1-0 1
--10 1
111- 1
.names a b ci co
11- 1
1-1 1
-11 1
.end
```

Each .names section describes a single output function. The first section describes *Sum* in terms of *A*, *B*, *CI* (carry in), and *CO* (carry out). The latter is defined in the second section as a function of *A*, *B*, and *CI*. In terms of Boolean algebra, the multilevel equations for *Sum* and *CO* are as follows:

$$Sum = A \bullet \overline{CO} + B \bullet \overline{CO} + CI \bullet \overline{CO} + A \bullet B \bullet CI$$

$$CO = A \bullet B + A \bullet CI + B \bullet CI$$

The expression for CO is identical to the one derived by *espresso*. However, the expression for *Sum* is quite different. Let's look at this in more detail.

Recall that the full adder *Sum* is $A \oplus B \oplus CI$. The generic *misII* script we are using cannot make use of XOR gates. Expressed in sum of products form, *Sum* becomes $\overline{A}\,\overline{B}\,CI + A\overline{B}\,\overline{CI} + \overline{A}B\,\overline{CI} + AB\,CI$. The *misII* expression for *Sum*, by using $\overline{CO}$, effectively reduces the number of literals from 12 to 9. There is an obvious performance penalty, however. The two-level expression for *Sum* in the standard sum of products form has been replaced by a five-level expression (see Figure 3.23).

Our second example is the 2-bit binary adder. Recall that the inputs are two 2-bit binary numbers to be summed, represented by the inputs *A*, *B* and *C*, *D*, respectively. The output is a 3-bit binary number *X*, *Y*, *Z*. The *misII* output is as follows:

```
.model 2bit.adder
.inputs a b c d
.outputs x y z
.names a c z [22] x
---1 1
11-- 1
-10- 1
.names a b c d x z [22] y
1---0-- 1
--1---1 1
-11-0-- 1
--110-- 1
---100- 1
.names a b c d z
-0-1 1
-1-0 1
0-10 1
.names a d z [22]
110 1
.end
```

You can see that there are four `.names` sections, even though the function has three outputs. *MisII* has introduced a single new intermediate result, denoted by [22]. Outputs *X* and *Y* have been expressed as functions of *Z* and the new intermediate function [22] (*Y* is also a function of *X*):

$$Z = \overline{B}D + B\overline{D} + \overline{A}C\overline{D}$$

$$[22] = AD\overline{Z}$$

$$X = [22] + AC + C\overline{Z}$$

$$Y = AX + C[22] + BC\overline{X} + CD\overline{X} + D\overline{X}\,\overline{Z}$$

This solution represents considerable savings of literals compared to the solution we found in Chapter 2. In sum of products form, X required 8 literals, Y used 22, and Z was expressed in 4, a total of 34. The multilevel implementation described above uses only 28 literals! Of course, there are performance implications of the multilevel implementation. The worst-case delay in the sum of products form is two gate levels, not counting inverted literals. In the multilevel form, it is eight gate levels (see Figure 3.24).

Our last example is the BCD increment by 1 function. The *misII* output looks like this:

```
.model bcd.increment
.inputs a b c d
.outputs w x y z
.names a b c d z w
1---1 1
0111- 1
.names a b c w z x
01-0- 1
0-100 1
```

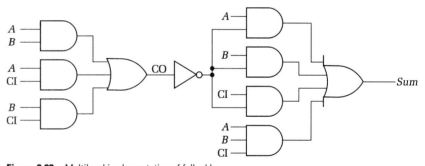

Figure 3.23   Multilevel implementation of full adder.

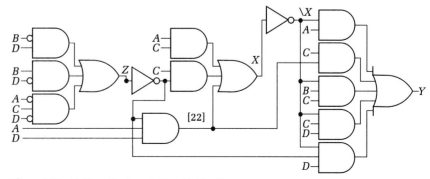

Figure 3.24   Multilevel implementation of 2-bit adder.

```
.names a c z y
-11 1
000 1
.names a b c d z
0--0 1
-000 1
.end
```

This leads to the following collection of equations:

$$Z = \overline{A}\overline{D} + \overline{B}\overline{C}\overline{D}$$

$$Y = CZ + \overline{A}\overline{C}\overline{Z}$$

$$W = AZ + \overline{A}BCD$$

$$X = \overline{A}B\overline{W} + \overline{A}C\overline{W}\overline{Z}$$

W and Y are functions of Z. X is a function of W and Z. The collection of functions is implemented with 23 literals. The schematic is shown in Figure 3.25. Worst-case delay is seven gate levels, not counting zeroth level inversions.

3.2.4   Summary

Our purpose in this section was to give you a flavor of the approaches to multilevel logic synthesis. The key idea is to identify common Boolean subexpressions across a collection of equations. If we can factor these out and share them among several functions, we can reduce the total number of literals needed to realize the functions. Fewer literals mean fewer wires, an important criterion in determining the complexity of a circuit.

We introduced the basic operations for manipulating multilevel networks: decomposition, extraction, factoring, substitution, and collapsing.

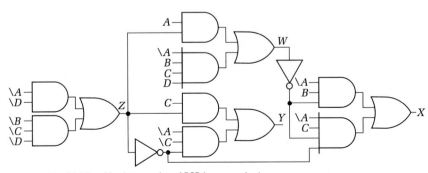

Figure 3.25   Multilevel implementation of BCD increment by 1.

A powerful system for multilevel logic manipulation, called *misII*, was introduced, and we showed how it could process these operations to simplify the full adder network.

Because it takes a sophisticated designer to use *misII* to best effect in its interactive mode, we also showed how it could be used in a batch mode, with prespecified scripts, to do a reasonable job of deriving technology-independent multilevel implementations. The key is to reduce literal counts, although this usually has the effect of increasing the number of levels of gates.

We applied *misII* and its generic script to the full adder, the 2-bit binary adder, and the BCD increment by 1 circuit. We were able to reduce the literal counts from the two-level implementations, although the worst-case gate delays were substantially increased. These multilevel realizations will require less circuit area, but they will not be as fast as the two-level implementations.

3.3   Time Response in Combinational Networks

Our analysis of circuits so far has concentrated on the static behavior of combinational networks. The analysis adequately describes a circuit in steady state, but it is not enough to tell us about a circuit's dynamic behavior. Remember that the propagation of signals through a network is not instantaneous. This characteristic can be useful, for example, when creating circuits that output pulse signals. But it causes problems if the momentary changes of signals at the outputs lead to logical errors. Such transient output changes are called glitches. A logic circuit is said to have a hazard if it has the potential for these glitches. We'll discuss glitches and hazards in Section 3.4.

As a hardware designer, it is extremely important to be able to visualize the behavior of a circuit as a function of time—that is, to be able to look at a circuit and see how signals move through it, recognizing asymmetric delays along paths that can lead to transitory behavior at the outputs. This is not an easy skill to acquire, even after extensive design experience. Fortunately, simulation tools can offer great assistance in visualizing the time-based behavior of circuits.

3.3.1   Gate Delays

Outputs in combinational logic are functions of the inputs and some delay. As we stated in Chapter 2, gate delay is the amount of time it takes for a change at the gate input to cause a change at its output. Most circuit families define delays in terms of minimum (best case), typical (average), and maximum (worst case) times. A corollary to Murphy's law, well known to experienced digital designers, is that if a circuit can run at its worst-case delay, it will. Never assume that your design will be able to run with minimum delay.

What would happen if you depended on a portion of your design running with minimum delay? If its delay is longer than you designed for, you may examine its output too soon, incorrectly computing the final output of your overall system.

The various families of TTL exhibit trade-offs between delay and power. The faster a component, the more power it consumes. Table 3.1 shows some timing information for typical TTL gates. Did you notice that propagation delays often depend on whether the output is going from low to high, written as t_{pLH}, or from high to low, t_{pHL}?

Table 3.1   Gate Delays for Typical TTL Families

TTL component	Maximum		Typical	
	t_{pHL}	t_{pLH}	t_{pHL}	t_{pLH}
7400	15	22	7	11
74H00	10	10	6.2	5.9
74L00	60	60	31	35
74LS00	15	15	10	9
74S00	5	4.5	3	3
74LS02	15	15	10	10
74LS86A	22	30	13	20

For two-input NAND gates, 74X00, the lower-power TTL families (L, LS), are substantially slower than higher-speed logic (H, S). Two-input NOR gates, 74X02, exhibit comparable delays. For a given TTL family, such as LS, more complex components tend to be slower. This is shown in Table 3.1 for the 74LS86A two-input XOR gate.

3.3.2   Timing Waveforms

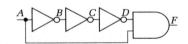

Figure 3.26   Pulse shaper circuit.

Let's consider the circuit shown in Figure 3.26. An input signal A passes through three inversions, leaving it in its inverted state, which is then ANDed with the original input. This appears to implement a rather useless function: $A \cdot \overline{A} = 0$. However, the timing diagram of Figure 3.27 tells us a different story. After the input A goes high, the output waveform goes high for a short time before going low. Such a circuit is called a *pulse shaper* because a change at its input causes a short-duration pulse at the output.

The circuit of Figure 3.26 operates as follows. Let's assume that the initial state has $A = 0$, $B = 1$, $C = 0$, $D = 1$, and $F = 0$, as shown in Figure 3.27 at time step 0. Further, we assume that each gate has a propagation delay of 10 time units. When input A changes from 0 to 1 at time 10, it takes 10 time units, a gate delay, before B changes from 1 to

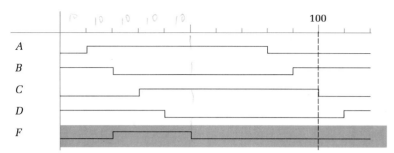

Figure 3.27   Pulse shaper waveform.

0 (time step 20). After a second gate delay, C changes from 0 to 1 (time step 30). D changes from 1 to 0 after a third gate delay (time step 40). However, between time 10 and time 40, both A and D are logic 1. If the AND gate also has a 10-unit gate delay, the output F will be high between time steps 20 and 50. This is exactly what is shown in the timing diagram. In effect, the three inverters stretch the time during which A and D are both logic 1 after A changes from 0 to 1. Eventually, the change in A propagates to D as a 0, causing F to fall after another gate delay. It is no surprise that the pulse is exactly three inverter delays wide. If we increased the number of inverters to five, the width of the pulse would be five gate delays instead.

A pulse shaper circuit exploits the propagation asymmetries in signal paths with the explicit purpose of creating short-duration changes at the output. It generates a periodic waveform that could be used, for example, as a clock in a digital system. It operates much like a stopwatch. With its switch in one position, the circuit does nothing. In the second position, the circuit generates a periodic sequence of pulses.

Application 3.3.3   Analysis of a Pulse Shaper Circuit

In this section, we will analyze the operation of the simple pulse shaper circuit of Figure 3.28. The circuit has a single input A that is connected to a logic 1 when the switch is open and to a logic 0 when the switch is closed. This is because the path to ground has lower resistance than the path to the power supply when the switch is closed (switches are discussed in more detail in Section 3.5.3). We will assume that the propagation delay of all gates is 10 time units.

Let's suppose that at time step 0, the switch has just been closed. We begin by determining the initial value for each of the circuit's nets. A goes to 0 instantly. Since a NAND gate will output a 1 whenever one of its inputs is 0, B goes to 1, but after a gate delay of 10 time units. So we say that B goes to 1 at time step 10.

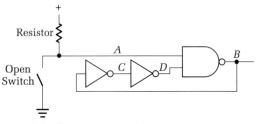

Figure 3.28   Pulse shaper example.

C is set to the complement of B, but once again only after an inverter propagation delay. Thus C goes to 0 at time step 20. D becomes the complement of C after another inverter delay. So it goes to 1 at time step 30. Since A is 0 and D is 1, the output of the NAND gate stays at 0. The circuit is said to be in a *steady state*.

What happens if the switch opens at time step 40? The input A immediately goes to 1. Now both inputs to the NAND gate are 1, so after a gate propagation of 10 time units, B will go low. This happens at time step 50.

The change in B propagates to C after another inverter delay. Thus at time step 60, C goes to 1. In a similar fashion, D goes to 0 at time step 70. Now the NAND gate has one of its inputs at 0, so at time step 80 B will go to 1.

Note that B first goes low at time step 50 and goes high at time step 80—a difference of 30 time units. This is exactly three gate delays: the delay through the NAND gate and the two inverter gates on the path from signal B to D.

Now that B is at 1, C will go to 0 at time step 90, D will go to 1 at time step 100, and B will return to 0 at time step 110. The circuit is no longer in steady state. It now oscillates with B, C, and D varying between 1 and 0, staying at each value for three gate delays (30 time units). The behavior of the circuit is summarized in the timing diagram of Figure 3.29.

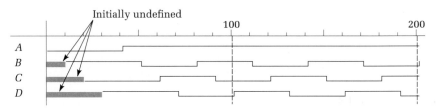

Figure 3.29   Timing waveform for pulse-shaping circuit.

3.4   Hazards/Glitches and How to Avoid Them

A *glitch* is an unwanted pulse at the output of a combinational logic network. A circuit with the potential for a glitch is said to have a *hazard*. In other words, a hazard is something intrinsic about a circuit; a circuit with a hazard may or may not glitch, depending on the input patterns and the electrical characteristics of the circuit. In this section we will develop a procedure that leads to hazard-free circuits.

3.4.1   The Problem with Hazards

Hazards are a problem for digital systems in two cases. In the first case, time-sensitive logic makes a decision based on the output of a function without allowing the output to settle to a final steady-state value. This problem can be solved by increasing the interval between the time when inputs first begin to change and the time when the outputs are examined by the decision-making logic. For example, you can lengthen this interval by increasing your system's clock period. We will discuss the topic of clocking methodologies in considerably more detail in Section 6.2.

In the second case, a hazardous output is connected to a component with asynchronous inputs. *Asynchronous inputs* take effect as soon as they change, rather than when sampled with a standard reference clock. This can be solved by avoiding clocked parts with asynchronous inputs.

In most cases, we can use these techniques to avoid the need to design hazard-free circuits. However, some very useful components unavoidably have asynchronous inputs. For example, many components that implement counting functions or storage elements have asynchronous inputs to reset them or initiate their operation. Therefore, if you ever design circuits that interface to such components (and you will!), you must understand how to design hazard-free.

Static and Dynamic Hazards   Methods for eliminating hazards always depend on the assumption that the unexpected changes in the outputs are in response to *single-bit changes* in the inputs. This assumption is equivalent to moving along an edge in the Boolean cube that describes the function's truth table. The techniques simply do not apply when more than one input bit changes at the same time.

The various kinds of hazards are summarized in Figure 3.30. A *static hazard* occurs when it is possible for an output to undergo a momentary transition when it is expected to remain unchanged. A *static 1-hazard* occurs when the output momentarily goes to 0 when it should remain at 1. Similarly, a *static 0-hazard* occurs when the output should remain at 0 but momentarily changes to 1. We will develop techniques that can eliminate static hazards from two-level and multilevel circuits.

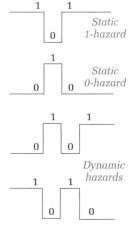

Figure 3.30   Kinds of hazards on an output function.

Dynamic hazards occur when the output signal has the potential to change more than once when it is expected to make a single transition from 0 to 1 or 1 to 0. Dynamic hazards cause glitches in multilevel circuits, where there are multiple paths with different delays from the inputs to the outputs. Unfortunately, it is quite difficult to eliminate dynamic hazards in general. The best approach to dealing with this problem is to transform a multilevel circuit with a dynamic hazard into a static hazard-free two-level circuit.

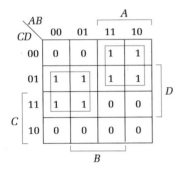

Figure 3.31 K-map for example circuit.

3.4.2 Hazard Detection and Elimination in Two-Level Networks

Consider the four-variable function $F(A,B,C,D) = \Sigma\, m(1,3,5,7,8,9,12,13)$. Its K-map is shown in Figure 3.31. The minimum sum of products form for the function is $A\overline{C} + \overline{A}D$.

The gate-level implementation of F is given in Figure 3.32. Let's examine what happens when the inputs change from $ABCD = 1100$ to 1101. When the inputs are 1100, the output of gate G1 is 1 while G2's output is 0. Thus, the output from G3 is 1. When the input changes by a single bit to 1101, the outputs of the gates remain unchanged. G1 implements the prime implicant that covers both of the input configurations we considered; it remains asserted despite the input changes. A glitch cannot happen in this case.

Now consider an input change from 1101 to 0101, another single-bit change in the inputs. When A goes low, $\overline{A}$ goes high, but only after a gate delay. For a short time, both A and $\overline{A}$ are low. This allows the outputs from G1 and G2 to be low at the same time, and thus F goes low. When $\overline{A}$ finally does go high, G2 will go high and F will return to 1. A glitch has happened! The step-by-step process is shown in Figure 3.33.

A close examination of the K-map of Figure 3.31 suggests what caused the problem. When the initial and final inputs are covered by the same prime implicant, no glitch is possible. But when the input change spans prime implicants, a glitch can happen. Of course, if G1 is much slower to change than G2, you might not see the glitch on F. The hazard is always there. Whether you actually see the glitch depends on the timings of the individual gates.

A strategy for eliminating the hazard is to add redundant prime implicants to guarantee that all single-bit input changes are covered by one such implicant. Suppose we add the implicant $\overline{C}D$ to the implementation for F. This strategy does not change the function's truth table. By adding the term $\overline{C}D$, F remains asserted for the inputs 1101 and 0101, independent of the change to input A.

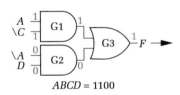

$ABCD = 1100$

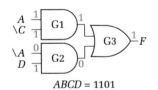

$ABCD = 1101$

Figure 3.32 Effect of input change from 1100 to 1101.

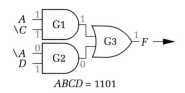

ABCD = 1101

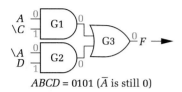

ABCD = 0101 ($\overline{A}$ is still 0)

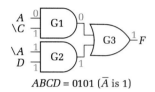

ABCD = 0101 ($\overline{A}$ is 1)

Figure 3.33 Effect of input change from 1101 to 0101.

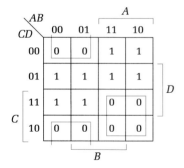

Figure 3.34 K-map for example circuit.

This method eliminates the static 1-hazard, but what about static 0-hazards? First, reexpress the function F in minimum product of sums form:

$$F = (\overline{A} + \overline{C})\,(A + D)$$

The K-map in Figure 3.34 clearly indicates that a static 0-hazard exists when the input changes from 1110 to 0110.

The solution is to add the redundant prime implicant $(\overline{C} + D)$ to the product of sums expression for F. The resulting expression is equivalent to the sum of products form that eliminates the static 1-hazard:

$$F = (\overline{A} + \overline{C})\,(A + D)\,(\overline{C} + D)$$
$$= (\overline{C} + \overline{A}D)\,(A + D)$$
$$= A\overline{C} + A\overline{A}D + \overline{C}D + \overline{A}D$$
$$= A\overline{C} + \overline{C}D + \overline{A}D$$

Alternatively, we can use a shortcut to analyze the function for 0-hazards. We start with the expression that is free of static 1-hazards and work with its complement. We can then superimpose the analysis on the original K-map, looking at the zeros of the original function. A static 0-hazard exists if the implicants of the complement do not cover all adjacent 0's.

The revised expression for F is $A\overline{C} + \overline{A}D + \overline{C}D$. Working with its complement, we get the following:

$$\overline{F} = \overline{A\overline{C} + \overline{A}D + \overline{C}D}$$
$$= (\overline{A} + C)\,(A + \overline{D})\,(C + \overline{D})$$
$$= AC + AC\overline{D} + C\overline{D} + \overline{A}C\overline{D} + \overline{A}\,\overline{D}$$
$$= AC + C\overline{D} + \overline{A}\,\overline{D}$$

This collection of terms does indeed cover all adjacent 0's in the K-map for the revised F. This expression is free of both static 1-hazards and 0-hazards.

General Strategy for Static Hazard Elimination The preceding example leads to a general strategy for eliminating static hazards in two-level networks. Let's consider static 1-hazards first. Starting with the K-map, we examine it to make sure that all adjacent elements of the on-set are covered by a prime implicant. If they are not, we add redundant prime implicants until all elements of the on-set are covered.

We follow a similar procedure to eliminate static 0-hazards. Given the sum of products form for the function that eliminates the static 1-hazards, we write it in product of sums form using Boolean algebra. Then we verify that adjacent elements of the off-set are covered by a common prime implicant in the product of sums form. If necessary, we add more prime implicants to cover any uncovered adjacencies.

3.4.3   Detecting Static Hazards in Multilevel Networks

We can generalize the techniques described in the previous section for multilevel circuits. We begin by mapping the multilevel function into a two-level form called the *transient output function*. In forming the transient output function, we treat a variable and its complement as independent variables. This means that we can no longer make use of the Boolean laws that state that $X \bullet \overline{X} = 0$ and $X + \overline{X} = 1$. The former introduces static 0-hazards, while the latter leads to static 1-hazards. Further, we can no longer use any of the simplification theorems derived from these Boolean laws, such as simplification theorems 9 and 11 and the consensus theorem of Chapter 2.

Example   A Multilevel Function   Let's consider the following multilevel Boolean function:

$$F = ABC + (A + D)\,(\overline{A} + \overline{C})$$

A quick application of the distributive law yields

$$F_1 = ABC + A\overline{A} + A\overline{C} + \overline{A}D + \overline{C}D$$

This is the transient output function in sum of products form. Since A and its complement are treated as independent variables, the term $A \bullet \overline{A}$ is kept in the transient output function.

Once the function is in two-level form, we follow the procedure described in the previous subsection. First we check for static 1-hazards in the function. Note that the term $A \bullet \overline{A}$ can never cause a 1-hazard (it does indicate that a 0-hazard exists), so it can be eliminated from consideration when analyzing for 1-hazards. The K-map for the remaining terms is shown in Figure 3.35. The function contains static 1-hazards, such as an input transition from $ABCD = 1111$ to 0111 or 1111 to 1101.

The remedy is to add the necessary redundant prime implicants. In the K-map of Figure 3.35, this is achieved by adding the terms AB and BD to the sum of products form of F:

$$F_2 = A\overline{C} + \overline{A}D + \overline{C}D + AB + BD$$

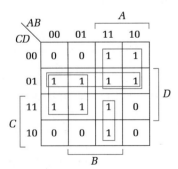

Figure 3.35   K-map for circuit with 1-hazards.

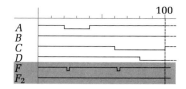

Figure 3.36 Waveform with 1-hazards.

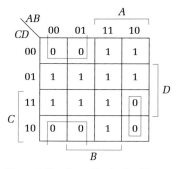

Figure 3.37 K-map for circuit with 0-hazards.

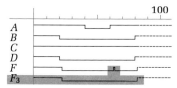

Figure 3.38 Waveform with 0-hazards.

Because AB completely covers the term ABC, we have eliminated it from F_2.

Figure 3.38 compares the timing behavior of the original function F and its revised expression F_2. Notice that F glitches on the input transitions 1111 to 0111 and 1111 to 1101, while F_2 eliminates the glitches.

We use the shortcut method to verify that the new expression is free of static 0-hazards. For the original function F, $\overline{F}$ is

$$\begin{aligned} \overline{F} &= \overline{ABC} + (A+D)\,(\overline{A}+\overline{C}) \\ &= (\overline{A}+\overline{B}+\overline{C})\,(\overline{A}\overline{D}+A C) \\ &= \overline{A}\overline{D} + \overline{A}\overline{B}\overline{D} + \overline{A}\overline{C}\overline{D} + A\overline{B}C \\ &= \overline{A}\overline{D} + A\overline{B}C \end{aligned}$$

This expression corresponds to the circled 0's in the K-map of Figure 3.37. The function has a 0-hazard on the transition from 1010 to 0010, as shown in the timing waveform of Figure 3.38. This problem can be fixed by adding the implicant $\overline{B}C\overline{D}$ to $\overline{F}$. The following is a two-level expression for F that is free of static 0-hazards:

$$F_3 = (A+D)\,(\overline{A}+B+\overline{C})\,(B+\overline{C}+D)$$

Expanding F_3 to place it into sum of products form yields F_2. Both expressions are simultaneously free of static 0- and 1-hazards.

3.4.4 Designing Static-Hazard–Free Circuits

The procedure for *designing* a static-hazard–free network is a straightforward application of the concepts we have just described. The key is to place the function in such a form that the transient output function guarantees that every set of adjacent 1's in the K-map are covered by a term, and that no terms contain both a variable and its complement. The former condition eliminates 1-hazards and the latter eliminates 0-hazards.

Following this procedure will eliminate dynamic hazards, at least for two-level implementations. We start with the truth table or the expression of the function in minterm shorthand form. Then we express the function in terms of prime implicants which ensure that adjacent 1's are covered by a single term. We factor the resulting expression using the laws and theorems of Boolean algebra, but treating a variable and its complement as independent variables. For example, the distributive law can never introduce a hazard, so it can be used freely to simplify the function. The complementarity laws, on the other hand, cannot be used to simplify the function. As long as no terms in the resulting expression contain a variable and its complement, the function will be hazard-free.

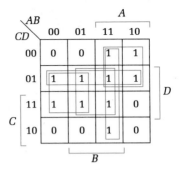

Figure 3.39   K-map for hazard-free function.

Returning to the example function of this section, its shorthand minterm form is

$$F(A,B,C,D) = \Sigma\, m(1,3,5,7,8,9,12,13,14,15)$$

The K-map with circled terms is shown in Figure 3.39. This yields the expression

$$F = AB + \overline{A}D + BD + A\overline{C} + \overline{C}D$$

This result is the same as the expression for F_2 in the previous subsection. Factoring via the distributive law yields the following multilevel static-hazard–free expression:

$$F = (\overline{A} + B + \overline{C})\,D + A\,(B + \overline{C})$$

This expression requires five gates, as was the case for the original expression for F given at the beginning of this section.

3.4.5   Dynamic Hazards

Dynamic hazards are defined as output transitions from 0 to 1 or 1 to 0, undergoing more than one change along the way. Dynamic hazards happen because of multiple paths in the underlying multilevel network, each with its own asymmetric delay. If there are three or more paths from an input or its complement to the output, the circuit has the potential for a dynamic hazard.

Figure 3.40 gives an example of a circuit with a dynamic hazard. Note that there are three different paths from B or $\overline{B}$ to the outputs. The following sequence of events can lead to a dynamic hazard at the output. Suppose that the initial inputs are $ABC = 000$, $F = 1$ and the final configuration is 010 with $F = 0$. In the starting configuration, G1 = 0, G2 = 1, G3 = 1, G4 = 1, and G5 = 1. The initial gate inputs and outputs are shown in plain text in the figure.

Now suppose that B changes from a 0 to 1. We assume that G1 is a slow gate, G4 is a very slow gate, and G2, G3, and G5 are fast. G2 changes from 1 to 0, followed by G3 going to 0 and G5 following it to 0 a short time later. So far, the input has changed from 1 to 0. This situation is shown by the bold values in the figure.

Now G1 catches up. Its output goes to 1, causing G3 to go high, followed by G5 going high. At this point, the output has changed from 1 to 0 to 1. This is shown by plain italics in the figure.

Finally, G4's output changes from 1 to 0. This causes G5 to go low, reaching its final output. The output has changed from 1 to 0 to 1 to 0. This is shown by bold italics in the figure.

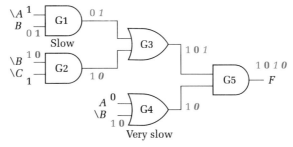

Figure 3.40 Circuit with a dynamic hazard.

Although it is possible to extend the techniques for static hazard elimination to dynamic hazards, the process is rather complicated and goes beyond the scope of this text. It is not enough to eliminate the static hazards—a multilevel network free of static hazards may still have dynamic hazards. If you need a hazard-free network, it is best to design it as a two-level network using the techniques of Section 3.4.4.

3.5 Practical Matters

We now turn from the theory of digital circuits to some more practical engineering aspects. In this section, we will first learn how to read a component data sheet. Then we will see how to perform some simple electrical calculations on the data it presents. We will be using the data sheet for the 74LS00 quad two-input NAND gate component as a running example. Finally, we will see how to connect inputs and outputs to our circuits by using simple switches and light-emitting diodes.

3.5.1 Elements of the Data Sheet

A data sheet contains all the relevant documentation that you need to use the component. The basic elements include (1) an English-language description of the function performed by the component, (2) a function/ truth table, (3) a logic schematic with labeled inputs and outputs, (4) Boolean expressions defining the outputs in terms of logic functions of the inputs, (5) alternative package pin-outs, (6) internal transistor schematics, (7) operating specifications for the component, (8) recommended operating conditions, (9) electrical characteristics, and (10) switching characteristics. Not every data sheet will have all of these pieces, but most of these will be present. Let's look at each of these for the 74LS00.

English-Language Description "These devices contain four independent two-input NAND gates."

The description tells you succinctly what the component does. In the case of a simple logic gate, the description is quite brief. For more complex MSI components, the description can go on for several paragraphs.

Inputs		Output
A	*B*	*Y*
H	H	L
L	X	H
X	L	H

Figure 3.41   Function table for 74LS00.

Function/Truth Table   The function table describes the operation of the component by tabulating all input and output combinations. To avoid confusion over positive and negative logic, the truth table is defined in terms of signal levels, H and L, rather than logic levels, 0 and 1.

Figure 3.41 shows the functional table for the NAND gate. When both inputs are high, the output is low. When an input is low, independent of the other input, the output is high. Writing the truth table for the NAND function in this way is a nice shorthand. For more complex functions, it is more common to take this functional approach than to write down a complete truth table.

Figure 3.42   Logic diagram for 74LS00.

Logic Schematics   Our example is the simple gate shown in Figure 3.42. Even in this simple case, the labeling is important because it ties together the functional table and the package pin-out.

Boolean Expression   The Boolean expression for the gate is in positive logic. The expression is written in two alternative forms: $Y = \overline{A \bullet B}$ or $Y = \overline{A} + \overline{B}$.

Package Pin-Out   Figure 3.43 shows the standard package pin-out for the 74LS00. Note that there are several alternative package types, so it is always important to refer to the one that matches your particular component. The 74LS00 comes in a 14-pin dip package. The inputs and outputs are labeled by gate number (1 through 4) and the signal names derived from the function table and the logic schematic.

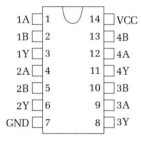

Figure 3.43   Package pin-out for the 74LS00.

Transistor Schematics   The next section of the data sheet describes the internal transistor configurations. These are not important for the purposes of this text.

Absolute Maximum Ratings   These ratings are the absolute worst-case conditions under which the component can operate or be stored. They should never be exceeded. The maximum supply voltage for an LS component is 7 V, the maximum input voltage is 5.5 V, the operating free-air temperature is from 0 to 70°C, and the storage temperature can range from −65 to 150°C.

Recommended Operating Conditions   These specifications describe the normal operating conditions for the supply voltage, input voltages, output currents, and temperature. Supply voltages are described in terms of minimum, nominal (normal), and maximum settings. For all 74LS components, these are 4.75, 5, and 5.25 V, respectively. This is why TTL is often described as a 5 V technology.

The input voltages, V_{IH} and V_{IL}, describe the minimum voltage that is recognized as a logic 1 and the maximum voltage that is recognized as a logic 0, respectively. For 74LS components, anything above 2 V is a logic 1 and anything below 0.8 V is a logic 0. Voltages between these values will not be recognized as a 1 or a 0.

The output currents, I_{OH} and I_{OL}, describe the maximum currents the gate can supply to maintain the output at a voltage that will be recognized as a logic 1 or 0, respectively. For LS TTL, these are −0.4 mA (current flows from the output pin) and 8 mA (current flows into the output pin). Faster logic families usually have larger absolute values for their output currents.

The operating temperature, T_A, defines the recommended temperature range over which to operate the gate. For 74LS components, the operating range is 0 through 70°C.

Electrical Characteristics This section defines several voltages and currents that can be observed at the inputs and outputs of the components. The entries are V_{OH}, the minimum output high voltage, V_{OL}, the maximum output low voltage, I_{IH}, the maximum current into an input pin when the input is high, I_{IL}, the maximum current into an input pin when the input is low, I_{CCH}, the package's power supply current when all outputs are high, and I_{CCL}, the package's power supply current when all outputs are low. The latter two values are per package and must be divided by the number of gates in the package to obtain the current per gate.

For the 74LS components, an output high voltage is 2.7 V minimum, 3.4 V typical. The output low voltage is 0.4 V maximum, 0.25 V typical. These values determine the noise margin. 74LS TTL enjoys a 0.7 V noise margin on logic 1 (2.7–2.0 V) and a 0.4 noise margin on logic 0 (0.8–0.4 V).

The input currents are a maximum of 20 μA for I_{IH} and −0.4 mA for I_{IL}. The power supply currents are 0.8 mA typical, 1.6 mA worst case for high outputs. For low outputs, the supply currents are 2.4 mA typical and 4.4 mA worst case.

Switching Characteristics This section gives the typical and maximum gate delays under specified test conditions of output resistance and capacitance. For example, the test conditions for the 74LS00 entries are a load resistance of 2000 Ω and a capacitance of 15 pF. Two different values are specified, t_{PLH}, the propagation delay to switch the output from a low to a high voltage, and t_{PHL}, the propagation time to switch it from high to low. The low-to-high and high-to-low delays are rarely symmetric. For the 74LS00, the respective specifications are 9 ns and 10 ns typical and 15 ns worst case. Most LS gates have typical delays of approximately 10 ns per gate level.

3.5.2   Simple Performance Calculations

In this subsection we describe some simple calculations you can use to determine the performance of your circuit.

Typical Propagation Delay   To compute the typical propagation delay through a gate, take the average of the typical low-to-high and high-to-low propagation delays. For the 74LS00, this would be 9.5 ns. Using typical delays is always somewhat controversial. A truly conservative design would always use the maximum propagation delays.

It is important to note that the delays quoted in the data book are for specific test conditions. Under conditions of increased resistance or capacitance, the delay will be worse than that described in the data book.

Power Consumption   Compute steady-state power consumption by multiplying the gate current in holding outputs high or low by the power supply voltage. The nominal power supply voltage is 5 V. The currents are I_{CCH} and I_{CCL}. For the 74LS00, the typical average package power consumption will be

$$\frac{I_{CCH} + I_{CCL}}{2} \times V_{CC} = \frac{0.8 \text{ mA} + 2.4 \text{ mA}}{2} \times 5 \text{V} = 8 \text{ mW}$$

This is the typical power consumption per package. It should be divided by 4 to obtain the power consumption per gate.

Once again, we have computed typical power consumption. A conservative designer would use maximum supply currents to compute worst-case power consumption.

Fan-Out   A given TTL output can drive only a finite number of inputs before the output signal levels become degraded and are no longer recognized as good logic 0's or logic 1's. Determining the fan-out is fairly straightforward. First, examine the (absolute value of) I_{OH} of the driving gate. This value must exceed the sum of the I_{IH} values of the inputs that the gate is driving. Similarly, the I_{OL} of the gate must exceed the (absolute value of the) sum of the I_{IL} values of the inputs to which it is connected.

As an example, let's calculate the fan-out of the 74LS00 NAND gate driving similar gates. The I_{IH} is 20 μA and the I_{OH} is −0.4 mA. This means that an LS NAND gate can drive 20 similar gates to a logic 1. I_{IL} is −0.4 mA while I_{OL} is 8 mA. Once again, an LS NAND gate can drive 20 similar gates to a logic 0.

Let's repeat the calculation for standard TTL. I_{OH} is −0.4 mA and I_{IH} is 40 μA. This indicates that the fan-out is only 10. I_{IL} is −1.6 mA and I_{OL} is 16 mA, also indicating that the fan-out is 10.

Now suppose we have a system with a mixture of LS TTL and standard TTL components. A portion of our design has an LS TTL NAND gate driving some standard TTL inputs. What is the correct maximum fan-out for the LS gate?

When driving the outputs high, the I_{OH} of LS TTL is –0.4 mA. The I_{IH} of standard TTL is 40 μA. This is a fan-out of 10. When driving the outputs low, the I_{OL} of LS TTL is 8 mA. The I_{IL} of standard TTL is –1.6 mA. This is only a fan-out of 5! This example illustrates the importance of determining the correct fan-out of gates, especially when you are using a mixture of TTL technologies.

3.5.3 Inputs and Outputs with Switches and LEDs

A combinational logic circuit is of no use unless you can provide it with inputs and observe its outputs. In this subsection, we will examine how to use switches to provide inputs to a circuit, while a light-emitting diode (LED) can be used to observe the circuit's output.

Single-Pole/Single-Throw Switches A single-pole/single-throw switch has two point connections to the outside. The switch can make or break the connection between these two points.

To implement a useful source of logic 1's and 0's, the switch can be configured as in Figure 3.44. It works as follows. The symbol that looks like a top is a standard way to represent ground. When the switch is open, ground is disconnected from the output node. The resistor is called a "pull-up" because it brings the voltage on the output node up to something that will be recognized as a logic 1. The box with a number inside it represents a logic probe, and we use it to indicate the logic value on the circuit node it is connected to.

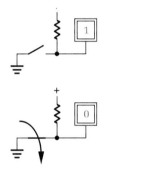

When the switch is closed, the ground potential brings the output node down to a logic 0 voltage. The resistor should be chosen to limit the current between the power supply and ground when the switch is closed. Too small a resistance will cause too much power to be consumed when the switch is closed. If the resistance is set too large, the drop across the resistor may yield a voltage at the circuit input node that is too small to be recognized as a logic 1. A good compromise resistor value for these kinds of pull-ups is 10,000 Ω.

Figure 3.44 Single-pole/single-throw switches.

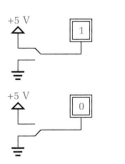

Figure 3.45 Single-pole/double-throw switches.

Single-Pole/Double-Throw Switches A single-pole/double-throw (SPDT) switch has three connections to the outside. Internal mechanics make it possible to connect selectively one of two of the connections to the third connection.

Figure 3.45 shows the SPDT switch configuration. One connection point is wired to the power supply and the other is connected to ground. The switch can be placed in one of two positions. When in the

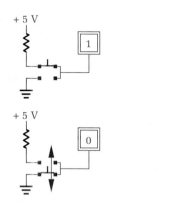

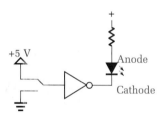

Figure 3.46 Single-pole/double-throw push-button.

up position, the switch connects the power supply to the output node. The output node is driven to a logic 1 voltage. In the other position, ground is connected to the output. Now the output node is driven to a logic 0 voltage.

Single-Pole/Double-Throw Push-Button A variation on the single-pole/double-throw switch is the momentary contact push-button. This is shown in Figure 3.46. A distinguished input pole is connected through to the output when the push-button is at rest. When the push-button is pressed, the switch makes a connection between the second input pole and the output. When you release the button, it immediately returns to its rest position.

Light-Emitting Diodes Light-emitting diodes, or LEDs, are electronic elements that emit light whenever a current flows across them. Thus, they are ideal optical output devices. An LED has two connections, called the *anode* and the *cathode*. The device is illuminated whenever the anode voltage exceeds the cathode voltage by a certain threshold. The LED is a unidirectional element, so it is important to be able to distinguish between the two connections. The cathode is usually the longer lead or the lead closest to the flat side of the LED's plastic housing.

Figure 3.47 shows one of the many ways in which a TTL gate can drive an LED. In a schematic, an LED is represented as a black triangle facing a line. The anode is the blunt edge of the triangle and the cathode is the flat line.

The LED is illuminated when the switch is set to its upper position. In this case, the inverter's input is a logic 1 and its output is at logic 0. This position ensures that the cathode potential is less than the anode potential.

The LED is dark when the switch is set to its lower position. This position gates a logic 0 to the inverter's input, yielding an output of logic 1. A TTL logic 1 output places too high a voltage on the cathode to allow the LED to light up.

The resistor between the LED and the power supply is called a *current-limiting resistor*. An unprotected LED wired directly between ground and the power supply would burn out and could destroy the output circuitry of the TTL gate.

We can compute the value for the current-limiting resistor as follows. We size the resistor so that the current across it comes close to but does not exceed the I_{OL} value for the gate that will drive the LED. For example, the I_{OL} of a standard TTL 7404 Inverter gate is 16 mA. The right resistance is 330 Ω because across a 5 V power supply, a 330 Ω resistor has a current of 5 V/330 Ω or 15 mA.

Figure 3.47 Light-emitting diode driven by a TTL gate.

Chapter Review

In this chapter, we have built on top of the simple gate logic introduced in Chapter 2. In particular, we examined the conversion of AND/OR and OR/AND networks into NOR-only and NAND-only logic. Under certain conditions, an additional inverter must be added at the output, so these conversions change two-level logic to a three-level form.

We introduced our first form of complex logic: AND-OR-Invert and OR-AND-Invert gates. Using these building blocks, it is possible to reduce significantly the number of packages needed to implement some functions of moderate levels of complexity.

We examined the concept of multilevel logic and introduced its advantages in terms of reduced literal counts and simplified wiring complexity. Of course, multilevel logic introduces the possibility of increased circuit delay by placing additional levels of gates between inputs and outputs. In general, two-level logic yields the fastest implementations and multilevel logic results in circuits with fewer wires.

We described a tool for multilevel logic optimization, *misII*, and discussed how it can be used to assist in multilevel circuit designs. To use the tool to its best effect, you really must understand the underlying mathematical structure of factored Boolean expressions. However, with standard command scripts supplied with *misII*, even novice designers can use the tools to create good multilevel designs.

We looked at time response in combinational logic networks and introduced the concept of timing hazards and methods for building hazard-free logic circuits. It should be pointed out that hazards are a problem primarily in circuits without a global clock. We will have more to say about clocked circuits in Chapter 6.

The final section dealt with several important practical matters. These were reading component specifications from a data book; performing simple calculations to determine delays, power consumption, and circuit fan-out; and wiring up switches and LEDs as circuit inputs and outputs.

Further Reading

For a detailed presentation of multilevel logic optimization techniques, the following papers are highly recommended: K. Bartlett, W. Cohen, A. DeGeus, G. Hachtel, "Synthesis and Optimization of Multi-Level Logic under Timing Constraints," *IEEE Transactions on Computer-Aided Design*, CAD-5, 4, 582–596 (October 1986), and R. K. Brayton, R. Rudell, A. Sangiovanni-Vincentelli, A. R. Wang, "MIS: A Multiple-Level Logic Optimization System," *IEEE Transactions on Computer-Aided Design*, CAD-6, 6, 1062–1081 (November 1987). The latter is the definitive theoretical treatment of the algorithms at the heart of *misII*'s approach to multilevel logic optimization.

We have based our discussion of hazards on Unit 26 of the classical text by C. H. Roth, Jr., *Fundamentals of Logic Design*, 3rd Edition, West Publishing Co., St. Paul, MN, 1985. Even he goes lightly over the discussion of dynamic hazards. A more detailed discussion of this topic can be found in E. J. McCluskey's earlier textbook, *Introduction to the Theory of Switching Circuits*, McGraw-Hill, New York, 1965.

All manufacturers provide data books for their components. The standard reference for TTL components can be obtained from Texas Instruments, the manufacturer that has most popularized the 74XX series. The most critical volumes of their five-volume set are Volume 2, which describes standard, S, and LS TTL, and Volume 3, which describes ALS and AS components.

Exercises

This is not exercise, it's flagellation!

—Noel Coward

3.1   *(Conversion Between Forms)*   Use Boolean algebra to verify the following:

   a. The AND-OR expression of Figure 3.4 is equivalent to the NAND/NAND expression of that figure.

   b. The AND-OR expression of Figure 3.5 is equivalent to the NOR/NOR expression of that figure.

   c. The OR/AND expression of Figure 3.6 is equivalent to the NOR/NOR expression of that figure.

   d. The OR/AND expression of Figure 3.7 is equivalent to the NAND/NAND expression of that figure.

3.2   *(AND-OR/NAND-NAND Mappings)*   Draw schematics for the following expressions, mapped into NAND-only networks. You may assume that literals and their complements are available:

   a. $A\overline{B}\,\overline{C} + \overline{A}C + \overline{A}B$

   b. $(\overline{A} + \overline{B} + \overline{C})\,(\overline{A} + B)\,(\overline{A} + C)$

   c. $\overline{A}B + A + \overline{C} + \overline{D}$

   d. $(\overline{AB})\,(\overline{\overline{AC}})$

   e. $\overline{AB + \overline{A}\,\overline{C}}$

3.3   *(OR-AND/NOR-NOR Mappings)*   Draw schematics for the following expressions, mapped into NOR-only networks. You may assume that literals and their complements are available:

   a. $(A + B)\,(\overline{A} + C)$

   b. $\overline{(A + B)} \bullet \overline{(\overline{A} + C)}$

   c. $\overline{(A + B)} \bullet \overline{(\overline{A} + C)}$

    d. $(A + B) \bullet (\overline{A} + C + D) \bullet (\overline{A} + \overline{C})$

    e. $(A + B) \bullet (\overline{B} \bullet C) \bullet (\overline{A} + \overline{C})$

3.4   *(Multilevel Network Mappings)* Draw schematics for the following expressions, using mixed NAND and NOR gates only:

    a. $(AB + CD) E + F$

    b. $(AB + C) E + DG$

    c. $\{A + [(B + C)(D + E)]\} \{[(F + G)(\overline{B} + \overline{E})] + \overline{A}\}$

    d. $(A + B)(C + D) + EF$

    e. $A\overline{B}(\overline{B} + C)\overline{D} + \overline{A}$

3.5   *(Canonical Forms)* Given the following function in sum of products form (not necessarily minimized):

$$F(A, B, C, D) = \overline{A}BC + AD + AC$$

Reexpress the function in:

    a. Canonical product of sums form. Use ΠM notation.

    b. Minimized product of sums form.

    c. $\overline{F}$ in minimized product of sums form.

    d. $\overline{F}$ in minimized sum of products form.

    e. Implement F and $\overline{F}$ using NAND gates only. You may assume that literals and their complements are available.

    f. Implement F and $\overline{F}$ using NOR gates only. You may assume that literals and their complements are available.

    g. Implement F and $\overline{F}$ using a single AND-OR-Invert gate. You may assume that literals and their complements are available.

    h. Implement F and $\overline{F}$ using a single OR-AND-Invert gate. You may assume that literals and their complements are available.

3.6   *(AND-OR-Invert Logic)* Implement the following functions using AND-OR-Invert gates. Assume no limitations on inputs or the number of stacks. You may assume that literals and their complements are available.

    a. $f(A,B,C) = A \oplus B \oplus C$

    b. $f(A,B,C) = AB + BC + AC$

    c. $f(A,B,C,D) = \Sigma\, m(1,3,5,7,9) + \Sigma\, d(6,12,13)$

    d. $f(A,B,C,D) = \Pi\, M(0,1,6,7)$

    e. $f(A,B,C,D) = \Sigma\, m(0,2,4,6)$

3.7   *(OR-AND-Invert Logic)*   Implement the same functions as in Exercise 3.4, but this time use OR-AND-Invert gates. Assume no limitations on inputs or the number of stacks. You may assume that literals and their complements are available.

3.8   *(Multilevel Logic)*   Factor the following sum of products expressions:

a. $ABCD + ABDE$

b. $ACD + BC + ABE + BD$

c. $AC + ADE + BC + BDE$

d. $AD + AE + BD + BE + CD + CE + AF$

e. $ACE + ACF + ADE + ADF + BCE + BCF + BDE + BDF$

3.9   *(Multilevel Logic)*   Write down the function represented by the circuit network in Figure Ex3.9 in a multilevel factored form using AND, OR, and NOT operations only—that is, no NAND or NOR operations:

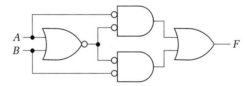

Figure Ex3.9

Derive the simplest Boolean expression (minimum number of literals and fewest gates) for the function represented by this schematic. You may use any kind of logic gates described in Chapter 2.

3.10   *(Multilevel Logic)*   Using Boolean algebra, K-maps, or truth tables, verify that the multilevel forms for the full adder *Sum* and *CO* (carry-out) obtained in Section 3.1 are logically equivalent to the two-level forms found in Chapter 2.

3.11   *(Multilevel Logic)*   Using Boolean algebra, K-maps, or truth tables, verify that the multilevel forms for the 2-bit binary adder outputs, X, Y, and Z, of Section 3.1 are logically equivalent to the two-level forms found in Chapter 2.

3.12   *(Multilevel Logic)*   Using Boolean algebra, K-maps, or truth tables, verify that the multilevel forms for the BCD increment by 1 outputs, W, X, Y, and Z, of Section 3.1 are logically equivalent to the two-level forms found in Chapter 2.

3.13   *(Time Response)*   Consider the circuit in Figure Ex3.13(a). Write down its functions in minimized form. Given that XOR/

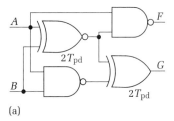

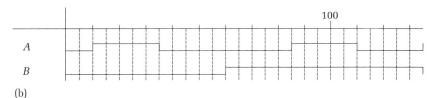

(a)

(b)

Figure Ex3.13

XNOR gates have twice the delay of the NAND gates, what is the circuit's output response to the input waveforms in Figure Ex3.13(b)? (Each 5-time-unit division represents one NAND gate delay.)

3.14 *(Time Response)* Consider the circuit with a single input in Figure Ex3.14(a). At time t_0 the switch is moved to the closed (connected) position, and at time t_1 the switch is returned to its original open (disconnected) position. Fill in a timing diagram showing the behavior of the internal signals B and C, and the output signal, in response to this input waveform. Assume all gates have an identical propagation delay T_{pd}, which corresponds to a single division on the chart in Figure Ex3.14(b).

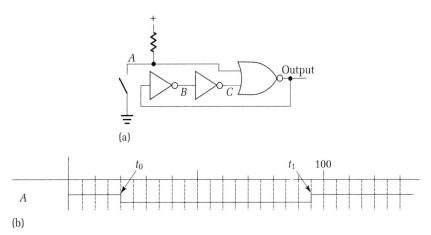

(a)

(b)

Figure Ex3.14

3.15   *(Time Response)*   Construct a timing diagram for the behavior of the circuit schematic in Figure Ex3.15.

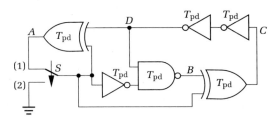

Figure Ex3.15

a. Start by finding a nonoscillating starting condition for the circuit with switch S in position 1 (up) as shown. Fill in the timing waveform with an initial steady-state condition for the circuit nodes labeled A, B, C, and D. *Warning:* It is very easy to choose an initial configuration that oscillates. A unique nonoscillating configuration does exist. Start your reasoning with the tightest loop, or make an educated guess and verify that the assumed state is indeed nonoscillating.

b. At time *T*, the switch is moved from position 1 to position 2 (down). Fill in the rest of the timing diagram with the logic values of the signals at points A, B, C, and D in the given circuit.

3.16   *(Hazard-Free Design)*   Given the following specification of Boolean functions, implement them in a hazard-free manner:

a. $F(A, B, C) = B\overline{C} + \overline{A}C$

b. $F(A, B, C, D) = \Sigma\, m(0, 4, 5, 6, 7, 9, 11, 13, 14)$

c. $F(A, B, C) = (A + B)\,(\overline{B} + C)$

d. $F(A, B, C, D) = \Pi\, M(0, 1, 3, 5, 7, 8, 9, 13, 15)$

e. $F(A, B, C, D, E) = \Sigma\, m(0, 1, 3, 4, 7, 11, 12, 15, 16, 17, 20, 28)$

3.17   *(TTL Data Book)*   To answer this question, you will need access to a TTL data book, preferably one published by Texas Instruments, Inc. Someone has constructed a giant 32-input AND gate from a cascaded tree of 2-input AND gates of type 74S08. This circuit is to drive an output net with 50 picofarads (pF) of capacitance. Assume that the typical capacitance of internal circuit nodes is more like 15 pF. See Figure Ex3.17.

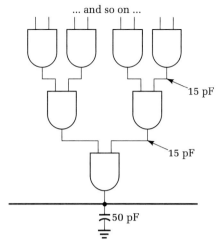

... and so on ...

15 pF

15 pF

50 pF

Figure Ex3.17

    a. What is the typical average delay through this circuit?

    b. What is the typical average DC power consumption of this circuit?

3.18 *(TTL Data Book)* To answer this question, you will need access to a TTL data book. Compute the typical propagation delay and power consumption of the following TTL components:

    a. 7400 and 74S00

    b. 7402, 74S02, and 74LS02

    c. 7404, 74S04, and 74LS04

3.19 *(TTL Data Book)* To answer this question, you will need access to a TTL data book. Compute the following fan-outs:

    a. An S TTL NAND gate driving other S TTL NAND gates

    b. An LS TTL NAND gate driving S TTL NAND gates

    c. A standard TTL NAND gate driving LS TTL NAND gates

    d. A standard TTL NAND gate driving S TTL NAND gates

3.20 *(TTL Gates)* It is never a good idea to allow inputs to a TTL gate to "float," that is, to be left unconnected. Give four ways to wire up the unused input of a TTL NAND gate to ensure proper operation of the gate.

4 Programmable and Steering Logic

*When you have eliminated
the impossible, whatever
remains, however
improbable, must be
the truth.*

—Sir Arthur Conan Doyle

Introduction

In Chapter 3, you learned the methods for realizing Boolean functions as multilevel networks. A multilevel network potentially reduces the wiring complexity of a Boolean function's implementation. You also met our first complex gate, the AND-OR-Invert gate. In this chapter, you will learn about more customizable and complex building blocks that can realize Boolean functions with fewer components and wires:

■ *Design with structured circuit implementation styles based on programmable array logic and memories.* We introduce PALs/PLAs and ROMs, which are particularly useful general-purpose digital building blocks that can be customized to implement specific functions. They are used to implement complex functions in very little space.

■ *Design with logic building blocks that are different from traditional logic gates.* In this chapter, we introduce several new components: multiplexers, selectors, decoders, and demultiplexers. These are Boolean functions that are often easier to visualize as switching networks than as truth tables or logic gates. You will learn the design methods for using them in digital systems. In addition, we will look at tri-state and open-collector gates, classes of logic whose outputs are not always 0 and 1.

■ *Word problems.* We will develop a design procedure for transforming English-language descriptions into hardware implementations and will illustrate the method with several case studies.

4.1   Programmable Arrays of Logic Gates

Integrated circuit (IC) manufacturers have been phenomenally successful in packing millions of transistor switching elements into microcomputers. We see how this technology can be exploited to reduce the component count of the digital system in this section.

4.1.1   Motivation for Programmable Logic

The key is to find logic building blocks that are sufficiently general purpose to be used in many designs. It is easy to identify generally useful building blocks with primitive structures, such as a handful of gates implementing an AND-OR-Invert structure. But such building blocks reduce the component count by only a modest amount. We could get a significant reduction if we could use a building block that contained the equivalent of hundreds of gates. But what should this building block look like?

The ingenious solution to this dilemma is to arrange the AND and OR gates (or NOR or NAND gates) into a generalized array structure whose connections can be *personalized* or *programmed* to implement a specific function. Such general-purpose logic building blocks are called PALs (*programmable array logic*) or PLAs (*programmable logic arrays*).

4.1.2   PALs and PLAs

Figure 4.1 shows a general block diagram for an array logic component. Such components are multi-input/multi-output devices, typically organized into an AND subarray and an OR subarray. The AND subarray maps the inputs into particular product terms, depending on the programmed connections. The OR subarray takes these terms and ORs them together to produce the final sum of products expression.

Example   A PLA device can implement a modest collection of functions of considerable complexity. This complexity is determined by the number of inputs, the number of product terms (number of AND gates), and the number of outputs (number of OR gates) that the PLA can support.

For example, a typical TTL field-programmable logic array (FPLA) might have 16 inputs, 48 product terms, and 8 outputs. In a package

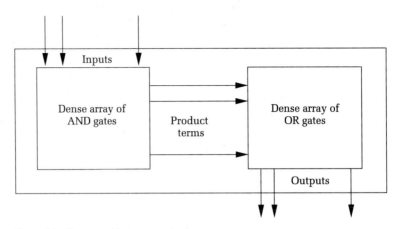

Figure 4.1   Programmable array organization.

with 24 data pins, this PLA contains the equivalent of forty-eight 16-input AND gates and eight 48-input OR gates. When you consider that a 12-data-pin SSI package gives you only four 2-input gates, you can see the real package efficiency of array logic.

Suppose you want to implement the following Boolean equations, defined for A, B, and C:

$$F_0 = A + \overline{B}\,\overline{C} \qquad F_2 = \overline{B}\,\overline{C} + AB$$

$$F_1 = A\overline{C} + AB \qquad F_3 = \overline{B}C + A$$

We can characterize them by the number of variables (A, B, C), the unique product terms $(A, \overline{B}\,\overline{C}, A\overline{C}, AB, \overline{B}C)$, and the functions (F_0, F_1, F_2, F_3). These correspond to the number of inputs to the AND array, the number of outputs from the AND array (which are the inputs to the OR array), and the number of outputs from the OR array. To implement these functions, you would need (at least) a 3-input, 5-product term, 4-output PLA device.

A convenient way to describe the functions is by a *personality matrix*, a minor reformulation of the truth table, shown in Figure 4.2. It describes which input literals should be connected to each AND gate to form the desired product term (1 = asserted variable, 0 = complemented variable, - = no connection), and which of these should be ORed together to form the final outputs (1 = connect product term to OR, 0 = no connection). Rows determine product terms; columns represent inputs and outputs. A product term participates in more than one function if there is more than one 1 in its row in the personality matrix's output columns. In Figure 4.2, it is easy to see that $\overline{B}C$, AB, and A are used by more than one function.

Product term	Inputs A B C	Outputs F₀	F₁	F₂	F₃	
$A\,B$	1 1 -	0	①	①	0	
$\overline{B}\,C$	- 0 1	0	0	0	①	Reuse
$A\,\overline{C}$	1 - 0	0	①	0	0	of
$\overline{B}\,\overline{C}$	- 0 0	①	0	①	0	terms
A	1 - -	①	0	0	①	

→ 5 minterms → AND Gates

Figure 4.2 PLA personality matrix.

↓   ↓   4 OR gates.

Gate-Equivalent Representation Figure 4.3 and Figure 4.4 show gate-equivalent diagrams of the implementation of our example functions in programmable array logic. Figure 4.3 shows the array before programming, with all possible connections between inputs and gates prewired

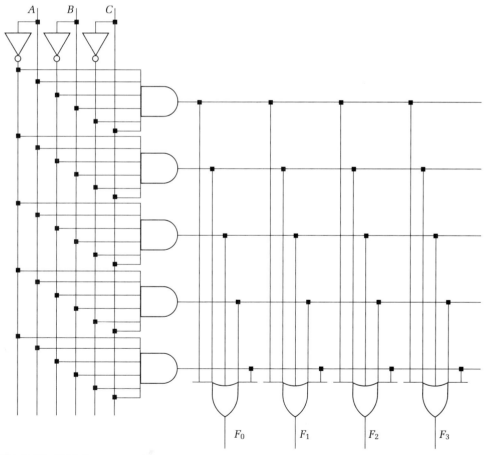

Figure 4.3 PLA before programming.

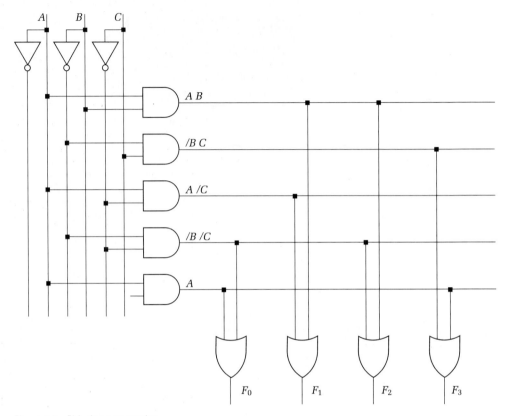

Figure 4.4 PLA after programming.

"at the factory." You personalize the array by using a hardware device called a *programmer*.

The details of the programming process depend on the particular integrated circuit. A frequently used technique places fuses between all possible inputs to a gate and the gate itself. A fuse is an electrical connection specially designed to break down or "blow" under high current. By placing a high current across selected fuses, the programmer hardware breaks those connections. The programmer software analyzes your Boolean equations to determine which fuses should be blown and which should be left alone. Figure 4.4 shows the same array after it has been personalized.

Figure 4.5 gives a commonly used notation for representing the topology of array logic. You should interpret the single wires entering the AND and OR gates as representing multiple inputs. The X's represent the fuse locations.

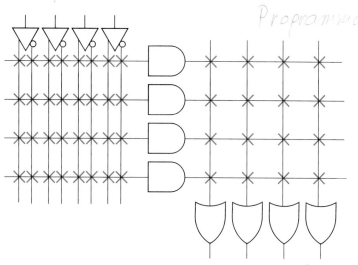

Programmable

Figure 4.5   Notation for four-input, four-output, four-product-term array.

different

PLA

Example   Now let's consider the design of a function generator of three inputs. The circuit should implement the logic functions AND, OR, NAND, NOR, XOR, and XNOR:

$$F_1 = ABC$$

$$F_2 = A + B + C$$

$$F_3 = \overline{ABC} = \overline{A} + \overline{B} + \overline{C}$$

$$F_4 = \overline{A + B + C} = \overline{A}\,\overline{B}\,\overline{C}$$

$$F_5 = A \oplus B \oplus C = \overline{A}\,\overline{B}C + \overline{A}B\overline{C} + A\overline{B}\,\overline{C} + ABC$$

$$F_6 = \overline{A \oplus B \oplus C} = AB\overline{C} + \overline{A}BC + A\overline{B}C + \overline{A}\,\overline{B}\,\overline{C}$$

next ? page?

Figure 4.6 shows how this collection of functions is implemented in a PLA. The terms ABC and $\overline{A}\,\overline{B}\,\overline{C}$ are shared among more than one output function. ABC is used to implement F_1, AND, and F_5, XOR, while $\overline{A}\,\overline{B}\,\overline{C}$ is used by F_4, NOR, and F_6, XNOR.

4.1.3   The Difference Between PLAs and PALs

Figure 4.5 implies that both the AND and OR subarrays can be personalized in any way the designer wants. Devices with this generality are called *programmable logic arrays* (PLAs).

PLA: OF 16 MINTERMS
2 ARE SHARED, SO
TOTAL WE HAVE 14
UNIQUE MINTERMS

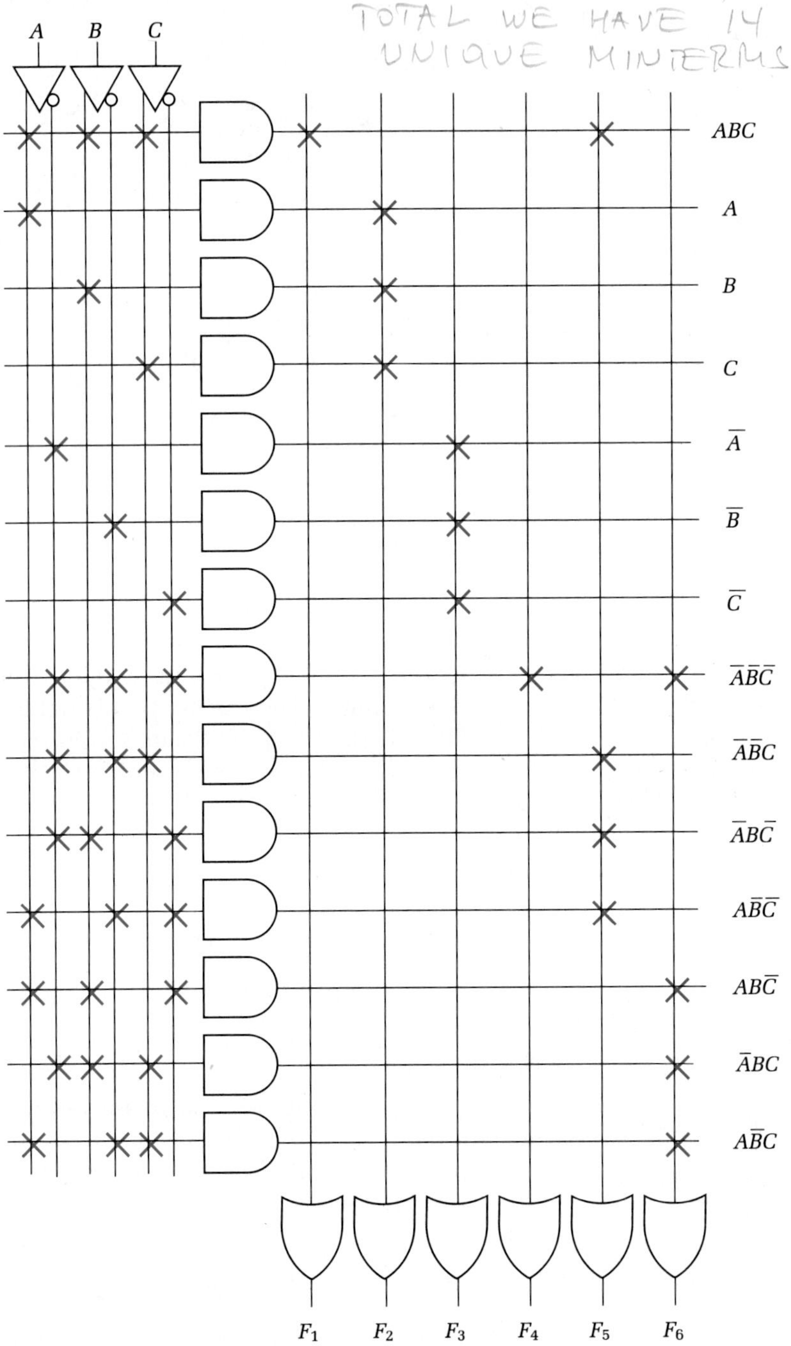

Figure 4.6 Example implementation.

PAL:
Will need to compute all of 16 minterms

However, not all programmable logic supports full programmability. For instance, Monolithic Memories' *programmable array logic* (PAL) devices have a programmable AND array, but the connections between product terms and specific OR gates are hardwired. The number of product term inputs to an OR gate is usually limited to 2, 4, 8, or 16.

There is a fundamental trade-off in PAL devices between the complexity of the functions in terms of the product terms per OR gate and the number of independent functions the device can implement. The higher the OR gate fan-ins, the fewer the functional outputs from the PAL.

For example, a PAL family might include three alternative devices, each with 16 inputs and 16 product terms, but differing in their OR array organization: four OR gates with 4 inputs each, two OR gates with 8 inputs each, and one OR gate with 16 inputs. The AND subarrays remain completely programmable. Figure 4.7 shows a 4-input/4-product-term/2-output PAL organization with a particular fixed choice for the OR array. In this case, the OR gates are limited to two product terms each.

The key difference between PLAs and PALs is that the former can take advantage of shared product terms and the latter cannot. Let's think back to the function generator design of the previous subsection. Since no product terms can be shared among the PAL outputs, the functions need a PAL that can compute 16 product terms (ABC, $\overline{ABC}$ are duplicated). A PLA needs to compute only 14 product terms, the number of unique terms. For devices with comparable internal resources, a PLA should be able to implement a more complex collection of functions than a PAL if many product terms are shared.

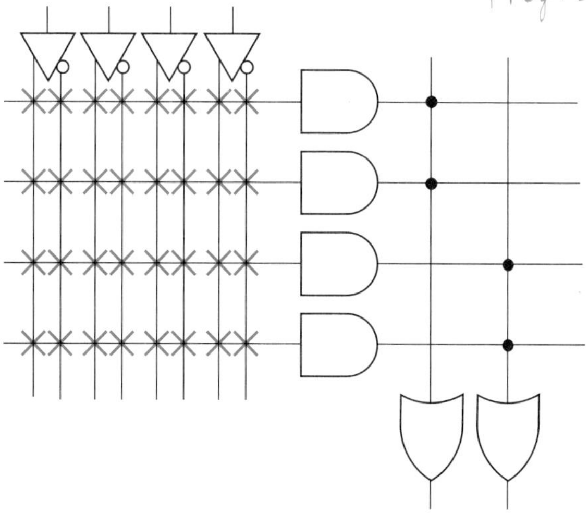

PAL is faster: it has less programmable fuses which are slow.

Programmable   *NOT Program.*

Figure 4.7 Example of a PAL organization with a constrained OR array and programmable AND array.

On the other hand, the PLA will be slower because of the relative resistances of programmable and hardwired connections. Programmable, fuse-based connections have higher resistance than standard wired connections. Thus, signals pass through two programmable connections in the PLA, incurring worse delays than the single programmable connection in the PAL.

4.1.4   Design Examples

We examine two different design examples in this subsection, a code converter and a magnitude comparator. They illustrate the various alternatives for implementing combinational logic in terms of PALs, PLAs, or multilevel logic.

BCD-to-Gray-Code Converter   In this example, we will design a code converter that maps a 4-bit BCD number into a 4-bit Gray code number. Each number in a Gray code sequence differs from its predecessor by exactly 1 bit. The circuit has four inputs, $A\ B\ C\ D$, representing the BCD number, and four outputs, $W\ X\ Y\ Z$, the 4-bit Gray code word.

The truth table and K-maps for the translation logic are shown in Figure 4.8 and Figure 4.9, respectively. The prime implicants are circled in Figure 4.9, resulting in the following reduced equations:

A	B	C	D	W	X	Y	Z
0	0	0	0	0	0	0	0
0	0	0	1	0	0	0	1
0	0	1	0	0	0	1	1
0	0	1	1	0	0	1	0
0	1	0	0	0	1	1	0
0	1	0	1	1	1	1	0
0	1	1	0	1	0	1	0
0	1	1	1	1	0	1	1
1	0	0	0	1	0	0	1
1	0	0	1	1	0	0	0
1	0	1	0	X	X	X	X
1	0	1	1	X	X	X	X
1	1	0	0	X	X	X	X
1	1	0	1	X	X	X	X
1	1	1	0	X	X	X	X
1	1	1	1	X	X	X	X

Figure 4.8   Truth table for the BCD-to-Gray-code converter.

$$W = A + BD + BC$$

$$X = B\overline{C}$$

$$Y = B + C$$

$$Z = \overline{A}\,\overline{B}\,\overline{C}D + BC\overline{D} + A\overline{D} + \overline{B}C\overline{D}$$

Since there are no shared product terms, these functions are best suited for a PAL implementation.

The implementation is shown in Figure 4.10. The PAL contains four 4-input OR gates. You can see that many of the AND gates are being wasted. The same function could be implemented with a less complex PLA, but it would be slower.

The programmable logic approach implements the functions in a single integrated circuit package. Let's consider an equivalent implementation with discrete TTL gates. We will restrict ourselves to NAND gates and inverters only.

The resulting discrete gate circuit is shown in Figure 4.11. The figure included a parts list at the lower right. We have labeled gates from the same package with the same number. The circuit uses 15 gates partitioned across five packages. Clearly, the programmable logic approach has a big advantage. Of course, only one of the four gates in package 5 is being used, leaving three gates that could be used by other circuits.

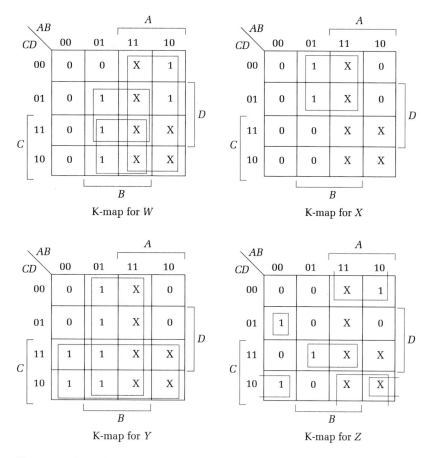

Figure 4.9 K-maps for code converter.

Two-Bit Magnitude Comparator Our next task is to design a comparator circuit. The circuit takes two 2-bit binary numbers as inputs, denoted by *AB* and *CD*, and computes the four functions $AB = CD$ *(EQ)*, $AB \neq CD$ *(NE)*, $AB < CD$ *(LT)*, and $AB > CD$ *(GT)*.

Figure 4.12 shows the K-maps for the four functions with boxed prime implicants. This yields the following reduced equations for the output functions:

$$EQ = \overline{A}\overline{B}\overline{C}\overline{D} + \overline{A}B\overline{C}D + ABCD + A\overline{B}C\overline{D}$$

$$NE = A\overline{C} + \overline{A}C + \overline{B}D + B\overline{D}$$

$$LT = \overline{A}C + \overline{A}\overline{B}D + \overline{B}CD$$

$$GT = A\overline{C} + AB\overline{D} + B\overline{C}\overline{D}$$

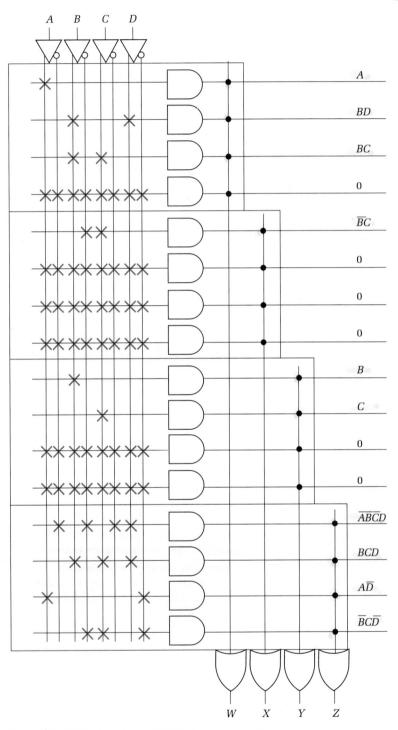

Figure 4.10 - PAL Implementation of BCD-to-Gray-code converter.

BCD — GRAY

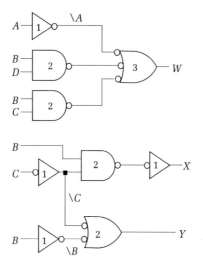

Figure 4.11 Discrete gate implementation of code converter.

1: 7404 hex inverters
2,5: 7400 quad 2-input NAND
3: 7410 tri 3-input NAND
4: 7420 dual 4-input NAND

no reduction

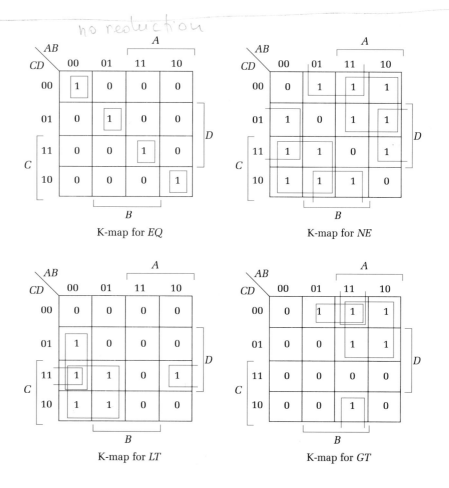

K-map for EQ

K-map for NE

K-map for LT

K-map for GT

Figure 4.12 K-maps for magnitude comparator.

The functions use 14 product terms, of which 2 terms ($A\overline{C}$ and $\overline{A}C$) are used twice. Because product terms are shared, a PLA-based implementation is more attractive than the PAL-based method. The programmed PLA is shown in Figure 4.13. This single-chip implementation compares very favorably with a multichip implementation formed using TTL SSI gates.

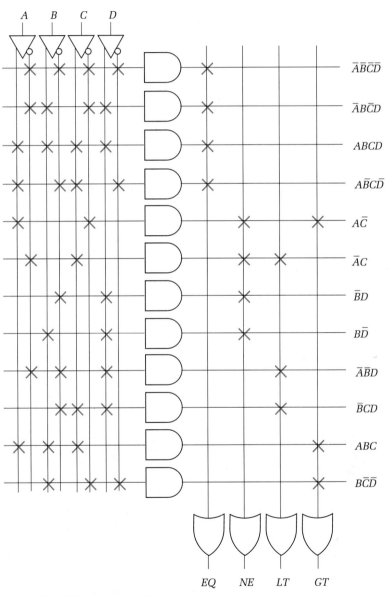

Figure 4.13 PLA implementation of magnitude comparator.

It is not unusual for a PAL or PLA implementation to replace 5 to 15 TTL packages of 10 to 30 gates. This is why many real-world designs make extensive use of programmable logic devices. It is an effective way to reduce an implementation's component count and thus its manufacturing costs as well.

4.2 Beyond Simple Logic Gates

Chapters 2 and 3 concentrated on the design of combinational logic functions with simple gates. PALs and PLAs are an IC package-efficient method for designing with simple gates.

In this section we go beyond simple gates, concentrating on how to make use of higher-level, more complex logic building blocks. The idea is to do more work, that is, compute a more complex function, without increasing the number of connections to the outside world. Such logic components are often called *medium-scale integration* or MSI. A typical MSI component implements a function that would require from 10 to 100 discrete gates to do the same thing. If you can use these components as general-purpose logic building blocks, you can usually achieve an implementation with a smaller package count. As examples of these kinds of components, we will examine *multiplexer/selector functions* and *decoder/demultiplexer functions*.

We will also look at two classes of building blocks that do not behave exactly like logic gates. The function of the first class of components cannot always be described easily as logic equations. We tend to think about them in terms of switching networks. Examples of these kinds of circuits include *CMOS transmission gates* and *read-only memories* (ROMs).

The second class are unlike simple gates because they have output values that are different from 0 and 1. These are *tri-state* and *open collector* gates. We begin by looking at transistor switches in more detail.

4.2.1 Switch and Steering Logic

Section B.4 in Appendix B describes the basic electrical behavior of MOS transistors and how they can be combined to form standard logic gates. In this subsection, we examine alternative ways to implement logic functions as networks of CMOS switching elements, based on CMOS transmission gates.

Switching networks provide an alternative to discrete gates for constructing digital systems. They operate by steering or directing inputs to outputs through a network of switching paths rather than by computing a Boolean function. You have actually seen this before in Chapter 2. The switching networks for standard gates like NAND and NOR route 0 or 1 to the output under the control of the data inputs.

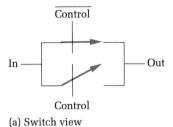

(a) Switch view

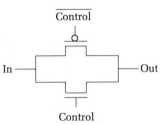

(b) Transistor view

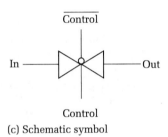

(c) Schematic symbol

Figure 4.14 CMOS transmission gate.

For general-purpose switching networks, the primitive component is the CMOS transmission gate. It is constructed from a normally open switch (nMOS transistor) wired in parallel with a normally closed switch (pMOS transistor), with complementary control signals. Figure 4.14 shows the switch, transistor, and schematic representations of the transmission gate. A transmission gate is equally good at passing a 0 or 1 when an external control signal is asserted.

Transmission gates are not equivalent in function to any of the logic gates you have encountered so far. They are not available to TTL logic designers, only to those designing directly in CMOS technologies.

So why bother with transmission gates? They are of interest because some important digital functions can be implemented in many fewer transistors if we use transmission gates. These are usually functions that can be recast in terms of steering networks, such as shifters (more on these in Chapter 7) and multiplexer/demultiplexer circuits, which we will tackle in Section 4.2.2.

CMOS Transmission Gate Transmission gates provide an efficient way to build steering logic. *Steering logic circuits* are circuits that route data inputs to outputs based on the settings of control signals. As an example of such a circuit, consider the following. The circuit has two data inputs, I_0 and I_1, a single output Z, and a control input S. The function steers I_0 to Z when S is 0 and I_1 to Z when S is 1.

We call this a *selector function* or a *multiplexer*. It operates just like a switch in a railroad yard. Two independent pieces of track have to be merged into a single track. In a similar way, we often need to merge signal paths in digital logic.

Steering logic implements the selector as shown in Figure 4.15. When S is asserted, the lower transmission gate conducts and the upper gate does not. Thus I_1 is gated to Z. When S becomes unasserted, the upper transmission gate conducts and the lower gate breaks the connection. Thus, I_0 is steered to Z. This multiplexer or selector function will be described in greater detail in the next subsection.

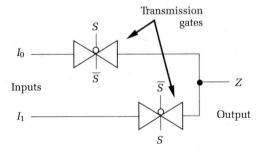

Figure 4.15 Selector function implemented with transmission gates.

We make two observations about steering logic. First, for any combinations of the control inputs, there must be at least one conducting path from an input to the output. In other words, the output node should always be driven from some input. It should not be left floating. Second, there should never be more than one conducting path between the inputs and an output. If more than one path could exist, one of the paths might attempt to drive the output node to logic 1 while another drives it to logic 0. The resulting conflict would yield neither a logic 1 nor a logic 0 at the output node.

We give a second example of steering logic in Figure 4.16. This network steers its single input to Z_1 if S is asserted and Z_0 when S is unasserted. This function is called a *demultiplexer* because it performs the reverse operation of a multiplexer. Multiplexers and demultiplexers are used to implement multiple connections between components, as shown in Figure 4.17. The figure shows connection paths between A and Z and B and Y. When the control settings are changed, the paths connect A to Y and B to Z. Once again, the structure looks just like the switches in a railroad yard.

There is one problem in the circuit of Figure 4.16. It violates one of our conditions for a properly functioning network. When S is asserted, I is steered to Z_1, but what value is placed on the output Z_0? Unfortunately, the output Z_0 is neither 0 nor 1, but floats. The same problem exists for Z_1 when S is unasserted. A solution with the correct behavior is given in Figure 4.18. When the input steers to Z_1, an additional transmission gate steers a 0 to Z_0. We do something similar for output Z_1 when the input steers to Z_0.

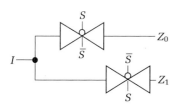

Figure 4.16 Possible implementation of demultiplexer functions.

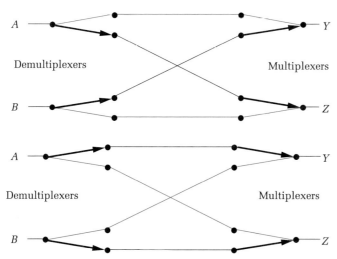

Figure 4.17 Multiplexer/demultiplexer functions.

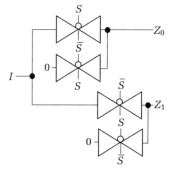

Figure 4.18 Correct implementation of demultiplexer function.

I_1	Zero	One
0	1	0
1	0	1

Figure 4.19   Truth table and gate implementation of single-input tally function.

A Complex Steering Logic Example   We are now ready to look at a more complex design example of what steering logic can do. Let's examine a function called the Tally circuit. A Tally circuit has N inputs (I_1, I_2, ..., I_n) and $N + 1$ outputs (Zero, One, ..., N). The circuit counts the number of its inputs that are at logic 1. Only one of the outputs is asserted at any time: if none of the inputs are 1, the output Zero is asserted; if one is 1, then the output One is asserted, and so on.

Figure 4.19 gives the truth table and gate-level implementation for a single-input Tally function. It has the single input I_1 and the two outputs Zero and One. The truth table makes it clear that Zero is simply the complement of I_1 and One is identical to I_1.

How would we implement this function with steering logic? Remember that steering logic is good at routing inputs to outputs under the direction of control signals, so we must rethink the definition of the Tally circuit in these terms. While it may seem counterintuitive at first, in steering logic it is quite acceptable to use data signals to control transmission gates.

Figure 4.20(a) shows the switch network for a single-input Tally function implemented from transmission gates. The inputs are 0 and 1, I_1 is used as a control signal, and the outputs are labeled Zero and One. Each output is connected to two transmission gates controlled by complementary signals. This guarantees that the network is well formed: it is not possible for both transmission gates to be conducting at the same time if their control signals are complementary.

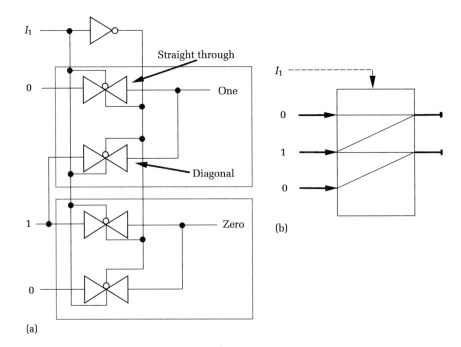

Figure 4.20   Single-input tally circuit implemented via transmission gates.

We'll call the upper of these the "straight-through" transmission gate, and the lower the "diagonal" transmission gate. Depending on the setting of the control signals, the inputs can be steered straight through the network or can be shifted diagonally. The steering paths can be seen more clearly in the block diagram of Figure 4.20(b).

When I_1 is unasserted, the straight-through gates are conducting and the diagonal gates are not. Thus, the input 0 steers to the output One while 1 steers to Zero. This is shown in Figure 4.21.

When I_1 is asserted, the opposite is the case. The straight-through gates are nonconducting while the diagonal gates conduct. This causes a 1 to be steered to the One output and a 0 to the Zero output. This is shown in Figure 4.22.

The transmission gate implementation is significantly more complex than the simple gate implementation, so it offers no real advantage. However, it does become more attractive when we have a larger number of inputs. Let's turn our attention to a two-input Tally circuit. The truth table and logic gate implementation are given in Figure 4.23.

The transmission gate implementation builds on the design of the single-input case for the two-input circuit. In essence, we decompose a two-input Tally circuit into two cascaded single-input networks. The inputs to the second stage are the Zero and One outputs from the first stage. The transmission gate implementation is given in Figure 4.24(a). Figure 4.24(b) gives its block diagram representation.

The four different cases of the two inputs and the resulting paths through the switching network are shown in Figure 4.25. Figure 4.25(a)

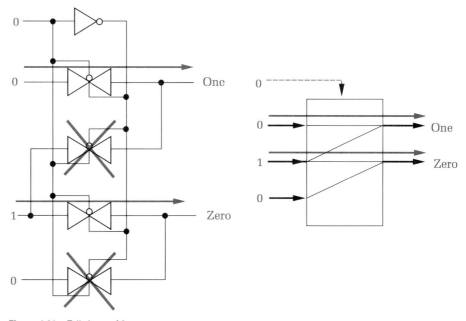

Figure 4.21   Tally input of 0.

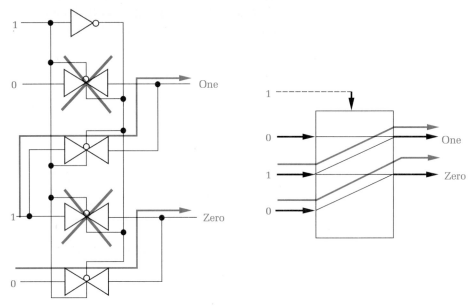

Figure 4.22 Tally input of 1.

I_1	I_2	Zero	One	Two
0	0	1	0	0
0	1	0	1	0
1	0	0	1	0
1	1	0	0	1

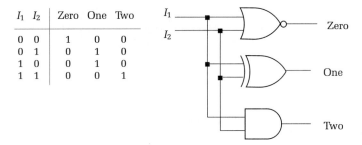

Figure 4.23 Truth table and gate implementation of the two-input tally function.

shows what happens when both inputs are 0. The straight-through gates are enabled, setting the Zero output to 1 and the One and Two outputs to 0.

Figure 4.25(b) shows the situation when I_1 is 0 and I_2 is 1. The first stage passes through while the second stage shifts diagonally. The intermediate One and Zero signals are set to 0 and 1, respectively, and these are shifted up by the second stage. The second stage's One output is asserted while the Two and Zero outputs are 0.

Figure 4.25(c) illustrates what happens when I_1 is 1 and I_2 is 0. The network behaves symmetrically. The One and Zero intermediate outputs read 1 and 0, respectively; these are passed directly through by the second stage.

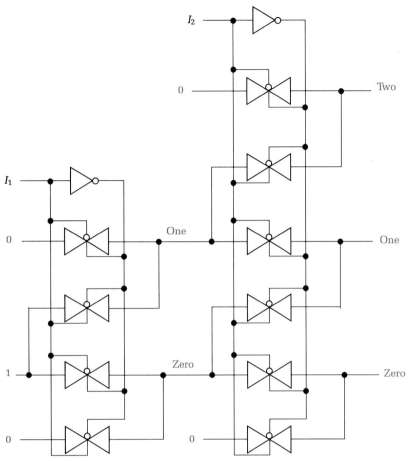

(a) Construction from transmission gates

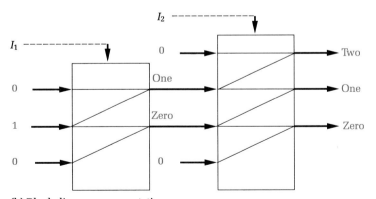

(b) Block diagram representation

Figure 4.24   Two-input tally function.

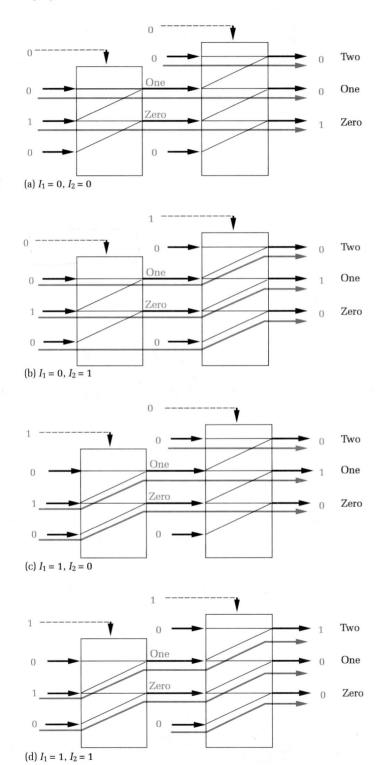

(a) $I_1 = 0, I_2 = 0$

(b) $I_1 = 0, I_2 = 1$

(c) $I_1 = 1, I_2 = 0$

Figure 4.25   Operation of the two-input tally circuit.

(d) $I_1 = 1, I_2 = 1$

The final case is shown in Figure 4.25(d), when both inputs are 1. All of the diagonal transmission gates are enabled. The One and Zero outputs at the first stage are driven to 1 and 0, respectively. These are shifted once again by the second stage, yielding 1, 0, 0 on the Two, One, and Zero outputs.

The transmission gate implementation still looks more complicated than the approach using discrete gates. But which method is more transistor efficient? The switching network makes use of 2 inverters and 10 transmission gates: a total of 24 transistors. The gate method actually uses 26 transistors! Here is how we counted them. The two-input NOR gate is implemented with four transistors. We assume that the AND gate is implemented with an inverter and a two-input NAND gate, for six more transistors. The XOR gate actually consists of four interconnected two-input NAND gates. That's 16 more transistors. The total is 26. Thus, the switching network makes use of fewer transistors than the gate network to implement the same function. The advantage would be even more pronounced for a three- or four-input Tally circuit.

4.2.2   Multiplexers/Selectors

We next examine two very important kinds of digital building blocks. They are very much in the spirit of steering logic just described. A *multiplexer/selector* chooses one of many inputs to steer to its single output under the direction of its control inputs. If the input to a circuit can come from several places, a multiplexer is one possible way to funnel the multiple sources selectively to a single input. In contrast, a demultiplexer takes its single data input and steers it to one of its many outputs under the direction of its control inputs. This is a useful building block for distributing an output to one of several different nodes, as long as only one of those is to be driven at any time.

More formally, a multiplexer, or *mux*, is a combinational logic network with 2^n data inputs, n control inputs, and one data output. Depending on the settings of the control inputs, a single data input is selected and steered to the output. The 0's and 1's on the control inputs form the binary index of the input that is to be connected to the output. Because a multiplexer does nothing more than select an input for connection to the output, the terms *multiplexer* and *selector* are used interchangeably.

A *demultiplexer*, or *demux*, steers its one data input to exactly one of its many outputs. This is the reverse of the multiplexer. *Decoder* is another name for the component. We use the latter term when the data input is considered to be a special signal used to enable one of many similar components. This is useful, for example, in a memory system to enable one of several memory chips to place its contents on shared data wires.

Figure 4.26 shows how these components could be used in a simple adder subsystem. There are two sources for each of the adder's inputs A and B and two destinations for the resulting sum. The control input S_a

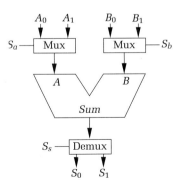

Figure 4.26   Illustration of the use of multiplexers and demultiplexers.

A	Z
0	I_0
1	I_1

I_1	I_0	A	Z
0	0	0	0
0	0	1	0
0	1	0	1
0	1	1	0
1	0	0	0
1	0	1	1
1	1	0	1
1	1	1	1

Figure 4.27   2:1 multiplexer truth tables.

chooses between the inputs A_0 and A_1, while S_b selects between B_0 and B_1. For example, to add A_0 to B_1, we would set $S_a = 0$ and $S_b = 1$. By placing the appropriate signal on S_s, the sum can be connected to one of the output nodes S_0 or S_1.

General Concept   Figure 4.27 gives a "functional" truth table on the left and a more conventional truth table on the right for a multiplexer with two data inputs, I_0 and I_1, and one control input, A. Both communicate the same information, but the functional truth table is much easier to write down. It really communicates the idea that we are passing a selected input to the output, independent of the value of that input. Restated as a Boolean equation, the two-input multiplexer can be described as

$$Z = \overline{A}I_0 + AI_1$$

If A is left unasserted, the output is driven by I_0. If A is asserted, I_1 is steered to the output.

Multiplexers are described by the number of data inputs, since you can infer the number of control inputs from this. Thus, a 2:1 multiplexer has two data inputs, one data output, and one control input, while a 4:1 multiplexer has four data inputs, one output, and two control inputs. Figure 4.28 contains block diagrams for 2:1, 4:1, and 8:1 multiplexers. The Boolean equations for the 4:1 and 8:1 multiplexers generalize from the equation for the 2:1 multiplexer:

$$Z = \overline{A}\overline{B}I_0 + \overline{A}BI_1 + A\overline{B}I_2 + ABI_3$$
$$Z = \overline{A}\overline{B}\overline{C}I_0 + \overline{A}\overline{B}CI_1 + \overline{A}B\overline{C}I_2 + \overline{A}BCI_3 + A\overline{B}\overline{C}I_4 + A\overline{B}CI_5$$
$$+ AB\overline{C}I_6 + ABCI_7$$

The most general expression for the multiplexer, based on the minterm form of Chapter 2, is

$$Z = \sum_{k=0}^{2^n - 1} m_k \bullet I_k$$

Alternative Implementations   As we saw in the previous subsection, there are two ways to implement a 2:1 multiplexer function: logic gates or transmission gates. These alternatives generalize for functions with larger numbers of inputs.

The Boolean equations give us guidelines for the logic gate implementation. Figure 4.29 has the gate schematic for the 4:1 multiplexer. The circuit requires four 3-input gates (one for each data input), one 4-input gate, and two inverters (one for each control input), a total of

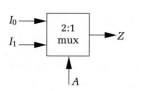

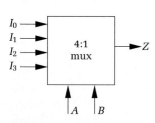

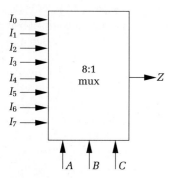

Figure 4.28   Multiplexer block diagrams.

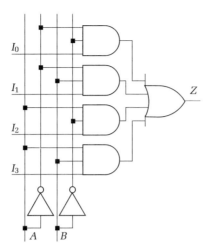

Figure 4.29   Gate-level implementation of 4:1 multiplexer.

seven discrete gates. Assuming these are implemented in CMOS logic, the circuit requires 36 transistors (6 transistors for each of four 3-input gates, 8 transistors for the 4-input gate, and 2 transistors for each of the two inverters). An 8:1 multiplexer requires eight 4-input gates, one 8-input gate, and three inverters (86 transistors). In standard gate libraries, such as the TTL catalog, the largest multiplexer is limited to 16 inputs. This is due in part to packaging limitations (we need 16 data pins, 4 control pins, 1 output pin, and power and ground, a total of 23 pins) and in part to limited fan-ins of the internal circuitry (16-input OR gates are hard to find because of electrical problems due to high fan-ins).

Contrast this with the transmission gate implementation of Figure 4.30. When the control inputs A and B are both at 0, the transmission gates in the first row conduct and I_0 is steered to the output Z. The transmission gate in the second row controlled by A and the gate in the third row controlled by B are also conducting, but no complete path is established between an input and Z. If A is 0 and B is 1, the second row of transmission gates is turned on, steering I_1 to Z. Other transmission gates are also conducting, but there is just one completed path from the inputs to the output. When A is 1 and B is 0, the path through the third row of gates is conducting, and when both control inputs are 1, the conducting path to the output weaves through the fourth row. For the 4:1 multiplexer, only eight transmission gates and two inverters are needed, a total of 20 transistors. For functions like the multiplexer, transmission gates provide a more transistor-efficient implementation than discrete gates.

It is possible to construct an N:1 multiplexer from several multiplexers with fewer inputs. Figure 4.31 shows an implementation of an 8:1 multiplexer from two 4:1 and one 2:1 multiplexers. The first stage selects one input from the range I_0 through I_3 and one from I_4 through I_7 using the

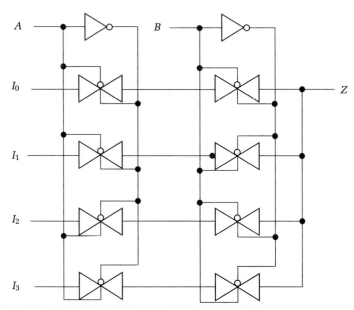

Figure 4.30 Transmission gate implementation of 4:1 multiplexer.

control inputs B and C. The second-stage multiplexer selects which first stage output should be gated to the final output using control input A.

This is not the only way to construct an 8:1 multiplexer, as Figure 4.32 shows. It makes use of four 2:1 multiplexers and one 4:1 multiplexer. Control signal C chooses among the even or odd inputs of the 2:1 multiplexers. The remaining control signals, A and B, choose among the outputs of the first-level multiplexers.

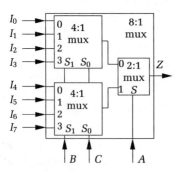

Figure 4.31 Hierarchically constructed 8:1 multiplexer.

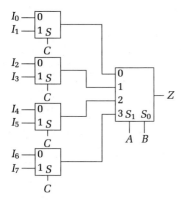

Figure 4.32 Alternative implementation of 8:1 multiplexer.

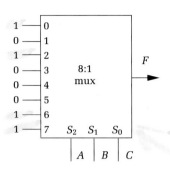

Figure 4.33 Implementation of a Boolean function with a look-up table.

Even if the component library limits you to multiplexers with a restricted number of inputs, these techniques can be used to build complex multiplexers from more primitive multiplexer building blocks.

Multiplexer as a Logic Building Block Multiplexers certainly provide a useful function for implementing signal selection, but we have not yet shown how a multiplexer implements a general-purpose logic building block. In fact, a multiplexer is one way to implement a truth table directly in hardware. A multiplexer is sometimes called a hardware *look-up table*.

Consider the function $F(A,B,C) = m_0 + m_2 + m_6 + m_7$. We can implement it directly by an 8:1 multiplexer as shown in Figure 4.33. The input variables A, B, and C are connected to the multiplexer selection inputs. We simply wire I_i to 1 if the function includes minterm m_i. All other inputs are set to 0. For the example, I_0, I_2, I_6, and I_7 are set to 1, while I_1, I_3, I_4, and I_5 are set to 0.

To see how this works, let's consider the case $A = B = C = 0$. This corresponds to the minterm m_0. Given these selection inputs, the multiplexer will select I_0 and F is set to 1. If $A = B = 0$ and $C = 1$, then I_1 is selected and F is set to 0. This continues for all other combinations of the inputs.

We can get by with an even less complex multiplexer to implement this function. We can use two of the variables, say A and B, for the selection inputs and connect the multiplexer data inputs to 0, 1, and the third variable C or its complement.

Consider the truth table for F given in Figure 4.34. It is arranged so that F is partitioned into groups of rows that share the same values of A and B. F can then be expressed as 0, 1, or a function of C for each of the four row groups defined by the values of A and B. This is equivalent to rewriting F as

$$F = \overline{A}\,\overline{B}\,(\overline{C}) + \overline{A}B\,(\overline{C}) + A\overline{B}\,(0) + AB\,(1)$$

We can now implement F with a 4:1 multiplexer, as shown in Figure 4.35.

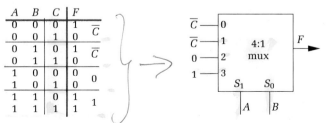

Figure 4.34 Expressing F as a function of 0, 1, and C.

Figure 4.35 Multiplexer as a programmable building block.

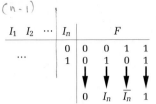

Figure 4.36 Truth table to multiplexer input mapping.

The strategy presented here is easy to generalize. By selecting $n-1$ variables as control inputs to a 2^{n-1}-input multiplexer, we can implement any Boolean function of n variables. Each choice of values for the $n-1$ variables selects exactly two rows of the truth table. The two truth table rows have exactly one of the four possible values, as shown in Figure 4.36. If the truth table rows are both 0 or both 1, the input is the constant 0 or 1, respectively. Otherwise the truth table rows correspond to the variable or its complement, and the input should be wired to the variable or its complement, respectively.

As another example, consider the function $G(A,B,C,D)$ whose K-map is given in Figure 4.37. Since it is a function of four variables, it can be implemented by an eight-input multiplexer. Let's select A, B, and C as the control inputs. This immediately partitions the K-map into eight pairs of K-map entries, each sharing common values for the three control inputs. Each pair can be replaced by the appropriate function of the remaining variable D, as shown in the truth table template of Figure 4.36. In essence, we are rewriting the equation:

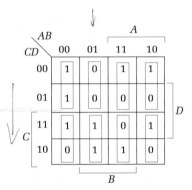

Figure 4.37 K-map for multiplexer implementation.

$$G = \overline{A}\,\overline{B}\,\overline{C}(1) + \overline{A}\,\overline{B}C(D) + \overline{A}B\overline{C}(0) + \overline{A}BC(1)$$
$$+ A\overline{B}\,\overline{C}(\overline{D}) + A\overline{B}C(D) + AB\overline{C}(\overline{D}) + ABC(\overline{D})$$

The multiplexer that realizes this function is shown in Figure 4.38.

An 8:1 multiplexer is available in a single TTL package. Now let's suppose an additional inverter is needed to form the complement of D, yielding at most two packages to implement the function. Using the usual methods for forming a minimized sum of products implementation of F, we get

$$F = \overline{A}\,\overline{B}C + \overline{A}CD + \overline{B}CD + A\overline{C}\,\overline{D} + BC\overline{D}$$

This requires five 3-input gates and one 5-input gate plus four inverters, a total of 10 gates available in perhaps three to four TTL packages. Internally, the multiplexer may use many more gates, but in terms of TTL packages (or standard cell library elements) the use of a complex building block like the multiplexer can be more efficient.

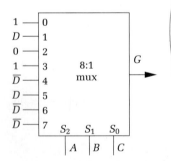

Figure 4.38 Implementation of the K-map of Fig. 4.37 by an 8:1 multiplexer.

TTL Multiplexer Components When you examine real digital component catalogs, the devices you find are slightly different from those described thus far. The catalog versions have one or more control inputs whose purpose is to enable the device for operation.

Figure 4.39 contains schematic shapes for the TTL 74157 and 74158 quad 2:1 multiplexers. The inputs and outputs of the four multiplexers are labeled with the indices 1 through 4. The inputs are A and B, and the output is Y. The four multiplexers share the same select line (SEL). SEL plays the same role as control input A in Figure 4.27. The A inputs

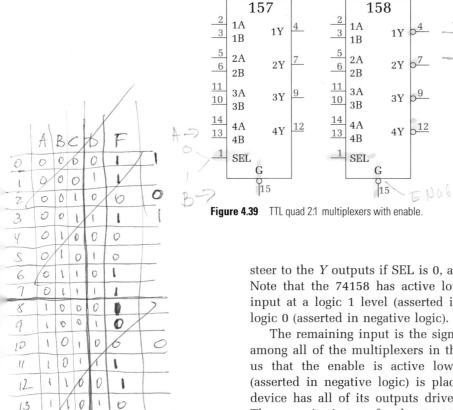

Enable G	Select SEL	Input A	Input B	'157 Y	'158 Y
1	X	X	X	0	1
0	0	0	X	0	1
0	0	1	X	1	0
0	1	X	0	0	1
0	1	X	1	1	0

Figure 4.39   TTL quad 2:1 multiplexers with enable.

steer to the Y outputs if SEL is 0, and the B's steer to the Y's if SEL is 1. Note that the 74158 has active low/negative logic outputs. A selected input at a logic 1 level (asserted in positive logic) will be output as a logic 0 (asserted in negative logic).

The remaining input is the signal G. This is an enable signal shared among all of the multiplexers in the package. The bubble notation tells us that the enable is active low: the device is enabled when a 0 (asserted in negative logic) is placed on G. For the 74157, a disabled device has all of its outputs driven low (unasserted in positive logic). The opposite is true for the 74158: when it is disabled, all of the outputs are driven to high (unasserted in negative logic). This behavior is summarized in the truth table of Figure 4.39.

4.2.3   Decoder/Demultiplexer

A demultiplexer is the opposite of a multiplexer: a single input is gated to exactly one of the outputs. It is also an excellent device for generating mutually exclusive signals. Consider the following design situation. We have several digital subsystems, each of which implements its own particular function. But the overall system is designed so that only one of these is to be active at any given time. Now let's suppose that each subsystem has a special "enable" signal which indicates that it has been selected to perform its function. We have seen exactly such signals in the multiplexer components just described.

A demultiplexer is exactly the correct device to use in this situation. First we set the demultiplexer input to the asserted value of the enable signal. Then we drive the demultiplexer control inputs with the binary index of the output signal to be steered from the input. This signal carries the enable signal to the selected subsystem, while the remaining outputs are left unasserted. When used in this manner, the demultiplexer is often called a *decoder.*

General Concept   A decoder/demultiplexer takes as input a single data input (an enable signal) and n control signals and uses the latter to assert one of 2^n output lines. For example, a 1:2 decoder/demultiplexer has two inputs, G (enable) and S (select), and two outputs, O_0 and O_1. The Boolean equations for the outputs are as follows:

$$O_0 = G \bullet \bar{S}$$

$$O_1 = G \bullet S$$

If G is left unasserted, both outputs are at 0. Otherwise the value of S determines which of the two outputs will be driven high. The equations for the 2:4 and 3:8 decoders are obvious generalizations.

A decoder/demultiplexer is typically named by the number of control signals and the number of output signals (for example, 1:2, 2:4, 3:8). Contrast this with the multiplexer naming: the number of data inputs and the number of data outputs (for example, 2:1, 4:1, 8:1).

Alternative Implementations   Figure 4.40 gives a gate-level implementation of a 1:2 decoder. The two inputs are G, the enable signal, and a control signal Select. When Select is unasserted, G is gated to $Output_0$ and $Output_1$ is driven to 0. When Select is asserted, the opposite happens: G steers to $Output_1$ and $Output_0$ is set to 0. If G is unasserted, both outputs are left unasserted no matter what the value of Select. We can say that the decoder has an active high enable (the selected output is a logic 1 when G is asserted in positive logic) and uses AND gates for its implementation.

This is not the only way to construct such a decoder. Figure 4.41 shows the same function implemented with NOR gates. In this case, the enable signal, $\bar{G}$, is active low. If Select is unasserted (logic 0/positive logic) and $\bar{G}$ is asserted (logic 0/negative logic), then $Output_0$ is asserted in positive logic. When Select is asserted, if $\bar{G}$ is also asserted, $Output_1$

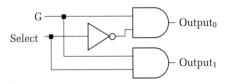

Figure 4.40   1:2 decoder: active high enable, AND gate implementation.

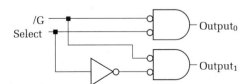

Figure 4.41   1:2 decoder: active low enable, NOR implementation.

will become asserted. Once again, if $\overline{G}$ is not asserted, both outputs are left unasserted.

The implementation of decoders with larger numbers of select lines and outputs generalizes from the 1:2 decoder. Figure 4.42 gives two implementations, one with AND gates and one with NOR gates, for a 2:4 decoder. The inverters generate the four possible combinations of the two select lines: $\overline{Select}_0$, $\overline{Select}_1$; $\overline{Select}_0$, $Select_1$; $Select_0$, $\overline{Select}_1$; and $Select_0$, $Select_1$. For given values of the select lines only one of these combinations will be asserted. Each combination is input to one of the AND gates, along with the enable input G. When G is asserted, the output associated with the one asserted combination will be driven to 1. All other outputs will be driven to 0.

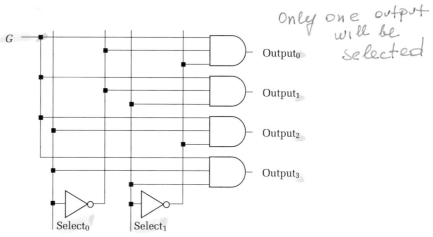

Only one output will be selected

(a) Active high enable, AND gate implementation

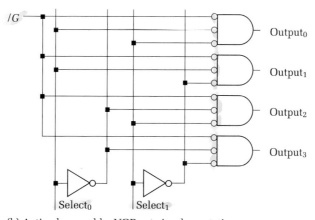

(b) Active low enable, NOR gate implementation

Figure 4.42   2:4 decoders.

Note that the NOR implementation requires the complements of the select line combinations, as well as an active low enable signal $\overline{G}$. For example, in the AND implementation, the inputs to the Output_0 gate are $\overline{\text{Select}_0}$, $\overline{\text{Select}_1}$, and G. In the NOR case, these become Select_0, $\overline{\text{Select}_1}$, and $\overline{G}$.

As you may expect, it is also possible to implement decoder and demultiplexer logic using CMOS transmission gates. After all, a decoder simply directs the enable signal to the correct output based on the select line settings. You may have already seen this implementation in Figure 4.18. Simply substitute G for I and Select for S to have a switch implementation of the decoder.

For the 1:2 decoder, the gate implementation is less transistor efficient than the transmission switch implementation. The two NOR gates and the inverter use 10 transistors while the four transmission gates use only 8 transistors. Of course, the inverter for $\overline{S}$ adds another two transistors in the second approach.

Now let's consider the 2:4 decoder. Figure 4.43 shows its transmission gate implementation. The path from G to each of the four outputs passes through two transmission gates. Each path is controlled by a different combination of the Select lines. A path is disabled if one or both of the transmission gates are not conducting. Note that each output is also connected to two parallel transmission gates whose inputs are 0. These are controlled by complementary signals to the transmission gate immediately above them. Thus, if the upper path is disrupted, one of the lower paths will conduct. This guarantees that G will be steered to the output node if the upper path conducts and will be driven to a logic 0 otherwise. The figure shows the conducting paths to the output nodes when $\text{Select}_0 = \text{Select}_1 = 0$. This implementation requires 16 transmission gates and 2 inverters, a total of 36 transistors. The discrete gate implementation, four 3-input NOR gates and two inverters, needed only 28 transistors. For this function, the transmission gate implementation is inferior to the discrete gate approach.

MINTERM GENERATOR =

Decoder/Demultiplexer as a Logic Building Block   A decoder can also be viewed as a "minterm generator." Figure 4.44 shows a block diagram of a 3:8 decoder where the select lines are labeled with the signals A, B, C. Each output can be labeled with the select line combination that causes that output to be asserted. For example, suppose the control signals A, B, and C are set to 0, 1, and 0, respectively. This corresponds to the minterm $\overline{A}B\overline{C}$ and output 2 is enabled. In other words, if the inputs correspond to minterm m_i then decoder output_i will be the single asserted output.

Although the decoder is not intended as a general-purpose combinational logic building block, it can be used in such a manner. Any function expressed in sum of products form over n variables can be implemented by an $n{:}2^n$ decoder in conjunction with OR gates.

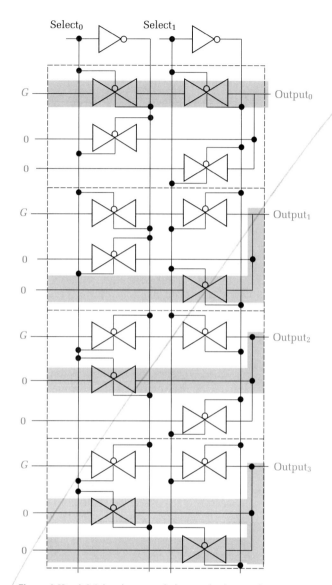

Figure 4.43 A 2:4 decoder: transmission gate implementation.

To see how this can be accomplished, let's consider the following three functions of the Boolean variables A, B, C, D:

$$F_1 = \overline{A}B\overline{C}D + \overline{A}\overline{B}CD + ABCD$$

$$F_2 = AB\overline{C}\overline{D} + ABC$$

$$F_3 = (\overline{A} + \overline{B} + \overline{C} + \overline{D})$$

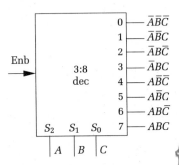

Figure 4.44   A 3:8 decoder.

It is more convenient to reexpress the functions as

$$F_1 = \overline{A}B\overline{C}D + \overline{A}\overline{B}CD + ABCD$$

$$F_2 = AB\overline{C}\overline{D} + ABC\overline{D} + ABCD \qquad = \quad ABC$$

$$F_3 = \overline{ABCD} \qquad = \quad (\overline{A} + \overline{B} + \overline{C} + \overline{D})$$

F_1 is already in canonical sum of products form. To get F_2 into canonical sum of products form, we expand the term ABC to two 4-variable terms: $ABC\overline{D} + ABCD$. Finally, we represent F_3 as the complement of the function $ABCD$, which is in the appropriate sum of products form.

Figure 4.45 shows how to implement these functions using a 4:16 decoder. F_1 is asserted whenever any of its three minterms are asserted. By connecting A, B, C, and D to the decoder select lines, the output O_5 ($\overline{A}B\overline{C}D$), O_3 ($\overline{A}\,\overline{B}CD$), or O_{15} ($ABCD$) will be asserted if the inputs correspond to the desired minterms. F_1 can then be implemented by an OR gate connected to these decoder outputs. For example, if $A = B = C = D = 0$, the decoder output O_0 is asserted and F_1 is not asserted. But if $A = B = C = D = 1$, the decoder output O_{15} is asserted and now F_1 is asserted.

Similarly, F_2 can be implemented by a three-input OR gate connected to the decoder outputs O_{12} ($AB\overline{C}\overline{D}$), O_{14} ($ABC\overline{D}$), and O_{15} ($ABCD$). F_3 is implemented by an inverter driven by the O_{15} decoder output.

This approach to implementing logic is most advantageous for functions of a relatively small number of variables (decoders of more than

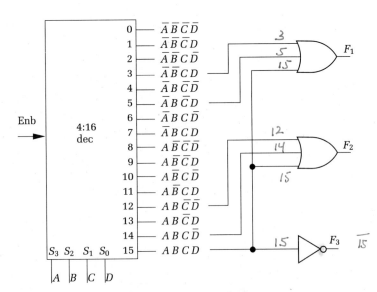

Figure 4.45   Combinational logic implemented by a decoder.

four select inputs are not available in a single package) and a small number of minterms per function.

TTL Decoder/Demultiplexer Components   Figure 4.46 shows two TTL decoder components, the 74139 dual 2-line to 4-line decoders/demultiplexers and the 74138 3-line to 8-line decoder/demultiplexer. We begin by discussing the 74139. A close examination of the schematic indicates that the enable signal $\overline{G}$ is active low, as are the decoder outputs $\overline{Y}_0$ through $\overline{Y}_3$. This means that a disabled 74139 (the $\overline{G}$ input is high) will have all of its outputs at a logic 1. When it is enabled (the $\overline{G}$ input is low), exactly one of these outputs will be driven low, that is, asserted in negative logic, while the remaining outputs go high. The select inputs, A and B, determine which output is asserted: $B = A = 0$, Y_0 is asserted; $B = 0$, $A = 1$, Y_1 is asserted; $B = 1$, $A = 0$, Y_2 is asserted; $B = 1$, $A = 1$, Y_3 is asserted. The high-order selection bit is B and A is the low-order bit. The function is described by the truth table in Figure 4.46.

The 74138 comes with three enable inputs, G, $\overline{G}_{2A}$, and $\overline{G}_{2B}$; three select inputs, A, B, and C; and eight outputs $\overline{Y}_0$ through $\overline{Y}_7$. Once again, two of the enable inputs and all of the outputs are active low. The 74138 is enabled when G is at a logic 1 while both $\overline{G}_{2A}$ and $\overline{G}_{2B}$ are 0. C is the high-order selection bit, A is the low-order bit. The function is summarized by the truth table in Figure 4.46.

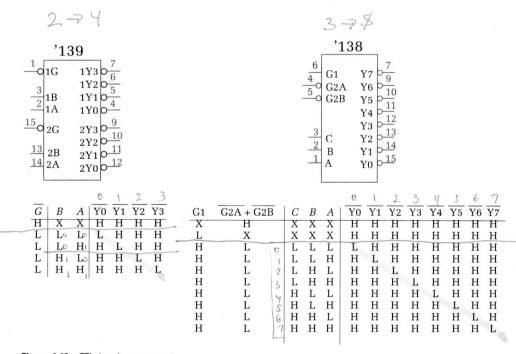

$\overline{G}$	B	A	Y0	Y1	Y2	Y3
H	X	X	H	H	H	H
L	L	L	L	H	H	H
L	L	H	H	L	H	H
L	H	L	H	H	L	H
L	H	H	H	H	H	L

G1	G2A + G2B	C	B	A	Y0	Y1	Y2	Y3	Y4	Y5	Y6	Y7
X	H	X	X	X	H	H	H	H	H	H	H	H
L	X	X	X	X	H	H	H	H	H	H	H	H
H	L	L	L	L	L	H	H	H	H	H	H	H
H	L	L	L	H	H	L	H	H	H	H	H	H
H	L	L	H	L	H	H	L	H	H	H	H	H
H	L	L	H	H	H	H	H	L	H	H	H	H
H	L	H	L	L	H	H	H	H	L	H	H	H
H	L	H	L	H	H	H	H	H	H	L	H	H
H	L	H	H	L	H	H	H	H	H	H	L	H
H	L	H	H	H	H	H	H	H	H	H	H	L

Figure 4.46   TTL decoder components.

We can often combine standard multiplexers and decoders to build even larger multiplexer and decoder blocks. Figure 4.47 shows two alternative methods for implementing a 32:1 multiplexer. In Figure 4.47(a), we simply select among the outputs of four 8:1 multiplexers with a 4:1 multiplexer. Alternatively, as in Figure 4.47(b), we can use a 2:4 decoder to enable one of the four 8:1 multiplexers. A disabled multiplexer will always output a 0. So the four outputs can be ORed together to obtain the multiplexer function. The active low decoder outputs match up with the active low enable signals on the multiplexers for proper bubble matching.

Just as with multiplexers, it is possible to build larger decoders by cascading smaller decoders. Figure 4.48 shows one possible strategy, implemented with a 2:4 decoder and four 3:8 decoders. The single active low enable signal directly enables the 2:4 decoder. It is inverted to provide the active high enable signals to the four 3:8 decoders. The active low outputs from the 2:4 decoder are wired directly to the enable signals of the second-level decoders. Only one of the 3:8 decoders is enabled, based on the selection inputs S4 and S3. And only one of this decoder's outputs will be enabled, based on the selection inputs S2, S1, and S0.

4.2.4   Tri-State Versus Open-Collector Gates

Multiplexers allow us to build circuits in which more than one signal can be gated to a particular wire under the influence of control signals. This is important, because in most technologies it is not possible to tie more than one gate to the same wire without dire results. If one gate attempts to draw the line to 0 while another actively pulls it to 1, a battle ensues in which one or both of the gates are likely to "melt down." This circuit configuration makes a relatively low-resistance path between power and ground, leading to dangerously high currents within the gates. We now examine alternatives to the multiplexer for sharing a circuit node among multiple outputs.

Tri-State Outputs   So far, we have seen only two possible logic values: 0 and 1. A third value we often encounter during design is the *don't-care* value, denoted by X. Of course, any realization of a circuit involving don't-care values in the output maps these into some assignment of 0's and 1's. So we should never encounter a don't-care value in a real circuit.

Besides 0 and 1, we find a third signal value in digital systems: the *high-impedance state*, usually denoted by the symbol Z. When a gate's output is in a high-impedance state (that is, a very high, essentially infinite, resistance exists between the power supply and ground lines and the output), it is as though the gate were disconnected from the output. Gates that can be placed in such a state are called *tri-state gates*: they can produce as outputs the three values 0, 1, and Z. In addition to its conventional inputs, a tri-state has one more input called *output enable*. When this input is unasserted, the output is in its high-impedance state and the gate is effectively

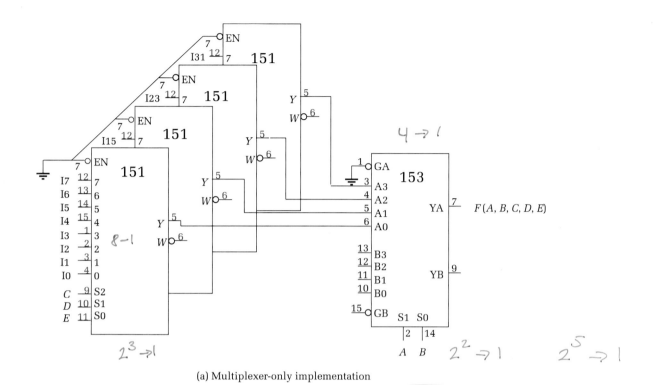

(a) Multiplexer-only implementation

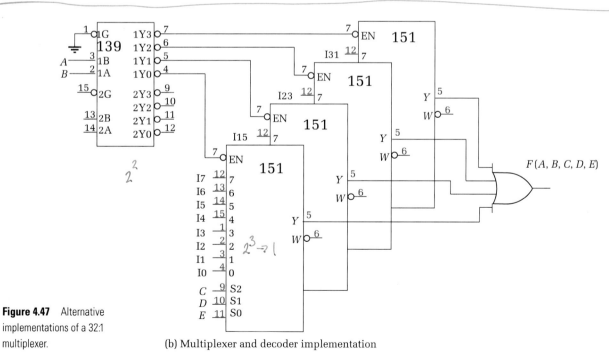

Figure 4.47   Alternative implementations of a 32:1 multiplexer.

(b) Multiplexer and decoder implementation

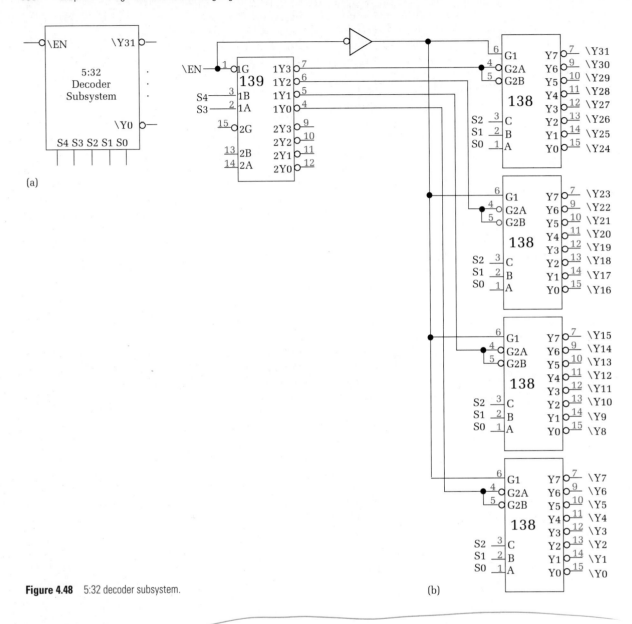

Figure 4.48 5:32 decoder subsystem.

(a)

(b)

A	OE	F
X	0	Z
0	1	0
1	1	1

Figure 4.49 Truth table for tri-state buffers.

disconnected from the output wire. When the output enable is asserted, the gate's output is determined by its data inputs.

For example, the truth table of a tri-state buffer gate is shown in Figure 4.49. When the output enable (OE) signal is unasserted, no matter what the input is, the output will be Z. When the OE input is asserted, the buffer simply passes its input to the output.

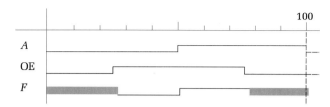

Figure 4.50 Waveform with high-impedance output.

Figure 4.50 gives a timing waveform for a buffer with a tri-state output. The input signal A changes from 0 to 1 and back between time unit 0 and 100. The OE signal is asserted between time units 25 and 75. A high-impedance output is represented by a patterned waveform, as shown in the figure. When OE is low, F is in its high-impedance state, regardless of the value of A. When OE is high, F outputs the same value as that presented at A.

Application of Tri-State Gates   Let's consider the circuit fragment shown in Figure 4.51, constructed from tri-state buffers (with active high enables) and a conventional inverter. The control signal SelectInput determines which of $Input_0$ or $Input_1$ steers to the output node F: if SelectInput is 0 then $Input_0$ steers to F; if it is 1 then $Input_1$ steers to F instead.

The circuit works in the following way. A tri-state buffer passes its input to its output when the output enable signal is driven high. Otherwise, the output is high impedance (disconnected). The $Input_1$ tri-state is controlled by SelectInput, while $\overline{\text{SelectInput}}$ controls the $Input_0$ gate.

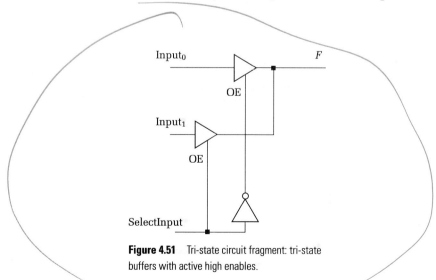

Figure 4.51 Tri-state circuit fragment: tri-state buffers with active high enables.

When SelectInput goes high, the Input$_1$ tri-state is enabled and the Input$_0$ tri-state is disabled, effectively disconnected from the output node F. When SelectInput goes low, the roles are reversed, and now the Input$_1$ tri-state is disabled/disconnected and the Input$_0$ tri-state drives the output node.

To complicate matters a bit, suppose we constructed a functionally identical circuit from inverting tri-state buffers with active low enables. Tri-state gates often come in this more complicated form. Figure 4.52 gives the revised circuit. This provides us with a good opportunity to test our understanding of positive and negative logic, for both data and control signals.

The tri-stated inverters now have active low output enable signals $\overline{OE}$. When the active low enable signal is driven to 1, the output is high impedance, and when it is driven to 0, the output becomes the complement of the input. SelectInput is now the wrong logic polarity for enabling the Input$_1$ tri-state: it is a positive logic control signal, but the gate expects negative logic. This is easily corrected by placing an inverter between SelectInput and the $\overline{OE}$ signal for the Input$_1$ tri-state. Now, when SelectInput is asserted in positive logic, the inverter maps it into an asserted signal in negative logic, thus enabling the tri-state buffer. The relationship between SelectInput and the Input$_0$ tri-state's enable is complementary. If SelectInput is not asserted in positive logic, it is asserted in negative logic, and it is already in the desired form for controlling the Input$_0$ tri-state.

The second complexity of Figure 4.52 is that the input data are complemented by the tri-state gate. To revert to positive logic, we can place a second-stage inverter between the tri-states and the output node F.

Figure 4.53 shows a switching network implementation of an inverting tri-state gate with active low enable. It looks very much like the

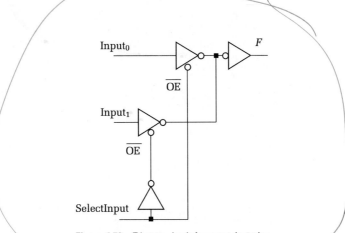

Figure 4.52 Tri-state circuit fragment: inverting tri-state buffers with active low enables.

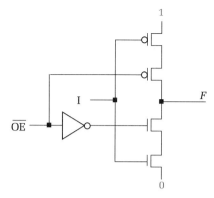

Figure 4.53   Switch implementation of tri-state gate.

CMOS implementation of an inverter, but with one critical difference. Switches controlled by the output enable signal and its complement isolate the output node. Let's suppose the $\overline{OE}$ signal is at logic 1, unasserted in negative logic. Then the pMOS transistor controlled by $\overline{OE}$ is nonconducting and the nMOS transistor controlled by its complement is also nonconducting. This leaves the output node F floating. Now let's suppose that the $\overline{OE}$ signal is driven low, becoming asserted in negative logic. The switches controlled by $\overline{OE}$ and its complement are now both closed and conducting. If I is a logic 1, F is connected to 0; if I is 0, then F is connected to 1.

The principle of using tri-state gates to connect selectively an input to an output wire generalizes for connecting n input signals to the same output wire. For large n, this represents a considerable savings in gates. Figure 4.54 shows one way to implement a multiplexer with a decoder

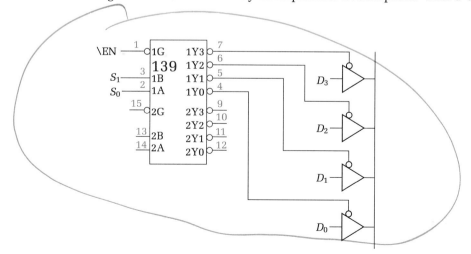

Figure 4.54   Implementation of a 4:1 multiplexer with tri-state buffers and a decoder.

and tri-state gates. Based on the values of S_1 and S_0, only one of D_3, D_2, D_1, or D_0 will be gated through to the shared output wire.

Open-Collector Outputs   There is one more way to implement multiple simultaneous connections to a single wire. The idea is to provide a gate that can only pull its output down to 0. If the output is to be 1, the voltage on the wire is left floating. To make this behave properly, the output wire must be attached to a resistor that pulls it to a logic 1 voltage if none of the connected gates are attempting to pull the wire low. The resistor is chosen to be large enough that it can be easily overcome by the pull-down resistances of any attached gates. These gates are called *open-collector* gates.

Figure 4.55 shows the switch-level circuitry for an open-collector NAND gate. The output is 0 only when A and B are both asserted. Otherwise the node F is floating. The resistor will pull it up to a logic 1 voltage.

Figure 4.56 shows two open-collector NAND gates in what is called a "wired-AND" configuration. When both inputs to the NAND gate are 1, the output is low and node F is pulled low. In the other input configurations, the gate's output floats and is pulled up to 1 by the resistor.

The open-collector output is active only in cases in which the NAND gate is unasserted! The configuration is called a wired-AND because the effect on F is just as though both NAND gates had been ANDed together: if either gate has an output 0 or both do (that is, both inputs to the gate are 1), then F will be at 0; only when both gates have their outputs asserted is F at a logic 1 (that is, any input combination other than both inputs at 1). This is clearly shown in the timing diagram of Figure 4.57.

We show a possible circuit to implement a mux in Figure 4.58. The decoder maps its two selection inputs, S_1 and S_0, into one of its four outputs to be asserted active low. Note that the data inputs, $\bar{I}_0$, $\bar{I}_1$, $\bar{I}_2$, and $\bar{I}_3$, are also active low. Suppose the decoder selects the topmost OR gate ($\bar{Y}_3$ is driven to 0) and $\bar{I}_3$ is also asserted (active low). The OR gate pulls the shared wire low, and the inverter asserts the output F active high. If $\bar{I}_3$ is not asserted, the shared wire stays high and the output is driven low.

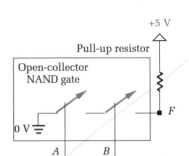

Figure 4.55   Switch representation of open-collector NAND gate.

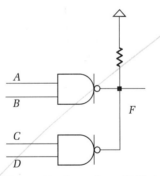

Figure 4.56   Open-collector NANDs in wired-AND configuration.

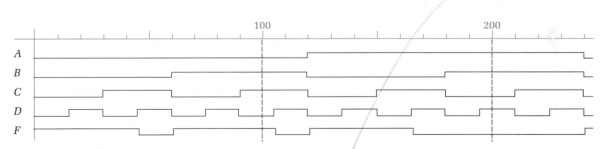

Figure 4.57   Timing waveform of open-collector NANDs in wired-AND configuration.

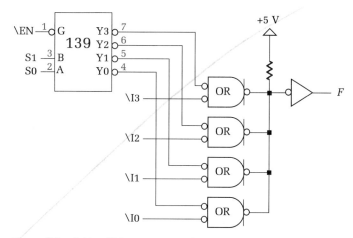

Figure 4.58   A 4:1 multiplexer constructed from open-collector OR gates.

We can think of the wire shared by the OR gates as active low. A signal is asserted onto the wire by pulling it low. The pull-up provides an unasserted default value. It pulls the wire high if none of the OR gates pull it low. The inverter hanging off the wire restores the signal to positive logic. This is a common usage with open-collector circuit nodes: they are designed to be active low, with inverters converting the signals back to positive logic where needed.

In general, open-collector gates and tri-state gates are used for the same kinds of functions. But tri-states are more economical because they do not require the external resistor. They have largely replaced open-collector gates in modern designs.

TTL Tri-State and Open-Collector Components   Figure 4.59 shows two different TTL tri-state buffer components. The 74240 octal buffer with three-state outputs is organized into two independent 4-bit sections, each with its own enable, data inputs, and data outputs. The enable inputs are $\overline{1G}, \overline{2G}$, the data inputs are 1A1–1A4 and 2A1–2A4, and the eight data outputs are $\overline{1Y1}-\overline{1Y4}$ and $\overline{2Y1}-\overline{2Y4}$. The enable signals are active low while the outputs are inverted. For example, output $\overline{1Y1}$ is high impedance when enable $\overline{1G}$ is high. When $\overline{1G}$ goes low, $\overline{1Y1}$ is driven to the complement of the value on the 1A1 input.

The function of the 74244 is identical to that of the 74240, except that the outputs are not inverted. Once again, the enables are active low. A logic 1 on $\overline{1G}$ yields high impedance on output 1Y1. When $\overline{1G}$ is driven to logic 0, 1Y1 receives whatever logic value is placed on 1A1.

Open-collector gates are available in packages similar to those of conventional discrete gates. The TTL components 7406 and 7407 contain six

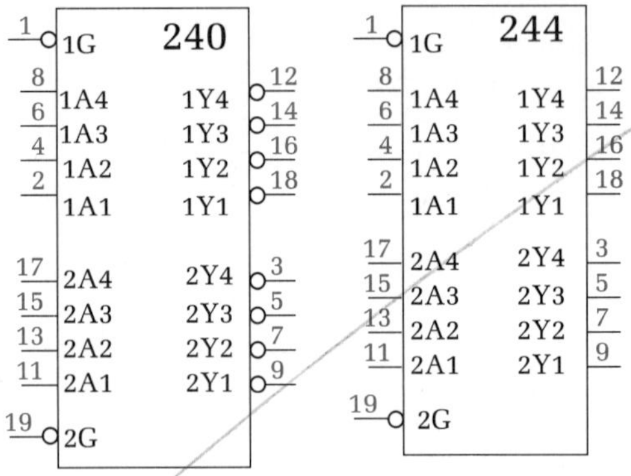

Figure 4.59   TTL tri-state buffers.

open-collector inverting and noninverting buffers, respectively. The 7426 and 7433 contain four 2-input NAND and NOR gates, respectively.

4.2.5   Read-Only Memories

Perhaps the ultimate form of look-up table logic is the read-only memory, or ROM. A ROM is really nothing more than a circuit that implements a two-dimensional array of 0's and 1's. The internal storage elements of the ROM are set to their values once and after that are only read. (This is not completely true because some technologies, called *EPROM* or erasable programmable ROM, allow the contents to be erased and rewritten at a later time. Since the process of erasure takes minutes or even hours, you should think of any kind of ROM as something you write very infrequently and read mostly.) Each row of the array is called a *word* and is selected by the control inputs, which are called the *address*. The number of columns in the array is called the *bit-width* or *word size*. The number of words and the word sizes of commercially available ROMs are almost always powers of 2.

General Concept   Figure 4.60 gives a block diagram view of a ROM. The ROM contains its own internal decoder that maps the address lines into word select lines. Each line selects a unique ROM word, which in turn is gated onto the output lines. As we know from our discussion of decoders, the selection lines correspond to each of the unique minterms of the variables at the address lines. This is not very different from the product terms formed by the AND array of a PAL. At least conceptually, a ROM is just like a PAL with a *fully decoded* AND array. There is a word line for every possible product term combination of input variables at the address lines.

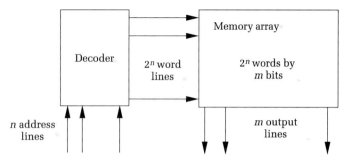

Figure 4.60 Internal organization of a ROM.

Figure 4.61 shows the ROM in more detail. The n-input address decoder asserts one of the 2^n selection lines. These are also called *word lines*. Each vertical wire, representing an output from the ROM, is called a *bit line*. You can think of the bit lines as being connected to open-collector inverters. A transistor controlled by the word line pulls down the bit line if a zero is to be stored in that word. If there is no pull-down transistor for that word and bit line, a one is stored instead. Based on the placement of the pull-downs, the word_i contains the value 0011 while word_j stores 1010.

Figure 4.62(a) shows a block diagram of an 8-word by 4-bit wide ROM. A ROM is frequently used to store the truth tables of a set of functions, as in the sample ROM contents of Figure 4.62(b). The variables over which the

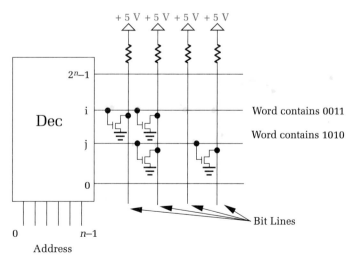

Figure 4.61 ROM internals.

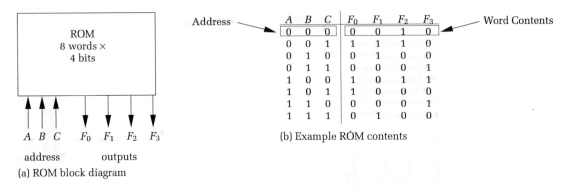

(a) ROM block diagram

(b) Example ROM contents

Figure 4.62   An 8-word by 4-bit ROM.

functions are defined, in this case A, B, and C, form the address. Depending on their values, the appropriate row of the truth table, and the corresponding ROM word, are selected. Each output function is associated with a column or bit position in the ROM. If the function is a true for that combination of inputs, a 1 is stored in the selected word at the bit position for that function. Otherwise a 0 is stored. By examining Figure 4.62(b), we get the following set of Boolean equations for the outputs:

$$F_0 = \overline{A}\overline{B}C + A\overline{B}\overline{C} + A\overline{B}C$$

$$F_1 = \overline{A}\overline{B}C + \overline{A}B\overline{C} + ABC$$

$$F_2 = \overline{A}\overline{B}\overline{C} + \overline{A}B\overline{C} + A\overline{B}\overline{C}$$

$$F_3 = \overline{A}BC + A\overline{B}\overline{C} + AB\overline{C}$$

ROMs Versus PALs/PLAs   Recall Figure 4.8, which shows a truth table for a conventional circuit mapping from BCD to Gray code. To implement this as a read-only memory, we need a 4 address line (16 words) by 4-bit ROM. Each row of the truth table maps to a ROM location holding a 4-bit Gray code word, addressed by the input word in 4-bit BCD code. Don't-care entries, such as the input configurations 1010 through 1111, are of no particular advantage in reducing the hardware needed for the implementation, since the ROM comes with locations for those words whether we store 1's and 0's there or not.

Code converters are used to translate from one data representation to another. For example, a calculator uses standard binary codes for its internal calculations. But it may convert these codes into BCD for input/output and display.

Code conversions are a particularly ideal application for ROMs, since most if not all combinations of the inputs need to be generated anyway and the decoder can do this quite efficiently. So how do you choose between a ROM and a PAL/PLA-based implementation?

The answer depends on the structure of the functions being implemented. This can be quantified in terms of (1) the number of unique product terms that must be generated to implement all the output functions, (2) the degree to which these terms can be shared among multiple output functions, and (3) the number of terms that must be ORed together to implement a given output function.

PLAs are effective when the number of unique terms is small and a given term generated in the AND array can be shared among multiple outputs (this contributes to keeping down the number of unique terms). You should remember that PAL/PLA structures do not always provide enough outputs from the AND array if you need to generate many terms. And PALs are limited in the number of terms that can contribute to realizing any single output function. It will take longer to design a circuit with a PAL or PLA, since minimization methods are needed to reduce the number of terms and to maximize the number of terms that can be shared.

ROMs are effective when the number of unique terms is large. You can reduce your design time because there is no need to perform minimization: the size of the ROM is determined solely by the number of inputs and outputs, not by the number of product terms. However, the size of the ROM doubles with each additional input, so the output functions had better be of a form that requires all possible product terms if this approach is to make sense.

In the BCD to Gray code example, 10 of 16 minterms were needed, the rest being don't-cares. Boolean minimization reduced the number of literals in the terms but not the number of unique terms, which was still 10. This is a good tipoff that a ROM-based implementation is probably the best.

ROM Components   ROMs come in a variety of sizes and word widths. The upper limit is represented by the 27512 EPROM, which provides 2^{16} 8-bit words, or one-half million ROM bits in a single 28-pin package!

As an example, let's concentrate on the 2764 8192 (2^{13}) word by 8-bit ROM, whose schematic symbol is shown in Figure 4.63. The 2764 component has 13 address lines, to identify each of the possible 8192 words, and 8 tri-state output lines, one for each bit in the ROM word. There are four additional inputs for control. The outputs are enabled by an active low output enable ($\overline{\text{OE}}$) signal. The component also comes with an active low chip select input ($\overline{\text{CS}}$). This can be used to cascade smaller/narrower ROMs to form larger/wider memories. We will see how this can be used in a moment. Since EPROMs are programmed by electrical pulses, an additional input places the ROM in programming mode rather than reading mode ($\overline{\text{PGM}}$), while the final input (VPP) provides the necessary high-voltage source used during the programming process. Outside the actual PROM programming station, these inputs are hardwired to the power supply.

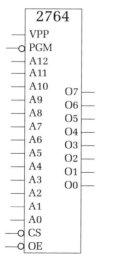

Figure 4.63   2764 EPROM schematic shape.

Figure 4.64 shows how the chip select lines can be used to construct a larger memory. Suppose that we are to build a memory that is 2^{14} by 16 bits wide using the 2764 EPROM. Such a subsystem has 14 address lines (A13:A0) and 16 data lines (D15:D0). An additional $\overline{OE}$ signal enables the entire subsystem for output.

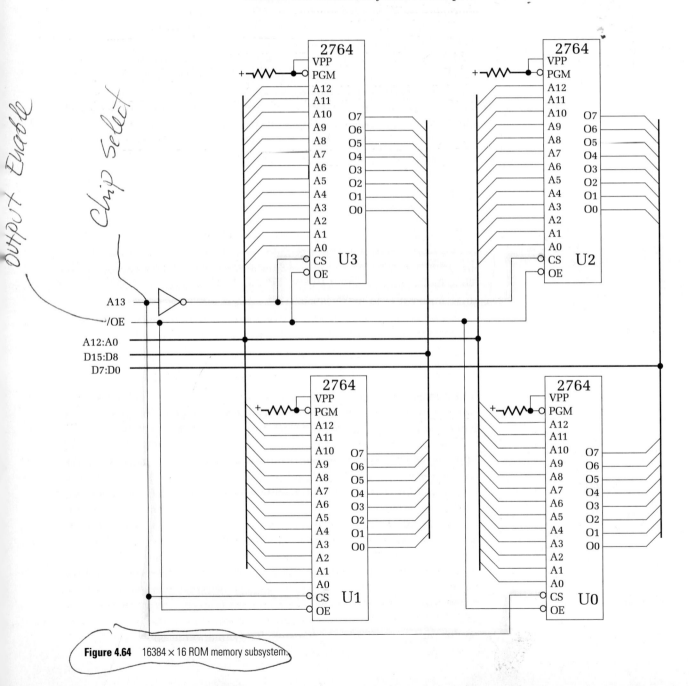

Figure 4.64   16384 × 16 ROM memory subsystem.

Because this has twice the width and twice the number of words of a single 2764, we will need four of them to implement the subsystem. These components are labeled U0 through U3. The thick lines in the figure denote *buses*, several logically related wires that share a common function. For example, buses are used to transmit related data and address bits. This is a shorthand notation used to avoid drawing individual signal lines.

The high-order address bit, A13, selects between the higher 8192 ROM words (addresses 8192 through 16383) and the lower 8192 words (addresses 0 through 8191). Address line A13, if low, enables U1 and U0. If high, it enables U3 and U2. The remaining address lines, A12:A0, are wired directly to the address line inputs of the ROM chips, as is the output enable signal. The output of the ROM will be driven only if the chip is selected and the output is enabled. Because the outputs are tri-stated and the upper and lower ROM chips are never asserted at the same time, it is perfectly acceptable to wire their outputs together. U3 and U1 are connected to D15:D8, while U2 and U0 are connected to D7:D0.

4.3   Combinational Logic Word Problems

Few things are harder to put up with than the annoyance of a good example.

—*Mark Twain*

In this section, we will look at a few case studies that illustrate the "art" of mapping circuit specifications into gate-level realizations. Sometimes the problems may seem more like puzzles than anything having to do with digital design. The art is in understanding the problem and formulating the solution; the implementation might well be very simple.

4.3.1   Design Procedure

In tackling word problems, we recommend following a standard "procedure" for extracting the key points and constraints of the problem and formulating its solution. Our method consists of the following steps. First, try to understand the problem. Second, reformulate it in terms of a standard digital design representation. Third, decide on how you will implement your design. And last, follow an implementation algorithm suitable for your chosen implementation approach. It is not possible to give a precise algorithm for some of these steps; you will need to rely on practice and experience. Let's look at each of them in more detail.

Step 1: Understand the Problem   The very first thing you must do is to understand the problem. There is no single approach for understanding a complex problem statement. Word problems are inherently difficult because they are presented in imprecise, wordy, ambiguous, and confusing statements. In the real world of design, the function being designed may not be particularly well understood or clearly defined. The place to start is with the input/output behavior of the object being designed. Can you identify the inputs, outputs, and control signals? How do the control signals operate on the inputs to generate the outputs? If the problem gives example output behaviors based on certain input streams, make sure you understand how those outputs are derived from the inputs. Sometimes it is helpful to draw a diagram, relating inputs, outputs, and control, to obtain a better understanding of the problem. Or perhaps the diagram can help you understand the different configurations of the inputs you are supposed to recognize.

For example, suppose you are asked to design a logic circuit to control a hall light, with light switches at either end of the hall. It should be possible to turn the light on from either end of the hall, then walk through the hall and turn it off at the other end.

You start by identifying the inputs and outputs. The inputs are the two light switches and the output is the light. Let's call the switches A and B. Sometimes you just need to make reasonable starting assumptions. We will assume that when the light switch is in the down position the input is 0, and when the switch is up the input is 1. The light is on when the logic function is 1. Otherwise it is off.

Let's assume that the system begins with both light switches in the down position. Clearly, the light should be off when both switches are down. When one switch goes up, the light should go on. At the other end of the hall, placing the second switch in the up position should turn the light off.

So if both switches are up, the light is off. What happens when you walk back through the hall? Putting one switch down, the light should go on. Putting the far switch down should turn the light off.

Step 2: Formulate in a Standard Representation   Once we have a feeling for what the combinational logic circuit is supposed to do, we must describe it more formally. Digital design representations are the precise ways of representing a digital system. For combinational logic word problems the appropriate representations are almost always Boolean equations or truth tables. These representations capture the relationships among inputs, control, and output as algebraic statements or as tabulations of input/output behavior. The key challenge is to extract these relationships from the word statement of the problem.

For the hall light example, simply tabulate the input conditions. When both switches are in the same position, the light is off. When they are in different positions, the light is on.

Step 3: Choose an Implementation   A Boolean equation or a truth table is an abstract representation of the digital system. The next step is to map this into something more concrete, like logic gates. Before you can implement the system, however, you must make a critical design decision: you must choose a technology for implementation. The kinds of choices available are two-level combinational networks of discrete gates or PALs/PLAs, multilevel networks, memories such as ROMs, transmission gate networks, or use of "complex gate logic" like AND-OR-Invert gates. The detailed choice is usually based on economics or performance, but it may be constrained by the kind of technology available to you. For example, if you only have TTL components, transmission gate networks are pretty much eliminated.

The hall light circuit is simple enough to implement with a small number of discrete gates.

Step 4: Apply the Design Procedure   The last step is perhaps the most mechanical. You have formulated the solution in terms of Boolean equations or truth tables, you have chosen an implementation approach, and now you must follow the algorithm to map your digital representation into an actual implementation. For two-level networks, you will apply the techniques of Chapter 2 to derive a circuit with the fewest number of product terms. The approach is the same whether the implementation target is discrete gates or programmable logic. For a ROM-based design, only the truth table is needed; there is no need to minimize your logic description first. If you choose a multilevel implementation approach, your best bet is to use computer-aided design tools to factor the Boolean equations into their best form to minimize gate and literal counts.

The hall light circuit can be implemented with a single XOR gate.

Introduction to the Case Studies   In the following sections, we will tackle four different word problems/case studies, applying the four-step approach we have just outlined. The first problem is a simple process control application. You must determine the particular Boolean conditions, as indicated by the condition of input light sensors, which characterize the condition of rods on an assembly line. When the right rod condition is detected, the logic must generate a signal to move a mechanical arm. The second case study is a decoder application: the combinational logic circuit must map encoded input signals to specified output signals for the desired effects. In this case, the circuit must illuminate certain segments of a seven-segment light display based on the inputs. The third problem describes a logical function unit that implements several different logic functions of its inputs. This kind of system could be of use in a simple microprocessor. The outputs are defined as combinational logic functions of the inputs and control signals. The last problem presents a digital subsystem that takes an 8-bit input and shifts it any number of positions. Follow along and try the design problems on your own. Then compare your solution with the ones presented. Yours may well be better than the solutions we show.

Case Study	4.4	A Simple Process Line Control Problem

Rods of varying length (± 10%) travel one at a time in the direction of their longest axis on a conveyor belt. A mechanical arm pushes rods that are within specification (± 5%) off the belt to one side. A second arm pushes rods that are too long to the other side. Rods that are too short remain on the belt. Use three light barriers (light source + photocell) as sensors, and design the combinational circuits that activate the two arms.

Step 1:   Understand the problem.

In a problem like this, it is important to make sure that you understand the problem specification. Suppose the perfect length is 100 inches. All rods will be within 10% of this specification, or from 90 to 110 inches in length. "Too long" rods are longer than the specified length by more than 5%—more than 105 inches but less than or equal to 110 inches. These rods are supposed to be pushed to one side of the conveyor belt. "Too short" rods are more than 5% shorter than the desired length—greater than or equal to 90 inches but less than 95 inches. These are destined to remain on the belt. Rods in the range 95 to 105 inches are "within spec" and will be pushed to the other side by a second arm. A picture should make this more obvious. (See Figure 4.65.)

Next, let's identify the inputs and outputs. The only inputs we have are the readings from the three light sensors. The outputs are the signals that actuate the two positioning arms. Since it is not explicitly stated in the problem, let's assume that the light barriers operate by reading out a 0 when the light beam is uninterrupted and a 1 when it is tripped by the passing rod. The inputs and outputs are fairly straightforward. The key design question becomes how to arrange the placement of the sensors so we can distinguish between the three different classes of rods.

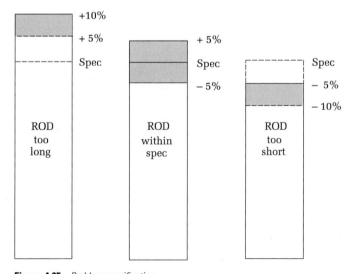

Figure 4.65   Problem specification.

We will call the light barriers A, B, and C and arrange them so that the sensor C is the first to be tripped by the passing rod, then B, and finally A. Let's make one critical assumption: we will fix the placement of barrier A and arrange barriers B and C so as to be able to decide on the rod length when the rod breaks the light barrier at A. A second assumption is that the rods are adequately spaced on the conveyor belt, at least a maximum rod length, so that it is never possible to interpret two rods accidentally as a single rod.

By redrawing Figure 4.65 slightly, this time incorporating the light barriers, it becomes a little clearer where to place B and C to distinguish the rod types. See Figure 4.66. We will use barrier B to identify rods that are too short and barrier C to detect those that are too long. B should be placed just far enough from A so that a too-short rod will trip A but not B. Thus, A and B should be separated by the specified length minus 5%. For our hypothetical specification of 100 inches, this means that A and B should be placed 95 inches apart.

Now we must place barrier C to detect the rods that are too long. Let's place it a distance that is the specification plus 5% from A (105 inches in our example). The barriers now distinguish between the three cases. If A is tripped, but not B or C, then the rod is clearly too short ($ABC = 100$). If A, B, and C are tripped simultaneously, the rod is too long ($ABC = 111$). This condition activates the arm to move the rod to one side of the belt. The remaining case is handled by A and B being tripped but not C ($ABC = 110$). Then the rod is within the desired specification. This is the condition to move the rod to the other side of the belt.

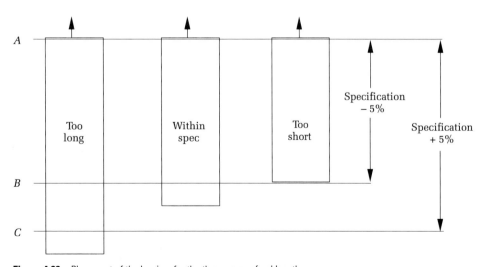

Figure 4.66   Placement of the barriers for the three cases of rod length.

This represents only three of the eight possible barrier configurations. Because of our first assumption, that we will make our decision as soon as barrier A is triggered, the rod must still be in transit if the barrier configuration is $ABC = 0XX$. Since we also assume that the rods are separated by a maximum rod length, the remaining input condition, $ABC = 101$, can never occur.

Step 2: Formulate the problem in terms of a truth table or other suitable design representation.

At this point, most of the hard work has been done. A summary truth table, derived from the discussion above, appears in Figure 4.67.

Step 3: Choose implementation technology.

The actual logic is really quite simple, so we can implement it as straightforward gate logic.

Step 4: Follow implementation procedure.

The "too long" condition is represented by the function $F = ABC$. The "within spec" condition is represented by the function $G = AB\overline{C}$. These can be implemented via two 3-input AND gates.

A	B	C	Function
0	0	0	X
0	0	1	X
0	1	0	X
0	1	1	X
1	0	0	too short
1	0	1	X
1	1	0	in spec
1	1	1	too long

Figure 4.67 Rod control function.

Case Study   4.5   BCD-to-Seven-Segment Display Controller

You are to design a combinational circuit that maps a 4-bit BCD digit to the signals that control a seven-segment display. The display element contains seven light-emitting diodes (LEDs). When the appropriate LED control line is asserted, the associated LED segment lights. We assume that the LED driver inputs are active high (most of the actual LED driver components are really active low). Otherwise, the LED segment is off. The seven segments are controlled independently; there is no limit to the number of segments that could be illuminated at the same time. Figure 4.68 shows the seven-segment display and its configurations displaying each of the 10 possible BCD digits.

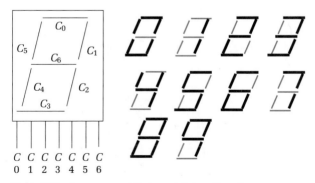

Figure 4.68 Seven-segment display and digit configurations.

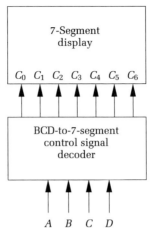

Figure 4.69   Controller block diagram.

Step 1:   Understand the problem.

Begin by asking yourself what the circuit is supposed to do. What are the inputs and outputs? There are four input signals, representing the 4-bit BCD digit. There should be seven outputs, one for each of the LED segments that must be controlled. At this point, it might be helpful to draw a block diagram, with the inputs and outputs clearly identified. A high-level block diagram is given in Figure 4.69. In more complex systems, you might apply a divide-and-conquer approach to break the high-level blocks into smaller, more primitive blocks that are easier to understand. In this case, the decomposition is reasonably straightforward: each LED segment control line is a Boolean function of the four inputs.

Step 2:   Formulate the problem in terms of a truth table or other suitable design representation.

For a problem like this one, it is best to tabulate the input values with the desired outputs. For example, the BCD representation for the digit 0 should cause the LED segments 0, 1, 2, 3, 4, and 5 to be illuminated. Thus, associated with the input combination 0000 we would assert the control signals C_0 through C_5, leaving C_6 unasserted. For the input combination 0001, segments 1 and 2 are turned on, while segments 0 and 3 through 6 are left off. In the table entry for 0001, C_1 and C_2 are asserted, while the remaining outputs are left unasserted. In this fashion we can fill in the whole truth table. Since BCD digits consist of the bit patterns 0000 through 1001, the outputs associated with the remaining input patterns can be left as don't cares. This should help reduce the complexity of our actual implementation. The complete truth table is shown in Figure 4.70.

A	B	C	D	C_0	C_1	C_2	C_3	C_4	C_5	C_6
0	0	0	0	1	1	1	1	1	1	0
0	0	0	1	0	1	1	0	0	0	0
0	0	1	0	1	1	0	1	1	0	1
0	0	1	1	1	1	1	1	0	0	1
0	1	0	0	0	1	1	0	0	1	1
0	1	0	1	1	0	1	1	0	1	1
0	1	1	0	1	0	1	1	1	1	1
0	1	1	1	1	1	1	0	0	0	0
1	0	0	0	1	1	1	1	1	1	1
1	0	0	1	1	1	1	0	0	1	1
1	0	1	0	X	X	X	X	X	X	X
1	0	1	1	X	X	X	X	X	X	X
1	1	0	0	X	X	X	X	X	X	X
1	1	0	1	X	X	X	X	X	X	X
1	1	1	0	X	X	X	X	X	X	X
1	1	1	1	X	X	X	X	X	X	X

Figure 4.70   BCD-to-seven segment display decoder truth table.

Step 3:   Implementation target

Now we must decide on our implementation technology. If we choose to implement the system with a read-only memory, we can stop now. All we need to do is to place the truth table of Figure 4.70 into a 16-word by 7-bit ROM (such a ROM is not likely to exist, but you should be able to find a 2^n by 8-bit ROM).

Suppose your boss tells you that a programmable ROM is too expensive to be used in this subsystem. You may have noticed the 74LS48 component in the TTL catalog. This implements a BCD-to-seven-segment display controller in a single MSI package. In fact, the catalog contains several alternative single-package implementations for this function. Unfortunately, your boss doesn't like the way these decoders display the digit "6," so you will have to implement your own decoder from scratch. This function, with its seven outputs, is complex enough that a discrete gate implementation will probably require quite a few gates and packages to realize. Therefore, let's make the decision that the target is a PAL or PLA structure, and our goal is to realize the function in a single package. Obviously, we will need a minimized two-level network.

Step 4:   Implementation procedure

Since the target is a two-level network, we can use either the K-map techniques of Chapter 2 or a CAD tool like *espresso* directly. Since this particular problem involves only four-variable maps, let's look at both approaches. It will turn out that even in a relatively simple problem such as this, *espresso* still does much better than our pencil-and-paper techniques!

K-Map Method   The K-map method requires seven 4-variable K-maps, one for each truth table column. By this point, it should be second nature for you to fill in the K-map from the truth table. The maps are shown in Figure 4.71(a) through (g). We've gone ahead and boxed the prime implicants, taking advantage of don't cares wherever possible. Read out from Figure 4.71, the equations for the LED segment control outputs become:

$$C_0 = A + BD + C + \overline{B}\overline{D}$$
$$C_1 = A + \overline{C}\overline{D} + CD + \overline{B}$$
$$C_2 = A + B + \overline{C} + D$$
$$C_3 = \overline{B}\overline{D} + C\overline{D} + B\overline{C}D + \overline{B}C$$
$$C_4 = \overline{B}\overline{D} + C\overline{D}$$
$$C_5 = A + \overline{C}\overline{D} + B\overline{D} + B\overline{C}$$
$$C_6 = A + C\overline{D} + B\overline{C} + \overline{B}C$$

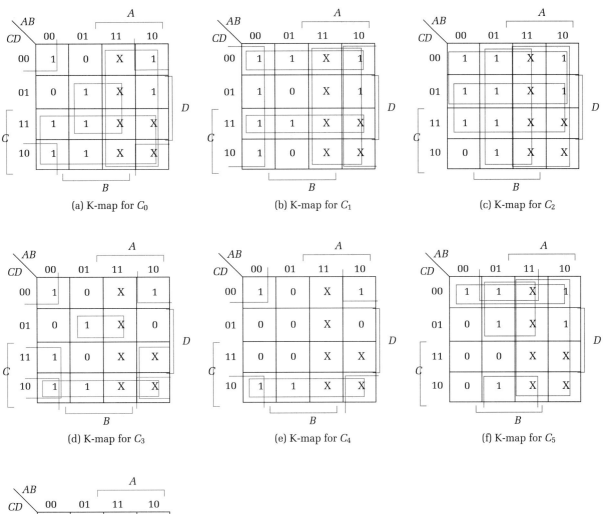

(a) K-map for C_0

(b) K-map for C_1

(c) K-map for C_2

(d) K-map for C_3

(e) K-map for C_4

(f) K-map for C_5

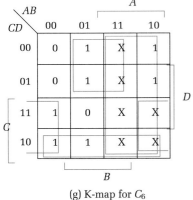

(g) K-map for C_6

Figure 4.71   K-maps for C_0 through C_6.

We would need a four-input, seven-output PAL with at least four product terms per output to implement this function. A P16H8 PAL, for example, has sufficient resources to implement it: ten external inputs plus six feedback inputs (more on this in Chapter 7), eight outputs, and seven product terms per output. The simpler P14H8 PAL cannot do the job. It has 14 inputs and eight outputs, but only two of the outputs are computed as the OR of four product terms while the remaining six outputs have only two product terms each. See Figures 4.72 and 4.73 for the PAL programming maps.

Suppose the target implementation is for a PLA structure rather than a PAL. The limiting factor in a PLA is the number of unique product terms to implement the outputs. These correspond to the number of horizontal "wires" in the PLA circuit array. We have fifteen unique product terms in the above set of equations. A typical PLA component can handle sixteen inputs, eight outputs, and forty-eight product terms (for example, see Figure 4.74 for the F100 PLA programming map).

Two-Level Logic Optimization Method The *espresso* input file is given in Figure 4.75. The *espresso* output is shown in Figure 4.76. This maps onto the following set of Boolean equations:

$$C_0 = B\overline{C}D + CD + \overline{B}\,\overline{D} + A + BC\overline{D}$$

$$C_1 = \overline{B}D + \overline{C}D + CD + \overline{B}\,\overline{D}$$

$$C_2 = \overline{B}D + B\overline{C}D + \overline{C}\,\overline{D} + CD + BC\overline{D}$$

$$C_3 = \overline{B}C + B\overline{C}D + \overline{B}\,\overline{D} + BC\overline{D}$$

$$C_4 = \overline{B}\,\overline{D} + BC\overline{D}$$

$$C_5 = B\overline{C}D + \overline{C}\,\overline{D} + A + BC\overline{D}$$

$$C_6 = B\overline{C} + \overline{B}C + A + BC\overline{D}$$

Remarkably, *espresso* appears to have come up with more complex expressions for the outputs than the K-map method. However, a closer inspection reveals that the number of unique product terms has been reduced from 15 to only 9. Although the individual expressions now have more product terms, there is greater sharing of terms among the outputs. Remember that the size of the PLA is determined primarily by the number of unique product terms, so the better design is the one with fewer terms.

Term sharing provides no assistance for a PAL-based implementation, since the topology of a PAL makes it impossible to share terms among the different output functions. (Note that this statement is not true for the more complex programmable logic structures we will cover in Chapter 7.) In fact, by increasing the number of terms per output, the *espresso* method may force us to use a more complicated PAL than is

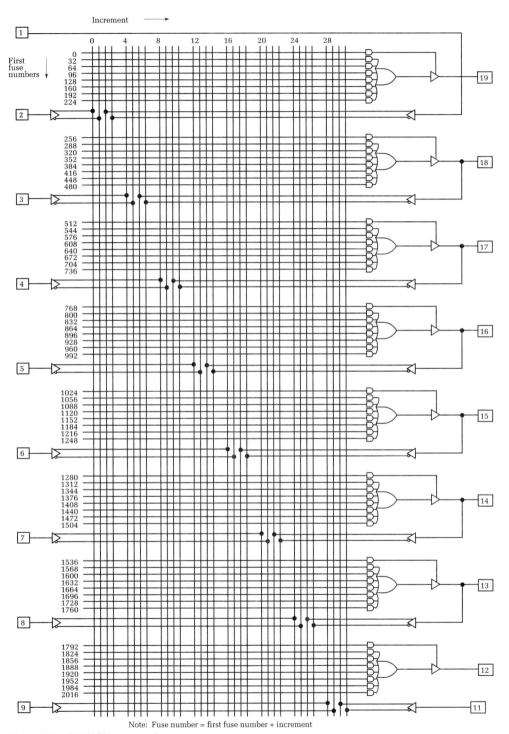

Figure 4.72   P16H8 PAL programming map.

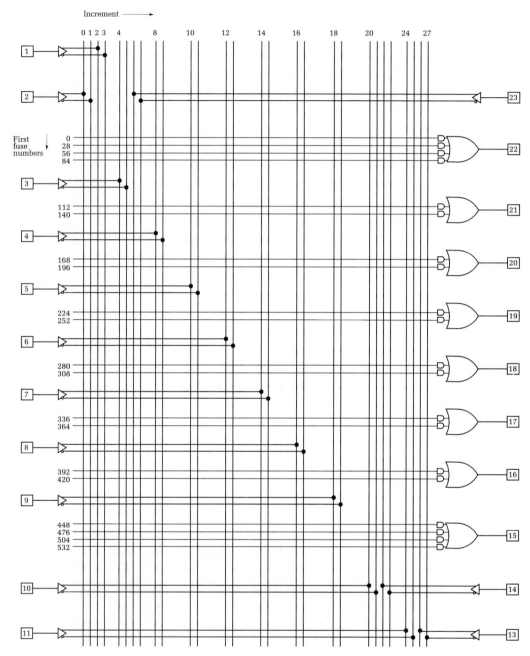

Figure 4.73 P14H8 PAL programming map.

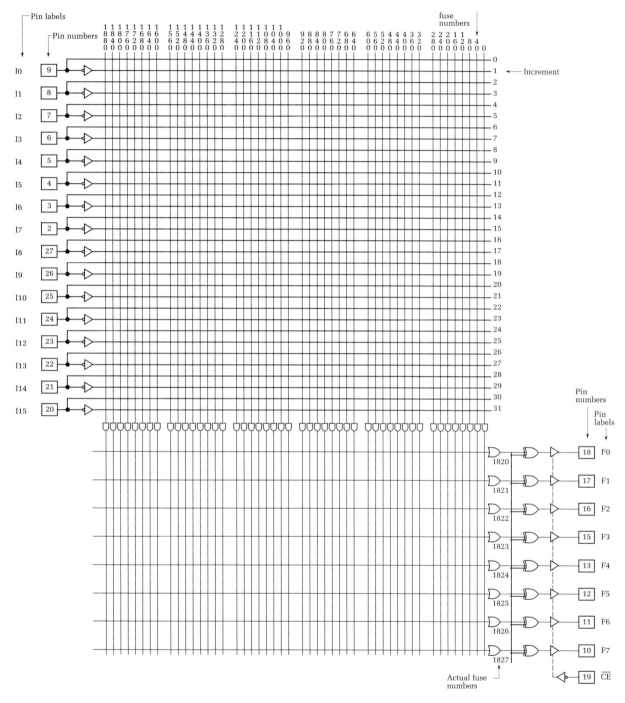

Note: Fuse number = first fuse number + increment

Figure 4.74 F100 PAL programming map.

really needed (it is possible to ask *espresso* to perform its optimization on the basis of an individual output, and this approach should be followed if the implementation technology is going to be a PAL). Figure 4.77 shows the programming map for a PLA implementation.

Multilevel Optimization Method   How does this compare with a multilevel solution, such as one that could be produced using *misII*? Multilevel logic is not well suited to PAL or PLA implementation, so let's have a look at discrete gate implementations, to compare *misII* and *espresso*. First, let's examine the complexity of the solution derived by *espresso* in a little more detail. The number of literals is 63. The number of gates is 7 (an OR gate for each output) plus 8 (an AND gate for each unique product term except the simple term A) plus 3 (an inverter for the inputs B, C, D), for a total of 18 gates. Each output is at the second level of the network, experiencing two to three gate delays.

Running a standard *misII* script on the *espresso* input file yields the following set of equations (note that hand optimization may do better):

$$X = \overline{C} + \overline{D}$$
$$Y = \overline{B}\,\overline{C}$$
$$C_0 = C_3 + \overline{A}B\overline{X} + ADY$$
$$C_1 = Y + \overline{A}\,\overline{C_5} + \overline{C}\,\overline{D}C_6$$
$$C_2 = C_5 + \overline{A}\,\overline{B}D + \overline{A}CD$$

$$C_3 = C_4 + BDC_5 + \overline{A}\,\overline{B}X$$
$$C_4 = \overline{D}Y + \overline{A}C\overline{D}$$
$$C_5 = \overline{C}C_4 + AY + \overline{A}BX$$
$$C_6 = AC_4 + CC_5 + \overline{C_4}C_5 + \overline{A}\,\overline{B}C$$

```
.i 4
.o 7
.ilb a b c d
.ob c0 c1 c2 c3 c4 c5 c6
.p 16
0000 1111110
0001 0110000
0010 1101101
0011 1111001
0100 0110011
0101 1011011
0110 1011111
0111 1110000
1000 1111111
1001 1110011
1010 -------
1011 -------
1100 -------
1101 -------
1110 -------
1111 -------
.e
```

Figure 4.75   *Espresso* input for the decoder circuit.

```
.i 4
.o 7
.ilb a b c d
.ob c0 c1 c2 c3 c4 c5 c6
.p 9
-10- 0000001
-01- 0001001
-0-1 0110000
-101 1011010
--00 0110010
--11 1110000
-0-0 1101100
1--- 1000011
-110 1011111
.e
```

Figure 4.76   *Espresso* output for the decoder circuit.

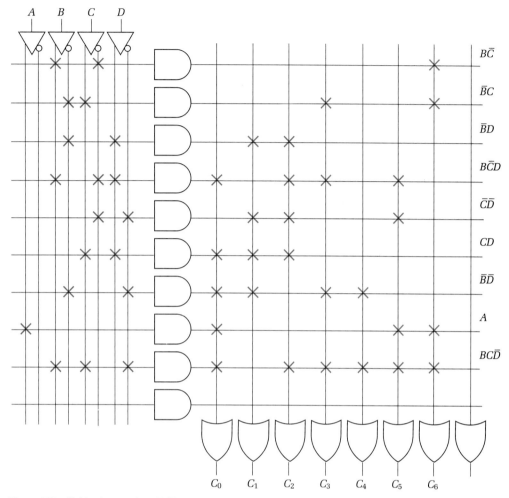

Figure 4.77   PLA implementation of BCD-to-seven-segment display decoder.

X and Y are intermediate terms inserted into the logic network by *misII*. This yields a total of 52 literals and 33 gates (one for each of outputs C_0 through C_6, X and Y, plus seven inverters including $\overline{X}$, $\overline{C_4}$, and $\overline{C_5}$, plus 17 other product terms). In terms of delay, the slowest output is C_1, since it is a function of C_6, which is a function of C_5, which in turn is a function of C_4. C_4 already experiences three gate delays since it is a function of Y. Thus C_1 experiences 9 or 10 gate delays! Although *misII* has done an admirable job of reducing the number of wires (as measured by the number of literals), it has not done so well on reducing the gate count, and its implementation will be quite a bit slower than the two-level realization derived by *espresso*. The primary reason is that this version of *misII* is not yet sophisticated enough to make use of don't-care conditions. The important lesson here is to understand the limitations of the computer-aided design tools you are using.

Case Study   4.6   A Logic Function Unit

You are to design a logic network that has two data inputs, A and B, and three control inputs, C_0, C_1, and C_2. The network should implement the logical function F specified in Figure 4.78. Components of this type find wide application in microprocessor data paths, for computing a variety of bitwise logic functions of two operands.

Step 1: Understand the problem.

The problem specification mentions three control inputs (C_0, C_1, C_2), two data inputs (A, B), and a single output function (F). Thus, F is a combinational logic function of these five variables.

Step 2: Formulate the problem in terms of truth table or other suitable design representation.

The natural thing to do next is to create a five-variable truth table, in preparation for solving a five-variable K-map. In terms of the truth table representation, there really is no distinction between control and data inputs. We begin by listing the 32 different combinations of five variables. Next, let's partition the truth table into eight groups of four rows each. Each group represents a unique setting of the three control inputs (000 through 111), and each row within the group represents a unique configuration of the data inputs A and B (00 through 11). Since the first truth table group ($C_0C_1C_2 = 000$) represents the constant function 1, we fill in all four rows with a 1. The second group ($C_0C_1C_2 = 001$) is the function OR. We fill in the first row ($AB = 00$) with a 0 and the remaining three rows ($AB = 01$, 10, 11) with a 1. Continuing in this fashion, we can complete the rest of the table. This is shown in Figure 4.79.

C_0	C_1	C_2	F	Comments
0	0	0	1	always 1
0	0	1	$A + B$	logical OR
0	1	0	$\overline{A \cdot B}$	logical NAND
0	1	1	A XOR B	logical XOR
1	0	0	A XNOR B	logical XNOR
1	0	1	$A \cdot B$	logical AND
1	1	0	$\overline{A + B}$	logical NOR
1	1	1	0	always 0

Figure 4.78   Specification of logic function unit.

C_0	C_1	C_2	A	B	F
0	0	0	0	0	1
0	0	0	0	1	1
0	0	0	1	0	1
0	0	0	1	1	1
0	0	1	0	0	0
0	0	1	0	1	1
0	0	1	1	0	1
0	0	1	1	1	1
0	1	0	0	0	1
0	1	0	0	1	1
0	1	0	1	0	1
0	1	0	1	1	0
0	1	1	0	0	0
0	1	1	0	1	1
0	1	1	1	0	1
0	1	1	1	1	0
1	0	0	0	0	1
1	0	0	0	1	0
1	0	0	1	0	0
1	0	0	1	1	1
1	0	1	0	0	0
1	0	1	0	1	0
1	0	1	1	0	0
1	0	1	1	1	1
1	1	0	0	0	1
1	1	0	0	1	0
1	1	0	1	0	0
1	1	0	1	1	0
1	1	1	0	0	0
1	1	1	0	1	0
1	1	1	1	0	0
1	1	1	1	1	0

Figure 4.79 Truth table for logic function unit.

Step 3: Choose an implementation technology.

The basic choice is whether to implement the function with a gate-oriented approach or with memories. Note that using discrete (or even programmable) gates is not the only "gate-oriented" approach. An implementation based on a multiplexer might be worth considering. See the block diagram in Figure 4.80. We could have come up with this implementation without even deriving the truth table of step 2.

To a large extent, the implementation decision depends on two factors: design time versus component cost. ROM–based designs usually require less time for design and implementation. For one thing, a ROM-based design starts with the same truth table as a discrete gate design, plus it has the advantage that we need not minimize the function. However, a ROM package is about five times as expensive as a discrete gate package (of course, this depends on the number of bits in the ROM). On the positive side, the function can be implemented in a single ROM but it will take several packages to implement it using discrete gates. For example, the multiplexer-based design of Figure 4.80 requires four TTL packages: four 2-input NAND, four 2-input NOR, two 2-input XOR, and an 8:1 multiplexer (inverters can be formed from leftover NAND, NOR, or XOR gates). If the cost differential is a factor of 5, the multiplexer-based design is still less expensive than ROM. Yet the multiplexer-based design takes up more circuit area than the ROM-based one, with more opportunities for wiring errors and component failures.

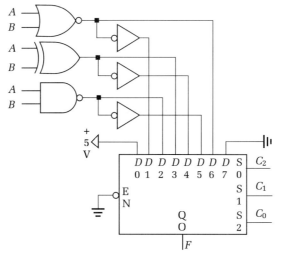

Figure 4.80 Multiplexer-based implementation of logic unit.

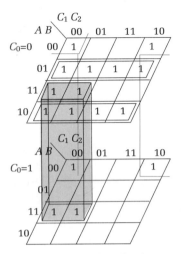

Figure 4.81   K-map for logic unit.

If cost is the overriding criterion, we will choose packaged logic. But which requires fewer packages, the discrete gate design or the multiplexer design? The minimized gate-level design cannot be evaluated without performing the K-map minimization, which we do next.

Step 4: Follow the implementation procedure.

To continue the analysis, we will minimize the function's K-map. This is shown in Figure 4.81, and the function for F turns out to be a rather simple equation:

$$F = \overline{C_2}\,\overline{A}B + \overline{C_0}A\overline{B} + \overline{C_0}\,\overline{A}B + \overline{C_1}AB$$

In packaged logic like TTL, this requires five gates (four 3-input, one 4-input), plus five inverters. This can be implemented in three TTL packages (one package of three 3-input gates, one package of two 4-input gates, and one package of six inverters), so there is a slight advantage for the gate approach.

Note that the function can be simplified further, assuming that XOR gates are available:

$$F = \overline{C_2}\,\overline{A}B + \overline{C_0}\,(A \oplus B) + \overline{C_1}AB$$

We still need five inverters and five more gates: three 3-input, one 2-input, and one 2-input XOR. This time we need four packages: one package of three 3-input gates, one package of four 2-input gates, one package of two 2-input XOR gates, and one package of six inverters. This simplification actually increases the implementation costs unless the leftover gates can be used for other purposes.

If the criterion is circuit area rather than cost, the clear winner is the ROM-based implementation, since it requires a single package. In a gate array design style, the 10-gate version probably has the area advantage. This is because it would be difficult to implement a 32-word ROM in an equivalent area using the primitive gate structures available in a typical gate array.

Case Study   **4.7**   **An Eight-Input Barrel Shifter**

A barrel shifter is a digital subsystem that can shift any number of bit positions at once. In a single pass through the shifter, the input can rotate from 0 to 7 positions. Barrel shifters are useful for implementing bit extraction operations supported in many computer instruction sets.

To be more precise, you are to design a digital subsystem that implements the following function. The subsystem has eight data inputs, D_7, D_6, ..., D_0, eight data outputs, O_7, O_6, ..., O_0, and three control inputs,

S_2, S_1, S_0. The control inputs specify the number of positions to shift the input to the left. Inputs that "fall off the end" are rotated around to the low-order bits of the output.

For example, when $S_2 = S_1 = S_0 = 0$, the inputs are simply gated straight through to the outputs: $O_7 = D_7$, $O_6 = D_6$, ..., $O_1 = D_1$, $O_0 = D_0$. When $S_2 = S_1 = 0$, $S_0 = 1$, the input bits are shifted one place toward the left: $O_7 = D_6$, $O_6 = D_5$, ..., $O_1 = D_0$, $O_0 = D_7$. Note that D_7 is rotated around to the 0th output position. When $S_2 = S_1 = S_0 = 1$, the input is shifted seven positions to the left, with the high-order bits wrapping around to the low-order output positions: $O_7 = D_0$, $O_6 = D_7$, ..., $O_1 = D_2$, $O_0 = D_1$. This is the same as shifting one position to the right, with the inputs wrapping from the low-order to the high-order positions.

Step 1:   Understand the problem.

The subsystem consists of eight output functions, each depending on 11 inputs: S_2, S_1, S_0, D_7, D_6, ..., D_0. Probably the easiest way to understand the subsystem's behavior is to tabulate the values of the outputs as a function of the control settings. This is shown in Figure 4.82. The inputs shift to the left by an increasing number of positions as the binary index of the control inputs increases. The inputs wrap around from the left to the right of the table.

Step 2:   Formulate the problem in terms of a truth table or other suitable design representation.

At this point, it is best to describe each of the outputs in terms of the 11 inputs:

$$O_7 = \bar{S}_2\bar{S}_1\bar{S}_0 D_7 + \bar{S}_2\bar{S}_1 S_0 D_6 + \cdots + S_2 S_1 S_0 D_0$$

$$O_6 = \bar{S}_2\bar{S}_1\bar{S}_0 D_6 + \bar{S}_2\bar{S}_1 S_0 D_5 + \cdots + S_2 S_1 S_0 D_7$$

$$\vdots$$

$$O_0 = \bar{S}_2\bar{S}_1\bar{S}_0 D_0 + \bar{S}_2\bar{S}_1 S_0 D_7 + \cdots + S_2 S_1 S_0 D_1$$

Step 3:   Choose implementation technology.

S_2	S_1	S_0	O_7	O_6	O_5	O_4	O_3	O_2	O_1	O_0
0	0	0	D_7	D_6	D_5	D_4	D_3	D_2	D_1	D_0
0	0	1	D_6	D_5	D_4	D_3	D_2	D_1	D_0	D_7
0	1	0	D_5	D_4	D_3	D_2	D_1	D_0	D_7	D_6
0	1	1	D_4	D_3	D_2	D_1	D_0	D_7	D_6	D_5
1	0	0	D_3	D_2	D_1	D_0	D_7	D_6	D_5	D_4
1	0	1	D_2	D_1	D_0	D_7	D_6	D_5	D_4	D_3
1	1	0	D_1	D_0	D_7	D_6	D_5	D_4	D_3	D_2
1	1	1	D_0	D_7	D_6	D_5	D_4	D_3	D_2	D_1

Figure 4.82   Function table for barrel shifter.

Step 4:   Follow implementation procedure.

For this case study, we will combine the discussion of implementation choice and procedures for yielding the implementation. The basic implementation choices are discrete gates, MSI components, programmable logic, or switching networks. Let's start with a discrete gate implementation. A close examination of the Boolean equations should tell us that there is little chance of simplifying the functions. All of the combinations of the S_i inputs are needed for each function, and each D_j appears in exactly one product term. There is just no way to exploit the uniting theorem. This means that a discrete gate implementation will require eight 4-input gates and one 8-input gate per function, for a total gate count of sixty-four 4-input gates and eight 8-input gates. This requires 40 packages: 32 for the 4-input gates and 8 for the 8-input gates. An approach based on discrete gates does not look too promising.

One alternative is to use MSI components such as multiplexers or decoders. It is not too hard to see that each output can be implemented by an 8:1 multiplexer. Simply use the control inputs to select one of the eight data inputs. All we have to do is to wire up the data inputs as specified by the table in Figure 4.82. This implementation requires only eight packages, a considerable savings over the discrete gate approach.

We can implement the subsystem with a single package if we use either a ROM or a PAL/PLA with sufficient programmable resources. Since the functions have 11 inputs, the ROM requires 2048 (2^{11}) by 8-bit words. To use a PAL, we need a component with 11 inputs, 8 outputs, and 8 product terms per OR gate output. A quick look at the output functions should convince you that they share no product terms. So there is no particular advantage to using a PLA.

The final implementation alternative is to develop some form of switching network. This should be a reasonable approach, since the shifter is a natural application of steering logic. Depending on the control signal settings, the inputs will be steered to the appropriate outputs. Figure 4.83 shows a switching structure constructed from orthogonal sets of wires connected by nMOS transistors. The "crosspoints" are implemented as shown by the cutaway at the right of the figure. The structure has the ability to connect any input to any output depending on which transistor gates are turned on. It is often called a *crosspoint switch*.

For example, if the diagonal crosspoints are enabled by the signal S_{000}, then D_i is connected to O_i. To implement the barrel shifter behavior, we need a strategy for distributing the right control signals to the appropriate switches in the array.

Within the crosspoint switch, we will use the fully decoded signals S_{000} through S_{111} derived from the eight possible configurations of the control inputs S_2, S_1, and S_0. It's not too hard to see how to implement the remaining control connections. The diagonal switches implement the barrel shifter function when $S_2 = S_1 = S_0 = 0$. The switches immediately below the diagonal connect D_6 to O_7, D_5 to O_6, ..., D_0 to O_1. This is almost the correct functionality for $S_2 = S_1 = 0$, $S_0 = 1$. All we need in addition is to be able to connect D_7 to O_0. This is made possible by the switch in the upper right corner of the array, as shown in the figure. The set of switches is controlled by the decoded signal S_{001}.

Figure 4.84 shows the crosspoint connection scheme with the complete set of control signals distributed through the structure. To shift 0 bits, the signal S_{000} controls the transistors along the main diagonal. S_{001}, the signal to shift 1 bit, is split across two diagonals, one below the main

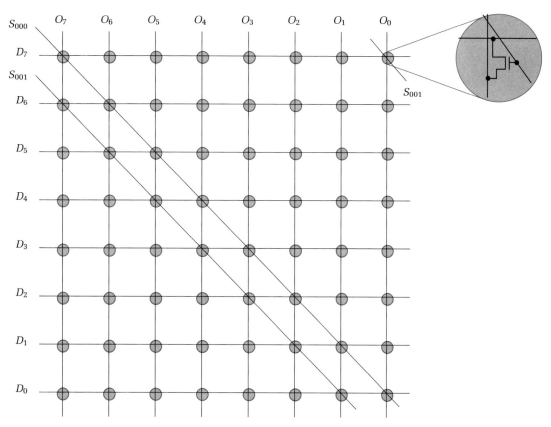

Figure 4.83   Crosspoint switch implementation of barrel shifter.

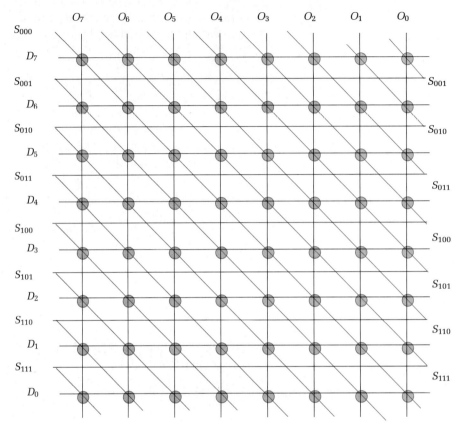

Figure 4.84 Completed crosspoint switch barrel shifter.

diagonal and one above. We use this strategy for each of the remaining control signals. With each increase in shift distance, the next control signal is routed to the diagonal immediately below and to the left of those controlled by the previous signal. For example, the switches controlled by S_{010} are immediately below and to the left of the switches controlled by S_{001}.

Clearly, the switch implementation is most efficient. It requires only 64 transistors (plus a decoder), although the signal routing is fairly complex. If you cannot implement the subsystem directly at the level of transistor switches, the best alternative is to use a ROM or PAL to complete implementation in a single integrated circuit package.

Case Study Summary In this section, you have followed a four-step design procedure for mapping a word specification of a combinational logic circuit into an actual implementation. First, you understand the problem specification by identifying inputs, outputs, and their relationships. A picture or diagram is often an indispensable aid to the process of understanding the problem. Second, you map your understanding of the problem onto a truth table or collection of Boolean equations. Without placing the design into one of these forms, you will be hard pressed to use the techniques learned in Chapter 2 and this chapter to derive an implementation. Third, you choose your implementation technology: discrete or programmable gates, memory-based designs, or perhaps alternative approaches based on multiplexers or other steering logic. The choice depends on many things: cost, availability of CAD tools or hardware programmers, circuit area. Memory-based designs require a truth table. The gate-oriented designs can start with either truth tables or Boolean equations, but they demand a minimization procedure to obtain an efficient implementation. With the availability of the appropriate computer-aided design tools, this should not represent too much of a problem, however. The fourth and final step is to apply the appropriate procedure to obtain the implementation: the K-map method or a CAD tool like *espresso* for a two-level logic network, Boolean factoring, or a tool like *misII* for a multilevel network.

Chapter Review

The theme of this chapter has been how to construct digital systems with more complex logic building blocks than the discrete gates of Chapters 2 and 3. We began with PALs and PLAs, particularly dense implementations of AND-OR logic defined over multiple inputs and outputs. PALs and PLAs have the important capability of being programmable: the connections among the gates can be wired "on demand" to implement a particular function.

ROMs are another form of programmable logic, implementing a collection of functions by placing their truth tables in an array of memory elements. PLAs are attractive when there is a high degree of sharing among the product terms of the multiple output functions. However, a two-level minimization method is critical for using PLAs (or PALs) effectively. ROM-based designs require nothing more than a truth table, but a ROM does not exploit don't-care conditions or shared product terms among output functions.

We examined switch logic in more detail. Building logic from individual transistors makes it is possible to implement some functions in a more transistor-efficient manner than with discrete gates. Steering logic devices, such as multiplexers and demultiplexers, are examples of logic of this form. Even complex functions, like the Tally circuit, can be implemented efficiently by casting them in terms of data signals routed through a network of switches.

We also looked at discrete gate implementations of multiplexers/selectors and demultiplexers/decoders and described methods for building general-purpose logic from such building blocks.

Some logic gates are not restricted to outputs of 1 and 0. A tri-state gate has a third state that is called high impedance and has the effect of disconnecting itself from its output circuit node. A gate with open-collector outputs can only drive its output to a 0; in conditions where its output would be a 1, the output actually "floats." A circuit node connected to an open-collector output must also be connected to a pull-up resistor. This guarantees that the node will be treated as a logic 1 when none of the connected gates are driving the node to a logic 0.

We closed this chapter by examining combinational word problems. The procedure is to understand the word statement of the problem and then to formulate it in terms of a suitable design representation, such as a truth table. Once an implementation strategy has been determined—for example, choosing whether to implement the circuit in terms of a ROM, two-level logic (PAL or PLA), or multilevel logic—the appropriate combinational logic design method is applied (ROM programming, K-maps, CAD tools for simplification) to obtain the circuit realization.

Further Reading

Books on digital design with programmable devices have appeared only in the past several years. R. Alford, *Programmable Logic Designer's Guide*, Sams and Co., Indianapolis, IN, 1989, provides a good discussion of programmable technology and design methods. Chapter 3 describes the wide range of programmable devices currently available, including more general logic structures than PALs and PLAs. Another good book on programmable logic is G. Bostock, *Programmable Logic Devices: Technology and Applications*, McGraw-Hill, New York, 1988. Chapter 2 describes the processing and electronic circuit technology of programmable devices. Chapter 4 covers logic design with PROMs, PLAs, and PALs.

The standard handbook on PLD components is Monolithic Memories' *Programmable Logic Handbook*, 4th edition, Monolithic Memories, Inc., Santa Clara, CA, 1985. The book contains a wealth of information on PLD parts from the company that invented the concept.

The section on switch logic in this chapter is based on the pioneering text by C. Mead and L. Conway, *Introduction to VLSI Systems Design*, Addison-Wesley, Reading, MA, 1979, especially Chapters 1 and 3. A more modern treatment of CMOS VLSI and its application to switching circuits and conventional gate logic can be found in E. D. Fabricius's textbook *Introduction to VLSI Design*, McGraw-Hill, New York, 1990. The basic concept of MOS switches is presented in Chapter 1, with a more detailed description of MOS implementations of Tally circuits, NAND, NOR, AOI, and multiplexers in Chapter 8.

No man who is occupied in doing a very difficult thing, and doing it very well, loses his self-respect.

—George Bernard Shaw

I_2	I_1	O_2	O_1
1	X	1	0
0	1	0	1
0	0	0	0

Figure Ex4.3 Two-input priority encoder truth table.

Exercises

4.1 *(PALs and PLAs)* Our third word problem case study described a logical "function unit" that computed the eight combinational functions of the inputs A and B: constant 1, A OR B, A NAND B, A XOR B, A XNOR B, A AND B, A NOR B, and constant 0. Show how to implement this using a programmable logic array (with five inputs and one output). Draw the AND array and OR array, and indicate which connections must be made to implement the function. For each output from the AND array, indicate along the wire the product term it is implementing.

4.2 *(PALs and PLAs)* Show how to implement the BCD-to-seven-segment LED decoder using a PAL such as that in the P16H8 structure: 10 inputs, 8 OR gate outputs, and 7 product terms per OR gate. Use the shorthand notation developed in Section 4.1.

4.3 *(Transmission Gates)* A priority encoder circuit has inputs and outputs that are numbered from 1 to N. The operation of the circuit is defined as follows. Determine the highest-numbered input that is asserted. Only the output with the same index as the highest-numbered input that is asserted should be asserted. If none of the inputs are asserted, all of the outputs read out a 0. A truth table for a two-input priority encoder circuit is shown in Figure Ex4.3.

a. Implement a two-input priority encoder circuit using discrete inverters and NAND gates only.

b. Implement the same function as in (a), except using CMOS transmission gates and inverters. Counting transistors, which implementation is more transistor efficient?

4.4 *(Transmission Gates)* Consider the description of the following circuit, often called a function generator. The circuit has two data inputs, A and B, four control inputs, G_0, G_1, G_2, and G_3, and one output F. F is defined as

$$F = G_0\bar{A}\bar{B} + G_1\bar{A}B + G_2A\bar{B} + G_3AB$$

a. Describe how to "program" this function to implement the following 10 functions: A AND B, A OR B, A NAND B, A NOR B, 0, 1, A, B, A XOR B, and A XNOR B by placing the appropriate values on the G_i inputs.

b. Implement this function using CMOS transmission gates and inverters only. (*Hint*: Use the inputs A and B to control the transmission gates; consider how to route the appropriate G_i to the output F.)

4.5 *(Switch Logic Implementation)* Show how to implement a two-input by two-stack AND-OR-Invert gate with a minimum number of nMOS and pMOS transistors.

4.6 *(Multiplexers vs. Demultiplexers)*

    a. Briefly define and differentiate between the following terms: *decoder, demultiplexer, multiplexer.* Mention the number of inputs, outputs, enable, and select bits, if any.

    b. Using AND and OR gates, design a circuit to gate a single data input to one of four output lines, determined by the binary-encoded index on the two control lines. Which of the above parts did you design?

    c. Repeat step (b) using a transistor "switching network" instead of AND and OR gates. Compare the discrete gate implementation versus the transmission gate implementation. Give one advantage and one disadvantage of each of the approaches.

4.7 *(Multiplexer Implementation)* The 2:1 multiplexer function has two data inputs A and B, a select control input S, and a single positive-logic output Z that operates as follows. When S is unasserted, input A is gated to the output. When S is asserted, input B is gated to the output Z. Draw schematics that implement the multiplexer function using *only* the following components:

    a. Inverting tri-state buffers and conventional inverters.

    b. Open-collector NAND gates, conventional inverters, and pull-up resistors.

    c. Repeat parts (a) and (b) for a four-input multiplexer. S_1, $S_0 = 00$ gates A to Z; S_1, $S_0 = 01$ gates B to Z; S_1, $S_0 = 10$ gates C to Z; S_1, $S_0 = 11$ gates D to Z.

4.8 *(Multiplexer Logic)* Implement the function $f(A, B, C, D, E) = A + \overline{C}D + B\overline{D} + \overline{B}D + \overline{B}CE$ using a multiplexer and no other logic. The constants logic 1, logic 0, and the variables, but not their complements, are available.

4.9 *(Multiplexer Logic)* Implement the 2-bit adder function (i.e., 2-bit binary number AB plus 2-bit binary number CD yields 3-bit result XYZ) using three 8:1 multiplexers. Show your truth table and how you derived the inputs to the multiplexers.

4.10   *(Multiplexer Logic)*   Because 32:1 multiplexers do not exist in standard component catalogs, design a two-stage multiplexer network that realizes the six-variable function

$$f(A, B, C, D, E, F) = \Sigma\, m(3, 7, 12, 14, 15, 19, 23, 27, 28, 29, 31, 35, 39,$$
$$44, 45, 46, 48, 49, 50, 52, 53, 55, 56, 57, 59)$$

a. How many TTL packages are used?

b. How many TTL packages are required to implement this function using conventional inverters and NAND gates in a two-level network?

4.11   *(Multiplexer Logic)*   You are working for a company that produces clones of famous name computers. Your assignment is to copy the circuit shown in Figure Ex4.11, which is a component of the computer. Because of copyright laws, your boss is very emphatic that the new circuit not resemble the old one. Also, your boss's brother-in-law's electronics wholesale firm has a special deal on multiplexers. So the boss wants you to use only 4:1 multiplexers in your circuit.

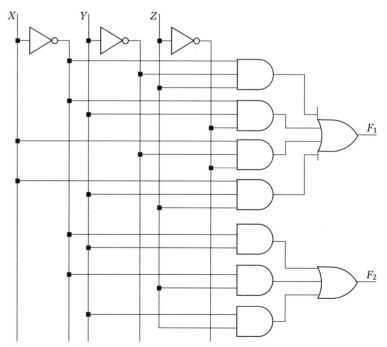

Figure Ex4.11   Circuit to be re-engineered with multiplexers.

4.12 *(Decoder Implementation)*   Demonstrate how to implement a 6:64 decoder using generic 2:4 and 4:16 decoders.

4.13 *(Decoder Implementation)*   We have seen how to implement decoders using AND gates and NOR gates. Show how to implement the truth table of the 74138 4:16 decoder, including the three-input enable logic, G_1, $\overline{G}_{2A}$, $\overline{G}_{2B}$, using only NAND gates and inverters.

4.14 *(Decoder Implementation)*   A decoder together with an OR gate connected to its output terminals can be used in the synthesis of combinational networks.

  a. Implement the function $f(A, B, C, D) = \overline{A}\overline{B}D + \overline{A}BD + AC\overline{D} + AC\overline{D}$ (not necessarily in minimized form) using one 4:16 decoder and a very large fan-in OR gate.

  b. Compare the resulting number of ICs with a solution using discrete gates only.

4.15 *(Implementation Methods)*   Given the following function in sum of products form (not necessarily minimized):

$$F(A, B, C, D) = \overline{A}BC + AD + AC$$

Implement the function F using

  a. An 8:1 multiplexer.

  b. A 4:16 decoder with a 16-input OR gate.

  c. A 16-word ROM.

  d. A PLA-like structure using the notation of Section 4.1.

4.16 *(Implementation Methods)*   Given a four-input Boolean function, $f(A, B, C, D) = \Sigma\, m(0, 3, 5, 7, 11, 12, 13, 15)$

  a. Implement the function using a 16:1 multiplexer.

  b. Implement using an 8:1 multiplexer (use D, $\overline{D}$ as MUX data inputs and A, B, C as MUX control inputs).

  c. Implement the function using a 4:1 multiplexer. (*Hint:* Place A and B on the select inputs. Assume $\overline{C}$, $\overline{D}$ are available and use an OR gate to form one of the inputs to the multiplexer.)

  d. Implement the function using a 4:16 decoder and an OR gate.

4.17 *(Implementation Methods)* Given the function $f(A, B, C, D) = (\bar{A} + B)(\bar{A} + C + D)(A + \bar{C} + D)$ in minimized product of sums form and the don't-care set $D = \{M_0, M_2, M_9, M_{10}\}$, do the following:

    a. Write f in canonical product of sums form.

    b. Write f in canonical sum of products form.

    c. Write f in minimized sum of products form.

    d. Show how to implement f with a single three-stack by three-input AND-OR-Invert gate.

    e. Show how to implement f with an 8:1 multiplexer.

4.18 *(Implementation Methods)* Given the three functions X, Y, and Z, defined by $X(A, B, C, D) = \Sigma\, m(1, 2, 3, 5, 7, 9, 11, 13, 15)$, $Y(A, B, C, D) = \Pi\, M(2, 3, 4, 5, 6, 7, 8, 10, 12, 14)$, and $Z(A, B, C, D) = \Sigma\, m(0, 1, 2, 3, 5, 7)$,

    a. Find the minimum sum of products form for each of these functions. How many unique product terms are there in your answer?

    b. Find an alternative sum of products form for X, Y, and Z that minimizes the number of unique product terms to implement all three functions simultaneously. How many unique product terms do you find in this implementation?

    c. Show how to implement your solution to part (b) in a PLA structure.

4.19 *(Implementation Methods)* Consider the implementation of a circuit with four data inputs, A, B, C, D, two outputs, F and G, and two control inputs S_1 and S_0. The block diagram and functional truth table are shown in Figure Ex4.19.

    a. Assume that S_1, $\bar{S}_1$, S_0, and $\bar{S}_0$ are available. Implement F and G using AND and OR gates only.

    b. Assume that S_1, $\bar{S}_1$, S_0, and $\bar{S}_0$ are available. Draw the schematic implementing the functions using NAND gates and non-inverting tri-state buffers with active low enables. (Your solution should not be a simple restatement of your answer for part (a).)

    c. Assume that S_1, $\bar{S}_1$, S_0, and $\bar{S}_0$ are available. Draw the schematics that implement F and G using open-collector NAND gates and conventional inverters only.

    d. Implement F and G using transmission gates only.

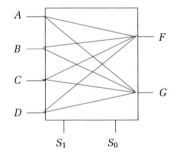

S_1	S_0	F	G
0	0	A	D
0	1	B	C
1	0	C	B
1	1	D	A

Figure Ex4.19 Specification for Exercise 4.19.

4.20   *(ROM-based Implementation)*   Design a schematic for a read-only memory subsystem of size 65536 words by 8 bits wide, using 2764 8K by 8-bit ROMs.

  a. Use a single 3:8 decoder and inverters.

  b. Use a single 2:4 decoder and inverters. Is there a clever way to make use of the output enable inputs to the ROM as well as the chip select lines?

4.21   *(Word Problems)*   A logic network has four inputs ($Input_0$, $Input_1$, $Input_2$, $Input_3$) and two outputs ($Output_0$, $Output_1$). At least one of the inputs is always asserted high. If a given input line has a logic 1 applied to it, the output signals will encode its index in binary. For example, if $Input_2$ is asserted, the output reads $Output_1 = 1$, $Output_0 = 0$. If two or more inputs are at logic 1, the output will be set according to which input has the highest index ($Input_3 > Input_2 > Input_1 > Input_0$).

  a. Fill in the truth table for this function.

  b. Fill in K-maps for $Output_1$ and $Output_0$, and find the Boolean expression for the minimum sum of products implementation.

4.22   *(Word Problems)*   You are to implement a combinational multiplier. It has two 2-bit inputs and a 4-bit output. The first 2-bit input is represented by the variables A, B; the second 2-bit input is represented by C, D. The outputs are W, X, Y, Z, from the most significant bit to the least.

  a. Complete a truth table that describes the functional behavior of the multiplier.

  b. Find the minimum sum of products forms for the outputs using the K-map method.

4.23   *(Word Problems)*   An n-input majority function asserts its output whenever more than half of its inputs are asserted. You are to implement a seven-input majority function, which will assert its output whenever four or more of its inputs are asserted.

Don't panic just because this is a seven-variable function. Build it up as a multilevel function whose subfunctions each have less than six variables. As a block diagram, it looks like Figure Ex4.23. Circuits #1 and #2 tally the number of their inputs that are asserted, providing the count in binary on the outputs (V, Y are the most significant bits; W, Z are the least significant bits). Based on these second-level inputs, Q determines if more than four or more of the original inputs are 1.

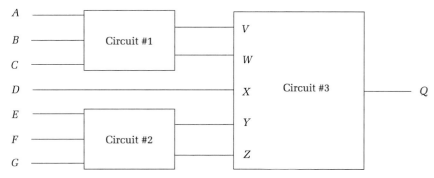

Figure Ex4.23 Block diagram for the tally circuit.

> **a.** Find the minimized sum of products form for circuit #1 (circuit #2 is identical). The functions V and W should look familiar. What do they implement?
>
> **b.** Complete a five-variable truth table for circuit #3.
>
> **c.** Find the minimum sum of products form for Q using the K-map method.
>
> **d.** Find the minimum product of sums form for Q using the K-map method.

4.24 *(Word Problems)* You are to design a converter that maps a 4-bit binary code into a 4-bit Gray code. The 4-bit Gray code sequence is defined as follows: 0000, 0001, 0011, 0010, 0110, 0111, 0100, 1100, 1101, 1111, 1110, 1010, 1011, 1001, 1000. Give the truth table, and show how to implement this code converter as a ROM circuit and as a PLA circuit.

4.25 *(Case Studies)* How close can the rods be placed on the conveyor belt without invalidating the solution to Case Study 1?

4.26 *(Case Studies)* Verify that the *misII* equations for the BCD-to-seven-segment LED decoder really do map onto the same on-set as the *espresso* equations. This can be accomplished by expanding the equations into two-level sum of products form and filling in four-variable K-maps from the equations thus derived. How do the K-maps compare with those of Figure 4.71?

4.27 *(Case Studies)*   We wish to extend the BCD-to-seven-segment LED display decoder to become a hexadecimal LED display decoder. The LED representations of the hex digits 0, 1, 2, 3, 4, 5, 6, 7, 8, and 9 are exactly the same as for the equivalent BCD digits. Figure Ex4.27 shows how the segment displays should be illuminated to denote the hex digits A (1010), B (1011), C (1100), D (1101), E (1110), and F (1111).

a. Obtain the minimized sum of products implementations for the display inputs.

b. Show how to implement the logic for the extended design as a PLA with four inputs and seven outputs. Draw the AND array and OR array, and indicate which connections must be made to implement the function. For each output from the AND array, indicate along the wire the product term it is implementing.

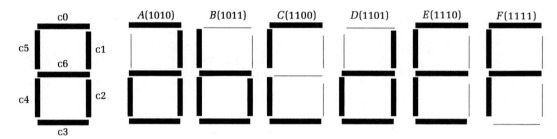

Figure Ex4.27   Hexadecimal displays.

4.28 *(Case Studies)*   Design to the gate level an arithmetic and logic function unit based on the circuit of Case Study 3. The modifications to the specification are as follows. We add one additional input *Cin* and one extra output *Cout*. When the control inputs $C_0C_1C_2 = 000$, F generates the function A plus B plus *Cin* and *Cout* is the carry-out result from the binary addition. The rest of the control signal settings generate the same functions as before. (*Cout* is a don't care for these.)

4.29 *(Case Studies)*   In the function table for the barrel shifter (Figure 4.82), the input data rotates from right to left. How does the implementation change if the data are rotated from left to right instead? Your answer should consider both the logic gate and transmission gate implementation styles.

4.30 *(Tally Circuit)* Examine the truth table for the two-input Tally function (Figure 4.23) very carefully. Is there a way to implement the three outputs without using an XOR gate? (*Hint*: Think of a way to implement the One output in terms of the Zero and Two functions.) How does this revised gate-level implementation compare with the switch implementation?

5 Arithmetic Circuits

Arithmetic is where the answer is right and everything is nice and you can look out the window and see the blue sky—or the answer is wrong and you have to start all over and try again and see how it comes out this time.

—Carl Sandberg

Introduction

In this chapter we will examine arithmetic circuits as detailed case studies of the principles of combinational logic design. Up to this point, we have concentrated on circuits that manipulate binary numbers as unsigned magnitudes only. We begin this chapter looking at ways to represent both positive and negative numbers in the binary system, and at the various schemes for adding and subtracting signed numbers. Then we will revisit the circuits for the half and full adder, as these form the basis for just about every arithmetic circuit we will meet.

Arithmetic circuits provide excellent examples of the trade-offs between circuit speed and complexity. We will examine two approaches for high-speed addition, *carry lookahead logic* and *carry select addition*. These allow us to sum numbers very quickly, but at the cost of a much more complex network with many more gates.

We will also learn how to design one of the most important subsystems in a digital computer: the *arithmetic logic unit* or *ALU*. The ALU comprises the combinational logic that implements logic operations, such as AND and OR, and arithmetic operations, such as ADD and SUBTRACT. It is at the heart of the instruction execution portion of every computer that has ever been built.

5.1 Number Systems

Within digital systems, all data, whether characters or numbers, are represented by strings of binary digits. This is fine as long as you never have negative numbers. Unfortunately, this is not normally the case.

Over the years, hardware designers have developed three different schemes for representing negative numbers: *sign and magnitude, ones complement,* and *twos complement.* In this section, we will examine these schemes and their implications for addition and subtraction of signed binary numbers.

5.1.1 Representation of Negative Numbers

In mathematics, there are infinitely many positive and negative integers. However, in a practical hardware system only a fixed number of integers can be represented, based on the number of bits allocated to the representation. In most modern computer systems, numbers are represented in 32 bits. This means that over 4 billion unique numbers can be represented—quite a few, but certainly not infinite! An *overflow* occurs when an arithmetic operation results in a number outside the range of those that can be represented.

Throughout this subsection we will assume that our system operates on 4-bit binary quantities. Thus we can represent 16 unique binary numbers. Roughly half of these will represent positive numbers and zero, while the remainder will be negative numbers. Each of the three representation schemes handles negative numbers slightly differently, as we now examine.

Sign and Magnitude   In *sign and magnitude* systems, the most significant bit represents the number's sign, while the remaining bits represent its absolute value as an unsigned binary magnitude. If the *sign bit* is a 0, the number is positive. If the sign bit is a 1, the number is negative. We negate a number simply by replacing the sign bit with its complement.

Figure 5.1 depicts a "number wheel" representation of our 4-bit number system. The figure shows the binary numbers and their decimal integer equivalents, assuming that the numbers are interpreted as sign and magnitude. The largest positive number we can represent in three data bits is $+7 = 2^3 - 1$. By a similar calculation, the smallest negative number is -7. Zero has two different representations, even though $+0$ and -0 don't make much sense mathematically.

Adding two positive or two negative numbers is straightforward. We simply perform the addition and assign the result the same sign as the original operands. When the signs of the two operands are not the same, addition becomes more complex. In this case, we should subtract the smaller magnitude from the larger. The resulting sign is the same as that of the number with the larger magnitude.

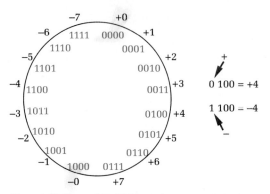

Figure 5.1 Sign and magnitude number representation.

This is what makes arithmetic operations with sign and magnitude numbers so cumbersome—any adder circuit must also include a subtractor and a comparator. Because of this burdensome complexity, hardware designers have proposed other schemes for representing negative numbers.

Ones Complement Numbers A *ones complement* approach represents the positive numbers just as in the sign and magnitude system. The only difference is in how it represents negative numbers.

We use the following procedure to derive a negative ones complement integer, denoted $\overline{N}$, from a positive integer, denoted N. If the word length is n bits ($n = 4$ in our case), then $\overline{N} = (2^n - 1) - N$. For example, in a 4-bit system, +7 is represented as 0111. We compute –7 as

$$
\begin{array}{rr}
2^4 = & 10000 \\
\text{Subtract 1} & -\ \underline{0001} \\
& 01111 \\
\text{Subtract 7} & -\ \underline{0111} \\
& 01000 \qquad \text{Representation of } -7
\end{array}
$$

This rather complicated method is just one way to compute the negative of a ones complement number. A simpler method forms the ones complement by taking the number's bitwise complement. Thus, +7 = 0111 and –7 = 1000, +4 = 0100 and –4 = 1011, and so on.

The number wheel representation of the 4-bit ones complement number system is shown in Figure 5.2. All negative numbers have a 1 in their sign bit, making it easy to distinguish between positive and negative numbers. Note that we still have two different representations of zero.

The advantage of ones complement numbers is the ease with which we can compute negative numbers. Subtraction is implemented by a combination of addition and negation: $A - B = A + (-B)$. Thus, we don't need a separate subtractor circuit. However, addition is still complicated by the two zeros, and that leads us to twos complement numbers.

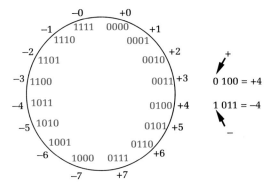

Figure 5.2 Ones complement number representation.

Twos Complement Numbers The *twos complement* scheme is similar to ones complement, except that there is only one representation for zero. Figure 5.3 shows how the twos complement numbers are derived from the ones complement representation. We've taken the negative numbers and shifted them one position in the clockwise direction. This allows us to represent one more negative number, −8, than we were able to represent in ones complement. The negative numbers still have a 1 in their highest-order bit, the sign bit.

More formally, a twos complement negative number, denoted N^*, is derived from its positive number, N, by the equation $N^* = 2^n - N$, where n is the number of bits in the representation. This equation omits the ones complement step that subtracts 1 from 2^n.

Let's compute the twos complement of +7, represented as 0111_2:

$$
\begin{array}{rl}
2^4 = & 10000 \\
\text{subtract 7} & -\underline{\ 0111} \\
& 0\underline{1001} \qquad \text{Representation of} -7
\end{array}
$$

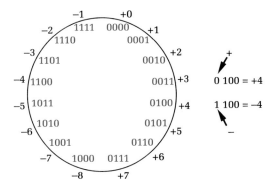

Figure 5.3 Twos complement number representation.

Note that the calculation works equally well in deriving the twos complement of −7:

$$
\begin{array}{r}
2^4 = \quad 10000 \\
\text{subtract } -7 \quad -\ \underline{1001} \\
0\overline{0111} \quad \text{Representation of 7}
\end{array}
$$

It should come as no surprise that the same shortcut we used to find ones complement numbers also applies for the twos complement system, but with a twist. The number wheel suggests the scheme. Simply form the bitwise complement of the number and then add one to form its twos complement. For example, $+7 = 0111_2$, its bitwise complement is 1000_2, plus 1 is 1001_2. This is the same twos complement representation of −7 we derived by the last calculation. For the number −4, represented as 1100_2, its bitwise complement is 0011_2, plus 1 is 0100_2. This is exactly the twos complement representation of +4.

As with ones complement, twos complement allows subtraction to be implemented with addition and negation. Even though it is a little harder to compute the twos complement, this is the form used almost universally in today's digital systems. In the next subsection, we will see how easily we can compute addition and subtraction by using twos complement numbers.

5.1.2   Addition and Subtraction of Numbers

In this section, we will examine how addition and subtraction are performed in the three different number systems.

Sign and Magnitude Calculations   Continuing with our 4-bit number scheme, let's look at some examples of addition and subtraction with sign and magnitude numbers. We need only consider addition, because subtraction is implemented by adding the negative of the subtracted number. Here are some examples adding and subtracting 3 and 4:

$$
\begin{array}{lll}
\text{(a)} & \begin{array}{rr} 4 & 0100 \\ +3 & +\ 0011 \\ \hline 7 & 0111 \end{array} &
\text{(b)} & \begin{array}{rr} -4 & 1100 \\ +(-3) & +\ 1011 \\ \hline -7 & 1\,111 \end{array}
\end{array}
$$

$$
\begin{array}{lll}
\text{(c)} & \begin{array}{rrr} 4 & 0100 & 0100 \\ -3 & -\ 0011 = & +1011 \\ \hline 1 & & 0001 \end{array} &
\text{(d)} & \begin{array}{rrr} -4 & -\ 0100 & 1100 \\ +3 & +\ 0011 = & +\ 0011 \\ \hline -1 & & 1001 \end{array}
\end{array}
$$

Examples (a) and (b) are cases in which the signs are the same. The result is simply the sum of the magnitudes, and the sign of the result is the same as the signs of the operands.

Examples (c) and (d) represent the more complex situations in which the signs of the two operands differ. In (c), we have converted $4 - 3$ to $4 + (-3)$. The smaller magnitude, 3, is subtracted from the larger magnitude, 4, to obtain the magnitude of the result, 1. Since 4 is greater than 3, its sign is given to the result. This makes the result +1.

Case (d) looks at the operation $(-4) + 3$. The subtraction of the smaller magnitude from the larger yields a result of 1. The larger magnitude is negative, so the result must also be negative.

Sign and magnitude calculations are complicated because we need both an adder and a subtractor even to implement addition. The adder is used when the signs are the same, the subtractor when they differ. Subtraction is just as complicated.

Ones Complement Calculations   Let's repeat the examples with ones complement arithmetic:

(e)
$$
\begin{array}{rl}
4 & 0100 \\
+3 & +\,0011 \\
\hline
7 & 0111
\end{array}
$$

(f)
$$
\begin{array}{rl}
-4 & 1011 \\
+(-3) & +\,1100 \\
\hline
-7 & 1\;0111 \\
& \quad\;\;\llcorner\!\!\rightarrow 1 \\
\hline
& 1000
\end{array}
$$

(g)
$$
\begin{array}{rl}
4 & 0100 \qquad 0100 \\
-3 & -\,0011 = +\,1100 \\
\hline
1 & \qquad\qquad 1\;0000 \\
& \qquad\qquad\;\;\llcorner\!\!\rightarrow 1 \\
\hline
& \qquad\qquad 0001
\end{array}
$$

(h)
$$
\begin{array}{rl}
-4 & -\,0100 \qquad 1011 \\
+3 & +\,0011 = +\,0011 \\
\hline
-1 & \qquad\qquad 1110
\end{array}
$$

Adding two positive numbers, case (e), gives the same result as before. This should not be too surprising, since positive numbers are represented in the same fashion in all three systems.

Example (f) introduces one considerable difference between sign and magnitude addition and ones complement addition: the concept of *end-around* carry. In ones complement, -4 is represented as 1011_2 and -3 as 1100_2. When we add these two numbers, we get a carry-out of the high-order bit position. Whenever this occurs, we must add the carry bit to the result of the sum. $1011_2 + 1100_2$ yields $1\;0111_2$. When the carry-out is added to the 4-bit result, we get $0111_2 + 1 = 1000_2$. This is the representation of -7 in ones complement.

The end-around carry also happens in example (g). The sum of 4 (0100_2) and -3 (1100_2) yields $1\;0000_2$. Adding in the carry gives 0001_2, the ones complement representation of 1.

The last example, (h), obtains the sum 1110_2. This is precisely the ones complement representation of -1.

Why does the end-around carry scheme work? Intuitively, the carry-out of 1 means that the resulting addition advances through the origin of the number wheel. In effect, we need to advance the result by 1 to avoid counting zero twice.

More formally, the operation of the end-around carry is the equivalent of subtracting 2^n and adding 1. Consider the case in which we compute the sum $M + (-N)$ where $M > N$:

$$M - N = M + \overline{N} = M + (2^n - 1 - N) = (M - N) + 2^n - 1$$

This is exactly the situation of example (g). The end-around carry subtracts off 2^n and adds 1, yielding the desired result of $M - N$.

Now consider the case shown in the second example. The sum to be formed is $-M + -N$, where $M + N$ is less than 2^{n-1}. This results in the following sequence of equations:

$$-M + (-N) = \overline{M} + \overline{N} = (2^n - M - 1) + (2^n - N - 1)$$
$$= 2^n + [2^n - 1 - (M + N)] - 1$$

After the end-around carry, the result of the sum becomes $[2^n - 1 - (M + N)]$. This is the correct form for representing $-(M + N)$ in ones complement form.

Twos Complement Calculations Twos complement calculations behave very much like the ones complement method, but without the end-around carry. Let's revisit the four examples:

(i)		4	0100	(j)	−4	1100
		+3	+ 0011		+(−3)	+ 1101
		7	0111		−7	1$\lfloor$1001

(k)	4	0100	0100	(l)	−4	− 0100	1100
	−3	− 0011 =	+ 1101		+3	+ 0011 =	+ 0011
	1		1$\lfloor$0001		−1		1111

Subtraction is handled as before: we negate the operand and perform addition. Carry-outs can still occur, but in twos complement arithmetic we ignore them.

Example (i), summing two positive numbers, is identical to the two previous representation schemes. Summing two negative numbers is also straightforward. We simply perform binary addition, ignoring any carry-outs. Since we no longer have two representations for zero, there is no need to worry about correcting the summation. Mixed addition of positive and negative numbers is handled exactly like the other cases.

Why is it all right to ignore the carry-out? The same kind of analysis we used in the ones complement case can be applied here. Consider the sum $-M + N$ when $N > M$. This can be rewritten as

$$M^* + N = (2^n - M) + N = 2^n + (N - M)$$

Ignoring the carry-out is equivalent to subtracting 2^n. Doing this to the foregoing expression yields the result $N - M$, which is exactly what we desire. Consider another case: $-M + -N$ where $M + N$ is less than or equal to 2^{n-1}. This can be rewritten as

$$-M + (-N) = M^* + N^* = (2^n - M) + (2^n - N)$$
$$= 2^n - (M + N) + 2^n$$

By subtracting 2^n, the resulting form is exactly the representation of $(M + N)^*$, the desired twos complement representation of $-(M + N)$.

The trade-off between twos complement and ones complement arithmetic should now be a little clearer. In the twos complement case, addition is simple but negation is more complex. For the ones complement system, it is easy to perform negation but addition becomes more complicated. Because twos complement only has one representation for zero, it is preferred for most digital systems.

5.1.3   Overflow Conditions

Overflow occurs whenever the sum of two positive numbers yields a negative result or when two negative numbers are summed and the result is positive. We can use the number wheel to illustrate overflow. Think of addition as moving clockwise around the number wheel. Subtraction moves counterclockwise. Using the twos complement number representation, we can divide the number wheel into two halves, one representing positive numbers (and zero), the other representing the negative numbers. Whenever addition or subtraction crosses the positive/negative line, an overflow has occurred.

This concept is illustrated in Figure 5.4, with the two example calculations $5 + 3$ and $-7 - 2$. On the number wheel, starting with the representation for +5, we advance three numbers in the clockwise direction. This yields −8; an overflow has occurred. Similarly for subtraction. Starting with the representation for −7, we move two numbers in the counterclockwise direction, obtaining the representation for +7. Once again, we have an overflow.

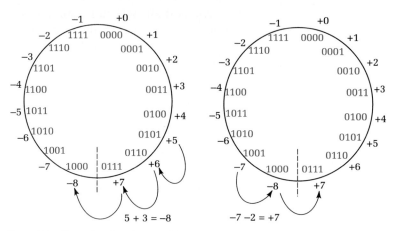

Figure 5.4 Illustration of overflow conditions.

There is another way to detect when overflow has taken place. Let's look at the detailed calculations:

Carry-in ≠ carry-out, overflow   Carry-in = carry-out, no overflow

$$
\begin{array}{rl}
& \boxed{0\ 1}1\ 1 \\
5 & \quad 0\ 1\ 0\ 1 \\
3 & +0\ 0\ 1\ 1 \\
\hline
-8 & \quad 1\ 0\ 0\ 0
\end{array}
\qquad
\begin{array}{rl}
& \boxed{1\ 0}0\ 0 \\
-7 & \quad 1\ 0\ 0\ 1 \\
-2 & +1\ 1\ 1\ 0 \\
\hline
7 & 1_{\,}0\ 1\ 1\ 1
\end{array}
\qquad
\begin{array}{rl}
& \boxed{0\ 0}0\ 0 \\
5 & \quad 0\ 1\ 0\ 1 \\
2 & +0\ 0\ 1\ 0 \\
\hline
7 & \quad 0\ 1\ 1\ 1
\end{array}
\qquad
\begin{array}{rl}
& \boxed{1\ 1}1\ 1 \\
-3 & \quad 1\ 1\ 0\ 1 \\
-5 & +1\ 0\ 1\ 1 \\
\hline
-8 & 1_{\,}1\ 0\ 0\ 0
\end{array}
$$

The carry-ins are shown at the top of each column of bits. In the first calculation, 5 + 3, the carry-in to the high-order bit is 1 while the carry-out is 0. In the second calculation, −7 + −2, once again the carry-in to the final bit is different from the carry-out. In two cases in which overflow does not occur, 5 + 2 and −3 + −5, the carry-in and the carry-out of the final stage are identical.

In general, overflow occurs when the carry-in and carry-out of the sign bit are different.

5.2   Networks for Binary Addition

In this section, we review the half adder and full adder circuits and show how these can be cascaded to form adder circuits over multiple bits. These circuits have no difficulty working with the twos complement number scheme we described in the previous section.

5.2.1   Half Adder/Full Adder

In this subsection, we reexamine the adder structures first introduced in Chapter 1.

Half Adder   The *half adder* is the most primitive of the arithmetic circuits. It has two inputs—the bits to be added—and two outputs—the sum and a carry-out. Figure 5.5 shows the schematic for the half adder.

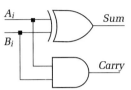

Figure 5.5   Half adder schematic.

Full Adder   If we want to do multibit additions, a half adder isn't enough. When we do addition with pencil and paper, the carry from one column of digits is added to the sum of the column to its left. The same works for binary addition. We form the ith sum from the addition of the ith bits and the carry-out of the $(i-1)$st sum.

The idea is shown in Figure 5.6 for a 4-bit adder. The rightmost "adder slice" can be a half adder, but each of the adders to the left has three inputs: A_i, B_i, and the carry-out of the preceding stage. The best way to construct this multibit adder is to use a single building block that can be cascaded to form an adder of any number of bits: the *full adder*.

The full adder has three inputs—A, B, and CI (carry-in)—and two outputs—S (sum) and CO (carry-out). S is written as

$$S = CI \oplus A \oplus B$$

while CO can be expressed in two-level and multilevel forms as

$$CO = B \bullet CI + A \bullet CI + A \bullet B$$
$$= CI \bullet (A + B) + A \bullet B$$

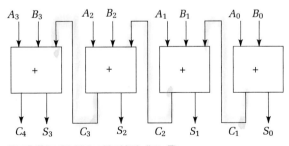

Figure 5.6   Multibit adder block diagram.

The implementation of the full adder suggested by the multilevel expressions is shown in Figure 5.7. This implementation requires six gates.

In Chapter 1, we saw how to implement a full adder in terms of cascaded half adders. In this scheme, we need only five gates for this implementation of the full adder: two for each of the two half adders and one OR gate for the carry-out. This is one fewer than in Figure 5.7. However, with cascaded half adders, the carry output passes through three gate levels: an XOR (first-stage sum), an AND gate (second-stage carry), and a final stage OR gate (final carry). This compares with an OR, AND, OR path in Figure 5.7. Since an OR gate is considerably faster than an XOR gate in most technologies, the multiple half adder implementation is probably slower.

Adder/Subtractor   Figure 5.8 shows the circuit for a 4-bit adder/subtractor constructed from full adder building blocks. Besides the A_i and B_i

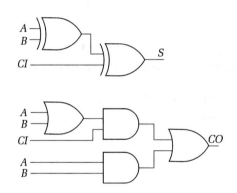

Figure 5.7   Schematic for multilevel full adder implementation.

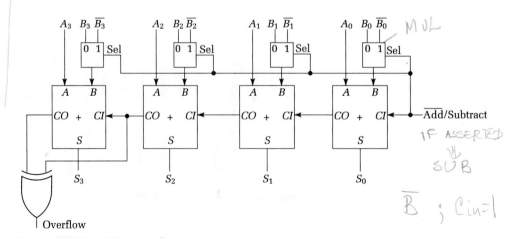

Figure 5.8   A 4-bit adder/subtractor.

inputs, we have introduced a control input $\overline{\text{Add}}$/Subtract. When this signal is 0, the circuit performs addition. When it is 1, the circuit becomes a subtractor.

The $\overline{\text{Add}}$/Subtract input feeds the low-order carry-in and the selection input of four 2:1 multiplexers. When it is asserted, the multiplexers deliver the complements of the B_i inputs to the full adders and set the low-order carry-in to 1. This is exactly the way to form $A + \overline{B} + 1$, the sum of A and the twos complement negation of B.

The circuit includes an XOR gate whose inputs are the carry-in and carry-out of the highest-order (leftmost) adder stage. When these bits differ, an overflow has occurred. We use the XOR to signal that an overflow has taken place.

5.2.2   Carry Lookahead Circuits

Carry lookahead circuits are special logic circuits that can dramatically reduce the time to perform addition. We study them next.

Critical Delay Paths in Adder Circuits   The adder of Figure 5.8 sums the A_i and B_i bits in parallel. But for the S_i outputs to be correct, the adder requires serial propagation of the carry outputs from the rightmost, lowest-order stage to the leftmost, highest-order stage. The "rippling" of the carry from one stage to the next determines the adder's ultimate delay.

Let's analyze the delays in the ripple adder by counting gate delays. We will assume that the adder stages are implemented as in Figure 5.7 and, for simplicity, that all gates have the same delay. At time 0 the inputs A_i, B_i, and C_0 are presented to the adder. Within two gate delays, one delay for each XOR gate, S_0 will be valid.

The carry signal is more complex, and we must examine it on a case-by-case basis. When $A_i = B_i = 1$, the carry is computed in two gate delays and is independent of the carry-in (carry-out will always be 1 in this case). When $A_i = B_i = 0$, the carry is also valid after two gate delays and is still independent of the carry-in (carry-out will always be 0). When $A_i \neq B_i$, the calculation of the carry takes three gate delays (carry-out depends on the carry-in).

This is the base case for the zeroth bit. When adders are cascaded, the critical delay is the time to compute the carry-out after the arrival of a valid carry-in. If the carry-in arrives after N gate delays, the carry-out will be computed by time $N + 2$. This is shown in Figure 5.9(a). The @ notation indicates the number of gate delays before a given signal is valid.

Figure 5.9(b) shows the delays in the cascaded logic for the worst-case addition, $1111_2 + 0001_2$, since each bit sum generates a carry into the next position. With the inputs arriving at time 0, the zeroth-stage sum and carry are generated at time 2. In the first stage, the sum is computed after one delay and the carry-out takes two. The valid carry-out of stage 1 at time 4 generates a valid sum and carry-out at times 5 and 6,

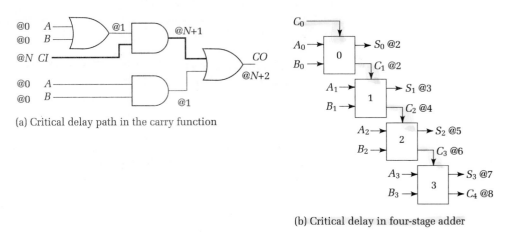

(a) Critical delay path in the carry function

(b) Critical delay in four-stage adder

Figure 5.9   Critical delay paths.

respectively, for the third stage. This leads to a final stage sum and carry at times 7 and 8, respectively.

In general, the sum output from stage i, S_i, will be valid after two gate delays if $i = 0$ and $(2*i + 1)$ if $i > 0$. For $i \geq 0$, the carry-out C_{i+1} will be valid one delay after the sum is valid.

Because this analysis assumes that each stage experiences the worst-case delay, it is often called the *upper bound*. The timing waveforms for the worst case are shown in Figure 5.10. The actual delay depends on the particular pattern of the inputs. For example, for the 4-bit sum $0101_2 + 1010_2$, the output will be valid after only two gate delays, since there are no carries between stages.

Although an eight-gate delay may not seem so bad for a 4-bit adder, the cascaded delays become intolerable for adders of greater widths, such as 32 or 64 bits. An 8-stage adder takes 16 gate delays, a 16-stage

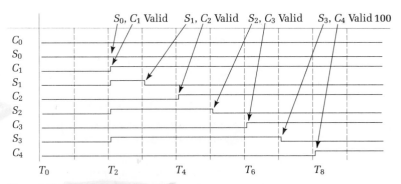

Figure 5.10   Waveforms for 1111 + 0001.

adder 32 gate delays, and a 32-stage adder 64 gate delays (to final stage carry-out) in the worst case. This observation led hardware designers to develop *carry lookahead schemes*. These are ways to calculate the carry inputs in parallel rather than in series. We look at these next.

Carry Lookahead Logic   In the 4-bit "ripple" adder, the carry-out of each stage, C_{i+1}, is expressed as a function of A_i, B_i, and C_i. The basic idea of carry lookahead logic is to express each C_i in terms of A_i, A_{i-1}, ..., A_0, B_i, B_{i-1}, ..., B_0, and C_0 directly. This is a much more complicated Boolean function, but it can always be expressed in two-level logic form. Thus, it should never take more than two gate delays to compute any of the carry outputs.

We begin by introducing two new functions from which we will construct the lookahead carry. These are called *carry generate*, written G_i, and *carry propagate*, written P_i. They are defined as

$$G_i = A_i \bullet B_i \qquad P_i = A_i \oplus B_i$$

In our previous analysis of the carry function, when A_i and B_i are both 1, a carry must be generated, independent of the carry-in. Hence, we call the function "carry generate." If one of A_i and B_i is 1 while the other is 0, then the carry-out will be identical to the carry-in. In other words, when the XOR is true, we pass or "propagate" the carry across the stage.

Interestingly, sum and carry-out can be expressed in terms of the carry generate and carry propagate functions:

$$S_i = A_i \oplus B_i \oplus C_i = P_i \oplus C_i$$

$$C_{i+1} = A_i B_i + A_i C_i + B_i C_i$$
$$= A_i B_i + C_i (A_i + B_i)$$
$$= A_i B_i + C_i (A_i \oplus B_i)$$
$$= G_i + C_i P_i$$

When the carry-out is 1, either the carry is internally generated within the stage (G_i) or the carry-in is 1 (C_i) and it is propagated (P_i) through the stage.

Expressed in terms of carry propagate and generate, we can rewrite the carry-out logic as follows:

$$C_1 = G_0 + P_0 C_0$$
$$C_2 = G_1 + P_1 C_1 = G_1 + P_1 G_0 + P_1 P_0 C_0$$
$$C_3 = G_2 + P_2 C_2 = G_2 + P_2 G_1 + P_2 P_1 G_0 + P_2 P_1 P_0 C_0$$
$$C_4 = G_3 + P_3 C_3 = G_3 + P_3 G_2 + P_3 P_2 G_1 + P_3 P_2 P_1 G_0 + P_3 P_2 P_1 P_0 C_0$$

The ith carry signal is the OR of $i + 1$ product terms, the most complex of which has $i + 1$ literals. This places a practical limit on the number of stages across which the carry lookahead logic can be computed. Four-stage lookahead circuits are commonly available in parts catalogs and cell libraries. Eight-stage lookahead circuits are difficult to find because of the scarcity of nine-input gates.

Implementing Carry Lookahead Logic   Figure 5.11 shows the schematic for an adder stage with propagate and generate outputs. The carry lookahead circuits for a 4-bit adder are given in Figure 5.12. If the inputs to the 0th adder stage are available at time 0, it takes one gate delay to compute the propagate and generate signals and two gate delays to compute the sum. When the P_i and G_i are available, the subsequent carries, C_1, C_2, C_3, and C_4, are computed after two more gate delays (three gate delays total). The sum bits can be computed in just one more gate delay.

The cascaded delay for the 4-bit adder with carry lookahead is shown in Figure 5.13. The final sum bit is available after four gate delays, compared with seven gate delays in the adder without carry lookahead. This analysis assumes that five-input gates have the same delay as two-input gates, which is not usually the case. Based on this simplifying assumption, we have been able to cut the add time in half.

Direct calculation of the carry lookahead logic beyond 4 bits becomes impractical because of the very high fan-ins that would be required. So how would we apply carry lookahead techniques to something like a 16-bit adder?

We take a hierarchical approach. We can implement 16-bit sums with four 4-bit adders, each employing its own internal 4-bit carry lookahead logic. Each 4-bit adder computes its own "group" carry propagate and generate: the group propagate is the AND of P_3, P_2, P_1, P_0, while the group generate is the expression $G_3 + G_2 P_3 + G_1 P_3 P_2 + G_0 P_3 P_2 P_1$.

A second-stage circuit computes the lookaheads and the output carries between first-stage 4-bit adders. The logic is identical to that of Figure 5.12. Figure 5.14 shows the block diagram. The propagate and generate functions are computed from the inputs in just one gate delay. For each 4-bit adder, the group propagate incurs one more delay while

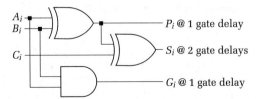

Figure 5.11   Add with propagate and generate.

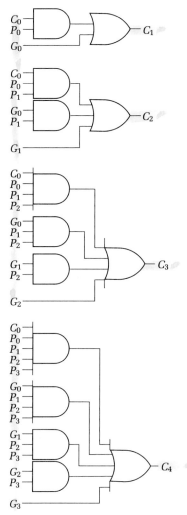

Figure 5.12 Four-bit carry lookahead logic.

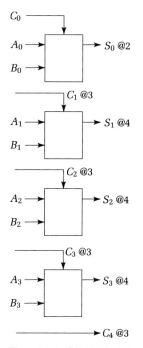

Figure 5.13 Critical delay in four-stage adder with carry lookahead.

the group generate incurs two delays. These signals are presented to the second-level carry lookahead logic at times 2 and 3, respectively.

Once the carry-in to a 4-bit adder is known, the internal carry lookahead logic computes the sums in four more gate delays for the lowest-order stage and three gate delays in the higher-order adder stages. The zeroth stage takes longer because its sums must wait one gate delay for the propagates and generates to be computed in the first place. The other stages overlap the propagate and generate computations with the

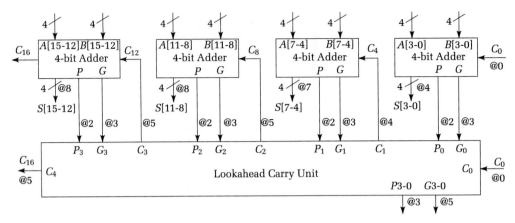

Figure 5.14 Sixteen-bit adder using hierarchical carry lookahead.

carry calculations in the external carry lookahead unit. Given this reasoning, the sums for bits 3 through 0 are valid after four gate delays.

To the external second-level carry lookahead, C_0 arrives at time 0, P_i arrives at time 2, and G_i arrives at time 3. Using the schematics of Figure 5.12, C_4 becomes valid at time 4, while C_8, C_{12}, and C_{16} become valid at time 5. The sums of the second, third, and fourth adder stages are computed in three more gate delays. Thus sum bits 7 through 4 become valid at time 7, while bits 15 through 8 are available at time 8.

So in eight delays we can calculate a 16-bit sum, compared with 32 delays in a simple 16-bit ripple adder. We can generalize the approach for adders spanning any number of inputs. For example, a 64-bit adder can be constructed from sixteen 4-bit adders, four 4-bit carry lookahead units at the second level, and a single 4-bit carry lookahead unit at the third level.

5.2.3   Carry Select Adder

The circuits of the last subsection trade more gates and hardware complexity for a faster method to compute the interstage carries. In this section, we examine the *carry select adder*, an adder organization that introduces redundant hardware to make the carry calculations go even faster.

Figure 5.15 illustrates the concept by showing the organization of an 8-bit carry select adder. The 8-bit adder is split in half. The upper half is implemented by two independent 4-bit adders, one whose carry-in is hardwired to 0 ("adder low"), another whose carry-in is hardwired to 1 ("adder high"). In parallel, these compute two alternative sums for the higher-order bits. The carry-out of the lower-order 4-bit adder controls multiplexers that select between the two alternative sums.

The circuit for C_8 could be a 2:1 multiplexer, but a simpler circuit that reduces the gate count also does the job. In the figure, C_8 is selected

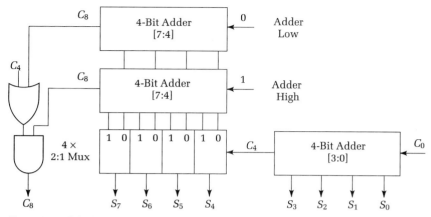

Figure 5.15   Eight-bit carry select adder.

from adder high when C_4 is 1 and is the AND of the carries of adder low and high when C_4 is 0. Adder low can never generate a carry when adder high does not. So either their carry-outs are the same or adder high's carry-out is 1 while adder low's carry-out is 0. By ANDing the two carries, we obtain the correct carry when C_4 is 0.

How long does the carry select adder take? Assuming internal carry lookahead logic is used, the 4-bit adders in Figure 5.15 take four gate delays to compute their sums and three gate delays to compute the stage carry-out. The 2:1 multiplexers add two further gate delays to the path of the high-order sum bits. Thus the 8-bit sum is valid after only six gate delays. This saves one gate delay over the standard two-level carry lookahead implementation for an 8-bit adder.

5.2.4   TTL Adder and Carry Lookahead Components

Adders and carry lookahead components are readily available as standard TTL building blocks.

Adders   The TTL catalog contains several adder components. Representative of these are the 7482 two-bit binary full adder and the 7483 four-bit binary full adder with fast carry. The schematics are shown in Figure 5.16.

The 7482 contains two cascaded stages of full adder circuits with a ripple carry implemented between the stages. The inputs are two sets of 2 bits to be summed, a carry input, two sum outputs, and a carry-output.

The 7483 is a 4-bit adder and contains the full carry lookahead logic within the chip. It has two sets of four input bits, four sum bit outputs, a carry-in, and a carry-out. Because of the effectiveness of the carry lookahead logic, the 4-bit adder is actually faster than the 2-bit adder. The 74183 has two independent single-bit full adders on the same chip.

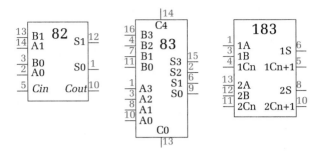

Figure 5.16 TTL adder components.

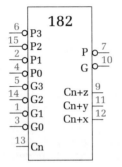

Figure 5.17 Carry lookahead unit.

Carry Lookahead Units The 74182 is a 4-bit carry lookahead unit. Its schematic shape is given in Figure 5.17. The '182 component has four generate inputs (active low), four propagate inputs (active low), and carry-in (C_n). Its outputs are the three intermediate carries, C_{n+x}, C_{n+y}, C_{n+z}, as well as group P and G (both active low). The latter two outputs make it possible to build multilevel carry lookahead networks. The '182 component is specially designed to work with the 74181 arithmetic logic unit, to be introduced in the next section.

5.3 Arithmetic Logic Unit Design

An arithmetic logic unit, or ALU (sometimes pronounced "Al Loo"), is a combinational network that implements a function of its inputs based on either logic or arithmetic operations. ALUs are at the heart of all computers as well as most digital hardware systems. In this section, we learn how to design these very important digital subsystems.

5.3.1 A Sample ALU

An n-bit ALU typically has two input words, denoted by $A = A_{n-1}, ..., A_0$ and $B = B_{n-1}, ..., B_0$. The output word is denoted by $F = F_n, F_{n-1}, ..., F_0$, where the high-order output bit, F_n, is actually the carry-out. In addition, there is a carry-in input C_0.

Besides data inputs and outputs, an ALU must have control inputs to specify the operations to be performed. One input is M, a mode selector. When $M = 0$, the operation is a logic function; when $M = 1$, an arithmetic operation is indicated. In addition, there are operation selection inputs, S_i, which determine the particular logic or arithmetic function to be performed.

To make the discussion more concrete, Figure 5.18 contains the specification of a simple ALU *bit slice*, that is, the behavior of a single bit of the ALU. The list of operations is partitioned into three sections:

M → Mode Select

M = 0 → Logic Op.

M = 1 → Arith. op.

M = 0, Logic Bitwise Operations

S_1	S_0	Function	Comment
0	0	$F_i = A_i$	Input A_i transferred to output
0	1	$F_i = $ not A_i	Complement of A_i transferred to output
1	0	$F_i = A_i$ XOR B_i	Compute XOR of A_i, B_i
1	1	$F_i = A_i$ XNOR B_i	Compute XNOR of A_i, B_i

M = 1, $C_0 = 0$, Arithmetic Operations

0	0	$F = A$	Input A passed to output
0	1	$F = $ not A	Complement of A passed to output
1	0	$F = A$ plus B	Sum of A and B
1	1	$F = $ (not A) plus B	Sum of B and complement of A

M = 1, $C_0 = 1$, Arithmetic Operations

0	0	$F = A$ plus 1	Increment A
0	1	$F = $ (not A) plus 1	Twos complement of A
1	0	$F = A$ plus B plus 1	Increment sum of A and B
1	1	$F = $ (not A) plus B plus 1	B minus A

Figure 5.18 Tabular specification of an ALU.

logic operations, arithmetic operations where the carry-in is 0, and arithmetic operations where the carry-in is 1. Some of the operations do not appear to be useful, such as the sum of B and the ones complement of A. However, if we set carry-in to 1, we obtain a very useful operation indeed: B minus A (B plus the twos complement of A).

Implementation of an ALU ALUs are relatively simple to implement: design a 1-bit slice and cascade as many of these as you need to build a multibit structure. Of course, the limiting performance factor will be the propagation of carries among the ALU stages.

Using the specification of Figure 5.18, a single bit slice has six inputs, A_i, B_i, C_i, M, S_1, and S_0, and two outputs, F_i and C_{i+1}. This may appear daunting, but the truth table shows a relatively simple structure with many don't cares (see Figure 5.19).

We can use *espresso* to find an optimized two-level implementation. Figure 5.20 shows the reduced truth table it produces. This result is still complicated. The F_i output requires 18 product terms. A PLA-based design is feasible, but a design based on discrete gates is probably too complex even to consider.

MisII does a bit better. *MisII*'s output on the *espresso* truth table is shown in Figure 5.21. The circuit it derives appears in Figure 5.22. It requires 12 gates plus 5 inverters, which are not shown in the schematic.

The schematic in Figure 5.23 offers an alternative multilevel implementation for the ALU. We obtained it by hand after a careful evaluation of how operations are encoded by the M and selection inputs. This implementation is based on the observation that when S_1 is 0, B_i is blocked from affecting the outputs by gate $A1$. This happens whenever the operation deals only

M	S_1	S_0	C_i	A_i	B_i	F_i	C_i+1
0	0	0	X	0	X	0	X
			X	1	X	1	X
	0	1	X	0	X	1	X
			X	1	X	0	X
	1	0	X	0	0	0	X
			X	0	1	1	X
			X	1	0	1	X
			X	1	1	0	X
	1	1	X	0	0	1	X
			X	0	1	0	X
			X	1	0	0	X
			X	1	1	1	X
1	0	0	0	0	X	0	X
			0	1	X	1	X
	0	1	0	0	X	1	X
			0	1	X	0	X
	1	0	0	0	0	0	0
			0	0	1	1	0
			0	1	0	1	0
			0	1	1	0	1
	1	1	0	0	0	1	0
			0	0	1	0	1
			0	1	0	0	0
			0	1	1	1	0
1	0	0	1	0	X	1	0
			1	1	X	0	1
	0	1	1	0	X	0	1
			1	1	X	1	0
	1	0	1	0	0	1	0
			1	0	1	0	1
			1	1	0	0	1
			1	1	1	1	1
	1	1	1	0	0	0	1
			1	0	1	1	1
			1	1	0	1	0
			1	1	1	0	1

Figure 5.19 ALU truth table.

```
.i 6
.o 2
.ilb m s1 s0 ci ai bi
.ob fi co
.p 23
111101 10
110111 10
1-0100 10
1-1110 10
10010- 10
10111- 10
-10001 10
010-01 10
-11011 10
011-11 10
--1000 10
0-1-00 10
--0010 10
0-0-10 10
-0100- 10
001-0- 10
-0001- 10
000-1- 10
-1-1-1 01
--1-01 01
--0-11 01
--110- 01
--011- 01
.e
```

Figure 5.20 *Espresso* output for the ALU design example.

with A_i. The same is true for C_i when M is 0 (gate $A2$). These are exactly the nonarithmetic operations.

Addition is indicated whenever $M = 1$. In these cases, B_i (assuming $S_1 = 1$) and C_i are passed to the inputs of the XOR gates X3 and X2. When S_0 is 0, the topmost XOR gate, X1, simply passes A_i. When S_0 is 1, it passes A_i's complement. Thus, the three cascaded XOR gates form a proper sum of A_i or its complement, B_i (or 0 if $S_1 = 0$), and C_i whenever the ALU is in its arithmetic mode.

How about the carry output? When the ALU is in the arithmetic mode, the output of gate O1 is the function $A_i \bullet C_i + B_i(A_i \oplus C_i)$. The first product term is formed from gate $A3$, the second from $A4$. This is a valid form of the carry. If $S_1 = 0$, we simply replace B_i by 0 in this expression to obtain the correct carry function.

```
.model alu.espresso
.inputs m s1 s0 ci ai bi
.outputs fi co
.names m ci co [30] [33] [35] fi
110--- 1
-1-11- 1
--01-1 1
--00-0 1
.names m ci [30] [33] co
-1-1 1
--11 1
111- 1
.names s0 ai [30]
01 1
10 1
.names m s1 bi [33]
111 1
.names s1 bi [35]
0- 1
-0 1
.end
```

Figure 5.21   *MisII* output for the ALU design example.

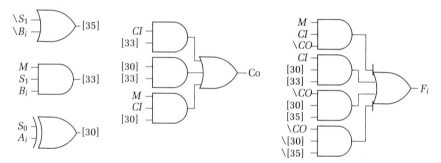

Figure 5.22   Multilevel schematic derived by *misII*.

When the ALU is in the logic mode, $M = 0$, we can concentrate on the cascaded XOR gates. When S_0 and S_1 are both 0, A_i is passed through to the output. If S_0 is 1 while S_1 is 0, the complement of A_i is passed. When S_0 is 0 while S_1 is 1, the inputs to X3 are A_i and B_i, and their XOR is computed. In the last case, $S_0 = 1$, $S_1 = 1$, the inputs to X3 are $\overline{A}_i$ and B_i. This function is equivalent to the XNOR function. The circuit does the right thing!

A careful hand design can sometimes do better than a sophisticated CAD tool. *MisII* did not come up with this schematic, in part because of its inability to exploit don't-care conditions or to use XOR functions effectively.

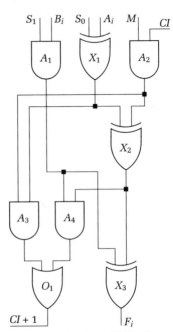

Figure 5.23 Multilevel ALU bit slice.

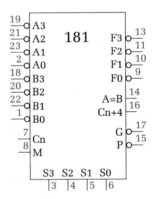

Figure 5.24 ALU schematic shape.

5.3.2 TTL ALU Components

The most widely used ALU in TTL designs is the 74181. Its schematic shape is shown in Figure 5.24. The '181 has two groups of 4-bit data inputs, a carry-in (C_n), a single 4-bit data output, and a carry-out (C_{n+4}). Many of the inputs and outputs are active low.

The component also has four function select bits, S_3, S_2, S_1, S_0, and a mode bit M. This allows the ALU to compute 32 different functions of its inputs. The component can also be used as a comparator, and it has an open-collector $A = B$ output for easy cascading across multiple stages.

Figure 5.25 shows the function table for the device, assuming negative logic data inputs and outputs. The ALU implements the logic functions NAND, NOR, AND, OR, XOR, and XNOR, as well as arithmetic plus and minus. The chip contains internal logic that implements a 4-bit carry lookahead. It outputs group generate and propagate signals, making it possible to cascade ALU stages and carry lookahead units to construct arithmetic units of larger bit widths.

Quite a few of the functions implemented by the 74181 are unlikely to be used in practice. After all, what does AB plus A implement? These are in the function table because they fall out of the internal implementation of the more interesting functions of the ALU.

The 74181 can also be used with positive logic inputs and outputs. The function table is the same, but the carry-in and out are complemented to maintain the proper sense of the function. In other words, to select the first column of arithmetic functions in positive logic, the carry-in, $\overline{C_n}$, must be set to 1. Similarly, the second column of arithmetic functions is selected when $\overline{C_n}$ is set to 0.

Figure 5.26 shows how to use a carry lookahead unit in conjunction with the 74181 to construct a 16-bit ALU. The figure assumes that the ALUs and the carry lookahead unit are being used in negative logic mode (C_N, C_{N+1} are active high, G and P are active low). As long as the sense of the carries is maintained, this interconnection scheme works whether the ALU is being used in negative or positive logic modes.

5.4 BCD Addition

BCD, or *binary-coded decimal*, represents the 10 decimal digits in terms of binary numbers. It is possible to build digital hardware that manipulates BCD directly, and such hardware could be found in early computers and many hand-held calculators. The BCD system was chosen for the internal number system in these machines because it is easy to convert it to alphanumeric representations for printouts and displays. The compelling advantages of BCD have waned over time, and these digits are supported by more modern hardware simply to provide backward compatibility with earlier generations of machines. In this

Selection				$M = 1$	$M = 0$, Arithmetic Functions	
S_3	S_2	S_1	S_0	Logic Function	$C_n = 0$	$C_n = 1$
0	0	0	0	$F = $ not A	$F = A$ minus 1	$F = A$
0	0	0	1	$F = A$ nand B	$F = A B$ minus 1	$F = A B$
0	0	1	0	$F = ($not $A) + B$	$F = A$ (not B) minus 1	$F = A$ (not B)
0	0	1	1	$F = 1$	$F = $ minus 1	$F = $ zero
0	1	0	0	$F = A$ nor B	$F = A$ plus $(A + $ not $B)$	$F = A$ plus $(A + $ not $B)$ plus 1
0	1	0	1	$F = $ not B	$F = A B$ plus $(A + $ not $B)$	$F = A B$ plus $(A + $ not $B)$ plus 1
0	1	1	0	$F = A$ xnor B	$F = A$ minus B minus 1	$F = (A + $ not $B)$ plus 1
0	1	1	1	$F = A + $ not B	$F = A + $ not B	$F = A$ minus B
1	0	0	0	$F = ($not $A) B$	$F = A$ plus $(A + B)$	$F = A$ plus $(A + B)$ plus 1
1	0	0	1	$F = A$ xor B	$F = A$ plus B	$F = A$ plus B plus 1
1	0	1	0	$F = B$	$F = A$ (not B) plus $(A + B)$	$F = A$ (not B) plus $(A + B)$ plus 1
1	0	1	1	$F = A + B$	$F = (A + B)$	$F = (A + B)$ plus 1
1	1	0	0	$F = 0$	$F = A$	$F = A$ plus 1
1	1	0	1	$F = A$ (not B)	$F = A B$ plus A	$F = AB$ plus A plus 1
1	1	1	0	$F = A B$	$F = A$ (not B) plus A	$F = A$ (not B) plus A plus 1
1	1	1	1	$F = A$	$F = A$	$F = A$ plus 1

Figure 5.25 74181 ALU truth table.

section, we briefly examine the approaches for constructing BCD arithmetic elements.

5.4.1   BCD Number Representation

We have met BCD representation in the previous chapters. The decimal digits 0 through 9 are represented by the 4-bit binary strings 0000 through 1001. The remaining 4-bit encodings, 1010_2 through 1111_2, are treated as don't cares.

Just as in conventional decimal addition, BCD addition is performed one decimal digit at a time. The question is, what happens when the sum exceeds what can be represented in 4 bits? Stated differently, what are the conditions under which a carry is generated to the next highest-order BCD digit?

For example, let's consider the addition of the two BCD digits 5 and 3:

$$
\begin{array}{rl}
5 = & 0101 \\
3 = & \underline{0011} \\
& 1000 = 8
\end{array}
$$

Now consider the sum of 5 and 8:

$$
\begin{array}{rl}
5 = & 0101 \\
8 = & \underline{1000} \\
& 1101 = 13!
\end{array}
$$

The sum is $1101_2 = 13$, but this result should be correctly represented as 0001 0011 in BCD notation. Fortunately, there is a simple way to find

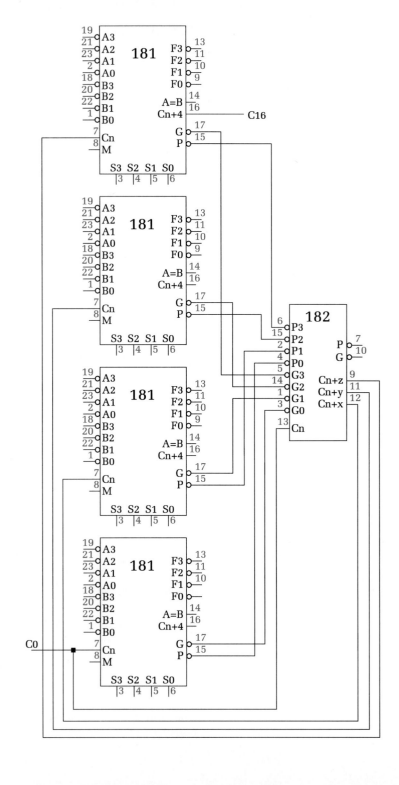

Figure 5.26 Sixteen-bit adder with carry lookahead.

the correct result. We add 6 (0110_2) to the digit sum if it exceeds 9. Let's examine the following cases:

$$5 = \quad 0101$$
$$8 = \quad \underline{1000}$$
$$\qquad 1101 = 13 \text{ in decimal}$$
$$\qquad \underline{+\ 0110}$$
$$1\,0011 = 1\ 3 \text{ in BCD}$$

$$9 = \quad 1001$$
$$7 = \quad \underline{0111}$$
$$1\ 0000 = 16 \text{ in decimal}$$
$$\underline{+\ 0110}$$
$$1\,0110 = 1\ 6 \text{ in BCD}$$

In both cases, by adding six we obtain the correct answer in BCD. This observation is critical to the design of a BCD adder, as we shall see in the next subsection.

5.4.2 BCD Adder Design

Figure 5.27 gives a block diagram implementation for a BCD adder. The first row of full adders implements a conventional 4-bit binary adder. The second row provides the capability to add 0110_2 when the sum obtained by the first row exceeds 9 (1001_2).

Here is how it works. The adders of the second row add the carry-out bit to the sum bits S_2 and S_1. Carry-out should be asserted in cases in which we need to add the correction factor. What are these cases?

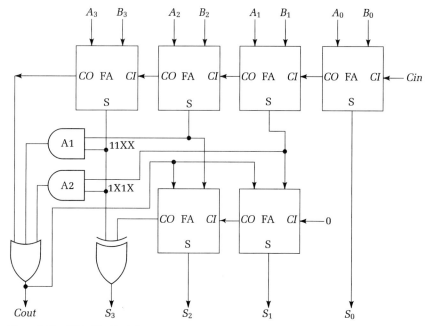

Figure 5.27 BCD adder block diagram.

The AND gates labeled A_1 and A_2 detect the conditions under which the first-level sum matches the patterns $11XX_2$ and $1X1X_2$. These are exactly the cases in which this sum exceeds 9. When carry-out is asserted, the XOR gate and the adders in the second row effectively add 0110_2 to the first row's sum.

There is one further case to consider. The correction factor should also be applied whenever the first-row sum exceeds 15. We saw such an example with the sum of 9 and 7 above. This case is easy to detect: the carry-out of the first-row adders will be asserted.

Thus the sum exceeds 9 if either the first-row carry-out is asserted, or the sum matches the pattern $11XX_2$, or the sum matches the pattern $1X1X_2$. These are precisely the inputs to the OR gate that computes the BCD carry-out.

A BCD adder requires over 50% more hardware than a comparable binary adder. Since faster binary adders are now available, it is no surprise that they have replaced BCD adders in almost all applications.

5.5 Combinational Multiplier

In this section we look at the design of multiplier circuitry. The methods we introduce are combinational, although alternative methods based on circuits with state are also possible. However, the fastest circuits for multiplication use just the techniques we will be discussing here.

Basic Concept Throughout this section, we will look only at multiplication techniques for unsigned numbers. Alternatively, the hardware we present is suitable for sign and magnitude multiplication, but we concentrate on the manipulation of the magnitude part. Recall that the two numbers involved in a multiplication are called the *multiplicand* and the *multiplier*.

The process of binary multiplication is best illustrated with an example. In this case, the multiplicand is 1101_2 (13) and the multiplier is 1011_2 (11):

$$
\begin{array}{lrl}
\text{multiplicand} & 1101 & (13) \\
\text{multiplier} & * \ 1011 & (11) \\
\hline
 & 1101 & \\
 & 1101 & \\
 & 0000 & \\
 & 1101 & \\
\hline
 & 10001111 & (143)
\end{array}
$$

$$128 + 8 + 4 + 2 + 1 = 143$$

Each bit of the multiplier is multiplied against the multiplicand, the product is aligned according to the position of the bit within the multiplier, and the resulting products are then summed to form the final result. One attraction of binary multiplication is how easy it is to form these intermediate products: if the multiplier bit is a 1, the product is an appropriately shifted copy of the multiplicand; if the multiplier bit is a 0, the product is simply 0.

For an n-bit multiplicand and multiplier, the resulting product will be $2n$ bits. Stated differently, the product of 2^n and 2^n is $2^{n+n} = 2^{2n}$, a $2n$-bit number. Thus, the product of two 4-bit numbers requires 8 bits, of two 8-bit numbers requires 16 bits, and so on.

Partial Product Accumulation We can construct a combinational circuit that directly implements the process described by the preceding example. The method is called *partial product accumulation*.

First, we rewrite the multiplicand bits as A_3, A_2, A_1, A_0 and the multiplier bits as B_3, B_2, B_1, B_0. The multiplication of A and B becomes

$$
\begin{array}{ccccccc}
 & & A_3 & A_2 & A_1 & A_0 \\
 & & B_3 & B_2 & B_1 & B_0 \\
\hline
 & & A_3 \bullet B_0 & A_2 \bullet B_0 & A_1 \bullet B_0 & A_0 \bullet B_0 \\
 & A_3 \bullet B_1 & A_2 \bullet B_1 & A_1 \bullet B_1 & A_0 \bullet B_1 \\
 A_3 \bullet B_2 & A_2 \bullet B_2 & A_1 \bullet B_2 & A_0 \bullet B_2 \\
A_3 \bullet B_3 & A_2 \bullet B_3 & A_1 \bullet B_3 & A_0 \bullet B_3 \\
\hline
S_6 & S_5 & S_4 & S_3 & S_2 & S_1 & S_0 \\
\end{array}
$$

Each of the ANDed terms is called a *partial product*. The resulting product is formed by accumulating down the columns of partial products, propagating the carries from the rightmost columns to the left.

A combinational circuit for implementing the 4-bit multiplier is shown in Figure 5.28. The first level of 16 AND gates computes the individual partial products. The second- and third-level logic blocks form the accumulation of the products on a column-by-column basis. The column sums are formed by a mixture of cascaded half adders and full adders.

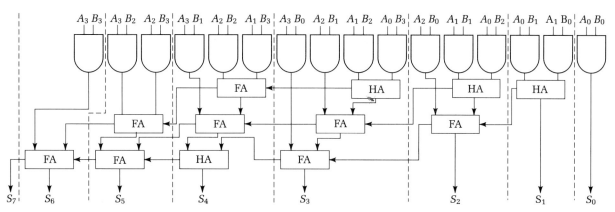

Figure 5.28 4 × 4 combinational adder.

In the figure, inputs from the top are the bits to be added and the input from the right is the carry-in. The output from the bottom is the sum and to the left is the carry-out.

To see how the partial products are accumulated, let's look at the circuit of Figure 5.28 in a little more detail. S_1 is the straightforward sum of just two partial products, $A_1 \bullet B_0$ and $A_0 \bullet B_1$. S_2 is the sum of three products. We implement this with two cascaded adders, one of which takes the carry-out from S_1's column.

S_3 is a little more complicated, because there are two different carry-outs from the previous column. We use three cascaded adders, two full adders and one half adder, to implement the sum. The two carry-outs from S_2 are accumulated through the carry-in inputs of the two full adders.

S_4 is the sum of three products and three possible carry-outs from S_3. The carries make this case more complicated than the S_2 sum. The solution is to implement the sum with three adders—two full adders and one half adder. The two full adders sum the three products and two of the carry-outs. The half adder adds to this result the third possible carry-in.

The logic for S_5 is similar. Here we must sum two products and three carries. Two full adders do the job. Note that the second full adder sums two of the three carries from the previous column with the result of the first full adder. A similar analysis applies to S_7 and S_6.

The delay through the multiplier is determined by the ripple carries between the adders. We can use a carry lookahead scheme to reduce these delays.

Clearly, the full combinational multiplier uses a lot of hardware. The dominating costs are the adders—four half adders and eight full adders. To simplify the implementation slightly, a designer may choose to use full adders for all of the adder blocks, setting the carry input to 0 where the half adder function is required. Given the full adder schematic of Figure 5.7, this is 12 adders of six gates each, for a total of 72 gates. When we add to this the 16 gates forming the partial products, the total for the whole circuit is 88 gates. It is easy to see that combinational multipliers can be justified only for the most high performance of applications.

A slightly different implementation of the 4-by-4 combinational multiplier is shown in Figure 5.29. Figure 5.29(a) gives the basic building block, a full adder circuit that sums a locally computed partial product ($X \bullet Y$), an input passed into the block from above *(Sum In)*, and a carry passed from a block diagonally above. It generates a carry-out *(Cout)* and a new sum *(Sum Out)*. Figure 5.29(b) shows the interconnection of 16 of these blocks to implement the full multiplier function. The A_i values are distributed along block diagonals and the B_i values are passed along rows. This implementation uses the same gate count as the previous one: 16 AND gates and 12 adders (the top row does not need adders).

TTL Multiplier Components   The TTL components 74284 and 74285 provide a two-chip implementation of a 4-by-4 parallel binary multiplier. Figure 5.30 illustrates their use. The 74284 component implements the

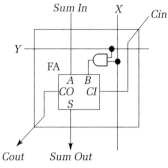

(a) Basic building block

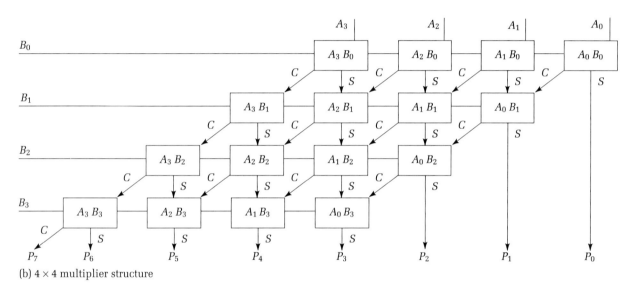

(b) 4×4 multiplier structure

Figure 5.29 4×4 combinational multiplier.

high-order 4 bits of the product, while the 74285 implements the low-order bits. Both chips have dual active low output enable signals, $\overline{G_A}$ and $\overline{G_B}$. When both enables are 0, the outputs are valid. Otherwise, they are in the high-impedance state.

Case Study   5.6   **An 8-by-8 Bit Multiplier**

In this section, we will see how to apply the principles and components of arithmetic circuits to implement a subsystem of moderate complexity. Our objective is to design a fast 8-by-8 bit multiplier using 4-by-4 bit multipliers as building blocks, along with adders, arithmetic logic, and carry lookahead units.

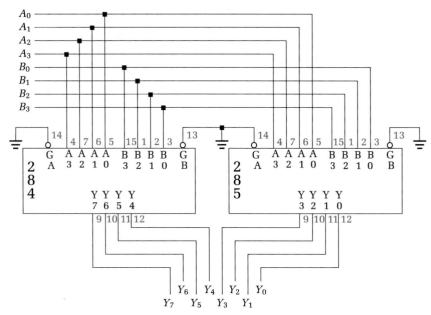

Figure 5.30 TTL two-chip multiplier.

5.6.1 Theory of Operation

In the last section, we saw how to express an 8-bit product as a series of sums of 1-bit products, so-called *partial product accumulation*. We can exploit the same principle to construct multipliers of wider bit widths using primitive 4-by-4 multiplier blocks.

First, we denote the two 8-bit magnitudes to be multiplied as A_{7-0} and B_{7-0} and the 16-bit product that results as P_{15-0}. We can partition A and B into two 4-bit groups, A_{7-4}, A_{3-0}, B_{7-4}, B_{3-0}, and form their 16-bit product as a sum of several 8-bit products:

$$
\begin{array}{rrrr}
 & & A_{7-4} & A_{3-0} \\
 & * & B_{7-4} & B_{3-0} \\
\hline
 & & A_{3-0} * B_{3-0} & = PP_0 \\
 & A_{7-4} * B_{3-0} & & = PP_1 \\
 & A_{3-0} * B_{7-4} & & = PP_2 \\
 A_{7-4} * B_{7-4} & & & = PP_3 \\
\hline
 P_{15-12} & P_{11-8} & P_{7-4} & P_{3-0}
\end{array}
$$

To see how this works, let's examine the multiplication of the 8-bit binary numbers 11110010_2 and 10001100_2. These correspond to the decimal numbers 242 and 140, respectively.

$$
\begin{array}{r}
1111\ 0010 \\
*\ \ 1000\ 1100 \\
\hline
0001\ 1000 \\
1011\ 0100 \\
0001\ 0000 \\
0111\ 1000 \\
\hline
1000\ 0100\ 0101\ 1000
\end{array}
$$

$= 0010 * 1100$
$= 1111 * 1100$
$= 0010 * 1000$
$= 1111 * 1000$

As a check, we see that $242 * 140 = 33880$, which is equal to 1000010001011000_2. (See Appendix A to review base conversions.)

The hardware implementation follows directly from this observation. It requires four 4-by-4 multipliers, implemented as in Figure 5.31, plus logic to sum the four-bit wide slices of the partial products.

Let's call the four 8-bit partial products PP0, PP1, PP2, and PP3. Then the final product bits are computed as follows:

$$P_{3\text{-}0} = \text{PP0}_{3\text{-}0}$$

$$P_{7\text{-}4} = \text{PP0}_{7\text{-}4} + \text{PP1}_{3\text{-}0} + \text{PP2}_{3\text{-}0}$$

$$P_{11\text{-}8} = \text{PP1}_{7\text{-}4} + \text{PP2}_{7\text{-}4} + \text{PP3}_{3\text{-}0}$$

$$P_{15\text{-}12} = \text{PP3}_{7\text{-}4}$$

Of course, any carry-out of the calculation of $P_{7\text{-}4}$ must be added to the sum for $P_{11\text{-}8}$, and likewise for the carry-out of $P_{11\text{-}8}$ to $P_{15\text{-}12}$.

5.6.2   Implementation

The basic blocks of the implementation are (1) the calculation of partial products, (2) the summing of the 4-bit product slices, and (3) the carry lookahead unit. We examine each of these in turn.

Calculation of Partial Products   Each of the 8-bit partial products is implemented by a 74284/74285 pair. The subsystem has 16 inputs, the multiplicand and multiplier, and 32 outputs, constituting the four 8-bit partial products. The partial product subsystem is shown in Figure 5.31.

Calculation of Sums   The low-order 4 bits of the final product, $P_{3\text{-}0}$, are the same as PP0$_{3\text{-}0}$ and do not participate in the sums. $P_{7\text{-}4}$ and $P_{11\text{-}8}$ are sums of three 4-bit quantities. How do we compute these?

Figure 5.32 shows a way to cascade full adders to implement a function that sums three 4-bit quantities, denoted $A_{3\text{-}0}$, $B_{3\text{-}0}$, and $C_{3\text{-}0}$. (Watch that you don't confuse the variable C_i with adder carry-ins.) The first level of full adders sums 1 bit from each of the three numbers to be added. We accomplish this by using the carry input as a data input. The second-level adders combine the carry-out from the next lower order stage with the sum

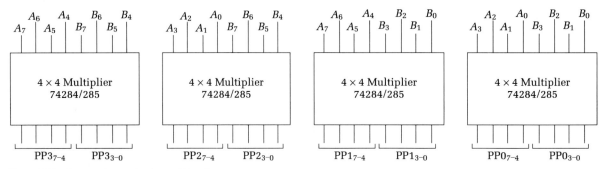

Figure 5.31 Computation section for partial products.

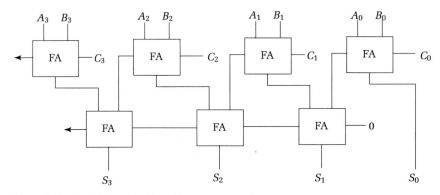

Figure 5.32 Four-bit three-at-a-time adder.

from the first-level adder. The carries simply propagate from right to left among the second-level adders. This is just like the carry propagations we needed in the 4-by-4 multiplier of Figure 5.28.

Figure 5.33 shows how the logic of Figure 5.32 can be implemented with TTL components. The first-level full adders are provided by 74183 dual binary adders. The second-level adders are implemented by a 74181 arithmetic logic unit, configured for the adder function. This has the extra performance advantage of internal carry lookahead logic. Note that the ALU block is written in its positive logic form, with positive logic data inputs and outputs and negative logic carry-in and carry-out.

Figure 5.33 provides the basic building block we can use to implement bit slices P_{7-4} and P_{11-8} for the result products. This is shown in Figure 5.34. The rightmost 74181 component and its two associated 74183s implement bit slice P_{7-4}. The logic is cascaded with an identical block of components to implement bit slice P_{11-8}.

Figure 5.34 also includes the implementation of slice P_{15-12}. The final slice is formed from the partial product $PP3_{7-4}$, plus any carry-outs from lower-order sums. We implement this using a 74181 component configured

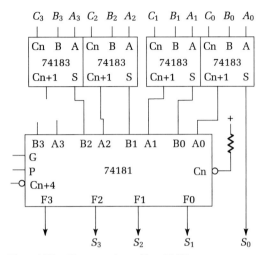

Figure 5.33 Three-at-a-time adder with TTL components.

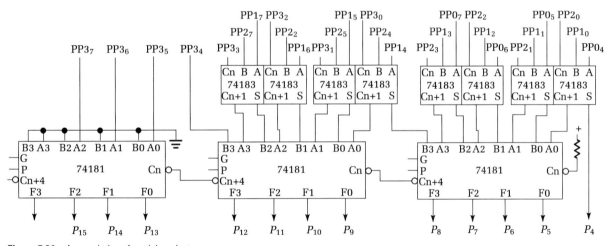

Figure 5.34 Accumulation of partial products.

as an adder, with the B data inputs set to 0, the A inputs set to the partial product, and the carry-in coming from the adjacent adder block.

Putting the Pieces Together The last step in the design combines the multiplier block with the accumulation block. To further improve the performance, the carries between the 74181s can be replaced with a 74182 carry lookahead unit.

This is shown in Figure 5.35. The generate/propagate outputs of the three 74181s are wired to the corresponding inputs of the 74182 carry lookahead unit. The component is drawn with positive logic generate

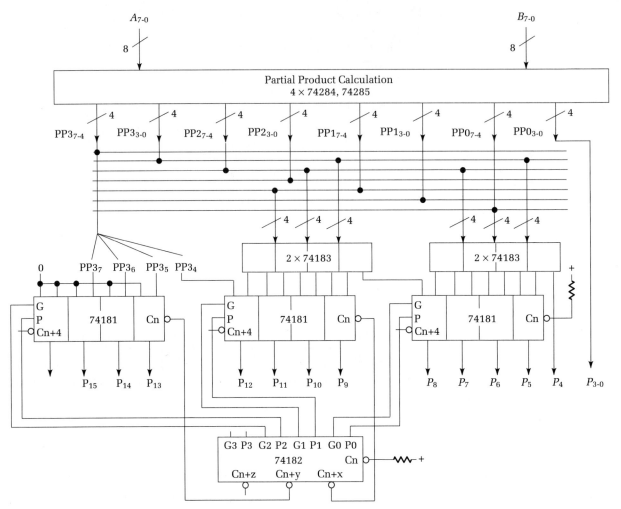

Figure 5.35 Complete 8 × 8 multiplier system.

and propagate inputs and negative logic carries. This matches the notation used for the ALUs. The C_n input is wired high, matching the carry-in to the lowest order 74181. The generated C_{n+x} and C_{n+y} carries are routed to the carry-in of the middle and high-order 74181s, respectively.

Package Count and Performance In terms of package count, the complete implementation uses four 74284/74285 multipliers (eight packages), four 74183 full adder packages, three 74181 arithmetic logic units, and one 74182 carry lookahead unit. This is a total of 16 packages.

A circuit this complex is far too complicated to analyze by simply counting gate delays. We start by identifying the *critical delay path*.

This is the sequence of propagated signals that limits the performance of the circuit. Once we have determined the critical path, the TTL catalog will provide us with signal delays associated with the individual packages in our implementation.

The first step in the critical path is the calculation of the partial products by the 74284/285 multipliers. Assuming standard TTL components, the typical delay from the arrival of the inputs to valid outputs is 40 ns (60 ns maximum).

The next step in the critical path is the formation of the intermediate sums by the 74183s. We assume LS TTL for these packages. Since the typical adder delay is sensitive to the final value of the sum output, 9 ns for a low-to-high transition and 20 ns for a high-to-low output transition, it is reasonable to average these to get 15 ns. For worst-case delay, we should use the worst-case maximum, which is 33 ns.

The final leg of the critical path is the calculation of the second-stage sums using the carry lookaheads. This consists of three pieces: (1) calculation of the group propagates/generates in the 74181s, (2) calculations of the carry-outs by the 74182 after the propagates and generates become valid, and (3) calculation of the final sums in the 74181s once the carries are valid.

We assume LS TTL for the 74181 and standard TTL for the 74182. For the 74LS181, from inputs valid to group propagate/generate valid takes 20 ns typical (30 ns maximum). In this case, the propagate is slightly slower than the generate, so this is the signal that really determines the delay.

Using a standard TTL 74182, the delay from group propagate/generate in to valid carry-outs is 13 ns typical, 22 ns worst case. Returning to the 74LS181, the last piece of the critical path is the delay from carry-in valid to sums valid. This is 15 ns typical, 26 ns worst case.

So the typical delay is 40 (multipliers) + 15 (full adders) + 20 (generate/propagate) + 13 (carry-outs) + 15 (sums) = 103 ns. The worst-case delay is 60 + 33 + 30 + 22 + 26 = 171 ns. There is a significant difference between the worst case and the typical performance. Also, the delay can be significantly reduced by using a faster TTL family, such as S or AS logic.

Chapter Review

In this chapter, we have examined the basic representations of numbers within digital systems and the primitive circuits for their arithmetic manipulation. In all digital systems, positive integers are represented in the same way. The difference is in how negative numbers and zero are represented. The primary representation schemes are (1) sign and magnitude, (2) ones complement, and (3) twos complement. Twos complement is the most pervasively used representation, because of the single representation for zero and the ease with which a binary adder can be used to implement both addition and subtraction operations. The latter is accomplished simply by adding the twos complement of the number to be subtracted.

Digital systems that implement multiplication (and division) hardware also need to support the sign and magnitude representation. All of the circuits we have shown for multiplication are based on number magnitudes. This means that a system that uses twos complement for addition/subtraction and sign and magnitude for multiplication and division must provide additional circuitry to convert between the forms and handle the sign correctly.

A half or full adder will be found at the center of all arithmetic circuits. The full adder can be constructed from cascaded half adders. Multibit adders are constructed from cascaded full adders. Since the performance of such adders is limited by the serial "rippling" of the carry from one adder stage to the next, designers have developed parallel carry lookahead circuits for fast adders. This is a very good example of the trade-off between hardware and speed. The ripple adder is much slower than the lookahead adder, but the latter achieves its high speed at the expense of many more gates.

Adders for binary-coded decimal numbers are built from cascaded full adders. They look much like conventional binary adders, with extra circuitry to correct the sum of two BCD digits when it exceeds nine. A 4-bit BCD adder needs six full adders.

Multipliers are also formed by combining cascaded full and half adders. We saw how to construct a 4-by-4 bit multiplier using 12 full adders. We also looked at ways to use the 4-by-4 multiplier as a fundamental building block, in conjunction with even more adders, to build multipliers of larger bit widths. The 8-by-8 multiplier we designed used a considerable amount of logic, but much less than if we had built the multiplier directly rather than using 4-by-4 multiplier building blocks.

The arithmetic logic unit, or ALU, is an ubiquitous circuit component that implements both logic and arithmetic operations over data inputs. ALUs can be found embedded in just about every digital system that manipulates numbers. Any of the design strategies covered in Chapters 2 through 4 can be used to implement ALUs, including two-level, multilevel, and even ROM-based approaches.

Further Reading

Elements of this chapter were drawn from several previous logic design textbooks, primarily C. H. Roth's *Fundamentals of Logic Design*, West, St. Paul, 1985, and Johnson and Karim's *Digital Design: A Pragmatic Approach*, PWS, Boston, 1987. The 8-by-8 bit multiplier case study is based on the application note associated with the 74284/285 data sheet in the Texas Instruments' *TTL Data Book,* Volume 2, 1985.

Computer arithmetic is a complex topic worthy of its own advanced course. There are several comprehensive textbooks on the underlying mathematics of number systems and the hardware to implement arithmetic operations over them. K. Hwang's *Computer Arithmetic*, Wiley, New York, 1979 is one of the best known.

Exercises

5.1   *(Sign and Magnitude Numbers)* Perform the following binary additions assuming the numbers are in sign and magnitude form:

   a. 0001 + 0100

   b. 1111 + 0010

   c. 0011 + 1010

   d. 1011 + 1010

5.2   *(Ones Complement Numbers)* Perform the same binary additions as in Exercise 5.1, but this time assuming the numbers are in ones complement form.

5.3   *(Twos Complement Numbers)* Perform the same binary additions as in Exercise 5.1, but this time assuming the numbers are in twos complement form.

5.4   *(Number Representations)* Implement a combinational logic circuit that converts 4-bit sign and magnitude numbers into corresponding 4-bit twos complement numbers. Draw an input/output conversion truth table, intermediate K-maps, and your minimized two-level logic description.

5.5   *(Number Representations)* Implement a combinational logic circuit that converts 4-bit sign and magnitude numbers into corresponding 4-bit ones complement numbers. Draw an input/output conversion truth table, intermediate K-maps, and your minimized two-level logic description.

5.6   *(Number Representations)* Implement a combinational logic circuit that converts 4-bit ones complement numbers into corresponding 4-bit twos complement numbers. Draw an input/output conversion truth table, intermediate K-maps, and your minimized two-level logic description.

5.7   *(Number Representations)* Implement a combinational logic circuit that converts 4-bit ones complement numbers into corresponding 4-bit sign plus magnitude numbers. Assume that −0 in ones complement maps into −0 in sign plus magnitude. Draw an input/output conversion truth table, intermediate K-maps, and your minimized two-level logic description.

5.8   *(Number Representations)*   Sign and magnitude and ones complement representations have two zeros, while twos complement numbers have only one representation for zero. What problem does this present for converting from twos complement to either of the other representations? How might this be handled in a practical conversion circuit?

5.9   *(Subtraction Logic)*   The truth table for a 1-bit combinational binary subtractor, analogous to the half adder, computing D(ifference) $= A$ minus B, with BL (borrow-from-left), is

A	B	D	BL
0	0	0	0
0	1	1	1
1	0	1	0
1	1	0	0

a. Design a 1-bit combinational binary subtractor, comparable to the full adder, with two data inputs (A, B), a borrow from the right input (BI), a borrow request to the left output (BL), and a difference output (D).

b. Show how your design can be cascaded to form multibit subtractors.

c. Does the subtractor work correctly for negative twos complement numbers?

d. How is a subtraction *underflow* condition indicated?

5.10   *(Adder/Subtractor Logic)*   Design a fully combinational adder/subtractor that can be cascaded to form a multibit circuit. The inputs are data inputs A, B, carry-in CI, and borrow in BI. The outputs are data output F, carry-out CO, and borrow from left BL. A mode input $M = 0$ indicates addition and $M = 1$ indicates subtraction. Can the carry and borrow inputs and outputs be combined?

5.11   *(Adder Design)*   Using comparators, multiplexers, and binary adder/subtractor logic blocks, design a 4-bit sign and magnitude adder (that is, one sign bit and three data bits). Include an overflow indicator in your design.

5.12   *(Remainder Function)*   Design a combinational circuit with three data inputs D_2, D_1, D_0, two control inputs C_1, C_2, and two outputs R_1, R_0. The R_1, R_0 should be the remainder after dividing the unsigned binary number formed from D_2, D_1, D_0 by the unsigned binary number formed by C_1, C_0. For example, D_2, D_1, $D_0 = 111$, C_1, $C_0 = 10$, then R_1, $R_0 = 01$ (7 divided by 2 yields a remainder of 1).

Note: Division by zero will never occur—take advantage of don't-care conditions in this case.

a. Write the truth table for R_1 and R_0.

b. Fill in K-maps and write Boolean expressions for R_1 and R_0.

c. Draw a schematic that implements the functions for R_1 and R_0 using a minimum number of NAND gates. Assume complemented literals are available and that there are no limits on NAND gate fan-ins.

5.13 *(Multi-Bit Adders)* Figure 5.14 shows how to use 4-bit adders and a 4-bit carry lookahead unit to implement a fast 16-bit adder. Using these as primitive building blocks, show how to construct 32- and 64-bit adders with carry lookahead.

a. Draw block diagrams for the 32- and 64-bit adders, showing all interconnections.

b. Analyze the worst-case gate delays encountered in 32- and 64-bit addition. Use the simple delay models as in Section 5.2.2.

c. Using 74LS181 ALUs and 74182 carry lookahead units for your implementation in part (a), determine the typical and worst-case delays in nanoseconds by referring to your TTL databook.

5.14 *(Carry Select Adder)* Consider a 16-bit adder implemented with the carry select technique described in Section 5.2.3. The adder is implemented with three 8-bit carry lookahead adders and eight 2:1 multiplexers. Estimate the gate delay and compare it against a conventional 16-bit ripple adder and a 16-bit carry lookahead adder.

5.15 *(Carry Select Adder)* Argue why, using explicit 8-bit test cases, the implementation of C_8 in Figure 5.15 is correct.

5.16 *(ALU Design)* Implement to the gate level an ALU bit slice with three operation selection inputs, S_2, S_1, S_0, that implements the following eight functions of the two data inputs A and B (and carry-in Cn):

S_2	S_1	S_0	ALU operation
0	0	0	$F_i = 0$
0	0	1	$F_i = B$ minus A
0	1	0	$F_i = A$ minus B
0	1	1	$F_i = A$ plus B
1	0	0	$F_i = A$ XOR B
1	0	1	$F_i = A$ OR B
1	1	0	$F_i = A$ AND B
1	1	1	$F_i = 1$

Assume a simple ripple carry scheme between bit slices.

5.17   *(ALU Design)*   Implement to the gate level an ALU bit slice with three selection inputs, S_2, S_1, S_0, and a logic/arithmetic mode input M, that implements the following 16 functions of the two data inputs A and B (and carry-in Cn):

S_2	S_1	S_0	ALU operation	S_2	S_1	S_0	ALU operation
\multicolumn{4}{l}{$M = 0$, logic mode}				
0	0	0	$F_i = 0$	0	0	0	$F_i = $ not A
0	0	1	$F_i = A$ XOR B	0	0	1	$F_i = $ not B
0	1	0	$F_i = A$ XNOR B	0	1	0	$F_i = A$ minus B
0	1	1	$F_i = A$ OR B	0	1	1	$F_i = B$ minus A
1	0	0	$F_i = A$ AND B	1	0	0	$F_i = A$ plus B
1	0	1	$F_i = A$ NOR B	1	0	1	$F_i = A$ plus 1
1	1	0	$F_i = A$ NAND B	1	1	0	$F_i = B$
1	1	1	$F_i = 1$	1	1	1	$F_i = A$

Assume a simple ripple carry scheme between bit slices.

5.18   *(ALU Design)*   Revise your design for the ALU of Exercise 5.16 to include carry lookahead logic that can operate across 4 bits.

5.19   *(ALU Design)*   Revise your design for the ALU of Exercise 5.17 to include four-bit carry lookahead logic.

5.20   *(ROM-Based ALU Design)*   Describe how a two-output ROM can be used to implement the ALU bit slice of Figure 5.19. Give a block diagram showing how a 4-bit ALU can be implemented from four cascaded ROMs. In terms of the total count of ROM bits, how does the bit slice approach compare with a solution that uses a single ROM with full 4-bit data inputs and outputs?

5.21   *(ALU Design)*   Verify that the multilevel circuit of Figure 5.23 implements the ALU specification of Figure 5.18. Do this by expanding the circuit into its equivalent two-level sum of products expressions for C_0 and F_i. Then show that the truth table/K-map for these expressions is compatible with the truth table of Figure 5.19.

5.22   *(BCD Addition)*   Perform the following binary additions assuming the numbers are in BCD form:

a.   0001 + 0100

b.   1000 + 1001

c.   0111 + 0011

d.   1001 1001 + 0001 0001

5.23 *(BCD/Binary Adder Design)*   Design a 4-bit circuit that can perform either BCD or binary addition under the control of a mode setting, M. When $M = 0$, the circuit's outputs implement binary addition. When $M = 1$, the outputs are BCD addition. Your solution should require minimal changes to the circuit of Figure 5.27.

5.24 *(Combinational Multiplier)*   Verify that the operation of the combinational multiplier of Figure 5.28 is correct by tracing all intermediate signals for the multiplication of 11 (1011_2) by 13 (1101_2).

5.25 *(Combinational Multiplier)*   Verify that the operation of the combinational multiplier of Figure 5.29 is correct by tracing all intermediate signals for the multiplication of 11 (1011_2) by 13 (1101_2).

5.26 *(Combinational Multiplier)*   Verify that the hardware of Figure 5.35 correctly computes the product of 242 by 140 by labeling all outputs with the actual bit patterns that would be computed at each stage of the circuit.

5.27 *(Combinational Multiplier)*   What is the worst-case propagation delay through the combinational multiplier of Figure 5.28, assuming the hardware is implemented with 12 full adders as in Figure 5.7?

5.28 *(Combinational Multiplier)*   Suppose that the 8-by-8 multiplier of Figure 5.35 is implemented with three 74S181 ALUs and a 74S182 carry lookahead unit (the multipliers and the full adders remain unchanged). Analyze the typical and worst-case delays by referring to your TTL databook. How does the delay compare with those computed at the end of Section 5.6?

5.29 *(Combinational Multiplier)*   Assume that you have a 4-by-4 magnitude multiplier available as a primitive building block. Discuss the design issues in building a 4-by-4 twos complement multiplier. Consider such issues as (a) determining the signs of the inputs and outputs, (b) putting the inputs into the appropriate form for the magnitude multiplier, and (c) putting the magnitude multiplier's output into a form suitable for twos complement representation.

5.30 *(Combinational Divider)*   Design a combinational divider, following the same general approach as used for the combinational multiplier of Section 5.6. Of course, this time you will use binary subtractors rather than adders.

6 Sequential Logic Design

O, for an engine to keep back all clocks
—Ben Jonson

And thus the whirligig of time brings in his revenges
—Shakespeare

Introduction

To this point, we have concentrated on circuits whose outputs are solely a function of their inputs. These are the *combinational* logic circuits. We are now ready to expand the discussion to circuits, such as the traffic light controller we studied in Chapter 1, whose outputs are a function of the current as well as the past sequence of inputs. Such circuits store information about the previous history of inputs: these are called *storage* or *memory elements*. The structure and behavior of the most primitive elements will be our primary topic. These are building blocks for more complex circuits with state to be introduced in the next chapter. In particular, we shall cover:

- *Simple circuits with memory.* A primitive storage element can be constructed from a small number of gates connecting the outputs back as inputs. We will examine how to build two such memory elements: *latches* and *flip-flops*.

- *Use of clocks.* Memory elements can replace their current state with a new state in a controlled and predictable way. A *clock* is a periodic signal distributed throughout a circuit that can ensure that all memory elements change state at approximately the same instant of time. Systems with a clock are called *synchronous*. We will examine alternative methods of providing the synchronizing clock signal to elements of the circuit.

■ *Building more complex circuits from flip-flops.* We will develop design methods for implementing clocked circuits from the various kinds of primitive building blocks introduced in this chapter.

■ *The metastability problem.* A problem often arises when two clocked circuits, synchronized by different clocks, need to communicate with one another. The output from one may be in transition when the other samples it as an input. The problem is intrinsic in communicating systems, but we will present design techniques that can reduce its effect.

■ *Self-timed circuits.* By following special signaling conventions, some design methods allow circuits to communicate without a global synchronizing clock. The idea is to include among the outputs a signal indicating that the outputs are valid. We will describe some of the methods for building such self-timed circuits.

6.1   Sequential Switching Networks

In Chapter 1 we defined sequential circuits as those in which some outputs feed back as inputs. Feedback is a necessary condition for sequential circuits, forcing the outputs to depend on the entire history of input sequences.

A digital alarm clock is a sequential circuit. The output of the clock is the current time of day, updated every second. The current setting of the clock determines the next output. The circuitry uses an independent, periodic reference signal to determine exactly when to change to a new output. This signal could be provided by an internal crystal that oscillates at a known frequency, or it could be (and frequently is) the 60-cycles-per-second alternating current that is delivered to your house by the power company. A sequential circuit counts the number of transitions in the reference signal to determine when to perform some action, such as advancing the clock. Interestingly, this independent signal oscillating at a known frequency is often called a *clock*.

Now let's recall the traffic light controller of Chapter 1. This circuit must "remember" the current light configuration before it can determine which configuration to advance to next. The unique configurations of the circuit are called its *states*. The traffic light controller has exactly four states (north-south green/east-west red, north-south yellow/east-west red, north-south red/east-west green, north-south red/east-west yellow), stored in special circuit structures called *memory elements*. Although the traffic light controller is a sequential circuit in its own right, these memory elements are the simplest, most *primitive* sequential circuits.

6.1.1   Simple Circuits with Feedback

We can implement a simple memory element from cascaded inverters. This is the basic circuit structure used in all static RAM (random-access memory) designs. Alternatively, we can build a simple memory structure from cross-coupled NOR and NAND gates. These two types of memory elements form the basic building blocks of the latch and flip-flop memory elements we will introduce in this chapter. We begin our examination of sequential logic with these very primitive structures.

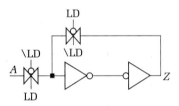

Figure 6.1   Cascaded inverters as a storage element.

Figure 6.2   Storage element with load and refresh paths.

Inverter Chains   Consider the almost trivial circuit of Figure 6.1. It contains nothing more than two inverters in series, with the output of the second-stage inverter fed back as input to the first-stage inverter. A logic 1 at the input of the first inverter becomes a 0 at its output. The 0 is mapped to a logic 1 at the output of the second stage, which reinforces the value at the first inverter's input. A similar argument holds for a 0 at the input. Once a value is inserted at the input, it can be held indefinitely by the circuit.

Of course, the problem with this circuit is how to get a value into the memory element in the first place. Some value will be there when power starts up, but for this circuit to be an effective building block, we must be able to select the value to be stored. We need extra logic to set the memory element to a specific value. The feedback path must be broken while a new value is connected to the input. One way to build such a memory element is shown in Figure 6.2, where CMOS transmission gates are used to implement a 2:1 multiplexer on the inputs to the memory element. When we assert LD (load), the feedback path is broken, and the value at input A can be stored in the element. When LD is unasserted, the input from A is broken, and the feedback path is reestablished. Note that because of the critical nature of the timing of the signals in these kinds of circuits, many logic simulators have difficulty in modeling such signal flows, even though the physical circuit would operate without difficulty.

Cascaded inverters can serve a purpose besides storage. They can be used to build circuits whose outputs oscillate between low and high voltages. Such circuits are called *ring oscillators*. Figure 6.3(a) shows an inverter chain, and Figure 6.3(b) gives the associated timing waveform. The timing waveform begins with node A (also labeled X) about to switch from 0 to 1.

The odd number of inverters leads to oscillatory behavior that repeats every t_p time units. This is called the *period* of the signal. *Duty cycle* is defined as the percentage of time a signal is high during its period. In the figure, the signal has a 50% duty cycle.

In the ring oscillator, the duration of the period depends on the number of inverters in the chain. In this case, we have five inverters with unit delay (that is, a gate delay of 1 time unit). The high time of

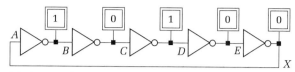

(a) Ring oscillator

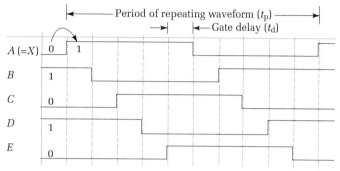

(b) Timing waveform

Figure 6.3   Inverter chain and timing waveform.

the waveform is five time units: five times the gate delay of a single stage. If we had a seven-inverter chain, the period would be 14 time units: seven units high, seven units low.

To see why this is the case, let's examine Figure 6.4. Each row gives the logic state associated with the nodes of the circuit. The rows differ in time by a single gate delay. Starting with a 1 at the input to the first stage, the signal propagates through the inverters, alternating its logic value between the stages. Once the signal emerges from the last stage, it is fed back to the first stage as the complemented value. The propagation repeats. In examining any node in the circuit, we discover that it stays high or low for exactly five gate delays.

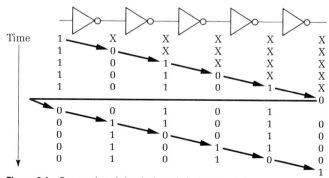

Figure 6.4   Propagation of signals through the inverter chain.

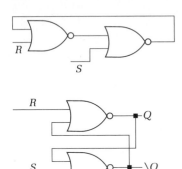

Figure 6.5 *R-S* latches.

Cross-Coupled NOR Gates as a Basic Memory Element An alternative method for building circuits with state is to use cross-coupled NOR gates (NAND gates can be used in a similar fashion). Figure 6.5 shows two alternative ways to represent cross-coupled NORs. Recall that a NOR gate with a 0 input acts like an inverter with respect to the other input: if the nonzero input is 1, the NOR's output is 0, and if it is 0, the NOR's output is 1. Similarly, if one of the NOR's inputs is 1, the output is always 0. One of the NOR gates of Figure 6.5 acts like an inverter while the other injects a 0, depending on the settings of the R and S inputs.

Suppose $R = 1$ and $S = 0$. Since the R input is 1, the Q output is *reset* to 0 independent of the $\overline{Q}$ input to the first NOR gate. With S at 0, the Q input is inverted to form the $\overline{Q}$ output. R is called the reset input.

Now suppose that $R = 0$ and $S = 1$. The same arguments apply as in the previous case. $\overline{Q}$ is reset to 0. When this output is fed back to the first NOR gate, it is inverted, and Q is *set* high. Hence S is called the set input. When R and S are both 0, the NOR gates behave like chained inverters and will hold their current output values indefinitely. This configuration of NOR gates is called an *R-S latch*.

Timing Behavior of the Cross-Coupled NOR Gates The timing behavior of these gates is shown in the timing waveform of Figure 6.6. Q is set high when S is asserted and is reset low when R is asserted. Whenever R and S are both zero, the outputs remain unchanged.

What happens when both R and S are asserted? Q cannot be both 1 and 0 simultaneously! This input condition is *forbidden* in normal operating conditions. Both Q and $\overline{Q}$ are driven to 0, violating the assumption that the two outputs are always complements of each other.

When one of R or S is returned to the unasserted state, the remaining asserted signal determines the steady-state output values of Q and $\overline{Q}$. In the first case of forbidden inputs in Figure 6.6, R remains asserted while S is left unasserted. Q stays at 0, while $\overline{Q}$ goes to 1. Comparable behavior will be observed if R becomes unasserted while S stays asserted.

Now suppose that R and S return to 0 simultaneously. This is the second case of forbidden inputs in Figure 6.6. The outputs actually

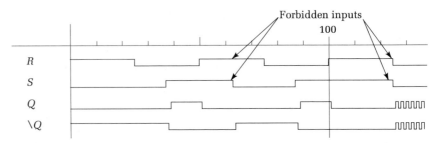

Figure 6.6 Cross-coupled NOR gate timing waveform.

oscillate. Q and $\overline{Q}$ are initially 0. When R and S go to 0, the NOR gate outputs go to 1. But when these are fed back to the inputs, the NOR gates behave like inverters, switching the outputs back to 0. This oscillatory behavior is called a *race condition*.

Theoretically, the race condition can continue as long as R and S are 0. However, the delay through the two NOR gates is not perfectly matched, and one of Q and $\overline{Q}$ will be driven to a new value before the other, stopping the oscillations. To avoid the race condition, we restrict the R and S inputs never to be 1 at the same time.

We summarize the behavior of the cross-coupled NOR gates in the functional truth table of Figure 6.7. When $R = S = 0$, the circuit holds its current output—in other words, the output is the same as it was for the last setting of the inputs. When one of R or S is set to 1, the output is forced to 0 or 1, respectively. When both inputs are 1, the outputs oscillate between 0 and 1.

Another representation of the behavior of cross-coupled gates is called the *state diagram*. The diagram consists of nodes and arcs. The nodes represent unique configurations or states of the circuit. The arcs are labeled with the input combinations that cause a transition from one state to another.

Figure 6.8 shows the state diagram for the cross-coupled NOR gates. The circuit's state depends on the values of the outputs Q and $\overline{Q}$, so there are four possible states, one for each combination of possible values for the two outputs. Since there are two inputs, S and R, there are

S	R	Q
0	0	hold
0	1	0
1	0	1
1	1	unstable

Figure 6.7 Functional truth table of cross-coupled NOR gates.

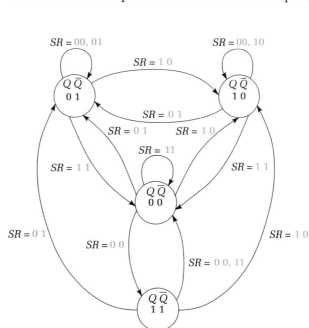

Figure 6.8 Theoretical state diagram of cross-coupled NOR gates.

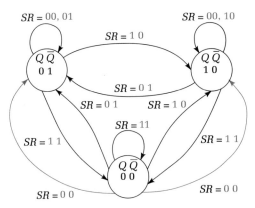

Figure 6.9   observed behavior of cross-coupled NOR gates.

exactly four transitions from each state, one for each of the possible input combinations.

The states labeled 01 and 10 are the normal configurations of the circuit. When set (S) is asserted, we enter state 10 $(Q = 1,\ \overline{Q} = 0)$. When reset (R) is asserted, we change to state 01 $(Q = 0,\ \overline{Q} = 1)$. When S and R are both 0, we hold in the current state.

When we encounter the forbidden input configuration $S = R = 1$, the circuit enters state 00. It stays in this state as long as these inputs are asserted. As soon as one input returns to 0, the circuit returns to state 01 or 10.

If the current state is 00 and $S = R = 0$, the circuit enters state 11. It does not stay there very long, immediately returning to state 00 if S and R remain 0. If the delays through the gates are perfectly matched, the circuit can oscillate between these two states forever. Of course, this does not make a very useful memory element.

Figure 6.9 gives a state diagram we constructed by observing the behavior of a real cross-coupled NOR gate circuit. The actual circuit does not oscillate between 00 and 11 indefinitely, but rather ends up sometimes in state 10 and sometimes in state 01. This is the true meaning of a race condition in sequential logic: the resulting state depends on the circuit's time-dependent behavior and cannot be predicted in advance. The race condition is most easily avoided by never putting the circuit into state 00 in the first place.

6.1.2   State, Clock, Setup Time, and Hold Time

We are now ready to introduce some definitions about the timing waveforms of sequential networks. The output of a sequential circuit is a function of the current inputs and any signals that are fed back to the inputs. We call these feedback signals the *current state* of the circuit. A periodic external event, called a *clock*, determines when the circuit will decide to change the current state to a new state. When the clocking event occurs, the circuit samples its current inputs and state and computes its new state.

As an example, consider the digital alarm clock we already discussed. Part of its state is the current time of day. Other parts of the state include such aspects of the clock's configuration as whether or not the alarm is set and the time the alarm should go off. Suppose that the oscillating reference signal, the true clock, becomes asserted once every second. When the clock is asserted, the digital clock advances the display by 1 second and checks whether it matches the alarm time. If it does and the alarm is set, then the sequential circuit sounds the alarm. The digital clock's new state now indicates that the alarm is on.

We can designate the *clocking event* as either the low-to-high or high-to-low transitions of the clock. It is important that the inputs determining the new state remain unchanged around the clocking event. We define a special window of time by two constraints: the *setup* time before the clock event and the *hold* time after the event. If the inputs do not change within this window, the state will be updated in a correct and unambiguous way. If they do change, the effect on the state is undefined.

Let's be more precise. The setup time, T_{su}, is the minimum time interval preceding the event during which the input must be stable to be validly recognized. The hold time, T_h, is the minimum time interval after the edge of the event during which the input signal must be stable to be validly recognized.

These concepts are shown in Figure 6.10 for a rising clock edge event. The input must remain stable at least a setup time before the reference clock edge and at least a hold time after the edge for the input signal to be recognized as a logic 1. If these constraints are not satisfied, the input may be interpreted as a 1 or a 0 or some unrecognizable value between 0 and 1. It is extremely dangerous to allow input signals to change very close to the sampling event, as we shall see in Section 6.4.

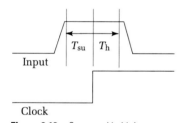

Figure 6.10 Setup and hold times.

Latches and Flip-Flops Let's return to the concept of the sampling event. Think of this event as an enable signal that instructs the memory element to examine its input to change its state. We can use a single clock to synchronize the update of many memory elements in our system.

Figure 6.5 already showed the basic *R-S* latch. Primitive memory elements actually fall into two broad classes: *latches* and *flip-flops*. When the memory element's outputs immediately change in response to input changes, they are called *transparent* outputs. The *R-S* latch has transparent outputs.

If a latch has only data inputs, like *R* and *S*, it is called an *unclocked* latch. *Level-sensitive* latches have an additional enable input, sometimes called the *clock*.

Level-sensitive latches continuously sample their inputs while they are enabled. Any change in the level of the input is propagated through

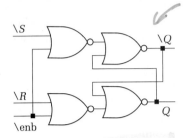

Figure 6.11 Level-sensitive R-S latch.

to the output. The circuit shown in Figure 6.11 is a level-sensitive latch. The holding state occurs when both inputs are 1, the forbidden state when both inputs are logic 0, the latch is set when $\overline{S} = 0$, $\overline{R} = 1$, and the latch is reset when $\overline{S} = 1$, $\overline{R} = 0$. The enable signal is also active low. When it is high, the output from the first stage of NOR gates is forced to 0, thus placing the cross-coupled second stage in the holding state.

When the enable signal is unasserted, the last value of the inputs determines the state held by the latch. The "latched" value is determined by the window formed from the setup and hold times around the falling (high-to-low) edge of the enable signal.

Flip-flops differ from latches in that their outputs change only with respect to the clock, whereas latches change output when their inputs change. We can characterize flip-flops on the basis of the clock transition that causes the output change: there are *positive edge-triggered*, *negative edge-triggered*, and *master/slave* flip-flops.

A positive edge-triggered flip-flop samples its inputs on the low-to-high clock transition. To be properly recognized, the input must be stable within the setup and hold time window around the clock edge. The outputs change a propagation delay after the rising clock transition.

A negative edge-triggered device works in a similar fashion, with the input sampled on the high-to-low clock transition. The outputs change a propagation delay after the falling edge of the clock. Under this classification, a master/slave flip-flop is indistinguishable from the negative edge-triggered device, except that it exhibits a strange behavior called "ones catching," which we will discuss later. Table 6.1 summarizes the different attributes of latches and flip-flops.

Timing Examples To better understand the terms just introduced, let's consider two memory elements: a positive edge-triggered flip-flop (such

Table 6.1 Input/Output Behavior of Latches and Flip-Flops

Type	When inputs are sampled	When outputs are valid
Unclocked latch	Always	Propagation delay from input change
Level-sensitive latch	Clock high (T_{su}, T_h around falling clock edge)	Propagation delay from input change
Positive-edge flip-flop	Clock low-to-high transition (T_{su}, T_h around rising clock edge)	Propagation delay from rising edge of clock
Negative-edge flip-flop	Clock high-to-low transition (T_{su}, T_h around falling clock edge)	Propagation delay from falling edge of clock
Master/slave flip-flop	Clock high-to-low transition (T_{su}, T_h around falling clock edge)	Propagation delay from falling edge of clock

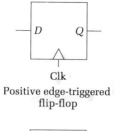

Positive edge-triggered
flip-flop

Level-sensitive
latch

Figure 6.12 Flip-flops versus latches.

as a TTL 74LS74) and a level-sensitive latch (such as a 74LS76). Each has a single data input D, a clock input C, and an output Q. The block diagrams are shown in Figure 6.12. We normally represent edge-triggered devices with the clock input as a triangle. A negative edge-triggered device has an additional negative logic bubble at the clock input.

We compare the timing behavior of the two types of devices in Figure 6.13. The outputs differ only when the input changes while the clock is asserted. This is because the latch immediately responds to changes in the input while the clock is high but the flip-flop does not.

The definitions of the setup and hold times are quite different for these two devices. Figure 6.14 gives the timing waveforms for the 74LS74 positive edge-triggered flip-flop. T_{su} is 20 ns and T_h is 5 ns. In addition, the clock signal has a minimum duration, $T_w = 25$ ns. The figure also defines T_{phl}, the propagation delay between the rising edge of the clock and the change in the output from high to low, and T_{plh}, the propagation delay from the rising clock edge to a low to high change in the output. T_{phl} is 40 ns maximum, 25 ns typical, and T_{plh} is 25 ns maximum, 13 ns typical.

Figure 6.15 displays the timing specifications for the 74LS76 clocked transparent latch. As for the flip-flop, the quantities T_{su}, T_h, and T_w are

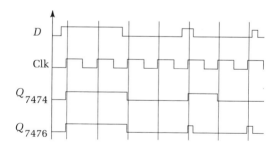

Figure 6.13 Waveform behavior of a positive edge-triggered flip-flop versus a level-sensitive latch.

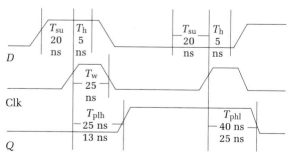

Figure 6.14 Timing constraints and specifications for the 74LS74 positive edge-triggered flip-flop.

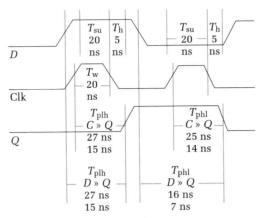

Figure 6.15 Timing constraints and specifications for the 74LS76 clocked transparent latch.

defined to be 20 ns, 5 ns, and 20 ns, respectively. However, the setup and hold times are defined relative to the falling edge. The specifications for T_{phl} and T_{plh} are more complex, because they must be defined for two different events: from when the input changes to a corresponding change in the output ($D \gg Q$) and from when the clock becomes asserted to when the output changes ($C \gg Q$). Of course, the clock must be asserted before the input can influence the output. T_{phl} ($D \gg Q$) is 16 ns maximum, 7 ns typical; T_{phl} ($C \gg Q$) is 25 ns maximum, 14 ns typical; T_{plh} ($D \gg Q$) is 27 ns maximum, 15 ns typical; and T_{plh} ($C \gg Q$) is 27 ns maximum, 15 ns typical.

6.1.3 The *R-S* Latch

The *R-S* latch can hold its current state, reset the state to 0, or set the state to 1. The detailed truth table for the *R-S* latch is shown in Figure 6.16. Note that the inputs are *S*, *R*, and *Q* at a given time *t*, and the output is *Q* at time $t + \Delta$, where Δ represents a small increment in time. $Q(t)$ is the *current state* of the latch, and $Q(t + \Delta)$ is the *next state*.

A *K*-map for the truth table is given in Figure 6.17. We can derive the following so-called *characteristic equation* to describe the next state in terms of the inputs and current state:

$$Q(t + \Delta) = S(t) + \overline{R}(t) \bullet Q(t)$$

$$Q^+ = S + \overline{R}Q$$

This equation is a convenient shorthand for describing the memory element's behavior. For example, if $S = 1$ and $R = 0$, the next state Q^+ becomes 1 independent of the current state. When $S = 0$ and $R = 1$, the next state is forced to be 0, independent of the current state.

$S(t)$	$R(t)$	$Q(t)$	$Q(t + \Delta)$	
0	0	0	0	HOLD
0	0	1	1	
0	1	0	0	RESET
0	1	1	0	
1	0	0	1	SET
1	0	1	1	
1	1	0	X	Not allowed
1	1	1	X	

Figure 6.16 *R-S* latch truth table.

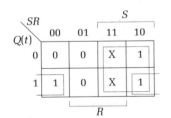

Figure 6.17 K-map for $Q(t + \Delta)$.

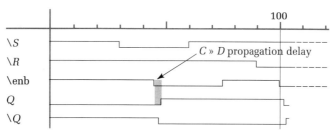

Figure 6.18 Timing diagram for the level-sensitive R-S latch.

Level-Sensitive R-S Latch The *gated R-S* latch is an extension of the basic R-S latch that we saw in Figure 6.11. This device adds the ability to latch a new state under the control of an external enable signal. When the enable signal is asserted, the circuit's R and S inputs affect the state. When enable is not asserted, the latch holds its current state.

The timing behavior of the level-sensitive R-S latch is shown in Figure 6.18. The propagation delay from when the clock is asserted to when the output changes ($C \gg D$) is shown in the diagram.

6.1.4   The *J-K* Flip-Flop

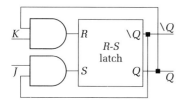

Figure 6.19 *J-K* latch.

It would be useful if we could eliminate the forbidden inputs to the R-S latch. Consider the circuit diagram of Figure 6.19. By feeding the Q and $\overline{Q}$ outputs back to the inputs and gating these with external set and reset control inputs (now called J and K, respectively), we guarantee that the internal R and S are never simultaneously 1 (this assumes that Q and $\overline{Q}$ are never both 1).

In addition to avoiding the forbidden state, we introduce a new capability: complementing the current state, or *toggling*. For example, if Q is 1, $\overline{Q}$ is 0, and J and K are both 1, then the inputs presented to the internal latch are $R = 1$, $S = 0$. This flips Q to 0 and $\overline{Q}$ to 1. If Q starts out as 0, then $\overline{Q}$ is asserted, as is the internal S signal. Once again, this will cause Q to toggle its value to 1.

This is shown in the truth table of Figure 6.20. All input combinations lead to useful functions for the J-K latch: hold, reset, set, and toggle. The characteristic equation is

$$Q^+ = Q\overline{K} + \overline{Q}J$$

$J(t)$	$K(t)$	$Q(t)$	$Q(t+\Delta)$	
0	0	0	0	HOLD
0	0	1	1	
0	1	0	0	RESET
0	1	1	0	
1	0	0	1	SET
1	0	1	1	
1	1	0	1	TOGGLE
1	1	1	0	

Figure 6.20   *J-K* latch truth table.

Notice how nicely the characteristic equation summarizes the behavior of the J-K flip-flop. When $J = 1$, $K = 0$, $Q^+ = Q + \overline{Q}$, which is always 1 (set). Q^+ is always 0 when $J = 0$, $K = 1$ (reset). Finally, when $J = 1$, $K = 1$, $Q^+ = \overline{Q}$ (toggle).

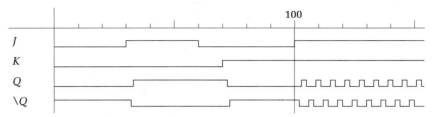

Figure 6.21 *J-K* latch timing waveform.

Problems with the Basic *J-K* Flip-Flop If we actually built this circuit, we would find an interesting problem as soon as the circuit is placed into the toggle mode. The output toggles forever (or at least until one of *J* or *K* returns to 0), as we show in Figure 6.21. The problem is that the toggle signal remains asserted while the outputs change, thus flipping the values of *R* and *S* presented to the internal latch, causing it to toggle again. The process continues until the toggle condition is removed.

Solution: Master/Slave Flip-Flop This leads us to an alternative way to build a *J-K* memory element, called a *master/slave* flip-flop. The basic idea is to build the memory element in two stages. The first stage, the *master*, accepts new *R-S* inputs and generates the outputs *P* and $\bar{P}$ on the rising edge of a clock signal. The second stage, the *slave*, accepts *P* and $\bar{P}$ as inputs on the falling edge of the clock and changes its outputs after the falling edge. By the time the outputs propagate back to the first stage, the clock signal has been removed, guaranteeing that the outputs cannot toggle again (at least not until the next rising clock edge). The schematic for this flip-flop is shown in Figure 6.22 and its associated timing diagram is given in Figure 6.23.

The timing diagram illustrates some important points about *J-K* master/slave flip-flops. First, the P, $\bar{P}$ outputs of the first stage track the Q, $\bar{Q}$ outputs of the second stage. The latter outputs change a propagation delay *after* the falling edge of the clock signal. Second, a general property of master/slave flip-flops is called *ones catching*. If an input is high

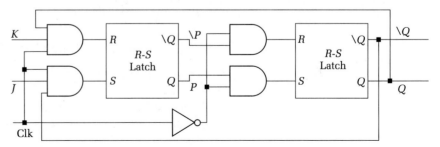

Figure 6.22 Schematic for *J-K* master/slave flip-flop.

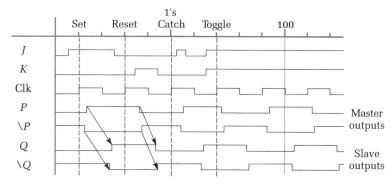

Figure 6.23 Timing diagram for *J-K* master/slave flip-flop.

any time during the clock period, it will be interpreted as a one for computing the output.

To see this behavior, let's trace the inputs and their effect on the outputs. Initially the flip-flop has 0 as its output. *J* goes high, and after the clock also goes high, *P* comes high. When the clock goes low, *P* and $\overline{P}$ are gated across to the second stage, causing its output *Q* to go high. On the next rising clock edge, *J* and *K* are both low, so the first stage holds its state. Midway through the clock period, however, *K* comes high, causing the first stage to reset. The 0 output is passed on to the second stage, whose output goes low after the falling edge of the clock.

The ones catching phenomenon is clearly shown in the next input condition, where *J* changes from low to high to low while the clock is asserted. Even though the input is back to zero by the time the clock goes low, the output is still set. You must be careful when using master/slave flip-flops with combinational logic that suffers from 0-hazards. Any glitch at the inputs to the flip-flops could cause unintended state changes.

If the latches are constructed from the NAND gates (that is, $\overline{R}$-$\overline{S}$ latches), there is an analogous problem with *zeros catching*. If the clock is asserted and the *J* or *K* input temporarily changes through zero, the associated set or reset operation will take place.

The rest of the input configurations cause the outputs to toggle from 1 to 0 to 1 to 0. Note that the outputs make only one state change per clock period and that the output changes only after the falling edge of the clock.

6.1.5 Edge-Triggered Flip-Flops: *D* Flip-Flops, *T* Flip-Flops

J-K flip-flops solve the forbidden state problem by guaranteeing that the inputs to the internal latches are never asserted simultaneously. The resulting toggle function can lead to oscillating outputs. The master/slave flip-flop solves the oscillation problem by sampling inputs only when the clock is high, generating new outputs just after the clock goes low. But now we have the problem of ones or zeros catching.

To solve this new problem, designers created *edge-triggered flip-flops*. Rather than sample inputs during the high time of the clock, edge-triggered devices sample inputs only on a rising (*positive edge-triggered*) or falling (*negative edge-triggered*) clock edge.

Let's look at the circuit schematic for a negative edge-triggered D flip-flop in Figure 6.24 (this can be changed to a positive edge-triggered device by using the clock's complement). Unlike R-S and master/slave J-K devices, a D flip-flop has only one data input. It stores the value presented on this input when the clock signal performs the appropriate transition. Its characteristic equation is simply $Q^+ = D$. Let's see how it works.

Operation of the D Flip-Flop   The operation of an edge-triggered device is considerably more complex than that of the master/slave flip-flop. The circuit of Figure 6.24 contains three communicating latches. The bottom latch samples the D input while the top stage holds $\overline{D}$. The output from the bottom latch drives the set input of the final stage latch, while the top latch provides its the reset input.

The figure shows the state of the circuit when the clock is high. The clock forces the outputs of the top and bottom latches to zero, thus keeping the final stage R-S latch in its holding state. Any change in the D input will be sampled by the top and bottom latches, but these changes are inhibited from affecting the final stage latch.

Figure 6.25 shows what happens when the clock initially changes from high to low. The output NOR gates in the top and bottom latches now act like inverters. The previously sampled value of D is presented

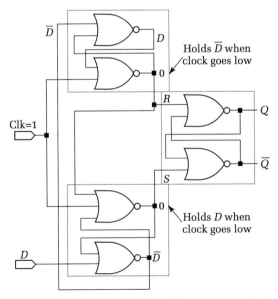

Figure 6.24   Negative edge-triggered D flip-flop when clock is high.

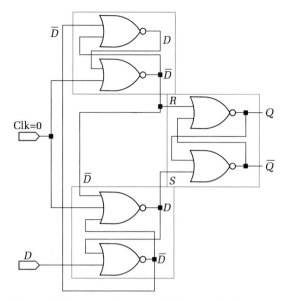

Figure 6.25   Negative edge-triggered D flip-flop when clock goes from high to low.

to the S input, while $\overline{D}$ drives the R input. If $D = 1$, the R-S latch outputs a 1. Otherwise it outputs a 0.

What happens when the clock is low, but D changes? Figure 6.26 shows the state when the input changes to D', which is different from the previously sampled value D. This new input forces the output of the

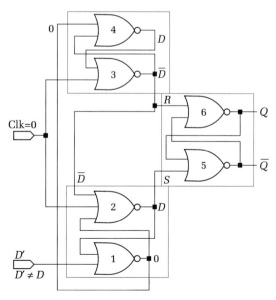

Figure 6.26   Negative edge-triggered D flip-flop when clock is low.

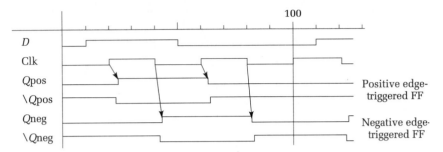

Figure 6.27   Timing diagram for positive and negative edge-triggered D flip-flops.

NOR gate to change from 1 to 0, since one input must be a 1 and the other a 0. By driving this circuit node to 0, gates 2, 4, and 5 are guaranteed to hold their previous values. D' can affect the circuit only when the outputs of gates 2 and 4 are forced to 0. This will happen only when the clock next goes high.

An examination of this circuit should make you appreciate the need for setup and hold time specifications for flip-flops. If the D input changes too close to the appropriate clock edge, its value may not be held correctly by the top and bottom latches. Also, you can see why the propagation delays may be rather substantial for these kinds of devices.

We give a timing diagram for both positive and negative edge-triggered devices in Figure 6.27. The outputs change after a small propagation delay from the rising or falling edge. The last transition (time step 110) shows how edge-triggered devices sample their inputs. In this case, the input changes from a 0 to a 1 midway through the clock period. The change goes undetected by the positive edge-triggered device—no ones catching here—but is recognized by the negative edge-triggered flip-flop.

Toggle Flip-Flop   There is still one more kind of flip-flop: the *toggle flip-flop*, or *T flip-flop*. The toggle flip-flop has a single input that causes the stored state to be complemented when the input is asserted. Toggle flip-flops are not usually found in standard parts catalogs because they are so easy to construct from other flip-flop types. For example, a *J-K* flip-flop with both inputs tied together will implement a *T* flip-flop. If the input is 0, both *J* and *K* are 0 and the flip-flop holds its state; if the input is 1, both *J* and *K* are 1 and the flip-flop complements its state.

6.1.6   TTL Latch and Flip-Flop Components

The TTL catalog contains a number of *R-S* latches and *J-K* and *D* flip-flops. Figure 6.28 shows three of the most popular of these: the 7473 *J-K* flip-flops and the 7474 *D* flip-flop. Each package contains dual independent flip-flops. The '73 comes with independent active-low clear signals (CLR/). When they are asserted, the flip-flop's state is set to 0,

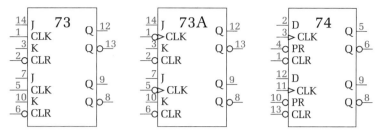

Figure 6.28 TTL flip-flop components.

independent of the current value of the inputs and the clock. The '74 has both preset (PR/) and clear (CLR/). In a similar way, when preset is asserted, the flip-flop's state is set to 1.

The 7473 component comes in two versions: the standard version contains master/slave flip-flops, and the "A" version contains negative edge-triggered devices. The notation on the 7473A's clocks shows you how to distinguish between edge-triggered and level-sensitive operation. Edge triggering is denoted by a small triangle on the clock signal. Negative edge triggering is denoted by the negation bubble on the clock line. Be sure you are selecting the correct component for the job at hand. The detailed timing behaviors of the 7473 and 7473A are not identical.

The 7474 is a positive edge-triggered D flip-flop. The edge triggering of the clock is indicated by the triangle on the clock signal. Without the bubble, the element is positive edge-triggered.

We usually form R-S latches from discrete cross-coupled NOR gates using 7402 components. However, you can find four $\overline{R}$-$\overline{S}$ latches in a single package if you use the 74279 component.

D flip-flops are almost universally available in positive edge-triggered configurations. What if you need a negative edge-triggered device? One solution is to invert the clock signal on the way into a D flip-flop like the 7474. An alternative is to use a negative edge-triggered J-$\overline{K}$ flip-flop, such as the 74276. By simply wiring the J and $\overline{K}$ inputs together, you can construct a D flip-flop.

6.2 Timing Methodologies

Timing in combinational circuits is straightforward, with the possible exception of glitches. Sequential logic, on the other hand, must examine both the current input and the current state to determine the outputs and next state. For this to work properly in synchronous systems, the input should not change while the state is changing. In effect, the circuit is constrained by setup and hold times, during which the inputs must be stable. In addition, outputs can change in response to clocking changes as well as input changes. This leads to more complex timing specifications.

In this section, we will describe timing methodologies associated with proper synchronous system design. A *timing methodology* is nothing more than a set of rules for interconnecting components and clock signals that, when followed, guarantee proper operation of the resulting system.

6.2.1   Cascaded Flip-Flops and Setup/Hold/Propagation

Timing methodologies guarantee "proper operation," but just what does this mean? For synchronous systems, we define *proper operation* as follows. For each clocking event, all flip-flops controlled by the same clock signal simultaneously examine their inputs and determine their new states. This means that (1) the correct input values, with respect to time, are provided to the flip-flops that are changing their states, and (2) no flip-flop should change its state more than once during each clocking event.

What rules should we follow for composing synchronous systems to guarantee these two properties? Figure 6.29 illustrates the problem. Here, we cascade two D flip-flops so that the output from the first stage feeds the input to the second stage. Both flip-flops are controlled by the same clock signal. The purpose of this circuit is to transfer the current state of the first stage to the second stage while the first stage receives a new value. In other words, the second stage contains the value stored in the first stage during the previous clock period. This is an example of a *shift register*, a multibit memory with a capability of exchanging a single memory element's contents with its neighbors. We will see more of shift registers in Chapter 7.

The proper logic operation of the circuit is shown in Figure 6.30, assuming that the flip-flops are positive edge-triggered and that the

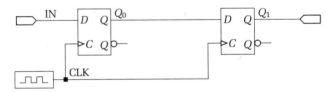

Figure 6.29   Cascaded D flip-flops to implement a two-stage shift register.

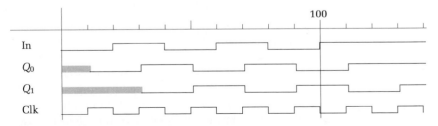

Figure 6.30   Timing diagram for the two-stage shift register.

input stream is 0101011. Initially, both flip-flops contain unknown values. On the first rising edge of the clock, the input is 0 and appears at output Q_0 a short propagation delay later. The state of the second flip-flop is still unknown.

On the second rising clock edge, the input is 1, and Q_0 takes on this value some propagation delay after the clock edge. However, at the clock edge, the second stage sees the old value of Q_0 as its input. Thus, Q_1 becomes zero shortly after the rising edge. The pattern continues through the diagram. Q_1 always displays the value that Q_0 had just before the rising clock edge.

We would not observe proper transfer of data between the stages if the first was positive edge-triggered while the second stage was negative triggered. After the first clock cycle, we would have 0 in both flip-flops. After the second cycle, both flip-flops would hold a 1, and so on. It is not good design practice to mix flip-flops that are sensitive to different timing events within the same circuit!

Proper Cascading of Flip-Flops   In general, we assume that the propagation of the clock signal is infinitely fast and that all flip-flops have identical timing. In real circuits, this isn't true. Some components may be faster than others, and the wire delay for distributing a signal to all points where it is needed may vary substantially. Let's suppose that the first-stage flip-flop has a very fast propagation delay, so fast in fact that the new value of Q_0 appears at the input to the second stage before it had a chance to observe the previous value of Q_0. We would not be properly passing the value from stage to stage in this case.

The same problem arises if the connection between the clocks of the two flip-flops is a long meandering wire, while the output of stage one and the input to stage two are connected by a very short wire. It is only after the first stage has changed its value that the second stage receives the clock transition. Thus, the stages will have incorrectly latched the same value. Such a circuit violates our basic assumption that all flip-flop inputs are examined simultaneously.

Fortunately, the designers of TTL components have built them so they can be cascaded without timing problems (this is true as long as the same families of TTL components and the same kinds of clocking events are used). It is important to remember that the inputs must be held stable for a setup time before and a hold time after the clock edge. For the 74LS74 positive edge-triggered flip-flop, these are 20 ns and 5 ns, respectively. Fortuitously, the propagation delay far exceeds the hold time. In the 74LS74 case, the typical delay for a low-to-high transition is 13 ns. Unless the clock signal to the second stage is delayed by more than 7 ns, the first stage cannot change its value and propagate it to the second stage before the hold time has expired. By then, the second stage has successfully latched the original Q_0 value. This timing behavior is shown in Figure 6.31.

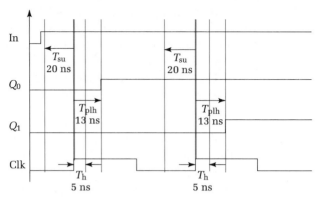

Figure 6.31   Timing behavior of cascaded positive edge-triggered flip-flops.

6.2.2   Narrow Width Clocking Versus Multiphase Clocking

When implementing a system in TTL logic, the memory element of choice is an edge-triggered flip-flop. These devices avoid the ones catching problem exhibited by master/slave devices and are easy to compose. If the system is being implemented in CMOS technology, designers tend to use level-sensitive latches, usually implemented as in Figure 6.2 and slightly redrawn in Figure 6.32. These latches are called *dynamic storage elements* because the clock must continue to run for the element to hold its current value. *Static storage elements*, such as the TTL flip-flops, hold their value independent of the oscillations of the clock and continue to do so as long as power is applied to the circuit.

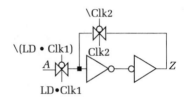

Figure 6.32   CMOS dynamic storage element.

Compare Figure 6.32, a dynamic *D*-type storage element, and Figure 6.24, a static edge-triggered *D* flip-flop. The former is much more transistor efficient than the latter. The two alternative approaches lead to quite different clocking strategies. Edge-triggered devices are easy to use and require only a simple oscillating clock signal. Level-sensitive latches, on the other hand, place special restrictions on the clock signal, as we will see next.

Clocked Sequential Systems with Latched State   Flip-flops are the most primitive form of circuits with feedback. There are several ways to generalize these to more complex sequential networks. Throughout this section, we will focus on more general *clocked sequential systems*, as shown in Figure 6.33.

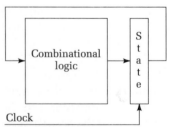

Figure 6.33   Generic block diagram for clocked sequential system.

Clocked sequential systems consist of a block of memory elements (*state*) driven by combinational logic whose inputs include the current contents of the memory elements. The feedback path from the state to the combinational logic inputs could cause multiple state changes unless we design the clocking method carefully. Proper operation of the circuit requires that the state changes only once per clock cycle.

To see how a problem can happen, let's consider an example. The arrival of the clocking event causes the new state to replace the current state. If there is some way that this new state can race through the combinational logic and cause a second new state to be computed, all within the same clock period, we have violated one of our requirements for proper operation. As in the *R-S* latch, the new state depends on the timing of the circuit, as well as the inputs and the current state. Sometimes the state may change once per clock period and sometimes more than once, depending on the delay paths through the logic. The new state cannot be determined unambiguously.

This problem will not occur in edge-triggered systems. The time that the clock edge is in transition is small compared to the clock period and any associated logic delays. So fast signals are not a problem.

However, if the state storage elements are implemented with level-sensitive latches, we must use a clocking methodology based on narrow clock widths. The clock high time is small compared to the clock period.

When implemented with a narrow-width clock, a clocked sequential system behaves as follows. Whenever the clock goes high, the current state is replaced by a new state as the state memory elements latch a new value. If the clock remains high long enough for the new state to race back to the input of the combinational logic and propagate through it, we could observe a double state change. To ensure that this never takes place, we must use a clock whose high time is *less than the fastest possible path through the combinational logic*. This is measured from the rising edge of the clock and should include the delay through the state latch.

To guarantee that the correct next state has been computed, we also make sure that *the period of the clock is longer than the worst-case propagation delay* through the combinational logic. Because the next state signal actually has until the end of the high time of the clock to be computed, this constraint can be measured up to the falling edge of the clock, as long as the latch setup time is included. The constraints are shown in Figure 6.34. T_{w} is the high time of the clock, T_{period} is the clock period, and T is the time from when the clock first goes high until it goes low in the next period.

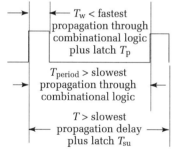

T_{w} < fastest propagation through combinational logic plus latch T_{p}

T_{period} > slowest propagation through combinational logic

T > slowest propagation delay plus latch T_{su}

Figure 6.34 Narrow-width clocking constraints.

An Alternative to Narrow-Width Clocking: Multiphase Clocking Narrow-width clocking forces the designer to think about fast as well as slow paths through the logic. Finding these critical delays is even more of a problem because they vary with temperature and other environmental factors. An alternative is to use multiple-phase nonoverlapping clocks, the simplest case being a two-phase scheme. An example of a two-phase clock waveform is shown in Figure 6.35.

If we apply the two-phase scheme to the general clocked sequential system block diagram of Figure 6.33, we get the system shown in Figure 6.36. Each feedback path passes through a pair of inverters. And each inverter

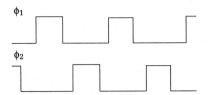

Figure 6.35   Two-phase nonoverlapping clocks.

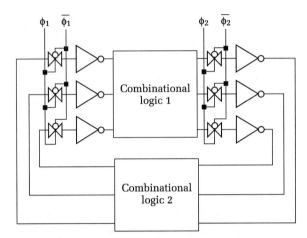

Figure 6.36   Two-phase clocked sequential system.

pair implements a dynamic storage element, as in Figure 6.32. (The second block of combinational logic is optional.)

By breaking every feedback path with both phases of the clock, we eliminate the possibility of signal races. Since both clocks are never high at the same time, a feedback signal cannot possibly pass through the combinational logic block more than once in any φ_1/φ_2 cycle. We need only ensure that the periods of φ_1 and φ_2 are greater than the worst-case delay found in combinational logic blocks 2 and 1 (plus the appropriate latch setup times).

This system is an improvement over narrow-width clocking. We need only worry about the slow signals. Unfortunately, the multiphase scheme requires more clock signals to be distributed and routed throughout the system.

Generating nonoverlapping clocks is not particularly difficult, as the circuit of Figure 6.37 and the timing diagram of Figure 6.38 demonstrate. The circuit works as follows. The rising edge of the external clock forces φ_1 to go low. The feedback from the φ_1 output to the lower NOR gate allows that phase to go high. When the external clock goes low, the process is repeated for the high-to-low transition of φ_2, feeding back to allow φ_1 to come high. In the timing diagram, the nonoverlap time is

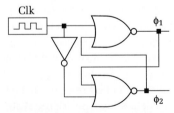

Figure 6.37   Two-phase clock generator.

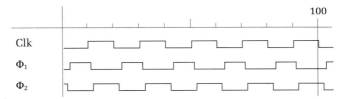

Figure 6.38 Timing diagram for clock generator.

only a single gate delay. This may not be sufficient to avoid offsets in the timing of the clock waveforms due to different wire distribution delays for the two phases. This problem is called *clock skew*, and it is discussed in the next subsection. To increase the nonoverlap time, we simply place additional delay in the feedback path. An even-numbered chain of inverters is a good way to implement this delay.

Summary Whereas latches may be transistor efficient in VLSI implementations, there is usually no area advantage in packaged logic like TTL. You get just about as many edge-triggered flip-flops per package as you get latches. Therefore, most modern TTL designs use edge-triggered flip-flops, and a single-phase clock is all you need. To avoid problems in transferring signals from one type of flip-flop to another, we strongly advise that the system be constructed from all positive edge-triggered or all negative edge-triggered devices.

6.2.3   Clock Skew

Proper operation of synchronous systems requires that the next state of all storage elements be determined at the same instant. In effect, the clock signal must appear at every storage device at the same time. Unfortunately, this condition cannot always be guaranteed. A single clock signal may fan out from more than one physical circuit, each with its own timing characteristics.

Example of the Skew Problem Clock skew can introduce subtle bugs into a synchronous system. As an example, refer back to the two-stage shift register of Figure 6.29. This time, think of the two flip-flops being clocked by signals CLOCK1 and CLOCK2 whose arrival is slightly skewed in time.

Suppose that the original state of both flip-flops is 1 and that the input to the first flip-flop is 0. If the circuit behaves correctly, the state of the first flip-flop should change from 1 to 0 while the second flip-flop stays at 1 (its current value of 1 is replaced by the old value of the first flip-flop, which is also 1).

The timing diagram of Figure 6.39 shows what really happens. The first flip-flop is reset to 0, but so is the second flip-flop! This occurs

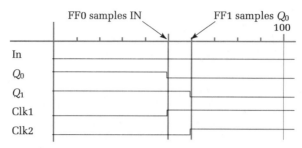

Figure 6.39   Timing diagram for cascaded flip-flops, illustrating the effects of clock skew.

because the second stage sees the new state of the first stage (0), rather than its current state (1), by the time CLOCK2 arrives.

Avoiding Clock Skew   One way to avoid clock skew is to route the clock signal in a direction opposite to the flow of data. For example, we could arrange the clock signal so that it arrives at the second flip-flop before the first. The second flip-flop would then change its state based on the current value of the first stage. There is no problem if the first stage changes its state well after the second stage.

Unfortunately, this may not be too helpful, since most communications move in both directions. This means that skew will be a problem in one of them.

Because the typical propagation delay for the LS family of TTL components is 13 ns, the skew needs to be rather substantial for the second stage to read the wrong value. (Of course, skew becomes more of a problem with faster systems or those that span a larger circuit area.) The best plan is to route the clock signals so that components that communicate with each other are connected via short clock lines.

6.3   Realizing Circuits with Different Kinds of Flip-Flops

Section 6.1 introduced four different flip-flop types: R-S, J-K, D, and T. In this section, we describe the methods for implementing one kind of flip-flop with another. The procedure is useful because a given flip-flop type may be the best choice to implement a given storage element, but flip-flops of that type may not be available to you.

We already know that a D flip-flop can be formed from a J-K flip-flop: simply tie the set input J to the data input D and the reset input K to $\overline{D}$. In similar fashion, a T flip-flop can be derived from a J-K flip-flop by connecting both the J and K inputs to T. But in this section, we will develop a general design procedure that will serve as the basis for designing a variety of synchronous sequential circuits in the next chapter.

6.3.1   Choosing a Flip-Flop Type

In this subsection, we examine the alternative kinds of storage elements for implementing state.

R-S Latch   The level-sensitive R-S latch has limited utility as a stand-alone building block for holding state. However, it is used as a component in implementing master/slave or edge-triggered flip-flops, and it serves some special functions for debouncing switches. (See Practical Matters at the end of this chapter.)

J-K Flip-Flops Versus D Flip-Flops   In real designs, the most frequently encountered flip-flops are the J-K and the D. The combinational logic associated with determining the next state will often require the fewest gates when the next state function is implemented with J-K flip-flops. However, each J-K flip-flop requires two inputs, and this could lead to more complex wiring. If the goal is to minimize wires, D flip-flops are attractive. In VLSI technologies, where the size of the wiring area is typically a greater concern than gate area, D flip-flops are used almost universally and are usually implemented as cross-coupled inverters as in Figure 6.32.

T Flip-Flops   T flip-flops are rarely available in packaged logic because they are so easily formed from J-K flip-flops. From the viewpoint of conceptual design, however, T flip-flops turn out to be good building blocks for special circuits called *counters*. These are clocked sequential systems that sequence through a periodic series of states, such as the binary numbers 0000 through 1111. We will learn the counter design strategy in the next chapter.

Summary of Flip-Flop Characteristic Equations   We have already introduced characteristic equations as a shorthand for describing flip-flop behavior. They are particularly useful when implementing next state logic, by making it possible to relate the desired flip-flop outputs (*state*) to the inputs that must be generated to obtain the necessary behavior.

If Q is the current state and Q^+ is the next state, the equations for the four flip-flop types are

$$R\text{-}S \text{ latch:} \qquad Q^+ = S + \overline{R}Q$$

$$D \text{ flip-flop:} \qquad Q^+ = D$$

$$J\text{-}K \text{ flip-flop:} \qquad Q^+ = J\overline{Q} + \overline{K}Q$$

$$T \text{ flip-flop:} \qquad Q^+ = T\overline{Q} + \overline{T}Q$$

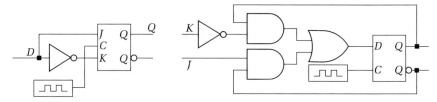

Figure 6.40   *D* flip-flop implemented by *J-K* flip-flop and *J-K* flip-flop implemented by *D* flip-flop.

6.3.2   Conversion of One Flip-Flop Type to Another

Any flip-flop can be implemented as combinational logic for the next state function in conjunction with a flip-flop of another type. As an example, Figure 6.40 shows how to implement a *D* flip-flop with a *J-K* flip-flop and, correspondingly, a *J-K* flip-flop with a *D* flip-flop.

Consider the leftmost circuit. If *D* is 1, we place the *J-K* flip-flop in its set input configuration ($J = 1$, $K = 0$). If *D* is 0, *J-K*'s inputs are configured for reset ($J = 0$, $K = 1$). In the case of the rightmost circuit, the *D* flip-flop's input is driven with logic that implements the characteristic equation for the *J-K* flip-flop, namely $J\overline{Q} + \overline{K}Q$.

General Procedure   We can follow a general procedure to map among the different kinds of flip-flops. It is based on the concept of an *excitation table*, that is, a table that lists all possible state transitions and the values of the flip-flop inputs that cause a given transition to take place.

Figure 6.41 gives excitation tables for *R-S*, *J-K*, *T*, and *D* flip-flops. If the current state is 0 and the next state is to be 0 too, then the first row of the table describes the flip-flop input to cause that state transition to take place. If an *R-S* latch is being used, it doesn't matter what value is placed on *R* as long as *S* is left unasserted. $R = 0$, $S = 0$ holds the current state at 0; $R = 1$, $S = 0$ resets the state to 0. The effect is the same.

If we are using a *J-K* flip-flop, the transition from 0 to 0 is accomplished by ensuring that *J* is left unasserted. The value of *K* does not matter. If $J = 0$, $K = 0$, the current state is held at 0; if $J = 0$, $K = 1$, the state is reset to 0.

If we are using a *T* flip-flop, the transition does not change the current state, so the input should be 0. If a *D* flip-flop is used, we set the input to the desired next state, which is 0 in this case. The same kind of analysis can be applied to complete the excitation table for the three other cases.

A flip-flop's next state function can be written as a *K*-map. For example, the next state *K*-map for the *D* flip-flop is shown in Figure 6.42(a). To realize a *D* flip-flop in terms of a *J-K* flip-flop, we simply remap the state transitions implied by the *D* flip-flop's *K*-map into equations for the *J* and *K* inputs. In other words, we express *J* and *K* as functions of the current state and *D*.

Q	Q^+	R	S	J	K	T	D
0	0	X	0	0	X	0	0
0	1	0	1	1	X	1	1
1	0	1	0	X	1	1	0
1	1	0	X	X	0	0	1

Figure 6.41   Excitation tables for *R-S*, *J-K*, *T*, and *D* flip-flops.

$$Q^+ = D$$

(a) K-map for *D* flip-flop and characteristic equation

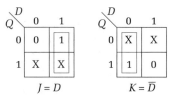

$$J = D$$ $$K = \overline{D}$$

(b) K-maps for *J* and *K* inputs

Figure 6.42   Implementing a given flip-flop by one of another type.

The procedure works as follows. First we draw K-maps for J and K, as in Figure 6.42(b). Then we fill them in the following manner. When $D = 0$ and $Q = 0$, the next state is 0. The excitation table tells us that the inputs to J and K should be 0 and X, respectively, if we desire a 0-to-0 transition. These values are placed into corresponding entries of the J and K K-maps. The inputs $D = 0$, $Q = 1$ lead to a next state of 0. This is a 1-to-0 transition, and J and K should be X and 1, respectively. For $D = 1$, $Q = 0$, the transition is from 0 to 1, and J must be 1 and K should be X. The final transition, $D = 1$, $Q = 1$, is from 1 to 1, and J and K are X and 0. A quick look at the K-maps confirms that $J = D$ and $K = \overline{D}$.

The implementation of a J-K flip-flop by a D flip-flop follows the same procedure. We start with a K-map to describe the next state in terms of the three variables J, K, and the current state Q. To obtain the transition from 0 to 0 or 1 to 0 requires that D be 0; similarly, D must be 1 to implement a 0-to-1 or 1-to-1 transition. In other words, the function for D is identical to the next state. The equation for D can be read directly from the next state K-map for the J-K flip-flop:

$$D = J\overline{Q} + \overline{K}Q$$

This K-map is shown in Figure 6.43.

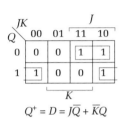

$$Q^+ = D = J\overline{Q} + \overline{K}Q$$

Figure 6.43 K-map for *J-K* flip-flop.

6.4 Metastability and Asynchronous Inputs

The problems of asynchronous inputs and their effects on state changes are covered next.

6.4.1 Asynchronous Circuits

So far, we have described only simple clocked synchronous circuits. These are circuits in which all components are driven from a common reference signal (this covers multiphase clocks as long as they are ultimately derived from a single common clock). The state of the circuit changes only in relation to the clock. The clock event determines when inputs are sampled and when outputs can change. If the setup, hold, and propagation delays are appropriately designed, there are no problems in composing components by connecting the output of one to the input of another.

An *asynchronous* circuit is one whose inputs, state, and outputs can be sampled or changed independently of any clock reference. Asynchronous circuits lie at the heart of every synchronous circuit. The basic *R-S* latch is an asynchronous circuit, whereas the edge-triggered *D* flip-flop, constructed from several such latches, is synchronous. The *J-K* master/slave flip-flop falls into something of a gray area because of its ones-catching behavior.

Synchronous Versus Asynchronous Inputs Even a supposedly synchronous circuit like the D flip-flop can have asynchronous inputs, such as preset and clear. These set the output (preset) or reset it (clear) whenever they are asserted, independent of the clock. *Synchronous inputs* are active only while the clock edge or level is active; at all other times, changes on these inputs are not noticed by the memory element. *Asynchronous inputs*, on the other hand, take effect immediately and are independent of the clock.

Glitches make asynchronous inputs extremely dangerous and should be avoided whenever possible. A glitch on the logic that drives an asynchronous input can cause a flip-flop to be cleared or set when no state change was called for. It is good design practice to choose components that have only synchronous inputs.

6.4.2   The Problem of Asynchronous Inputs

Sometimes asynchronous inputs cannot be avoided—for example, when a signal must pass from the outside world into the synchronous system. An example might be a reset signal, triggered by an operator pressing a push-button. It is particularly dangerous to fan out an asynchronous input to many points in the clocked system: if the input changes close to the clock event, it may be seen at some flip-flops but not others, leading to an "impossible" state.

An incorrect circuit for handling an asynchronous input is shown in Figure 6.44(a). Two positive edge-triggered D flip-flops are driven by the same asynchronous input. You would expect both devices to hold the same state, yet because of different wiring and other internal delays, one flip-flop

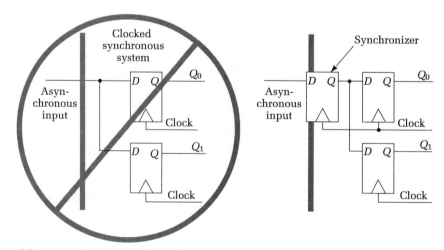

(a) Incorrect fan-out to multiple flip-flops   (b) Correct synchronization

Figure 6.44   Incorrect and correct circuits for handling an asynchronous input.

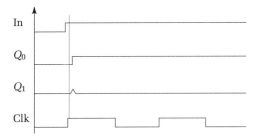

Figure 6.45   Outputs of two positive edge-triggered flip-flops when their input changes close to the clock edge.

is set while the other remains reset. The assumption that both flip-flops hold the same state is now invalid. The timing waveform in Figure 6.45 tells the sad tale.

A better way to deal with an asynchronous signal is to *synchronize* it to the clocked system. This synchronization is accomplished by placing a single D flip-flop between the input source and the rest of the system. The proper circuit is shown in Figure 6.44(b). The flip-flop's output Q will change only in relation to the clock and can be properly fanned out and distributed to other points in the circuit in a synchronous manner.

6.4.3   Metastability and Synchronizer Failure

What if the setup and hold times of the synchronizer flip-flop are not met by the asynchronous signal? Under such conditions, the output of the synchronizer is undefined.

Normally, we minimize this problem by choosing the synchronizer flip-flop from the fastest available logic family, with the shortest possible setup and hold times. Unfortunately, the problem cannot be eliminated completely. The behavior of this flip-flop is worse than unpredictable: it can result in input values injected into the system that cannot be interpreted as either a 1 or a 0. Figure 6.45 gives a hint of this: Q_1 exhibits a partial transition that falters back to 0. This "in-between" voltage is called the *metastable* state. Under the right (or wrong) conditions, the flip-flop can hang in this state indefinitely, a so-called *synchronizer failure*.

An Analogy for Understanding Metastability   Figure 6.46 provides a useful analogy for describing the nature of synchronizer failure. The states of the flip-flop are represented by two flat regions separated by a steep slope. The flat parts represent the stable states, logic 0 and logic 1. For the purpose of this analogy, we will represent the state of the flip-flop by a ball in one plateau or the other. To change the state, energy must be exerted to push the ball up and over the slope to the other side.

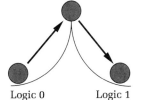

Logic 0   Logic 1

Figure 6.46   Analogy for explaining synchronizer failure.

When setup and hold time constraints are met, there is sufficient energy to cause the state change. If these constraints are not met, three cases are possible, two that yield acceptable behavior and one that does not. In the first case, there isn't enough energy to get the ball over the summit, and it rolls back—the state is not changed. In the second case, the energy might be just enough to get the ball over the top—and the state changes from 0 to 1. Both of these are acceptable outcomes. However, there is a small probability that just enough energy is imparted that the ball can be pushed up the slope but remains tottering at the top, not able to return to one or the other of the stable states. This is the metastable state.

Theoretically, a flip-flop can remain in the metastable state. However, thermal disturbances and asymmetries in signal delays within the transistor-level implementation of the flip-flop usually make it settle in one state or the other in some period of time.

Figure 6.47 shows a circuit with its data input and clock input tied together, a perfect circuit in which to violate setup constraints. A typical trace from an oscilloscope is shown in Figure 6.48. Even though a stable state is usually obtained (after a potentially long delay), this can still cause a system failure if the flip-flop has not left the metastable state by the end of the system's clock period.

Reducing the Chance of Synchronizer Failure   The only way to recover from synchronizer failure is to reset the entire circuit. While the probability of synchronizer failure can be made small, it can never be eliminated as long as there are asynchronous inputs.

One way to reduce the probability of synchronizer failure is to lengthen the system's clock period. This gives the synchronizer flip-flop more time to make its decision to enter a stable state. The longer the clock period is stretched, the lower the probability of failure. Unfortunately, this is not an adequate solution for high-performance systems in which a short clock period is critical.

A second strategy places two synchronizers in series between the asynchronous input and the rest of the synchronous system. Both flip-flops

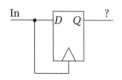

Figure 6.47   Circuit under test for Figure 6.48.

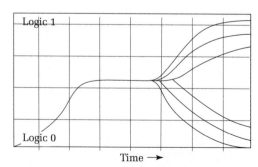

Figure 6.48   Oscilloscope sketch of metastable behavior.

must be metastable before the synchronization fails, an event with low probability.

A third strategy does away with the clock altogether and follows a timing strategy that is independent of the speed of the individual circuits. We examine this intriguing approach to digital design in the next section.

6.5 Self-Timed and Speed-Independent Circuits

Although synchronous system design is our preferred approach, it is not always possible to build a complete system this way. As digital systems become larger, incorporating more components, or faster, running at higher clock rates, the limiting problem becomes how to distribute a single global clock without introducing intolerable clock skew.

6.5.1 Locally Clocked, Globally Delay-Insensitive Approach

When a global clocking approach is inappropriate, the alternative is to partition the digital system into locally clocked pieces that communicate with each other using *delay-insensitive* signaling conventions.

A delay-insensitive protocol allows the sender and receiver to communicate with each other without the need for a global clock. Each proceeds at its own speed, synchronizing its communications when it needs to interact.

A good example of this locally clocked, globally delay-insensitive approach can be found in just about every digital system constructed from multiple printed circuit boards. Each board contains its own independent clock, and the logic on the board is designed to be fully synchronous. When one board needs to communicate with another, special signaling conventions are used that have been designed to be insensitive to delay. We examine these conventions next.

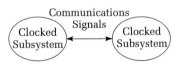

Figure 6.49 Independently clocked subsystems.

6.5.2 Delay-Insensitive Signaling

The concept of delay-insensitive signaling is shown graphically in Figure 6.49 and Figure 6.50. One subsystem is called the *requester*, *client*, or *master*, while the other is called the *provider*, *server*, or *slave*. It is common for a given component to contain logic that allows it to be

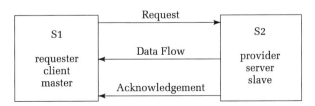

Figure 6.50 Request/acknowledgment signaling.

either a master or a slave. For data to flow from the slave to the master, the master must make an explicit request to the slave. If the master requests a read, the slave responds by providing the requested data and signals an acknowledgment when the data is ready for the master.

Synchronous Delay-Insensitive Signaling   There is no reason why the communication between the requester and the provider cannot proceed in a completely synchronous manner. This is demonstrated by the timing diagram of Figure 6.51. The protocol is synchronous because the request and acknowledgment signals are asserted with the rising edge of the clock. They can be sampled on the falling edge.

If it is known that the slave will respond in a certain number of cycles, an acknowledgment signal is not strictly needed. However, this method can be inefficient if there is a wide variation among the speeds of potential slaves. We would have to set the number of cycles to that of the slowest slave.

To provide at least some degree of speed independence, an alternative signaling convention allows the slave to delay the master by asserting a wait signal if it cannot satisfy the request in the allotted number of cycles. This is shown in Figure 6.52. When the slave unasserts this signal, it implicitly acknowledges that the data is available for the master. This signaling still assumes a single global clock and that all interface signals change synchronously with clock edges.

Delay Insensitivity Without a Clock: Four-Cycle Handshaking   True speed-independent signaling can no longer assume that signals change with

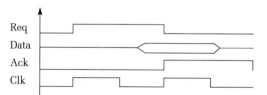

Figure 6.51   Synchronous request/acknowledgment signaling.

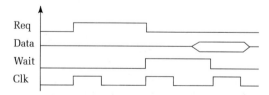

Figure 6.52   Synchronous request with wait signaling.

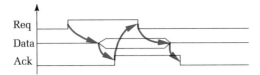

Figure 6.53   Four-cycle asynchronous signaling.

respect to a global clock. A component that asserts a signal must ensure that the signal has been observed by the component for which it is intended. This requires that the signals be *interlocked*: a request cannot be unasserted until the target acknowledges that it has been seen and acted on.

A four-cycle interlocked handshake, sometimes called *return-to-zero signaling*, is shown in Figure 6.53. Initially, both request and acknowledge are at 0. The request for data is initiated by asserting the request signal. Because the clocks of the master and slave are unrelated, the master can make no assumptions about how long it takes for the slave to notice the request. That the request has been seen and acted on is indicated only by the slave's assertion of its acknowledgment signal. This is driven high only after the requested data has been placed on the data signal lines.

Similarly, the slave cannot make assumptions about whether the master has seen its acknowledgment signal. It must wait, continuing to drive the data and the acknowledgment until the master communicates that the data has been latched by unasserting its request signal. Now the slave can stop driving the data and can reset its acknowledgment to 0. The acknowledgment signal must become unasserted before a new request can be made.

Four-cycle signaling guarantees that the master and slave will behave properly in all timing scenarios. The request signal is asynchronous to the slave and the acknowledgment is asynchronous to the master: both must be synchronized and provide the unavoidable potential for synchronizer failure.

Two-Cycle Handshaking   An alternative to four-cycle signaling is called two-cycle or *non-return-to-zero signaling*. The waveforms are shown in Figure 6.54. Initially, both request and acknowledge are at 0. The master

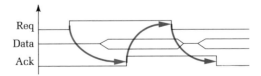

Figure 6.54   Two-cycle asynchronous signaling.

makes a request by complementing the request line, in this case driving it high. Eventually, the slave notices the change in request state, services the request, and acknowledges that the data is available by complementing its acknowledgment line, driving it high.

The master makes its next request by complementing the request line once again, driving it low. The slave stops driving the data lines with their old data, services the new request, places new data on the data lines, and signals that it has accomplished its task by complementing the acknowledge line, driving it low.

Although two-cycle signaling involves fewer transitions to accomplish the same function as four-cycle signaling, it requires that the master and slave contain an additional state to recognize a change in the request/acknowledge signal lines. Four-cycle signaling usually requires less hardware for its implementation.

Self-Timed Circuits   Using the request/acknowledgment signaling conventions just described, we can build internally clocked circuit components that communicate with each other in a speed-independent manner. It is also possible to build these components so that they do not contain any internal clocks.

These unclocked circuits are sometimes called *self-timed circuits*. A self-timed circuit can determine on its own when a given request has been serviced. This usually involves mimicking the worst-case propagation delay path by using special logic to delay the request signal.

This scheme for a self-timed combinational logic block is shown in Figure 6.55. The delay line merely slows down the acknowledgment signal, derived from the request signal, long enough to guarantee that the combinational logic has sufficient time to compute the correct output. If the worst-case delay path is n gate levels deep, the delay line should be a comparable number of gate levels.

Self-timed systems continue to interest designers as integrated circuits become denser and the problems of clock distribution become even more significant. Many complex VLSI circuits, such as dynamic memory chips, contain self-timed elements, and a whole microprocessor has been constructed in a self-timed manner. More information about self-timed circuits and systems can be found in the references at the end of this chapter.

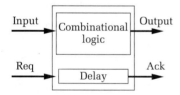

Figure 6.55   Self-timed combinational logic block.

6.6   Practical Matters

In this section, we look at two important practical issues related to the design of synchronous digital systems: methods for debouncing mechanical switches and the use of timer generating chips. Mechanical switches provide a very simple input device, but they must be used carefully because a single switch transition could appear as multiple transitions to internal logic. Programmable timer chips provide a simple way to generate clock signals within a system.

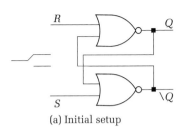

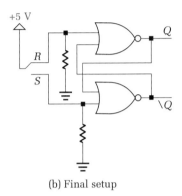

(a) Initial setup

(b) Final setup

Figure 6.56 Debouncing a switch.

6.6.1   Debouncing Switches

A problem with the use of mechanical switches in digital circuits is a phenomenon known as *bouncing*. When a switch is flipped from one terminal to another, it does not make a clean, solid contact with the new terminal. Instead, it bounces off the terminal into the air several times before finally coming to rest. Because of this and the fact that TTL chips treat floating inputs as logic 1's, a single flip of the switch that should cause a 1-to-0 transition in fact causes several transitions from 1 to 0. This can cause errors in the circuitry that is reading the switch's output.

The Solution   The simple R-S latch provides the solution for debouncing mechanical switches. We depend on the fact that the latch will hold its current state when both inputs are 0.

Figure 6.56(a) shows the initial setup, a single pole/double throw (SPDT) switch and an R-S latch. We should get a 0 at the output Q when we place the switch in one position and a 1 at Q when we place it in the opposite position. Since the holding state occurs when R and S are both 0, we want these to be the default values while the switch is in transition between its settings. The switch must be able to force one of these inputs to a 1 depending on its current setting.

This setup leads to the wiring diagram of Figure 6.56(b). The single contact side of the switch is connected to the power supply while the double contact side is connected to the R and S inputs of the latch. When the switch is connected to the top output, R is asserted and Q is reset to 0. When it is placed in the lower position, S is asserted and Q is set to 1.

This diagram does not yet solve the bounce problem. We must ensure that when the switch is not connected to one side, the latch input remains steady at 0. To accomplish this, we wire both R and S to ground through resistors. The resistors are sized so that the input can be pulled high when the switch is trying to do so. They also protect the circuit against a short circuit between ground and the power supply.

When the switch is in the reset position, the R input to the latch is set high and Q is low. Now suppose that the switch is in transition from the R to the S position. The switch breaks connection with the R terminal, and the ground connection pulls the latch input low. The latch is now in its holding state because both inputs are 0.

When the switch first touches the S contact, the S input to the latch goes high, and the latch is set with Q equal to 1. If the switch bounces, temporarily breaking the connection, the latch input returns to 0, leaving the latch in the holding state. If the switch bounces back, remaking the S connection, the latch is simply set again and no state change occurs.

As long as the switch does not bounce far enough to remake the R connection, the Q output will remain high as long as the switch is bouncing into its final setting position. The same analysis applies for a switch transition from resting at the S terminal to connecting the R terminal.

6.6.2   555 Timer Component

The 555 timer is a very useful component for the digital system designer, an example of a programmable timer chip. By *programmable*, we mean that the chip can be "tuned" to generate clocks of alternative periods and duty cycles.

The circuit diagram for the programmable timer is shown in Figure 6.57. The period and duty cycle are controlled by placing the appropriate resistors and capacitors between the 555 timer's pins, as shown in the figure. The following formulas describe the relationships between the resistors, the capacitor, and the generated clock's characteristics:

Clock high time $= 0.7(R_a + R_b)C_1$

Clock low time $= 0.7(R_b)C_1$

Clock period = high time + low time $= 0.7(R_a + 2R_b)C_1$

$$\text{Clock frequency} = \frac{1}{\text{clock period}} = \frac{1.44}{0.7\,(R_a + R_b)\,C_1}$$

$$\text{Duty cycle} = \frac{R_a + R_b}{R_a + 2R_b}$$

Example   Capacitance is measured in farads, resistance is in ohms, and $R \bullet C =$ farads $\bullet$ ohms = seconds (you may want to review Appendix B if this is foreign to you). Suppose we want to design a clock signal with a

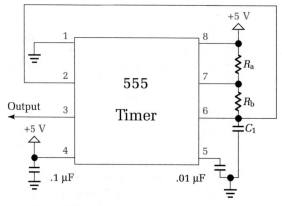

Figure 6.57   555 programmable timer.

period of approximately 500 μs and a 75% duty cycle. This is a frequency of 2000 hertz, written as 2 kHz.

The first step is to determine the ratio of the resistors needed to obtain the desired duty cycle. Substituting into the duty cycle formula, we obtain

$$0.75 = \frac{R_a + R_b}{R_a + 2R_b}$$

$$R_a = 2R_b$$

The duty cycle is completely determined by the ratio of the resistors, not their specific values.

To achieve the 75% duty cycle, R_a should have twice the resistance of R_b. Suppose that we choose $R_a = 5000\ \Omega$ and $R_b = 2500\ \Omega$. At a 75% duty cycle, the high time of the clock is 375 μs and the low time is 125 μs. Substituting the chosen resistances into one of the clock-time equations should give us the appropriate value for C_1:

$$500 \times 10^{-6}\ \text{s} = 0.7\,(5000\ \Omega + 2 \times 2500\ \Omega)\,C_1$$

$$0.0714 \times 10^{-6}\ \text{F} = C_1$$

In terms of practical design, it may not be possible to obtain exactly the desired clock signal with the resistors and capacitors at hand. Suppose we have only 0.1-μF capacitors. Substituting one of these in the equations yields a clock with period 700 μs and a high time of 525 μs. This is somewhat slower than our design goal.

Alternatively, we could replace R_a with a 3600-Ω resistor and R_b with an 1800-Ω resistor. Keeping C_1 a 0.1-μF capacitor, we obtain a clock with period 504 μs and a 75% duty cycle. This is quite close to our desired clock waveform.

Figure 6.58 gives a chart that plots the free-running timer frequency as a function of $R_a + 2R_b$ and C_1. This chart is useful for identifying approximate values for the resistors and capacitors to obtain a clock of a particular frequency. For example, it is easy to see that a 0.1-μF capacitor and resistors such that $R_a + 2R_b = 7200\ \Omega$ should yield a clock frequency close to 2 kHz.

A Practical Warning   The 555 timer draws large amounts of current for short periods of time when the output changes state. For this reason, it is important to put a 0.1-μF bypass capacitor from the 5-V pin, pin 4, on the 555 to ground. This capacitor will minimize spikes that can upset the rest of your circuit. In general, it is good practice to put bypass capacitors liberally throughout your design on the power pins of ICs.

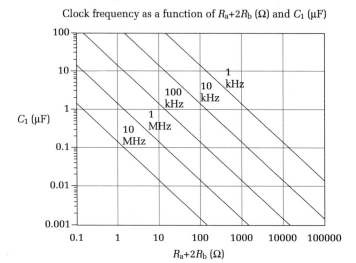

Figure 6.58 Free-running clock frequency of 555 timer.

Chapter Review

In this chapter, we have begun our study of circuits with state by looking at the fundamental building block of such circuits: the latch and its more complex derivative, the flip-flop. We introduced the basic R-S latch and the level-sensitive R-S latch. These devices suffer from a "forbidden state." Once this state is entered, the state you will go to next is unpredictable.

The J-K flip-flop attempts to eliminate the forbidden state, replacing it with an ability to toggle the state instead. However, simply feeding the outputs back to the inputs of a J-K flip-flop is not sufficient to correct the problem, and we introduce an alternative implementation approach, called the master/slave flip-flop. The flip-flop is constructed from two stages of latches, the first being set while the clock is high, the second when the clock goes low. This "two-phase" approach breaks any possible feedback paths. But master/slave flip-flops have their own problem: ones catching. We correct this problem in positive and negative edge-triggered flip-flops.

Next we discussed some issues related to clock methodologies, starting with the meaning of setup and hold time constraints as they relate to latches and flip-flops. If an input changes within the window formed by the setup time before the clocking event and the hold time after the clocking event, we do not know what value will be stored in the memory element. There is even a chance that the flip-flop will be caught in an in-between state, called the *metastable state*, should the input change too near the clock edge. Theoretically, it could be stuck in this state forever. Fortunately, when a system is constructed from a compatible family of logic, such as TTL LS logic, flip-flops can be cascaded without fear of setup and hold time violations.

We also described narrow-width clocking and two-phase nonoverlapped clocking, which are methodologies needed when building systems from latches. The two-phase clocking scheme, commonly used in some variation within VLSI systems, has the advantage that you need only worry about worst-case signal propagation delays. Narrow-width clocking has the disadvantage that you must also be concerned with "fast signals." This requires a careful analysis of best-case propagation delays as well as worst-case ones. Neither approach is necessary if edge-triggered flip-flops are used, since clock edges rather than levels are used to control state updates in the storage elements.

Finally, we briefly described asynchronous inputs and the dangers in using them. Unfortunately, they cannot be completely eliminated. We introduced the synchronizer concept to reduce their danger. We also showed the four-cycle signaling convention as a protocol for communication among independently clocked subsystems. We presented the concept of a self-timed circuit, which determines on it own when it has finished computing its function. These circuits will provide the basis for future systems that may have no clocks in them at all.

Further Reading

Most logic design textbooks provide an extensive discussion of flip-flops along the lines of the presentation we have given here. However, clocking issues and metastability are not usually covered as thoroughly. An unusual exception to this is T. R. Blakeslee's book, *Digital Design with Standard MSI & LSI*, 2nd edition, Wiley, New York, 1979. Chapter 6, "Nasty Realities I: Race Conditions and Hang-up States," formed the basis for our discussion of asynchronous inputs, clock skew, and metastable states.

The concept of narrow-width versus two-phase nonoverlapped clocking is best described in C. Mead and L. Conway's classic text *Introduction to VLSI Design*, Addison-Wesley, Reading, MA, 1980. Chapter 7, "System Timing," contributed by Professor C. Seitz of the California Institute of Technology, provided the motivation for the discussion of clocking strategies, metastable behavior, and self-timed circuits in this chapter. Although it is an advanced presentation, it should be read by every designer attempting to build a high-performance system.

Metastability has plagued digital designers for many years but was not well understood until the mid-1970s. The classic papers describing the phenomenon include Chaney, Ornstein, and Littlefield, "Beware the Synchronizer," *Proceedings of the Spring COMPCON Meeting*, San Francisco, September 1972, and Chaney and Molnar, "Anomalous Behavior of Synchronizer and Arbiter Circuits," *IEEE Transactions on Computers*, C-22:4, 421–422 (April 1973).

The concepts of self-timed circuits date back to the early days of computers, but the increased difficulty of building such systems has limited their application in digital design. Self-timed concepts, however, are used extensively in advanced dynamic memory components. The best place to start in finding out more about self-timed circuits is in Seitz's chapter in Mead and Conway's book referenced above. A research group, led by Professor Alain Martin of the California Institute of Technology, has succeeded in implementing a complete 32-bit microprocessor using self-timed techniques. Their work is reported in the *10th CALTECH Conference VLSI Proceedings*; the conference was held in March 1989 in Pasadena, CA.

Exercises

6.1 *(Simple Circuits with Feedback)* Build a feedback circuit with cross-coupled NAND gates. What input conditions cause the state of this latch-like device to be reset? To be set? Does this circuit have forbidden inputs? If so, what are they?

6.2 *(Simple Circuits with Feedback)* An *R-S* latch can be used to determine which of two events has occurred first. Design a circuit with three inputs and three outputs that determines which of three single pole/single throw switches connected to the inputs has been opened first. The circuit will produce a logic 1 on the output that corresponds to that input. Discuss how you would expand this circuit to a larger number of inputs, say 12 inputs or 30 inputs.

6.3 *(Setup and Hold Times)* Imagine that it is possible to have storage devices with negative setup and hold times. What do you think such a concept would be? Draw timing diagrams to illustrate your answer.

6.4 *(D Flip-Flop)* Add preset and clear inputs to the edge-triggered *D* flip-flop of Figure 6.24. Draw the logic schematic of the revised circuit.

6.5 *(D Flip-Flop)* How would you implement a negative edge-triggered *D* flip-flop using NAND gates only? What changes are necessary to make this a positive edge-triggered device?

6.6 *(J-K Flip-Flop)* How would you implement a *J-K* master/slave flip-flop, such as the circuit in Figure 6.22, using NAND gates only? Assume the master and slave latches are actually controlled by the signals $\overline{R}$ and $\overline{S}$.

6.7 *(J-K Flip-Flop)* Starting with the basic circuit schematic for the master/slave *J-K* flip-flop, show how to add asynchronous preset and clear inputs to force the flip-flop into a 1 (preset) or 0 (clear) state. Draw a timing waveform for the preset input, clear input, clock, master stage outputs (P, $\overline{P}$), and slave stage outputs (Q, $\overline{Q}$) showing the operation of preset and clear.

6.8 *(J-K Flip-Flop)* J-K master/slave flip-flops exhibit the phenomenon of ones catching. Briefly explain why this takes place. Can a master/slave flip-flop catch 0's? Explain why or why not.

6.9 *(Flip-Flops)* The basic functionality of a D flip-flop can be implemented by a J-K flip-flop simply by connecting the input signal D to the J-K flip-flop's J input and $\overline{D}$ to the K input.

   a. Show that this is true by comparing the characteristic equations for a D flip-flop and a J-K flip-flop.

   b. Draw a timing waveform for the clock, input D, and outputs Q_{pos}, Q_{neg}, and Q_{ms} that illustrates the differences in input/output behavior of a positive edge-triggered D flip-flop, negative edge-triggered D flip-flop, and master/slave D flip-flop (implemented from a J-K master/slave flip-flop as described in Figure 6.22). Include some transitions on D while the clock is asserted.

6.10 *(Flip-Flops)* Given the input and clock transitions given in Figure Ex6.10, draw a waveform for the output of a J-K device, assuming:

   a. It is a master/slave flip-flop.

   b. It is a positive edge-triggered flip-flop.

   c. It is a negative edge-triggered flip-flop. You may assume 0 setup, hold, and propagation times, and that the initial state of the flip-flop is 0.

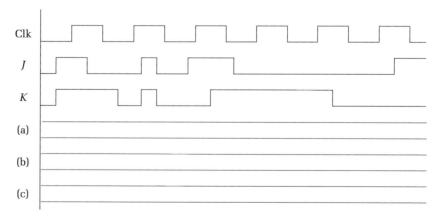

Figure Ex6.10   Timing diagram for Exercise 6.10.

6.11 *(Flip-Flops)* Given the input and clock transitions in Figure Ex6.11, indicate the output of a *D* device assuming:

a. It is a negative edge-triggered flip-flop.

b. It is a master/slave flip-flop.

c. It is a positive edge-triggered flip-flop.

d. It is a clocked latch. You may assume 0 setup, hold, and propagation times.

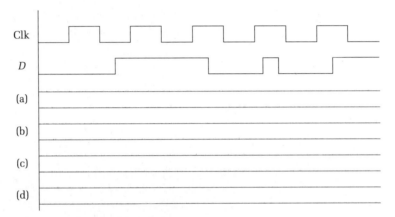

Figure Ex6.11 Timing diagram for Exercise 6.11.

6.12 *(Flip-Flops)* Identify the following statements as either true or false:

a. The inputs to a level-sensitive latch always affect its outputs.

b. Flip-flop delays from the change in the clock edge to the change in the output are typically shorter than flip-flop hold times, so shift registers can be constructed from cascaded flip-flops.

c. Assuming zero setup and hold times, clocked latches and flip-flops produce the same outputs as long as the inputs do not change while the clock is asserted.

d. A master/slave flip-flop behaves similarly to a clocked latch, except that its output can change only near the rising edge of the clock.

e. An edge-triggered *D* flip-flop requires more internal gates than a similar device constructed from a *J-K* master/slave flip-flop.

6.13 *(Flip-Flops)* Match each of the following five circuits (Figure Ex6.13) with the phrase that best describes it from the list: (1) clocked *R-S* latch, (2) clocked *D* latch, (3) master/slave *R-S*

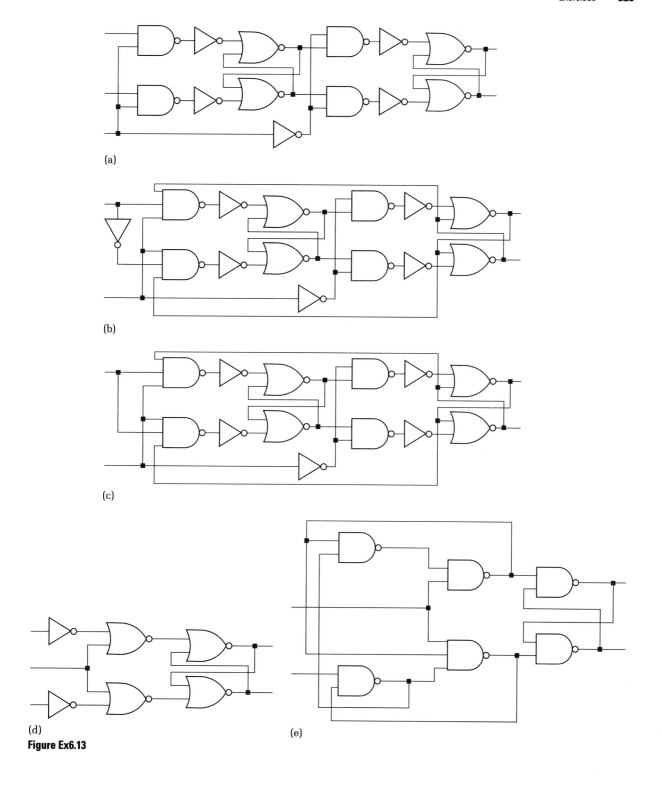

(a)

(b)

(c)

(d)

(e)

Figure Ex6.13

flip-flop, (4) positive edge-triggered *R-S* flip-flop, (5) negative edge-triggered *R-S* flip-flop, (6) master/slave *D* flip-flop, (7) positive edge-triggered *D* flip-flop, (8) negative edge-triggered *D* flip-flop, (9) master/slave *T* flip-flop, (10) positive edge-triggered *T* flip-flop, (11) negative edge-triggered *T* flip-flop, (12) master/slave *J-K* flip-flop, (13) positive edge-triggered *J-K* flip-flop, (14) negative edge-triggered *J-K* flip-flop.

6.14 *(Flip-Flops)* Any flip-flop type can be implemented from another type with suitable logic applied to the latter's inputs. Show how to implement a *J-K* flip-flop starting with a *D* flip-flop.

6.15 *(Flip-Flops)* Show how to implement a *J-K* flip-flop starting with a *T* flip-flop.

6.16 *(Flip-Flops)* Show how to implement a *D* flip-flop starting with a *J-K* flip-flop.

6.17 *(Flip-Flops)* Show how to implement a *D* flip-flop starting with a *T* flip-flop.

6.18 *(Flip-Flops)* Show how to implement a *T* flip-flop starting with a *J-K* flip-flop.

6.19 *(Flip-Flops)* Show how to implement a *T* flip-flop starting with a *D* flip-flop.

6.20 *(Clock Generator)* Extend the circuit of Figure 6.37 to generate a three-phase nonoverlapping clock. How would the circuit be extended to generate a four-phase nonoverlapping clock?

6.21 *(Clock Skew)* Given the timing specification of the 74LS74 flip-flop of Figure 6.14, what is the worst-case skew in the clock that could be tolerated when one 74LS74 needs to pass its value to another 74LS74, as in Figure 6.29?

6.22 *(Clocking Issues)* Given the sequential logic circuit of Figure Ex6.22, where the flip-flops have worst-case setup times of 20 ns, propagation delays of 13 ns, and hold times of 5 ns, answer the following questions:

a. Assuming 0 propagation delay through the combinational logic block, what is the maximum allowable frequency of the clock that controls this subsystem?

b. Assuming a typical combinational logic delay of 75 ns and a worst-case delay of 100 ns, how does your answer to part (a) change?

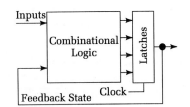

Figure Ex6.22 Sequential circuit for Exercise 6.22.

6.23 *(Two-Phase Clocking)* Consider the two-phased clocked sequential circuit of Figure Ex6.23. Assume that the ϕ_1 and ϕ_2 latches have 5-ns setup times, 5-ns hold times, and 10-ns propagation delays in the worst case. Given that the combinational logic block has a maximum delay of 100 ns and a typical delay of 75 ns, what is the shortest possible period between the rising edge of ϕ_1 and the falling edge of ϕ_2? Show how you obtained your result.

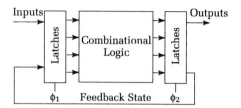

Figure Ex6.23   Two-phase clocked sequential circuit for Exercise 6.23.

6.24 *(Metastability)* You have designed a high-performance disk drive interface. The interface has an internal clock rate of 25 MHz, and asynchronous commands from a computer with a different clock are presented every 200 ns. It works fine, but every few days or weeks it has random operational failures that cause loss of data. There are no component failures, software bugs, or power glitches, and the errors occur mainly for customers who use the interface heavily. Suggest a possible cause of these failures and how you could change the design to reduce the failure rate.

6.25 *(Metastability)* One way to reduce the probability of synchronizer failure is to place two synchronizer flip-flops in series between the asynchronous input and the rest of the synchronous digital system. Why do you think this reduces the problem of metastability?

6.26 *(Delay Insensitive Handshaking)* Draw a simple flowchart for the master side and the slave side algorithms of the four-cycle handshake. Repeat for the two-cycle handshake. How does the complexity of the two approaches compare?

6.27 *(Practical Matters)* How would the debounce circuit of Figure 6.56 change if you were to use an $\overline{R}\text{-}\overline{S}$ latch instead of an $R\text{-}S$ latch?

6.28 *(Practical Matters)* Suppose you are to design a debouncing circuit using a single pole/single throw (SPST) switch. Can it be done? What problems do you face?

6.29   *(Practical Matters)*   Given the discussion of the 555 timer chip, is it possible to obtain duty cycles of less than 50%? If it is, give an example of resistor ratios needed to obtain such a duty cycle. If not, explain why and give a possible scheme for deriving a waveform with less than a 50% duty cycle from the 555's output.

6.30   *(Practical Matters)*   Use the equations given in Section 6.6.2 and the chart in Figure 6.58 to configure the 555 timer according to the following specifications. Show all of your intermediate work, coming as close to the specification as you can:

a. Choose resistors and a capacitor to obtain a 100-kHz clock with 67% duty cycle.

b. Choose resistors to obtain a 1 MHz clock with 75% duty cycle using a 0.1-μF capacitor.

c. Choose resistors and a capacitor to obtain a clock period of 140 μs and 75% duty cycle.

d. Given a clock period of 1 μs, $R_a = 9$ kΩ, $R_b = 1$ kΩ, what is the duty cycle and what size of capacitor should be used?

7 Sequential Logic Case Studies

Throw theory into the fire; it only spoils life.
—*M. A. Bakunin*

We must use time as a tool, not as a couch.
—*J. F. Kennedy*

Introduction

In this chapter, we illustrate some of the operational characteristics of sequential circuits by examining three particularly useful sequential logic components: registers, counters, and memories. Registers contain groups of storage elements that are read or written as a unit. *Register files* are multiple registers within a single integrated component. *Random-access memories* are generalizations of register files with very many storage elements. *Shift registers* contain logic to circulate the contents of the storage elements among themselves. *Counters* are registers with additional logic that cycle the register's contents through a predefined sequence of states. If these states are interpreted as a binary or BCD number, the state sequence may increase (an *up-counter*) or decrease (a *down-counter*). In particular, we shall cover:

■ *Construction of various kinds of registers and counters.* Starting with the flip-flop building blocks introduced in the previous chapter, we show how to build registers and counters.

■ *Counter design procedure.* We develop a procedure for mapping a behavioral description of a counter into an implementation based on flip-flops and combinational logic. This is a primitive form of the

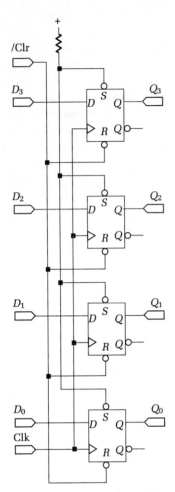

Figure 7.1 Possible implementation of a four-input register.

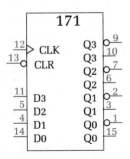

Figure 7.2 Schematic shape of the TTL 74171 register component.

more general finite-state machine design procedure we describe in the next chapter.

- *Counters available as packaged parts.* We will examine catalog counters and some of the pitfalls in their use.

- *Random-access memories.* We describe the function and timing behavior of logic components with very many storage elements.

7.1 Kinds of Registers and Counters

In this section, we will examine the basic kinds of storage elements found in digital logic: registers, RAMs, shifters, and counters.

7.1.1 Storage Registers

A *register* is a group of storage elements read or written as a unit. The simplest way to construct a register is by grouping together as many D flip-flops as you need to obtain your desired bit width. Figure 7.1 shows a four-input register built by wiring together the clocks of four flip-flops.

The individual flip-flops have active low reset (R) and set (S) inputs. Since they affect the outputs independently of the clock, they are asynchronous. On the other hand, the D data inputs are synchronous. They are sampled only in conjunction with clocking events.

Figure 7.1 gives the implementation of a TTL 74171 "Quadruple D-type Flip-flop with Clear" register component, and Figure 7.2 gives its schematic shape. The bubble notation shows which inputs and outputs are active low.

Circuits such as the one in Figure 7.1 are at the heart of almost all packaged registers. However, there are many variations on the basic theme, usually involving additional control signals for the inputs and outputs. One extension provides a load signal. The register's internal logic holds the current state on each clock as long as a load is not asserted. When a load is asserted, the new inputs are gated to the internal inputs of the flip-flops. These replace the current state when the clock edge arrives.

Another extension allows the register's outputs to be tri-state or open collector. In this way multiple registers can share common output wires. External logic selectively enables a single register to place its outputs on the shared wires.

As a concrete example, consider the TTL 74377 "Octal D-type Flip-flops with Enable" component. It is an eight-element register constructed from positive edge-triggered D flip-flops (see Figure 7.3(a)). It provides an active low input enable signal. When the load signal is low and the positive edge of the clock arrives, the flip-flops receive new data. Otherwise the current contents of the storage elements are held despite the clock transitions.

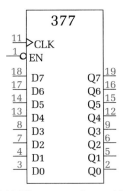

(a) TTL 74377 register with
input enable

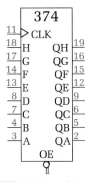

(b) TTL 74374 register with
output enable

Figure 7.3 Schematic shapes of other
register components.

The TTL 74374 "Octal D-type Flip-flops with Tri-state Outputs" component contains an additional active low output enable signal (see Figure 7.3(b)). When this signal is driven low, the contents of the register are visible at the outputs. Otherwise, the outputs are tri-state.

Register Files If registers group multiple storage elements into a unit, then register files extend the grouping to multiple registers. Each register in the register file is called a *word* and is identified by a unique index or *address*.

The component contains its own internal decoders. In conjunction with an externally specified address, the decoders select a specific register file word to be written. On a read, the selected word is multiplexed to the outputs.

An example is the TTL 74670 "4-by-4 Register File with Tri-State Outputs," whose schematic shape is shown in Figure 7.4. The device contains 16 D flip-flops organized into four words of four flip-flops each. The RB, RA and WB, WA inputs are driven with 2-bit binary encodings of one of four registers to be read or written, respectively.

The read enable ($\overline{\text{RE}}$) and write enable ($\overline{\text{WE}}$) inputs are active low. Because of the independent enable signals, it is possible to read and write this register file at the same time (presumably to different register words).

Interestingly, this device has no distinguished clock signal. It uses the $\overline{\text{WE}}$ signal and the write address bits to generate the clock inputs to the internal flip-flops. Because the component lacks an explicit clock, it should be used with great care. The write address lines must be stable before the $\overline{\text{WE}}$ signal arrives, otherwise the wrong word might be written. Any glitches on the $\overline{\text{WE}}$ signal could also lead to unwanted writes.

Random-Access Memories Registers are convenient for holding small amounts of information, usually in the range of 4 to 16 bits. However, many digital systems require substantially more storage elements than this. *Random-access memory*, or RAM, offers a solution. By using very transistor-efficient methods for implementing storage elements, RAM generalizes the register file concept to make many more words available in a single integrated circuit package. A small RAM might hold 256 four-bit words (1024 storage elements), a state-of-the-art device contains over 4 million storage elements, and 16-million-bit devices are on the way. Very fast but small-capacity RAMs are just as difficult to design as the very large but much slower memories. We cover RAMs in more detail in Section 7.6.

7.1.2 Shift Registers

Registers can be used for other applications besides simply storing bits. They are often used to circulate, or *shift*, values among the storage elements. In this subsection, we concentrate on register components that shift as well as store. These are called *shift registers*.

Figure 7.4 Schematic shape of the
TTL 74670 4-by-4 register file.

TO USE
THE D_f

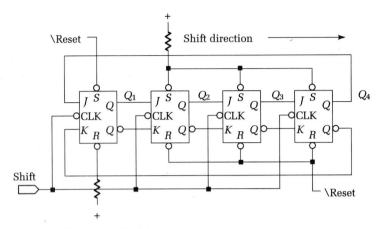

Figure 7.5   Quad right-shifting circular shift register.

Figure 7.5 shows the logic of a simple right-shifting *circular* shift register constructed from master/slave flip-flops. Data moves from left to right. On every shift pulse, the contents of a given flip-flop are replaced by the contents of the flip-flop to its left. The leftmost device receives its inputs from the rightmost. Because flip-flop propagation times far exceed hold times, the values are passed correctly from one stage to the next (we discussed cascaded flip-flops in Section 6.2.1).

The step-by-step operation of the shift register is shown graphically in Figure 7.6, for an initial configuration of $Q_1 = 1$, $Q_2 = 0$, $Q_3 = 0$, $Q_4 = 0$ followed by three shift pulses. The values move from the left to the right and wrap around from right to left. We also show this in the timing diagram of Figure 7.7.

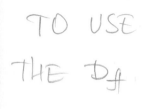

Figure 7.6   Circular shift behavior.

Variations: Parallel Versus Serial Inputs and Outputs   Although the circuit of Figure 7.5 provides a primitive ability to shift, we have no way to load the shift register with an initial value! Most shift registers contain

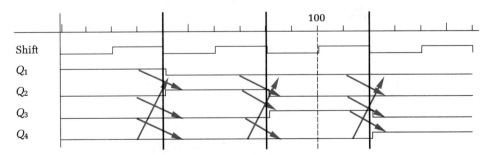

Figure 7.7   Timing diagram of the behavior of the shift register of Figure 7.5.

additional logic to load the internal flip-flops from external inputs. The two major ways to do this are through serial or parallel data inputs.

The *serial input* approach is the simpler of the two. Instead of having a feedback path between the rightmost and leftmost flip-flops, as in Figure 7.5, a shift register with serial inputs has an external connection to the leftmost flip-flop. The register is loaded by successively providing new values at the serial input, in conjunction with the shift pulse. Previously provided inputs shift through the elements of the register.

A shift register with *parallel inputs* contains multiplexing logic at the input to each internal flip-flop. The flip-flop receives a new value from its left neighbor when the shift register is in shift mode or from an external input when the register is in load mode.

A similar variation distinguishes between parallel and serial outputs. *Parallel outputs* mean that the outputs of the internal flip-flops are visible at the pins of the register's IC package. With *serial outputs*, only the value of the last element is visible outside the register, such as Q_4 in Figure 7.5. The primary motivation for serial outputs is to reduce the number of output connections, since the flip-flop outputs are always available inside the shift register.

Example   Universal Shift Register To illustrate these concepts, let's consider the 74194 "4-Bit Bidirectional Universal Shift Register" TTL component. Figure 7.8 shows its schematic shape and function table. This device can operate in four distinct modes, determined by the values at the control inputs S_1 and S_0: hold data (S_1, S_0 = 00), shift right Q_A toward Q_D (S_1, S_0 = 01), shift left Q_D toward Q_A (S_1, S_0 = 10), and parallel load from the A, B, C, D inputs (S_1, S_0 = 11). In addition, the register has an active low (asynchronous) reset signal CLR and two serial shift inputs LSI and RSI.

The parallel load takes place when S_1 and S_0 are both high and a rising edge arrives at the clock input. At the same time, the value at input

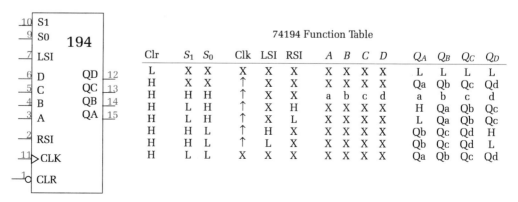

74194 Function Table

Clr	S_1	S_0	Clk	LSI	RSI	A	B	C	D	Q_A	Q_B	Q_C	Q_D
L	X	X	X	X	X	X	X	X	X	L	L	L	L
H	X	X	↑	X	X	X	X	X	X	Qa	Qb	Qc	Qd
H	H	H	↑	X	X	a	b	c	d	a	b	c	d
H	L	H	↑	X	H	X	X	X	X	H	Qa	Qb	Qc
H	L	H	↑	X	L	X	X	X	X	L	Qa	Qb	Qc
H	H	L	↑	H	X	X	X	X	X	Qb	Qc	Qd	H
H	H	L	↑	L	X	X	X	X	X	Qb	Qc	Qd	L
H	L	L	X	X	X	X	X	X	X	Qa	Qb	Qc	Qd

Figure 7.8 Schematic shape for the 74194 four-bit universal shift register.

A replaces the contents of the Q_A flip-flop, B replaces Q_B, and so on. This is called a *synchronous load* because it takes place in response to a clock event.

S_1 low and S_0 high indicate a right shift. On the rising edge of the clock, the value on the RSI input replaces Q_A, Q_A replaces Q_B, Q_B replaces Q_C, and Q_C replaces Q_D. The old value at Q_D is lost. We can construct a right circular shifter by wiring the Q_D output to the RSI input.

S_1 high and S_0 low specify a left shift. In this case, LSI replaces Q_D, Q_D replaces Q_C, Q_C replaces Q_B, and Q_B replaces Q_A, all on the rising edge of the clock. We can construct a left circular shifter by wiring Q_A to LSI.

S_1 and S_0 both low tell the shift register to hold its state. The outputs do not change even though the clock signal undergoes a low-to-high transition.

Sample Shifter Application Consider the problem of communicating between a terminal and a computer over phone lines. The terminal expects its data to appear in a byte-wide parallel form, but the data must be sent over the line in bit-serial form. Shift registers play a key role in such communication systems because they can convert between parallel and serial formats. We design the hardware to load the data from the computer in parallel and shift it out serially over the communications link. On the return trip, serial data from the terminal is captured by the shift register, bit by bit, and presented to the computer via the shift register's parallel outputs.

A partial implementation of this subsystem is shown in Figure 7.9. On the sender side, we load 8 bits of parallel data into the cascaded shift register by setting S_1, S_0 to 1, 1. The sender and receiver then enter their shift-left mode when S_1, S_0 are set to 0, 1. We do this for eight clock cycles, transmitting D_0 through D_7, 1 bit at a time. Once all 8 bits have been sent, we can place the receiver in its hold mode by setting S_1, S_0 to 0, 0.

7.1.3   Counters

Counters are sequential logic circuits that proceed through a well-defined sequence of states. We study them in more detail in this subsection.

Up-Counters and Down-Counters An *up-counter* proceeds from a value to the next larger value in the sequence in response to a count pulse. The counter outputs are identical to the state of the internal flip-flops. Once the largest possible value has been reached, the sequence restarts with the smallest value. For example, a 3-bit *binary up-counter* begins in state 000; goes through the sequence 001, 010, 011, 100, 101, 110, 111; and returns to 000, 001, and so on.

As you might expect, a *down-counter* operates similarly except that it sequences from large values to smaller values. The counter wraps from the smallest possible value back to the largest value in the sequence.

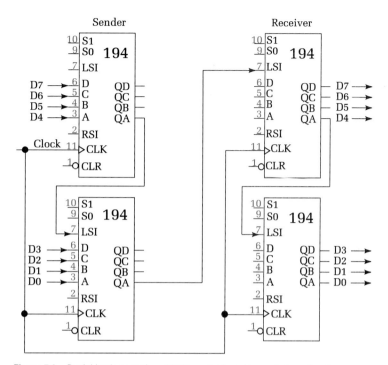

Figure 7.9   Partial implementation of 8-bit parallel/serial transmission subsystem.

Binary, Decade, Gray Code Counters   Although we have been describing binary counters, a counter can be designed to advance through any periodic sequence. Popular alternatives to binary counters are *decade* counters. These sequence through the BCD digits: 0000, 0001, 0010, 0011, 0100, 0101, 0110, 0111, 1000, and 1001.

In some applications, to avoid circuit hazards, it is important that only a single bit of the counter changes at a time. The binary and decade counters do not exhibit this property. However, a Gray code counter does. A 4-bit Gray code up-counter would sequence through the states 0000, 0001, 0011, 0010, 0110, 0111, 0101, 0100, 1100, 1101, 1111, 1110, 1010, 1011, 1001, 1000 and repeat.

Ring Counters   The shift register implementation of Figure 7.5 can also be used as a kind of primitive counter, a *ring counter*. The shifter sequences through the states 1000, 0100, 0010, 0001 and then repeats. The ring counter uses minimal hardware for its implementation, but it does not encode its states as efficiently as the counters we have just described. The four-element ring counter sequences through only 4 states, compared with the 16 states of the four-element binary counter.

A *Johnson counter* (also known as a Mobius counter) requires no more hardware than the basic ring counter but can represent twice as many states. The idea is to "twist around" the feedback outputs of the rightmost flip-flop to yield the shifter/ring counter. This has the effect of complementing the bit shifted out to the right before it is reinserted into the shifter from the left.

We show an implementation of the 4-bit Johnson counter with master/slave J-K flip-flops in Figure 7.10. We use the asynchronous set and reset inputs to force the flip-flops into the initial state 1000 when reset is asserted.

Figure 7.11 shows the timing diagram. The counter sequences through the states 1000, 1100, 1110, 1111, 0111, 0011, 0001, 0000 and repeats. It happens that this sequence satisfies the same property as the Gray code: only a single bit changes its value from one state to the next.

Applications and Example Catalog Counter   Counters are used in digital systems to count events and find many applications in tracking the passage of time. See Exercise 7.23 at the end of this chapter for some design problems.

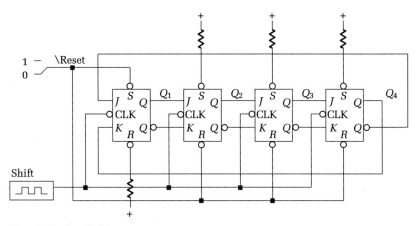

Figure 7.10   Four-bit Johnson counter.

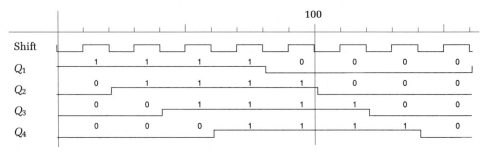

Figure 7.11   Timing waveforms for 4-bit Johnson counter.

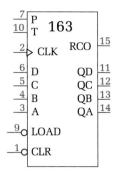

Figure 7.12 Schematic shape of 4-bit synchronous up-counter.

Let's examine a counter component from the TTL catalog. Figure 7.12 shows the schematic shape of the TTL 74163 synchronous 4-bit counter. The component has four data inputs, four data outputs, four control inputs (P, T, $\overline{\text{LOAD}}$, $\overline{\text{CLR}}$), one control output (RCO), and the clock.

When the $\overline{\text{LOAD}}$ signal is asserted, the data inputs replace the contents of the counter's internal flip-flops. Similarly, when $\overline{\text{CLR}}$ is asserted, all the flip-flops are reset to zero. These operations are synchronous. Although the load or clear signal must be asserted before the clock edge, the actual operation occurs on the positive transition of the clock. Contrast this with asynchronous operation, in which the load or clear takes place as soon as the appropriate control signal is asserted. We will say more about synchronous versus asynchronous counter operation in Section 7.5.

The P and T inputs cause the counter to advance to the next state in the binary sequence when both are asserted. Again, the count operation takes place when the clock undergoes a low-to-high transition. RCO is a ripple carry output that is asserted after the same rising clock edge that advances the counter to its largest value, 1111. This signal can be used as a count enable signal to a second cascaded counter (see Section 7.5.1).

The timing waveform of Figure 7.13 illustrates the interaction of these signals. When the clear signal is asserted, the counter's outputs are set to 0 on the next rising clock edge. When load is asserted, the counter is preset to 1100, the data on the parallel load inputs. When the count enable inputs, P and T, are enabled simultaneously, the counter counts up on each subsequent rising clock edge. As soon as the counter's output reaches 15, the RCO output is asserted. When either of P or T becomes unasserted, the counter stops counting and holds its current value through subsequent rising edges of the clock.

7.2 Counter Design Procedure

This section begins our study of designing an important class of clocked sequential logic circuits—*synchronous finite-state machines*. Like all sequential circuits, a finite-state machine determines its outputs and its next state from its current inputs and current state. A synchronous finite-state machine changes state only on the clocking event.

7.2.1 Introduction and an Example

Counter design is a good place for you to start understanding the design process for finite-state machines. Counters are the simplest possible finite-state machines. They typically have only a single input instructing them to count (often just the clock), and their outputs are nothing more than their current state.

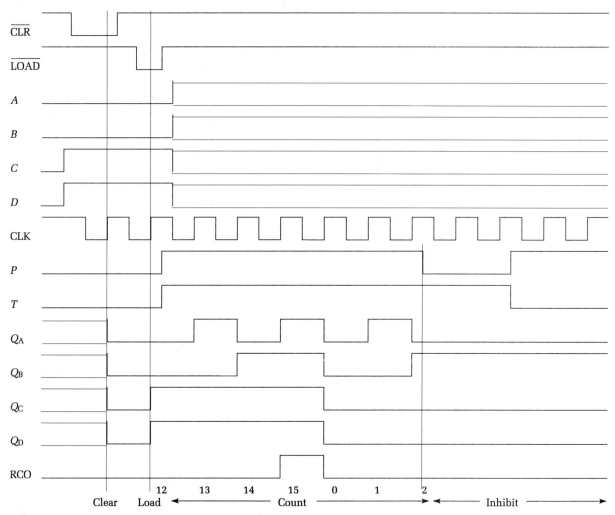

Figure 7.13 Timing waveform of 74163 synchronous 4-bit up-counter.

Three-Bit Up-Counter: State Transition Diagram Let's start with a simple counter, a 3-bit binary up-counter. We begin the design process by understanding how the counter is to operate. A convenient way to describe this is with a graphical specification called a *state transition diagram*.

The state transition diagram is a graph with nodes and directed arcs. Each node represents a unique state of the counter. A directed arc connects two nodes representing the present state and the next state. If the counter is in the state at the tail of the arc, it will advance to the state at the head of the arc at the next count request.

For the example design, we will dispense with a "count" input, and simply allow the counter to advance to the next state on each clock pulse.

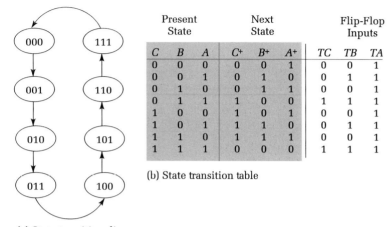

(a) State transition diagram

Present State / Next State / Flip-Flop Inputs

C	B	A	C+	B+	A+	TC	TB	TA
0	0	0	0	0	1	0	0	1
0	0	1	0	1	0	0	1	1
0	1	0	0	1	1	0	0	1
0	1	1	1	0	0	1	1	1
1	0	0	1	0	1	0	0	1
1	0	1	1	1	0	0	1	1
1	1	0	1	1	1	0	0	1
1	1	1	0	0	0	1	1	1

(b) State transition table

Figure 7.14 State transition diagram and table for a 3-bit binary up-counter.

Figure 7.14(a) shows a state transition diagram for the example. The nodes are labeled with the counter state they represent, and the arcs connect the nodes in the sequence implemented by the counter. We can describe the behavior of any finite-state machine with a state transition diagram, although the diagrams are typically more complex than those for counters.

Three-Bit Up-Counter: State Transition Table An alternative formulation of the state transition diagram is the *state transition table*, which shows the present state with the next state. Each row corresponds to an arc in the state transition diagram. The state transition table for the up-counter is given in Figure 7.14(b).

Each bit of the state is held by a single storage element. In this example, the counter proceeds through eight states. To assign binary codes to these states, we need exactly three storage elements. We have named the storage elements C, B, and A, from the highest- to the lowest-order bit.

Three-Bit Up-Counter: Flip-Flop Choice The next step is to choose a kind of flip-flop to implement the counter's storage elements. A close look at the state transition table suggests that toggle flip-flops might be an attractive choice. In essence, A toggles on every clock pulse, B on every second clock pulse, and C on every fourth clock pulse. This is a binary counter, after all.

The rightmost column of the state transition table of Figure 7.14(b) shows the inputs that must be presented to toggle flip-flops to implement the desired state transitions. For example, consider the state transition from 011 to 100. To get toggle flip-flops to implement these state changes, we must set the toggle input of each flip-flop to one. The transition will take place on the appropriate clock edge after the toggle inputs are set.

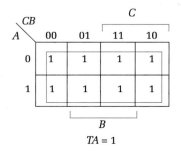

$TA = 1$

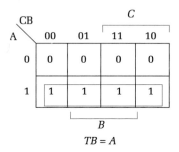

$TB = A$

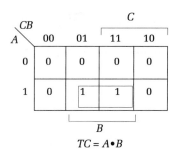

$TC = A \cdot B$

Figure 7.15 K-maps for up-counter toggle flip-flops.

Three-Bit Up-Counter: Next-State Logic Our task now is to design combinational logic whose input is the current state of the counter and whose output is the toggle inputs to the state flip-flops. For this simple example, we can determine the logic just by examining the transition table. Flip-flop A toggles on each state transition, B toggles whenever A is asserted, and C toggles whenever A and B are asserted.

For more complex examples, we can view the transition table as a truth table that specifies the flip-flops' inputs as a function of C, B, and A. We would use standard K-map methods to obtain the reduced Boolean expressions. The K-maps for TC, TB, and TA are shown in Figure 7.15. This leads immediately to the circuit design of Figure 7.16. The timing waveform of this implementation is given in Figure 7.17.

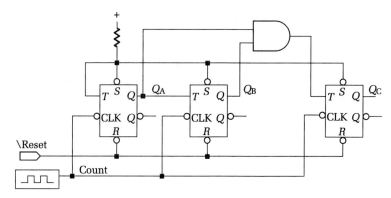

Figure 7.16 Circuit diagram of three-bit binary up-counter.

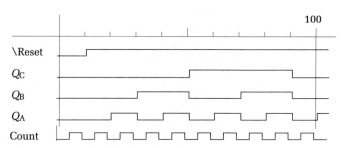

Figure 7.17 Timing waveform of the 3-bit up-counter.

7.2.2   Counters with More Complex Sequencing

The generalized design process consists of the following four steps:

Step 1:   From the written specification of the counter, we first draw a state transition diagram that shows the counter's desired sequence.

Step 2:   We next derive the state transition table from the state diagram, tabulating the current state with the next state in the count sequence. Each state bit is implemented by its own flip-flop.

Step 3:   We express each next-state bit as a combinational logic function of the current state bits.

Step 4:   We choose a flip-flop for implementation. Then we must "remap" the next-state mapping derived in step 3 to obtain the desired behavior from the selected flip-flop.

Example   **Generalized Counter Design**   To see this four-step process in action, let's look at another implementation of a counter. We will design a 3-bit counter that advances through the sequence 000, 010, 011, 101, 110, 000 and repeats. Not all of the possible combinations of the 3 bits represent a valid state. The unused states, 001, 100, and 111, can be used as don't-care conditions to simplify the logic.

Step 1:   Draw the state transition diagram. This is shown in Figure 7.18.

Step 2:   Derive the state transition table. This is shown in Figure 7.19.

Step 3:   Express each next-state bit as a combinational logic function of three current-state bits. Figure 7.20 shows the appropriate K-maps.

Step 4:   Choose a flip-flop type for implementation. Since this is almost a straight binary sequence, toggle flip-flops seem like a reasonable choice. We use the toggle flip-flop excitation table in Figure 7.21 to derive new next-state maps. Then we replace the desired state bits in the K-map with the values needed to control the selected flip-flops to perform the necessary state changes.

Figure 7.22 shows the toggle inputs needed to implement the state transitions of Figure 7.18. For example, counter state 000 advances to 010, so the inputs to the toggle flip-flops should be 0 (don't toggle) for C, 1 (toggle) for B, and 0 (don't toggle) for A. Similarly, state 110 returns to 000. In this case, the control for C, B, A is toggle, toggle, don't toggle, respectively, or 110.

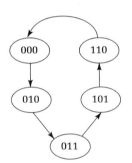

Figure 7.18   State transition diagram.

Present State			Next State		
C	B	A	C^+	B^+	A^+
0	0	0	0	1	0
0	0	1	X	X	X
0	1	0	0	1	1
0	1	1	1	0	1
1	0	0	X	X	X
1	0	1	1	1	0
1	1	0	0	0	0
1	1	1	X	X	X

Figure 7.19   State transition table.

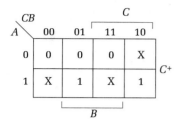

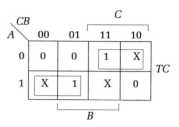

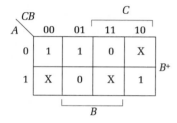

Q	Q^+	T
0	0	0
0	1	1
1	0	1
1	1	0

Figure 7.21   Toggle excitation table.

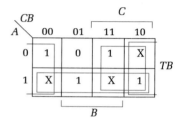

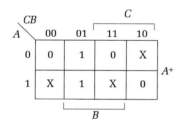

Present State			Toggle Inputs		
C	B	A	TC	TB	TA
0	0	0	0	1	0
0	0	1	X	X	X
0	1	0	0	0	1
0	1	1	1	1	0
1	0	0	X	X	X
1	0	1	0	1	1
1	1	0	1	1	0
1	1	1	X	X	X

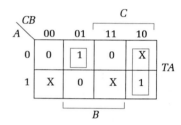

Figure 7.20   K-maps for next-state functions.

Figure 7.22   Remapped state transition table.

Figure 7.23   Remapped K-maps for toggle implementation.

Reflecting this remapping of functions, the K-maps become those of Figure 7.23. The minimized functions become

$$TC = \overline{A}C + A\overline{C} = A \oplus C$$

$$TB = A + \overline{B} + C$$

$$TA = \overline{A}B\overline{C} + \overline{B}C$$

Figure 7.24 shows the component-level implementation, with its associated timing waveform in Figure 7.25. To reduce wiring complexity, we simply label input and output nets rather than draw them as wires. Two nets with the same label are understood to be connected. The proper sequencing through the states 000, 010, 011, 101, 110, 000 should be clear from the waveform.

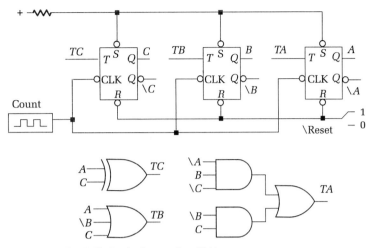

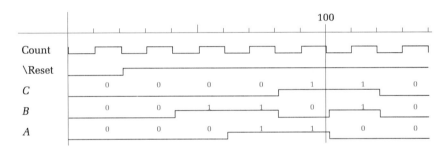

Figure 7.24 Toggle flip-flop implementation of 3-bit counter.

Figure 7.25 Timing waveform of 3-bit counter.

7.3 Self-Starting Counters

In drawing state transition diagrams for the example counters in the previous section, we assumed implicitly that they would begin the sequence in state 000. When working with real hardware, you should never assume that the counter will start in a particular state unless you design it to do so! At the time of power-up, the states of the flip-flops are undefined: they could be 0 or 1 at random.

This leads to a particularly nasty problem, especially for counters that do not use all state combinations of the storage elements, such as the last example. What would happen if, by chance, our example counter had entered state 001 on start-up? Of course, it depends on how don't cares have

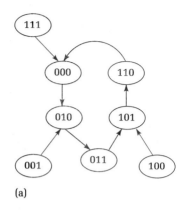

(a)

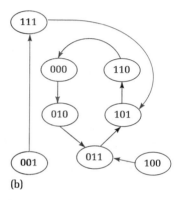

(b)

Figure 7.26   Two self-starting counter state diagrams.

been mapped into 0's and 1's by the implementation procedure, but the counter could sequence through the noncounter states, 001, 100, and 111, never entering the sequence it was designed for at all.

7.3.1   Verifying If a Counter Is Self-Starting

A *self-starting* counter is one in which every possible state, even those not in the desired count sequence, has a sequence of transitions that eventually leads to a valid counter state. This guarantees that no matter how the counter starts up, it will eventually enter the proper counter sequence.

Figure 7.26 shows two different state transition diagrams that lead to self-starting implementations for the counter of Figure 7.18. In the state diagram of Figure 7.26(a), the counter is guaranteed to be in sequence after one transition. In Figure 7.26(b), the counter may require up to two transitions before it is in the correct sequence.

In general, it is desirable to enter the counter sequence in as few transitions as possible, so we would prefer the state diagram in Figure 7.26(a). However, there may be an advantage in departing from this rule if a particular sequence of noncounter states can lead to reduced hardware.

The implementation of the counter given in Figure 7.24 leads to the state diagram of Figure 7.26(b). To see how this is derived, let's look at the step-by-step process, illustrated in Figure 7.27. First, we replace the don't cares in the K-maps of Figure 7.23 with the actually assigned 1's and 0's (these are underlined in Figure 7.27). Since these K-maps represent the inputs to the toggle flip-flops, we must remap them to express their effects on the flip-flops' state. The remapping is shown in the middle K-maps. For example, when $A = 0$, $B = 0$, $C = 1$, the input to the C toggle flip-flop is 1. Thus, the C^+ state will change from 1 to 0 under this input combination. By reading across the K-maps, it is easy to see that the current state $CBA = 100$ changes to the new state 011.

7.3.2   Counter Reset

In the preceding discussion, our primary goal was to enter the count sequence at a valid state. The particular starting state did not matter. Although this may be true in some applications, it is more usual to have a distinguished *starting* state for the counter or finite-state machine.

If this is the case, it is desirable to include additional hardware to *reset* the counter to this state. We can accomplish this with an explicit reset button or a special resistor/capacitor circuit that asserts the reset signal for a short time after power-up. Flip-flops typically come with preset and clear inputs. Thus, we can use an asserted reset signal to

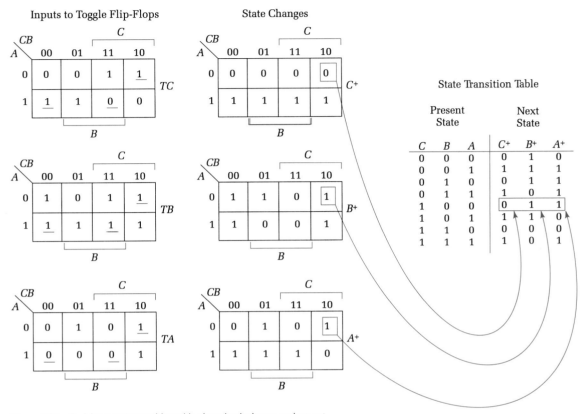

Figure 7.27 Deriving a state transition table given the don't-care assignment.

place the flip-flops in the desired starting state. The implementation in Figure 7.24 includes such circuitry to reset the flip-flops to state 000. Of course, by judicious use of preset inputs as well as clear, we can choose any state as the starting state.

7.4 Implementation with Different Kinds of Flip-Flops

Toggle flip-flops are a natural choice for implementing binary counters, but other flip-flop types may need less hardware for implementation. Also, the availability of computer-aided design software may influence our choice of flip-flop. Existing CAD software, such as *espresso*, favors designs with *D* flip-flops, in part because *D* storage elements are pervasive in VLSI design. However, *J-K* devices often require the fewest gates to implement a given state diagram. Admittedly, as the level of integration continues to increase, saving a gate here or there becomes less of an issue.

In Section 7.2.2 you saw how to implement the five-state up-counter of Figure 7.18 (state transition diagram) and Figure 7.19 (state transition table) using toggle flip-flops. In this section, you will see three more implementations of this counter, using R-S, J-K, and D storage elements.

7.4.1   Implementation with R-S Flip-Flops

We already performed the first three steps of the counter design procedure—the state transition diagram, the state transition table, and the next-state K-map—in Section 7.2.2 (see Figures 7.18, 7.19, and 7.20). Step 4, remapping the next state functions into control inputs for the chosen flip-flop, is the one step that depends on the type of flip-flop selected.

Q	Q^+	R	S
0	0	X	0
0	1	0	1
1	0	1	0
1	1	0	X

$$Q^+ = S + R\overline{Q}$$

Figure 7.28 R-S excitation table.

R-S Excitation Table   We start with the excitation table for the R-S flip-flop, which is given in Figure 7.28. The state transitions are now encoded in terms of the R and S inputs that cause the flip-flops to make those transitions. For example, if the flip-flop's current state is 0 and the next state is also to be 0, we can accomplish this by setting the S input to 0 and the R input to either 0 (hold current state) or 1 (reset current state). We complete the remaining three entries of the tables in a similar manner.

Remapped State Transition Table   The next step is to reexpress the state transition table in terms of the R and S inputs to the three state flip-flops C, B, and A. This is shown in Figure 7.29.

We complete the remapped state transition table as follows. First we examine how the state bit is to change—for example, from a 0 to a 1. We use this information and the R-S excitation table to determine the R and S inputs needed to make that transition happen. We repeat the procedure for each state bit (column) and each state transition (row) of the state transition table.

Present State			Next State			Remapped Next State					
C	B	A	C^+	B^+	A^+	RC	SC	RB	SB	RA	SA
0	0	0	0	1	0	X	0	0	1	X	0
0	0	1	X	X	X	X	X	X	X	X	X
0	1	0	0	1	1	X	0	0	X	0	1
0	1	1	1	0	1	0	1	1	0	0	X
1	0	0	X	X	X	X	X	X	X	X	X
1	0	1	1	1	0	0	X	0	1	1	0
1	1	0	0	0	0	1	0	1	0	X	0
1	1	1	X	X	X	X	X	X	X	X	X

Figure 7.29   State transition table and remapped next-state functions.

Let's see how we obtained the table of Figure 7.29. In the transition from state 000 to 010, C changes from 0 to 0, B from 0 to 1, and A from 0 to 0. The A and C transitions are implemented by the R and S inputs X and 0. The 0-to-1 transition for B is accomplished by setting R and S to 0 and 1, respectively. For the state transition 010 to 011, C goes from 0 to 0, B from 1 to 1, and A from 0 to 1. Based on the excitation table, C's R and S inputs should be X and 0, B's inputs are 0 and X, and A's are 0 and 1. We determine the rest of the transitions in a similar manner.

Remapped K-maps and Counter Schematic Figure 7.30 shows the remapped K-maps. The minimized next-state functions are

$$R_C = \overline{A} \qquad\qquad S_C = A$$
$$R_B = AB + BC \qquad S_B = \overline{B}$$
$$R_A = C \qquad\qquad S_A = B\overline{C}$$

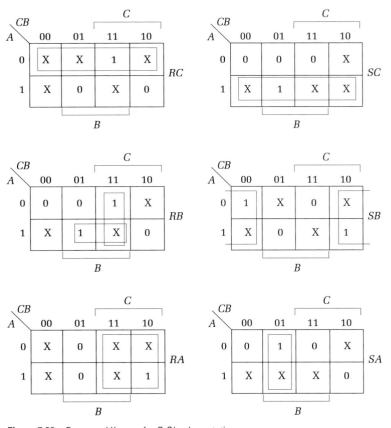

Figure 7.30 Remapped K-maps for $R\text{-}S$ implementation.

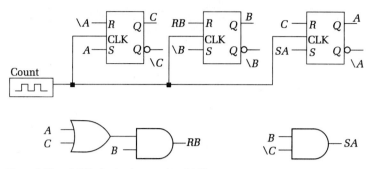

Figure 7.31 *R-S* flip-flop implementation of 3-bit counter.

This implementation requires 4 gates and 10 literals. If we factor the expression for R_B, that is, $R_B = B(A + C)$, we can save another gate and a literal. The implementation logic is shown in Figure 7.31: 3 gates, 9 literals, and a total of 12 wires if we consider the flip-flop inputs. We do not count the clock in this tabulation. The figure doesn't show the reset logic.

7.4.2   Implementation with *J-K* Flip-Flops

The first three design steps are exactly as in the previous subsection. The only difference is that we now use the excitation table for the *J-K* flip-flop. This is shown in Figure 7.32. For a transition from a current state of 0 to a next state of 0, the *J* input should be set to 0 and the *K* to 0 (hold) or 1 (reset). In a 0-to-1 transition, *J* should be set to 1 with *K* at 0 (set) or 1 (toggle). We handle the 1-to-0 transition and 1-to-1 transition similarly.

State Transition Table and Remapped Next-State Functions   The state transition table and the remapped next-state functions are given in Figure 7.33. Let's examine the first two state transitions, from 000 to 010 and from 010 to 011. For the first transition *C* stays at 0, *B* toggles from 0 to 1, and *A* holds at 0. For this transition *C*'s *J*, *K* inputs are 0, X (0-to-0 transition); *B*'s inputs are 1, X (0-to-1 transition); and *A*'s inputs are the same as *C*'s. For the second state transition, *C* holds at 0, *B* holds at 1, and *A* toggles from 0 to 1. The excitation table tells us that the *J*, *K* inputs should be 0, X for *C*; X, 0 for *B*; and 1, X for *A*.

Remapped K-maps and Counter Schematic   Because it eliminates the forbidden state, the *J-K* flip-flop's excitation table contains many more don't-care conditions than in the *R-S* case. As you would expect, this leads to an implementation with a reduced gate and literal count.

Q	Q^+	J	K
0	0	0	X
0	1	1	X
1	0	X	1
1	1	X	0

$$Q^+ = J\overline{Q} + \overline{K}Q$$

Figure 7.32   *J-K* flip-flop excitation table.

Present State			Next State			Remapped Next State					
C	B	A	C+	B+	A+	JC	KC	JB	KB	JA	KA
0	0	0	0	1	0	0	X	1	X	0	X
0	0	1	X	X	X	X	X	X	X	X	X
0	1	0	0	1	1	0	X	X	0	1	X
0	1	1	1	0	1	1	X	X	1	X	0
1	0	0	X	X	X	X	X	X	X	X	X
1	0	1	1	1	0	X	0	1	X	X	1
1	1	0	0	0	0	X	1	X	1	0	X
1	1	1	X	X	X	X	X	X	X	X	X

Figure 7.33 State transition table and remapped next-state functions.

Figure 7.34 shows the K-maps for the remapped next-state functions. The reduced expressions become

$$J_C = A \qquad K_C = \overline{A}$$

$$J_B = 1 \qquad K_B = A + C$$

$$J_A = B\overline{C} \qquad K_A = C$$

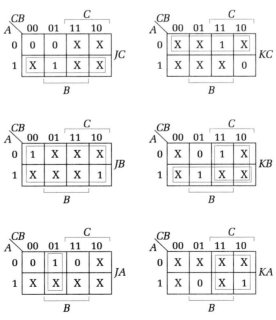

Figure 7.34 Remapped K-maps for *J-K* implementation.

This implementation reduces the gate count to two and the literals to seven. The implementation logic appears in Figure 7.35. The wire count for this implementation is nine (we don't count the hardwired input for J_B and again don't show the reset logic).

There is actually little to distinguish between the R-S and J-K implementations. This should come as no surprise, given the similar behavior of these two types of devices.

7.4.3   Implementation with *D* Flip-Flops

The choice of D flip-flops yields the most straightforward implementation. We dispense with the remapping step altogether. The D inputs are identical to the next-state outputs that are already tabulated in the state transition table.

We simply place the next state outputs into K-maps and find the minimized functions by the usual methods. The K-maps are identical to those of Figure 7.20, yielding the following minimized functions:

$$D_C = A$$
$$D_B = \overline{A}\,\overline{C} + \overline{B}$$
$$D_A = B\overline{C}$$

This implementation requires three gates and six literals and is shown in Figure 7.36 (reset logic is not shown). Again, the wire count is nine.

7.4.4   Comparison and Summary

Exactly the same state diagram led to somewhat different implementation costs:

T flip-flops:	5 gates, 10 literals, 15 wires (Figure 7.24)
R-S flip-flops:	3 gates, 5 literals, 12 wires (Figure 7.31)
J-K flip-flops:	2 gates, 4 literals, 9 wires (Figure 7.35)
D flip-flops:	3 gates, 5 literals, 9 wires (Figure 7.36)

Although it is difficult to generalize from a single example, J-K flip-flops usually yield the most gate- and literal-efficient implementations. Since the R-S flip-flop behavior is a proper subset of a J-K, there is never any advantage in using R-S devices as counter storage elements. In fact, you would be hard pressed to find them in the usual parts catalogs (although R-S latches are readily available).

T flip-flops are well suited for implementing straightforward binary counters, but their advantage is mitigated when the counter must follow a sequence that is not in direct binary order. In the example of this section, the T flip-flop implementation was worst by a wide margin.

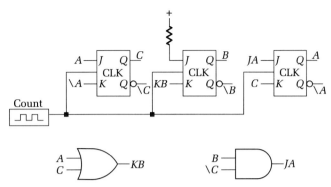

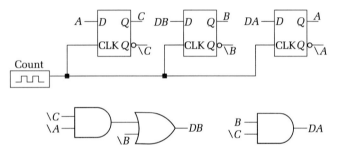

Figure 7.35   *J-K* flip-flop implementation of 3-bit counter.

Figure 7.36   *D* flip-flop implementation of 3-bit counter.

Although they do not often yield the most gate-efficient solution, *D* flip-flops have some important advantages. First, they simplify the design procedure, allowing you to skip the next-state remapping step. Tools like *espresso* and *misII* can be applied to the state transition table, treated as a truth table, to obtain a minimized implementation rapidly.

Second, if wiring complexity rather than gate count dominates the design, *D* flip-flops usually have the advantage (in our example, the *D* and *J-K* implementations had the same wiring complexity). Only a single input must be routed to a *D* flip-flop, compared to two inputs in the case of a *J-K* storage element.

Wiring complexity is especially important when using programmable logic technologies. Often the number of functional outputs supported by a programmable logic part is more constrained than the complexity of the logic that can be implemented, such as the number of product terms.

Finally, *D* storage elements are particularly transistor efficient in MOS VLSI technologies, as we saw in Chapter 6. *J-K* flip-flops require many more transistors for their implementation.

To summarize, for conventional packaged MSI/SSI TTL design, *J-K* flip-flops are usually preferable, especially when the design criterion is minimum gate and literal count. *D*-type devices are preferred when designing with programmable logic or in technologies more highly integrated than TTL, where minimum wire count or a simplified design procedure is the goal.

7.5   Asynchronous Versus Synchronous Counters

In the designs described in the previous sections, we used a *synchronous design style*. That is, we constructed all of the example counters from flip-flops controlled by a common clock signal (labeled *count* in the figures). In a fully synchronous counter, the storage elements simultaneously examine their inputs and determine new outputs. This is the preferred way to build counters, but there are other approaches we will examine in this section.

7.5.1   Ripple Counters

Some counters avoid the global clock altogether. These elements count by propagating or rippling the decision to change state from one storage element to an adjacent element. Hence these counters are called *ripple counters*, and we study them next.

Example   **Three-Bit Binary Ripple Counter**   Figure 7.37 shows a 3-bit binary ripple counter constructed from *T* flip-flops (the reset logic is not shown). The lowest-order (most rapidly changing) bit is the leftmost. The output from one stage drives the clock of the next stage to the right.

The timing waveform for a typical count sequence is shown in Figure 7.38. Compare it with Figure 7.17, the timing diagram of an equivalent synchronous counter. In the ripple counter the state changes do not all take place on the falling clock edge but continue into the next high time of the clock. This points out a serious problem with ripple-type circuits: the propagation through the counter takes longer to reach its next output state as more stages are added to the counter.

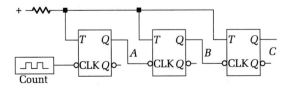

Figure 7.37   Three-bit ripple counter constructed from *T* flip-flops.

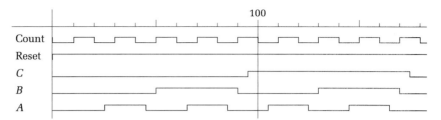

Figure 7.38 Timing waveform for 3-bit ripple counter.

In effect, the ripple counter computes its next state in a serial fashion, rather than in parallel as in the implementation of Figure 7.16. Since the state transitions are not crisp, external logic reading the current state as an input can glitch or "spike" in an undesirable manner. Despite the simpler hardware, you should never be tempted to implement a counter in this fashion.

Cascaded Counters Cascading is the process of combining several smaller-bit-width components into a larger-bit-width function. As you have seen, an 8-bit shift register can be constructed by wiring together two 4-bit registers. You can use a similar strategy to build wider counters from multiple 4-bit slices. Even though the counter components are implemented internally using synchronous techniques, the components are wired together in a series ripple fashion. These are *cascaded counters*.

Figure 7.39 shows an 8-bit cascaded counter. Shortly after the rising edge in which the low-order counter enters the state 1111, the RCO, *ripple*

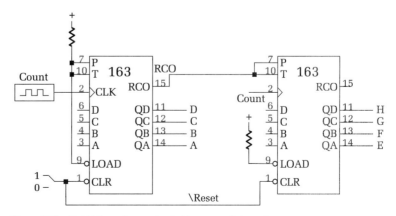

Figure 7.39 Eight-bit counter constructed from cascaded counters.

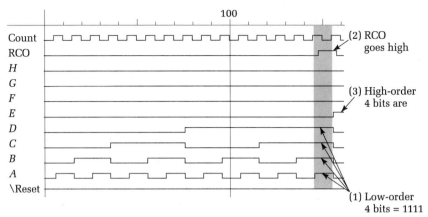

Figure 7.40   Timing waveform of cascaded counters.

carry output, is asserted. This signal enables the next higher stage for counting. On the next rising edge, the low-order bits enter state 0000, the high-order bits count by 1, and the first RCO signal is unasserted.

The detailed sequence of events is given in the timing waveform of Figure 7.40. First, the low-order counter enters the state 1111. Second, the RCO is asserted. Third, the higher-order stage counts by 1.

If ripple counters are such a bad idea, why do we allow rippling here? The answer is that the cascaded counters of Figure 7.39 are still synchronous. The counter's internal logic computes the RCO signal in parallel, simply by ANDing together the current-state bits. The count takes place on the rising edge of the clock. As long as there is enough time between rising edges for RCO to be asserted by the lower-order counter and recognized by the higher-order counter, the cascaded counters function properly. This is a perfectly acceptable use of a ripple signal.

7.5.2   Synchronous Versus Asynchronous Inputs

In Chapter 6 we described some of the dangers in using asynchronous inputs to otherwise synchronous systems. In general, you should try to avoid components with asynchronous inputs.

The ubiquitous 74163 counter illustrates the power of synchronous inputs. In addition to its internal synchronous implementation, it provides synchronous clear and load signals. This makes it ideal for implementing more complex count sequences with a beginning offset or limiting cutoff.

Example   Starting Offset Counter   Suppose we need to implement a counter that follows the sequence 0110 through 1111 and then repeats. The RCO signal, in conjunction with a synchronous load input, can implement this function easily.

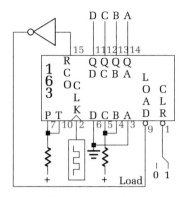

Figure 7.41 Counter with beginning offset.

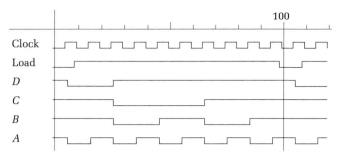

Figure 7.42 Count sequence 0110 through 1111 and repeat.

The logic is shown in Figure 7.41. The RCO signal, when asserted, is negated and used to drive the active low load input. If the desired starting state is placed at the parallel load inputs, it will be entered on the next rising edge of the clock.

This counter is self-starting. Resetting clears the counter to 0000. Although it starts off in an invalid state, it reaches the desired sequence within six clock periods.

The timing waveform is given in Figure 7.42. The $\overline{\text{LOAD}}$ signal (the complement of RCO) is asserted when the counter enters state 1111. On the next rising clock edge, the counter enters state 0110.

Example   Cutoff Limit Counter   Similarly, we can construct a counter with a cutoff limit by using the synchronous clear signal. For example, we can use the logic of Figure 7.43 to implement a counter that begins at 0000 and sequences through to 1101 before restarting. When the counter enters the cutoff state, the active low $\overline{\text{CLR}}$ signal is asserted. This forces the counter into the zero state on the next rising edge.

Figure 7.44 shows the timing diagram. When the counter reaches 1101, it enters the cutoff state, $\overline{\text{CLR}}$ goes low, and the next state is 0000.

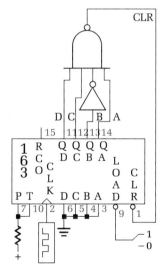

Figure 7.43 Counter with limit.

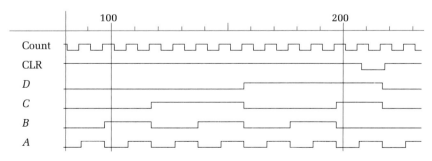

Figure 7.44 Timing waveform for offset limited counter.

Dangers of Asynchronous Inputs The designs of Figure 7.41 and Figure 7.43 would not be possible if the clear and load inputs were asynchronous. We use external logic to recognize the offset or cutoff state, to assert a control input that leads to an out-of-sequence new state. In these synchronous designs, the state does not change until the next rising clock edge.

If the control inputs were asynchronous, the state change would have happened as soon as the control input was asserted, independent of the clock. This violates a fundamental assumption of synchronous systems—that the state changes at clocking events and not at other times.

Let's reexamine the counter of Figure 7.43, but this time implemented with the TTL 74161 counter. This device is identical to the 74163, except that the clear signal is asynchronous.

Compare the timing diagram of Figure 7.45 with that of Figure 7.44. The $\overline{CLR}$ signal is obviously a short-duration pulse, and state 1101 is held for a much shorter time than any other state. In effect, if we consider the counter to advance from one state to the next on every rising clock edge, then the behavior of Figure 7.45 actually shows the counter advancing from 1100 to 0000, passing through 1101 in an instant. This is obviously not the behavior we desired.

Asynchronous inputs should be used only for situations like power-on reset. Never use them to implement state transitions. As a designer, you should always be aware of the behavior of the catalog parts you select. Remember to choose the right parts for the job at hand.

7.6   Random-Access Memories

In this section, we will examine memory components in more detail. In particular, we will focus on two important aspects of memory system design: the detailed timing waveforms for a static RAM component, and the design of the register and control logic that surrounds the memory subsystem, making it possible to interface the memory to the rest of the digital system. But first, we must begin with the basics.

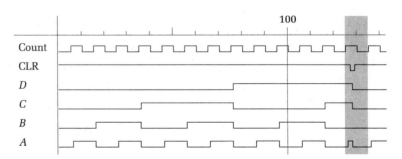

Figure 7.45   Sequence implemented with TTL 74161.

7.6.1   RAM Basics: A 1024 by Four-Bit Static RAM

We begin with a relatively simple memory component, a 1024 by 4-bit static RAM. The basic storage element of the static RAM is a six-transistor circuit, shown in Figure 7.46. The "static" storage element is provided by the cross-coupled inverters. This circuit configuration will hold a 1 or 0 as long as the system continues to receive power. There is no need for a periodic refreshing signal or a clock.

The nMOS transistors provide access to the storage element from two buses, denoted $Data_j$ and $\overline{Data}_j$. To write the memory element, special circuitry in the RAM drives the data bit and its complement onto these lines while the word enable line is asserted. When driven in this fashion, the data bit can overwrite the previous state of the element.

To read the contents of the storage element, the word enable line is once again enabled. Instead of being driven onto the data lines (also called *bit lines*), the data are "sensed" by a different collection of special circuits. These circuits, called *sense amplifiers*, can detect small voltage differences between the data line and its complement. If $Data_j$ is at higher voltage than $\overline{Data}_j$, the cell contained a logic 1. If the situation is reversed, the cell contained a logic 0.

RAMs are efficient in packing many bits into a circuit package for two reasons. First, only a small number of transistors are needed to implement the storage elements. And second, it is easy to arrange these elements into rows and columns. Each row of memory cells shares a common word enable line. Each column shares common bit lines. The number of columns determines the bit width of each word. Thus, you can find memory components that are 1, 4, or 8 bits wide and that read or write the bits of a single word in parallel.

Figure 7.47 shows the pin-out for our 1024 by 4-bit SRAM (static RAM). The pins can be characterized as address lines, data lines, and control lines.

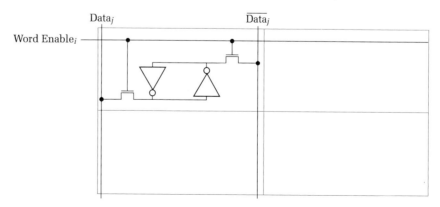

Figure 7.46   Static RAM storage elements.

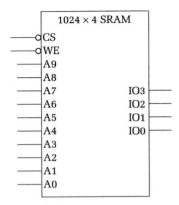

Figure 7.47 Schematic shape of the 1024 × 4-bit SRAM.

Since the RAM has 1024 words, there must be 10 lines to address them. Since each word is 4 bits wide, there are four data lines. The same pins are used for reading or writing and are called *bidirectional*. The value on the active low control signal Write Enable ($\overline{\text{WE}}$) determines their direction.

The final signal on the chip is the chip select control line ($\overline{\text{CS}}$). When this signal goes low, a read or write cycle commences, depending on the value of write enable. If write enable is also low, the data lines provide new values to be written into the addressed word within the RAM. If it is high, the data lines are driven with the contents of the addressed word.

Internal Block Diagram   From the preceding discussion, you might infer that the RAM is organized as an array with 1024 words and four columns. In terms of performance and packaging, this is not the best internal organization. A long thin array leads to long wires, which take more time to drive to a given logic voltage. Also, rectangular integrated circuits are more difficult to arrange on a silicon wafer for processing. A square configuration is much more desirable.

Figure 7.48 gives a more realistic block diagram of the internal structure of a typical 1024 by 4-bit SRAM. The RAM array consists of four banks of

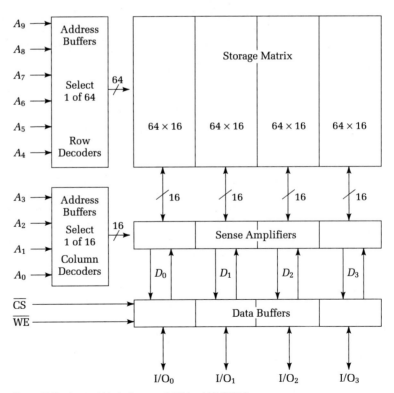

Figure 7.48   Internal block diagram of 1024 × 4-bit SRAM.

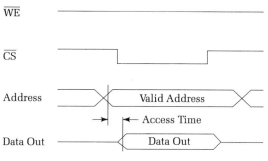

Figure 7.49 Read cycle logical sequencing.

64 words by 16 bits each. This makes the array square. Let's consider a read operation. The high-order 6 bits of the address select one of 64 words. Four groups of 16 bits each emerge from the storage array, one group for each of the possible data bits. The four low-order address bits select one of 16 bits from each of the four groups to form the 4-bit data word. Writes are similar, except with data flowing in the opposite direction.

This form of two-dimensional decode, with row and column decoders, is used universally in memory components. Not only does it keep the memory array square, it also limits the longest lines in the decoders.

Simplified Read Cycle and Write Cycle Timing   Controlling the function of a RAM chip requires precise sequencing of the address pins and control signals. Figure 7.49 gives a simplified logic timing diagram for the RAM read cycle (we defer a more precise description of RAM timing to Section 7.6.2). First, a valid address must be set up on the address lines. Then the chip select ($\overline{\text{CS}}$) line is taken low while the write enable ($\overline{\text{WE}}$) stays high. The *memory access time* is the time it takes for new data to be ready to appear at the output. It is measured from the last change in the address lines, although the output is not visible off-chip unless the chip select is low. Once the chip select line goes high again, deselecting the chip, the output on the data lines will no longer be valid.

Figure 7.50 gives the write cycle sequencing. Because an erroneous write could have destructive consequences, we must be especially careful during the sequencing of the write signals. To be conservative, $\overline{\text{WE}}$ should be brought low and the address and data lines should be stable before $\overline{\text{CS}}$ goes low. A similar sequence occurs in reverse to end the write cycle.

While conceptually correct, this specification is more restrictive than it needs to be. Technically speaking, the write cycle begins when both $\overline{\text{WE}}$ and $\overline{\text{CS}}$ go low. It ends when $\overline{\text{WE}}$ goes high. The only absolute requirement is that the address is stable a setup time before both signals go low and satisfies a hold time constraint after the first one goes high. The data setup and hold times are also measured from the first control signal to rise.

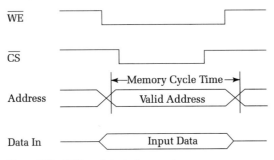

Figure 7.50   Write cycle logical sequencing.

Another important metric for RAMs is the *memory cycle time*. This is the time between subsequent memory operations. In general, the access time is less than or equal to the memory cycle time.

7.6.2   Dynamic RAM

Static RAMs are the fastest memories (and the easiest to interface with), but the densest memories are dynamic RAMs (DRAMs). Their high capacity is due to an extremely efficient memory element: the one-transistor (1-T) memory cell.

The 1-T memory cell, consisting of a single access transistor and a capacitor, works as follows (see Figure 7.51). The word line and bit line provide exactly the same function as in the SRAM. To write the memory cell, the bit line is charged to a logic 1 or 0 voltage while the word line is asserted. This enables the access transistor, making it possible to charge up the storage capacitor with the desired logic voltage.

The read operation takes place by asserting the word line. The access transistor is turned on, sharing the voltage on the capacitor with the bit line. Sensitive amplifier circuits detect small changes on the bit line to determine whether a 1 or 0 was stored in the selected memory element.

The destructiveness of the read operation makes DRAMs complex. To read the contents of the storage capacitor, we must discharge it across the bit line. Thus, external circuitry in the DRAM must buffer the values that have been read out and then write them right back.

The second problem with DRAMs, and the most significant one from your viewpoint as a system designer, is that their contents decay over time. Every once in a while (measured in milliseconds), the charge on the storage capacitors leaks off. To counteract this, the DRAM must be refreshed. Periodically, the memory elements must be read and written back to their storage locations.

To make this operation reasonably efficient, the DRAM's memory array is a two-dimensional matrix organized along the lines of the SRAM block diagram of Figure 7.48. Figure 7.52 shows the block diagram of a 4096 by

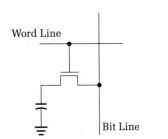

Figure 7.51   One-transistor memory cell.

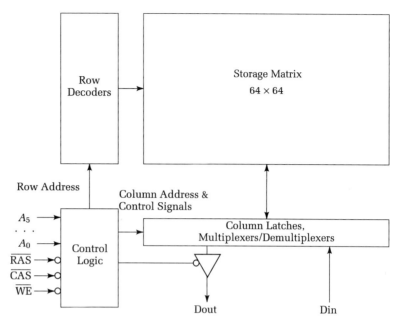

Figure 7.52 4096 × 1-bit DRAM block diagram.

1-bit DRAM. Rather than refresh individual bits, a refresh cycle reads out and writes back an entire row. This happens about once every few microseconds. Just as in the SRAM, the row is typically a multiple of the DRAM's word size. In this case, it is 64 bits wide. The refresh cycles are generated by an external memory controller.

DRAM Access with Row and Column Address Strobes Every time a single-bit word is accessed within the memory array of Figure 7.52, the DRAM actually accesses an entire row of 64 bits. The column latches select one of the 64 bits for reading or writing. The DRAM often accesses adjacent words in sequence, so it is advantageous if access is rapid.

Memory chip designers have developed clever methods to provide rapid access to the DRAM. The key is to provide separate control lines for DRAM row access, *RAS* (*row address strobe*), and column access, *CAS* (*column address strobe*). Normally, access involves specifying a row address followed by a sequence of column addresses. This has the extra advantage of reducing the number of address pins needed. A single (smaller) set of address lines are multiplexed over time to specify the row and column to be accessed. This becomes a critical issue as memory chips exceed 1 million bits (20 address pins).

In Figure 7.52 we have done away with the chip select signal and replaced it with two signals: $\overline{RAS}$ and $\overline{CAS}$. The address lines, normally 12 for a 4096-bit memory, can now be reduced to 6. Memory access consists of a RAS cycle followed by a CAS cycle. During the RAS cycle, the six address lines specify which of the 64 rows to access. In the following CAS cycle, the address lines select the column to access.

Figure 7.53 shows the RAS/CAS timing for a memory read. Throughout this sequencing, the $\overline{WE}$ line is held high. First the row address is provided on the address lines. When the $\overline{RAS}$ line is brought low, the row address is saved in a latch within the DRAM and the memory access begins. Meanwhile, the address lines are replaced by a column address. When $\overline{CAS}$ goes low, the column address is latched. At this point the output is enabled, although it is valid only after a propagation delay. When $\overline{RAS}$ goes high again, the accessed row is written back to the memory array, restoring its values. When $\overline{CAS}$ goes high, the output returns to the high-impedance state.

Figure 7.54 shows the RAS/CAS sequencing for a memory write. The signaling begins as before: the row address appears on the address lines and is internally latched when $\overline{RAS}$ goes low. The row is now read out from the memory array. While the address lines are changing to the column

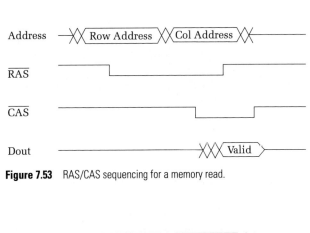

Figure 7.53 RAS/CAS sequencing for a memory read.

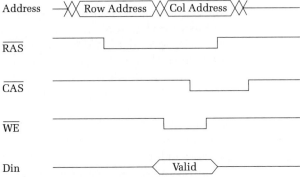

Figure 7.54 RAS/CAS sequencing for a memory write.

address, valid data is placed on the data input line and $\overline{WE}$ is taken low. Once the address lines are stable, $\overline{CAS}$ can also be taken low. This latches the column address and also replaces the selected bit with the DIN within the column latches. At this point, $\overline{WE}$ can be driven high. When $\overline{RAS}$ goes high again, the entire row, including the replaced bit, is written back to the memory array. Finally, $\overline{CAS}$ can be driven high, and another memory cycle can commence.

Refresh Cycle The storage capacitor at the heart of a DRAM memory cell is not perfect. Over time, it leaks away the charge it is meant to hold. Thus DRAMs must undergo periodic *refresh cycles* to maintain their state. In its simplest form, a refresh cycle looks like an abbreviated read cycle: data is extracted from the storage matrix and then immediately written back without appearing at the output pin.

Suppose every DRAM word must be refreshed once every 4 ms. This means that the 4096-word RAM would require a refresh cycle once every 976 ns. Assuming the cycle time is 120 ns, approximately one in every eight DRAM accesses would be a refresh cycle!

Fortunately, the two-dimensional organization of the storage matrix makes it possible to refresh an entire row at a time. Since the DRAM of Figure 7.52 has 64 rows, we can refresh the rows in sequence once every 62.5 μs, still meeting the overall 4-ms requirement. This is approximately one refresh cycle every 500 accesses. Larger-capacity DRAMs usually have 256 to 512 rows and require a refresh cycle once every 8 to 16 μs.

The RAS-only refresh cycle provides a simple form of refresh. It looks very much like the read timing with the CAS phase deleted. The row address is placed on the address lines and $\overline{RAS}$ is taken low. This causes the row to be read out of the storage matrix into the column latches. When $\overline{RAS}$ goes high again, the column latches are written back, refreshing the row's contents.

This refresh cycle requires an external memory controller to keep track of the last row to be refreshed. To simplify the memory controller design, some DRAMs have a refresh row pointer in the memory chip. A special CAS-before-RAS signaling convention implements the refresh. If $\overline{CAS}$ goes low before $\overline{RAS}$, the chip recognizes this as a refresh cycle. The indicated row is read, written back, and the internal indicator points to the next row to be refreshed.

7.6.3   DRAM Variations

We have described the basic internal functioning of a DRAM with RAS/CAS addressing, but have not shown how such an organization can improve DRAM performance. Variations on the basic DRAM model take advantage of the row-wide access to the storage matrix to reduce the time to access bits in the same DRAM row. These are called page mode, static column mode, and nibble mode DRAMs. All three support conventional RAS/CAS addressing. They differ in how they specify accesses to additional bits in the same row.

Page mode DRAMs can read or write a bit within the last accessed row without repeating the RAS cycle. The first time a bit within a row is accessed, the controller sequences through a RAS followed by a CAS cycle, as described earlier. To access a subsequent bit in the row, the controller simply changes the column address and pulses the CAS strobe ($\overline{\text{RAS}}$ is held low throughout). CAS pulsing can be repeated several times to access a sequence of bits in the row. The result is much faster access than is possible with complete RAS/CAS cycling.

Static column mode DRAMs provide a similar function but present a slightly simpler interface to the memory controller. Changing the column address bits accomplishes a static column read, eliminating multiple strobes on the $\overline{\text{CAS}}$ line altogether. Writes are a little more complicated. To protect against accidentally writing the wrong memory location, either $\overline{\text{CAS}}$ or $\overline{\text{WE}}$ must be driven high before the column address can be changed.

Nibble mode DRAMs are yet another variation on page mode. Most memory locations are accessed in sequence, and the DRAM can take advantage of this to reduce the complexity of the control sequencing. After the first RAS/CAS cycle, a subsequent CAS pulse accesses the next bit in sequence. This can be done three times, yielding 4 bits in sequence, before a RAS/CAS cycle is needed again. Thus the sequence is RAS/CAS, CAS, CAS, CAS, RAS/CAS, CAS, CAS, CAS, etc.

Video RAMs (*VRAMs*) are DRAMs that can be used as frame buffers for computer displays. A *frame buffer* is a display memory that allows new data to be written to storage without affecting how the screen is being refreshed from the old data. A VRAM has a conventional DRAM storage matrix and four serial-access memories (SAMs). Its signaling convention allows a data row to be transferred from the storage matrix to the SAMs. Once in a SAM, the data can be read out a bit at a time at a high rate even while new data is being written into the storage matrix. In this way, VRAMs support a kind of dual-port access to memory: one from the standard read/write interface and one from the serial memories.

In addition, some VRAMs support logical operations, such as XOR, between the current contents of the memory and the bit that is overwriting it. This is useful for certain graphics-oriented operations, such as moving items around smoothly on the display.

7.6.4   Detailed SRAM Timing

Here we expand on the discussion of SRAM components begun in the previous section. We will describe the detailed timing of a 1024 by 4-bit static RAM, the National 2114. We have already shown the basic pin-out in Figure 7.47: 10 address lines, 4 data input/output lines, and active low chip select ($\overline{\text{CS}}$) and write enable ($\overline{\text{WE}}$) control signals. The generic read and write cycle sequencings were shown in Figures 7.49 and 7.50.

Read Cycle Let's reexamine the read cycle timing in more detail. The following discussion assumes that $\overline{\text{WE}}$ is held high throughout the read operation. Any change on the address lines causes new data to be extracted from the storage matrix, independent of the condition of the chip select. Once $\overline{\text{CS}}$ goes low, the output buffers become enabled, latching the data from the storage array and driving the output pins.

An important metric of a memory component is the *access time*, t_A. This is the time it takes for an address change to cause new data to appear at the output pins (the memory has already been selected by driving $\overline{\text{CS}}$ low). The MM2114 has an access time of 200 ns, which is relatively slow by today's standards. High-speed static RAMs, such as the Cypress CY2148, have an access time of 35 ns.

An equally important metric is the *read cycle time*, t_{RC}. This is the time between the start of one read operation and a subsequent read operation. In the case of the MM2114, it is also 200 ns. In modern SRAM components, the access time and cycle time are usually the same. However, this is not the case for DRAMs, where cycle times are often longer than access times.

Figure 7.55 shows the read cycle timing waveform. It shows two back-to-back read cycles, the first commencing before $\overline{\text{CS}}$ goes low and the second while $\overline{\text{CS}}$ is low.

The first cycle begins with a change on the address lines. Valid data cannot appear on the output lines before an access time, 200 ns, has

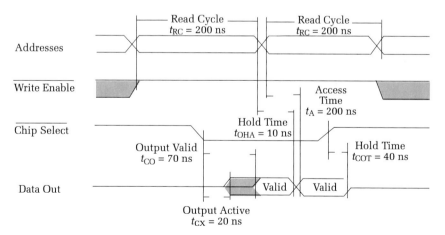

Figure 7.55 MM2114 read cycle timing.

expired. The timing waveform assumes that the limiting condition is not the access time, but rather the time from when the chip is selected. T_{CX}, the time from chip select to output active, is 20 ns. This means that the memory chip will begin to drive its outputs no sooner than 20 ns after chip select goes low, although the data is not yet valid. Any other components driving the same wires as the RAM's output lines must become tri-state within this time.

T_{CO}, the time from chip select to output valid, is 70 ns. Thus, the time to data valid is determined by which is longer: 200 ns from the last address line change or 70 ns from when the chip is selected.

Once the address lines begin to change for the next read cycle, the outputs are guaranteed to remain valid for another 10 ns, the output-hold-from-address-change time, t_{OHA}. External logic latching the output of the RAM must factor this into its timing before it can allow the addresses to change.

Once the address lines are stable, it takes another 200 ns for valid data to appear at the outputs. If a third read cycle were to commence now, by changing the address lines, the output data would remain valid for 10 ns. However, the read cycle is terminated in the waveform by deselecting the chip. In this case, the hold time is determined by t_{COT}, the time from chip select to output tri-state. For the MM2114, t_{COT} is a minimum of 0 ns and a maximum of 40 ns. Thus external logic must wait at least 40 ns before it can begin to drive the wires at the RAM's I/O pins.

Write Cycle   As in all RAMs, the write cycle timing is more complex and requires more careful design. The write operation is enabled whenever $\overline{CS}$ and $\overline{WE}$ are simultaneously driven low. This is called the *write pulse*. To guard against incorrect writes, one or both of the signals must be driven high before the address lines can change.

Figure 7.56 gives the timing waveform for the write operation. Once the address lines are stable, we must wait an address setup time before driving the last of the chip select and write enable signals low. This is the address-to-write setup time, t_{AW}, and is 20 ns. The write cycle time, t_{WC}, is defined from address change to address change and must be at least 200 ns for this component. The write pulse width, t_{WP}, is at least 100 ns.

The write cycle ends when the first of the two control signals goes high. Thus, data setup and hold times are measured with respect to this event. The data setup time, t_{DS}, is at least 100 ns. The data hold time, t_{DH}, is 0 ns.

The write recovery time—the time between the end of the write pulse and when the address lines are allowed to change—is denoted by t_{WR}. For this RAM component, the recovery time is 0 ns.

The bottommost waveform in Figure 7.56, labeled Data Out, illustrates the interaction between read and write cycles. The writing circuitry must realize that the outputs could take as long as 40 ns to be tri-stated, so this

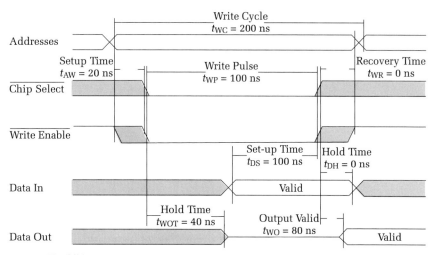

Figure 7.56 MM2114 write cycle timing.

amount of time must pass before the data to be written can be placed on the I/O pins. This is indicated by t_{WOT}, the time from write enable to output tri-state.

The final timing specification, t_{WO}, the write-enable-to-output-valid time, is the time between the end of the write cycle and when the RAM turns around to drive the output lines with the data just written (write enable high). In this case, it is 80 ns.

7.6.5 Design of a Simple Memory Controller

At the heart of most digital systems is a data path consisting of one or more interconnection pathways (called *buses*) and several registers, arithmetic circuits, and memory attached to some or all of these interconnections. This is the "switchyard," which routes data items from memory to a unit that executes some operation on them and then back into memory.

In this subsection, we will design a simple memory controller, using the TTL register and counter components introduced in this chapter, as well as a 2114 RAM chip. We will develop control circuitry for sequencing through the write enable and chip select signals to implement read and write operations.

Memory Subsystem Data Path   Figure 7.57 gives a block diagram view of the data and address paths of a simple memory subsystem. To keep it simple, the address and data paths are just 4 bits wide. We can read data from four input switches and store them in the 2114 RAM when the tri-state buffer is enabled. Data stored in the RAM can be read out, latched into a

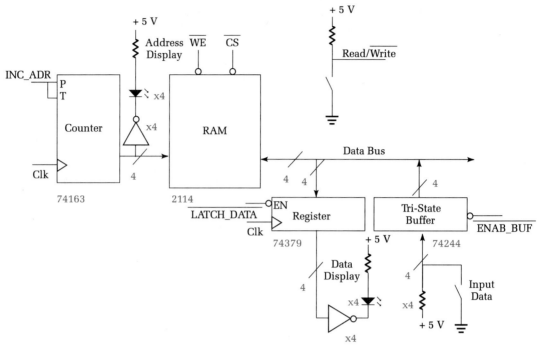

Figure 7.57 Data path of simple memory subsystem.

register, and then displayed on LEDs attached to the register's outputs (inverter drivers are used to buffer the LEDs). We use a 4-bit binary counter to access locations in memory sequentially for reading or writing. We also use LEDs to monitor memory addresses.

Figure 7.58 provides the schematic representation for the data path, using TTL components to implement the logic blocks of Figure 7.57. We implement the address counter with a 74163 four-bit binary up-counter. For the tri-state buffers and output latches we use one-half of a 74244 and a 74379 component, respectively. The 74379 is a 4-bit version of the 74377 introduced in Figure 7.3(a). For the purposes of the schematic, we have replaced the output LEDs by symbols for hexadecimal displays and the input switches by a hex keypad.

Memory Controller   The following signals control the data path:

INC_ADR	Add one to address.
$\overline{WE}$	Write Enable on 2114.
$\overline{CS}$	Chip Enable on 2114.
LATCH_DATA	Latch valid data on data bus in display register during read cycle.

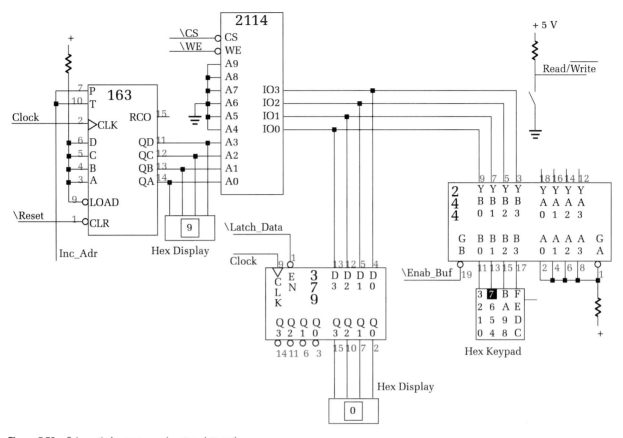

Figure 7.58 Schematic for memory subsystem data path.

| $\overline{\text{ENAB\_BUF}}$ | Enable buffer to put switch data on data bus during write cycle. |
| $\text{READ}/\overline{\text{WRITE}}$ | User input to select read or write mode. |

In addition, we need a global reset signal to force the counter to the 0000 state.

The memory controller reads from or writes to the current address, then increments the counter to point to the next address. First, a sequence of write cycles fills the RAM with data. Then the controller is reset, setting the address counter back to 0. A sequence of read cycles then views the data that has been stored in the RAM.

Figure 7.59 shows a skeletal sequencer circuit diagram. The timing waveform it generates is given in Figure 7.60. Pressing the momentary push-button switch generates a $\overline{\text{GO}}$ signal that lasts for one clock cycle. The $\overline{\text{GO}}$ signal enables the 74194 shift register, which shifts right, generating overlapping clock signals Φ_1, Φ_2, Φ_3, Φ_4. The circuit halts when

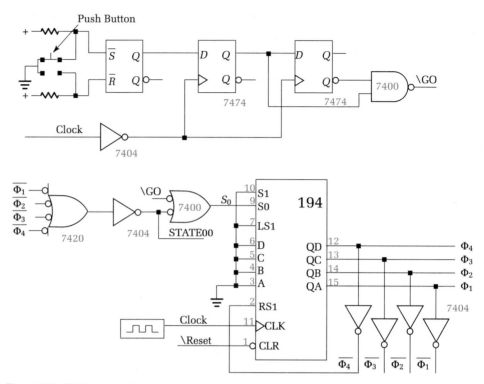

Figure 7.59 Multiphase clock for sequencer.

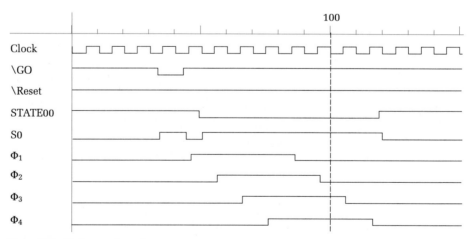

Figure 7.60 Timing waveforms for sequencer.

all of the clock signals return to 0. This sequencer could be driven with a slow clock, such as the 555 timer described in the last chapter.

We can use simple combinational logic to derive pulses of the correct start time and length for the various control signals from the multiphase clock. Figure 7.61 shows how this is accomplished.

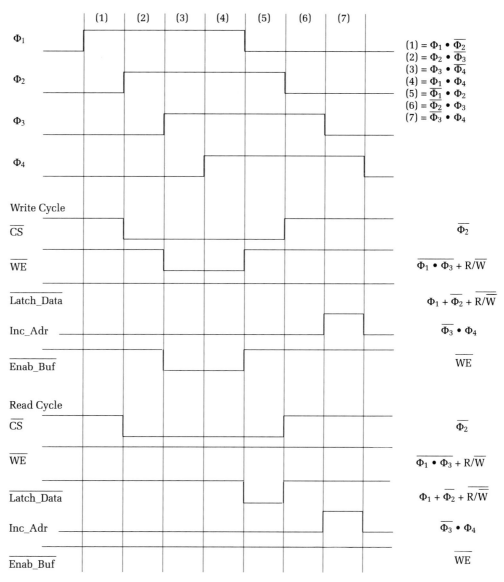

Figure 7.61   Generation of control signals from overlapping clocks.

We start by partitioning the overlapping clocks into seven periods, each of which is defined as a unique function of two of the clock phases. By combining these functions, we can obtain equations for the individual control signals. For example, we choose to implement $\overline{CS}$ simply as the inversion of clock phase Φ_2. To be safe, we will design the high-to-low-to-high transitions on the $\overline{WE}$ signal to be properly nested within the $\overline{CS}$ transitions.

$\overline{WE}$ should be low exactly during the time that clock phases Φ_1 and Φ_3 overlap (periods 3 and 4 in Figure 7.61). This is easy to generate with combinational logic:

$$\text{WE} = \Phi_1 \bullet \Phi_3 \bullet \overline{R/\overline{W}} \qquad \overline{\text{WE}} = \overline{(\Phi_1 \bullet \Phi_3)} + R/\overline{W}$$

The write enable signal should be asserted whenever clock phases Φ_1 and Φ_3 are asserted simultaneously and the READ/$\overline{\text{WRITE}}$ signal is low. Since $\overline{\text{WE}}$ is active low, we invert this logic to obtain the current sense of the signal.

We assert $\overline{\text{LATCH\_DATA}}$ during period 5, when Φ_1 is low and Φ_2 is high. Since the signal is active low, the implementation for the control signal becomes

$$\overline{\overline{\Phi_1} \bullet \Phi_2 \bullet \overline{R/\overline{W}}} = \Phi_1 + \overline{\Phi_2} + \overline{R/\overline{W}}$$

INC_ADR is active during period 7, so its implementation becomes $\overline{\Phi_3} \bullet \Phi_4$. Finally, $\overline{\text{ENAB\_BUF}}$ is identical to the signal $\overline{\text{WE}}$.

Of course, alternative implementations are possible as long as they lead to valid sequencing of the control signals. Also, the logic must be designed so that the sequence meets the setup and hold time requirements for the 2114 RAM.

Chapter Review

In this chapter, we have focused on a variety of sequential circuits used mostly as storage elements: registers, counters, and RAMs. We saw how to construct registers for storage and shifting from simple D-type flip-flops sharing common clock lines.

Random-access memories provide a large number of storage elements in a single integrated circuit package. Static RAMs are based on a storage element constructed from cross-coupled inverters. These devices tend to be very fast. Dynamic RAMs are based on a single transistor storage element. They have higher capacity than SRAMs but longer access times.

Counters are an important class of sequential circuits, not only because they count events but also because they can be used to generate a periodic sequence. This has important implications for controller design, which we will examine in more detail in the next chapter.

We introduced a design procedure for mapping a state transition diagram, describing the count sequence, into actual hardware. The steps involved deriving the state diagram from the written specification for the counter, deducing a state table from the diagram which tabulates current and next states, expressing each next-state bit as a combinational logic function of the current-state bits, and remapping these next-state functions according to the kind of flip-flop chosen as a storage element. Excitation tables provide the information for remapping the next-state truth tables into truth tables for the selected flip-flops' inputs.

In general, *J-K* flip-flops yield counter implementations with the fewest gates. However, we often choose *D* flip-flops because of the simplified design procedure. No remapping step is necessary, and fewer wires are needed to control a *D* flip-flop.

Because real hardware does not necessarily come up in a known state, we described the concept of self-starting counters. Self-starting design methods can be used to get a counter (eventually) into a known, valid state.

We presented counters without a global clock, asynchronous counters, and pointed out that their use should be avoided. We also demonstrated the advantages of counters with synchronous load and clear inputs, especially for the design of counters with starting or ending offsets.

In the final section, we looked at the timing behavior of a typical SRAM component in more detail. The important performance metrics are the memory access time and the memory cycle time. In addition, we introduced a simple memory controller design to illustrate the "glue" logic that must surround a RAM subsystem to interface it to the rest of the digital system.

We are now ready to study the design of more general circuits that follow a prescribed sequence other than the counters we have studied up to now. These *finite-state machines* will be the topic of the next chapter.

Further Reading

Just about any textbook on digital design will describe register and counter components and design strategies that employ them. It is more difficult to find good descriptions of memory components. J. Wakerly, *Digital Design: Principles and Practices*, Prentice-Hall, Englewood Cliffs, NJ, 1990 and Johnson and Karim, *Digital Design: A Pragmatic Approach*, PWS Publishers, Boston, 1987, are notable exceptions.

Perhaps the best way to learn about digital components is to study the relevant data books. For example, Cypress Semiconductor's *CMOS/BiCMOS Data Book*, San Jose, CA, 1989, describes their product line of very fast CMOS SRAMs in considerable detail.

An excellent survey and tutorial on memory system design using general-purpose and special-purpose RAMs can be found in Jean-Daniel Nicoud's paper "Video RAMs: Structure and Applications," which appeared in *IEEE MICRO* (February 1988), pp. 8–27. Nicoud describes how to apply video RAMs in the design of graphical frame buffers and compares the designs with those employing conventional RAMs.

For a system-level perspective on interfacing hardware to memory systems, see M. Slater's textbook *Microprocessor-Based Design*, published by Prentice-Hall in 1989.

Exercises

7.1 *(Shift Register Design)* Design the basic cell of a universal shift register to the following specifications. The internal storage elements will be positive edge-triggered D flip-flops. Besides the clock, the shifter stage has two external control inputs, S_0 and S_1, and three external data inputs, SR, SL, and DI. SR is input data being shifted into the cell from the right, SL is data being shifted from the left, and DI is parallel load data. The current value of the flip-flop will be replaced according to the following settings of the control signals: $S_0 = S_1 = 0$: replace D with DI; $S_0 = 0$, $S_1 = 1$: replace D with SL; $S_0 = 1$, $S_1 = 0$: replace D with SR; $S_0 = S_1 = 1$: hold the current state. Draw a schematic for this basic shifter cell.

7.2 *(Shift Register Design)* Shifters are normally used to shift data in a *circular* pattern (the data that shifts out at one end of the shifter is shifted back into the other end), or as a *logic* shift (fill the shifted positions with 0's) or an *arithmetic* shift (propagate the high-order sign bit to the right or shift in 0's to the left). For example, if a 4-bit register contains the data 1110, the effects of the six kinds of shifts are the following:

Circular shift right: 1110 becomes 0111.

Circular shift left: 1110 becomes 1101.

Logical shift right: 1110 becomes 0111.

Logical shift left: 1110 becomes 1100.

Arithmetic shift right: 1110 becomes 1111.

Arithmetic shift left: 1110 becomes 1100.

Show how to wire up a 4-bit universal shift register (TTL component 74194) to perform the following kinds of shifts:

a. Circular shift right

b. Circular shift left

c. Logic shift right

    d. Logic shift left

    e. Arithmetic shift right

    f. Arithmetic shift left

7.3 *(Shift Register Design)* Your task is to design a shift register subsystem based on the TTL 74194 component that can implement the six kinds of shifts described in Exercise 7.2. The subsystem has three control inputs, S_2, S_1, S_0 that are interpreted as follows: S_2, S_1, $S_0 = 000$ is hold; 001 is circular shift right; 010 is circular shift left; 011 is logic shift right; 100 is logic shift left; 101 is arithmetic shift right; 110 is arithmetic shift left; 111 is parallel load.

    a. Show the data path for the shifter subsystem. You may use multiplexers at the shift inputs to the 74194.

    b. Show the combinational logic (equations or schematics) to decode the global S_2, S_1, S_0 control inputs into the appropriate detailed control signals for the 74194 shifter and the external data path logic for handling the serial shift inputs.

7.4 *(Register Design)* A FIFO (first in, first out) queue is a special-purpose register file n words deep and m bits wide that operates as follows (see the block diagram in Figure Ex7.4(a)). When a PUSH_DATA control input is asserted, new data at the inputs at the right is read into the end of the queue. When a POP_DATA control input is asserted, existing data at the head of the queue becomes available at the outputs at the left. Since the FIFO has finite capacity, two status outputs indicate whether the FIFO is empty or full. PUSH_DATA is inhibited in a full FIFO, while POP_DATA is inhibited in an empty FIFO. On reset, the FIFO should be set to empty.

    a. A "flow-through" FIFO is the simplest form of this kind of device. The FIFO must fill up with data before any data can be removed. Furthermore, the FIFO must be completely emptied before new data can be placed in it. Using only shift register components and combinational logic, design a flow-through 4 word by 4 bit FIFO. Consider carefully how to represent the empty/full status of the FIFO. (*Hint*: Consider adding an (m + 1)st bit to the FIFO to indicate whether the FIFO word is valid.)

    b. A more flexible version of the FIFO can be implemented with counter and register components. Two counters represent the Q_HEAD and Q_TAIL respectively. These can be used as an index to a register file or an array of registers for reading from the head of the FIFO or writing to its tail. (b) shows one way to implement the PUSH_DATA and POP_DATA operations. POP_DATA delivers $word_2$ to the outputs and advances the Q_HEAD pointer. PUSH_DATA advances the tail pointer and writes the input to $word_0$. Notice how the queue wraps around on itself. Your task is to implement a 4 word by 4 bit FIFO using two 2-bit counters for the Q_HEAD and Q_TAIL. Think carefully about how you determine whether the FIFO is empty or full. Don't forget to consider the starting configuration of the head and tail pointers on FIFO reset.

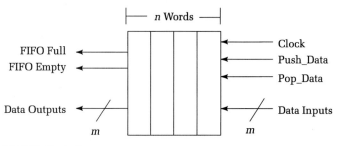

(a) FIFO block diagram

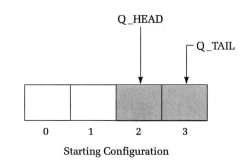

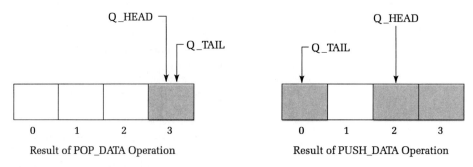

(b) PUSH_DATA and POP_DATA FIFO operations

Figure Ex7.4

7.5   *(Register Design)*   A LIFO (last in, first out) stack is similar in concept to the FIFO queue, except that the most recently pushed data is the first to be popped. The block diagram is identical to the FIFO, except that the data inputs and outputs are the same lines. Design a 4 word by 4 bit LIFO stack using shift registers and combinational logic only. Draw your schematic, indicating the components used. How do you distinguish between a full stack and an empty stack in this implementation?

7.6   *(Register Design)*   Repeat Exercise 7.5, this time using registers and counters. Draw the schematic. How do you distinguish between a full stack and an empty stack? What is the initial condition of the pointers at reset?

a.   *(Register Design)*   One way to compute the twos complement of a number is examine the number bit by bit from the lowest-order bit to the highest-order bit. In scanning from right to left, find the first bit that is one. All bits to the left of this should now be complemented to form the twos complement number. For example, the twos complement of 0010 is formed as follows:

$$0010 \longrightarrow 1101 \quad \text{(ones complement)}$$
$$\downarrow \qquad\qquad \underline{+\,1}$$
$$1110 \qquad\quad 1110 \quad \text{(twos complement)}$$

b.   Your task is to draw a schematic for a 4-bit register with parallel inputs and outputs and the synchronous control signals HOLD, CLEAR, LOAD, and COMPLEMENT. When the complement signal is asserted, the register's contents will be replaced by its twos complement.

c.   *(Shifter Application)*   Figure 7.9 shows the partial implementation of a bit-serial transmission subsystem. This subsystem is unidirectional: it can transmit only from the left shift registers to the right.

i.   Extend this data path implementation to make it bidirectional. Under external control, include logic (such as multiplexers) thatComposition 2 allows the subsystem to transmit from right to left as well as left to right.

ii.   The subsystem also needs a counter that can raise a signal after 8 bits have been transmitted. Show how a counter such as the TTL 74163 synchronous up-counter can be used to perform this function.

7.7   *(Shifter Application)*   In this exercise, you will generate control logic for use with the data path you developed in Exercise 7.6. You are given the control signals DIRECTION (0 = left to right, 1 = right to left), LOAD (load parallel data), XMIT (transmit bits in the indicated direction). External logic first sets the DIRECTION, then asserts LOAD to load parallel data, and finally asserts XMIT to begin the data transfer. Your logic will use these inputs to (a) parallel load the appropriate shifter registers, (b) shift 8 bits in the correct direction, and (c) place the receiving registers in the hold state when the transfer is complete. State all assumptions, and show your equations or logic schematics.

7.8   *(Counter Design)*   Design a 2-bit counter that behaves according to the two control inputs I_0 and I_1 as follows: $I_0, I_1 = 0, 0$: stop counting; $I_0, I_1 = 0, 1$: count up by one; $I_0, I_1 = 1, 0$: count down by one; $I_0, I_1 = 1, 1$: count by two.

    a. Draw the state diagram and state transition table.

    b. Implement the counter using T flip-flops, D flip-flops, and *J-K* flip-flops.

    c. Which choice of flip-flops leads to the minimum gate count? Assume that only two-input NAND, NOR, XOR, and XNOR gates are available. Draw the schematic for your minimum gate count implementation.

    d. Which choice of flip-flops leads to the minimum wire count? The same kinds of gates are available as in part (c). Draw the schematic for your minimum wire count implementation. Indicate how you have counted the interconnections.

7.9   *(Counter Design)*   Design a three flip-flop counter that counts in the following sequence: 000, 010, 111, 100, 110, 011, 001, and repeat. Design the counter using toggle flip-flops. Verify that your implementation is self-starting.

7.10   *(Counter Design)*   Consider the design of a 4-bit BCD counter that counts in the following sequence: 0000, 0001, 0010, 0011, 0100, 0101, 0110, 0111, 1000, 1001, and then back to 0000, 0001, etc.

    a. Draw the state diagram and next-state table.

    b. Implement the counter using D flip-flops, toggle flip-flops, *S-R* flip-flops, and *J-K* flip-flops.

    c. Implement the counter making it self-starting just for the D flip-flop case.

7.11 *(Counter Design)* Consider the design of a 4-bit Gray code counter (that is, only one of the state bits changes for each transition) that counts in the following sequence: 0000, 0001, 0011, 0010, 0110, 0111, 0101, 0100, 1100, 1101, 1111, 1110, 1010, 1011, 1001, 1000, and then back to 0000, 0001, 0011, etc.

  a. Draw a state diagram and next-state table.

  b. Implement the counter using *D* flip-flops, toggle flip-flops, *R-S* flip-flops, and *J-K* flip-flops.

  c. Do you have to worry about self-starting? Why or why not?

7.12 *(Counter Design)* The 4-bit Johnson counter advances through the sequence 0000, 1000, 1100, 1110, 1111, 0111, 0011, 0001, and repeat. Using the standard counter design process, show how to implement this count sequence using (a) *D* flip-flops and (b) *T* flip-flops. How does your solution compare with the *J-K* implementation of Figure 7.10, in terms of gates and wiring complexity?

7.13 *(Self-Starting Counters)* Analyze your solutions to Exercise 7.12(a) and (b) to check whether or not they are self-starting. Draw complete state diagrams and show all states and transitions implied by your implementation.

7.14 *(Reverse Engineering)* What is the counter state diagram implied by the flip-flop implementation of Figure Ex7.14?

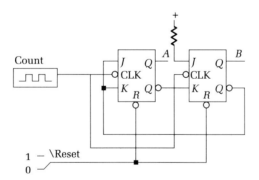

Figure Ex7.14   Counter implementation to reverse engineer in Exercise 7.14.

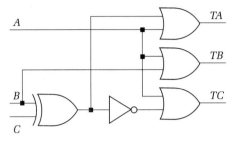

Figure Ex7.15   Next-state function to be reversed engineered in Exercise 7.15.

7.15   *(Reverse Engineering)*   Consider a counter implemented with three toggle flip-flops, labeled C, B, A from highest-order bit to lowest. The next-state function is implemented by the logic in Figure Ex7.15. Assuming the counter can be reset to state 000, what is the state diagram for this counter?

7.16   *(Ripple Counters)*   Figure 7.37 shows a 3-bit ripple up-counter. What simple change can you make to this circuit to convert it to a down-counter? Show your logic circuit and associated timing diagram. Explain why your circuit operates correctly.

7.17   *(Asynchronous Inputs)*   Can you think of any cases in which an asynchronous load or reset signal is acceptable in a digital design?

7.18   *(Offset Counters)*   Figure 7.41 shows a possible implementation for a counter with a beginning offset. The counter will eventually enter the correct sequence, but in some applications this may not be acceptable. How might you add a reset signal that will force the counter into a valid state when it is asserted? What assumptions must be made about the duration of the reset signal?

7.19   *(Offset Counters)*   Use two cascaded synchronous up-counters (for example, a TTL 74163 component) to implement a 6-bit offset counter that counts from 000010 to 110011 and repeats. Make sure the counter begins in state 000010 when the external reset signal is asserted.

7.20   *(Self-Starting Counters)*   Determine whether the counter implementation shown in the K-maps of Figure 7.34 is self-starting. Show the complete state diagram including the illegal states.

7.21   *(Self-Starting Counters)*   Determine whether the counter implementation indicated by the logic schematic of Figure 7.36 is self-starting. Show the complete state diagram including the invalid states. How does it compare with the complete state diagram of Exercise 7.20?

7.22 *(Counter/Register Applications)* Consider the design of a bit-serial adder. This circuit uses a single full adder to add two binary numbers presented in serial fashion, 1 bit at a time.

    a. Draw the schematic for a 4-bit version of this circuit. Two 4-bit shift registers are loaded with the data to be added in parallel. These are shifted out a bit at a time, starting with the lowest-order bit, into the A and B inputs of the full adder. The partial sum is shifted into a third register. How should the carry out be handled between subsequent bits?

    b. Define your control signals for the bit-serial adder subsystem. Draw a timing diagram that illustrates the sequencing of these signals to implement the 4-bit addition. What happens on reset?

7.23 *(Counter/Register Applications)* Flip-flops, registers, and counters can be used to implement a variety of useful clocking functions.

    a. Design a system that will generate a single clock pulse one period long each time a push-button is pressed (you may assume that an external reference clock is available).

    b. Design a system using an MSI counter that will assert a signal for exactly 13 clock pulses each time a push-button is pressed (once again, an external reference clock is available).

    c. In many applications, it is desirable to single step the clock as well as to halt a free-running clock signal and later restart it. Design a circuit that will generate a single clock pulse each time a STEP push-button is pressed. Provide a separate circuit, independent of STEP, that will cleanly turn the clock on when a RUN switch is in the ON position and off when RUN is in its off position. No marginal/partial clock outputs are allowed.

7.24 *(Counter/Register Applications)* Design a 2-bit binary up-counter to the following specification. The counter has five inputs (not including the clock) and three outputs. The inputs are CLR, LOAD, COUNT, L_B, and L_A. CLR takes precedence over LOAD, which in turn takes precedence over COUNT. The outputs are B, A, and RCO.

7.25 When CLR is asserted, the flip-flops of the counter in Exercise 7.24 are reset to 0. If LOAD is asserted (when CLR is not asserted), the flip-flops' contents are replaced by the L_B and L_A inputs. If COUNT is asserted (when CLR and LOAD are not asserted), the flip-flops' contents are incremented: 00 becomes 01, 01 becomes 10, 10 becomes 11, and 11 becomes 00. When the counter is in state 11, RCO is asserted.

7.26   Implement the counter in Exercise 7.24 using D flip-flops and as few logic components as possible. *Hint*: Use 4-to-1 multiplexers to implement your next-state function. You may also use XOR gates, as well as standard AND, OR, and NOT gates.

7.27   *(Random-Access Memories)*   A microprocessor with an 8-bit-wide data bus uses RAM chips of 4096 by 1-bit capacity. How many chips are needed and how should their address lines be connected to provide a memory capacity of 16 Kbytes (1 byte = 8 bits).

7.28   *(Random-Access Memories)*   Consider a 1-megabit dynamic memory component. The memory is organized into 512 rows of 2048 bits each. Assume that every bit must be refreshed within 4 ms. How frequently should a row refresh operation be scheduled? If the memory has an 80 ns access time, approximately what fraction of memory accesses must be dedicated for refresh?

7.29   *(Random-Access Memories)*   Consider the memory controller design described in Section 7.6.5. Show an alternative implementation of the control signals INC_ADR, $\overline{\text{LATCH\_DATA}}$, and $\overline{\text{ENAB\_BUF}}$ that leads to a different detailed sequencing of the signals that is still logically correct.

7.30   *(Random-Access Memories)*   Consider the read and write timing of the 2114 memory component in Figures 7.55 and 7.56. What is the minimum clock width for the overlapping clocks generated by the memory controller that will still meet the memory's timing specification? Justify your answer.

8   Finite State Machine Design

Introduction

In this chapter we begin our examination of the most important kind of sequential circuit: the finite state machine. *Finite state machines* are so named because the sequential logic that implements them can be in only a fixed number of possible states. The counters of Chapter 7 are rather simple finite state machines. Their outputs and states are identical, and there is no choice of the sequence in which states are visited.

More generally, the outputs and next state of a finite state machine are combinational logic functions of their inputs and present state. The choice of next state can depend on the value of an input, leading to more complex behavior than that of counters. Finite state machines are critical for realizing the control and decision-making logic in digital systems.

In this and the following chapter we extend the counter design procedure of Chapter 7 to the more general case of finite state machines. In this chapter, we shall emphasize:

■ *Methods for describing the behavior of finite state machines.* These include abstract state machine notation, state diagrams, state tables, and hardware description languages.

■ *Techniques for mapping word specifications into more formal descriptions of finite state machine behavior.* We will examine four representative finite state machine design problems to illustrate the techniques for performing these mappings.

8.1   The Concept of the State Machine

We begin our study of finite state machines with an example logic function that depends on its history of inputs to determine its output. We will see the complete process of transforming a specification of the function, through a variety of equivalent representations, resulting in an actual implementation of gates and flip-flops.

Application   8.1.1   Odd or Even Parity Checker

Consider the design of a logic circuit that counts the number of 1's in a bit-serial input stream. If the circuit asserts its output when the input stream contains an odd number of 1's, it is called an *odd parity checker*. If it asserts its output when it has seen an even number of 1's, it is an *even parity checker*. The circuit is clearly sequential: the current output depends on the complete history of inputs.

State Diagram   The first step of our design process is to develop a state diagram that describes the behavior of the circuit. It's not too hard to see that the circuit can be in one of two different states: either an even or an odd number of 1's has been seen since reset. Whenever the input contains a 1, we switch to the opposite state. For example, if an odd number of 1's has already been seen and the current input is 1, we now see an even number of 1's. If the input is 0, we stay in the current state.

The state diagram we derive is shown in Figure 8.1. We name the two unique configurations of the circuit Even and Odd. The outputs are explicitly associated with the states and are shown in square brackets. When an odd number of 1's has been seen, the output is 1. Otherwise it is 0. We associate the input values that cause a transition to take place with the arcs in the state diagram.

State Transition Table   A reformulation of the state diagram is the *symbolic state transition table*. This is shown in Figure 8.2. We give meaningful symbolic names to the inputs, outputs, and present and next states. We cannot implement the circuit just yet. We must first assign binary encodings to all the state, input, and output symbols in the transition table.

Figure 8.3 shows the revised representation, called the *encoded state table*. We have assigned the encoding 0 to state Even and 1 to state Odd. The table now looks more like a truth table.

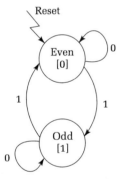

Figure 8.1   Example state diagram.

Present State	Input	Next State	Output
Even	0	Even	0
Even	1	Odd	0
Odd	0	Odd	1
Odd	1	Even	1

Figure 8.2   Symbolic state transition table.

Present State	Input	Next State	Output
0	0	0	0
0	1	1	0
1	0	1	1
1	1	0	1

Figure 8.3   Encoded state transition table.

Next State and Output Functions   At this point, we have the next state (NS) and output (OUT) expressed as logic functions of the present state (PS) and present input (PI). Based on a quick examination of the encoded state table, we write the functions as

$$NS = PS \oplus PI$$

$$OUT = PS$$

Implementation   Now we are ready to implement the circuit. The state of the finite state machine is held by flip-flops. Since we have only two states, we can implement the circuit with a single flip-flop. The next-state function determines the input to this flip-flop.

We show an implementation using a D flip-flop in Figure 8.4(a). The XOR gate directly computes the D input as a function of the present state and the input.

A close inspection of the state transition table should suggest to you an alternative implementation. Whenever the input is 0, the circuit stays in the same state. Whenever the input is 1, the state toggles. An implementation based on a T flip-flop is given in Figure 8.4(b). This eliminates the XOR gate. By judicious selection of the flip-flop type, you can simplify the implementation logic.

Figure 8.5 shows the abstract timing behavior of the finite state machine for the input stream 100110101110. Each input bit is sampled on the rising edge of the clock because the state register is implemented by a positive edge-triggered flip-flop. The output changes soon after the rising edge. You should be able to convince yourself that the output is 1 whenever the input stream has presented an odd number of 1's, and is 0 otherwise.

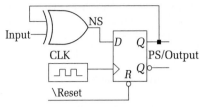

(a) *D* flip-flop implementation

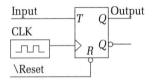

(b) *T* flip-flop implementation

Figure 8.4 Parity checker hardware.

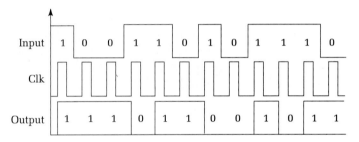

Figure 8.5 Waveforms for input/output behavior.

8.1.2 Timing in State Machines

In designing our finite state machines, we will follow a rigorous *synchronous design methodology*. This means that we will trigger the state changes with a global reference signal, the *clock*. It is important for you to understand when inputs are sampled, the next state is computed, and the outputs are asserted with respect to the clock signal.

State Time We define *state time* as the time between related *clocking events*. For edge-triggered systems, the clocking events are the low-to-high (positive edge) or high-to-low (negative edge) transitions on the clock. In a positive edge-triggered system, the state time is measured from one rising clock edge to the next. In negative edge-triggered systems, the state time is measured between subsequent falling edges.

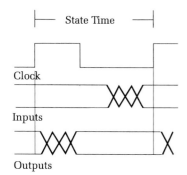

Figure 8.6 Input/output behavior of a positive edge-triggered state machine.

In response to a clocking event, the state and the outputs change, based on the current state and inputs. To be safe, and to meet propagation delays and setup times in the next-state logic, the inputs should be stable before the clocking event. After a suitable propagation delay, the finite state machine enters its next state and its new outputs become stable.

Figure 8.6 illustrates the state change, input sampling, and output changes for a positive edge-triggered synchronous system. On the rising edge, the inputs and current state are sampled to compute the new state and outputs.

Output Validity An output is not valid until after the edge, and inputs are sampled just before the edge. As an example of detailed state machine timing behavior, Figure 8.7 gives fragment state diagrams for two communicating finite state machines (FSMs). We assume that both are positive edge-triggered synchronous systems and the output from each state machine is the input to the other. The interaction between these machines is illustrated by the timing diagram of Figure 8.8.

To start, the clock is in the first period with FSM_1 about to enter state A with its output $X = 0$. FSM_2 is entering state C with its output $Y = 0$. In the second clock period, FSM_1 is in state A and asserts its output X. FSM_2 is in state C with its output Y unasserted. On the rising edge that starts the third clock period, FSM_1 stays in state A since its input is 0. FSM_2 advances to state D, asserting Y, but too late to affect the state change in FSM_1. The input value before the clock edge is the one that matters.

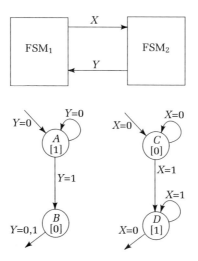

Figure 8.7 Communicating FSM fragments.

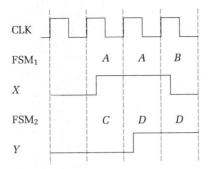

Figure 8.8 State and output changes associated with the FSM fragments of Figure 8.7.

Now that Y is 1, FSM_1 goes to state B on the next rising edge. In this state, it will output a 0, but this is too late to affect FSM_2's state change. It remains in state D.

8.2 Basic Design Approach

The counter design procedure presented in the last chapter forms the core of a more general procedure for arbitrary finite state machines. You will discover that the procedure must be significantly extended for the general case.

8.2.1 Finite State Machine Design Procedure

Step 1: *Understand the problem.* A finite state machine is often described in terms of an English-language specification of its behavior. It is important that you interpret this description in an unambiguous manner. For counters, it is sufficient simply to enumerate the sequence. For finite state machines, try some input sequences to be sure you understand the conditions under which the various outputs are generated.

Step 2: *Obtain an abstract representation of the FSM.* Once you understand the problem, you must place it in a form that is easy to manipulate by the procedures for implementing the finite state machine. A state diagram is one possibility. Other representations, to be introduced in the next section, include algorithmic state machines and specifications in hardware description languages.

Step 3: *Perform state minimization.* Step 2, deriving the abstract representation, often results in a description that has too many states. Certain paths through the state machine can be eliminated because their input/output behavior is duplicated by other functionally equivalent paths. This is a new step, not needed in the simpler counter design process.

Step 4: *Perform state assignment.*   In counters the state and the output were identical, and we didn't need to worry about encoding a particular state. In general finite state machines, this is not the case. Outputs are derived from the bits stored in the state flip-flops (plus the inputs), and a good choice of how to encode the state often leads to a simpler implementation.

Step 5: *Choose flip-flop types for implementing the FSM's state.*   This is identical to the decision in the counter design procedure. *J-K* flip-flops tend to reduce gate count at the expense of more connections. *D* flip-flops simplify the implementation process.

Step 6: *Implement the finite state machine.*   The final step is also found in the counter design procedure. Using Boolean equations or K-maps for the next state and output combinational functions, produce the minimized two-level or multilevel implementation.

In this chapter, we concentrate on the first two steps of the design process. We will cover steps 3 through 6 in Chapter 9.

Application   **8.2.2**   A Simple Vending Machine

To illustrate the basic design procedure, we will advance through the implementation of a simple finite state machine that controls a vending machine.

Here is how the control is supposed to work. The vending machine delivers a package of gum after it has received 15 cents in coins. The machine has a single coin slot that accepts nickels and dimes, one coin at a time. A mechanical sensor indicates to the control whether a dime or a nickel has been inserted into the coin slot. The controller's output causes a single package of gum to be released down a chute to the customer.

One further specification: We will design our machine so it does not give change. A customer who pays with two dimes is out 5 cents!

Understanding the Problem   The first step in the finite state machine design process is to *understand the problem*. Start by drawing a block diagram to understand the inputs and outputs. Figure 8.9 is a good example. *N* is asserted for one clock period when a nickel is inserted into the coin slot. *D* is asserted when a dime has been deposited. The machine asserts Open for one clock period when 15 cents (or more) has been deposited since the last reset.

The specification may not completely define the behavior of the finite state machine. For example, what happens if someone inserts a penny into the coin slot? Or what happens after the gum is delivered to

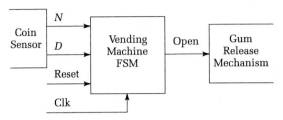

Figure 8.9   Vending machine block diagram.

the customer? Sometimes we have to make reasonable assumptions. For the first question, we assume that the coin sensor returns any coins it does not recognize, leaving N and D unasserted. For the latter, we assume that external logic resets the machine after the gum is delivered.

Abstract Representations   Once you understand the behavior reasonably well, it is time to *map the specification into a more suitable abstract representation*. A good way to begin is by enumerating the possible unique sequences of inputs or configurations of the system. These will help define the states of the finite state machine.

For this problem, it is not too difficult to enumerate all the possible input sequences that lead to releasing the gum:

Three nickels in sequence: N, N, N

Two nickels followed by a dime: N, N, D

A nickel followed by a dime: N, D

A dime followed by a nickel: D, N

Two dimes in sequence: D, D

This can be represented as a state diagram, as shown in Figure 8.10. For example, the machine will pass through the states S_0, S_1, S_3, S_7 if the input sequence is three nickels.

To keep the state diagram simple and readable, we include only transitions that explicitly cause a state change. For example, in state S_0, if neither input N or D is asserted, we assume the machine remains in state S_0 (the specification allows us to assume that N and D are never asserted at the same time). Also, we include the output Open only in states in which it is asserted. Open is implicitly unasserted in any other state.

State Minimization   This nine-state description isn't the "best" possible. For one thing, since states S_4, S_5, S_6, S_7, and S_8 have identical behavior, they can be combined into a single state.

To reduce the number of states even further, we can think of each state as representing the amount of money received so far. For example,

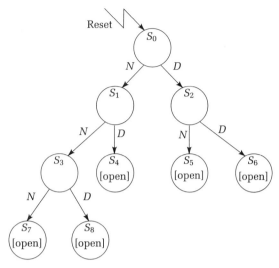

Figure 8.10 Vending machine state diagram.

it shouldn't matter whether the state representing 10 cents was reached through two nickels or one dime.

A state diagram derived in this way is shown in Figure 8.11. We capture the behavior in only four states, compared with nine in Figure 8.10. Also, as another illustration of a useful shorthand, notice the transition from state 10¢ to 15¢. We interpret the notation "N, D" associated with this transition as "go to state 15¢ if N is asserted OR D is asserted."

In the next chapter, we will examine formal methods for finding a state diagram with the minimum number of states. The process of minimizing the states in a finite state machine description is called *state minimization*.

State Encoding At this point, we have a finite state machine with a minimum number of states, but it is still symbolic. See Figure 8.12 for the symbolic state transition table. The next step is *state encoding*.

The way you encode the state can have a major effect on the amount of hardware you need to implement the machine. A natural state assignment would encode the states in 2 bits: state 0¢ as 00, state 5¢ as 01, state 10¢ as 10, and state 15¢ as 11. A less obvious assignment could lead to reduced hardware. The *encoded* state transition table is shown in Figure 8.13.

In Chapter 9 we present a variety of methods and computer-based tools for finding an effective state encoding.

Implementation The next step is to implement the state transition table after choosing storage elements. We will look at implementations based on D and J-K flip-flops.

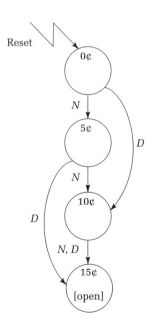

Figure 8.11 Minimized vending machine state diagram.

Present State	Inputs D N	Next State	Output Open
0¢	0 0	0¢	0
	0 1	5¢	0
	1 0	10¢	0
	1 1	X	X
5¢	0 0	5¢	0
	0 1	10¢	0
	1 0	15¢	0
	1 1	X	X
10¢	0 0	10¢	0
	0 1	15¢	0
	1 0	15¢	0
	1 1	X	X
15¢	X X	15¢	1

Figure 8.12   Minimized vending machine symbolic state transition table.

Present State Q_1 Q_0	Inputs D N	Next State D_1 D_0	Output Open
0 0	0 0	0 0	0
	0 1	0 1	0
	1 0	1 0	0
	1 1	X X	X
0 1	0 0	0 1	0
	0 1	1 0	0
	1 0	1 1	0
	1 1	X X	X
1 0	0 0	1 0	0
	0 1	1 1	0
	1 0	1 1	0
	1 1	X X	X
1 1	0 0	1 1	1
	0 1	1 1	1
	1 0	1 1	1
	1 1	X X	X

Figure 8.13   Encoded vending machine state transition table.

The K-maps for the D flip-flop implementation are shown in Figure 8.14. We filled these in directly from the encoded state transition table. The minimized equations for the flip-flop inputs and the output become

$$D_1 = Q_1 + D + Q_0 \bullet N$$

$$D_0 = N \bullet \overline{Q}_0 + Q_0 \bullet \overline{N} + Q_1 \bullet N + Q_1 \bullet D$$

$$\text{OPEN} = Q_1 \bullet Q_0$$

The logic implementation is shown in Figure 8.15. It uses eight gates and two flip-flops.

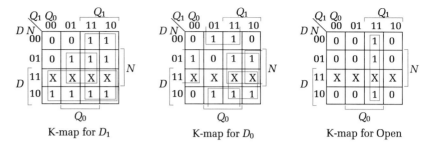

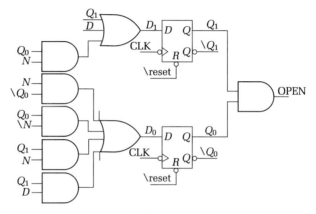

Figure 8.14 K-maps for D flip-flop implementation of vending machine.

Figure 8.15 Vending machine FSM implementation based on D flip-flops.

To implement the state machine using *J-K* flip-flops, we must remap the next-state functions as in Chapter 7. The remapped state transition table for *J-K* flip-flop implementation is shown in Figure 8.16. We give the K-maps derived from this table in Figure 8.17. The minimized equations for the flip-flop inputs become

$$J_1 = D + Q_0 \bullet N \qquad K_1 = 0$$
$$J_0 = \overline{Q}_0 \bullet N + Q_1 \bullet D \qquad K_0 = \overline{Q}_1 \bullet N$$

Figure 8.18 shows the logic implementation. Using *J-K* flip-flops moderately reduced the hardware: seven gates and two flip-flops.

Discussion We briefly described the complete finite state machine design process and illustrated it by designing a simple vending machine controller. Starting with an English-language statement of the task, we first described the machine in a more formal representation. In this case, we used state diagrams.

Present State Q_1 Q_0		Inputs D N		Next State D_1 D_0		J_1	K_1	J_0	K_0
0	0	0	0	0	0	0	X	0	X
		0	1	0	1	0	X	1	X
		1	0	1	0	1	X	0	X
		1	1	X	X	X	X	X	X
0	1	0	0	0	1	0	X	X	0
		0	1	1	0	1	X	X	1
		1	0	1	1	1	X	X	0
		1	1	X	X	X	X	X	X
1	0	0	0	1	0	X	0	0	X
		0	1	1	1	X	0	1	X
		1	0	1	1	X	0	1	X
		1	1	X	X	X	X	X	X
1	1	0	0	1	1	X	0	X	0
		0	1	1	1	X	0	X	0
		1	0	1	1	X	0	X	0
		1	1	X	X	X	X	X	X

Figure 8.16   Remapped next-state functions for the vending machine example.

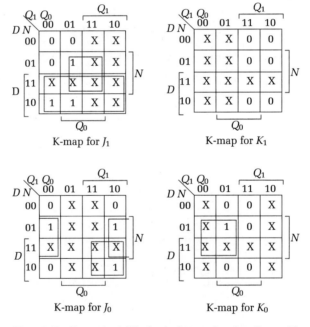

Figure 8.17   K-maps for *J-K* flip-flop implementation of vending machine.

Since more than one state diagram can lead to the same input/output behavior, it is important to find a description with as few states as possible. This usually reduces the implementation complexity of the finite state machine. For example, the state diagram of Figure 8.10 contains nine states and requires four flip-flops for its implementation. The minimized state

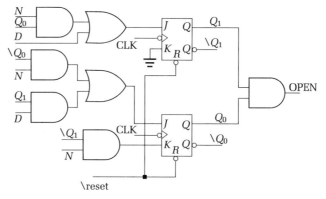

Figure 8.18 *J-K* flip-flop implementation for the vending machine example.

diagram of Figure 8.11 has four states and can be implemented with only two flip-flops.

Once we have obtained a minimum finite state description, the next step is to choose a good encoding of the states. The right choice can further reduce the logic for the next-state and output functions. In the example, we used only the most obvious state assignment.

The final step is to choose a flip-flop type for the state registers. In the example, the implementation based on D flip-flops was more straightforward. We did not need to remap the flip-flop inputs, but we used more gates than the *J-K* flip-flop implementation. This is usually the case.

Now we are ready to examine some alternatives to the state diagram for describing finite state machine behavior.

8.3 Alternative State Machine Representations

You have already seen how to describe finite state machines in terms of state diagrams and tables. However, it can be difficult to describe complex finite state machines in this way. Recently, hardware designers have shifted toward using alternative representations of FSM behavior that look more like software descriptions. In this section, we introduce algorithmic state machine (ASM) notation and hardware description languages (HDLs). ASMs are similar to program flowcharts, but they have a more rigorous concept of timing. HDLs look much like modern programming languages, but they explicitly support computations that can occur in parallel.

You may wonder what is wrong with state diagrams. The problem is that they do not adequately capture the notion of an *algorithm*—a well-defined sequence of steps that produce a desired sequence of actions based on input data. State diagrams are weak at capturing the structure behind complex sequencing. The representations discussed next do a better job of making this sequencing structure explicit.

8.3.1   Algorithmic State Machine Notation

The ASM notation consists of three primitive elements: the state box, the decision box, and the output box, as shown in Figure 8.19. Each major unit, called an ASM block, consists of a state box and, optionally, a network of condition and output boxes. A state machine is in exactly one state or ASM block during the stable portion of the state time.

State Boxes   There is one state box per ASM block, reached from other ASM blocks through a single state entry path. In addition, for each combination of inputs there is a single unambiguous exit path from the ASM block. The state box is identified by a symbolic state name—in a circle—and a binary-encoded state code, and it contains an output signal list.

The output list describes the signals that are asserted whenever the state is entered. Because signals may be expressed in either positive or negative logic, it is customary to place an "L." or "H." prefix before the signal name, indicating whether it is asserted low or high. You can also specify whether the signal is asserted immediately (I) or is delayed (no special prefix) until the next clocking event. A signal not mentioned in the output list is left unasserted.

Condition Boxes   The condition box tests an input to determine an exit path from the current ASM block to the block to be entered next. The order in which condition boxes are cascaded has no effect on the determination of the next ASM block. Figure 8.20(a) and (b) show functionally equivalent ASM blocks: state B is to be entered next if I_0 and I_1 are both 1; otherwise state C is next.

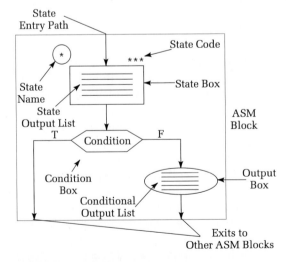

Figure 8.19   Elements of the ASM notation.

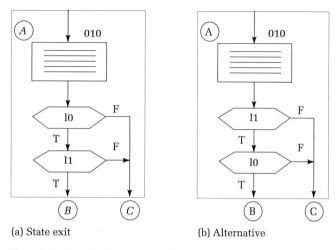

(a) State exit   (b) Alternative

Figure 8.20 Functionally equivalent ASM blocks.

Output Boxes Any output boxes on the path from the state box to an exit contain signals that should be asserted along with the signals mentioned in the state box. The state machine advances from one state to the next in discrete rather than continuous steps. In this sense, ASM charts have different timing semantics than program flowcharts.

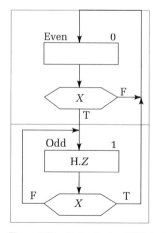

Figure 8.21 Parity checker ASM chart.

Example   The Parity Checker As an example, we give the parity checker's ASM chart in Figure 8.21. It consists of two states, Even and Odd, encoded as 0 and 1, respectively. The input is the single bit X; the output is the single bit Z, asserted high when the finite state machine is in the Odd state.

We can derive the state transition table from the ASM chart. We simply list all the possible transition paths from one state to another and the input combinations that cause the transition to take place. For example, in state Even, when the input is 1, we go to state Odd. Otherwise we stay in state Even. For state Odd, if the input is 1, we advance to Even. Otherwise we remain in state Odd. The output Z is asserted only in state Odd. The transition table becomes:

Input X	Present State	Next State	Output Z
F	Even	Even	Not asserted
T	Even	Odd	Not asserted
F	Odd	Odd	Asserted
T	Odd	Even	Asserted

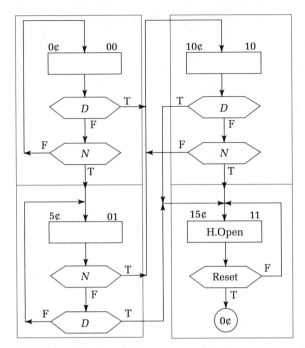

Figure 8.22 Vending machine ASM chart.

Example   Vending Machine Controller We show the ASM chart for the vending machine in Figure 8.22. To extract the state transition table, we simply examine all exit paths from each state. For example, in the state 0¢, we advance to state 10¢ when input D is asserted. If N is asserted, we go to state 5¢. Otherwise, we stay in state 0¢. The rest of the table can be determined by looking at the remaining states in turn.

8.3.2   Hardware Description Languages: VHDL

Hardware description languages provide another way to specify finite state machine behavior. Such descriptions bear some resemblance to a program written in a modern structured programming language. But again, the concept of timing is radically different from that in a program written in a sequential programming language. Unlike state diagrams or ASM charts, specifications in a hardware description language can actually be simulated. They are executable descriptions that can be used to verify that the digital system they describe behaves as expected.

VHDL (VHSIC hardware description language) is an industry standard. Although its basic concepts are relatively straightforward, its detailed syntax is beyond the scope of this text. However, we can illustrate its capabilities for describing finite state machines by examining a description of the parity checker written in VHDL:

```
ENTITY parity_checker IS
    PORT (
        x, clk: IN BIT;
        z: OUT BIT);
END parity_checker;

ARCHITECTURE behavioral OF parity_checker IS
    BEGIN
        main: BLOCK (clk = '1' and not clk'STABLE)

        TYPE state IS (Even, Odd);
        SIGNAL state_register: state := Even;

        BEGIN state_even:
            BLOCK ((state_register = Even) AND GUARD)
                BEGIN
                state_register <= Odd WHEN x = '1'
                ELSE Even
            END BLOCK state_even;

        BEGIN state_odd:
            BLOCK ((state_register = Odd) AND GUARD)
                BEGIN
                state_register <= Even WHEN x = '1'
                ELSE Odd;
            END BLOCK state_odd;

        z <= '0' WHEN state_register = Even ELSE
             '1' WHEN state_register = Odd;
    END BLOCK main;
END behavioral;
```

Every VHDL description has two components: an *interface description* and an *architectural body*. The former defines the input and output connections or "ports" to the hardware entity being designed; the latter describes the entity's behavior.

The architecture block defines the behavior of the finite state machine. The values the *state register* can take on are defined by the type *state*, consisting of the symbols *Even* and *Odd*. We write VHDL statements that assign new values to the state register and the output Z, depending on the current value of input X, whenever we detect a rising clock edge.

Checking for events like a clock transition is handled through the VHDL concept of the *guard*, an expression that enables certain statements in the description when it evaluates to true. For example, the expression

```
clk = '1' and not clk'stable
```

is a guard that evaluates to true whenever the clock signal has recently undergone a 0-to-1 transition. The main block is enabled for evaluation when this particular guard becomes true.

The description contains two subblocks, *state_even* and *state_odd*, that are enabled whenever the main guard is true and the machine is in the indicated state. Within each subblock, the state register receives a new assignment depending on the value of the input. Outside the subblocks, the output becomes 0 when the machine enters state Even and 1 when it enters state Odd.

8.3.3 ABEL Hardware Description Language

ABEL is a hardware description language closely tied to the specification of programmable logic components. It is also an industry standard and enjoys widespread use. The language is suitable for describing either combinational or sequential logic and supports hardware specification in terms of Boolean equations, truth tables, or state diagram descriptions. Although the detailed syntax and semantics of the language are beyond our scope, we can highlight its features with the parity checker finite state machine.

Let's look at the ABEL description of the parity checker:

```
module parity
title 'odd parity checker state machine
    Joe Engineer, Itty Bity Machines, Inc.'
u1    device   'p22v10';

"Input Pins
   clk, X, RESET pin 1, 2, 3;

"Output Pins
    Q, Z       pin 21, 22;
    Q, Z       istype 'pos,reg';

"State registers
SREG   =  [Q, Z];
EVEN   =  [0, 0]; " even number of 0's
ODD    =  [1, 1]; " odd number of 0's
```

```
equations
   [Q.ar, Z.ar] = RESET;"Reset to state S0

state_diagram SREG
state EVEN:
   if X then ODD
   else EVEN;
state ODD:
   if X then EVEN
   else ODD;

test_vectors ([clk, RESET, X] -> [SREG])
   [0,1,.X.] -> [EVEN];
   [.C.,0,1] -> [ODD];
   [.C.,0,1] -> [EVEN];
   [.C.,0,1] -> [ODD];
   [.C.,0,0] -> [ODD];
   [.C.,0,1] -> [EVEN];
   [.C.,0,1] -> [ODD];
   [.C.,0,0] -> [ODD];
   [.C.,0,0] -> [ODD];
   [.C.,0,0] -> [ODD];
end parity;
```

An ABEL description consists of several sections: *module*, *title*, *descriptions*, *equations*, *truth tables*, *state diagrams*, and *test vectors*, some of which are optional. Every ABEL description begins with a `module` statement and an optional `title` statement. These name the module and provide some basic documentation about its function.

These are followed by the `description` section. The elements of this section are the kind of device being programmed, the specification of inputs and outputs, and the declaration of which signals constitute the state of the finite state machine.

We must first describe the device selected for the implementation. It is a P22V10 PAL, with 12 inputs, 10 outputs, and embedded flip-flops associated with the outputs. For identification within the schematic, we call the device *u1*.

Next come the pin descriptions. The finite state machine's inputs are the clock *clk*, data *X*, and the *RESET* signal. The outputs are the state *Q* and the output *Z*. These are assigned to specific pins on the PAL. For example, pin 1 is connected to the clock inputs of the internal flip-flops.

Many of the attributes of a PAL are selectable, so the description may need to make explicit choices. The next line of the description tells ABEL that *Q* and *Z* are POSitive logic outputs of the PAL's internal flip-flops (REG) associated with particular output pins. The P22V10 PAL also supports negative logic outputs as well as outputs that bypass the internal flip-flops.

The state of the finite state machine is represented by the outputs Q and Z. EVEN is defined as the state where Q and Z are 0. ODD is defined as the state where Q and Z are 1.

The `equation` section defines outputs in terms of Boolean equations of the inputs. In this case, the asynchronous reset (`.ar`) inputs of the Q and Z flip-flops are driven high when the RESET signal is asserted.

The `state_diagram` section describes the transitions among states using a programming language–like syntax. If we are in EVEN and the input X is asserted, we change to ODD. Otherwise we stay in EVEN. Similarly, if we are in ODD and X is asserted, we return to EVEN. Otherwise we stay in state ODD. ABEL supports a variety of control constructs, including such things as case statements.

The final section in this example is for `test_vectors`. This is a tabular listing of the expected input/output behavior of the finite state machine. The first entry describes what happens when RESET is asserted: independent of the current value of X, the machine is forced to EVEN. The rest of the entries describe the state sequence for the input string 111011000. The ABEL system simulates the description to ensure that the behavior matches the specified behavior of the test vectors.

The major weakness of an ABEL description is that it forces the designer to understand many low-level details about the target PAL. Nevertheless, the state diagram description is an intuitively simple way to describe the behavior of a state machine.

8.4   Moore and Mealy Machine Design Procedure

There are two basic ways to organize a clocked sequential network:

■ *Moore machine*: The outputs depend only on the present state. See the block diagram in Figure 8.23. A combinational logic block maps the inputs and the current state into the necessary flip-flop inputs to store the appropriate next state. The outputs are computed by a combinational logic block whose only inputs are the flip-flops' state outputs. The outputs change *synchronously* with the state transition and the clock edge. The finite state machines you have seen so far are all Moore machines.

■ *Mealy machine*: The outputs depend on the present state and the present value of the inputs. See Figure 8.24. The outputs can change immediately after a change at the inputs, independent of the clock. A Mealy machine constructed in this fashion has *asynchronous* outputs.

Moore outputs are synchronous with the clock, only changing with state transitions. Mealy outputs are asynchronous and can change in response to any changes in the inputs, independent of the clock. This

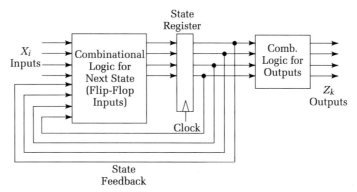

Figure 8.23   Moore machine block diagram.

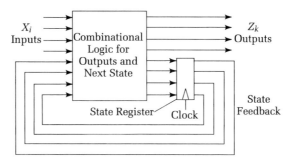

Figure 8.24   Mealy machine block diagram.

gives Moore machines an advantage in terms of disciplined timing methodology. However, there is a synchronous variation of the Mealy machine, which we describe later.

8.4.1   State Diagram and ASM Chart Representations

An ASM chart intended for Moore implementation would have no conditional output boxes. The necessary outputs are simply listed in the state box. Conditional output boxes in the ASM chart usually imply a Mealy implementation.

Figure 8.25 shows the notations for Mealy and Moore state diagrams, using the vending machine example. For Moore machines, the outputs are associated with the state in which they are asserted. Arcs are labeled with the input conditions that cause the transition from the state at the tail of the arc to the state at its head. Combinational logic functions are perfectly acceptable as arc labels.

In Mealy machines, the outputs are associated with the transition arcs rather than the state bubble. A slash separates the inputs from the

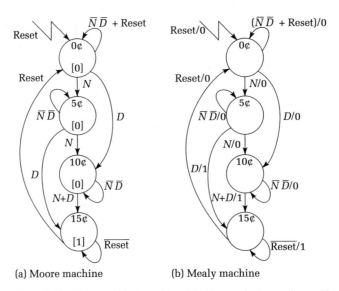

(a) Moore machine   (b) Mealy machine

Figure 8.25   Moore and Mealy machine state diagrams for the vending machine FSM.

outputs. For example, if we are in state 10¢ and either N or D is asserted, Open will be asserted. Any glitch on N or D could cause the gum to be delivered by mistake.

The state diagrams in this figure are labeled more completely than our previous examples. For example, we make explicit the transitions that cause the machine to stay in the same state. We usually eliminate such transitions to simplify the state diagram. We also associate explicit output values with each transition in the Mealy state diagram and each state in the Moore state diagram. A common simplification places the output on the transition or in the state only when it is asserted. You should clarify your assumptions whenever you draw state diagrams.

8.4.2   Comparison of the Two Machine Types

Because it can associate outputs with transitions, a Mealy machine can often generate the same output sequence in fewer states than a Moore machine.

Consider a finite state machine that asserts its single output whenever its input string has at least two 1's in sequence. The minimum Moore and Mealy state diagrams are shown in Figure 8.26. The equivalent ASM charts are in Figure 8.27.

To represent the 1's sequence, the Moore machine requires two states to distinguish between the first and subsequent 1's. The first state has output 0, while the second has output 1. The Mealy machine accomplishes this with a single state reached by two different transitions. For the first 1, the transition has output 0. For the second and subsequent 1's, the transition has output 1. Despite the Mealy machine's timing complexities, designers like its reduced state count.

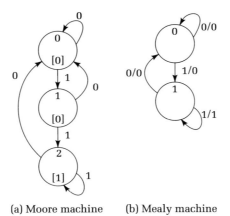

(a) Moore machine   (b) Mealy machine

Figure 8.26   Two state diagrams with the same I/O behavior but different number of states.

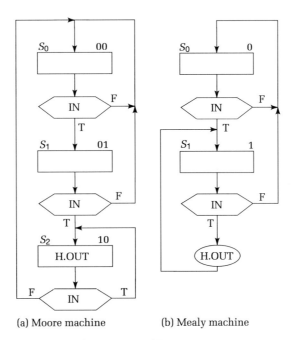

(a) Moore machine   (b) Mealy machine

Figure 8.27   ASM equivalents of Figure 8.26.

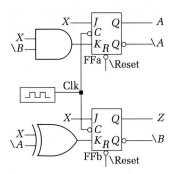

Figure 8.28   Mystery Moore finite state machine.

8.4.3   Examples of Moore and Mealy Machines

Example   Moore Machine Description   To better understand the timing behavior of Moore and Mealy machines, let's begin by *reverse engineering* some finite state machines. We will work backward from a circuit-level implementation of the finite state machine to derive an ASM chart or state diagram that describes the machine's behavior.

Figure 8.28 shows schematically a finite state machine with single data input X and output Z. The FSM is a Moore machine because the output is a combinational logic function (in this case a trivial one) of the state alone. The state register is implemented by two master/slave J-K flip-flops, named A and B, respectively. The machine can be in any one of up to four valid states. The output Z and the state bit B are the same.

Signal Trace Method   There are two systematic approaches to determining the state transitions: *exhaustive signal tracing* and *extraction of the next state/output functions*. We examine the former here and the latter in the next subsection.

Signal tracing uses a collection of input sequences to exercise the various state transitions of the machine. To see how it works, let's start by generating a sample input sequence.

It is reasonable to assume that the FSM is initially reset and that it has been placed in state $A = 0$, $B = 0$. Figure 8.29 contains the timing waveform you would see after presenting the input sequence 1 0 1 0 1 0 to the machine. Because the FSM is implemented with master/slave flip-flops, the state time begins with the falling edge of the clock. Input X must be stable throughout the high time of the clock to guard against ones catching problems.

The sequence of events in Figure 8.29 is as follows. The asserted reset signal places the FSM in state 00. After the falling edge, input X goes high just after time step 20. At the next rising edge, the input is sampled and the next state is determined, but this is not presented to

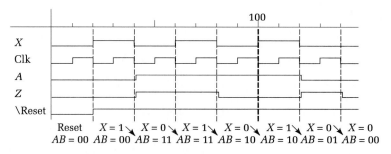

Figure 8.29   A timing trace of the mystery Moore machine.

A	B	X	A⁺	B⁺	Z
0	0	0	?	?	0
		1	1	1	0
0	1	0	0	0	1
		1	?	?	1
1	0	0	1	0	0
		1	0	1	0
1	1	0	1	1	1
		1	1	0	1

Figure 8.30 Partial state transition table derived from the signal trace.

the outputs until the falling edge at time step 40. After a short propagation delay, the state becomes 11. We express the transition as "a 1 input in state 00 leads to state 11."

During the next state time, X is 0, and the FSM stays in state 11 as seen at time step 60. X now changes to 1, and at the next falling edge the state changes to 10.

The input next changes to 0, causing the state machine to remain in state 10 at time step 100. A transition to 1 causes it to change to state 01 after time step 120. The final transition to 0 leaves the machine in state 00.

Figure 8.30 contains the partial transition table we deduce from this input sequence. We would have to generate additional input sequences to fill in the missing transitions. For example, an input sequence from the reset state starting with a 0 would fill in the missing transition from state 00. The sequence 1 1 1 1, tracing from state 00 to 11 to 10 to 01, would catch the remaining transition.

Next State/Output Function Analysis Signal tracing is acceptable for a small FSM, but it becomes intractable for more complex finite state machines. With a single input and 2 bits of state, the example FSM has eight different transitions, two from each of four states. And the number of combinations doubles for each additional input bit and doubles again for each state bit.

Our alternative method derives the next-state functions directly from the combinational logic equations at the flip-flop inputs and the output function from the flip-flop outputs. For the mystery machine, these are

$$J_a = X \qquad K_a = X \bullet \overline{B} \qquad Z = B$$
$$J_b = X \qquad K_b = X \oplus \overline{A}$$

We can now express the flip-flop outputs, A^+ and B^+, in terms of the excitation equations for the J-K flip-flop. We simply substitute the logic functions at the inputs into the excitation equations:

$$A^+ = J_a \bullet \overline{A} + \overline{K_a} \bullet A = X \bullet \overline{A} + (\overline{X} + B) \bullet A$$
$$B^+ = J_b \bullet \overline{B} + \overline{K_b} \bullet B = X \bullet \overline{B} + (X \bullet \overline{A} + \overline{X} \bullet A) \bullet B$$

The next-state functions, A^+ and B^+, are now expressed in terms of the current state, A and B, and the input X. We show the K-maps that correspond to these functions in Figure 8.31.

The missing state transitions are now obvious. In state 00 with input 0, the next state is $A^+ = 0$ and $B^+ = 0$. In state 01 with input 1, the next state is $A^+ = 1$, $B^+ = 1$. With its behavior no longer a mystery, we show the ASM chart for this finite state machine in Figure 8.32. In the figure, we assume the following symbolic state assignment: $S_0 = 00$, $S_1 = 01$, $S_2 = 10$, $S_3 = 11$.

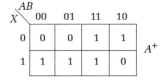

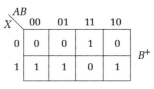

Figure 8.31 Next-state K-maps.

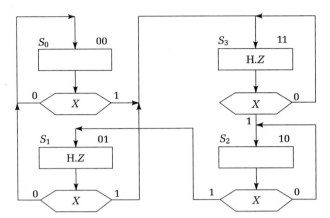

Figure 8.32 ASM chart for the mystery Moore machine.

Example   Mealy Machine Description   Continuing with our reverse engineering exercise, consider the circuit of Figure 8.33. Once again, the FSM has one input, X, and one output, Z. This time the output is a function of the current state, denoted by A and B, *and* the input X. The state register is implemented by one D flip-flop and one master/slave J-K flip-flop.

Before examining a signal trace, we must understand the conditions under which the Mealy machine's inputs are sampled and the outputs are valid. The next state is computed from the current state and the inputs, so exactly when are the inputs sampled? The answer depends on the kinds of flip-flops used to implement the state register. In the example, our use of a master/slave flip-flop dictates that the inputs must

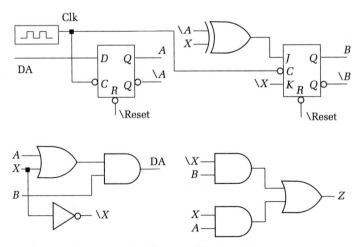

Figure 8.33 Circuit schematic of the mystery Mealy machine.

be stable during the high time of the clock (to avoid ones catching) and must be valid a setup time before the falling edge.

Technically, the outputs are valid only at the end of the state time, determined by the falling edge of the clock. In other words, the output for the current state is valid just as the machine enters its next state! If we are using a master/slave flip-flop and if the inputs do not change during the high time of the clock, then the outputs may also be valid during the clock high time.

Negative edge-triggered systems require that the inputs be stable before the falling edge that delineates the state times. This means that the outputs cannot be determined until just before the falling edge. The output remains valid only as long as it takes to compute a new output in the new state.

Similarly, for positive edge-triggered systems the outputs are valid at the rising edge. Again, the output is considered valid just before the clock edge that causes the machine to enter its new state.

Figure 8.34 gives the timing waveform that corresponds to the input sequence 10101, after a reset to state 00. In state 00, reading a 1 keeps the machine in state 00 (time step 40).

Reading a 0 then advances the machine to state 01 (time step 60). The waveform for output Z has a glitch. The valid output is determined only at the end of the state time. In this case, the output is 0.

A 1 in state 01 leads to state 11 (time step 80). Again, the output in this state is the value of Z at the falling edge and thus is 1.

Reading a 0 in state 11 moves us to state 10 (time step 100), with the output continuing to be asserted despite the momentary glitch.

A 1 in state 10 leads us to state 01 (time step 120). The output goes low and will stay that way as long as the input X stays high.

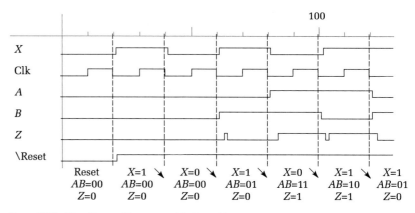

Figure 8.34   Signal trace of the mystery Mealy machine.

A	B	X	A^+	B^+	Z
0	0	0	0	1	0
		1	0	0	0
0	1	0	?	?	?
		1	1	1	0
1	0	0	?	?	?
		1	0	1	1
1	1	0	1	0	1
		1	?	?	?

Figure 8.35 Partial state transition table derived from the signal trace.

A^+:

X \ AB	00	01	11	10
0	0	0	1	0
1	0	1	1	0

B^+:

X \ AB	00	01	11	10
0	1	0	0	0
1	0	1	1	1

Z:

X \ AB	00	01	11	10
0	0	1	1	0
1	0	0	1	1

Figure 8.36 Next-state and output K-maps.

We show the partial state transition table in Figure 8.35. The input sequence produced only five of the eight state transitions. To complete the state diagram, we would have to generate additional sequences to traverse the missing transitions.

Alternatively, we can discover the complete set of transitions by analyzing the next-state and output functions directly, just as we did in the Moore machine:

$$A^+ = B\,(A + X) = A \bullet B + B \bullet X$$

$$B^+ = J_b \bullet \overline{B} + \overline{K_b} \bullet B = (\overline{A} \oplus X) \bullet \overline{B} + X \bullet B$$

$$= (\overline{A} \bullet \overline{X} + A \bullet X)\,\overline{B} + X \bullet B$$

$$= A \bullet \overline{B} \bullet X + \overline{A} \bullet \overline{B} \bullet \overline{X} + B \bullet X$$

$$Z = A \bullet X + B \bullet \overline{X}$$

Since A is a D flip-flop, the function for A^+ is exactly the combinational logic function at its input. B is a J-K flip-flop, so we determine the function for B^+ by substituting the logic functions at the J and K inputs into the J-K excitation function.

We give the next-state and output K-maps in Figure 8.36. The missing transitions are from state 01 to 00 on input 0, 10 to 00 on input 0, and 11 to 11 on input 1. The respective outputs are 1, 0, and 1. Assuming that S_0, S_1, S_2, and S_3 correspond to encoded states 00, 01, 10, 11, we show the ASM chart for the mystery machine in Figure 8.37.

States, Transitions, and Outputs in Mealy and Moore Machines Suppose that a given state machine has M inputs and N outputs and is being implemented using L flip-flops. You might ask a number of questions to bound the complexity of this state machine. For example, what are the minimum and maximum numbers of states that such a machine might have? With L flip-flops, the implementation has the power to represent 2^L states. But for a specific FSM as few as 1 and as many as 2^L of these might be valid states.

What are the minimum and maximum numbers of state transitions that can begin in a given state? Since there must be an exit transition for each possible input combination, the minimum and the maximum are the same: 2^M transitions.

A similar question involves the minimum and maximum numbers of state transitions that can end in a given state. Because we can have start-up states reachable only on reset, the minimum number of input transitions is 0. Since a single state could conceivably be the target of all the transitions of the finite state machine, the maximum number of input transitions is $2^M * 2^L$, the number of possible input combinations multiplied by the number of states.

A final question is the minimum and maximum numbers of patterns that can be observed on the machine's outputs. The minimum number of unique output patterns is 1, of course. Every state and every transition can be associated with the same pattern.

The maximum number depends on the kind of machine. For a Mealy machine, the maximum number of output patterns is the smaller of the number of transitions, $2^M * 2^L$, or the number of possible output patterns, 2^N. If the number of transitions exceeds the number of possible output patterns, then some must be repeated. In the Moore machine, the maximum is the smaller of the number of states, 2^L, and the number of possible output patterns, 2^N. If the number of states exceeds the number of output patterns, then some patterns will also need to be repeated.

As an example, consider a Moore machine with two inputs, one flip-flop, and three outputs. The state, transition, and output bounds are:

Minimum number of states: 1

Maximum number of states: 2

Minimum number of output transitions (per state): 4

Maximum number of output transitions (per state): 4

Minimum number of input transitions (per state): 0

Maximum number of input transitions (per state): 8

Minimum number of observed output patterns: 1

Maximum number of observed output patterns: 2

In this case, the output patterns are limited by the number of states.

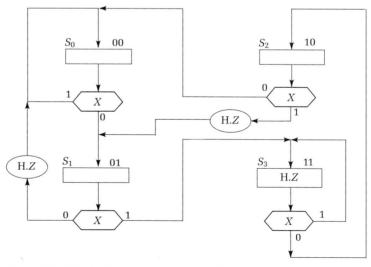

Figure 8.37   ASM chart for the mystery Mealy machine.

Synchronous Mealy Machines The glitches in the output in Figure 8.34 are inherent in the asynchronous nature of the Mealy machine. As you have already seen, glitches are undesirable in real hardware controllers. But because Mealy machines encode control in fewer states, saving on state register flip-flops, it is still desirable to use them.

This leads to alternative *synchronous* design styles for Mealy machines. Simply stated, the way to construct a synchronous Mealy machine is to break the direct connection between inputs and outputs by introducing storage elements.

One way to do this is to synchronize the Mealy machine outputs with output flip-flops. See Figure 8.38. The flip-flops are clocked with the same edge as the state register. This has the effect of converting the Mealy machine into a Moore machine, by making the outputs part of the state encoding! However, this machine does not have exactly the same input/output behavior as the original Mealy machine (can you figure out why?). We will have more to say about synchronous Mealy machines in Chapter 10.

Discussion In general, fully synchronous finite state machines are much easier to implement and debug than asynchronous machines. If you were using discrete TTL components, you would usually prefer the Moore machine organization, even though it may require more states. You should use edge-triggered flip-flops for the state registers.

Synchronous Mealy machines can be constructed in TTL logic, but the designer must be careful. The approach leads to more complex designs that may affect the input/output timing of the FSM. You should use asynchronous Mealy machines only after very careful analysis of the input/output timing behavior of the finite state machine.

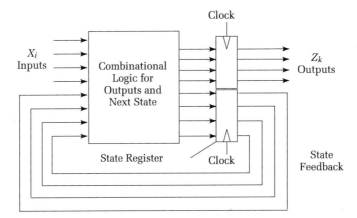

Figure 8.38 Synchronous Mealy machine block diagram.

8.5 Finite State Machine Word Problems

Perhaps the most difficult problem the novice hardware designer faces is mapping an imprecise behavioral specification of an FSM into a more precise description (for example, an ASM chart, a state diagram, a VHDL program, or an ABEL description). In this section we will illustrate the process by examining several detailed case studies: an FSM that can recognize patterns in its inputs, a complex counter, a traffic light controller, and a digital combination lock.

8.5.1 A Finite String Recognizer

Finite state machines are often used to recognize patterns in an input sequence.

Problem Specification Consider the following finite state machine specification: "A finite state recognizer has one input (X) and one output (Z). The output is asserted whenever the input sequence ...010... has been observed, as long as the sequence 100 has never been seen."

Understanding the Specification For problems of this type, it is a good idea to write down some sample input and output behavior to make sure you understand the specification. Here are some input and output strings:

X: 00101010010 ...

Z:　00010101000 ...

X: 11011010010 ...

Z:　00000001000 ...

In the first pair of input/output strings, we find three overlapping instances of 010 (...0101010...) before detecting the termination string (...100). Once this is found, additional 010 strings in the input cause no changes in the output. We have written the outputs so they lag behind the inputs. This is the kind of 0000timing we would expect to see in the real machine.

Similar behavior is illustrated in the second pair of strings. The detected sequence ...010 is immediately followed by another 0. Since this is the terminating string, the output stays at 0 despite further 010 strings in the input.

Formal Representation Now that we understand the desired behavior of the finite state machine, it is time to describe its function by a state diagram or ASM chart. Suppose we choose to represent this example FSM with a state diagram for a Moore machine. It is a good idea to start by drawing state diagram fragments for the strings the machine must recognize: 010 and 100.

Figure 8.39(a) shows the initial Moore state diagram, assuming state 0 is reached on an external *reset* signal. One path in the diagram leads to a state with the output asserted when the string 010 has been encountered. The other path leads to a looping state for the string 100.

Given that there is only one input, each state should have two exit arcs: when the input is 0 and when it is 1. To refine the state diagram, the trick is to add the remaining arcs, and perhaps additional states, to make sure the machine recognizes all valid strings.

For example, what happens when we exit state S_3? To get to S_3, we must have recognized the string 010. If the next input is 0, then the machine has seen …0100, the termination string. The correct next state is therefore S_6, our termination looping state.

What if the input had been a 1 in state S_3? Then we have seen the string …0101. This is a prefix of …010 if the next input turns out to be a 0. We could introduce a new state to represent this case. However, if we carefully examine the state diagram, we find that an existing state, S_2, serves the purpose of representing all prefix strings of the form …01. The new transition from S_3 to S_2 is shown in Figure 8.39(b).

Continuing with this approach, let's examine S_1. You should realize that any number of zeros before the first 1 is a possible prefix of …010. So we can loop in this state as long as the input is 0. We define S_1 to represent strings of the form …0 before a 1 has been seen.

State S_4 plays a similar role for strings of 1's, which may represent a prefix of the terminating string 100. So we can loop in this state as long

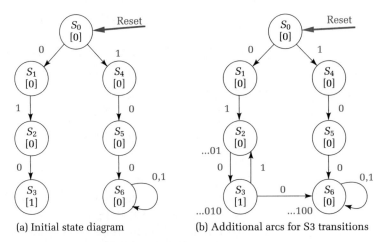

(a) Initial state diagram   (b) Additional arcs for S3 transitions

Figure 8.39   State diagrams for the finite string recognizer.

as the input is 1. The next refinement of the state diagram, incorporating these changes, is shown in Figure 8.40(a).

We still have two states with incomplete transitions: S_2 and S_5. S_2 represents strings of the form ...01, a prefix of the string 010. If the next input is a 1, it can no longer be a prefix of 010 but instead is a prefix of the terminating string 100. Fortunately, we already have a state that deals with this case: S_4. It stands for strings whose last input was a 1 which may be a prefix of 100. So all we need to do is add a transition arc between S_2 and S_4 when the input is a 1.

The final state to examine is S_5. It represents strings consisting of a 1 followed by a 0. If the next input is a 1, the observed string is of the form ...101. This could be a prefix for 010. S_2 already represents strings of the form ...01. So we add the transition between S_5 and S_2 when the input is a 1.

We show the completed state diagram in Figure 8.40(b). You should run through the sample input strings presented at the beginning of this subsection to make sure you obtain the same output behavior. It is always a good strategy to check your final state diagram for proper operation.

ABEL Description It is straightforward to map the state diagram of Figure 8.40(b) into an ABEL finite state machine description. The description becomes

```
module string
title '010/100 string recognizer state machine
    Joe Engineer, Itty Bity Machines, Inc.'
u1   device   'p22v10';
```

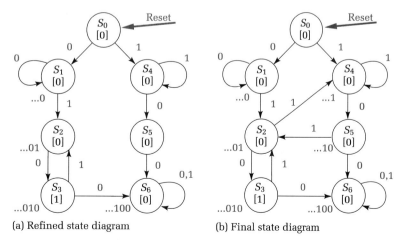

(a) Refined state diagram   (b) Final state diagram

Figure 8.40 Refinement of the state diagrams.

```
"Input Pins
   clk, X, RESET    pin    1, 2, 3;

"Output Pins
   Q0, Q1, Q2, Z    pin    19, 20, 21, 22;
   Q0, Q1, Q2, Z    istype 'pos,reg';

"State registers
SREG = [Q0, Q1, Q2, Z];
S0   = [0,0,0,0];  " Reset state
S1   = [0,0,1,0];  " strings of the form ...0
S2   = [0,1,0,0];  " strings of the form ...01
S3   = [0,1,1,1];  " strings of the form ...010
S4   = [1,0,0,0];  " strings of the form ...1
S5   = [1,0,1,0];  " strings of the form ...10
S6   = [1,1,0,0];  " strings of the form ...100

equations
   [Q0.ar, Q1.ar, Q2.ar, Z.ar] = RESET;"Reset to S0

state_diagram SREG
state S0: if X then S4 else S1;
state S1: if X then S2 else S1;
state S2: if X then S4 else S3;
state S3: if X then S2 else S6;
state S4: if X then S4 else S5;
state S5: if X then S2 else S6;
state S6: goto S6;

test_vectors ([clk, RESET, X] -> [Z])
   [0,1,.X.] -> [0];
   [.c.,0,0] -> [0];
   [.c.,0,0] -> [0];
   [.c.,0,1] -> [0];
   [.c.,0,0] -> [1];
   [.c.,0,1] -> [0];
   [.c.,0,0] -> [1];
   [.c.,0,1] -> [0];
   [.c.,0,0] -> [1];
   [.c.,0,0] -> [0];
   [.c.,0,1] -> [0];
   [.c.,0,0] -> [0];
end string;
```

Since the finite state machine is encoded in seven states, (at least) three registers must be assigned for its representation. These are named Q_0, Q_1, and Q_2. The output Z is also registered and forms part of the state encoding. This is shown in the state register description section.

The state transitions are described in the `state_diagram` section, using simple IF-THEN-ELSE and GOTO statements. For example, if the FSM is currently in state S_0 and the input X is 1, the machine's next state is S_4. If the input is 0, the next state is S_1.

The `test_vectors` section first verifies that the machine should output a 0 when reset. It then presents the machine with the sample input string 00101010010 to check that the expected output, 00010101000, is obtained.

Discussion   Let's briefly review the steps you should follow to arrive at the final state diagram:

1. Write sample inputs and outputs to make sure you understand the statement of the problem.

2. Next, write sequences of states and transitions for the distinguished strings your FSM is expected to recognize.

3. Most likely, step 2 will not cover all transitions. You then add the missing transitions, taking advantage of states you have already introduced wherever possible. You should view the states as "remembering" certain input string sequences. In this example, the FSM in state S_1 means that a string of all zeros has been seen so far; S_2 represents all strings in which the last two inputs are a 0 followed by a 1; and so on.

4. Finally, verify that the input/output behavior of your state diagram matches the specified behavior of the FSM. You may need to juggle some transitions or introduce additional states when you encounter a "counterexample" input string that does not yield the expected outputs.

In this case study, we used state diagrams rather than ASM charts. Either technique could be used, although state diagrams are better suited for *recognizers* whereas ASM charts are more appropriate for *controllers*. We shall use both state diagrams and ASM charts in our next case study, the complex counter.

8.5.2   A Complex Counter

As we saw in the previous chapter, counters are a special case of finite state machines: their state and their outputs are always identical. In this case study, we will combine a simple control function with basic sequencing.

Problem Specification   The task is to create a complex counter that can count in binary or in Gray code, depending on the value of a mode input: "A synchronous 3-bit counter has a mode control input m. When $m = 0$, the counter steps through the binary sequence 000, 001, 010, 011, 100, 101, 110, 111, and repeat. When $m = 1$, the counter advances through the Gray code sequence 000, 001, 011, 010, 110, 111, 101, 100, and repeat."

Understanding the Specification   Start by making sure you understand the interaction of the control input and the counter's sequence. Let's label the control input as signal M and the outputs as signals Z_2, Z_1, and Z_0. To check our understanding, let's write down a sample counter sequence as the M input varies. The following is one example of a valid count sequence:

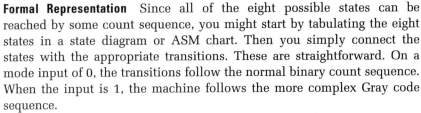

Mode Input (M)	Current State	Next State ($Z_2 Z_1 Z_0$)
0	000	001
0	001	010
1	010	110
1	110	111
1	111	101
0	101	110
0	110	111

Formal Representation   Since all of the eight possible states can be reached by some count sequence, you might start by tabulating the eight states in a state diagram or ASM chart. Then you simply connect the states with the appropriate transitions. These are straightforward. On a mode input of 0, the transitions follow the normal binary count sequence. When the input is 1, the machine follows the more complex Gray code sequence.

Figure 8.41 shows the state diagram. The states are named according to the binary encoding of the state's output. State S_0 has output 000, state S_2 has output 010, and so on. Reset places the finite state machine into state S_0.

The equivalent ASM chart is shown in Figure 8.42. It looks very much like a flowchart you might use to implement a program with the specified input/output behavior. For example, when in state S_1, if M is 0, the next state is S_2, otherwise the next state is S_3.

You should notice how the outputs are specified. Z_1 high in S_2 means that the Z_1 output is asserted while Z_2 and Z_0 are not. Also, observe that the conditional boxes between S_0 and S_1, and again between S_6 and S_7, have been eliminated. This is because these transitions are independent of the input.

ABEL Description   The machine's state sequencing is quite easy to capture in terms of IF-THEN-ELSE descriptions. The ABEL description follows:

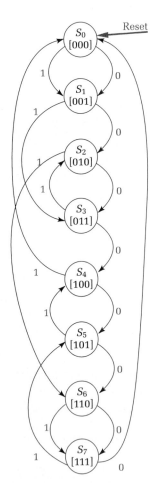

Figure 8.41   State diagram for complex counter.

```
module counter
title 'combination binary/gray code up-counter
    Joe Engineer, Itty Bity Machines, Inc.'
u1    device    'p22v10';

"Input Pins
   clk, M, RESET    pin    1, 2, 3;

"Output Pins
   Z0, Z1, Z2        pin    19, 20, 21;
   Z0, Z1, Z2        istype 'pos,reg';
```

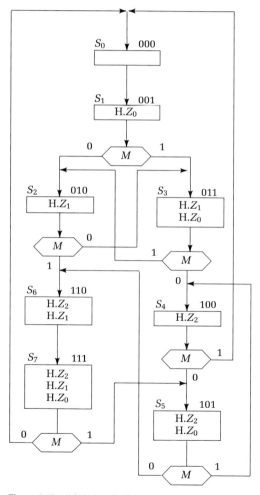

Figure 8.42   ASM chart for the complex counter.

```
"State registers
SREG = [Z0, Z1, Z2];
S0   = [0,0,0];
S1   = [0,0,1];
S2   = [0,1,0];
S3   = [0,1,1];
S4   = [1,0,0];
S5   = [1,0,1];
S6   = [1,1,0];
S7   = [1,1,1];

equations
    [Z0.ar, Z1.ar, Z2.ar] = RESET; "Reset to state S0

state_diagram SREG
state S0: goto S1;
state S1: if M then S3 else S2;
state S2: if M then S6 else S3;
state S3: if M then S2 else S4;
state S4: if M then S0 else S5;
state S5: if M then S4 else S6;
state S6: goto S7;
state S7: if M then S5 else S0;

test_vectors ([clk, RESET, M] -> [Z0, Z1, Z2])
    [0,1,.X.] -> [0,0,0];
    [.c.,0,0] -> [0,0,1];
    [.c.,0,0] -> [0,1,0];
    [.c.,0,1] -> [1,1,0];
    [.c.,0,1] -> [1,1,1];
    [.c.,0,1] -> [1,0,1];
    [.c.,0,0] -> [1,1,0];
    [.c.,0,0] -> [1,1,1];
end counter;
```

The test vectors verify that the state machine can be reset to state S_0 and that the counter will sequence through the same states as our test sequence at the beginning of this subsection.

Discussion   When working with circuits that follow periodic sequences, like counters, it is always a good strategy to begin by writing down the states and connecting them in the order of the sequence. You can add unusual/exceptional sequencing among the states later.

The choice of describing the FSM as a state diagram or an ASM chart depends on the complexity of the control. In this case study, the control was rather simple and the state diagram is probably easier to understand. We will see a more complex control function in the next case study, the traffic light controller. It will illustrate some of the advantages of the ASM charts for describing more complex state sequencing.

8.5.3   A Traffic Light Controller

The following description of a traffic light controller represents a relatively complex control function: "A busy highway is intersected by a little-used farmroad, as shown in Figure 8.43. Detectors are placed along the farmroad to raise the signal C as long as a vehicle is waiting to cross the highway. The traffic light controller should operate as follows. As long as no vehicle is detected on the farmroad, the lights should remain green in the highway direction. If a vehicle is detected on the farmroad, the highway lights should change from yellow to red, allowing the farmroad lights to become green. The farmroad lights stay green only as long as a vehicle is detected on the farmroad and never longer than a set interval to allow the traffic to flow along the highway. If these conditions are met, the farmroad lights change from green to yellow to red, allowing the highway lights to return to green. Even if vehicles are waiting to cross the highway, the highway should remain green for a set interval. You may assume there is an external timer that, once set via the control signal ST (set timer), will assert the signal TS after a short time interval has expired (used for timing yellow lights) and TL after a long time interval (for green lights). The timer is automatically reset when ST is asserted."

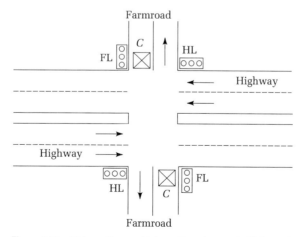

Figure 8.43   Highway/farmroad intersection: placement of lights and sensors.

Understanding the Specification   To understand the problem statement, a good way to begin is to identify the inputs and outputs and the unique configurations of the controller. The inputs and outputs are as follows:

Input signal	Description
Reset	place controller in initial state
C	detects vehicle on farmroad in either direction
TS	short timer interval has expired
TL	long timer interval has expired

Output signal	Description
HG, HY, HR	assert green, yellow, red highway lights
FG, FY, FR	assert green, yellow, red farmroad lights
ST	commence timing a long or short interval

In terms of the unique states, you might think there should be one for each possible output, but this is not the case. If the highway is green or yellow, the farmroad must be red, and similarly when the farmroad is green or yellow. The controller has four unique configurations:

State	Description
S0	highway green (farmroad red)
S1	highway yellow (farmroad red)
S2	farmroad green (highway red)
S3	farmroad yellow (highway red)

Formal Representation   A complex finite state machine such as this is a good candidate for description in terms of an ASM chart. We begin with a skeletal chart and expand it with more details as we go along, stopping when we obtain the complete chart in its final form.

Figure 8.44 shows an initial ASM chart. It captures the basic state sequencing: S_0, S_1, S_2, S_3, and repeat. The setting of the outputs for controlling the lights is straightforward. To complete the ASM chart, our major challenge is to determine the conditions under which the state transitions should take place.

First, we should list our assumptions. We assume that a reset signal places the controller in state S_0, with the highway green and the farmroad red. Reset should also cause the timer to commence its timing function.

From the problem specification, the controller should stay in state S_0 as long as no vehicle is waiting on the farmroad. Even if a vehicle is waiting, the highway is guaranteed to stay green for the long time interval. Thus, the conditions for advancing from S_0 to S_1 are that TL is asserted and C is asserted. In all other cases, the controller should remain in S_0.

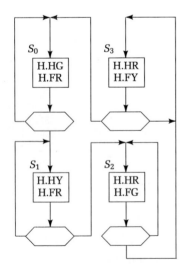

Figure 8.44   Initial ASM chart for the traffic light controller.

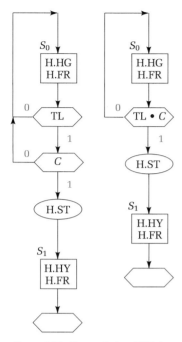

Figure 8.45   Two equivalent ASM chart representations.

We show two alternative methods for representing this transition in Figure 8.45. The chart fragment at the left of the figure first checks TL and then C. If both are asserted, the ST output is asserted and the machine advances to state S_1. Unlike a program flowchart, the order in which TL and C are checked does not matter. The decision boxes could just as easily have been written the other way around. The fragment at the right of the figure has combined the two decision boxes into a single box containing the essential exit condition: TL $\bullet$ C.

Next, let's consider the transition from S_1 to S_2. According to the specification, the controller should remain in S_1 for the short time interval before advancing to S_2. The exit condition is an asserted TS signal. Otherwise, the machine stays in S_1. The chart fragment for S_1 is shown in Figure 8.46. The behavior of S_3, with its transition to S_0, is very similar.

Now all that remain are the transitions for S_2, the farmroad green state. The exit conditions are: a long time interval has expired, whether or not any cars are still waiting, or there are no more vehicles waiting to cross the intersection. This can be expressed as the condition TL $+ \overline{C}$. Under any other circumstances, we remain in state S_2.

Figure 8.47 contains the completed ASM chart. ST is asserted on exiting each state to reset the timers. For comparison, an equivalent state diagram is shown in Figure 8.48 (the traffic light outputs are not shown). The conditions for remaining in states S_0 and S_2 are less clear in the state diagram, although they are nothing more than the complement of the exit conditions.

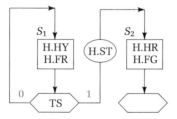

Figure 8.46   S1-to-S2 transition.

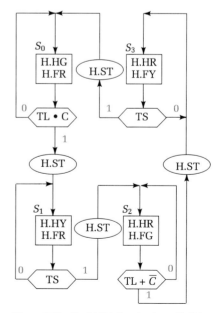

Figure 8.47   Final ASM chart for the traffic light controller.

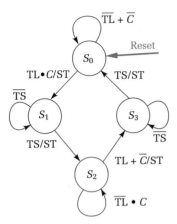

Figure 8.48 Traffic light state diagram.

ABEL Description The ASM chart for the traffic light controller combines some aspects of Mealy machines and Moore machines. The set timer signal ST is asserted on state transitions (Mealy behavior), while the traffic light signals are decoded from the state (Moore behavior). Fortunately, the ABEL language is powerful enough to describe such mixed behavior. It describes the traffic lights in terms of combinational equations of the current state, and asserts ST in conjunction with state transitions within IF-THEN-ELSE statements. An ABEL description for the traffic light controller follows:

```
module traffic
title 'traffic light state machine
    Joe Engineer, Itty Bity Machines, Inc.'
u1    device    'p22v10';

"Input Pins
    clk, C, RESET, TS, TL
        pin   1, 2, 3, 4, 5;

"Output Pins
    Q0, Q1, HG, HY, HR, FG, FY, FR, ST
        pin   14, 15, 16, 17, 18, 19, 20, 21, 22;

    Q0, Q1                          istype 'pos,reg';
    ST, HG, HY, HR, FG, FY, FR      istype 'pos,com';

"State registers
SREG = [Q0, Q1];
S0    = [ 0,   0];
S1    = [ 0,   1];
S2    = [ 1,   0];
S3    = [ 1,   1];

equations
    [Q0.ar, Q1.ar] = RESET;
    HG = !Q0 & !Q1;
    HY = !Q0 & Q1;
    HR = (Q0 & !Q1) # (Q0 & Q1);
    FG = Q0 & !Q1;
    FY = Q0 & Q1;
    FR = (!Q0 & !Q1) # (!Q0 & Q1);

state_diagram SREG
state S0: if (TL & C) then S1 with ST = 1
            else S0 with ST = 0
state S1: if TS then S2 with ST = 1
            else S1 with ST = 0
state S2: if (TL # !C) then S3 with ST = 1
            else S2 with ST = 0
```

```
state S3: if TS then S0 with ST = 1
          else S3 with ST = 0

test_vectors
([clk,RESET, C, TS, TL] ->
                            [SREG,HG,HY,HR,FG,FY,FR,ST])
 [.X.,    1,.X.,.X.,.X.] -> [ S0, 1, 0, 0, 0, 0, 1, 0];
 [.C.,    0,  0,  0,  0] -> [ S0, 1, 0, 0, 0, 0, 1, 0];
 [.C.,    0,  1,  0,  1] -> [ S1, 0, 1, 0, 0, 0, 1, 0];
 [.C.,    0,  1,  0,  0] -> [ S1, 0, 1, 0, 0, 0, 1, 0];
 [.C.,    0,  1,  1,  0] -> [ S2, 0, 0, 1, 1, 0, 0, 0];
 [.C.,    0,  1,  0,  0] -> [ S2, 0, 0, 1, 1, 0, 0, 0];
 [.C.,    0,  1,  0,  1] -> [ S3, 0, 0, 1, 0, 1, 0, 0];
 [.C.,    0,  1,  1,  0] -> [ S0, 1, 0, 0, 0, 0, 1, 0];
end traffic;
```

In this description, the state is described by the internal registers Q_0 and Q_1. These are asynchronously reset to 0 when the external RESET signal is asserted.

The equations for the traffic light outputs, HG, HY, HR, FG, FY, and FR, are written as combinational functions of the states in which these lights should be illuminated. For example, HG is asserted in S_0. This is written as !Q0 & !Q1 (note that ! is NOT, & is AND, # is OR). Similarly, FR is asserted in states S_0 and S_1, which is written as (!Q0 & !Q1) # (!Q0 & Q1).

The state_diagram section describes the state transitions. The with statement associates signal changes with state transitions. Thus, if we are in S_0 and TL and C are both asserted, we move to state S_1 with the signal ST asserted.

The test_vectors section provides the verification test cases for the state machine. The first vector verifies that the machine will enter S_0 when reset is asserted. The second and third vectors check that the machine stays in S_0 until TL and C are asserted. Note that it is not possible to check on the assertion of ST. In the third vector, ST is asserted just before the rising clock edge. After the edge, the machine enters S_1 while unasserting ST. The vectors describe the state of the outputs only after the clock edge, not at the edge.

The fourth and fifth vectors check the conditions for leaving state S_1, namely that TS is asserted. The sixth and seventh vectors perform a similar check on S_2. One of the conditions for leaving the state is that TL is asserted, even if C is still asserted.

The final vector verifies the exit condition for S_3. When TS is asserted, we return to S_0. The collection of test vectors is not exhaustive, but it describes one possible scenario for the sequence of events for one complete cycling of the traffic lights. Additional vectors can be added to check other cases, such as leaving state S_2 as soon as C becomes unasserted.

Discussion   This case study illustrates the basic strength of ASM charts. They let us concentrate on the paths and conditions we follow to exit a state. As in the leftmost chart in Figure 8.45, we can build up the exit conditions incrementally, as in a program flowchart. Later we can combine them into a smaller number of Boolean exit expressions, as at the right of Figure 8.45. Although it is subjective, the description in Figure 8.47 seems to be easier to understand as an algorithm than the state diagram of Figure 8.48.

8.5.4   Digital Combination Lock

Here we are asked to design a 3-bit serial digital lock. By "serial," we mean that the bits representing the key are entered as a sequence, one at a time, rather than all at once.

Problem Specification   We are given the following description: "A 3-bit serial lock is used to allow entry to a locked room. The lock has a RESET button, an ENTER button, and a two-position switch to represent the key value being entered. When the signal UNLOCK is asserted, an electromechanical relay is released, allowing the door to open. The unlock process begins when the operator presses RESET. He or she then sets the input switch, followed by pressing the ENTER button. This is repeated for the second and third key digits. An ERROR light should be illuminated if, after entering the three binary digits, the operator has not matched the key. The process can be retried by hitting RESET again."

Understanding the Specification   Problem specifications, like the preceding one, are often incomplete. As the hardware designer, you have to resolve the ambiguities and make fundamental design choices. For example, there is no discussion of how the FSM knows the key value that opens the lock. It could be hardwired into the next state logic, although this is not very flexible. Changing the combination would require a whole new FSM. A better design decision is to store the key values in a register inside the lock hardware.

An additional mechanism, not discussed here (see Exercises 8.29 and 8.30), could be provided to change the key value in the register. In this way you can design the finite state machine once, yet have it operate with any key combination. We will assume a fixed register-based key value in this study.

Let's begin by listing the FSM's inputs and outputs. This machine has a number of human-generated inputs, and an understanding of their timing behavior is critical for a correct design.

The operator-controlled inputs are RESET, ENTER, and a single-bit KEY-IN. We can assume that RESET is a debounced switch, ENTER is a debounced and synchronized push-button (when pressed, it will assert a

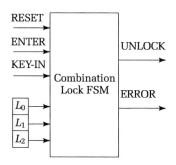

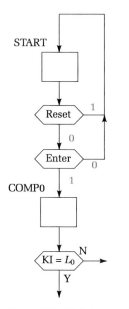

Figure 8.49 Combination lock finite state machine.

Figure 8.50 Digital combination lock starting states.

signal for exactly one clock period), and the KEY-IN value is set before the operator presses ENTER. It is fair to assume that the clock of the FSM runs much faster than human interaction times, which are typically measured in tenths of a second.

The LOCK values, L_0, L_1, L_2, are available as inputs from an internal lock register. The outputs are the UNLOCK signal and the ERROR light control. Figure 8.49 shows the final FSM block diagram.

Formal Representation Now we are ready to enumerate the machine's states while refining the ASM chart. Let's start by listing states that will lead to unlocking the door. We will come back to the error conditions on a second pass.

There must be some starting state, START, that is always entered when RESET is asserted. Since the key length is 3 bits, there should also be one state for each key bit comparison. To enter the first comparison state—let's call it $COMP_0$—ENTER must be pressed and RESET must not be asserted. This is shown in Figure 8.50.

What is the condition to exit $COMP_0$? Obviously, KEY-IN (abbreviated KI from here on) must match L_0. You might be tempted to include ENTER, with the intention of exiting to a state COMP1 that checks the second key bit when ENTER is asserted. However, this would not be correct. Once we know the key bit is correct, we should exit to an *idle* state to wait for ENTER to be asserted again. We cannot check KI and ENTER simultaneously, since the operator will change KI before pressing ENTER. And since the time between subsequent ENTER presses could be quite long, we need to loop in some state until ENTER is pressed again.

With the insertion of idle states, we give the set of states for unlocking the door in Figure 8.51. We remain in the DONE state, asserting UNLOCK, until RESET is asserted.

Our ASM chart is only partially complete. We still have to handle cases in which the entered key bit does not match the lock bit. A simple strategy would have all such state exits change to an ERROR state that asserts ERROR and remains in that state until RESET. Unfortunately, this makes it very easy to "pick" the lock, since the FSM will assert ERROR as soon as it detects the first incorrect bit.

A better strategy is to detect errors as soon as they happen, but to assert ERROR only after a full sequence of key bits has been input. The structure of this part of the ASM chart is similar to that of the unlock path and is given in Figure 8.52. $COMP_0$ exits to $IDLE_0'$ on error (that is, when KI does not equal L_0), $COMP_1$ error exits to $IDLE_1'$, and $COMP_2$ error exits to $ERROR_3$.

Stitching together the various ASM charts should now be straightforward. For comparison, we give a complete state diagram for the FSM in Figure 8.53.

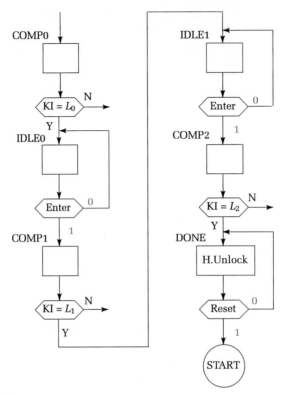

Figure 8.51 Digital combination lock path to unlock.

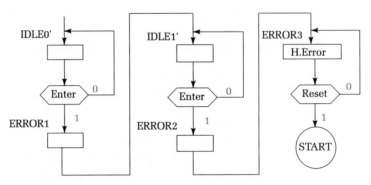

Figure 8.52 Digital combination lock path to error.

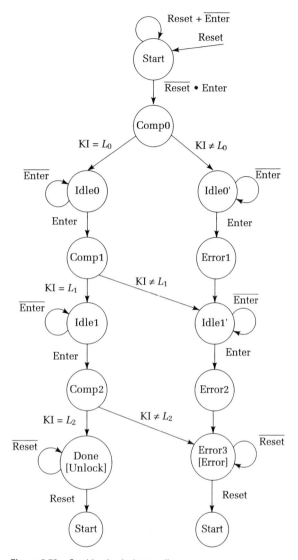

Figure 8.53   Combination lock state diagram.

ABEL Description   At this point, you should be reasonably familiar with the ABEL syntax. Here is the description for the combination lock finite state machine:

```
module lock
title '3 bit combination lock state machine
     Joe Engineer, Itty Bity Machines, Inc.'
u1    device   'p22v10';
```

```
"Input Pins
        clk, RESET, ENTER, L0, L1, L2, KI
   pin  1,   2,     3,     4,  5,  6,  7;

"Output Pins
      Q0, Q1, Q2, Q3, UNLOCK, ERROR
   pin 16, 17, 18, 19, 14,        15;

   Q0, Q1, Q2, Q3    istype 'pos,reg';
   UNLOCK, ERROR      istype 'pos,com';

"State registers
SREG   = [Q0, Q1, Q2, Q3];
START  = [ 0,  0,  0,  0];
COMP0  = [ 0,  0,  0,  1];
IDLE0  = [ 0,  0,  1,  0];
COMP1  = [ 0,  0,  1,  1];
IDLE1  = [ 0,  1,  0,  0];
COMP2  = [ 0,  1,  0,  1];
DONE   = [ 0,  1,  1,  0];
IDLE0p = [ 0,  1,  1,  1];
ERROR1 = [ 1,  0,  0,  0];
IDLE1p = [ 1,  0,  0,  1];
ERROR2 = [ 1,  0,  1,  0];
ERROR3 = [ 1,  0,  1,  1];

equations
   [Q0.ar, Q1.ar, Q2.ar, Q3.ar] = RESET;
   UNLOCK = !Q0 & Q1 & Q2 & !Q3;   "asserted in DONE
   ERROR = Q0 & !Q1 & Q2 & Q3;      "asserted in ERROR3

state_diagram SREG
state START:  if (RESET # !ENTER)
   then START else COMP0;
state COMP0:  if (KI == L0) then IDLE0 else IDLE0p;
state IDLE0:  if (!ENTER) then IDLE0 else COMP1;
state COMP1:  if (KI == L1) then IDLE1 else IDLE1p;
state IDLE1:  if (!ENTER) then IDLE1 else COMP2;
state COMP2:  if (KI == L2) then DONE else ERROR3;
state DONE:   if (!RESET) then DONE else START;
state IDLE0p: if (!ENTER) then IDLE0p else ERROR1;
state ERROR1: goto IDLE1p;
state IDLE1p: if (!ENTER) then IDLE1p else ERROR2;
state ERROR2: goto ERROR3;
state ERROR3: if (!RESET) then ERROR3 else START;

test_vectors
([clk,RESET,ENTER,L0,L1,L2,KI] -> [SREG,UNLOCK,ERROR])
```

```
    [.X., 1, .X.,.X.,.X.,.X.,.X.] -> [ START,   0,   0];
    [.C., 0,   1,   1,   0,   1,   1] -> [ COMP0,   0,   0];
    [.C., 0,   0,   1,   0,   1,   1] -> [ IDLE0,   0,   0];
    [.C., 0,   1,   1,   0,   1,   0] -> [ COMP1,   0,   0];
    [.C., 0,   0,   1,   0,   1,   0] -> [ IDLE1,   0,   0];
    [.C., 0,   1,   1,   0,   1,   1] -> [ COMP2,   0,   0];
    [.C., 0,   0,   1,   0,   1,   1] -> [  DONE,   1,   0];

    [.C., 1,   0,   1,   0,   1,   0] -> [ START,   0,   0];
    [.C., 0,   1,   1,   0,   1,   0] -> [ COMP0,   0,   0];
    [.C., 0,   0,   1,   0,   1,   0] -> [IDLE0p,   0,   0];
    [.C., 0,   1,   1,   0,   1,.X.] -> [ERROR1,   0,   0];
    [.C., 0,   0,   1,   0,   1,.X.] -> [IDLE1p,   0,   0];
    [.C., 0,   1,   1,   0,   1,.X.] -> [ERROR2,   0,   0];
    [.C., 0,   0,   1,   0,   1,.X.] -> [ERROR3,   0,   1];
end lock;
```

Since the UNLOCK and ERROR outputs are asserted in only one state each, the combinational logic equations for these are straightforward. The state transitions are nothing more than mapping the state charts or diagrams into ABEL's IF-THEN-ELSE syntax. The "==" notation represents an equality operation.

The `test_vectors` show two sequences, one leading to UNLOCK and the other leading to ERROR. In both cases, the lock combination is 101. In the first sequence, RESET brings us to the START state. When ENTER is pressed, we advance to COMP$_0$. KI is compared to L_0. Since they match, we advance to IDLE$_0$. KI changes to 0 and ENTER is asserted. This moves us to COMP$_1$, where KI and L_1 are compared. Since these match, we go to IDLE$_1$ next. KI changes to 1 and ENTER is again asserted. This moves us to COMP$_2$. Since KI matches L_2, we enter DONE and assert UNLOCK.

The lock is reset when the RESET signal is asserted. The rest of the test vector sequence verifies that when KI does not match L_0 in state COMP$_0$, we advance through the states IDLE$_0$', ERROR$_1$, IDLE$_1$', ERROR$_2$, terminating in ERROR$_3$ with the ERROR signal asserted.

Discussion These are the steps you should follow in deriving a design such as the digital combination lock:

1. First, understand the problem, perhaps by first understanding the inputs or outputs. Drawing a figure or a block diagram usually helps.

2. Not all specifications are complete. Make reasonable assumptions about input/output behavior or internal state.

3. Start by deriving the states and state transitions that lead to the goal of the FSM—in this case, unlocking the door. This allows you to focus on

one critical sequence of state transitions. Try to reuse states you have already enumerated whenever possible.

4. Finally, remember to consider the error conditions and the transitions that lead to error states. Make sure there is a state transition for every combination of inputs.

Chapter Review

In this chapter, we have concentrated on understanding the basic timing behavior of a finite state machine: when inputs are sampled, when the next state and outputs undergo transition, and when these become stable. We presented the Moore and Mealy machine organizations, the latter in both asynchronous and synchronous forms. The basic idea is that you can represent a finite state machine by combinational logic functions of the current state (both Moore and Mealy machines) and inputs (Mealy machine) for the next state and output. Flip-flop storage elements hold the current state.

We introduced a six-step process for finite state machine design, and the body of this chapter concentrated on the first two of these steps: *understanding the problem* and *obtaining an abstract representation of the finite state machine from an imprecise description of its behavior*. We cover the remaining four steps, *state minimization*, *state assignment*, *implementation of the state registers*, and *implementation of the next state and output combinational functions*, in Chapter 9.

In terms of abstract FSM representations, we presented the algorithmic state machine (ASM) notation as a precise way to describe FSM behavior using a flowchart-like description. In addition, we gave example descriptions in popular hardware description languages, VHDL and ABEL.

We illustrated the process of mapping a word specification to a state diagram or ASM chart with four detailed case studies: a finite string recognizer, a complex counter, a traffic light controller, and a digital combination lock. The mapping strategies are founded on (1) understanding the input/output behavior of the specified FSM, (2) drawing diagrams to help understand the problem statement, (3) enumerating states and developing state transitions for the expected or "goal" cases, (4) expanding the description to include the exceptional or error states and transitions, and (5) carefully reusing states whenever possible.

We are now ready to examine the process of finite state machine optimization and implementation in the next two chapters.

Further Reading

The concept of algorithmic state machines (ASMs) has appeared in several recent books. A very good, albeit brief, description can be found in Prosser and Winkel, *The Art of Digital Design*, Prentice-Hall, Englewood Cliffs, NJ, 1987. A more detailed mathematical description is to be found in Green, *Modern Logic Design*, Addison-Wesley, Wokingham, England, 1986.

VHDL is a government-backed industry standard hardware description language. Several vendors of computer-aided design tools now provide VHDL simulator support. Armstrong, *Chip-Level Modeling with VHDL*, Prentice-Hall, 1989 provides an excellent tutorial introduction to modeling hardware systems with VHDL. The language's capabilities are presented in a step-by-step fashion as the reader advances through the text. A more exhaustive (and exhausting) description can be found in Coehlo, *The VHDL Handbook*, Kluwer, Boston, MA, 1989. This book includes voluminous example VHDL models for standard TTL components, such as gates, multiplexers, counters, and ALUs, and also contains the description of a complete RISC (reduced instruction set computer) processor.

Exercises

8.1 *(Timing Methodology)* In this chapter, we have encouraged you to think of implementing all state registers of a finite state machine with flip-flops that are clocked in the same way. Consider the combinations of flip-flop types in (a) to (c) and describe briefly what (if anything) could go wrong if they were used to implement an FSM state register:

a. A positive edge-triggered D flip-flop and a negative edge-triggered D flip-flop.

b. A positive edge-triggered D flip-flop and a master/slave J-K flip-flop.

c. A negative edge-triggered D flip-flop and a master/slave J-K flip-flop.

d. Can you change a master/slave J-K flip-flop to behave like a positive edge-triggered device by inverting its clock input signal?

8.2 *(Parity Checker)* Redesign the odd parity checker FSM of Section 8.1.1 to make it check for even parity (that is, assert the output whenever the input contains an even number of 1's). Show your state diagram and implement the machine using either a D or T flip-flop.

8.3   *(Vending Machine)*   Reimplement the vending machine controller of Section 8.2.2 using T flip-flops.

8.4   *(Parity Checker Subsystem)*   The odd parity checker of Section 8.1.1 generates a 1 whenever a bit stream of serial inputs contain an odd number of 1's. This is useful in a data communication subsystem for checking that transmitted data has been sent correctly. Data is transmitted as 8 data bits appended with a ninth parity bit. The 9-bit sequence must be in odd parity. That is, if the data bits have an odd number of 1's, the parity bit is 0. If the data bits have an even number of 1's, the parity bit is 1. You are to design a parity checker that asserts OK if the 9-bit sequence is correct in odd parity and ERROR otherwise.

a. Is it possible to write a state diagram with a small number of states to describe the behavior of this finite state machine? Does your state diagram need to track all possible sequences of 9 bits?

b. Consider implementing the subsystem using the parity checker FSM of Figure 8.4 in conjunction with a synchronous 4-bit counter like the TTL 74163. Draw a schematic using logic gates, a single flip-flop, and the counter. Draw a timing diagram including a bit sequence that leads to ERROR and one that leads to OK. Make sure you are using components with the same kind of timing behavior!

8.5   *(Mealy Machines)*   Suppose you are told that a Mealy machine is implemented with three flip-flops, two inputs, and six asynchronous outputs. Consider the *complete* state diagram for this machine (that is, there are no don't cares). Answer the following questions:

a. What are the minimum and maximum numbers of states in the state diagram?

b. What are the minimum and maximum numbers of transition arrows starting at a particular state?

c. What are the minimum and maximum numbers of transition arrows that can end in a particular state?

d. What are the minimum and maximum numbers of different binary patterns that can be displayed on the outputs?

8.6   *(Moore Machines)*   Suppose you are told that a Moore machine has five flip-flops, three inputs, and nine outputs. Answer the following questions:

    a. What are the minimum and maximum numbers of states in the state diagram?

    b. What are the minimum and maximum numbers of transition arrows starting at a particular state?

    c. What are the minimum and maximum numbers of transition arrows that can end in a particular state?

    d. What are the minimum and maximum numbers of different binary patterns that can be displayed on the outputs?

8.7   *(Reverse Engineering)*   Given the Mealy machine in Figure Ex8.7, implemented with one toggle flip-flop and one D flip-flop, with single input I and single output Z, draw its complete state diagram.

8.8   *(Reverse Engineering)*   Derive the complete state diagram for the finite state machine implemented in Figure Ex8.8.

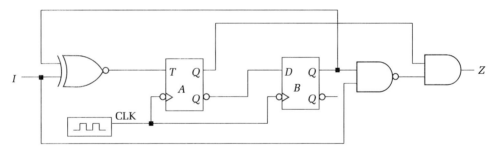

Figure Ex8.7   Mealy machine implementation.

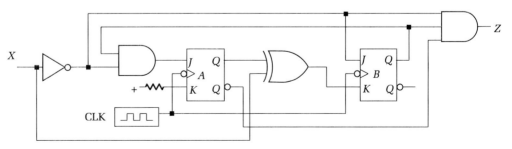

Figure Ex8.8   Mealy machine implementation.

8.9   *(Reverse Engineering)*   Derive the state transition table for the schematic implementation of the finite state machine of Figure Ex8.9 (the next-state and output functions are implemented by a PLA structure). The machine has one input *I* and one output *Z*.

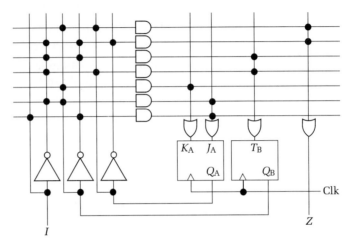

Figure Ex8.9   PLA-based Mealy implementation.

8.10   *(Reverse Engineering)*   The circuit of Figure Ex8.10 is the implementation of a finite state machine. Derive its state diagram through the process of reverse engineering. The machine has two flip-flops with state bits *A* and *B*, two inputs *X* and *Y*, and the single output *Z*.

    a. Start by writing the input equations to the flip-flops as a function of *X*, *Y*, *A*, and *B*. (*Hint:* Simplify the output from the multiplexer before you proceed!)

    b. Using the excitation table for the *J-K* flip-flop, derive the functions for A^+ and B^+ in terms of *X*, *Y*, *A*, *B*.

    c. Complete the state transition table for the state machine.

8.11   *(Synchronous Mealy Machine)*   Section 8.4.3 describes the basic architecture of a synchronous Mealy machine. Implement the vending machine controller of Figure 8.25 as a synchronous Mealy machine and as an asynchronous Mealy machine using negative edge-triggered *D* flip-flops (the Moore machine implementation appears in Figure 8.15). Draw a timing diagram that shows a difference in the detailed timing behavior of the three implementations.

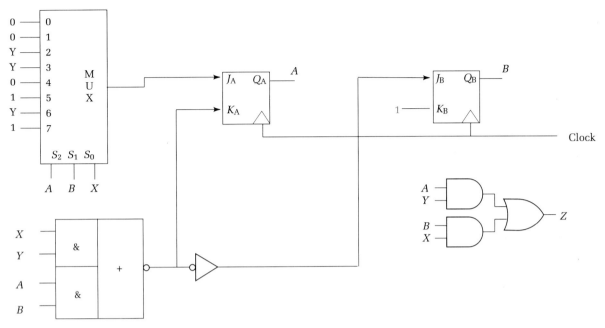

Figure Ex8.10 Machine implementation to be reverse engineered in Exercise 8.10.

8.12 *(Word Problem)* Implement a two-input Mealy machine that produces a 1 at its single output when the values of the two inputs differ *at the time of the previous clock pulse*. Show your state diagram or ASM chart. Describe what each of your states is supposed to represent.

8.13 *(Word Problem)* A finite state machine has one input and one output. The output becomes 1 and remains 1 thereafter when at least two 0's and at least two 1's have occurred as inputs, regardless of the order of occurrence. Assuming this is to be implemented as a Moore machine, draw a state diagram or ASM chart for the machine. (*Hint*: You can do this in nine states.)

8.14 *(Word Problem)* A finite state machine has one input (X) and two outputs (Z_1 and Z_2). An output $Z_1 = 1$ occurs every time the input sequence 101 is observed, provided the sequence 011 has never been seen. An output $Z_2 = 1$ occurs every time the input 011 is observed. Note that once $Z_2 = 1$, $Z_1 = 1$ can never occur. Assuming the machine is to be implemented in the Mealy design style, draw the corresponding state diagram or ASM chart. (*Hint*: The minimum number of states is eight.)

8.15   *(Word Problem)*   A Moore machine has two inputs (X_1, X_2) and one output (Z). Produce the state diagram or ASM chart for the machine, given the following specification. The output remains a constant value unless one of the following input sequences occurs:

a. The input sequence $X_1 X_2 = 00$, 11 causes the output to become 0.

b. The input sequence $X_1 X_2 = 01$, 11 causes the output to become 1.

c. The input sequence $X_1 X_2 = 10$, 11 causes the output to change value.

8.16   *(Word Problem)*   A sequential circuit has one input (X) and one output (Z). Draw a Mealy state diagram or an ASM chart for each of the following cases:

a. The output is $Z = 1$ if and only if the total number of 1's received is divisible by 3 (for example, 0, 3, 6, ...).

b. The output is $Z = 1$ if and only if the total number of 1's received is divisible by 3 and the total number of 0's received is an even number greater than zero (nine states are sufficient).

8.17   *(Word Problem)*   A sequential circuit has two inputs and two outputs. The inputs ($X_1 X_2$) represent a 2-bit binary number, N. If the present value of N is greater than the previous value, then $Z_1 = 1$. If the present value of N is less than the previous value, then $Z_2 = 1$. Otherwise, Z_1 and Z_2 are 0.

a. Derive a Mealy machine state diagram. (*Hint*: The machine needs only five states.)

b. Derive a Moore machine state diagram. (*Hint*: The machine needs at least 11 states.)

8.18   *(Word Problem)*   A Moore machine has one input and one output. The output should be 1 if the total number of 0's received at the input is odd and the total number of 1's received is an even number greater than 0. This machine can be implemented in exactly six states. Draw a complete state diagram. Indicate what each state is meant to represent.

8.19   *(Word Problem)*   Two two-way streets meet at an intersection controlled by a four-way traffic light. In the east and west directions, the lights cycle from green to yellow to red. The south-facing lights do the same thing, except that they are red when the east-west lights are green or yellow, and vice versa. However, the north-facing lights are augmented with a green left turn arrow. They cycle red–green arrow–yellow arrow–green–yellow–red. Consider the following additional problem specifications:

a. When the green or yellow left turn arrows are illuminated, the lights in the other three directions are red.

b. The timings for the north-facing lights are as follows: red, 60 seconds; green arrow, 20 seconds; yellow arrow, 10 seconds; green, 45 seconds; and yellow, 15 seconds.

c. The timings for the other lights can be derived from specifications (a) and (b). Assume you have as many programmable timers as you need. These can be loaded with a time constant (in seconds) and assert an output when they count down to zero.

Construct a chart that shows the timing behavior of the lights in each of the four directions (Y-axis). List the illuminated lights for east, west, south, and north along the Y-axis. The X-axis is calibrated in the elapsed time in seconds. Show what happens in one complete cycle of the lights. How many unique configurations of the lights are there? Draw an ASM chart, explicitly listing all input and output control signals needed to implement the traffic light system.

8.20 *(Word Problem)* Consider the following variation on the classical traffic light controller. The intersection is shown in Figure Ex8.20. A Street runs north-south, B Street runs east-west, and C Street enters the intersection from the southeast. A Street is quite busy, and it is frequently difficult for cars heading south on A to make the left turn onto either B or C. In addition, cars rarely enter the intersection from C Street. Design a traffic light state diagram for this three-way intersection to the following specifications:

a. There are five sets of traffic lights, facing cars coming from A north, A south, B east, B west, and C southeast, respectively.

b. The red, yellow, and green lights facing cars from A north are augmented with a left turn arrow that can be lit up as either green or yellow or not lit up at all.

c. The normal sequencing of lights facing the cars coming from A north is arrow green, arrow yellow, traffic light green, traffic light yellow, traffic light red, and repeat. In other words, the left arrow light is illuminated in every complete cycle of the lights.

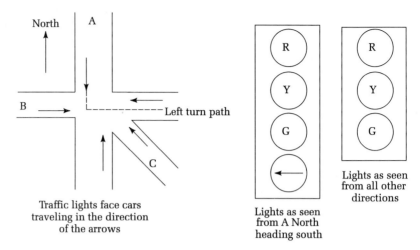

Figure Ex8.20 Traffic light problem specification.

d. However, it should be possible for traffic going from north to south on A Street to cross the intersection even when the left turn arrow is illuminated. Therefore, the traffic light green should also be illuminated while the turn arrow is lit up.

e. Cars traveling from south to north on A Street (and all directions on B and C Streets) must see a red light while the left turn arrow is illuminated for the traffic heading south.

f. A car sensor C is embedded in C Street to detect whether a car is waiting to enter the intersection from the southeast.

g. A timer generates a long interval signal TL and a short interval signal TS when set by an ST signal.

h. Red and green lights are lit up for at least a TL unit of time. Yellow lights, the green arrow, and the yellow arrow are lit up for exactly a TS unit of time.

i. The C Street lights cycle from red to green only if the embedded car sensor indicates that a car is waiting. The lights cycle to yellow and then red as soon as no cars are waiting. Under no circumstances is the C Street green light to be lit for longer than a TL unit of time.

Draw an ASM chart for the traffic light controller. Indicate the logical conditions for remaining in the current state and for exiting it to the next state. Also, create a table that indicates precisely which lights are illuminated for each of your states.

8.21   *(Word Problem)*   You are to develop a state diagram for a washing machine. The machine starts when a coin is deposited. It then sequences through the following stages: soak, wash, rinse, and spin. There is a "double wash" switch, which, if turned on, causes a second wash and rinse to occur. There is one timer—you may assume that each stage should take the same amount of time. The timer begins ticking as soon as the coin is deposited, generates a T signal at the end of the time period, and then resets itself and starts again. If the lid is raised during the spin cycle, the machine stops spinning until the lid is closed. You may assume that the timer suspends ticking while the lid is raised. Identify your inputs and outputs, and draw the ASM chart that implements this finite state machine.

8.22   *(Word Problem)*   You are to design the control for an automatic candy vending machine. The candy bars inside the machine cost 25 cents, and the machine accepts nickels, dimes, and quarters only. The inputs to the control are a set of three signals that indicate what kind of coin has been deposited, as well as a reset signal. The control should generate an output signal that causes the candy to be delivered whenever the amount of money received is 25 cents or more (no change is given). Once the candy has been delivered, some external circuitry will generate a reset signal to put the control back into its initial state. Identify your inputs and outputs, and draw the ASM chart that implements this finite state machine.

8.23   *(Word Problem)*   You are to design a Mealy state diagram for a digital lock. Assume that two debounced push-buttons, A and B, are available to enter the combination. An electromechanical interlock guarantees that the buttons cannot be activated simultaneously. The lock should have the following features:

a. The combination is A-A-B-A-B-A. If this sequence is correctly entered, an output signal is asserted that causes the lock to open.

b. For any state, three B pulses in a row should guarantee to reset the control to its initial state.

c. When any out-of-sequence use of the A push-button occurs, an output is asserted that rings a bell to warn that the lock is being tampered with.

Once the lock is open, pressing either A or B will cause the lock to close without signaling an error. Draw a Mealy state diagram for this finite state machine. Indicate what each state represents and what input conditions cause state and output changes. Not everything may have been specified, so write down any assumptions you make.

8.24   *(Word Problem)*   Design a state diagram to perform the following function. There are two data inputs A and B, a check input C, and an output D. The FSM takes as input two continuous, synchronous streams of 4-bit twos complement numbers in a bit-serial form with the most significant (sign) bit first. The least significant bit is marked by a 1 on the check line (C). During the time slot in which C is asserted, the output D should go to a 1 if the twos complement number on A is larger than the twos complement number on B.

a. Complete the timing diagram in Figure Ex8.24 to make sure you fully understand the statement of the problem.

b. Draw a state diagram that implements this specification using as few states as possible. (*Note:* It is possible to implement this machine in six or fewer states.)

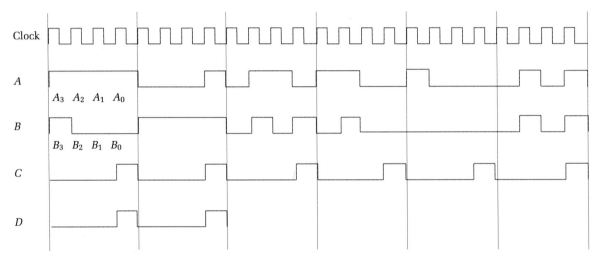

Figure Ex8.24   Timing diagram for serial number comparator.

8.25   *(Word Problem)*   You are to design a finite state machine to control the position of a mechanical arm. Your inputs include two registers, R_0 and R_1, that contain the current position of the arm and the target position, respectively, encoded as 32-bit twos complement numbers. R_0 is automatically updated by external logic on every clock pulse.

The machine should operate as follows. The FSM commences operation when a START pulse is asserted. If the current position is less than the target, the machine should assert a FORWARD signal. If the position is greater than the target, a REVERSE signal should be asserted. If the position is already correct, return to the initial off state. When the arm has moved seven eighths of the way to the target from its initial position, an additional SLOW output should be activated to brake the motion of the arm. You may assume that the arm moves slowly enough with respect to your FSM's clock rate that you need not worry about overshooting the target.

You will probably need additional data path objects besides registers R_0 and R_1. Draw a register diagram of your data path, showing the elements and how they are interconnected. Then draw the controller's state diagram, showing the high-level register transfer operations that are asserted in each state or transition (you may choose Moore or Mealy implementation, at your own discretion).

8.26 *(Word Problem)* Your task is to design the control for a sequential 4-bit multiplier. The data path is shown in Figure Ex8.26. It consists of a 4-bit adder, a 4-bit register, and a 9-bit shift register. The latter shifts right when its Sh input is asserted (assume that 0's are entered at the left for this operation). A new value is loaded into the high-order 5 bits of the shift register when Ld is asserted. The same 5 bits are zeroed when Cl is asserted. These signals are synchronous.

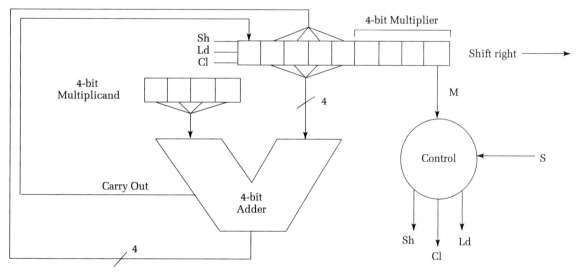

Figure Ex8.26 Multiplier data path for Exercise 8.26.

As a simple example, consider the 2-bit version of the device forming the product of 11_2 and 10_2.

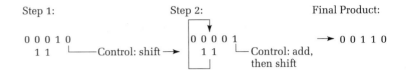

Step 1:   Step 2:   Final Product:

0 0 0 1 0   0 0 0 0 1   → 0 0 1 1 0
  1 1 └──Control: shift →   1 1 └─Control: add,
                                                    then shift

Draw a Mealy machine state diagram for a 4-bit multiply. The inputs are S (a multiply start signal) and M (the low-order bit of the multiplier). The outputs are the Sh, Ld, and Cl signals.

8.27   *(Word Problem)*   Your task is to design the control for a newspaper vending machine to the following specification. The newspaper costs 35 cents. The vending machine accepts nickels, dimes, and quarters. The customer presses a START button and then begins entering coins. Coin sorter logic indicates to the FSM whether a nickel (N), dime (D), or quarter (Q) has been deposited. (Assume that the FSM advances from one state to the next when a coin is deposited.) If exact change is entered, a latch is released so the customer can get the paper. If the amount of money deposited exceeds 35 cents, change is given if possible. Otherwise, deposited coins are refunded to the customer.

Assume that the money just deposited is kept separated from previously accepted coins. The latter are held in a coin repository. Change is given in dimes and nickels. If one nickel is in the repository, a signal N1 is asserted. If two nickels are there, N2 is true (note: N1, N2 will both be asserted if the repository contains two or more nickels), and so on for the number of nickels and dimes in the repository. If sufficient change is available, the FSM pulses a nickel release (NR) or dime release (DR) signal to release one coin of change at a time (it would jam the machine to release more than one coin at a time).

If insufficient change is available, the coins just deposited are refunded by the FSM, asserting a refund (REF) signal. Otherwise, the deposited coins join the repository as the FSM asserts a release (REL) signal. The block diagram for the FSM is shown in Figure Ex8.27.

Consider for a moment the signals that indicate the number of nickels and dimes available to make change. What is the maximum number of nickels needed at any time? What is the maximum number of dimes needed? Understanding the answers to these questions may help to simplify your state diagram.

Complete a Mealy machine state diagram for the vending machine's control.

Figure Ex8.27 Inputs/outputs for newspaper vending machine.

8.28 *(Word Problem)* You are to design the state diagram for a simple controller that turns a lamp on and off at preset times. This is a *timed light switch*. The finite state machine has six inputs: RESET, SetTime, SetLiteOn, SetLiteOff, RUN, and ADVANCE. The first five inputs are generated by a five-position rotary switch that advances through RESET, SetTime, SetLiteOn, SetLiteOff, and RUN (the inputs are mutually exclusive and are encountered in the specified order). The ADVANCE input is a push-button. See Figure Ex8.28(a). When you hold the ADVANCE button down (asserted), the displayed time rapidly advances through 24 hours, a minute at a time.

The typical operation of the timed light switch works as follows. It is normally in RUN mode. The lamp is turned on whenever the internal clock matches an internal register (LiteOn) that holds the time to turn the light on. The lamp is turned off whenever the internal clock matches an internal register (LiteOff) that holds the time to turn the light off.

To operate the timed light switch, you must set the current time, then the time on, and finally the time off. This is accomplished as follows. The mode switch is moved from RUN to RESET. This causes an internal timer register to be loaded with the time 08:00. Next, the mode switch is moved to the SetTime position. Whenever ADVANCE is pushed and held down, the timer register rapidly cycles through the minutes and hours. You "pulse" or single step ADVANCE as it gets close to the current time. When you move the switch to SetLiteOn, the current value in the timer register overwrites the value in the internal clock register. At the same time, the internal timer register is reset to 08:00.

By working with the ADVANCE button, you set a new time at which the light is to be turned on. Moving the mode switch to SetLiteOff causes the LiteOn register to be overwritten by the timer register.

Using the ADVANCE button once again, you advance the timer from its last value (the "lights on" time) to the desired time to turn the lights off. Once the mode switch is set to RUN, the timed light switch goes into its running mode.

The data path associated with the timed light switch is shown in Figure Ex8.28(b). The block diagram is given in Figure Ex8.28(c).

Complete a Moore state diagram for the timed light switch controller.

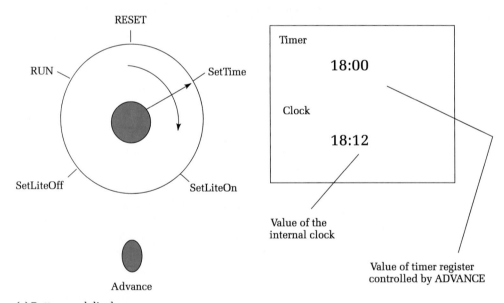

(a) Buttons and displays

Figure Ex8.28   The timed light switch.

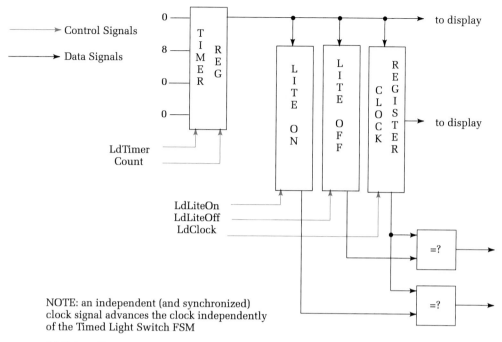

⟶ Control Signals

⟶ Data Signals

NOTE: an independent (and synchronized) clock signal advances the clock independently of the Timed Light Switch FSM

(b) Data path

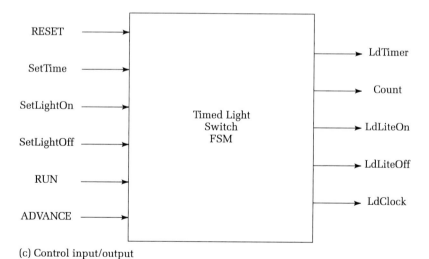

(c) Control input/output

Figure Ex8.28   *(Continued.)*

8.29   *(Word Problem)*   Consider the combination lock finite state machine of Section 8.5.4. Add another input, CHANGE COMBINATION, similar to ENTER, that makes it possible to change the lock value once the door has been unlocked. Assume that the new combination is available on three switches. Draw a new state chart incorporating this change.

8.30   *(Word Problem)*   Given the combination lock of Section 8.5.4, describe how you would design a combination lock with a variable number of bits in the key. *Hint*: How could you use a counter to assist in this? Draw a block diagram showing signals between the finite state machine and the counter. Draw a revised ASM chart incorporating your design change.

9 Finite State Machine Optimization

*Nature is as complex as it
needs to be . . . and no more.*
—*A. Einstein*

Introduction

We are now ready to complete the finite state machine design process introduced in Chapter 8. The steps of Chapter 8 yield an abstract description of the state machine. This may be a state diagram, an ASM chart, or a hardware description language specification. Deriving a symbolic state transition table from one of these is straightforward. In this chapter, we concentrate on state minimization, state assignment, and choice of flip-flops.

We show why finite state machine "optimization" (*improvement* might be a better word) is still important, even in today's era of very large scale integrated circuits. We present pencil-and-paper methods, as well as more formal techniques suitable for computer implementation, for reducing the number of states and for choosing a state encoding.

Then we examine the approaches for choosing the machine's flip-flops and how the choice affects the next-state and output combinational functions. The right choice of flip-flop leads to a smaller gate count and thus fewer components to implement the machine.

Finally, we develop techniques for partitioning complex finite state machines into simpler, smaller, communicating machines. You may be forced to partition your state machine because it cannot fit into a given programmable logic component. This could arise, for example, because of limited logic resources, such as input/outputs, product terms, or flip-flops.

In this chapter, we emphasize the following techniques and concepts:

- *Procedures for optimizing a finite state machine.* You will learn the methods for state minimization and state assignment.

- *Application of modern computer-aided design tools for state assignment.* CAD tools make it possible for you to evaluate the implementation complexity of alternative state assignments very rapidly.

- *Partitioning methods.* You will learn the techniques for breaking finite state machines into smaller, communicating state machines that are well suited for implementation with programmable logic.

9.1   Motivation for Optimization

To review, the finite state machine design process consists of (1) understanding the problem, (2) obtaining a formal description (ultimately, a *symbolic state transition table*), (3) minimizing the number of states, (4) encoding the states, (5) choosing the flip-flops to implement the state registers, and finally (6) implementing the finite state machine's next-state and output functions. This chapter starts at step 3 and carries us through to the final implementation at step 6, using methods based on discrete logic gates. We discuss the use of programmable logic for finite state machine implementation in the next chapter.

9.1.1   Two State Diagrams, Same I/O Behavior

In the age of very large scale integrated circuits, why should we bother to minimize a finite state machine implementation? After all, as long as the input/output behavior of the machine is correct, it really doesn't matter how it is implemented. Or does it?

Figure 9.1 shows two different state diagrams for the odd parity checker of Section 8.2. They have identical output behavior for all input strings. You should try some inputs to convince yourself. We define *equivalence* of finite state machines as follows. Two machines are equivalent if their input/output behavior is identical for all possible input strings.

For a particular finite state machine, there are many equivalent forms. Rather than reusing states while deriving the state diagram, you could simply introduce a new state whenever you need one (to keep the number of states finite, you will need to reuse some of them, of course).

The two implementations of the state diagrams of Figure 9.1 are certainly not the same. The machine with more states requires more flip-flops and more complex next-state logic.

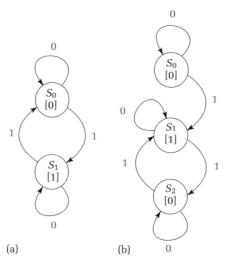

Figure 9.1   Two equivalent state diagrams for the odd parity checker.

9.1.2   Advantages of Minimum States

In general, you will find it is worthwhile to implement the finite state machine in as few states as possible. This usually reduces the number of logic gates and flip-flops you need for the machine's implementation.

Similarly, judicious mapping between symbolic and encoded states can reduce the implementation logic. For the parity checker, our implementation in Chapter 8 required no gates because we made a good state assignment that naturally matched the control input to the toggle flip-flop.

A state diagram with n states must be implemented with at least k flip-flops, where $2^{k-1} < n \leq 2^k$. By reducing the number of states to 2^{k-1} or less, you can save a flip-flop. For example, suppose you are given a finite state machine with five state flip-flops. This machine can represent up to 32 states. If you can reduce the number of states to 16 or less, you save a flip-flop.

Even when reducing the number of states is not enough to eliminate a flip-flop, it still has advantages. With fewer states, you introduce more don't-care conditions into the next-state and output functions, making their implementation simpler. Less logic usually means shorter critical timing paths and a higher clock rate for the system.

More important, today's programmable logic provides limited gate and flip-flop counts on a single programmable logic chip. A typical programmable logic part might have "2000 gate equivalents" (rarely approached in practice) yet provide only 64 flip-flops! An important goal of state reduction is to make the implementation "fit" in as few components as possible. The fewer components you use, the shorter the design time and the lower the manufacturing cost.

State reduction techniques also allow you to be sloppy in obtaining the initial finite state machine description. If you have introduced a few redundant states, you will find and eliminate them by using the state reduction techniques introduced next.

9.2   State Minimization/Reduction

State reduction identifies and combines states that have equivalent "behavior." Two states have *equivalent* behavior if, for all input combinations, their outputs are the same and they change to the same or equivalent next states.

For example, in Figure 9.1(b), states S_0 and S_2 are equivalent. Both states output a 0; both change to S_1 on a 1 and self-loop on a 0. Combining these into a single state leads to Figure 9.1(a). On all input strings, the output sequence of either state diagram is exactly the same.

Algorithms for state reduction begin with the symbolic state transition table. First, we group together states that have the same state outputs (Moore machine) or transition outputs (Mealy machine). These are potentially equivalent, since states cannot be equivalent if their outputs differ.

Next, we examine the transitions to see if they go to the same next state for every input combination. If they do, the states are equivalent and we can combine them into a renamed new state. We then change all transitions into the newly combined states. We repeat the process until no additional states can be combined.

In the following two subsections, we examine alternative algorithms for state reduction: *row matching* and *implication charts*. The former is a good pencil-and-paper method, but does not always obtain the best reduced state table. Implication charts are more complex to use by hand, but they are easy to implement via computer and do find the best solution.

We can always combine the two approaches. Row matching quickly reduces the number of states. The more complicated implication chart method, now working with fewer states, finds the equivalent states missed by row matching more rapidly.

9.2.1   Row-Matching Method

Let's begin our investigation of the row-matching method with a detailed example. We will see how to transform an initial state diagram for a simple sequence detector into a minimized, equivalent state diagram.

Four-Bit Sequence Detector: Specification and Initial State Diagram   Let's consider a sequence-detecting finite state machine with the following specification. The machine has a single input X and output Z. The output is asserted after each 4-bit input sequence if it consists of one of the binary strings 0110 or 1010. The machine returns to the reset state after each 4-bit sequence.

We will assume a Mealy implementation. Some sample behavior of the finite state machine is

X = 0010 0110 1100 1010 0011 ...

Z = 0000 0001 0000 0001 0000 ...

The output is asserted only after the previous four serial inputs match one of the specified strings. Also, the input patterns do not overlap: the machine makes a decision to assert its output after each group of 4 bits.

Because this finite state machine recognizes finite length strings, we can place an upper bound on the number of states needed to recognize any particular binary string of length four. Figure 9.2 shows the state diagram. There are 16 unique paths through the state diagram, one for each possible 4-bit pattern. This adds up to 15 states and 30 transitions. We highlight the paths leading to recognition of the strings 0110 and 1010 in the figure. Only two of the transitions have a 1 output, representing the accepted strings.

Four-Bit Sequence Detector: State Table and Row-Matching Method We can combine many of the states in Figure 9.2 without changing the input/output behavior of the finite state machine. But how do we find these equivalent states in a systematic fashion?

First, we look at the state transition table, as shown in Figure 9.3. This table is in a slightly different format than we have seen so far. It contains one row per state, with multiple next-state and output columns based on the input combinations. It gives exactly the same information as a table with separate rows for each state and input combination.

The input sequence column is a documentation aid, describing the partial string as seen so far. When read from left to right, it describes the sequence of input bits that lead to the given state.

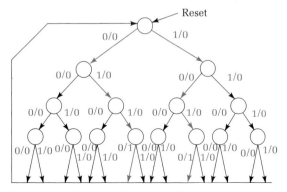

Figure 9.2 Original state diagram for 4-bit string recognizer.

Input Sequence	Present State	Next State X=0	X=1	Output X=0	X=1
Reset	S_0	S_1	S_2	0	0
0	S_1	S_3	S_4	0	0
1	S_2	S_5	S_6	0	0
00	S_3	S_7	S_8	0	0
01	S_4	S_9	S_{10}	0	0
10	S_5	S_{11}	S_{12}	0	0
11	S_6	S_{13}	S_{14}	0	0
000	S_7	S_0	S_0	0	0
001	S_8	S_0	S_0	0	0
010	S_9	S_0	S_0	0	0
011	S_{10}	S_0	S_0	1	0
100	S_{11}	S_0	S_0	0	0
101	S_{12}	S_0	S_0	1	0
110	S_{13}	S_0	S_0	0	0
111	S_{14}	S_0	S_0	0	0

Figure 9.3   Initial state transition table for the 0110 or 1010 sequence detector.

Next we examine the rows of the state transition table to find any with identical next-state and output values (hence the term "row matching"). For this finite state machine, we can combine S_{10} and S_{12}. Let's call the new state S_{10}' and use it to rename all transitions to S_{10} or S_{12}. The revised state table is shown in Figure 9.4.

Four-Bit Sequence Detector: Row-Matching Iteration   We continue matching rows until we can no longer combine any. In Figure 9.4, S_7, S_8, S_9, S_{11}, S_{13}, and S_{14} all have the same next states and outputs. We combine them into a renamed state S_7'. The table, with renamed transitions, is shown in Figure 9.5.

Input Sequence	Present State	Next State X=0	X=1	Output X=0	X=1
Reset	S_0	S_1	S_2	0	0
0	S_1	S_3	S_4	0	0
1	S_2	S_5	S_6	0	0
00	S_3	S_7	S_8	0	0
01	S_4	S_9	S_{10}'	0	0
10	S_5	S_{11}	S_{10}'	0	0
11	S_6	S_{13}	S_{14}	0	0
000	S_7	S_0	S_0	0	0
001	S_8	S_0	S_0	0	0
010	S_9	S_0	S_0	0	0
011 or 101	S_{10}'	S_0	S_0	1	0
100	S_{11}	S_0	S_0	0	0
110	S_{13}	S_0	S_0	0	0
111	S_{14}	S_0	S_0	0	0

Figure 9.4   Revised state transition table after S_{10} and S_{12} combined.

Input Sequence	Present State	Next State		Output	
		$X=0$	$X=1$	$X=0$	$X=1$
Reset	S_0	S_1	S_2	0	0
0	S_1	S_3	S_4	0	0
1	S_2	S_5	S_6	0	0
00	S_3	S_7'	S_7'	0	0
01	S_4	S_7'	S_{10}'	0	0
10	S_5	S_7'	S_{10}'	0	0
11	S_6	S_7'	S_7'	0	0
not (011 or 101)	S_7'	S_0	S_0	0	0
011 or 101	S_{10}'	S_0	S_0	1	0

Figure 9.5 Revised state transition table after S_7, S_8, S_9, S_{11}, S_{13}, S_{14} combined.

Input Sequence	Present State	Next State		Output	
		$X=0$	$X=1$	$X=0$	$X=1$
Reset	S_0	S_1	S_2	0	0
0	S_1	S_3'	S_4'	0	0
1	S_2	S_4'	S_3'	0	0
00 or 11	S_3'	S_7'	S_7'	0	0
01 or 10	S_4'	S_7'	S_{10}'	0	0
not (011 or 101)	S_7'	S_0	S_0	0	0
011 or 101	S_{10}'	S_0	S_0	1	0

Figure 9.6 Final reduced state transition table after S_3, S_6 and S_4, S_5 combined.

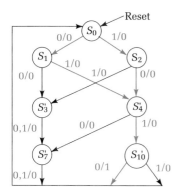

Figure 9.7 Reduced state diagram for 4-bit string recognizer.

Now states S_3 and S_6 can be combined, as can S_4 and S_5. We call the combined states S_3' and S_4', respectively. The final reduced state transition table is shown in Figure 9.6. In the process, we have reduced 15 states to just 7 states. This allows us encode the state in 3 bits rather than 4. The reduced state diagram is given in Figure 9.7.

Limitations of the Row-Matching Method Unfortunately, row matching does not always yield the most reduced state table. We can prove this with a simple counterexample. Figure 9.8 shows the state table for the three-state odd parity checker of Figure 9.1. Although states S_0 and S_2 have the same output, they do not have the same next state. Thus, they cannot be combined by simple row matching. The problem is the self-loop transitions on input 0. If we combined these two states, the self-loop would be maintained, but this is not found by row matching. We need another, more rigorous method for state reduction.

Present State	Next State		Output
	$X=0$	$X=1$	
S_0	S_0	S_1	0
S_1	S_1	S_2	1
S_2	S_2	S_1	0

Figure 9.8 State table for three-state odd parity checker.

9.2.2   Implication Chart Method

The implication chart method is a more systematic approach to finding the states that can be combined into a single reduced state. As you might suspect, the method is more complex and is better suited for machine implementation than hand use.

Three-Bit Sequence Detector: Specification and Initial State Table   We illustrate its use with another example. Your goal is to design a binary sequence detector that will output a 1 whenever the machine has observed the serial sequence 010 or 110 at the inputs. We call this machine a 3-bit sequence detector. Figure 9.9 shows its initial state table.

Data Structure: The Implication Chart   The method operates on a data structure that enumerates all possible combinations of states taken two at a time, called an *implication chart*. Figure 9.10(a) shows the chart with an entry for every pair of states. This form of the chart is more complicated than it needs to be. For example, the diagonal entries are not needed: it does not reduce states to combine a state with itself! And

Input Sequence	Present State	Next State		Output	
		$X=0$	$X=1$	$X=0$	$X=1$
Reset	S_0	S_1	S_2	0	0
0	S_1	S_3	S_4	0	0
1	S_2	S_5	S_6	0	0
00	S_3	S_0	S_0	0	0
01	S_4	S_0	S_0	1	0
10	S_5	S_0	S_0	0	0
11	S_6	S_0	S_0	1	0

Figure 9.9   Initial state transition table for the 3-bit sequence detector.

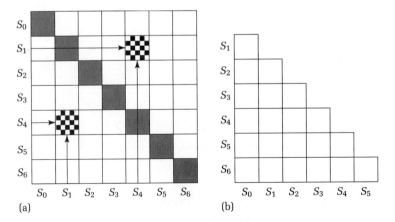

(a)   (b)

Figure 9.10   Matrix for state combinations and the corresponding implication chart.

the upper and lower triangles of entries are symmetric. The chart entry for S_i and S_j contains the same information as that for S_j and S_i. Thus, we work with the reduced structure of Figure 9.10(b).

We fill in the implication chart as follows. Let X_{ij} be the entry whose row is labeled by state S_i and whose column is labeled by state S_j. If we were able to combine states S_i and S_j, it would imply that their next-state transitions for each input combination must also be equivalent. The chart entry contains the next-state combinations that must be equivalent for the row and column states to be equivalent. If S_i and S_j have different outputs or next-state behavior, an X is placed in the entry. This indicates that the two states can never be equivalent.

Three-Bit Sequence Detector: Initial Implication Chart The implication chart for the example state table is shown in Figure 9.11. S_0, S_1, S_2, S_3, and S_5 have the same outputs and are candidates for being combined. Similarly, states S_4 and S_6 might also be combined. Any combination of states across the two groups, such as S_1 and S_4, is labeled by an X in the chart. Since their outputs are different, they can never be equivalent.

To fill in the chart entry for (row) S_1 and (column) S_0, we look at the next-state transitions. S_0 goes to S_1 on 0 and S_2 on 1, while S_1 goes to S_3 and S_4, respectively. We fill the chart in with S_1–S_3, the transitions on 0, and S_2–S_4, the transitions on 1. We call these groupings *implied state pairs*. The entry means that S_0 and S_1 cannot be equivalent unless S_1 is equivalent to S_3 and S_2 is equivalent to S_4. The rest of the entries are filled in similarly.

At this point, the chart already contains enough information to eliminate many impossible equivalent pairs. For example, we already know that S_2 and S_4 cannot be equivalent: they have different output behavior. Thus there is no way that S_0 can be equivalent to S_1.

Finding these cases is straightforward. We visit the entries in sequence. For example, start with the top square in the first column and advance from top to bottom and left to right. If square S_i, S_j contains the implied state pair S_m-S_n and square S_m, S_n contains an X, then mark S_i, S_j with an X as well.

Sequence Detector Example: First Marking Pass Figure 9.12 contains the results of this first marking pass. Entry S_2, S_0 is marked with an X because the chart entry for the implied state pair S_2-S_6 is already marked with an X. Entry S_3, S_0 is also marked, because entry S_1, S_0 (as well as S_2, S_0) has just been marked. The same is true for S_5, S_0. By the end of the pass, the only entries not marked are S_2, S_1; S_5, S_3; and S_6, S_4.

Sequence Detector Example: Second Marking Pass We now make a second pass through the chart to see if we can add any new markings. Entry S_2, S_1 remains unmarked. Nothing in the chart refutes that S_3 and S_5 are equivalent. The same is true of S_4 and S_6.

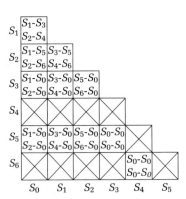

Figure 9.11   Initial implication chart for the 3-bit sequence detector.

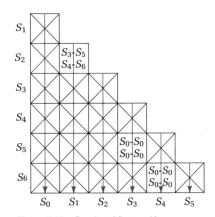

Figure 9.12   Results of first marking pass.

Continuing, S_3,S_5 and S_4,S_6 are now obviously equivalent. They have identical outputs and transfer to the same next state (S_0) for all input combinations.

Since no new markings have been added, the algorithm stops. The unmarked entries represent equivalences between the row and column indices: S_1 is equivalent to S_2, S_3 to S_5, and S_4 to S_6. The final reduced state table is shown in Figure 9.13.

Multi-Input Example: State Diagram and Transition Table   We can generalize the procedure for finite state machines with more than one input. The only difference is that there are more implied state pairs: one for each input combination.

Let's consider the state diagram for a two-input Moore machine shown in Figure 9.14. Each state has four next-state transitions, one for each possible input condition. The derived state transition table is given in Figure 9.15.

Multi-Input Example: Implication Chart Processing   Figure 9.16 shows the implication chart derived from the state transition table. Let's see how some of the entries are filled in. Since S_1 and S_0 have different state outputs, we place X in entry S_1,S_0. For the S_2,S_0 entry, we list the implied state pairs under the input conditions 00, 01, 10, 11. Because S_0

		Next State		Output	
Input Sequence	Present State	$X=0$	$X=1$	$X=0$	$X=1$
Reset	S_0	S_1'	S_1'	0	0
0 or 1	S_1'	S_3'	S_4'	0	0
00 or 10	S_3'	S_0	S_0	0	0
01 or 11	S_4'	S_0	S_0	1	0

Figure 9.13   Final reduced state transition table for the 3-bit sequence detector.

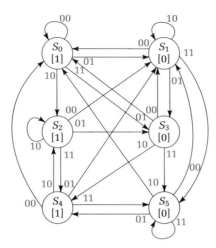

Figure 9.14 Multiple-input state diagram.

Present State	Next State				Output
	00	01	10	11	
S_0	S_0	S_1	S_2	S_3	1
S_1	S_0	S_3	S_1	S_5	0
S_2	S_1	S_3	S_2	S_4	1
S_3	S_1	S_0	S_4	S_5	0
S_4	S_0	S_1	S_2	S_5	1
S_5	S_1	S_4	S_0	S_5	0

Figure 9.15 Multiple-input state transition table.

stays in S_0 on input 00, while S_2 goes to S_1 on 00, we add the implied state pair S_0-S_1 to the entry. On input 01, S_0 goes to S_1, S_2 goes to S_3, and we add S_1-S_3 to the entry. Similarly, we add the pairs S_2-S_2 on 10 and S_3-S_4 on 11 to the entry and fill in the rest of the entries.

Now we begin the marking pass. Working down the columns, we cross out entry S_2-S_0 because S_0,S_1 is already crossed out. The same thing happens to the entries S_3,S_1; S_5,S_1; and S_4,S_2. This leaves S_4,S_0 and S_5,S_3 unmarked (these are highlighted in the figure). Their being unmarked implies that S_4 is equivalent to S_0 (renamed S_0') and S_3 is equivalent to S_5 (S_3'). The reduced state table is given in Figure 9.17.

Figure 9.16 Multiple-input implication chart.

Present State	Next State				Output
	00	01	10	11	
S_0'	S_0'	S_1	S_2	S_3'	1
S_1	S_0'	S_3'	S_1	S_3'	0
S_2	S_1	S_3'	S_2	S_0'	1
S_3'	S_1	S_0'	S_0'	S_3'	0

Figure 9.17 Multiple-input reduced state table.

Figure 9.18 Implication chart for three-state odd parity checker.

Example State Reduction of Parity Checker Finite State Machine The row-matching method could not combine states S_0 and S_2 in the three-state parity checker of Figure 9.1. Can the implication chart method do the job?

The implication chart for the state transition table of Figure 9.8 is given in Figure 9.18. S_1,S_0 and S_2,S_1 are marked immediately because their outputs differ. The remaining square is left unmarked, implying that S_0 and S_2 are equivalent. This is the correct reduced state transition table.

Implication Chart Summary The algorithm for state reduction using the implication chart method consists of the following steps:

1. Construct the implication chart, consisting of one square for each possible combination of states taken two at a time.

2. For each square labeled by states S_i and S_j, if the outputs of the states differ, mark the square with an X; these states are *not* equivalent. Otherwise, they may be equivalent. Within the square, write implied pairs of next states for all input combinations.

3. Systematically advance through the squares of the implication chart. If the square labeled by states S_i,S_j contains an implied pair S_m-S_n and square S_m,S_n is marked with an X, then mark S_i,S_j with an X. Since S_m and S_n are not equivalent, neither are S_i and S_j.

4. Continue executing step 3 until no new squares are marked with an X.

5. For each remaining unmarked square S_i,S_j, you can conclude that states S_i and S_j are equivalent.

9.3 State Assignment

The number of gates needed to implement a sequential logic network depends strongly on how we assign *encoded* Boolean values to *symbolic* states. Unfortunately, the only way to obtain the best possible assignment is to try every choice for the encoding, an extremely large number for real state machines. For example, a four-state finite state machine, such as the traffic light controller of the last chapter, has 4! (4 factorial) = 4 * 3 * 2 * 1 = 24 different encodings (see Figure 9.19).

9.3.1 Traffic Light Controller

To illustrate the impact of state encoding on the next-state and output logic, let's use the symbolic state transition table for the traffic light controller, shown in Figure 9.20. The input combinations that cause the state transitions are shown at the left of the table. The symbolic state names HG, HY, FG, FY represent the states highway green/farmroad red, highway yellow/farmroad red, highway red/farmroad green, and highway red/farmroad yellow. We have already encoded the traffic light outputs: 00 = Green, 01 = Yellow, and 10 = Red.

HG	HY	FG	FY		HG	HY	FG	FY
00	01	10	11		10	00	01	11
00	01	11	10		10	00	11	01
00	10	01	11		10	01	00	11
00	10	11	01		10	01	11	00
00	11	01	10		10	11	00	01
00	11	10	01		10	11	01	00
01	00	10	11		11	00	01	10
01	00	11	10		11	00	10	01
01	10	00	11		11	01	00	10
01	10	11	00		11	01	10	00
01	11	00	10		11	10	00	01
01	11	10	00		11	10	01	00

Figure 9.19 Alternative state encodings of the traffic light controller.

Inputs			Present State	Next State	Outputs			
C	TL	TS	Q_1 Q_0	P_1 P_0	ST	H_1 H_0	F_1 F_0	
0	X	X	HG	HG	0	00	10	
X	0	X	HG	HG	0	00	10	
1	1	X	HG	HY	1	00	10	
X	X	0	HY	HY	0	01	10	
X	X	1	HY	FG	1	01	10	
1	0	X	FG	FG	0	10	00	
0	X	X	FG	FY	1	10	00	
X	1	X	FG	FY	1	10	00	
X	X	0	FY	FY	0	10	01	
X	X	1	FY	HG	1	10	01	

Figure 9.20 Traffic light controller symbolic state transition table.

We can use *espresso* to examine the alternative state assignments rapidly. Figure 9.21 shows the generic truth table description that is input to *espresso*. We simply replace the symbolic state names HG, HY, FG, and FY with a particular encoding. Before we do a state assignment

```
.i 5
.o 7
.ilb c tl ts q1 q0
.ob p1 p0 st h1 h0 f1 f0
.p 10
0-- HG HG 00010
-0- HG HG 00010
11- HG HY 10010
--0 HY HY 00110
--1 HY FG 10110
10- FG FG 01000
0-- FG FY 11000
-1- FG FY 11000
--0 FY FY 01001
--1 FY HG 11001
.e
```

Figure 9.21 *Espresso* input for the traffic light controller.

and two-level minimization, the finite state machine requires 10 unique product terms (one for each row of Figure 9.21).

Figure 9.22 and Figure 9.23 show the results of *espresso* runs with the state assignments HG = 00, HY = 01, FG = 11, FY = 10 and HG = 00, HY = 10, FG = 01, FY = 11 respectively. A cursory glance shows that the second encoding uses fewer product terms, eight versus nine, and fewer literals, 21 versus 26.

Comparison of the Two Encodings   Let's look at the relative complexity of the two implementations. The logic equations implied by the two alternative encodings are the following.

First encoding:

```
.i 5
.o 7
.ilb c tl ts q1 q0
.ob p1 p0 st h1 h0 f1 f0
.p 10
0-- 00 00 00010
-0- 00 00 00010
11- 00 01 10010
--0 01 01 00010
--1 01 11 10110
10- 11 11 01000
0-- 11 10 11000
-1- 11 10 11000
--0 10 10 01001
--1 10 00 11001
.e
```
(a) *Espresso* input

```
.i 5
.o 7
.ilb c tl ts q1 q0
.ob p1 p0 st h1 h0 f1 f0
.p 10
0-- 00 00 00010
-0- 00 00 00010
11- 00 10 10010
--0 10 10 00110
--1 10 01 10110
10- 01 01 01000
0-- 01 11 11000
-1- 01 11 11000
--0 11 11 01001
--1 11 00 11001
.e
```
(a) *Espresso* input

```
.i 5
.o 7
.ilb c tl ts q1 q0
.ob p1 p0 st h1 h0 f1 f0
.p 9
11-00 0110000
10-11 1101000
--101 1010000
--010 1001001
---01 0100100
--110 0011001
---0- 0000010
0--11 1011000
-1-11 1011000
.e
```
(b) *Espresso* output

```
.i 5
.o 7
.ilb c tl ts q1 q0
.ob p1 p0 st h1 h0 f1 f0
.p 8
11-0- 1010000
--010 1000100
0--01 1010000
--110 0110100
--111 0011001
----0 0000010
---01 0101000
--011 1101001
.e
```
(b) *Espresso* output

Figure 9.22   First encoding.

Figure 9.23   Second encoding.

$$P_1 = C \bullet \overline{TL} \bullet Q_1 \bullet Q_0 + TS \bullet \overline{Q}_1 \bullet Q_0 + \overline{TS} \bullet Q_1 \bullet \overline{Q}_0 + \overline{C} \bullet Q_1 \bullet Q_0 + TL \bullet Q_1 \bullet Q_0$$

$$P_0 = C \bullet TL \bullet \overline{Q}_1 \bullet \overline{Q}_0 + C \bullet \overline{TL} \bullet Q_1 \bullet Q_0 + \overline{Q}_1 \bullet Q_0$$

$$ST = C \bullet TL \bullet \overline{Q}_1 \bullet \overline{Q}_0 + TS \bullet \overline{Q}_1 \bullet Q_0 + TS \bullet Q_1 \bullet Q_0 + \overline{C} \bullet Q_1 \bullet Q_0 + TL \bullet Q_1 \bullet Q_0$$

$$H_1 = C \bullet \overline{TL} \bullet Q_1 \bullet Q_0 + \overline{TS} \bullet Q_1 \bullet \overline{Q}_0 + TS \bullet Q_1 \bullet \overline{Q}_0 + \overline{C} \bullet Q_1 \bullet Q_0 + TL \bullet Q_1 \bullet Q_0$$

$$H_0 = \overline{Q}_1 \bullet Q_0$$

$$F_1 = \overline{Q}_1$$

$$F_0 = \overline{TS} \bullet Q_1 \bullet \overline{Q}_0 + TS \bullet Q_1 \bullet \overline{Q}_0$$

With conventional gate logic, the encoding requires 3 five-input gates, 2 four-input gates, 6 three-input gates, and 2 two-input gates, a total of 13 gates. We assume that variables and their complements are available to the network.

Second encoding:

$$P_1 = C \bullet TL \bullet \overline{Q}_1 + \overline{TS} \bullet Q_1 \bullet \overline{Q}_0 + \overline{C} \bullet \overline{Q}_1 \bullet Q_0 + \overline{TS} \bullet Q_1 \bullet Q_0$$

$$P_0 = TS \bullet Q_1 \bullet \overline{Q}_0 + \overline{Q}_1 \bullet Q_0 + \overline{TS} \bullet Q_1 \bullet Q_0$$

$$ST = C \bullet TL \bullet \overline{Q}_1 + \overline{C} \bullet \overline{Q}_1 \bullet Q_0 + TS \bullet Q_1 \bullet \overline{Q}_0 + TS \bullet Q_1 \bullet Q_0$$

$$H_1 = TS \bullet Q_1 \bullet Q_0 + \overline{Q}_1 \bullet Q_0 + \overline{TS} \bullet Q_1 \bullet Q_0$$

$$H_0 = \overline{TS} \bullet Q_1 \bullet \overline{Q}_0 + TS \bullet Q_1 \bullet \overline{Q}_0$$

$$F_1 = \overline{Q}_0$$

$$F_0 = TS \bullet Q_1 \bullet Q_0 + \overline{TS} \bullet Q_1 \bullet Q_0$$

This encoding requires 2 four-input gates, 8 three-input gates, and 3 two-input gates, for a total of 13 gates. This implementation uses the same number of gates, but it makes more extensive use of gates with smaller fan-ins. This reduces overall wiring and is one reason why it is often more useful to count literals than gates in comparing circuit complexity.

In the next two subsections, we present methods for finding good state encodings. These are suitable for pencil and paper, as well as computer-aided design tools.

9.3.2   Pencil-and-Paper Methods

Without computer-aided design tools, there is little you can do to generate a good encoding. Hand enumeration using trial and error becomes tedious even for a relatively small number of states. An n-state finite state machine has $n!$ different encodings. And this is only the lower bound. If the state is not densely encoded in the fewest number of bits, even more encodings are possible.

To make the problem more tractable when you must use hand methods, designers have developed a collection of heuristic "guidelines." These try to reduce the distance in Boolean n-space between related states. For example, if state Y is reached by a transition from state X, then the encodings should differ by as few bits as possible. The next-state logic will be minimized if you follow such guidelines. We examine them in this section.

State Maps *State maps*, similar in concept to K-maps, provide a means of observing adjacencies in state assignments. The squares of the state map are indexed by the binary values of state bits; the state given that encoding is placed in the map square. Obviously the technique is limited to situations in which a K-map can be used, that is, up to six variables.

Figure 9.24 presents an ASM chart for a five-state finite state machine. Figure 9.25 gives two alternative state assignments and their representations in state maps.

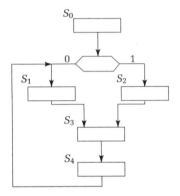

Figure 9.24 Five-state ASM chart.

Minimum-Bit-Change Heuristic One heuristic strategy assigns states so that the number of bit changes for all state transitions is minimized. For example, the assignment of Figure 9.25(a) is not as good as the one in Figure 9.25(b) under this criterion:

Transition	First Assignment Bit Changes	Second Assignment Bit Changes
S_0 to S_1:	2	1
S_0 to S_2:	3	1
S_1 to S_3:	3	1
S_2 to S_3:	2	1
S_3 to S_4:	1	1
S_4 to S_1:	2	2

The first assignment leads to 13 different bit changes in the next-state function, the second only 7 bit changes.

We derived the first assignment completely at random and the second assignment with minimum transition distance in mind. Here is how we did it. We made the assignment for S_0 first. Because of the way reset logic works, it usually makes sense to assign all zeros to the starting state. We make assignments for S_1 and S_2 next, placing them next to S_0 because they are targets of transitions out of the starting state.

Note how we used the edge adjacency of the state map. This is so we can place S_3 between the assignments for S_1 and S_2, since it is the target of transitions from both of these states.

Finally, we place S_4 adjacent to S_3, since it is the destination of S_3's only transition. It would be perfect if S_4 could also be placed distance 1

State Name	Assignment Q_2	Q_1	Q_0
S_0	0	0	0
S_1	1	0	1
S_2	1	1	1
S_3	0	1	0
S_4	0	1	1

Assignment

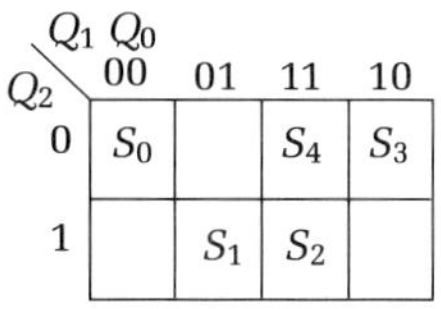

State Map

(a) First state assignment and map

State Name	Assignment Q_2	Q_1	Q_0
S_0	0	0	0
S_1	0	0	1
S_2	0	1	0
S_3	0	1	1
S_4	1	1	1

Assignment

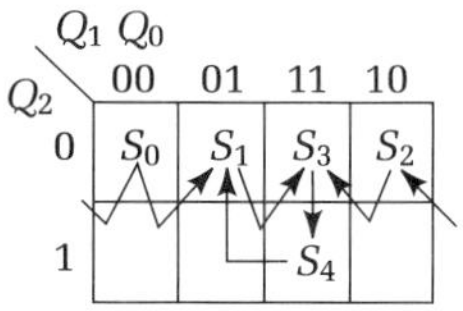

State Map

(b) Second state assignment and map

Figure 9.25 Five-state finite state machine.

from S_0, but it is not possible to do this and satisfy the other desired adjacencies.

The resulting assignment exhibits only seven bit transitions. There may be many other assignments with the same number of bit transitions, and perhaps an assignment that needs even fewer.

The minimum-bit-change heuristic, although simple, is not likely to achieve the best assignment. For a finite state machine like the traffic light controller, cycling through its regular sequence of states, the minimum transition distance is obtained by a Gray code assignment: HG = 00, HY = 01, FG = 11, FY = 10. This was the first state assignment we tried in the previous subsection, and it was not as good as the second assignment, even though the latter did not involve a minimum number of bit changes.

Guidelines Based on Next State and Input/Outputs Although the criterion of minimum transition distance is simple, it suffers by not considering the input and output values in determining the next state. A second set of heuristic guidelines makes an effort to consider this in the assignment of states:

Highest priority: States with the same next state for a given input transition should be given adjacent assignments in the state map.

Medium priority: Next states of the same state should be given adjacent assignments in the state map.

Lowest priority: States with the same output for a given input should be given adjacent assignments in the state map.

Highest Priority

Medium Priority

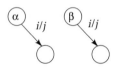

Lowest Priority

Figure 9.26 Adjacent assignment priorities.

The guidelines, illustrated in Figure 9.26 for the candidate states α and β, are ranked from highest to lowest priority. The first two rules attempt to group together ones in the next-state maps, while the third rule performs a similar grouping function for the output maps. We do a state assignment by listing all state adjacencies implied by the guidelines, satisfying as many of these as possible.

Example   Applying the Guidelines Consider the state transition table of Figure 9.13 for the 3-bit sequence detector. The corresponding state diagram is shown in Figure 9.27. Let's apply the state assignment guidelines to this state diagram.

The highest-priority constraint for adjacent assignment applies to states that share a common next state on the same input. In this case, states S_3' and S_4' both have S_0 as their next state. No other states share a common next state.

The medium-priority assignment is for states that have a common ancestor state. Again, S_3' and S_4' are the only states that fit this description.

The lowest-priority assignments are made for states that have the same output behavior for a given input. S_0, S_1', and S_3' all output 0 when the input is 0. Similarly, S_0, S_1', S_3', and S_4' output 0 when the input is 1.

The constraints on the assignments can be summarized as follows:

Highest priority: (S_3', S_4');

Medium priority: (S_3', S_4');

Lowest priority: 0/0: (S_0, S_1', S_3');
        1/0: (S_0, S_1', S_3', S_4');

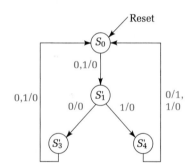

Figure 9.27 Reduced state diagram for 3-bit sequence detector.

Since the finite state machine has four states, we can make the assignment onto two state bits. In general, it is a good idea to assign the reset state to state map square 0. Figure 9.28 shows two possible assignments. Both assign S_0 to 00 and place S_3' and S_4' adjacent to each other.

Example   Applying the Guidelines in a More Complicated Case As another example, let's consider the more complicated state diagram of

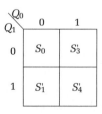

(a) First state assignment

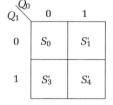

(b) Second state assignment

Figure 9.28 Two possible state assignments.

the 4-bit string recognizer of Figure 9.7. Applying the guidelines yields the following set of assignment constraints:

Highest priority: (S_3', S_4'), (S_7', S_{10}');

Medium priority: (S_1, S_2), $2 \times (S_3', S_4')$, (S_7', S_{10}');

Lowest priority: 0/0: $(S_0, S_1, S_2, S_3', S_4', S_7')$;
1/0: $(S_0, S_1, S_2, S_3', S_4', S_7', S_{10}')$;

Figure 9.29 shows two alternative assignments that meet most of these constraints. We start with Figure 9.29(a) and first assign the reset state to the encoding for 0. Since (S_3', S_4') is both a high-priority and medium-priority adjacency, we make their assignments next. S_3' is assigned 011 and S_4' is assigned 111.

We assign (S_7', S_{10}') next because this pair also appears in the high- and medium-priority lists. We assign them the encodings 010 and 110, respectively. Besides giving them adjacent assignments, this places S_7 near S_0, S_3', and S_4', which satisfies some of the lower-priority adjacencies.

The final adjacency is (S_1, S_2). We give them the assignments 001 and 101. This satisfies a medium-priority placement as well as the lowest-priority placements.

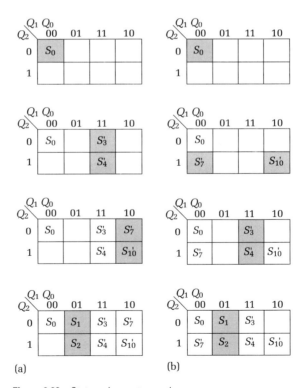

(a) (b)

Figure 9.29 State assignment example.

The second assignment is shown in Figure 9.29(b). We arrived at it by a similar line of reasoning, except that we assigned S_7' and S_{10}' the states 100 and 110. The second assignment does about as good a job as the first, satisfying all of the high- and medium-priority guidelines, as well as most of the lowest-priority ones.

Applying the Guidelines: Why They Work   The state assignment guidelines attempt to maximize the adjacent groupings of 1's in the next-state and output functions. Let P_2, P_1, and P_0 be the next-state functions, expressed in terms of the current state Q_2, Q_1, Q_0 and the input X. To see how effective the guidelines were, let's compare the assignment of Figure 9.29(a) with a more naive assignment: $S_0 = 000$, $S_1 = 001$, $S_2 = 010$, $S_3' = 011$, $S_4' = 100$, $S_7' = 101$, $S_{10}' = 110$.

Figure 9.30 compares the encoded next-state tables and K-maps for the two encodings. The 1's are nicely clustered in the next state K-maps for the assignment derived from the guidelines. We can implement P_2 with three product terms and P_1 and P_2 with one each.

In the second assignment, the 1's are spread throughout the K-maps, since we made the assignment with no attempt to cluster the 1's usefully. In this implementation, the next-state functions P_2, P_1, and P_0 each require three product terms, with a considerably larger number of literals overall.

9.3.3   One Hot Encodings

So far, our goal has been *dense* encodings: state encodings in as few bits as possible. An alternative approach introduces additional flip-flops, in the hope of reducing the next-state and output logic.

One form of this method is called *one hot encoding*. A machine with n states is encoded using exactly n flip-flops. Each state is represented by an n-bit binary code in which exactly 1 bit is asserted. This is the origin of the term "one hot."

Let's consider the traffic light finite state machine described earlier in this section. The following would be a possible one hot encoding of the machine's state:

$HG = 0001$

$HY = 0010$

$FG = 0100$

$FY = 1000$

The state is encoded in four flip-flops rather than two, and only 1 bit is asserted in each of the states.

Figure 9.31 shows the *espresso* inputs and outputs for this encoding. It yields eight product terms, as good as the result of Figure 9.23. However, the logic is considerably more complex:

Current State	Next State $X=0$	$X=1$
(S_0) 000	001	101
(S_1) 001	011	111
(S_2) 101	111	011
(S_3') 011	010	010
(S_4') 111	010	110
(S_7') 010	000	000
(S'_{10}) 110	000	000

P_2

Q_0X \ Q_2Q_1	00	01	11	10
00	0	0	0	X
01	1	0	0	X
11	1	0	1	0
10	0	0	0	1

P_1

Q_0X \ Q_2Q_1	00	01	11	10
00	0	0	0	X
01	0	0	0	X
11	1	1	1	1
10	1	1	1	1

P_0

Q_0X \ Q_2Q_1	00	01	11	10
00	1	0	0	X
01	1	0	0	X
11	1	0	0	1
10	1	0	0	1

Current State	Next State $X=0$	$X=1$
(S_0) 000	001	010
(S_1) 001	011	100
(S_2) 010	100	011
(S_3') 011	101	101
(S_4') 100	101	110
(S_7') 101	000	000
(S'_{10}) 110	000	000

P_2

Q_0X \ Q_2Q_1	00	01	11	10
00	0	1	0	1
01	0	0	0	1
11	1	1	X	0
10	0	1	X	0

P_1

Q_0X \ Q_2Q_1	00	01	11	10
00	0	0	0	0
01	1	1	0	1
11	0	0	X	0
10	1	0	X	0

P_0

Q_0X \ Q_2Q_1	00	01	11	10
00	1	0	0	1
01	0	1	0	0
11	0	1	X	0
10	1	1	X	0

Figure 9.30 State assignment example.

$$P_3 = \overline{C} \bullet \overline{Q}_3 \bullet Q_2 \bullet \overline{Q}_1 \bullet \overline{Q}_0 + TL \bullet \overline{Q}_3 \bullet Q_2 \bullet \overline{Q}_1 \bullet \overline{Q}_0$$
$$+ \overline{TS} \bullet \overline{Q}_3 \bullet \overline{Q}_2 \bullet Q_1 \bullet \overline{Q}_0$$

$$P_2 = C \bullet \overline{TL} \bullet \overline{Q}_3 \bullet Q_2 \bullet \overline{Q}_1 \bullet \overline{Q}_0 + TS \bullet \overline{Q}_3 \bullet \overline{Q}_2 \bullet Q_1 \bullet \overline{Q}_0$$

$$P_1 = C \bullet TL \bullet \overline{Q}_3 \bullet \overline{Q}_2 \bullet \overline{Q}_1 \bullet Q_0 + \overline{TS} \bullet \overline{Q}_3 \bullet \overline{Q}_2 \bullet Q_1 \bullet \overline{Q}_0$$

$$P_0 = \overline{TL} \bullet \overline{Q}_3 \bullet \overline{Q}_2 \bullet \overline{Q}_1 \bullet Q_0 + \overline{C} \bullet \overline{Q}_3 \bullet Q_2 \bullet \overline{Q}_1 \bullet Q_0$$
$$+ TS \bullet \overline{Q}_3 \bullet \overline{Q}_2 \bullet \overline{Q}_1 \bullet \overline{Q}_0$$

$$ST = C \bullet TL \bullet \overline{Q}_3 \bullet \overline{Q}_2 \bullet \overline{Q}_1 \bullet Q_0 + \overline{C} \bullet \overline{Q}_3 \bullet Q_2 \bullet \overline{Q}_1 \bullet \overline{Q}_0$$
$$+ TL \bullet \overline{Q}_3 \bullet Q_2 \bullet \overline{Q}_1 \bullet \overline{Q}_0 + TS \bullet \overline{Q}_3 \bullet \overline{Q}_2 \bullet Q_1 \bullet \overline{Q}_0$$

$$H_1 = C \bullet TL \bullet Q_3 \bullet Q_2 \bullet Q_1 \bullet Q_0 + C \bullet Q_3 \bullet Q_2 \bullet Q_1 \bullet Q_0$$
$$+ TL \bullet \overline{Q}_3 \bullet Q_2 \bullet \overline{Q}_1 \bullet \overline{Q}_0 + \overline{TS} \bullet \overline{Q}_3 \bullet \overline{Q}_2 \bullet Q_1 \bullet \overline{Q}_0$$
$$+ TS \bullet \overline{Q}_3 \bullet \overline{Q}_2 \bullet Q_1 \bullet \overline{Q}_0$$

$$H_0 = \overline{TS} \bullet \overline{Q}_3 \bullet \overline{Q}_2 \bullet Q_1 \bullet \overline{Q}_0 + TS \bullet \overline{Q}_3 \bullet \overline{Q}_2 \bullet Q_1 \bullet \overline{Q}_0$$

$$F_1 = C \bullet TL \bullet \overline{Q}_3 \bullet \overline{Q}_2 \bullet \overline{Q}_1 \bullet Q_0 + \overline{TL} \bullet \overline{Q}_3 \bullet Q_2 \bullet \overline{Q}_1 \bullet \overline{Q}_0$$
$$+ \overline{C} \bullet \overline{Q}_3 \bullet Q_2 \bullet \overline{Q}_1 \bullet Q_0 + \overline{TS} \bullet \overline{Q}_3 \bullet \overline{Q}_2 \bullet Q_1 \bullet \overline{Q}_0$$
$$+ TS \bullet \overline{Q}_3 \bullet \overline{Q}_2 \bullet Q_1 \bullet \overline{Q}_0$$

$$F_0 = \overline{TS} \bullet \overline{Q}_3 \bullet \overline{Q}_2 \bullet Q_1 \bullet \overline{Q}_0 + TS \bullet \overline{Q}_3 \bullet \overline{Q}_2 \bullet Q_1 \bullet \overline{Q}_0$$

```
.i 7
.o 9
.ilb c tl ts q3 q2 q1 q0
.ob p3 p2 p1 p0 st h1 h0 f1 f0
.p 10
0-- 0001 0001 00010
-0- 0001 0001 00010
11- 0001 0010 10010
--0 0010 0010 00110
--1 0010 0100 10110
10- 0100 0100 01000
0-- 0100 1000 11000
-1- 0100 1000 11000
--0 0010 1000 01001
--1 0010 0001 11001
.e
```

(a) *Espresso* input

```
.i 7
.o 9
.ilb c tl ts q3 q2 q1 q0
.ob p3 p2 p1 p0 st h1 h0 f1 f0
.p 8
10-0100 010001000
11-0001 001010010
-0-0001 000100010
0--0001 000100010
0--0100 100011000
-1-0100 100011000
--00010 101001111
--10010 010111111
.e
```

(b) *Espresso* output

Figure 9.31 *Espresso* input/output for the one hot encoding of the traffic light state machine.

The product terms are all five and six variables, with two to five terms per output. This is rather complex for discrete logic but would not cause problems for a PLA-based design.

9.3.4 Computer Tools: *Nova, Mustang, Jedi**

The previous subsections described various heuristic approaches for obtaining a good state encoding. None are guaranteed to obtain the best result. In this section, we examine three programs for computer-generated state assignments.

---

*This subsection requires access to software developed at the University of California, Berkeley. If you do not have access to it, you may want to skim this section, or skip it altogether.

The state assignment guidelines of Section 9.3.2 place related states together in the state map, thereby clustering the 1's in those functions. However, we cannot evaluate an assignment fully without actually minimizing the functions. When it comes to hand techniques, this means the K-map method. If we have to use K-maps to minimize the functions for each possible assignment, we are not likely to examine very many of them!

Tools are available that follow the basic kinds of heuristics described above. Unlike hand methods, they are not limited to six state bits, they can generate many alternative assignments rapidly, and they can evaluate the derived assignments by invoking minimization tools like *espresso* or *misII* automatically. Three tools that provide this function are *nova*, for two-level logic implementations, and *mustang* and *jedi*, for multilevel logic. *Jedi* is somewhat more general; it can be used for general-purpose symbolic encodings, such as outputs, as well as next states. We examine each of these programs in the following subsections.

***Nova:* State Assignment for Two-Level Implementation**   The inputs to *nova* are similar to the truth table format already described for *espresso*. The input file consists of the truth table entries for the finite state machine description. The latter are of the form:

inputs   current_state   next_state   outputs

Figure 9.32 shows the format for our example traffic light controller. The states are symbolic; the inputs and outputs are binary encoded. It is important to separate each section with a space. We interpret the first line as "if input 1 (car sensor) is unasserted and the state is HG (highway green), then the next state is HG (highway green) and the outputs are 00010 ($ST = 0$, $H_1:H_0 = 00$ "green," $F_1:F_0 = 10$ "red")."

Figure 9.33 gives the abbreviated *nova* output associated with the state machine of Figure 9.32, assuming you have requested a "greedy" state assignment. The "codes" section shows the state assignment: HG = 00, HY = 11, FG = 01, and FY = 10. The *espresso* truth table is included in the output, indicating that it takes nine product terms to implement the state machine.

Intuitively, the state assignment algorithms used by *nova* are much like the assignment guidelines of Section 9.3.2. States that are mapped by some input into the same next state and that assert the same output are partitioned into groups. In the terminology of state assignment, these are called *input constraints*. *Nova* attempts to assign adjacent encodings within the smallest Boolean cube to states in the same group. A related concept is *output constraints*. States that are next states of a common predecessor state are given adjacent assignments.

```
0--  HG  HG  00010
-0-  HG  HG  00010
11-  HG  HY  10010
--0  HY  HY  00110
--1  HY  FG  10110
10-  FG  FG  01000
0--  FG  FY  11000
-1-  FG  FY  11000
--0  FY  FY  01001
--1  FY  HG  11001
```

Figure 9.32   *Nova* inputs for the traffic light controller.

```
# .start_codes
.code HG 00
.code HY 11
.code FG 01
.code FY 10
# .end_codes
#
BLIF Representation
.i 5
.o 7
.p 9
10-01 0101000
11-00 1110000
--01- 1000000
--11- 0010000
---00 0000010
---10 0001001
0--01 1011000
-1-01 1011000
---11 0100110
.e
#
```

Figure 9.33   Abbreviated *Nova* outputs.

Nova implements a wide range of state-encoding strategies, any of which you can select when you invoke the program:

■ *Greedy:* makes its state assignment based on satisfying as many of the input constraints as it can. When using a greedy approach, *nova* looks only at new assignments that strictly improve on those it has already examined.

■ *Hybrid:* also makes its state assignment based on satisfying the input constraints. However, *nova* will examine some assignments that start off looking worse, but may eventually yield a better assignment. This yields better assignments than the greedy strategy.

■ *I/O Hybrid:* similar to hybrid, except it tries to satisfy input and output constraints. Its results are usually better than hybrid's.

■ *Exact:* obtains the best encoding that satisfies the input constraints. Since the output constraints are not considered, this is still not the best possible encoding.

■ *Input Annealing:* similar to hybrid, except it uses a more sophisticated method for improving the state assignment.

■ *One-Hot:* uses a one-hot encoding. This rarely yields a minimum product term assignment, but it may dramatically reduce the complexity of the product terms (in other words, the literal count may be greatly reduced).

■ *Random:* uses a randomly generated encoding. *Nova* will generate the specified number of random assignments. It will report on the best assignment it has found (the one requiring the smallest number of product terms).

For the traffic light controller, the various encoding algorithms yield the following assignments:

	HG	HY	FG	FY	Number of product terms	PLA Area
Greedy:	00	11	01	10	9	153
Hybrid:	00	11	10	01	9	153
Exact:	11	10	01	00	10	170
IO Hybrid:	00	01	11	10	9	153
I Annealing:	01	10	11	10	9	153
Random:	11	00	01	10	9	153

None of the assignments found by *nova* match the eight-product-term encoding we found in Figure 9.23. But we shouldn't despair just because the tool did not find the best possible assignment. The advantage of the

```
-  S0  S1   0
0  S1  S3   0
1  S1  S4   0
-  S3  S0   0
0  S4  S0   1
1  S4  S0   0
```

Figure 9.34 *Nova* inputs for the 3-bit string recognizer.

```
0  S0   S1   0
1  S0   S2   0
0  S1   S3   0
1  S1   S4   0
0  S2   S4   0
1  S2   S3   0
-  S3   S7   0
0  S4   S7   0
1  S4   S10  0
-  S7   S0   0
0  S10  S0   1
1  S10  S0   0
```

Figure 9.35 *Nova* inputs for the 4-bit string recognizer.

computer-based tool is that it finds reasonable solutions rapidly. Thus you can examine a variety of encodings and choose the one that best reduces your implementation task.

As another example, let's consider the 3-bit sequence recognizer of Figure 9.27. Its *nova* input file is shown in Figure 9.34. The state assignments found by *nova* are the following:

	S_0	S_1'	S_3'	S_4'	Number of product terms	PLA Area
Greedy:	00	01	11	10	4	36
Hybrid:	00	01	10	11	4	36
Exact:	00	01	10	11	4	36
IO Hybrid:	00	10	01	11	4	36
I Annealing:	00	01	11	10	4	36
Random:	00	11	10	01	4	36

Several of the assignments correspond to the ones found in Figure 9.28(a) and (b).

The last example is the 4-bit recognizer of Figure 9.7. The *nova* input file is given in Figure 9.35. *Nova* produced the following assignments:

	S_0	S_1	S_2	S_3'	S_4'	S_7'	S_{10}'	Number of product terms
Greedy:	100	110	010	011	111	000	001	7
Hybrid:	101	110	111	001	011	000	010	7
Exact:	101	110	111	001	011	000	010	7
IO Hybrid:	110	011	001	100	101	000	010	7
I Annealing:	100	101	001	111	110	000	010	6
Random:	011	100	101	110	111	000	001	7

None of these assignments match those derived in Figure 9.29, since S_0 has not been assigned 000. Figure 9.36 shows that the adjacencies that were highly desirable based on the guidelines—that is, S_3' adjacent to S_4', S_7' adjacent to S_{10}', and S_1 adjacent to S_2—are satisfied by the input annealing assignment.

Mustang The minimum number of product terms is a good criterion if you are going to implement the logic in a two-level form, such as a PLA. This is what *nova* uses. Literal count is better if you plan to implement the logic in multiple levels. *Mustang* takes this approach. Its optimization criterion is to minimize the number of literals in the multi-level factored form of the next-state and output functions.

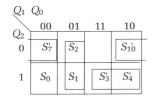

Figure 9.36 State map for the best *Nova* assignment of the finite state machine of Figure 9.7.

```
.i 3
.o 5
.s 2
0--    HG HG  00010
-0-    HG HG  00010
11-    HG HY  10010
--0    HY HY  00110
--1    HY FG  10110
10-    FG FG  01000
0--    FG FY  11000
-1-    FG FY  11000
--0    FY FY  01001
--1    FY HG  11001
```

Figure 9.37 *Mustang* input file for traffic light controller.

Mustang has an input format similar to that of *nova*. The only difference is that the number of inputs, outputs, and state bits must be explicitly declared with .i, .o, and .s directives. For example, the traffic light input file is shown in Figure 9.37.

Mustang implements several alternative strategies for state assignment, specified by the user on the command line. These include:

■ *Random:* chooses a random state encoding.

■ *Sequential:* assigns the states binary codes in a sequential order.

■ *One-Hot:* makes a one-hot state assignment.

■ *Fan-in:* works on the input and fan-in of each state. Next states that are produced by the same inputs from similar sets of present states are given adjacent state assignments. The assignment is chosen to maximize the common subexpressions in the next-state function. This is much like the high-priority assignment guideline of Section 9.3.2.

■ *Fan-out:* works on the output and fan-out of each state, without regard to inputs. Present states with the same outputs that produce similar sets of next states are given adjacent state assignments. Again, this maximizes the common subexpressions in the output and next-state functions. This approach works well for finite state machines with many outputs but few inputs. It is much like the medium- and low-priority assignment guidelines from Section 9.3.2.

Mustang derives the following assignments for the traffic light state machine:

	HG	HY	FG	FY	Number of product terms
Random:	01	10	11	00	9
Sequential:	01	10	11	00	9
Fan-in:	00	01	10	11	8
Fan-out:	10	11	00	01	8

The eight term encodings are actually better than any of those found by *nova*. To determine the multilevel implementation, you must invoke *misII* on the *espresso* file created by *mustang*.

For example, the *misII* output for the fan-in encoding of the traffic light controller is the following:

$$P_1 = H_0 \bullet TS + F_0 \bullet \overline{TS} + F_0 \bullet Q_1$$

$$P_0 = P_1 \bullet \overline{C} \bullet Q_1 + C \bullet TL \bullet \overline{Q_0} + \overline{TS} \bullet Q_0$$

$$ST = P_0 \bullet \overline{Q_0} + \overline{P_0} \bullet Q_0$$

$$H_1 = F_0 + Q_1 \bullet \overline{Q}_0$$

$$H_0 = \overline{Q}_1 \bullet Q_0$$

$$F_1 = \overline{Q}_1$$

$$F_0 = \overline{H}_0 \bullet Q_0$$

For comparison with *nova*, *mustang* obtains the following encodings for the 3-bit string recognizer:

	S_0	S_1	S_3'	S_4'	Number of product terms
Random:	01	10	11	00	5
Sequential:	01	10	11	00	5
Fan-in:	10	11	00	01	4
Fan-out:	10	11	00	01	4

The number of product terms to implement an encoding is comparable to the number needed for the *nova* encodings. However, don't forget that the goal of *mustang* is to reduce literal count rather than product terms.

As a final example, let's look at the *mustang* encodings for the 4-bit recognizer:

	S_0	S_1	S_2	S_3'	S_4'	S_7'	S_{10}'	Number of product terms
Random:	101	010	011	110	111	001	000	8
Sequential:	001	010	011	100	101	110	111	8
Fan-in:	100	010	011	000	001	101	110	8
Fan-out:	110	010	011	100	101	000	001	6

It is interesting that in all three cases, *mustang* obtained an encoding that is as good as any of the best encodings found by *nova*.

Jedi   The final encoding program we shall examine is *jedi*. It is similar to *mustang* in that its goal is to obtain a good encoding for a multilevel implementation. It is more powerful than *mustang* because it can solve *general encoding problems*: *jedi* can find good encodings for the outputs as well as the states.

Like the other programs, *jedi* implements several alternative encoding strategies that can be selected on the command line. Besides random, one hot, and straightforward, the program supports input dominant, output dominant, modified output dominant, and input/output combination algorithms.

The *jedi* input format is similar to, but slightly different from, the *mustang* input format. We can illustrate this best with an example. Figure 9.38 shows the *jedi* input file for the traffic light controller. The present state and next states each count as a single input, even though they may be encoded by several bits. The .enum States line tells *jedi* that there are four states and that they should be encoded in 2 bits and then gives the state names. The .enum Colors line tells *jedi* that there are three output colors and that these should also be encoded in 2 bits. You should think of these as enumerated types. The .itype and .otype lines define the types of the inputs and outputs, respectively.

The encodings obtained from *jedi* for the traffic light controller are:

	HG	HY	FG	FY	Grn	Yel	Red	Number of product terms
Input:	00	10	11	01	11	01	00	9
Output:	00	01	11	10	10	11	01	9
Combination:	00	10	11	01	10	00	01	9
Output′:	01	00	10	11	10	00	01	10

For the 3-bit string recognizer, the state assignments are:

	S_0	S_1	S_3'	S_4'	Number of product terms
Input:	01	00	11	10	4
Output:	11	01	00	10	4
Combination:	10	00	11	01	4
Output′:	11	01	00	10	4

Finally, for the 4-bit string recognizer, they are:

	S_0	S_1	S_2	S_3'	S_4'	S_7'	S_{10}'	Number of product terms
Input:	111	101	100	010	110	011	001	7
Output:	101	110	100	010	000	111	011	7
Combination:	100	011	111	110	010	000	101	7
Output′:	001	100	101	010	011	000	111	6

Let's look at one head-to-head comparison between *mustang* and *jedi*. We will use the *mustang* encoding in which $HG = 00$, $HY = 01$, $FG = 10$, $FY = 11$, Green = 00, Yellow = 01, and Red = 10 and the *jedi* encoding in which $HG = 00$, $HY = 01$, $FG = 11$, $FY = 10$, Green = 10, Yellow = 11, and Red = 01. The first encoding used eight product terms in a two-level implementation; the second used nine.

```
.i 4
.o 4
.enum States 4 2 HG HY FG FY
.enum Colors 3 2 GREEN RED YELLOW
.itype Boolean Boolean Boolean States
.otype States Boolean Colors Colors
0 - - HG HG 0 GREEN RED
- 0 - HG HG 0 GREEN RED
1 1 - HG HY 1 GREEN RED
- - 0 HY HY 0 YELLOW RED
- - 1 HY FG 1 YELLOW RED
1 0 - FG FG 0 RED GREEN
0 - - FG FY 1 RED GREEN
- 1 - FG FY 1 RED GREEN
- - 0 FY FY 0 RED YELLOW
- - 1 FY HG 1 RED YELLOW
```

Figure 9.38   *Jedi* input file.

The multilevel implementation for the *mustang* assignment was already shown in the *mustang* section. It requires 26 literals. The *jedi* multilevel implementation is

$$P_1 = H_1 \bullet C \bullet TL + H_0 + F_1 \bullet C \bullet TL$$

$$P_0 = H_0 \bullet TS + F_1 + F_0 \bullet \overline{TS}$$

$$ST = P_1 \bullet H_1 + \overline{P}_1 \bullet F_1 + \overline{H}_1 \bullet \overline{F}_0 \bullet TS$$

$$H_1 = \overline{Q}_1 \bullet \overline{Q}_0$$

$$H_0 = Q_1 \bullet \overline{Q}_0$$

$$F_1 = \overline{H}_0 \bullet Q_1$$

$$F_0 = \overline{H}_1 \bullet \overline{Q}_1$$

It has 27 literals. In terms of straight literal count, the *mustang* encoding is better. If we examine the wiring complexity, the *mustang* encoding is also slightly better.

9.4   Choice of Flip-Flops

After state reduction and state assignment, the next step in the design process is to choose flip-flop types for the state registers. The issues are identical to those in the counter case studies of Chapter 7.

Usually, we have to decide whether to use *J-K* flip-flops or *D* flip-flops. *J-K* devices tend to reduce the gate count but increase the number of connections. *D* flip-flops simplify the implementation process and are well suited for VLSI implementations, where connections are at more of a premium than gates. Because the CAD tools mentioned in the previous section were developed to assist in VLSI implementations, it is not surprising that they implicitly assume D flip-flops as the targets of the assignment. Their best assignment may not lead to the minimum logic for a J-K flip-flop implementation.

The following procedure completes the finite state machine implementation, given a particular choice of flip-flops:

1. Given the state assignments, derive the next-state maps from the state transition table.

2. Remap the next-state maps given the excitation tables for the flip-flops chosen to implement the state bits.

3. Minimize the remapped next-state function.

9.4.1   Flip-Flop Choice for the Four-Bit Sequence Detector

Let's illustrate the procedure with the 4-bit sequence detector, using the state assignment of Figure 9.39, the encoded state transition table. Each state has been replaced by its binary encoding given by the state assignment. Figure 9.40 is the encoded next-state map, organized according to the standard binary sequence and showing the don't cares.

D Implementation   To obtain the direct form for determining the state machine implementation with D flip-flops, represent the encoded next-state functions as K-maps. Figure 9.41 contains the four-variable K-maps for the next-state functions Q_2^+, Q_1^+, Q_0^+, given the current state Q_2, Q_1, Q_0 and the input I. The reduced equations that describe the inputs to the D flip-flops are

$$D_{Q2+} = \overline{Q}_2 \bullet Q_1 + Q_0$$

$$D_{Q1+} = Q_1 \bullet Q_0 \bullet I + \overline{Q}_2 \bullet \overline{Q}_0 \bullet \overline{I} + \overline{Q}_2 \bullet \overline{Q}_1$$

$$D_{Q0+} = \overline{Q}_2 \bullet Q_1 + \overline{Q}_2 \bullet \overline{I}$$

Present State	Next State $I=0$	$I=1$	Output $I=0$	$I=1$
000 (S_0)	011 (S_1)	010 (S_2)	0	0
011 (S_1)	101 (S_3')	111 (S_4')	0	0
010 (S_2)	111 (S_4')	101 (S_3')	0	0
101 (S_3')	100	100 (S_7')	0	0
111 (S_4')	(S_7')	110	0	0
100 (S_7')	100	(S_{10}')	0	0
110 (S_{10}')	(S_7')	000	1	0

Figure 9.39   Encoded state transition table for 4-bit sequence detector.

Present State	Next State $I=0$	$I=1$
000	011	010
001	XXX	XXX
010	111	101
011	101	111
100	000	000
101	100	100
110	000	000
111	100	110

Figure 9.40   Encoded next-state map.

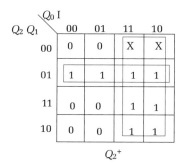

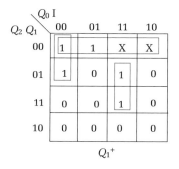

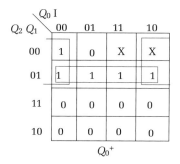

Figure 9.41   Next-state K-maps.

There are six unique product terms and 15 literals. In terms of discrete gates, the implementation requires 3 three-input gates, 5 two-input gates, and 4 inverters, a total of 12 gates.

J-K Implementation   For the J-K implementation, we begin by remapping the inputs based on the J-K excitation tables. Figure 9.42 gives the remapped next-state table, and Figure 9.43 shows the K-maps. The J-K logic equations become

$$J_{Q2+} = Q_1 \qquad\qquad K_{Q2+} = \overline{Q_0}$$

$$J_{Q1+} = \overline{Q_2} \qquad\qquad K_{Q1+} = \overline{Q_0} \bullet I + Q_0 \bullet \overline{I} + Q_2 \bullet \overline{Q_0}$$

$$J_{Q0+} = \overline{Q_2} \bullet Q_1 + \overline{Q_2} \bullet \overline{I} \qquad K_{Q0+} = Q_2$$

This implementation requires nine unique terms and 14 literals. The gate count is 1 three-input gate, 6 two-input gates, and 3 inverters, a total of 10 gates. This is slightly fewer than the D flip-flop implementation. However, when you use structured logic such as a PLA to implement the functions, the option with fewer product terms is better. In this case, it would be the D implementation.

9.5   Finite State Machine Partitioning

In the preceding sections, we described the design process for a single monolithic finite state machine. The approach is reasonable for many strategies for implementing a finite state machine, such as using discrete gates.

However, when using some forms of programmable logic, we may need to partition the machine. In some cases we cannot implement a complex finite state machine with a single programmable logic component. The machine might require too many inputs or outputs, or the number of terms to describe the next-state or output functions might be too large, even after state reduction and Boolean minimization.

			Remapped Next State			
	Next State		J	K	J	K
Present State	$I=0$	$I=1$	$I=0$	$I=0$	$I=1$	$I=1$
000	011	010	011	XXX	010	XXX
001	XXX	XXX	XXX	XXX	XXX	XXX
010	111	101	1X1	X0X	1X1	X1X
011	101	111	1XX	X10	1XX	X00
100	000	000	X00	1XX	X00	1XX
101	100	100	X0X	0X1	X0X	0X1
110	000	000	XX0	11X	XX0	11X
111	100	110	XXX	011	XXX	001

Figure 9.42   Remapped next-state table for J-K flip-flops.

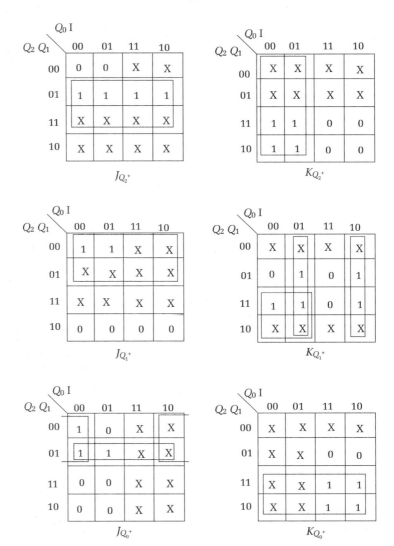

Figure 9.43   Remapped K-maps.

Example 1   FSM Partitioning   To illustrate the value of state machine partitioning, suppose we have a finite state machine with 20 inputs and 10 outputs (including next-state outputs). But we only have programmable logic components with 15 inputs and 5 outputs. We cannot implement this finite state machine with a single component.

Suppose we can arrange the outputs in two sets of five, each of which can be computed from different 15-element subsets of the original 20 inputs. Then we could partition the output functions among two programmable logic components, as shown in Figure 9.44. Of course, it isn't

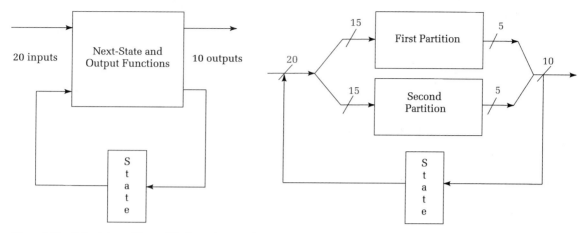

Figure 9.44 Finite state machine partitioning on inputs and outputs.

always possible to find such a fortuitous partitioning. For example, every output might be a function of 16 inputs.

If we cannot reduce the complexity of the finite state machine by simple input/output partitioning, another way to "make it fit" is to partition the single finite state machine into smaller, less complex, communicating finite state machines. We examine this approach in the next subsection.

9.5.1 Finite State Machine Partitioning by Introducing Idle States

Partitioning the finite state machine makes sense if the next-state logic is too complex to implement with the programmable logic components at hand. The problem is that PALs provide a fixed number of product terms per output function. We can make a trade-off between the number of flip-flops needed to encode the state and the complexity of these next-state functions. Our idea is to introduce additional "idle" states into the finite state machine in the hope of reducing the number of terms in the next-state functions.

Example 2   FSM Partitioning   For example, Figure 9.45 shows a subset of a state diagram. We have chosen to partition the state diagram into two separate machines, containing states S_1, S_2, S_3 and S_4, S_5, S_6, respectively. The symbols C_i associated with the transitions represent the Boolean conditions under which the transition takes place.

What happens if we partition the state diagram, but a transition must take place between the two pieces? We need to introduce idle states to synchronize the activity between the two finite state machines. In essence, the machine at the left hands control off to the machine at the

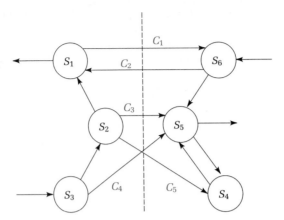

Figure 9.45 State diagram fragment before partitioning.

right when a transition from S_1 to S_6 takes place. The left machine must idle in some new state until it regains control, such as when there is a transition from S_6 back to S_1. In this event, the machine on the right must remain idle until it regains control.

The revised state diagrams are shown in Figure 9.46. We have introduced two new states, S_A and S_B, to synchronize the transitions across the partition boundary. Here is how it works for the state sequence S_1 to S_6 and back to S_1. Initially, the machines are in states S_1 and S_B. If condition C_1 is true, then the left-hand state machine exits S_1 and enters its idle state, S_A. At the same time, the right-hand machine exits S_B and enters S_6.

Suppose that the right-hand machine sequences through some states, eventually returning to S_6. Throughout this time, the left-hand machine

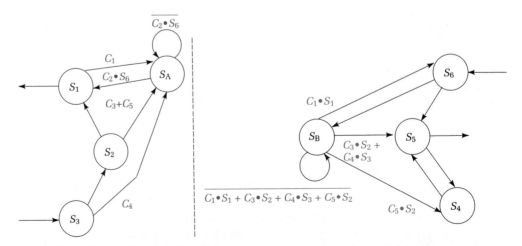

Figure 9.46 State diagram fragment after partitioning.

remains in its idle state. If the right-hand machine is in S_6 and C_2 is true, it next enters its idle state, S_B. At the same instant, the left-hand machine exits S_A, returning to S_1. While the left-hand machine sequences through states, the right-hand machine idles in S_B.

Rules for Partitioning   We are ready to describe the rules for introducing idle states into a partitioned finite state machine. We illustrate each rule with an example from the partitioned state machine of the previous subsection. All the rules involve transitions that cross the partition boundary.

The first rule applies for a state that is the source of a transition that crosses the boundary. The case is shown in Figure 9.47(a). The cross-boundary transition is replaced by a transition to the idle state, labeled by

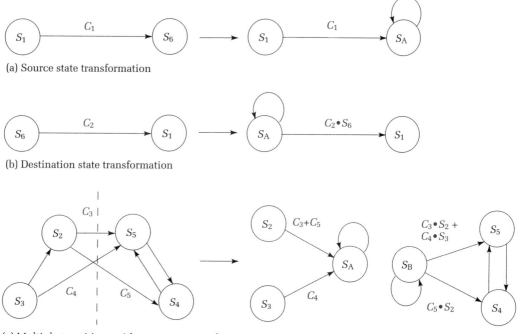

(a) Source state transformation

(b) Destination state transformation

(c) Multiple transitions with same source or destination

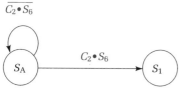

(d) Hold condition for idle state

Figure 9.47   Rules for partitioning.

the same exit condition as the original transition. For example, the S_1-to-S_6 transition is replaced by a transition with the same condition to S_A.

The second rule applies to the destination of a transition that crosses the partition boundary. This is shown in Figure 9.47(b). The transition is replaced with an exit transition from the idle state, labeled with the original condition ANDed with the source state. For example, the transition from S_6 to S_1 is replaced with a transition from S_A. We exit the idle state when both C_2 is true and the right-hand state machine is in S_6. Hence, the transition is labeled with the condition $C_2 \bullet S_6$.

The third rule applies when multiple transitions share the same source or destination. This case is illustrated in Figure 9.47(c). If a state is the source of multiple transitions across the partition boundary, all of these are collapsed into a single transition to the idle state. The exit conditions are ORed together to label the new transition. For example, S_2 has transitions to states S_5 and S_4. These are replaced with a single transition to S_A, labeled $C_3 + C_5$.

If a state is the target of multiple transitions across the boundary, a single transition is added from the idle state to this state. The transition is labeled with the OR of the conditions associated with the individual transitions in the original state machine. This case is illustrated by the transitions from S_2 and S_3 to S_5. These are replaced by a single transition from S_B to S_5, labeled $C_3 \bullet S_2 + C_4 \bullet S_3$.

When all these rules have been applied, the final rule describes the self-loop ("hold") condition for the idle states. Simply form the OR of all of the exit conditions and invert it. This is shown in Figure 9.47(d). Consider the idle state S_A. Its only exit condition is $C_2 \bullet S_6$. So its hold condition is the inverse of this, namely $\overline{C_2 \bullet S_6}$.

Example 3 FSM Partitioning Consider the six-state finite state machine of Figure 9.48(a). The machine implements a simple up/down counter. When the input U is asserted, the machine counts up. When D is asserted, it counts down. Otherwise the machine stays in its current state.

The goal is to partition the machine into two communicating four-state finite state machines. We might need to do this because the underlying logic primitives provide support for two flip-flops within the logic block, as in the Xilinx CLB to be introduced in the next chapter.

Figure 9.48(b) shows the result of the partitioning. States S_0, S_1, and S_2 form the core of one machine and S_3, S_4, and S_6 form the other. We also introduce the two idle states, S_A and S_B.

The machine at the left enters its idle state S_A when it is in S_0 and D is asserted or when it is in S_2 and U is asserted. It exits the idle state when the machine at the right is in S_5 with U asserted or in S_3 with D asserted. Otherwise it stays in its idle state. The machine at the right works similarly.

To see how the machines communicate, let's consider an up-count sequence from S_0 to S_5 and back to S_0. On reset, the machine on the left

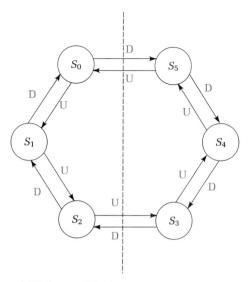

(a) Before partitioning

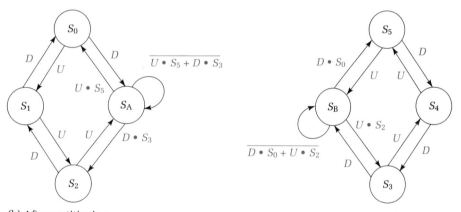

(b) After partitioning

Figure 9.48 Partitioning example.

enters S_0 while the machine on the right enters S_B. With U asserted, the left machine advances from S_0 to S_1 to S_2 to S_A. It will idle in this state until the right machine is ready to exit S_5.

Meanwhile, the right machine holds in S_B until the left machine enters S_2. At the same time that the left machine changes to S_A, the right one exits S_B to S_3. On subsequent clock transitions, it advances from S_3 to S_4 to S_5 to S_B, where it holds. When the right machine changes from S_5 to S_B, the left machine exits S_A to S_0, and the process repeats itself. Down-count sequences work in an analogous way.

Chapter Review

This chapter has concentrated on the optimization of finite state machines. We have emphasized the methods for state reduction, state assignment, choice of flip-flops, and state machine partitioning. For state reduction, we introduced the row matching and implication chart methods. These can be used to identify and eliminate redundant states, thus reducing the number of flip-flops needed to implement a particular finite state machine.

We then examined heuristic methods for state assignment, aimed at reducing the number of product terms or literals needed to implement the next-state and output functions. Since paper-and-pencil methods are not particularly effective, we introduced computer-aided design tools for state assignment that do a much better job in a fraction of the time: *nova*, *mustang*, and *jedi*.

The latter part of the chapter focused on choosing flip-flops for implementing the state registers of the finite state machine. *J-K* flip-flops tend to be most effective in reducing the logic, but they require logical remapping of the next-state functions and more wires than the simpler *D* flip-flops.

Finally, we discussed state machine partitioning methods, in particular partitioning based on inputs and outputs and partitioning by introducing idle states. These techniques are needed when we cannot implement a finite state machine with a single programmable logic component.

In the next chapter, we will examine implementation strategies in more detail. In particular, we will look at the methods for implementing finite state machines based on structured logic methods, such as ROM, programmable logic, and approaches based on MSI components.

Further Reading

The traffic light controller example used extensively in this chapter is borrowed from the famous text by C. Mead and L. Conway, *Introduction to VLSI Systems*, Addison-Wesley, Reading, MA, 1979. C. Roth's book, *Fundamentals of Logic Design*, West Publishing, St. Paul, MN, 1985, has an extensive discussion of state assignment guidelines that formed the basis of our Section 9.3.2. *Modern Logic Design* by D. Green, Addison-Wesley, 1986, has a highly readable, short, direct description of state assignment (pp. 40–43).

Nova's approach to state assignment is described in T. Villa and A. Sangiovanni-Vincentelli's paper "NOVA: State Assignment of Finite State Machines for Optimal Two-Level Logic Implementations," given at the 26th Design Automation Conference, Miami, FL (June 1989). A revised and expanded version of the paper appeared in *IEEE Transactions on Computer-Aided Design* in September 1990 (vol. 9, no. 9, pp. 1326–1334). *Mustang*'s method is described in "MUSTANG: State Assignment of Finite State Machines Targeting Multi-level Logic Implementations," by S. Devadas, B. Ma,

R. Newton, and A. Sangiovanni-Vincentelli, in *IEEE Transactions on Computer-Aided Design*, vol. 7, no. 12 (December 1988). *Jedi*'s method for symbolic assignment is described by Lin and Newton in "Synthesis of Multiple Level Logic from Symbolic High-Level Description Languages," which appeared in the *Proceedings of the VLSI'89 Conference*, Munich, West Germany, in August 1989.

These tools (along with *espresso* and *misII*) are available for a very modest charge from the Industrial Liaison Program Office of the Electrical Engineering and Computer Science Department, University of California, Berkeley. Detailed descriptions of how to invoke the tools, as well as examples of their use, can be found in the most current OCTTOOLS Manual distributed by that office.

Finite state machine partitioning is a topic that waxes and wanes in importance. The original work was done in the late 1950s, became less interesting during the era of VLSI, and is becoming more important again with pervasive use of programmable logic in digital designs. The topic is not well covered by most of today's textbooks. One exception is M. Bolton's book, *Digital System Design with Programmable Logic*, Addison-Wesley, Wokingham, England, 1990, which offers a section on the topic. The partitioning rules introduced in Section 9.5.1 were obtained from an applications note in the *Altera Applications Handbook*, Altera Corporation, Santa Clara, CA, 1988.

Exercises

9.1 *(State Reduction)* Use the implication chart method to reduce the 4-bit string recognizer state diagram of Figure 9.2.

9.2 *(State Reduction)* Given the state diagram in Figure Ex9.2, obtain an equivalent reduced state diagram containing a minimum number of states. You may use row matching or implication charts. Put your final answer in the form of a state diagram rather than a state table. Make it clear which states have been combined.

9.3 *(State Reduction)* Given the state diagram in Figure Ex9.3, determine which states should be combined to determine the reduced state diagram. You may use row matching or implication charts.

9.4 *(State Reduction)* Given the state diagram in Figure Ex9.4, draw the fully reduced state diagram. State succinctly what strings cause the recognizer to output a 1.

9.5 *(State Reduction)* Starting with the state diagram of Figure Ex9.5, use the implication chart method to find the minimum state diagram. Which of the original states are combined?

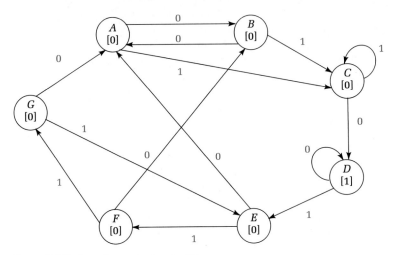

Figure Ex9.2 State diagram for Exercise 9.2.

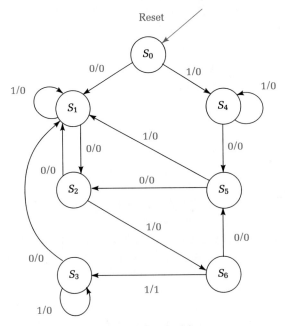

Figure Ex9.3 State diagram for Exercise 9.3.

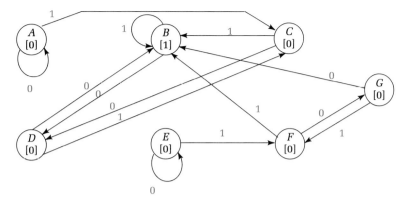

Figure Ex9.4 State diagram for Exercise 9.4.

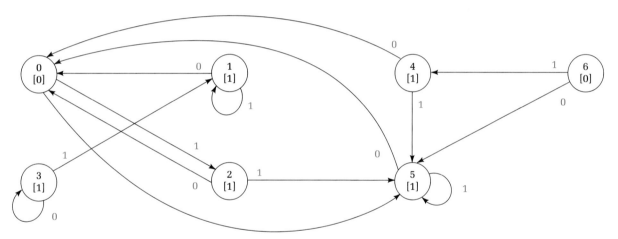

Figure Ex9.5 Original state diagram for Exercise 9.5.

9.6 *(State Assignment)* Given the state diagram in Figure Ex9.6, implement a state assignment using the following techniques:

a. Minimum bit change heuristic

b. State assignment guidelines

Show your assignment in a state map. Explain the rationale for your state assignment.

9.7 *(State Assignment)* Given the state diagram in Figure Ex9.7, select a good state assignment, justifying your answer in terms of the state assignment guidelines.

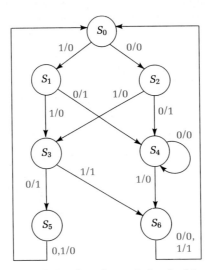

Figure Ex9.6   State diagram for Exercise 9.6.

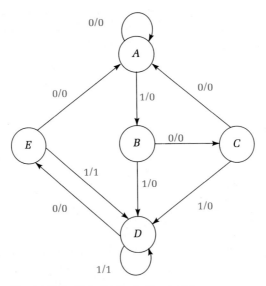

Figure Ex9.7   State diagram for Exercise 9.7.

9.8   *(State Assignment)*   One method for state assignment is to exhaustively enumerate all the possible state assignments. Given the traffic light controller symbolic state table of Figure 9.20, use *espresso* to evaluate all 24 possible 2-bit encodings of the states. Using literal count as your metric, what is the optimal encoding?

Q_3	Q_2	Q_1	Q_0	P_3	P_2	P_1	P_0
0	0	0	0	0	0	0	1
0	0	0	1	0	0	0	0
0	0	1	0	1	0	0	1
0	0	1	1	1	0	1	0
0	1	0	0	0	1	0	1
0	1	0	1	0	1	0	0
0	1	1	0	0	0	0	1
0	1	1	1	0	0	1	0
1	0	0	0	0	0	1	0
1	0	0	1	0	0	0	1
1	0	1	0	1	0	1	0
1	0	1	1	1	0	1	0
1	1	0	0	0	1	1	0
1	1	0	1	0	1	0	1
1	1	1	0	1	1	1	0
1	1	1	1	1	1	1	0

Figure Ex9.10 Next-state functions for Exercises 9.10, 9.11.

9.9   *(State Assignment)*   Using a logic minimization tool like *espresso*, try some random encodings of the traffic light controller that are *nondense*. That is, map the four states into eight (3 bits) or sixteen (4 bits) possible states. How do they compare in terms of literal count to the encodings found in the previous question? How many state assignments are possible in these two nondense encodings? Derive a formula for it if you can.

9.10   *(State Assignment)*   Given the next-state function of the finite state machine shown in Figure Ex9.10, use the implication chart method to find the most reduced state diagram.

9.11   *(State Partitioning)*   Show how to partition the next-state functions of Figure Ex9.10, P_3, P_2, P_1, P_0, into two groups, each of which depends on only three of the four possible current state bits, Q_3, Q_2, Q_1, Q_0.

9.12   *(State Partitioning)*   Given a 3-bit, eight-state Gray code up/down counter (similar to the state machine in Figure 9.48), show how the state diagram can be partitioned into two communicating finite state machines with five states each, including idle states.

9.13   *(State Partitioning)*   Given the state diagram in Figure Ex9.13, partition the state machine into two communicating finite state machines, one containing the states S_0, S_1, S_2, S_3, and the other containing S_4, S_5, S_6.

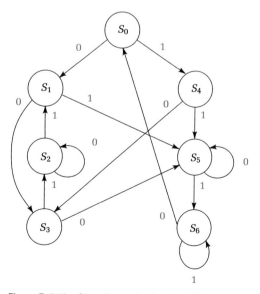

Figure Ex9.13   State diagram for Exercise 9.13.

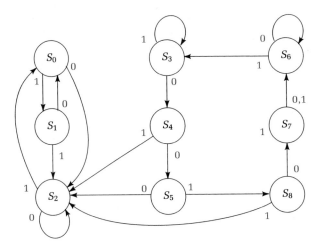

Figure Ex9.14   State diagram for Exercise 9.14.

9.14   *(State Partitioning)*   Figure Ex9.14 gives a state diagram with nine states. Show how to partition the state diagram into three communicating state machines, consisting of the state groups S_0, S_1, S_2; S_3, S_4, S_5; and S_6, S_7, S_8.

9.15   *(State Partitioning)*   The partitioning rules presented in Figure 9.47 describe only the transformations on states and transition conditions. Outputs are not considered.

    a. Describe how the partitioning rules should be modified to handle Mealy outputs. How are the transfers into the idle states affected?

    b. Describe how the partitioning rules should be modified to handle Moore outputs. How might the outputs from the partitioned machines be combined?

9.16   *(Flip-Flop Choice)*   Given the state diagram in Figure Ex9.16 and the state assignment $S_0 = 000$, $S_1 = 001$, $S_2 = 010$, $S_3 = 011$, $S_4 = 100$, and $S_5 = 101$, do the following:

    a. Write the encoded state table, and derive the minimized Boolean equations for implementing the next-state and output functions. Assume the state registers are implemented with D flip-flops.

    b. Repeat the above, but this time using *J-K* flip-flops.

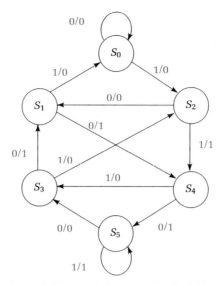

Figure Ex9.16   State diagram for Exercise 9.16.

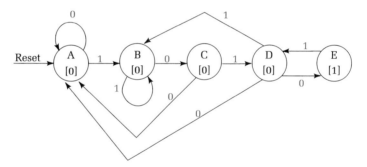

Figure Ex9.17   State diagram for Exercise 9.17.

9.17   *(Flip-Flop Choice)*   Given the state diagram in Figure Ex9.17 and the state assignment $A = 000$, $B = 001$, $C = 011$, $D = 111$, $E = 101$, implement the state machine using a minimum number of gates and *J-K* flip-flops. You may assume that an external RESET signal places the machine in state A (000).

9.18   *(Design Process)*   Implement the following finite state machine description using a minimum number of states and a good state assignment, assuming D flip-flops are used for the state registers. The machine has a single input X, a single output Z, and will assert $Z = 1$ for every input sequence ending in the string 0010 or 100.

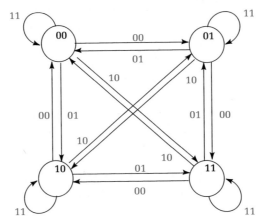

Figure Ex9.19   State diagram for Exercise 9.19.

9.19   *(Design Process)*   Your task is to implement a finite state machine with toggle flip-flops given the following state diagram. The finite state machine is actually a complex Gray code counter. The counter has two control inputs, I_1 and I_0, which determine the next state. The counter's functional specification is as follows. When $I_1 I_0 = 00$, it is a Gray code up-counter. When $I_1 I_0 = 01$, it is a Gray code down-counter. When $I_1 I_0 = 10$, it is a Gray code count by two. Finally, when $I_1 I_0 = 11$, the counter holds it current state. The state diagram is shown in Figure Ex9.19.

   a. Complete a state transition table, including the next-state bits (Q_1 and Q_0) and the needed inputs to the two toggle state flip-flops T_1 and T_0 to obtain that next state.

   b. Produce the four-variable K-maps for the next-state functions. Obtain the minimized two-level implementation.

   c. Draw an implementation schematic, using a minimum number of inverters and two-input NAND, NOR, XOR, and XNOR gates. Assume that complements are not available.

9.20   *(Design Process)*   Design a Mealy finite state machine with input X and output Z. The output Z should be asserted for one clock cycle whenever the sequence ...0111 or ...1000 has been input on X. The patterns may overlap. For example, $X = ...0000111000...$ should generate the output stream $Y = ...0000001001....$

   a. Complete the state diagram for the sequence detector, without concern for state minimization.

   b. Complete the state table for the state diagram derived in part (a).

c. Use row matching or implication charts to minimize the state table derived in part (b).

d. Use the state assignment guidelines to obtain a good state assignment for the reduced state machine of part (c). Justify your method in terms of the high-, medium-, and low-priority assignment guidelines.

e. Implement your encoded, reduced state table using D flip-flops.

f. Implement your encoded, reduced state table using T flip-flops.

g. Implement your encoded, reduced state table using J-K flip-flops.

10 Finite State Machine Implementation

Introduction

Once we have the logic equations for the next-state and output functions, the final step is to choose a method for their implementation. In the previous chapter, we assumed that the implementation method was based on *discrete logic*, such as TTL SSI gates. However, there are many alternative approaches based on higher levels of integration. These exploit MSI parts, such as counters/multiplexers/decoders, or programmable logic components like PALs/PLAs and ROMs. Programmable logic allows us to implement more complex finite state machines with dramatically fewer components.

Especially important is a new class of digital components, called *field-programmable gate arrays* (FPGAs). A gate array is a component that contains a large number of gates whose function and interconnect are initially uncommitted. Field programmable means that you can determine the function and interconnect "in the field" rather than when the parts are manufactured. You can even reprogram these components to revise their function or specify a new function altogether.

Many FPGAs combine flip-flops with discrete gates, making it possible to construct a complete finite state machine on a chip. They combine the economy of discrete gate designs with the dense integration and low parts count of programmable logic. Furthermore, they provide the key hardware technology for rapid prototyping: Given a logic description and the appropriate CAD tools, you can *personalize* or program an FPGA in fractions of a second.

In this chapter, we will examine the techniques for implementing finite state machines using MSI components and programmable logic. In particular, you will learn how to:

■ *Implement state machines with ROMs or PALs/PLAs.* The next-state and output functions are implemented with programmable logic connected to state flip-flops.

■ *Use MSI components to reduce component counts.* The next-state and output functions can be implemented with multiplexers and decoders, and counters can be used as the state register.

■ *Use field-programmable gate arrays.* You will see how to use devices like the Altera electronically programmed logic devices (EPLDs), Actel field-programmable gate arrays (FPGAs), and Xilinx logic cell arrays (LCAs) to implement finite state machines in a minimum number of components.

10.1   Finite State Machine Design with Programmable Logic

In this section, we examine alternative schemes for implementing finite state machines using programmable logic components.

10.1.1   Mapping a State Machine into a ROM Implementation

A ROM or PAL/PLA is a convenient way to implement the combinational logic of a finite state machine. The state is stored in an external register whose outputs are fed back as addresses to the ROM or inputs to the PAL/PLA. Figure 10.1 shows the general block diagram of a synchronous Mealy finite state machine and how this is mapped onto a ROM implementation.

In the figure, the finite state machine has n inputs, k outputs, and m state bits. The ROM address bits are at the left of the ROM block, with the data bits at the right. The $n + m$ input bits and next-state bits form the ROM's address lines. The $k + m$ output and state bits form the ROM's output lines. Thus, we need a ROM of 2^{n+m} words of $k + m$ bits each to implement this finite state machine.

It is easy for you to fill in the ROM contents, given an encoded state transition table organized as a truth table. Each row of the table, identified by the input and current state bits, selects a unique word of the ROM. You store the bit pattern for the next state and outputs in this word.

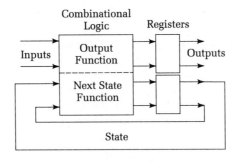

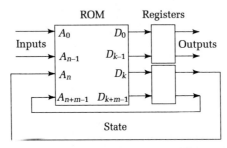

Figure 10.1 ROM implementation of a synchronous Mealy finite state machine.

Effect on the Design Process Using programmable logic for the finite state machine implementation has important implications for state assignment, choice of flip-flop, and state machine partitioning. Unlike discrete logic, which has few external constraints, programmable logic has many. For example, programmable logic devices have a fixed number of pins, preassigned to be inputs or outputs. The internal resources, be they product terms or ROM words, are severely limited. This leads to more complexity when mapping a design onto programmable logic.

It simplifies your design if the next-state and output functions can be made to "fit" within a single component. Unfortunately, this is not always possible for complex finite state machines. You may need the partitioning strategies of Chapter 9 to map the state machine onto as few components as possible.

Since a programmable logic component's outputs are limited, we prefer *D* flip-flops or MSI registers for the state. We rarely use *J-K* flip-flops, with their two wires per bit. This helps to simplify the flip-flop choice.

The choice of programmable logic also affects the state assignment process. Since the complexity of a ROM is determined solely by the number of inputs and outputs, the kind of ROM you need is the same regardless of the state assignment. However, a PAL/PLA, with its limited product terms, requires a good state assignment to keep manageable the number of terms to implement the next state and output logic.

| Application | 10.1.2 | ROM Versus PLA-Based Design |

Let's compare the implementation of the same finite state machine using a ROM and a PLA. The function to be implemented is a BCD-to-Excess-3 code converter. We obtain the Excess-3 code by adding 11_2 to the BCD number, as shown in Figure 10.2. We could easily implement this as a 4-bit combinational logic function. However, our machine will be designed to accept a bit-serial BCD number, starting with the least significant bit. The machine has one input X, the BCD bit, and one output Z, the corresponding Excess-3 bit.

Reduced State Diagram/Symbolic State Transition Table   We will not obtain the state transition table and state diagram here, but simply present them in Figure 10.3 and Figure 10.4. You should verify that the state diagram actually implements the conversion (see Exercise 10.1). By the way, you may wonder why state S_6 has only one transition. Since the input is always a BCD digit, if you get to this state, the next input can never be 1.

State Assignment for ROM-Based Implementation   We assume that the seven states of the finite state machine are encoded in 3 bits. Thus, the ROM-based implementation requires a 16-word ROM (four address bits: input X and three current-state bits, Q_2, Q_1, Q_0) with four data outputs (output Z and three next-state bits, D_2, D_1, D_0). Since the size of the ROM is independent of the state assignment, a straightforward assignment will be used (that is, $S_0 = 000$, $S_1 = 001$, etc.). This leads us to the truth table of Figure 10.5. The inputs at the left form the ROM's address and the outputs at the right are the contents of the ROM word at that address.

BCD	Excess 3 Code
0000	0011
0001	0100
0010	0101
0011	0110
0100	0111
0101	1000
0110	1001
0111	1010
1000	1011
1001	1100

Figure 10.2   BCD and excess-3 codes.

Present State	Next State $X=0$	Next State $X=1$	Output $X=0$	Output $X=1$
S_0	S_1	S_2	1	0
S_1	S_3	S_4	1	0
S_2	S_4	S_4	0	1
S_3	S_5	S_5	0	1
S_4	S_5	S_6	1	0
S_5	S_0	S_0	0	1
S_6	S_0	–	1	–

Figure 10.3   Symbolic state transition table for the code converter.

Figure 10.4   State diagram corresponding to Figure 10.3.

X	Q₂	Q₁	Q₀	Z	D₂	D₁	D₀
0	0	0	0	1	0	0	1
0	0	0	1	1	0	1	1
0	0	1	0	0	1	0	0
0	0	1	1	0	1	0	1
0	1	0	0	1	1	0	1
0	1	0	1	0	0	0	0
0	1	1	0	1	0	0	0
0	1	1	1	X	X	X	X
1	0	0	0	0	0	1	0
1	0	0	1	0	1	0	0
1	0	1	0	1	1	0	0
1	0	1	1	1	1	0	1
1	1	0	0	0	1	1	0
1	1	0	1	1	0	0	0
1	1	1	0	X	X	X	X
1	1	1	1	X	X	X	X

ROM Address / ROM Outputs

Figure 10.5   ROM truth table.

Hardware Implementation for the ROM-Based Design We choose a synchronous Mealy machine implementation, as shown in Figure 10.6. The ROM addresses are at the left of the converter ROM, with the outputs at the right. The 74175 is a TTL component with quad positive edge-triggered D flip-flops with common clear and clock signals.

It is important to understand the timing behavior of our implementation. Figure 10.7 gives the timing waveforms for the converter's output behavior, for the input strings 0000 (0) and 1110 (7). Don't forget that these arrive in the sequence from least significant bit to most significant bit.

Let's start with the first string, 0000. Inputs are sampled on the rising edge, with the output becoming valid just after the edge. After reset, a 0 at the input results in a 1 at the output after the clock edge. At the next rising edge, the input is still 0 and the output stays 1. The output falls and stays low for the next two positive edges. Thus, the string 0000 is converted to 1100, representing a binary three when read backward.

Similarly, the string 1110 generates the output 0101. On the first rising edge, the input is 1 and the output stays 0. On the next positive edge, the input is 1 but the output rises. The input stays 1 for the third positive edge, but the output goes low. Before the fourth and final edge, the input goes low, causing the output to come high. Thus, a backward seven has been converted to a backward ten.

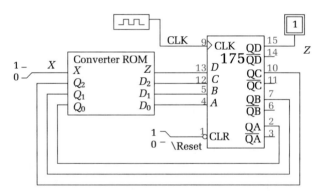

Figure 10.6 Excess 3 synchronous Mealy ROM-based implementation.

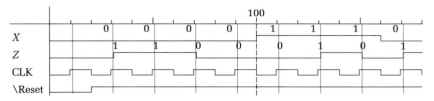

Figure 10.7 Timing behavior of ROM converter.

```
0  S0  S1  1
1  S0  S2  0
0  S1  S3  1
1  S1  S4  0
0  S2  S4  0
1  S2  S4  1
0  S3  S5  0
1  S3  S5  1
0  S4  S5  1
1  S4  S6  0
0  S5  S0  0
1  S5  S0  1
0  S6  S0  1
```

Figure 10.8   *Nova* input file.

```
.i 4
.o 4
.ilb x q2 q1 q0
.ob d2 d1 d0 z
.p 16
0 000 001 1
1 000 011 0
0 001 110 1
1 001 100 0
0 011 100 0
1 011 100 1
0 110 111 0
1 110 111 1
0 100 111 1
1 100 101 0
0 111 000 0
1 111 000 1
0 101 000 1
1 101 --- -
0 010 --- -
1 010 --- -
.e
```

Figure 10.9   *Espresso* input.

```
.i 4
.o 4
.ilb x q2 q1 q0
.ob d2 d1 d0 z
.p 9
0001 0100
10-0 0100
01-0 0100
1-1- 0001
-0-1 1000
0-0- 0001
-1-0 1000
--10 0100
---0 0010
.e
```

Figure 10.10   *Espresso* outputs.

State Assignment for PAL/PLA-Based Implementation   For a PAL/PLA based implementation, we must first perform a state assignment with a tool like *nova*, followed by a two-level minimization with *espresso*. We show the *nova* input file in Figure 10.8.

Suppose that the tool (or a pencil-and-paper method) yields the following state assignment (other assignments might be equally good):

$$S_0 = 000$$
$$S_1 = 001$$
$$S_2 = 011$$
$$S_3 = 110$$
$$S_4 = 100$$
$$S_5 = 111$$
$$S_6 = 101$$

To find the minimized two-level implementation, we next run *espresso*. The *espresso* input file that corresponds to this state assignment is given in Figure 10.9. We have added the don't-care transitions to obtain the best possible reductions. The *espresso* results, shown in Figure 10.10, lead to the following reduced logic:

$$D_2 = \overline{Q}_2 \bullet Q_0 + Q_2 \bullet \overline{Q}_0$$
$$D_1 = \overline{X} \bullet \overline{Q}_2 \bullet \overline{Q}_1 \bullet Q_0 + X \bullet \overline{Q}_2 \bullet \overline{Q}_0 + \overline{X} \bullet Q_2 \bullet \overline{Q}_0 + Q_1 \bullet \overline{Q}_0$$
$$D_0 = \overline{Q}_0$$
$$Z = X \bullet Q_1 + \overline{X} \bullet \overline{Q}_1$$

If we select a PLA to implement the logic, it must provide four inputs, four outputs, and at least nine product terms. The implementation schematic is shown in Figure 10.11. It shouldn't surprise you that it is essentially identical to Figure 10.6. We only replace the converter ROM with a PLA.

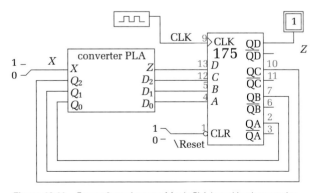

Figure 10.11   Excess 3 synchronous Mealy PLA-based implementation.

PAL Versus PLA-Based Implementations   As mentioned in Chapter 4, the delay in a PLA tends to be worse than that in a comparable PAL. Although PLAs are very popular in full custom VLSI designs, PALs are more likely to be used in conventional board-level designs.

If you select a PAL to implement the code converter finite state machine, then (at least) one of the gates of the OR plane must have a four-input fan-in. Not every PAL has this kind of internal architecture. For example, a 10H8 PAL (10 inputs, eight outputs, two inputs per OR gate) could not implement the next-state logic without some modification to the equations, but a 12H6 PAL (12 inputs, six outputs, two OR gates with four inputs each, four OR gates with two inputs each) could implement it without modification.

Suppose that as the designer, you have only the simpler 10H8 PAL available. It is not difficult to get the equations into the right form. You simply rewrite them as subexpressions that do not exceed the maximum product term count for the PAL. Here is the way to write the next-state function D_1 as expressions with no more than two product terms per function:

$$D_1 = D_{11} + D_{12}$$
$$D_{11} = \overline{X} \bullet \overline{Q_2} \bullet \overline{Q_1} \bullet Q_0 + X \bullet \overline{Q_2} \bullet \overline{Q_0}$$
$$D_{12} = \overline{X} \bullet Q_2 \bullet \overline{Q_0} + Q_1 \bullet \overline{Q_0}$$

Figure 10.12 shows the partial 10H8 PAL programming map for this logic.

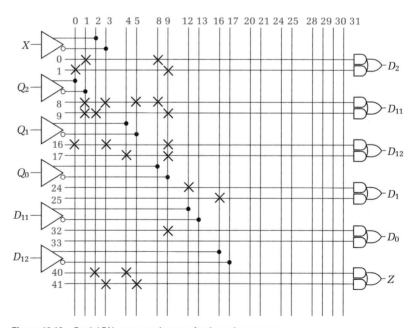

Figure 10.12   Partial PAL programming map for the code converter.

The programming map includes indices for the vertical input lines and the horizontal product term lines, to let you program down to the individual crosspoints. The horizontal rows correspond to the following product terms:

0.	$\overline{Q_2} \bullet Q_0$	24.	D_{11}
1.	$Q_2 \bullet \overline{Q_0}$	25.	D_{12}
8.	$\overline{X} \bullet \overline{Q_2} \bullet \overline{Q_1} \bullet Q_0$	32.	$\overline{Q_0}$
9.	$X \bullet \overline{Q_2} \bullet \overline{Q_0}$	33.	Not used
16.	$X \bullet Q_2 \bullet \overline{Q_0}$	40.	$X \bullet Q_1$
17.	$Q_1 \bullet \overline{Q_0}$	41.	$\overline{X} \bullet \overline{Q_1}$

The D_{11} and D_{12} outputs are simply fed back as inputs, which are ORed within the PAL to form the expression for D_1. Figure 10.13 shows the pinout and wiring. The PAL still has four inputs and two outputs that are uncommitted. These are available to implement other logic functions.

Partitioning functions in this way has some performance implications. The propagation delay to compute D_1 is essentially twice that of the other outputs, since it passes through the AND-OR network twice while they pass through only once. Thus, D_1 could easily determine the performance-limiting critical delay path.

One alternative is to use a more sophisticated PAL that provides interconnect for outputs to be fed back as inputs in the AND array. This is a little faster than the implementation suggested by Figure 10.13, but still results in a fundamentally multilevel logic circuit. If this is a serious problem for the performance of the system, you will need to choose a PAL containing OR gates with a sufficient number of product term fan-ins.

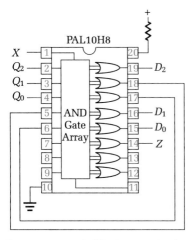

Figure 10.13   10H8 PAL pin-outs and wiring.

10.1.3   Alternative PAL Architectures

So far, we have examined PALs in their simplest form: relatively small fan-in structures suitable for implementing simple combinational logic. PAL architectures are actually much richer than this. For example, some members of the PAL family contain on-chip flip-flops, they can generate either positive or negative logic outputs, they can allow a pin to be selectively programmed for input or output, or they include XOR gates. Let's examine these alternatives.

Registered PALs   A *registered PAL* is a programmable AND array device with on-chip flip-flops associated with the output pins. These devices are particularly useful for implementing synchronous Mealy machines or Moore machines.

Part of the programming map for a registered PAL is shown in Figure 10.14. Positive edge-triggered D flip-flops latch the OR plane outputs. These are gated to the output pins through tri-state inverting buffers when the $\overline{OE}$ signal is asserted low.

Depending on the details of the PAL architecture, you may supply the $\overline{OE}$ signal by a dedicated input pin or drive it from a product term computed within the array. Similarly, you can provide the Clock signal from off-chip or compute it within the PAL.

Figure 10.14 shows the output of the flip-flop fed back to the AND array. If this is a next-state function, the signal fed back serves as the current-state input.

The feedback line is the negative logic output of the flip-flop. This isn't as confusing as it may seem. It is common practice to implement the negative logic form of the function within the AND array. The inverting tri-state buffer complements this function to get back to the positive logic form. The feedback buffer drives the function and its complement back into the AND array.

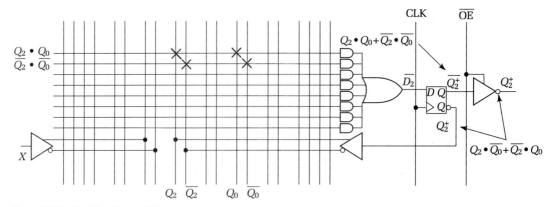

Figure 10.14   Partial registered PAL programming map.

The CAD software usually hides the issues of signal polarities from you. For example, the ABEL system understands the underlying PAL architecture and handles the polarities accordingly. This is why you need to identify the device in the ABEL description. The ABEL software implements sophisticated methods for mapping Boolean equations onto the specific PAL devices.

Example   Code Converter Implemented with a Registered PAL   The function implemented at the input of the flip-flop in the PAL fragment of Figure 10.14 is the negative logic for the next-state function D_2. ABEL handles the translation to negative logic directly; otherwise minimization tools let you find the optimized form of a function's complement. For example, you can specify the **-epos** option in *espresso* to minimize the complements of the functions specified in the input file.

In negative logic, the code converter next-state equations become

$$\overline{D}_2 = Q_2 \bullet Q_0 + \overline{Q}_2 \bullet \overline{Q}_0$$

$$\overline{D}_1 = Q_1 \bullet Q_0 + Q_2 \bullet Q_0 + X \bullet Q_0 + X \bullet Q_2 \bullet \overline{Q}_1 + \overline{X} \bullet \overline{Q}_2 \bullet \overline{Q}_1 \bullet \overline{Q}_0$$

$$\overline{D}_0 = Q_0$$

$$\overline{Z} = X \bullet \overline{Q}_1 + \overline{X} \bullet Q_1$$

Since both the positive and negative forms of the current-state bits are available to the AND plane, the detailed programming of the functions is much as before.

PALs with Programmable Outputs   More sophisticated PALs allow you to program the output's polarity, giving you the option of positive or negative logic outputs. Figure 10.15 shows how this is done in the PAL. An XOR gate is placed between the output of the OR gate and the input to

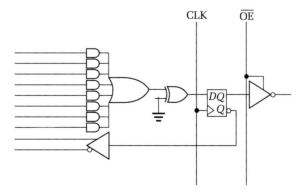

Figure 10.15   PAL architecture with programmable output polarity.

the D flip-flop. One of XOR's inputs can be programmed with a connection to ground. When this fused connection is blown, the input is treated as though it were high and the XOR behaves like an inverter. It passes the inverted signal to the D flip-flop, which inverts the signal one more time on the way to the output pin and the feedback path. When the connection is left intact, the input is 0 and the XOR behaves like a noninverting buffer.

Programmable polarity can also help you overcome the limited product term inputs to the OR gate. The complement of a function in sum of products form may use fewer terms than the function itself. You can implement the function in its complemented form, using the XOR gate to return the function to its true sense.

Additional Variations on PAL Architectures   PAL architectures continue to evolve, giving the basic PAL structure ever more function and flexibility. We mention some of the newer variations here.

XOR PALs (as distinct from PALs with programmable polarity) contain internal XOR gates whose inputs are fed from AND-OR array structures. They are well suited for computing certain arithmetic functions that would otherwise generate many product terms.

An example is the P20X10 PAL of Figure 10.16. It also illustrates some of the complexities of the detailed structure of a typical PAL. The 20X10 contains 10 data input pins and 10 output pins with internal D flip-flops. The outputs are fed back into the AND plane, a total of 20 possible AND array inputs. Pin 1 is a dedicated input that drives the flip-flop clocks. Pin 13 controls the tri-state enables of the inverting output buffers of the registered outputs. Two-input XOR gates at the inputs to the D flip-flops are driven by OR gates with two product terms each.

As an example, let's look at alternative PAL-based implementations of the expression $A \oplus B \oplus C \oplus D$. Using a conventional AND-OR PAL, we need 8 four-literal product terms. But we could also implement this in only four terms in an AND-OR-XOR structure. The two alternatives are shown in Figure 10.17.

Typical registered PALs have several limitations on their inputs and outputs. For example, an output pin is dedicated to the register even if it is used to hold state information that is never provided off-chip. One solution is to have "buried" registers, with the outputs decoupled from the registers. The register can feed back a signal to the AND array while the output pin carries a different signal. Or the outputs may be multiplexed, allowing the output pin to be connected to the combinational output from the array or the registered output from the flip-flop. An example of this more sophisticated PAL structure is the P22V10, to be shown in Figure 10.28. We will discuss it at that time.

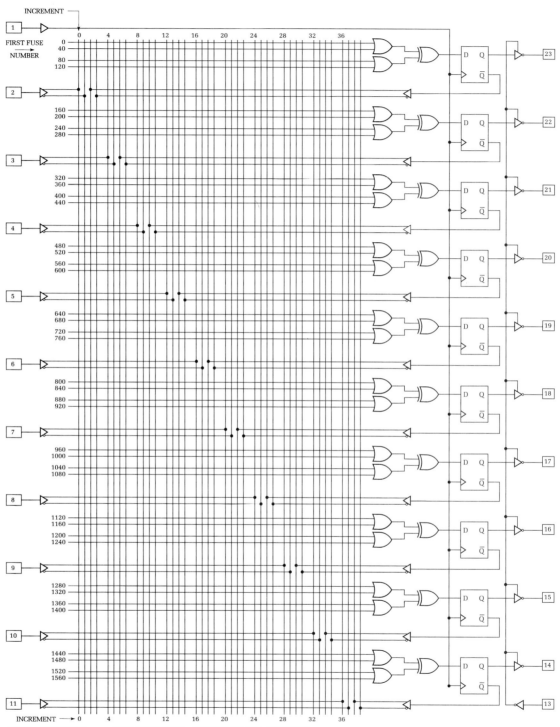

Figure 10.16 P20X10 PAL.

NOTE: FUSE NUMBER = FIRST FUSE NUMBER + INCREMENT

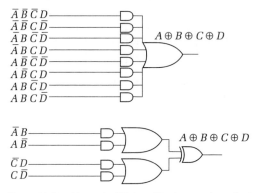

Figure 10.17   Alternative PAL-based implementations of a 4-variable XOR function.

10.1.4   Specifying PALs with ABEL

In this section, we describe how to specify PAL-based implementations of Boolean functions using ABEL. If you do not have access to this software, you may want to skim or skip this subsection.

An advantage of programmable logic is the power of the CAD tools provided with a particular PAL design environment. These map the positive logic equations into the form needed for a target PAL architecture. Many, but not all, of the device details are hidden from the designer.

In Chapter 8 we saw how ABEL can specify the behavior of finite state machines. ABEL maps the descriptions into the *programming map*, the list of fuses to be blown within the device. Your ABEL description must alert the software about the PAL you plan to use through the `device` statement.

In this subsection, we will examine mapping the BCD-to-Excess-3 code converter state machine onto various PAL devices.

Implementation with P10H8   ABEL's strength and weakness is its close relationship with the underlying PAL architecture. Let's look at the implementation of the state machine of Figure 10.13. Because this particular PAL has limited product term resources, you must describe the D_1 next-state function in terms of two simpler expressions, D_{11} and D_{12}. The software will not automatically perform this partitioning. The ABEL description must reflect your partitioning decisions:

```
module bcd2excess3
title 'BCD to Excess 3 Code Converter State Machine
    Joe Engineer, Itty Bitty Machines, Inc.'

u1 device 'p10h8';

"Input Pins
    X,Q2,Q1,Q0,D11i,D12i pin 1,2,3,4,5,6;
```

```
"Output Pins
    D2,D11o,D12o,D1,D0,Z pin 19,18,17,16,15,14;

INSTATE = [Q2, Q1, Q0];
S0 = [0, 0, 0];
S1 = [0, 0, 1];
S2 = [0, 1, 1];
S3 = [1, 1, 0];
S4 = [1, 0, 0];
S5 = [1, 1, 1];
S6 = [1, 0, 1];

equations
    D2 = (!Q2 & Q0) # (Q2 & !Q0);
    D1 = D11i # D12i;
    D11o = (!X & !Q2 & !Q1 & Q0) # (X & !Q2 & !Q0);
    D12o = (!X & Q2 & !Q0) # (Q1 & !Q0);
    D0 = !Q0;
    Z = (X & Q1) # (!X & !Q1);

test_vectors
([X, INSTATE, D11i, D12i]->[D2, D1, D0, D11o, D12o, Z])
    [0, S0,.X.,.X.] -> [0,.X., 1, 0,    0, 1];
    [0, S0,  0,  0] -> [0,  0, 1,.X.,.X., 1];
    [0, S1,.X.,.X.] -> [1,.X., 0, 1,    0, 1];
    [0, S1,  1,  0] -> [1,  1, 0,.X.,.X., 1];
    [0, S3,.X.,.X.] -> [1,.X., 1, 0,    1, 0];
    [0, S3,  0,  1] -> [1,  1, 1,.X.,.X., 0];
    [0, S5,.X.,.X.] -> [0,.X., 0, 0,    0, 0];
    [0, S5,  0,  0] -> [0,  0, 0,.X.,.X., 0];
end bcd2excess3;
```

The `device` statement specifies a P10H8 PAL. The input and output pin descriptions match the assignment of Figure 10.13. Since the P10H8 is purely combinational, the description simply consists of the Boolean equations for the PAL's outputs: D_2, D_1, D_{11}, D_{12}, D_0, and Z. Registers and clocking logic are external to the PAL (see Figure 10.11).

The test vectors are complex because D_1 is computed in two steps. D_{11} and D_{12} are computed first and then ORed to form D_1. We need two test vectors for each step: one for computing the intermediate values D_{11} and D_{12}, and one for the final value of D_1.

The first test vector has input X at 0 and the machine in state S_0. D_2, D_0, D_{11}, D_{12}, and Z are checked by the output vector, with D_1 left as a don't care. The second test vector takes the current value for the state and input and the values for D_{11} and D_{12} just checked by the previous vector. It then verifies that the next state outputs become 001, which is the encoding for S_1.

Similarly, the third and fourth vectors verify the transition from S_1 to S_3 on 0 generating a 1. The fifth and sixth vectors do the same for the S_3-to-S_5 transition on 0, generating a 0. The last two vectors handle the case of the transition from S_5 to S_0 on 0, still outputting a 0.

Implementation with a 12H6 PAL   To see how the PAL architecture can influence the ABEL description, let's examine the implementation of the converter state machine using a 12H6 PAL. This device has 12 inputs and six outputs. Two of the outputs are defined by four product terms (output pins 18 and 13). The ABEL description becomes

```
module bcd2excess3
title 'BCD to Excess 3 Code Converter State Machine
    Joe Engineer, Itty Bitty Machines, Inc.'

u1 device 'p12h6';

"Input Pins
    X, Q2, Q1, Q0 pin 1, 2, 3, 4;

"Output Pins
    D2, D1, D0, Z pin 17, 18, 16, 15;

INSTATE = [Q2, Q1, Q0]; OUTSTATE = [D2, D1, D0];
S0in = [0, 0, 0];       S0out = [0, 0, 0];
S1in = [0, 0, 1];       S1out = [0, 0, 1];
S2in = [0, 1, 1];       S2out = [0, 1, 1];
S3in = [1, 1, 0];       S3out = [1, 1, 0];
S4in = [1, 0, 0];       S4out = [1, 0, 0];
S5in = [1, 1, 1];       S5out = [1, 1, 1];
S6in = [1, 0, 1];       S6out = [1, 0, 1];

equations
    D2 = (!Q2 & Q0) # (Q2 & !Q0);
    D1 = (!X & !Q2 & !Q1 & Q0) # (X & !Q2 & !Q0) #
        (!X & Q2 & !Q0) # (Q1 & !Q0);
    D0 = !Q0;
    Z = (X & Q1) # (!X & !Q1);

test_vectors ([X, INSTATE] -> [OUTSTATE, Z])
    [0, S0in] -> [S1out, 1];
    [0, S1in] -> [S3out, 1];
    [0, S3in] -> [S5out, 0];
    [0, S5in] -> [S0out, 0];
end bcd2excess3;
```

This description is much more straightforward because we don't need the artificial partitioning of D_1. The test vectors are also less complicated.

Implementation with a 16R6 PAL   In our final case, we look at describing the state machine for a registered PAL, in this case a 16R6. The PAL structure is shown in Figure 10.18. It has eight data inputs, eight feedback inputs from the outputs, six registered outputs (pins 13, 14, 15, 16, 17, 18), two combinational outputs (pins 12 and 19), a clock input (pin 1), and an active low output enable (pin 11). Each output can be defined by up to eight product terms.

The embedded registers allow us to implement the state machine in a single device. However, we must add an input to reset the machine to state S_0, as well as the clock and output enable inputs. The ABEL description is

```
module bcd2excess3
title 'BCD to Excess 3 Code Converter State Machine
    Joe Engineer, Itty Bitty Machines, Inc.'

u1 device 'p16r6';

"Input Pins
    Clk, Reset, X,  !OE pin  1,  2,  3,  11;

"Output Pins
    D2,  D1,    D0, Z   pin  13, 14, 15, 12;

SREG = [D2, D1, D0];
S0 = [0, 0, 0];
S1 = [0, 0, 1];
S2 = [0, 1, 1];
S3 = [1, 1, 0];
S4 = [1, 0, 0];
S5 = [1, 1, 1];
S6 = [1, 0, 1];

state_diagram SREG
state S0: if Reset then S0
        else if X then S2 with Z = 0
        else S1 with Z = 1
state S1: if Reset then S0
        else if X then S4 with Z = 0
        else S3 with Z = 1
state S2: if Reset then S0
        else if X then S4 with Z = 1
        else S4 with Z = 0
state S3: if Reset then S0
        else if X then S5 with Z = 1
        else S5 with Z = 0
state S4: if Reset then S0
        else if X then S6 with Z = 0
        else S5 with Z = 1
```

```
state S5: if Reset then S0
        else if X then S0 with Z = 1
        else S0 with Z = 0
state S6: if Reset then S0
        else if !X then S0 with Z = 1

test_vectors ([Clk, Reset, !OE, X] -> [SREG, Z])
   [.c., 1, 0,.X.] -> [S0,.X.];
   [ 0, 0, 0,  0] -> [S0,  1];
   [.c., 0, 0,  0] -> [S1,.X.];
   [ 0, 0, 0,  0] -> [S1,  1];
   [.c., 0, 0,  0] -> [S3,.X.];
   [ 0, 0, 0,  0] -> [S3,  0];
   [.c., 0, 0,  0] -> [S5,.X.];
   [ 0, 0, 0,  0] -> [S5,  0];
   [.c., 0, 0,  0] -> [S0,.X.];
end bcd2excess3;
```

We use the `state_diagram` statement in this description. The next-state functions of this PAL are sequential, not combinational as in the previous cases. In each state, the `Reset` input is checked. If it is asserted, the machine returns to state S_0.

The active low signal $\overline{OE}$ is specially handled in the description. In the input pin description, the signal is declared to be active low by listing it as `!OE`. To retain the sense of the signal, we must use `!OE` in the test vector and list the signal's value as 0 in cases in which the output tri-states are turned on.

Take a close look at the way we have specified the test vectors. The ABEL description specifies the converter as an asynchronous Mealy machine: the output Z is combinational rather than registered. To make Z synchronous, we need to associate Z with one of the registered outputs, such as pin 17. Thus, for a given state transition, the output is valid at the next rising edge. We model this in the set of test vectors with two vectors. The first moves the machine into a new state, ignoring the output. The second verifies that the output is correct with the machine in a given state and the clock at 0.

The first vector in the description checks that reset works correctly. When the clock edge comes, if `Reset` is asserted, the machine enters state S_0. With an input of 0 and being in S_0, the machine outputs a 1. On the next clock edge, the machine advances to state S_1. We do not check the output until the clock falls. Since the input is still 0, the output is 1.

On the next edge, the machine goes to state S_3. The output is checked when the clock goes low, when it should be 0 if the input is still 0. On the next positive clock edge, the machine enters S_5. Since the input remains 0, the output stays at 0. Finally, the next clock edge leads the machine back to state S_0.

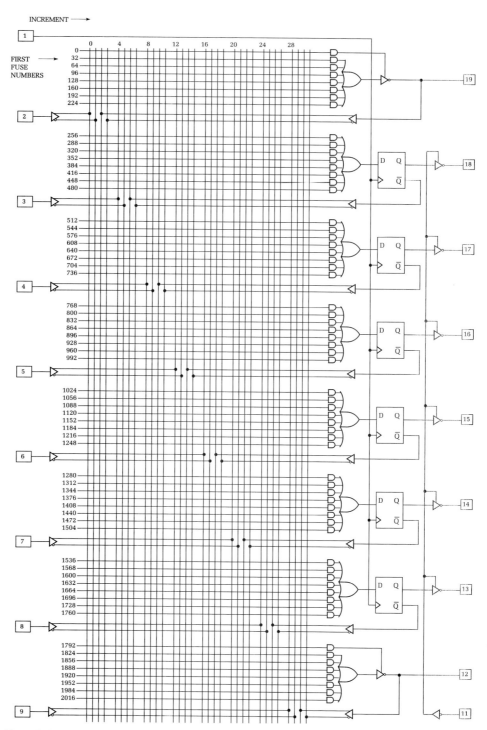

Figure 10.18 Registered 16R6 PAL.

10.2   FSM Design with Counters

Synchronous counters are potentially attractive for implementing finite state machines. In a single package they provide a state register with mechanisms for advancing the state (CNT), resetting it to zero (CLR), and "jumping" to a new state (LD). Rather than encode the next-state function as actual state bits, you can implement it by asserting the counter control signals CNT, LD, and CLR under the right conditions. We examine a counter-based implementation strategy in this section.

For correct operation in state sequencing, the counter must be implemented with synchronous LD and CLR signals, such as the TTL 74163 binary up-counter. As pointed out in Section 7.5.2, asynchronous control signals lead to invalid behavior of the state machine.

Figure 10.19 shows the kinds of state transitions supported by a counter. You should choose the state assignment to exploit the special sequencing capabilities of a counter. The state encodings you assign to sequential states should follow the binary sequence supported by the counter. Let's look at an MSI counter-based implementation of the BCD-to-Excess-3 converter next.

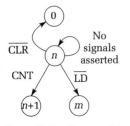

Figure 10.19   State transitions of a counter-based finite state machine.

10.2.1   BCD-to-Excess-3 Code Converter

Figure 10.20 gives a state assignment for the state diagram of the code converter. This assignment is reasonably well suited for a counter-based finite state machine implementation. As much as possible, we assign sequential state encodings to flows in the state diagram. We also try to reduce the number of transitions in which a jump (LD) to a state (other than 0) takes place. The figure shows three such jumps: from state 0 to 4, from 1 to 5, and from 5 to 3.

State Transition Table   To implement a finite state machine with a counter, we replace the next-state bits with logic to generate the counter control signals. This is like remapping the next-state functions to flip-flop control inputs that we saw in Chapter 6. However, we must still directly specify the next-state bits for the jump cases.

Figure 10.21 shows the finite state machine state transition table, extended with output columns for the counter control signals $\overline{\text{CLR}}$, $\overline{\text{LD}}$, EN (count), as well as the counter load inputs C, B, and A. Our basic procedure obtains minimized logic expressions for these signals rather than the next-state bits.

For the 74163 counter, the $\overline{\text{CLR}}$ signal has precedence over $\overline{\text{LD}}$, which in turn has precedence over EN (count). This makes it possible to exploit many more don't-care conditions within the K-maps.

We derive the state transition table in the following manner. We examine each state transition in turn. Consider the first transition, from

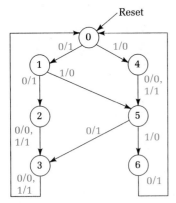

Figure 10.20   Code converter state diagram with counter-based state assignment.

Inputs/Current State				Next State			Outputs						
X	Q_2	Q_1	Q_0	Q_2^+	Q_1^+	Q_0^+	Z	$\overline{\text{CLR}}$	$\overline{\text{LD}}$	EN	C	B	A
0	0	0	0	0	0	1	1	1	1	1	X	X	X
0	0	0	1	0	1	0	1	1	1	1	X	X	X
0	0	1	0	0	1	1	0	1	1	1	X	X	X
0	0	1	1	0	0	0	0	0	X	X	X	X	X
0	1	0	0	1	0	1	0	1	1	1	X	X	X
0	1	0	1	0	1	1	1	1	0	X	0	1	1
0	1	1	0	0	0	0	1	0	X	X	X	X	X
0	1	1	1	X	X	X	X	X	X	X	X	X	X
1	0	0	0	1	0	0	0	1	0	X	1	0	0
1	0	0	1	1	0	0	0	1	0	X	1	0	1
1	0	1	0	0	1	1	1	1	1	1	X	X	X
1	0	1	1	0	0	0	1	0	X	X	X	X	X
1	1	0	0	1	0	1	1	1	1	1	X	X	X
1	1	0	1	1	1	0	0	1	1	1	X	X	X
1	1	1	0	X	X	X	X	X	X	X	X	X	X
1	1	1	1	X	X	X	X	X	X	X	X	X	X

Figure 10.21 Transition table for code converter implemented with a counter-based finite state machine.

state 0 to 1. If the machine is currently in state 0 with input 0, the finite state machine changes to state 1 with output 1. Thus, $\overline{\text{CLR}}$ and $\overline{\text{LD}}$ should be unasserted (left high) and EN asserted to cause the state register to count up from 0 to 1. These settings fill out the rest of the row in the transition table.

If the input is 1 in state 0, the next state is 4 with an output 0. This calls for a jump: $\overline{\text{CLR}}$ is left unasserted high, $\overline{\text{LD}}$ is asserted low, and EN can be a don't care. The value to be loaded, 1 0 0, must be available on the C, B, A signals. The collection of values fill out the ninth row of the state transition table.

An example of a return to state 0 is the 0 transition from state 3. In this case, the $\overline{\text{CLR}}$ signal is asserted low, while $\overline{\text{LD}}$ and EN can be don't cares. Rows 7 and 12 of the transition table provide other examples of these "return to 0" transitions.

Boolean Minimization of the Counter Control Signals Our next step is to minimize the functions for Z, $\overline{\text{CLR}}$, $\overline{\text{LD}}$, and EN. The *espresso* input file is shown in Figure 10.22 and the resulting output file in Figure 10.23.

Because we are already using the $\overline{\text{CLR}}$ signal for a control function, we need a separate RESET input to place the finite state machine in state 0 initially. Note that this is a synchronous reset; the reset on the 74175 quad registers used in some of the finite state machine implementations in this chapter is asynchronous. To be correctly "synchronous," we should include a reset signal as input to the ROM or PLA/PAL next-state logic (see Exercise 10.2).

```
.i 5
.o 7
.ilb res x q2 q1 q0
.ob z clr ld en c b a
.p 17
1---- -0-----
00000 1111---
00001 1111---
00010 0111---
00011 00-----
00100 0111---
00101 110-011
00110 10-----
00111 -------
01000 010-100
01001 010-101
01010 1111---
01011 10-----
01100 1111---
01101 0111---
01110 -------
01111 -------
.e
```

Figure 10.22 *Espresso* input.

```
.i 5
.o 7
.ilb res x q2 q1 q0
.ob z clr ld en c b a
.p 10
0-001 0101101
-0-01 1000000
-11-0 1000000
0-0-0 0101100
-000- 1010000
-0--0 0010000
0-10- 0101011
--11- 1000000
-11-- 0010000
-1-1- 1010000
.e
```

Figure 10.23   *Espresso* outputs.

Discussion   For this implementation of the BCD-to-Excess-3 code converter, the logic is more complex than the others: 10 product terms, an additional input, and three additional outputs. The schematic is shown in Figure 10.24. Since we are designing synchronous Mealy machines, we need a D flip-flop between the PLA and the output Z, adding yet another component. The timing behavior of this circuit is identical to that of Figure 10.7.

The counter-based implementation was a bad choice for this particular state machine. However, when the state diagram has fewer out-of-sequence jumps, a counter-based implementation can be very effective. We will see more applications of this technique in Section 10.4.3 as well as in Chapter 12 (see also Exercise 10.20).

10.3   FSM Design with More Sophisticated Programmable Logic Devices

The PAL concept was pioneered in the 1970s by Monolithic Memories (which has since merged with Advanced Micro Devices, also known as AMD). It was based on bipolar fuse technology developed for programmable ROMs (all connections are initially available; "blow" the connections you do not want). The primary goal of PAL-based designs was to reduce parts count by replacing conventional TTL logic with more highly integrated programmable logic. Designers frequently report that four TTL packages (10 to 100 "gate equivalents") can be replaced by a single PAL.

PAL-based designs also have the advantage of reduced parts inventory, since a PAL is a "universal" device. You don't need a large stock of

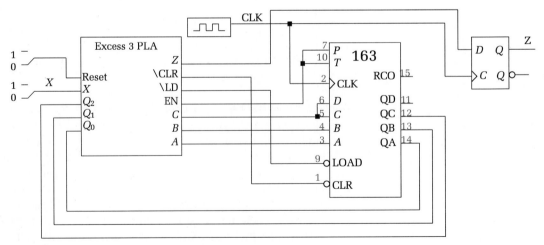

Figure 10.24   Counter-based implementation of code converter.

miscellaneous TTL components. In addition, PALs support rapid proto-typing, because they reduce the number of component-to-component interconnections. Designers can implement bug fixes and new functions within the PALs, often without making changes at the printed circuit board level.

10.3.1   PLDs: Programmable Logic Devices

A number of companies have extended the PAL concept by changing the underlying technology, as well as the component's array of gates and interconnections. Generically, these components are called *programmable logic devices* (PLDs), with the more sophisticated devices called *field-programmable gate arrays* (FPGAs). We will examine three representative PLD architectures in this section: Altera MAX, Actel programmable gate array, and Xilinx logical cell array.

10.3.2   Altera Erasable Programmable Logic Devices

Except for very high speed programmable logic, the general trend has been toward CMOS implementation, with its much higher levels of circuit integration and lower power demands than bipolar technologies. PALs were initially based on the same "program once" technology as bipolar PROMs. Altera pioneered the development of erasable programmable logic devices (EPLDs) based on CMOS erasable ROM technology. The EPLD can be erased simply by exposing it to ultraviolet (UV) light and then reprogrammed at a later time. Altera EPLDs are equivalent to 100 to 1000 conventional two-input gates, depending on the model selected.

EPLD Macrocell Architecture   The basic element of the EPLD is the macrocell, containing an eight-product-term AND-OR array and several programmable multiplexers. Multiplexers are particularly easy to implement in MOS technology, so it is no surprise that they are pervasive in CMOS-based programmable logic.

Figure 10.25 gives a block diagram/schematic view of the macrocell's contents. Its elements include a programmable AND array, a multiple fan-in OR gate to compute the logic function with programmable output polarity (via the XOR gate), a tri-state buffer driving an I/O pin, a programmable sequential logic block, and a programmable feedback section. Depending on the component, an EPLD may contain from 8 (EP300 series) to 48 (EP1800 series) such macrocells, each of which can be independently programmed.

Let's look at each of the programmable elements of the macrocell. As you will see, it offers more flexibility than any of the PAL architectures we have seen so far.

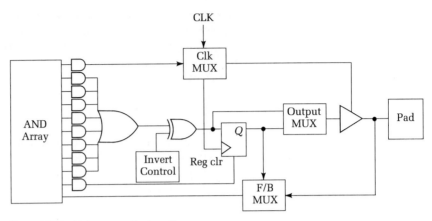

Figure 10.25 Altera macrocell schematic.

The macrocell's AND array is crossed with the true and complement of the EPLD's dedicated input and clock pin signals and the internal feedbacks from each of the component's outputs. Crosspoints are implemented by EPROM connections that are initially connected. Unwanted connections are broken by "blowing" the appropriate EPROM bits.

The multiplexers allow the feedback, output, and clock sections to be independently programmed. The MUX selection lines are controlled by their own EPROM bits. Under MUX control, the combinational function can bypass the flip-flop on the way to the output. Thus you can program any output to be either combinational or registered.

Similarly, macrocell feedback into the AND arrays can come from the registered output or from the external pin. You can program many of the pins to be either output or input.

Some variations on the macrocell architecture support dual feedback, making it possible to use the register for internal state while the pin is used as an independent input. This is an application of the concept of buried registers mentioned in Section 10.1.3.

The programmable clock section allows you to (1) clock the registers synchronously in groups by a dedicated clock input or (2) clock them by a local signal within the macrocell. Since the latter is a product term, the register's clock signal can be any combination of inputs or external clocks.

The two possible configurations of the clock multiplexer are shown in Figure 10.26. Depending on the value of the bit programmed within the EPROM cell, the flip-flop is controlled with the global clock while the AND array's product term selectively enables the output. This is called *synchronous mode* because the output register is clocked by a global clock signal, shared among all macrocells. This signal can cause all outputs to change at the same time.

Alternatively, the clock multiplexer can be configured so a local clock, computed from a distinguished AND array product term, controls the output register. In this mode, the output is always enabled, driving the output pin. Since every macrocell can generate its own local clock, the output can change at any time. This is called *asynchronous mode*.

The register embedded in the macrocell can be configured as a D or T flip-flop, either positive or negative edge-triggered. Since J-K or R-S flip-flops can be implemented in terms of D or T flip-flops, they are realized by providing the appropriate mapping logic in the AND-OR array.

The final programmable element of the macrocell is the register clear signal. One of the AND array's product terms is dedicated to provide this function.

Altera MAX Architecture The major problem with all AND-OR structures is the difficulty of sharing product terms among macrocells. In a conventional PAL, you cannot share the same product term across

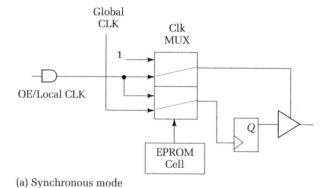

(a) Synchronous mode

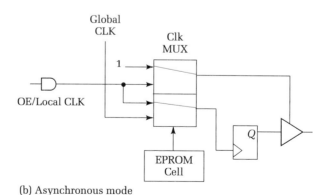

(b) Asynchronous mode

Figure 10.26 Clock MUX modes.

different OR gates. The term must be repeated for each output. This can lower the efficiency of the PAL, reducing the number of equivalent discrete gates it can replace.

As programmable logic devices become even more highly integrated, the architectures must evolve to provide more area for global routing of signals. It must be possible to share terms and outputs between macrocells more easily. Altera has addressed these problems in their *multiple array matrix* (MAX) family of parts. We describe the structure of MAX components in this subsection.

Macrocells, similar in structure to Figure 10.25, are grouped into *Logic Array Blocks* (LABs). Associated with each LAB is a group of additional product terms, usable by any of the macrocells within the LAB. These *Expander Product Terms* make it possible to implement a function with up to 35 product terms inside a single macrocell. This compares to only eight terms per function in most PAL families.

In addition, a *Programmable Interconnect Array* (PIA) can route the LAB's macrocell outputs globally throughout the device. Some lower-density devices also use the PIA to route the product term expanders.

Figure 10.27 shows the generic architecture of a MAX component, the EPM5128. The device has eight dedicated inputs (including the clock), 64 programmable I/O pins, eight LABs, 16 macrocells per LAB (128 macrocells total—not all macrocells are connected to an output pin), and 32 product term expanders per LAB (256 total). The dedicated input pins come in along the top and are distributed to each of the eight LABs. The PIA routes global signals. All on-chip signals have a connection path to the PIA. Only the signals needed by a particular LAB are connected to it under EPROM programming.

The newest top-of-the-line Altera MAX component is the EPM5192. This device contains 192 macrocells organized into 12 LABs. Altera claims that a single EPM5192 can replace up to 100 TTL SSI and MSI components or 20 P22V10 PALs (for the implementation power of this kind of PAL, see Figure 10.28). Altera has under development a 7000 series of parts that organizes the LABs into multiple rows and columns around the programmable interconnect. The plan is to develop a chip architecture offering 1500 to 20,000 gate equivalents.

Figure 10.29 shows more details of the LAB's internal organization. It consists of an array of macrocells sharing a product term expander array. All macrocell outputs and I/O block inputs are connected to the PIA. Selected signals from the PIA are input to the macrocells.

Figure 10.30 gives more details of the implementation of the expander product terms. The AND array is crossed by the dedicated inputs and the feedback signals from the macrocells. The expander terms also form some of the columns of the array. In other words, they appear like inputs to the macrocells. Any expander term can be shared by all of the macrocells in the LAB.

If you use expander terms you quickly get into multilevel logic structures. Optimization techniques such as those in *misII* are absolutely necessary to do a good job of mapping logic onto these structures.

Once you reach devices as complex as the advanced MAX family, you would be unlikely to try to generate the personality map by hand. Altera provides an extensive tool set for mapping logic schematics onto the primitives supported by their EPLD structures.

EEPROM Technology for EPLDs   Another class of erasable PLDs is based on the technology of *electrically erasable* programmable ROM (EEPROM). This has two advantages. First, less expensive packaging can be used because there is no chip window for the erasing UV light. Second, crosspoints can be reprogrammed individually, which can speed up the process if only a small number of changes are needed. The macrocell and chip architectures are similar to those described in this section.

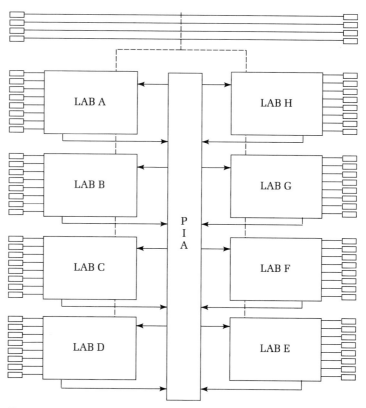

Figure 10.27   Altera EPM5128 block diagram.

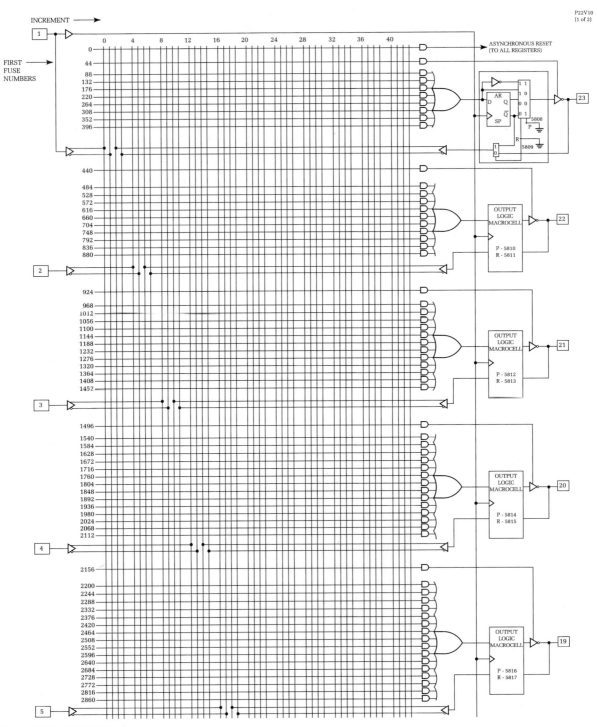

Figure 10.28 P22V10 PAL.

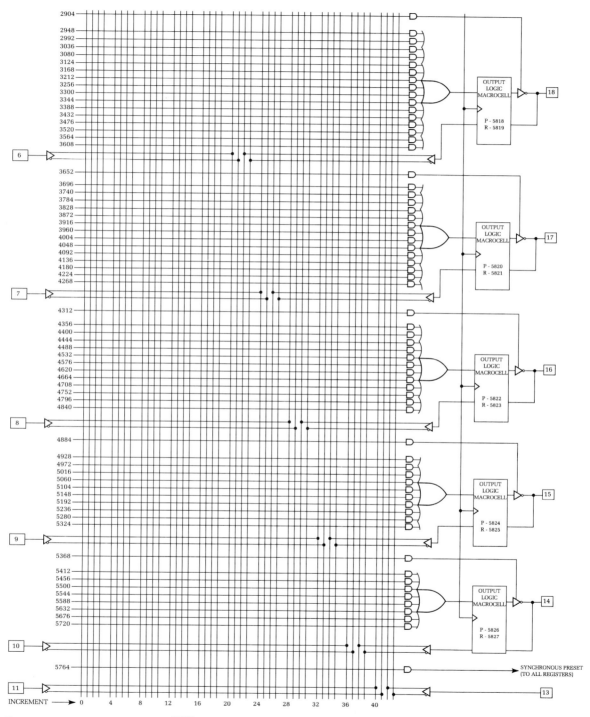

Figure 10.28   *(Continued.)*

NOTES:
1. INSIDE EACH MACROCELL, THE "P" FUSE NUMBER IS THE POLARITY FUSE, AND THE "R" FUSE IS THE REGISTER FUSE.
2. FUSE NUMBER = FIRST FUSE NUMBER + INCREMENT

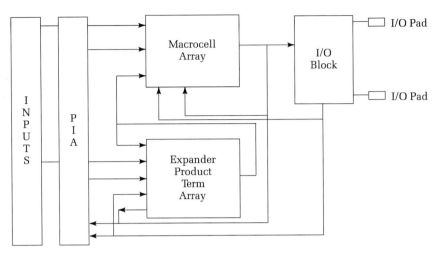

Figure 10.29 Internal architecture of the LAB.

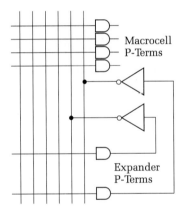

Figure 10.30 Expander product terms internal organization.

10.3.3 Actel Programmable Gate Arrays

Actel programmable logic chips provide what amounts to a field-programmable gate array structure. The chip contains rows of personalizable logic building blocks separated by horizontal routing channels. The programming method is a proprietary "antifuse" technology, so called because the connector's resistance changes from high to low when a high voltage is placed across it. This is the opposite of a conventional PAL or PROM based on fuse technology. The antifuses require a very small area, so the chip can have more connections than with other technologies. Unlike the EPLDs, Actel parts can be programmed only once.

The elements of the Actel architecture are I/O buffers, logic modules, and interconnect. Figure 10.31 shows a chip "floor plan" or block diagram. Programmable I/O buffers, and special programming and test logic are along the chip's edges. The I/O pins can be configured as input, output, tri-state, or bidirectional buffers, with or without internal latches.

Internally, the building blocks are organized into multiple rows of *logic modules* separated by wiring tracks. Each logic module is an eight-input, one-output configurable combinational logic function (the internal structure is described in the next subsection). You can program the module to implement a large number of two-, three-, and four-input logic gates, as well as two-level AND/OR and OR/AND gates. There are no dedicated flip-flops, although *D* and *J-K* storage elements can be constructed from two connected modules.

Horizontal wiring tracks provide the main interconnection. Although the tracks run across the length of the chip, a given wire can be partitioned into segments for several interconnections. In addition, vertical wires pass through the logic modules and span multiple wiring channels. Four inputs come from the track above the logic module and four from the track below.

The ACT 1 component family is organized around 25 horizontal and 13 vertical routing tracks. The arrays contain 1200 to 2000 gates, equivalent to two- or three-input NAND and NOR functions. Because of the flexibility of the routing and the personalization of the logic module,

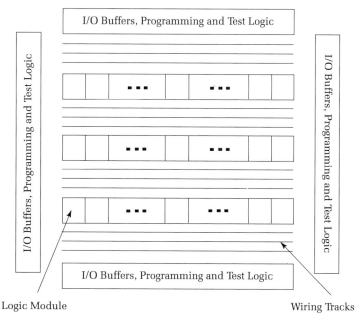

Logic Module

Wiring Tracks

Figure 10.31 Chip floorplan of Actel PGAs.

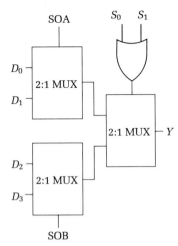

Figure 10.32 Actel logic module.

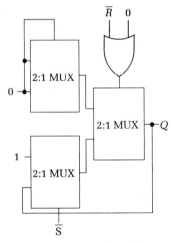

Figure 10.33 Actel logic module implementation of a simple latch.

Actel claims these are equivalent to 3000 to 6000 gates in a more typical PLD. A second-generation family, under development, will have more horizontal and vertical routing tracks. The new components will contain up to 8000 gates, which Actel claims are equivalent to 20,000 gates in a conventional PLD.

Actel Logic Module The logic module is a modified four-to-one multiplexer. Its block structure is shown in Figure 10.32. D_0, D_1, D_2, D_3, SOA, SOB, S_0, S_1 are inputs selected through programmable connections from the wiring tracks either above or below the logic block. Y is the single output. It can be routed to the horizontal tracks through programmable connections.

A remarkable number of logic functions can be implemented with this simple building block. For example, let's see how the module can be used to implement a two-input AND gate with inputs A and B. We simply wire A to D_1, 0 to D_0, and B to SOA. Then wire S_0 and S_1 to 0. If B is 1 then Y receives A; otherwise it receives 0. This is essentially an AND function.

The symmetry of the logic module makes it easy to implement functions whether the inputs are available above or below the module. For example, if the inputs to the AND "gate" are not available from the top of the module, the lower two-to-one multiplexer could easily be used to implement the function.

The logic module is not limited to implementing combinational functions. Let's look at how to implement an $\overline{S}\text{-}\overline{R}$ latch with a single module. The approach is shown in Figure 10.33. If $\overline{R}$ is 0, Q is set to 0, the output of the upper two-to-one multiplexer. If $\overline{R}$ is 1, then Q is set to the output from the lower multiplexer. This depends on $\overline{S}$. If $\overline{S}$ is 0, then Q is set to 1. Otherwise, Q is again set to its current value. This is exactly the function of the $\overline{S}\text{-}\overline{R}$ latch.

Actel Interconnect The routing of signals through the array is one of the most innovative features of the Actel architecture. Antifuses are placed wherever a horizontal and a vertical wire cross, as well as between adjacent horizontal and vertical wire segments.

The interconnection "fabric" and its relation to the logic modules are shown in Figure 10.34. The pass transistors and lines controlling their gates are used in programming to isolate a particular antifuse. Placing a high voltage across the antifuse establishes a bidirectional interconnection between the two crossing wires.

The logic modules must be carefully placed and then wired by routing interconnections through the network of antifuses. Because of the resistance and capacitance associated with crossing an antifuse, speed-critical signals pass through two antifuses. Most connections can be performed in two or three hops. The worst case might require four hops.

These concepts are illustrated in Figure 10.35. Every jog from a horizontal to a vertical wiring track and vice versa crosses an antifuse. To go from

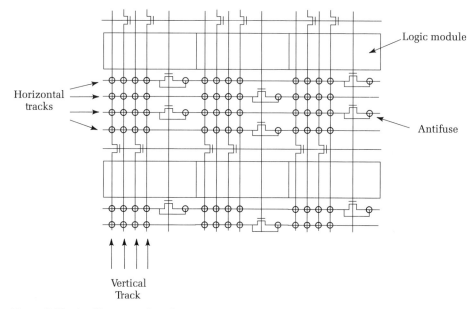

Figure 10.34   Actel interconnection scheme.

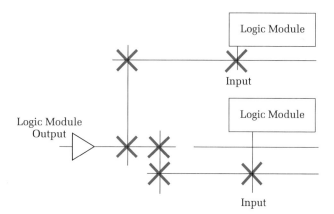

Figure 10.35   Interconnections among logic modules.

an output to the upper input requires one jog from horizontal to vertical, a second from vertical to horizontal, and a final jog to vertical again.

Some wire segments may be blocked by previously allocated segments. This is shown by the lower logic module input. To get to it, the output signal jogs vertically to a new horizontal line, to which the input vertical line can be connected. In general, a horizontal segment is made longer by jogging to another overlapping segment via an available vertical wire.

10.3.4   Xilinx Logic Cell Arrays

Xilinx takes another approach to bringing the PLD concept to higher levels of integration. Their programming method is based on CMOS static RAM technology: RAM cells sprinkled throughout the chip determine the personality of logic blocks and define the connectivity of signal paths. Static RAM circuits are important in integrated circuit technology and will continue to get denser and faster.

The RAM cells are linked into a long shift register, and the programming involves shifting in strings of ones and zeros to personalize the function of the chip. The devices come with an on-board hardwired finite state machine that allows the program to be downloaded from a standard ROM part. The Xilinx approach has the advantage of fast reprogrammability, although the chip loses its program each time it is powered down.

Figure 10.36 shows a portion of the chip architecture of the Xilinx logic cell array. The major components are I/O blocks (IOBs) and configurable logic blocks (CLBs). The programmable I/O blocks are placed around the periphery, while the CLBs are arrayed in the central part of

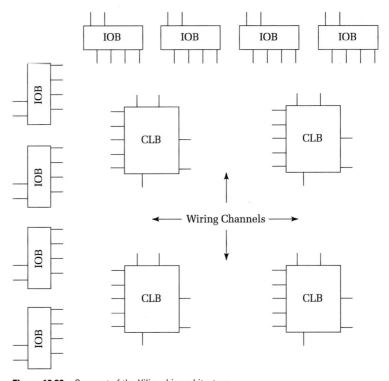

Figure 10.36   Segment of the Xilinx chip architecture.

the chip. Horizontal and vertical wiring channels separate the various components. We will examine these components in the following subsections.

Xilinx currently supports three component families, the 2000, 3000, and 4000 series. We will discuss the 3000 series, the one most commonly encountered in practice. The XC3020 component contains 64 IOBs and 64 CLBs arranged in an eight-by-eight matrix. Xilinx claims that the component contains 2000 equivalent logic gates. The largest member of the family, XC3090, contains 320 CLBs and 144 IOBs and is claimed to be equivalent to 9000 two-input gates.

Xilinx I/O Block Figure 10.37 shows the internal architecture of the I/O block. The inputs to the I/O block are a tri-state enable, the bit to be output (OUT) to the package pad, and the input and output clocks. The outputs from the block are the input (Direct In or Registered In) signals.

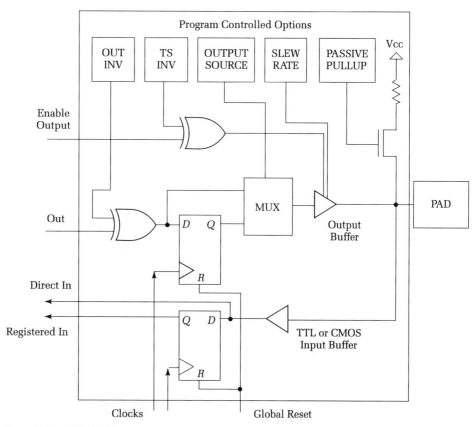

Figure 10.37 Xilinx I/O block architecture.

The block contains registers in both the input and output paths. These can be reset by a global reset signal provided to the block.

First, let's consider how the block can be used when it is associated with an output pad. The active high or low sense of the OUT signal and the output enable can be set by internal options, stored in RAM cells within the block. The output signal can be direct (combinational) or from the dedicated output register (registered). This register is an edge-triggered D flip-flop.

The slew rate control on the output buffer is used to slow down the rise time of output signals. It can reduce noise spikes in designs where large numbers of outputs change at the same time. Outputs can be fast (5 ns switching time) or slow (30 ns switching time).

Let's now consider the block with the pad used as an input. The input signal can come from the dedicated input register or directly from the input pad. The input register can be an edge-triggered flip-flop or a transparent latch. The input pull-up is intended for use with unused IOBs, so that internal signals are not permitted to float. It cannot be used by the output buffer.

Xilinx CLB Figure 10.38 gives the internal view of the CLB. It has five general purpose data inputs (A, B, C, D, E), one clock input, one clock enable input, data in (DIN), Reset, and two outputs, X and Y. The outputs can be registered or direct. In addition, the CLB has a combinational function generator, two storage elements, and five programmable multiplexers.

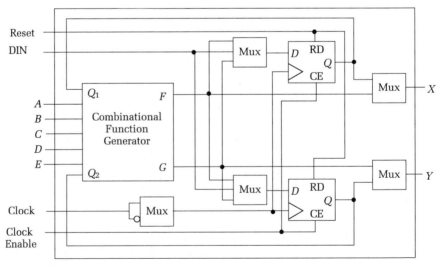

Figure 10.38 Xilinx CLB architecture.

The function generator takes seven inputs, five from the programmable interconnect (A, B, C, D, E), and two from internal flip-flop feedbacks (Q_1, Q_2). It also produces two internal outputs (F, G).

Personality RAM bits let us configure the function block in one of three different ways. With the first option, the function generator can compute any Boolean function of five variables. The distinct inputs are A, one of $B/Q_1/Q_2$, one of $C/Q_1/Q_2$, D, and E. Both F and G carry the same output value. For example, in this mode, a single combinational function generator can implement a 5-bit odd parity function: $F = \overline{A \oplus B \oplus C \oplus D \oplus E}$.

With the second option, the function generator can compute two independent functions of four variables each. The inputs are A, one of $B/Q_1/Q_2$, one of $C/Q_1/Q_2$, and one of D/E. F and G carry separate outputs. In this mode, a single function generator can compute a simple 2-bit comparator. Suppose the two 2-bit numbers are represented as A, B and C, D, respectively. Then the *greater than* (GT) and *equal* (EQ) functions can be computed as follows:

(GT) $F = A \bullet \overline{C} + A \bullet B \bullet \overline{D} + B \bullet \overline{C} \bullet \overline{D}$

(EQ) $G = \overline{A} \bullet \overline{B} \bullet \overline{C} \bullet \overline{D} + \overline{A} \bullet B \bullet \overline{C} \bullet D + A \bullet \overline{B} \bullet C \bullet \overline{D} + A \bullet B \bullet C \bullet D$

The final option implements certain restricted functions of more than five inputs. The variable E selects between two independent functions, each computed from the inputs A, one of $B/Q_1/Q_2$, one of $C/Q_1/Q_2$, and D. The three different options are summarized in Figure 10.39.

The internal flip-flops are positive edge triggered and can be controlled by the clock or its complement, depending on the configuration setting. They share a common clock signal. Their data sources are the internally generated functions F and G or the DIN input from the interconnect. An active high asynchronous reset signal can set both registers to zero. When the enable clock input is unasserted, the flip-flops hold their current state, ignoring the clock signals and the inputs. The flip-flop outputs, Q_1 and Q_2, are fed back as inputs to the function generator, making it possible to implement sequential functions within a single CLB.

The two outputs from the CLB, X and Y, can be driven from the flip-flops or directly from the F and G outputs of the function generator. The CLB organization is reasonably symmetric, making it possible to interchange the top or bottom inputs/outputs to reduce the complexity of interblock routing.

CLB Application Examples A small number of CLBs can implement a wide range of combinational functions. Figure 10.40 shows a few examples of majority logic and parity checking.

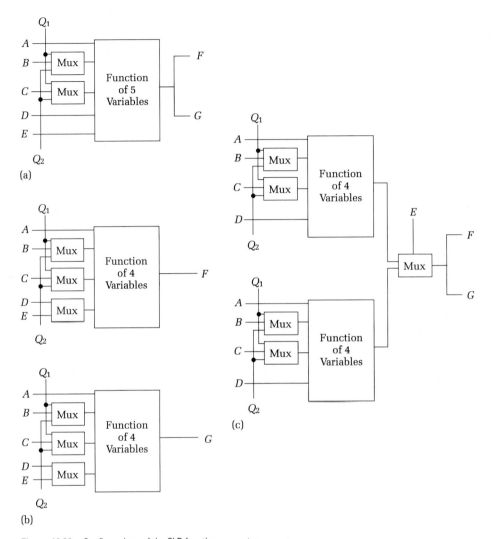

Figure 10.39 Configurations of the CLB function generator.

An n-input majority function asserts a 1 whenever $n/2$ or more inputs are 1. Clearly, a single CLB can implement a five-input majority circuit: this is nothing more than a combinational function of five variables!

Now consider a seven-input majority circuit. This can be implemented with three CLBs as shown in the figure. The first-level CLBs count the number of ones in their three inputs, outputting the patterns 00, 01, 10, or 11. Although the first-level CLBs are functions of only three inputs, they use both of their outputs. The second-level CLB sums its three sets of inputs (two 2-bit inputs and one 1-bit input); if these equal or exceed four, it asserts the majority output.

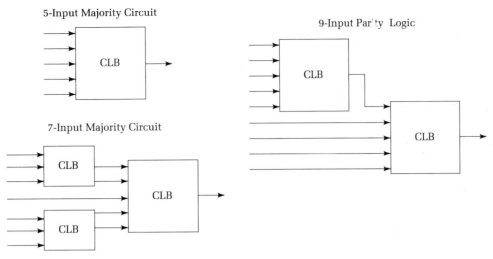

5-Input Majority Circuit

7-Input Majority Circuit

9-Input Parity Logic

Figure 10.40   Combinational logic implemented with CLBs.

Now consider a parity-checking circuit. A single CLB can implement a 5-bit-wide parity checker, as we have already seen. Cascading two CLBs, as shown in the figure, yields a nine-input circuit. With two levels of CLBs, we can extend the scheme to 25-bit-wide parity logic.

As another combinational logic example, consider how we might implement a 4-bit binary adder. A full adder can be implemented in a single CLB. The C_{out} and S_i outputs are functions of the three inputs A_i, B_i, and C_{in}. To get a 4-bit adder, we simply cascade four CLBs. This is shown in Figure 10.41(a).

An alternative approach is to use the 2-bit binary adder as a building block. This circuit has five inputs, A_1, A_0, B_1, B_0, and a C_{in}. The outputs S_1, S_0, and C_{out} are each functions of these five variables. Thus, the 2-bit adder can be implemented with three CLBs. To construct a 4-bit adder, we cascade two 2-bit units for a total of six CLBs. This is shown in Figure 10.41(b).

The second implementation may not look attractive, but it has some advantages. It incurs two CLB delays in computing the 4-bit sum, one to compute the carry between the low-order 2 bits and the high-order sums and one to compute the final sums of the high-order bits. This compares with four CLB delays in the implementation based on the standard full adders.

This example illustrates some of the trade-offs between CLB resources and delay. The delay through the logic block is fixed, independent of the function it is implementing. The first approach uses less CLB resources than the second, but actually is slower.

Obviously, the CLB structure is not limited to combinational circuits. Because of the two flip-flops per CLB, it is possible to construct 4-bit counters of various kinds using just two CLBs. The CLB inputs are the

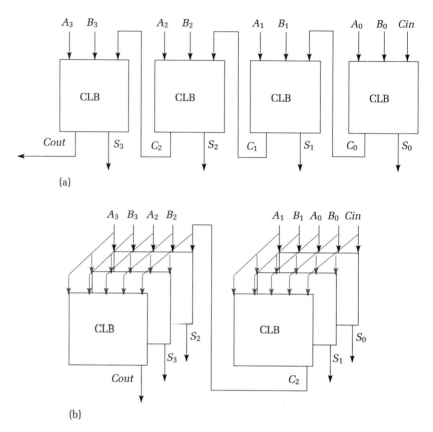

(a)

(b)

Figure 10.41 Alternative implementations of a 4-bit adder.

current state, Q_3, Q_2, Q_1, and Q_0. The outputs of the first CLB are the higher-order 2 bits of the counter. The output of the second is the lower-order 2 bits.

Xilinx Interconnect The Xilinx chip architecture supports three methods of interconnecting the CLBs and IOBs: (1) direct connections, (2) general-purpose interconnect, and (3) long line interconnections. With direct connections, adjacent CLBs are wired together in the horizontal or vertical direction. General-purpose interconnect is used for longer distance connections or for signals with a moderate fan-out. The long lines are saved for time-critical signals that must be distributed to many CLBs with minimum signal skew, such as clock signals.

Direct connections provide the fastest, shortest-distance form of interconnect. Thus, it is important for the software that assigns logic functions to available CLBs to place related logic in adjacent CLBs. The X output of a CLB can be connected to the B input of the CLB to its right or the C input of the CLB to its left. The Y output can be connected to the D input of the CLB above it and the A input of the CLB below it.

These direct connections are shown in Figure 10.42. We show four CLBs, with inputs A, CE (clock enable), DI (data in), B, C, K (clock), E, D, and R (reset) and outputs X and Y. The relative placement of connection pins on the CLBs is geometrically accurate.

CLB$_2$'s X output is connected to the B input of CLB$_3$. The X output of CLB$_1$ connects to the C input of CLB$_0$. All of the X connections are horizontal. Similarly, the Y output of CLB$_1$ is connected to the A input of CLB$_3$. The Y output of CLB$_2$ connects to the D input of CLB$_0$. The Y connections are vertical.

We can also use direct connections to wire CLBs and IOBs. There are two IOBs next to each CLB along the top or bottom row of the logic cell array. Along the top, the CLB A input can be driven from the output of one IOB, and the CLB Y output is connected to the other IOB's input. Along the bottom, the D input plays the same role as the A input along the top.

Along the right edge, the X output can be connected to one IOB while the Y output is connected to either of the adjacent IOBs. The C

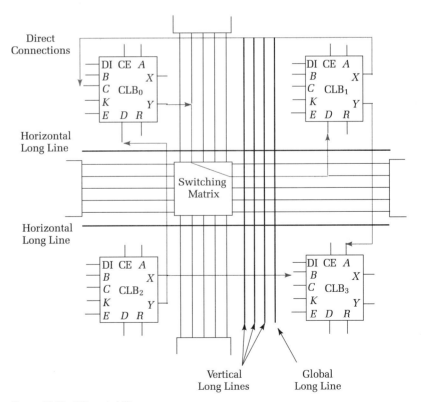

Figure 10.42   Xilinx wirability.

input is driven from one of the IOBs. Along the left edge, the B input can be driven from an IOB, and the IOB can be driven from the X output. CLBs in the corners can connect to IOBs in two dimensions.

Interleaved among the checkerboard of CLBs are the horizontal and vertical wiring channels of the Xilinx general-purpose interconnect. Each channel contains five wires. At the intersections, a programmable switching matrix connects the wires, as shown in Figure 10.42. The figure shows a connection path between the Y output of CLB_0 and the D input of CLB_1.

The general-purpose interconnect places many restrictions on what can be connected to what. For example, it is not possible to connect every switch matrix pin to every other pin. The pin we used, the second pin from the left on the top, is only connected to the top pins on the left and the right, the three leftmost pins on the bottom, and the second pin from the top on the right. As another example of wiring restrictions, the D input of a CLB can be connected to the second wire in the horizontal channel but not the top wire. Fortunately, Xilinx's software for placing and routing the LCA is aware of the restrictions in the wiring fabric and can hide most of these considerations from you.

The final forms of interconnect are the long lines. There are two such lines per row and three per column. In addition, a single global long line is driven by a special buffer and distributed to every column. It can be connected to the K input of every CLB.

One more special global signal is not shown in the wiring diagrams. A global reset line, connected to the chip reset pin, can force all flip-flops in the LCA to zero, independent of the individual CLB reset input.

Implementing the BCD-to-Excess-3 Converter with a Xilinx Logic Cell Array
In this subsection, we examine the implementation of the BCD-to-Excess-3 converter finite state machine using the LCA structure. The next-state and output equations are

$$Q_2^+ = \overline{Q}_2 \bullet Q_0 + Q_2 \bullet \overline{Q}_0$$

$$Q_1^+ = \overline{X} \bullet \overline{Q}_2 \bullet \overline{Q}_1 \bullet Q_0 + X \bullet \overline{Q}_2 \bullet \overline{Q}_0 + \overline{X} \bullet Q_2 \bullet \overline{Q}_0 + Q_1 \bullet \overline{Q}_0$$

$$Q_0^+ = \overline{Q}_0$$

$$Z = X \bullet Q_1 + \overline{X} \bullet \overline{Q}_1$$

Suppose we adopt a synchronous Mealy implementation style. Then each of the four functions requires its own flip-flop. Since no function is more complex than four variables, we can implement each one in one-half of a CLB.

To give you a feeling for the size of functions that can be implemented in a Xilinx chip, the smallest configuration contains 64 CLBs. The example finite state machine uses only 1/32 of the CLB resources of the array.

One critical issue is how to provide reset to the finite state machine. We will use the global reset signal derived from the dedicated reset pin on the LCA package. When this signal is asserted, all flip-flops in the array are set to zero.

Xilinx provides software to map a logic schematic into a placed and routed collection of CLBs, so designers rarely have to deal with the array at this level of detail. Still, it is instructive to understand some of the routing details, because they have a critical effect on performance. Xilinx permits you to hand route critical nets to tune circuit performance (or to help the automatic router complete a difficult routing), if desired.

Figure 10.43 shows a possible interconnection scheme. It uses global long lines, horizontal long lines, direct connections, and general-purpose connections. The global long line is dedicated to the clock signal, which drives the K input of the two CLBs. The horizontal long line

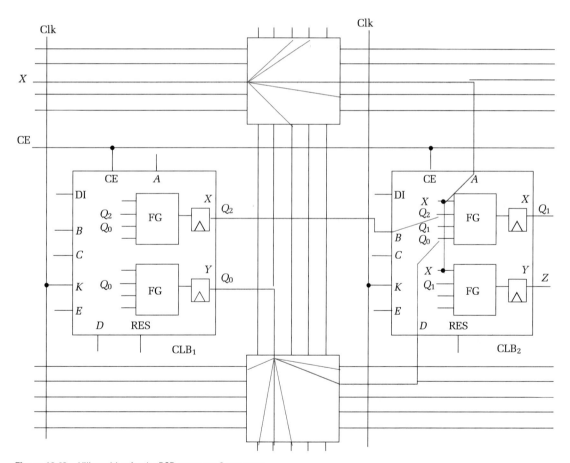

Figure 10.43 Xilinx wiring for the BCD-to-excess-3 converter.

carries the clock enable signal (CE). Xilinx makes it possible to attach the horizontal lines to pull-up resistors, so this wire can always carry a 1. The vertical long lines are not used in this example.

We have placed Q_2 and Q_0 in CLB_1, with Q_1 and Z in CLB_2. This partitioning helps to minimize the use of general-purpose interconnect. CLB_1 is implemented without any external inputs, by exploiting the connections inside the CLB.

Since the flow of signals is horizontal from left to right and only CLB_1's X output (Q_2) can be routed through horizontal direct interconnect, the Y output (Q_0) must go through general-purpose interconnect.

Normally, the Y output of CLB_2 (Z) would be wired to the vertical channel, eventually reaching an IOB at the periphery of the array of CLBs. If these CLBs are placed along the top row of the array, direct connections can be used to make the machine's inputs and outputs directly available. An input IOB, carrying the machine's X input, can be wired to the A input of CLB_2. Also, CLB_2's Y output, carrying the machine's Z output, can be connected to an adjacent IOB configured for output.

Case Study   **10.4   Traffic Light Controller**

In this section, we will examine several alternative implementations for the traffic light controller finite state machine. We start by decomposing the basic machine into its constituent subsystems. Besides the next-state and output functions, we also need logic for the timing of the lights and for detecting the presence of a car at the intersection.

10.4.1   Problem Decomposition: Traffic Light State Machine

Of course, there are many possible ways to organize the components of the traffic light system. Here is the decomposition we will use:

- Controller finite state machine
    next state/output combinational functions
    state register
- Short time/long time interval counter
- Car sensor
- Output decoders and traffic lights

System Block Diagram   A block diagram description for this decomposition is shown in Figure 10.44. The controller finite state machine takes as input the Reset, Clk, TL, and TS signals, as well as a synchronized C signal, and generates the ST signal and encoded light signals (00 = green, 01 = yellow, 10 = red). The interval counter subsystem takes Clk, Reset, and ST as inputs, generating TL and TS as outputs. The car sensor subsystem has an asynchronous sensor input C, which it outputs

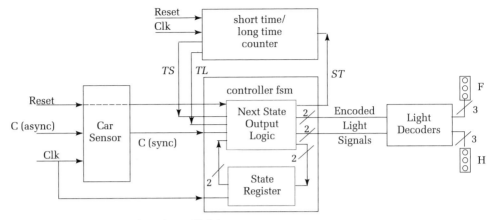

Figure 10.44   Block diagram of complete traffic light system.

as a synchronized signal. The light decoders translate the encoded light control signals into signals to drive the individual lights.

It is reasonable to generate outputs that directly control the lights, rather than the encoded scheme we have chosen. Since the actual traffic lights are probably relatively far from the traffic light controller hardware, the encoded scheme has the advantage of fewer wires that need to be routed that distance. But the approach requires additional logic to do the decoding near the lights.

In the way we have drawn Figure 10.44, the finite state machine is a Mealy machine. Is it synchronous or asynchronous? Because the inputs C (sync), TS, and TL change with the clock, it is a synchronous machine. To be thorough, Reset should also be synchronized.

In the following subsections, we look at the logic for the next state and outputs, the car detector, the light decoders, and the interval timer.

Next-State Logic and Outputs   The finite state machine has six inputs: Reset, C, TL, TS, and the current state (Q_1, Q_0); and seven outputs: the next state (P_1, P_0), ST, $H_{1,0}$ (encoded highway lights), and $F_{1,0}$ (encoded farmroad lights).

An *espresso* truth table file, such as that in Figure 9.21, can be used to specify the transition table for the state machine. From this, we can generate discrete gate, PAL, or PLA-style logic for the next state and other outputs.

Car Detector   The car detector logic is much like the debounced switch of Section 6.6.1. A two-position switch embedded in the road determines whether a car is present. This signal should be stable during the transition from one setting to the other, and this calls for a debouncing circuit.

Since a car can arrive at any time, the car detector is asynchronous with respect to the rest of the traffic light system. To synchronize the car sense signal, we must pass it through a synchronizer flip-flop, clocked by the system clock. The circuit is given in Figure 10.45.

Light Decoders The light decoder circuitry is reasonably straightforward. We can use 2-to-4 decoders, such as the TTL 74139. Figure 10.46 contains the necessary logic.

Interval Timer The last major component is the interval timer, designed to generate the signals *TL* and *TS* after being set by *ST*. We could implement this in many ways, perhaps the simplest being to use a counter and external decode logic. The counter is cleared when *ST* is asserted, and *TL* and *TS* are asserted by the external logic when the counter counts up to the appropriate threshold value. For this discussion, we will assume that *TS* is asserted when the 4-bit counter reaches 0111_2 and *TL* is asserted when it reaches 1111_2. Wider counters can be used for more realistic interval timings.

Figure 10.47 shows how the logic could be implemented using a 74163 synchronous up-counter. In the figure, the OR of *ST* and RESET is complemented to reset the counter. When either *ST* or RESET is

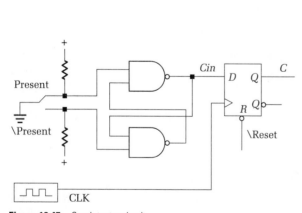

Figure 10.45 Car detector circuit.

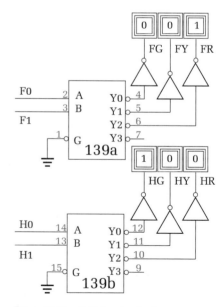

Figure 10.46 Light decoder circuitry.

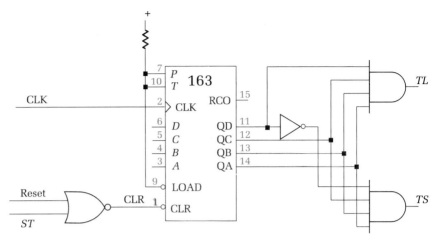

Figure 10.47   Simple interval timing.

asserted, the $\overline{\text{CLR}}$ input is asserted, and the counter is set to zero. This is not strictly necessary: whatever state the counter comes up in when powered on, it will eventually cycle through the states that cause *TS* and *TL* to be asserted.

10.4.2   PLA/PAL/ROM-Based Implementation

In this subsection, we will use the best encoding found in Section 9.3.1: HG = 00, HY = 10, FG = 01, and FY = 11. This yields an implementation for the next-state and output functions that requires eight unique product terms:

$$P_1 = C \bullet TL \bullet \overline{Q}_1 + \overline{TS} \bullet Q_1 \bullet \overline{Q}_0 + \overline{C} \bullet \overline{Q}_1 \bullet Q_0 + \overline{TS} \bullet Q_1 \bullet Q_0$$

$$P_0 = TS \bullet Q_1 \bullet \overline{Q}_0 + \overline{Q}_1 \bullet Q_0 + \overline{TS} \bullet Q_1 \bullet Q_0$$

$$ST = C \bullet TL \bullet \overline{Q}_1 + \overline{C} \bullet \overline{Q}_1 \bullet Q_0 + TS \bullet Q_1 \bullet \overline{Q}_0 + TS \bullet Q_1 \bullet Q_0$$

$$H_1 = TS \bullet Q_1 \bullet Q_0 + \overline{Q}_1 \bullet Q_0 + \overline{TS} \bullet Q_1 \bullet Q_0$$

$$H_0 = \overline{TS} \bullet Q_1 \bullet \overline{Q}_0 + TS \bullet Q_1 \bullet \overline{Q}_0$$

$$F_1 = \overline{Q}_0$$

$$F_0 = TS \bullet Q_1 \bullet Q_0 + \overline{TS} \bullet Q_1 \bullet Q_0$$

Any PLA component with five inputs, seven outputs, and eight product terms could implement these functions.

PLA/PAL Implementation   Because no function is more complex than four product terms, they can also be implemented by many of the available sequential PALs. For example, in Section 8.5.3 we gave an ABEL description for the traffic light state machine that used a P22V10 PAL (see Figure 10.28). This device has 11 dedicated inputs and 10 programmable input/outputs. When the latter are programmed as outputs, they can be either registered or combinational. The OR array varies from 8 to 14 product term inputs, sufficient to implement any of the functions above. The embedded registers can be reset through a dedicated reset line that is routed to each output register, so it is not necessary to include a Reset input signal in the equations.

ROM Implementation   A ROM-based implementation requires a complete tabulation of the state transition table. With five inputs and seven outputs, this is a 32-word by 8-bit ROM. If Reset is to be handled by the next-state logic directly, this should be included as one of the inputs to the ROM, thus doubling its size.

10.4.3   Counter-Based Implementation

Although the two-level implementation just described is appropriate for a PAL- or PLA-based approach, it is not necessarily the best strategy when using packaged components such as TTL. The equations in the preceding subsection require eight 3-input gates (three packages), two 4-input gates (one package), three 2-input gates (one package), four inverters (one package), and many wires. An MSI-based implementation could lead to fewer components and certainly fewer interconnections.

Counters, Multiplexers, Decoders   If you examine the traffic light finite state machine carefully, you should see that a counter could be used to implement the state register. After all, the machine either holds in its current state or advances to the next state in a well-defined sequence.

Let's make the state assignment HG = 00, HY = 01, FG = 10, and FY = 11. We will implement the state register with a 74163 synchronous up-counter. An external reset signal can be wired to the counter's synchronous clear input.

The question now becomes how to implement the counter's count input. Figure 10.48 reproduces the state diagram for the traffic controller. In state HG, the exit condition is $TL \cdot C$. In HY and FY, it is TS. In FG, it is $TL + \bar{C}$. We could use logic that takes the relevant condition of the current-state bits and ANDs it with the appropriate exit condition to form the count signal. Unfortunately, this would take a fair amount of discrete logic.

A better way is to use a multiplexer to implement the count signal. We drive a four-to-one multiplexer's selection lines with the current-state bits,

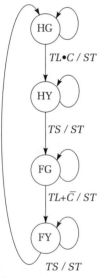

Figure 10.48   Traffic light controller finite state machine.

TL•C / ST

TS / ST

TL+C̄ / ST

TS / ST

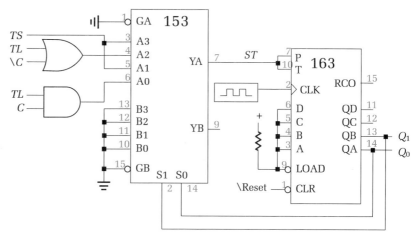

Figure 10.49   TTL MSI implementation of next-state function.

Q_1 and Q_0. The inputs are wired for the appropriate exit condition. This is shown in Figure 10.49. The count signal and the start timer signal, *ST,* are identical. As you can see, this approach represents a substantial reduction in package count.

As one final application of MSI components, it is possible to drive the traffic lights from signals that have been directly decoded from the current state. For example, if the machine is in state HG, the highway lights are green and the farmroad lights are red. Similarly, the highway lights are yellow and the farmroad lights are red when the machine is in state HY. Thus the highway green light and yellow light can be decoded directly from state 0 and 1, respectively, while the farmroad red light is driven by the OR of these decoded signals. The logic is shown in Figure 10.50.

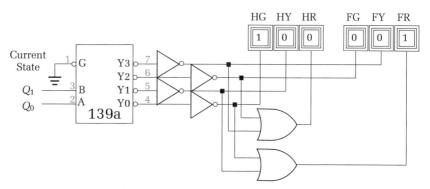

Figure 10.50   Traffic light decoder.

10.4.4   LCA-Based Implementation

Let's begin with the same set of equations we used for the PAL/PLA-based implementation. Fortunately, none of the next-state and output functions are more complex than five variables: P_1 and ST are five variables; P_0, H_1, H_0, and F_0 are three variables; and F_1 is one variable. Thus, we can implement the finite state machine in four and one half CLBs: one CLB each for the two 5-variable functions, and the remaining five functions grouped two apiece into the remaining CLBs.

Xilinx provides software that takes as input a schematic description of a circuit, automatically partitions the logic to the CLB components, chooses specific CLBs in the logic array to implement this partitioning, and selects a routing of the interconnections to complete the implementation. In general, the designer need not know in detail how the schematic is mapped into the array structure. Nevertheless, to illustrate more about the internal structure of the LCA, we will perform the partitioning, placement, and routing by hand (Xilinx provides an editor that lets you deal with this level of detail).

The first step is to map functions onto CLBs, especially when two functions are to be placed in the same CLB. To make the best use of the CLB's inputs, we should try to place functions of the same inputs in the same CLB. For example, H_1 and H_0 are both functions of TS, Q_1, and Q_0. These two functions can easily be placed in the same CLB.

A second goal is to minimize the amount of inter-CLB routing. For example, it makes sense to place P_0 and F_1 in the same CLB, because the latter is simply a function of the former. The remaining function, F_0, is placed in a CLB by itself.

The second step maps the five CLBs onto the array to make best use of direct interconnect and minimum use of global interconnect. We begin by placing the CLB for Q_1, since both its outputs X and Y will carry the same value. By placing other CLBs above, below, and to the right of this CLB, we can make good use of many direct connections.

Figure 10.51 shows one possible CLB placement and the routing of the inputs and state outputs. The Q_1 CLB is placed in the center at the left. Through direct connections, it drives the D input of F_0's CLB, the A input of ST's CLB, and the B input of the $H_{1,0}$ CLB. The Q_0 CLB is placed in the upper right-hand corner. It uses direct connections to drive the A input of the $H_{1,0}$ CLB.

We must use general-purpose interconnections to get Q_1 to the Q_0 CLB and Q_0 to the left-hand column of CLBs. The X output of the Q_1 CLB can be connected to the first vertical track. This is routed up through the switching matrix. The B input on the Q_0 CLB can be connected to this wire.

This interconnection illustrates some of the constraints on the general-purpose connections. The X output can be connected only to vertical tracks 1 and 4 (numbered from left to right), while the B input can be connected only to vertical tracks 1, 3, and 5, as well as horizontal tracks 1 and 5 in the channel below the CLB. It is not possible to wire up any input or output to any track.

The distribution of Q_0 is somewhat more complicated. It is initially connected to the third wire of the horizontal channel below its CLB. The middle switching matrix splits the signals onto the fourth vertical routing track while simultaneously passing it through on the third horizontal wire. Let's

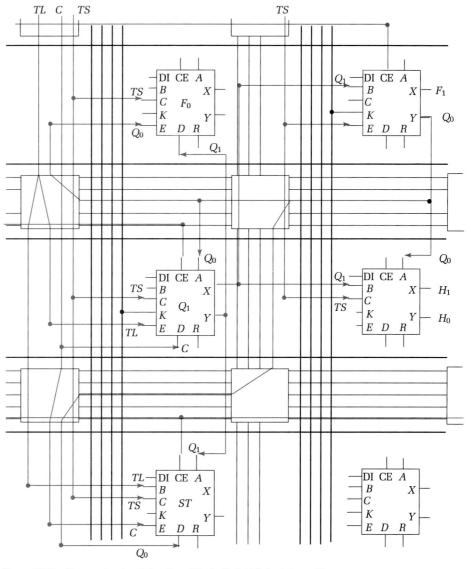

Figure 10.51   Placement and partial routing of the traffic light finite state machine.

follow the horizontal distribution first. The A input of Q_1's CLB can connect to this wire (as well as the first horizontal track and the first and third vertical tracks of the channel to its left). The next switching matrix routes the wire to the third vertical track, where it can be connected to the E input (E can also be connected to the fifth vertical track and the fifth horizontal track below it).

Now returning to the vertical distribution of Q_0, it passes through another switching matrix, which routes it onto the third vertical track. Since the ST CLB's A input is already directly connected to Q_1, we have to route Q_0 to the vertical channel to the left of the CLB. The next switching matrix places the signal on the fourth vertical track. From here it can be connected to the D input (which can also be wired to the third horizontal track below it).

The rest of the routing details are to get the C, TL, and TS signals to the appropriate CLB inputs. TS is routed along the fifth vertical track in both of the vertical channels shown in the figure. To keep the routing regular, we wire the C input to this track in each of the CLBs (C can be wired to vertical tracks 2, 4, and 5 and horizontal tracks 3 and 5 from the channel above the CLB), except Q_0's CLB. Recall from Figure 10.39 that if an internal flip-flop's output is to be used in computing a function, then one of the B or C inputs cannot be used.

C and TL are needed only in the computation of Q_0 and ST, so we only route them through the leftmost vertical track. C follows the fourth and then the third vertical track, from which it can be wired to Q_1's D input and ST's E input. TL starts on the second track, where it splits onto the first and third tracks by the first switching matrix. This allows it to be connected to the E input of Q_1 and the B input of ST.

It is worth making a few extra points. First, Q_1's B input is left floating. This is because the internal flip-flop's output is used as an input to the internal function generator. Second, the Q_0 and Q_1 CLBs are connected to the global clock line, and their clock enable inputs are wired to the fifth horizontal track. This track carries the clock enable signal. The global reset signal puts the state machine into its starting state.

In general, the designer need not see this level of detail. So why bother to understand it? Routing decisions can have a serious impact on performance, and no routing software is perfect, especially given the complex constraints imposed on the routing task by the Xilinx architecture. Each traversal of a switching matrix adds 1 to 3 ns to the signal delay. The worst-case routing for Q_0 passes it through three switching matrices, and this might represent the critical path in the circuit. By working at the detailed level of the interconnection fabric, you can do hand routing for critical signals or force them onto the smaller-delay long line interconnections.

Counter/Multiplexer It is also possible to think about our MSI implementation in terms of the primitives supported by the Xilinx LCA. The basic elements of our MSI approach are a four-to-one multiplexer and a 2-bit up-counter. Let's see how these map into CLBs.

We begin with the multiplexer. A general-purpose four-to-one multiplexer is a function of six variables: its four data inputs and two control inputs. Fortunately, this is exactly the kind of six-variable function that can be implemented by a single CLB. Think back to Figure 10.39(c). The CLB can be configured as a two-to-one multiplexer, controlled by input E, that selects among two functions of four variables. Of course, each of these functions could be its own two-to-one multiplexer.

This is not the best solution, however. We need a second CLB just to implement the terms $TL \bullet C$ and $TL + \overline{C}$ for input to the multiplexer. On closer examination, the function we want to implement is really five variables: TL, C, TS, Q_1, and Q_0. We can implement this in a single CLB.

Now consider the 2-bit counter that implements the state register. A full-blown 74163 is not really needed: we never use the load capability, and we can clear the counter using the global reset signal rather than a specific clear input. Thus, each bit of the counter is a function of three inputs: a count signal and the 2-bit current state. This too can be implemented in a single CLB.

Finally, let's look at the logic to decode the six light functions from the current state, as we did in the MSI example. All of these functions are defined over two variables: Q_1 and Q_0. We can pack two such functions per CLB, for a total of three additional CLBs.

By cleverly using MSI functions rather than discrete gates, we came up with a five-CLB implementation, including the output decoders. Many things you have learned about TTL MSI components remain valid in the new programmable logic technology!

Chapter Review

In this chapter, we have focused on alternative strategies for implementing finite state machines. We covered structured logic methods, based on ROM, PLA, and PALs, to compute the next-state and output functions. We also examined MSI-based implementation strategies, using components like counters, multiplexers, and decoders to implement the machine using a small number of component packages.

If the goal is minimum package count, the best solution is to use some of the more advanced programmable logic components, such as those provided by Altera, Actel, and Xilinx. Altera's architecture is a generalization of the more conventional PAL structures. Their major innovations are the ability to share product terms among multiple output functions and a more general method of interconnect.

Actel bases its architecture on a very simple building block, a generalization of the four-to-one multiplexer, and a flexible orthogonal wiring grid for interconnections. Whereas Altera and Xilinx parts can be reprogrammed, the Actel technology is program-once. Therefore, you must take care to fully simulate the design before the programming process. There are no second chances!

We concentrated on Xilinx technology, because it was the first in the programmable gate array business and, thus, is the most prevalent in industry today. The architecture is based on complex building blocks, the IOB and CLB, containing considerable logic, flip-flops, and interconnection resources. These blocks are interconnected by a network of vertical and horizontal tracks joined by switching matrices.

In the final section of the chapter, we looked at the detailed implementation of the traffic light controller, a running example throughout this book. In particular, we examined PAL/PLA/ROM implementations, counter/multiplexer/decoder implementations, and how they might be implemented within a Xilinx LCA. Interestingly, the MSI-inspired implementation yielded a much more elegant solution than the one obtained from discrete gates. Many MSI building blocks, or suitably modified versions of them, can map nicely onto the primitives provided by the LCA.

Further Reading

The best place to learn about special PAL/PLD architectures is in the data books available from the manufacturers. These are usually filled with excellent tutorial materials and detailed design examples in the applications notes. Here is a partial list of relevant databooks:

Actel, *ACT1 Family Gate Arrays* (June 1988).

Altera, *Applications Handbook* (July 1988).

Altera, *Data Book* (October 1990).

Cypress Semiconductor, *CMOS/BiCMOS Data Book* (February 1989).

Monolithic Memories, *Programmable Logic Handbook*, 4th ed. (1985).

Xilinx, *Programmable Gate Array Design Handbook*, 2nd ed. (1989).

Some books have recently been published that focus exclusively on digital design techniques for programmable logic. R. Sandige's book, *Modern Logic Design*, McGraw-Hill, 1990, focuses on PROM/PAL/PLA-based design. P. K. Lala, *PLD: Digital System Design Using Programmable Logic Devices*, Prentice-Hall, 1990, gives a very detailed description of the various PAL and PLD families and many excellent design examples. He includes discussions of the more modern components from Actel, Altera, and Xilinx. M. Boulton, *Digital Systems Design with Programmable Logic*, Addison-Wesley, 1990, covers similar ground.

The Actel databook mentioned above includes several technical paper reprints that describe the underlying technology in significant detail. Among these are K. A. El-Ayat et al., "A CMOS Electrically Configurable

Gate Array," originally published in the *IEEE Journal of Solid State Circuits*, 24 (3), 752–762 (June 1989), and A. El Gamal et al., "An Architecture for Electrically Configurable Gate Arrays," *IEEE Journal of Solid State Circuits*, 24 (2), 394–398 (April 1989).

Exercises

10.1 *(State Reduction)*   Verify that the code converter problem statement of Section 10.1.2 yields the reduced state transition table and state diagram of Figures 10.3 and 10.4. Start with a general state diagram derived directly from the problem statement, and show how it is reduced.

10.2 *(Reset in Finite State Machines)*   Consider the BCD-to-Excess-3 code converter state machine. In various implementations of this machine, reset was used to control the state register's clear signal directly. How does the next-state logic change when reset is treated as an explicit input, for the following implementations:

   a. The ROM-based approach of Figures 10.5 and 10.6

   b. A PLA-based approach as suggested by Figures 10.9 and 10.11

10.3 *(Actel Logic Module)*   Figure 10.32 showed the basic Actel logic module. Show how a single logic module can be used to implement the following functions:

   a. A two-input AND gate

   b. A two-input NAND gate

   c. A two-input NOR gate with one input inverted

   d. A two-input XOR gate

   e. The logic function $Y = (A \bullet B) + C$

   f. The logic function $Y = (A + B) \bullet C$

   g. The logic function $Y = (A \bullet B) + (A \bullet C) + (B \bullet C)$. This function is also known as the majority function.

10.4 *(Actel Logic Module)*   Describe how to implement the following functions using two Actel logic modules:

   a. A four-input AND-OR-Invert structure with two 2-input AND gates at the first level

   b. $Y = \overline{A} + \overline{B} + C + D$

10.5 *(Actel Logic Module)*   Show how to implement a half adder in terms of an Actel logic module (more than one module may be needed). How would you implement the full adder circuit? (*Hint*: This can be done in two logic modules if the carry-in and carry-out are designed to be active low.)

10.6 *(Actel Logic Module)*   Figure 10.33 showed how to implement an $\overline{R}\text{-}\overline{S}$ latch using the Actel logic module. Show how to implement an *R-S* latch using a similar structure. How would you implement a *D* flip-flop?

10.7 *(Xilinx CLB)*   The function generator within the Xilinx CLB can implement any combinational logic function of five inputs. This is equivalent to how many two-input gates? Explain how you derived your answer.

10.8 *(Xilinx CLB)*   A single Xilinx CLB can implement a five-input parity function.

   a. Show how a two-level CLB structure can implement a 25-input parity function.

   b. How many input parity functions can be implemented by a three-level CLB structure?

10.9 *(Xilinx CLB)*   The Xilinx CLB can implement any single combinational logic function $F(A,B,C,D,E)$ of five variables OR two independent functions $F(A,B,C,D)$ and $G(A,B,C,D)$ of four (or less) variables.

   a. Show how this might be implemented by wiring up a 32-input function generator (multiplexer/selector) using two 16-to-1 and three 2-to-1 multiplexers. Assume that $input_0$ is selected when $EABCD = 00000$, $input_{15}$ when $EABCD = 01111$, $input_{16}$ when $EABCD = 10000$, and $input_{31}$ when $EABCD = 11111$. Besides the five data inputs A, B, C, D, and E, there is a control input M such that when $M = 0$ the function generator generates the two independent four-variable functions F and G, and when $M = 1$ it generates the single five-variable function on both the F and G outputs.

   b. What must the input settings be to implement the five-variable function $F = A \oplus B \oplus C \oplus D \oplus E$?

   c. What must the input settings be to implement the two 3-variable functions $F(A,B,C) = A \oplus B \oplus C$ (full adder sum) and $G(A,B,C) = A \bullet B + B \bullet C + A \bullet C$ (full adder carry)?

10.10 *(Traffic Light Controller)*   The description of the traffic light controller in Section 10.4.1 assumes that the traffic light outputs from the state machine are encoded. This saves only two output lines, yet introduces the extra complexity (and parts count) of external decoders.

   a. Rederive the equations for the traffic light control signals, assuming fully decoded outputs from the state machine: HG, HY, HR, FG, FY, FR. Also show the revised state transition table.

b. How does this affect the PAL-based implementation? In particular, will you require a PAL with more product terms per output or fewer terms per output?

c. How does the change affect the ROM-based implementation?

10.11 *(Traffic Light Controller)* The traffic light controller as presented in Section 10.4.1 is a Mealy machine. Modify the description to make it part Moore/part Mealy by decoding the traffic light control signals directly from the state, as we did in Section 10.4.3.

a. What are the implications for a PAL-based implementation?

b. How does this affect the ROM-based implementation?

10.12 *(Traffic Light Controller)* The end of Section 10.4.4 described how to implement the traffic light controller finite state machine in terms of MSI-style components mapped onto Xilinx CLBs. Verify that the *ST* function can be implemented by a single CLB by giving the truth table for the five-variable function $ST(TL, TS, C, Q_1, Q_0)$.

10.13 *(Implementing Finite State Machines)* Follow the complete implementation process for the string recognizer finite state machine from Section 8.5.1. Choose a state assignment and determine the minimized next-state and output functions.

a. Given the equations you derived for the next-state and output functions, determine the kind of PAL you will need to complete the implementation. Consider such factors as number of inputs, number of registered versus combinational outputs, and number of product terms per output.

b. Repeat the analysis for Xilinx LCAs. How many CLBs will you need to realize the set of equations you derived?

10.14 *(Implementing Finite State Machines)* Repeat Exercise 10.13, but for the complex counter finite state machine of Section 8.5.2.

10.15 *(Implementing Finite State Machines)* Repeat Exercise 10.13, but this time for the 3-bit combination lock of Section 8.5.4.

10.16 *(Implementing Finite State Machines)* Repeat Exercise 10.13, but for the reduced state diagram of the 3-bit string recognizer of Figure 9.27. Use one of the good state assignments of Figure 9.28. What are the implications of choosing a state assignment in which the start state is not encoded as 0?

10.17 *(Implementing Finite State Machines)* Repeat Exercise 10.13, but for the reduced state diagram of the 4-bit string recognizer of Figure 9.7. Use one of the good state assignments from Figure 9.29.

10.18 *(Implementing Finite State Machines)* Repeat Exercise 10.13, but for the reduced multi-input state diagram of Figure 9.17. Use a straightforward state assignment: $S_0' = 00$, $S_1 = 01$, $S_2 = 10$, $S_3' = 11$.

10.19 *(Implementing Finite State Machines)* Implement an 8-bit register using the 20X10 PAL of Figure 10.16 to the following specifications:

   a. The register has three control inputs, $\overline{OE}$ (output enable), $\overline{LD}$ (load), and CLK (clock), and eight data inputs D_7-D_0. It has eight registered outputs Q_7-Q_0. When $\overline{OE}$ is unasserted, the outputs are in high impedance. When $\overline{LD}$ is unasserted, the register holds its current value. When $\overline{LD}$ is asserted, the register's contents are replaced by the data inputs on the next rising clock edge. What are the Boolean equations for each register input? Draw a wiring diagram, similar to Figure 10.13, for the PAL's pin inputs and outputs.

   b. The register has three control inputs: $\overline{OE}$ (output enable), $CLR/\overline{INC}$ (clear/increment), and CLK (clock), and eight data outputs, Q_7-Q_0. When $\overline{OE}$ is unasserted, the outputs are in high impedance. When CLR is asserted, the register is set to 0 on the next rising clock edge. When CLR is unasserted, the register is incremented by 1 on the next clock edge. In essence, the register is a free-running counter. What are the Boolean equations for each register input? Draw a wiring diagram like Figure 10.13 for the PAL's pin inputs and outputs. (*Hint:* consider the carry lookahead logic described in Chapter 5, except simplified for the specific case where the sum is $A + 1$.)

10.20 *(Implementing Finite State Machines)* In this exercise, you will design a memory controller finite state machine that implements a processor-memory handshake to the following specification. The processor initiates a transfer request by asserting REQ (request) while specifying a read or write (RW) operation. During a read operation (RW asserted), the processor waits for the memory controller to assert $\overline{DA}$ (data available). The processor can then sample the data. It unasserts the REQ line to end the memory cycle. During a write operation (RW unasserted), the processor drives data to the memory system, waiting for the memory controller to assert $\overline{WC}$ (write complete). When the processor sees this, it unasserts REQ to end the cycle. This is a variation of the four-cycle handshake described in Chapter 4.

The Moore state diagram for the memory controller is shown in Figure Ex10.20(a). Note that the read and write require multiple states for their execution. A timing diagram, showing the relationships between the critical control signals for a read and a write cycle, is given in Figure Ex10.20(b). The state control signal outputs are listed in Figure Ex10.20(c). Several of the memory controller's signals listed here are used to control the memory components. Their detailed meaning is not important, except that the appropriate signals should be asserted in the listed states.

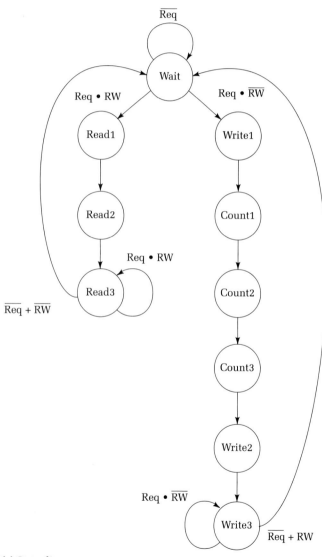

(a) State diagram

Figure Ex10.20 Memory controller.

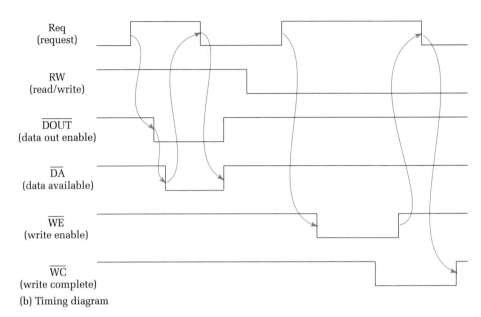

Req
(request)

RW
(read/write)

$\overline{\text{DOUT}}$
(data out enable)

$\overline{\text{DA}}$
(data available)

$\overline{\text{WE}}$
(write enable)

$\overline{\text{WC}}$
(write complete)

(b) Timing diagram

Figure Ex10.20 *(Continued.)*

a. Choose a good state assignment and implement using discrete gates and *D* flip-flops. What kind of PAL would you need to implement this machine in a single chip (in particular, number of inputs/outputs, flip-flops, product terms per output, etc.)?

b. How many Xilinx CLBs would it take to implement your solution to part (a)? Justify your answer.

c. Implement the state machine using a four-bit counter as a state register. Show your counter-based state assignment, and your implementation of the next state function in terms of clear, count, and load. What kind of PAL would you need to implement the next state control in a single chip (assume the state register is implemented externally with a 74163 synchronous up-counter)?

d. How many Xilinx CLBs would it take to implement your solution to part (c), including the counter state register and the output logic?

STATE	$\overline{\text{DOUT}}$	$\overline{\text{DA}}$	$\overline{\text{WE}}$	$\overline{\text{WC}}$	C_0	C_1
Wait	1	1	1	1	0	0
Read1	0	1	1	1	0	0
Read2	0	0	1	1	0	0
Read3	1	1	1	1	0	0
Count1	1	1	0	1	1	0
Count2	1	1	0	1	0	1
Count3	1	1	0	1	1	1
Write1	1	1	0	1	0	0
Write2	1	1	0	0	0	0
Write3	1	1	1	0	0	0

(c) State output behavior

Figure Ex10.20   *(Continued.)*

11 Computer Organization

From coupler-flange to spindle-guide I see Thy Hand, O God—
Predestination in the stride o' yon connectin'-rod.

—R. Kipling

Introduction

In Chapters 1 through 10, we examined the fundamental principles of digital design. In this chapter and the next, we will focus on applying these techniques to one major class of digital systems: the *stored program computer.*

A stored program computer consists of a *processing unit* and an attached *memory system.* Commands that instruct the processor to perform certain operations are placed in the memory along with the data items to be operated on. The processing unit consists of *datapath* and *control.* The datapath contains *registers* to hold data and *functional units,* such as arithmetic logic units and shifters, to operate on data. The control unit is little more than a finite state machine that sequences through its states to (1) fetch the next instruction from memory, (2) decode the instruction to interpret its meaning, and (3) execute the instruction by moving and/or operating on data in the registers and functional units of the datapath.

The critical design issues for a datapath are how to "wire" the various components together to minimize hardware complexity and the number of control states to complete a typical operation. For control, the issue is how to organize the relatively complex "instruction interpretation" finite state machine.

In this chapter, we will discuss how hardware components are organized into computers. In addition, we will apply the techniques we have already learned to design datapaths and processor control units. In particular, we will examine:

■ *Point-to-point, single-bus, and multiple-bus strategies for interconnecting the elements of the datapath.* There is a trade-off between datapath complexity and control complexity. A more complex datapath can simplify the control and vice versa.

■ *The structure of the controller finite state machine's state diagram.* The state diagram for computer control has a special structure that we will exploit in Chapter 12.

11.1   Structure of a Computer

Figure 11.1 shows a high-level block diagram of a computer. It is decomposed into a central processing unit (CPU), or *processor,* and an attached *memory system.* In turn, the processor is decomposed into *datapath* and *control units.*

The *datapath* (also called the *execution unit*) contains registers for storing intermediate results and combinational circuits for operating on data, such as shifting, adding, and multiplying. The latter are sometimes called *functional units* because they apply functions to data. Data is moved from memory into registers. It is then moved to the functional units, where the data manipulations take place. The results are placed

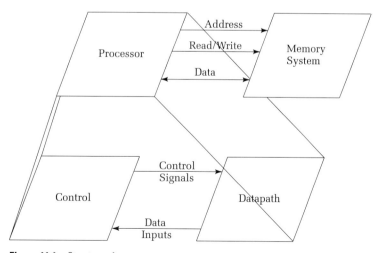

Figure 11.1   Structure of a processor.

back into registers and eventually put back into memory. The datapath implements the pathways along which data can flow from registers to functional units and back again.

The *control unit* (or *instruction unit*) implements a finite state machine that fetches a stream of instructions from memory. The instructions describe what operations, such as ADD, should be applied to which operands. The operands can be found in particular registers or in memory locations.

The control unit interprets or "executes" instructions by asserting the appropriate signals for manipulating the datapath, at the right time and in the correct sequence. For example, to add two registers and place the results in a third register, the control unit (1) asserts the necessary control signals to move the contents of the two source registers to the arithmetic logic unit (ALU), (2) instructs the ALU to perform an ADD operation by asserting the appropriate signals, and (3) moves the result to the specified destination register, again by asserting signals that establish a path between the ALU and the register.

Instructions can be grouped into three broad classes: data manipulation (add, subtract, etc.), data staging (load/store data from/to memory), and control (conditional and unconditional branches). The latter class determines the next instruction to fetch, sometimes conditionally based on inputs from the datapath. For example, the instruction may be to take the branch if the last datapath operation resulted in a negative number.

You are already familiar with the basic building blocks needed to implement the processor. You can interconnect NAND and NOR gates to build adder and logic circuits (Chapter 5) and registers (Chapters 6 and 7). The processor control unit is just another finite state machine (Chapters 8, 9, and 10). In the rest of this section, we will examine the components of a computer in a little more detail, as a prelude to the rest of this chapter.

11.1.1   Control

A processor control unit is considerably more complex than the kinds of finite state machines you have seen so far. A simple finite state machine is little more than next-state and output logic coupled to a state register. A control unit, on the other hand, needs access to its own datapath, a collection of registers containing information that affects the actions of the state machine.

Program Counter/Instruction Register   For example, the control unit may have a register to hold the address of the next memory word to fetch for instruction interpretation. This is frequently called the *program counter*, or PC. When the instruction is moved from memory into the control unit, it must be held somewhere while the control decodes the kind of instruction it is. This staging memory, often implemented by a register, is called the *instruction register* or IR. It is a special-purpose register and is usually not visible to the assembly language programmer.

Basic States of the Control Unit The control unit can be in one of four basic phases: *Reset*, *Fetch the Next Instruction*, *Decode the Instruction*, and *Execute the Instruction*. A high-level state diagram for a typical control unit is shown in Figure 11.2. Let's begin with the initialization sequence. An external reset signal places the finite state machine in its initial *Reset* state, from which the processor is initialized. Since the state of the processor contains more than just the state register of the finite state machine, several of the special registers must also be set to an initial value. For example, the PC must be set to some value, such as 0, before the first instruction can be fetched. Perhaps an accumulator register or a special register holding an indication of the condition of the datapath will be set to 0 as well. Although shown as a single state in the figure, the initialization process may be implemented by a sequence of states.

Next, the machine enters the *Fetch Instruction* state. The contents of the PC are sent as an address to the memory system. Then the control generates the signals needed to commence a memory read. When the operation is complete, the instruction is available on the memory's output wires and must be moved into the control unit's IR. Again, Fetch Instruction looks like a single state in the figure, but the actual implementation involves a sequence of states.

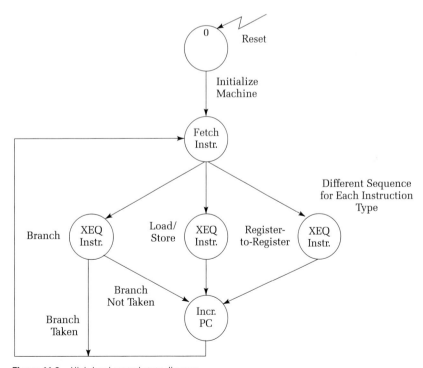

Figure 11.2 High-level control state diagram.

Once the instruction is available in the IR, the control examines certain bits within the instruction to determine its type. Each instruction type leads to a different sequence of execution states. For example, the basic execution sequence for a register-to-register add instruction is identical to one for a register-to-register subtract. The operands must be moved to the ALU and the result directed to the correct register destination. The only difference is the operation requested of the ALU. As long as the basic data movements are the same, the control sequences can be parameterized by the specific operation, decoded directly from the instruction.

The state machine in the figure partitions the instructions into three classes: Branch, Load/Store, and Register-to-Register. Of course, there could be more classes. In the limit, there could be a unique execution sequence for each instruction in the processor's instruction set.

The final state takes care of housekeeping operations, such as incrementing the PC, before branching back to fetch the next instruction. The execution sequence for a taken branch modifies the PC itself, so it bypasses this step. The sequence of instruction fetch, execute, and PC increment continues until the machine is reset.

While the details of the state diagram may vary from one instruction set to another, the general sequencing and the shape of the state diagram are generic to CPU state machines. The most distinguishing feature is the multiway decode branch between the instruction fetch and its execution. This influences the design of controllers for simple CPUs that we describe in the next chapter.

11.1.2   Datapath

The elements of the datapath are built up in a hierarchical and iterative fashion. Consider how we go about constructing a 32-bit arithmetic unit for inclusion in the datapath. At the most primitive level, we begin with the half adder that can add 2 bits. By interconnecting two of these, we create the full adder. Once we have a single "bit slice" for the datapath object, we create as many instances of it as we need for the width of the datapath. For example, we construct a 32-bit adder of the ALU by iteratively composing 32 instances of a 1-bit-wide adder.

As we saw in Chapter 5, an ALU bit slice is somewhat more complicated than this. It should also include hardware for logic operations and carry lookahead to perform arithmetic operations with reduced delay.

The datapath symbol for a typical arithmetic logic unit is shown in Figure 11.3. The 32-bit A and *B* data inputs come from other sources in the datapath; the *S* output goes to a datapath destination. The operation signals come from the control unit; the carry-out signal is routed back to the control unit so that it may detect certain exceptional conditions, such as overflow, that may disrupt the normal sequencing of instructions. We construct other datapath objects, such as shifters, registers, and register files, in an analogous manner.

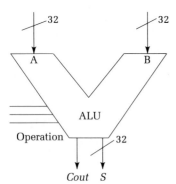

Figure 11.3 Iterative composition of datapath objects.

11.1.3   Block Diagram/Register Transfer

A computer with only a single data register, usually called the *accumulator* or AC, is the simplest machine organization. Figure 11.4 shows the block diagram for such a single accumulator machine.

Instructions for a single accumulator machine are called *single address instructions*. This is because they contain only a single reference to memory. One operand is implicitly the AC; the other is an operand in memory. The instructions are of the form AC := AC <operation> Memory (Address). <operation> could be ADD, SUBTRACT, AND, OR, and so on.

Let's consider an ADD instruction. The old value of the AC is replaced with the sum of the AC's contents and the contents of the specified memory location.

Data and Control Flows   Figure 11.4 shows the flow of data and control between memory, the control registers (IR, MAR, and PC), the data register (AC), and the functional units (ALU). The MAR is the *Memory Address Register*, a storage element that holds the address during memory accesses. Data flows are shown as bold arrowed lines; the other lines represent control.

The core of the datapath consists of the arithmetic logic unit and the AC. The AC is the source or destination of all transfers. These transfers

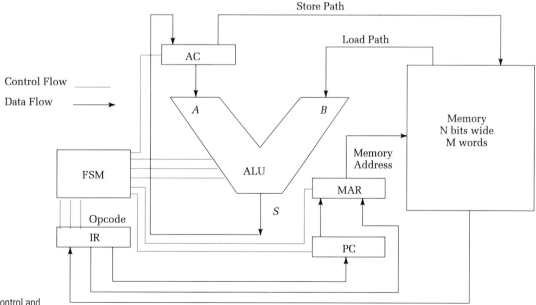

Figure 11.4 Control and data flows in a simple CPU.

are initiated by store, arithmetic, or load operations. Let's look at them in more detail.

The instruction identifies not only the operation to be performed but also the address of the memory operand. Store operations move the contents of the AC to a memory location specified by bits within the instruction. The sequencing begins by moving the specified address from the IR to the MAR. Then the contents of the AC are placed on the memory's data input lines while the MAR is placed onto its address lines. Finally, the memory control signals are cycled through a write sequence.

Arithmetic operations take as operands the contents of the accumulator and the memory location specified in the instruction. Again, the control moves the operand address from the IR to the MAR, but this time it invokes a memory read cycle. Data obtained from the load path is combined with the current contents of the AC to form the operation result. The result is then written back to the accumulator.

A load operation is actually a degenerate case of a normal arithmetic operation. The control obtains the *B* operand along the load path from memory, it places the ALU in a pass-through mode, and it stores the result in the AC.

Whereas load/store and arithmetic instructions manipulate the AC, branch instructions use the PC. If the instruction is an unconditional branch, the address portion of the IR replaces the PC, changing the next instruction to be executed. Similarly, a conditional branch replaces the PC if a condition specified in the instruction evaluates to true.

Placement of Instructions and Data There are two possible ways to connect the memory system to the CPU. The first is the so-called *Princeton architecture*: instructions and data are mixed in the same memory. In this case, the instruction and load/store paths are the same.

The alternative is the *Harvard architecture*. Data and instructions are stored in separate memories with independent paths into the processor.

The Princeton architecture is conceptually simpler and requires less connections to the memory, but the Harvard architecture has certain performance advantages. A Harvard architecture can fetch the next instruction even while executing the current instruction. If the current instruction needs to access memory to obtain an operand, the next instruction can still be moved into the processor. This strategy is called *instruction prefetching*, because the instruction is obtained before it is really needed. A Princeton architecture can prefetch instructions too. It is just more complicated to do so. To keep the discussion simple, we will assume a straightforward Princeton architecture in the rest of this chapter.

Detailed Instruction Trace As an example of the control signal and data flows needed to implement an instruction, let's trace a simple instruction that adds the contents of a specified memory location to the AC:

1. The instruction must be fetched from memory. The control does this by moving the PC to the MAR and then initiating a memory read operation. The instruction comes from memory to the IR along the instruction path.

2. Certain bits of the instruction encode the operation to be performed, that is, an ADD instruction. These are called the *op code* bits and are part of the inputs to the control finite state machine. We assume that the rest of the instruction's bits encode the address.

3. The control moves the operand address bits to the MAR and begins a second memory read operation to fetch the operand.

4. Once the data is available from memory along the load path, the control drives the ALU with signals instructing it to ADD its A and B operands to form the S result.

5. The control then moves the S result into the AC to complete the execution of the instruction.

6. The control increments the program counter to point at the next instruction. The machine returns to the first step.

Register Transfer Notation   As you have seen so far, most of what the control does is transfer data from one register to another, asserting the appropriate control signals at the correct times. Control sequences are commonly described in terms of a special *register transfer notation*. Without defining the notation formally, we can illustrate the concept of register transfer with the instruction execution sequence described above:

Instruction Fetch:

PC → MAR;	Move PC to MAR
Memory Read;	Assert Memory READ signal
Memory → IR;	Load IR from Memory

Instruction Decode:

IF IR<op code> = ADD_FROM_MEMORY

THEN

Instruction Execution:

IR<address bits> → MAR;	Move operand address to MAR
Memory Read;	Assert Memory READ signal
Memory → ALU B;	Gate Memory to ALU B
AC → ALU A;	Gate AC to ALU A
ALU ADD;	Instruct ALU to perform ADD
ALU S → AC;	Gate ALU result to AC
PC increment;	Instruct PC to increment

We write the operation statements in terms of the control signals to be asserted, such as *Memory Read, ALU ADD,* or *PC increment.* We write register-to-register transfers in the form *source register → destination register.* The detailed pathways between registers determine the more refined register transfer description. We will see more register transfer descriptions in Section 11.2.

11.1.4   Interface to Memory

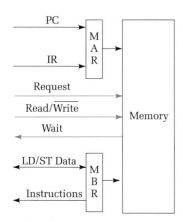

Figure 11.5   Memory interface.

Figure 11.4 showed a reasonably generic interface to memory. A more realistic view for a Princeton architecture machine is shown in Figure 11.5. The key elements are the two special registers, MAR and MBR, and the three control signals, Request, Read/$\overline{\text{Write}}$, and Wait. Let's start with the registers.

We have seen the MAR before. In Figure 11.5, it can be loaded from the program counter for instruction fetch or from the IR with a load or store address. To decouple the memory from the internal working of the processor, we introduce a second interface register, the *Memory Buffer Register,* or MBR. A bidirectional path for load/store data exists between the processor datapath and the MBR, while the pathway for instructions between the MBR and IR is unidirectional.

Besides the address and data lines, the interface to memory consists of three control signals. The Request signal notifies the memory that the processor wishes to access it. The Read/$\overline{\text{Write}}$ signal specifies the direction: read from memory on a load and write to memory on a store. The Wait signal lets memory stall the processor, in effect, notifying the processor that its memory request has not yet been serviced. We can think of Wait as the complement of an acknowledgment signal.

Processor-Memory Handshaking   In their most general form, the memory system and the processor do not share a common clock. To ensure proper transfer of data, we should follow the four-cycle signaling convention of Section 6.5.2. The processor asserts the read/write direction, places data in the MAR (and the MBR if a write), and asserts Request. The memory normally asserts Wait, unasserting it when the read or write is complete.

When the processor notices that Wait is no longer asserted, it latches data into the MBR on a read or tri-states the data connection to memory on a write. The processor unasserts its Request line and must wait for the Wait signal to be reasserted by the Memory before it can issue its next memory request.

The signaling waveforms are shown in Figure 11.6. The four-cycle handshake of the Request and Wait signals for the read sequence work as follows:

Cycle 1: Request asserted. Read data placed on memory data bus.

Cycle 2: Wait unasserted. CPU latches read data into MBR.

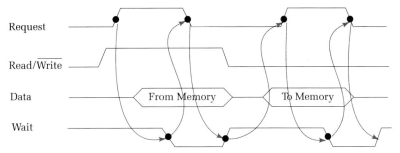

Figure 11.6 Memory interface timing waveforms.

Cycle 3: Request unasserted.

Cycle 4: Wait asserted.

In this signaling convention, a new request can be made only after the Wait signal is asserted. The write cycle is analogous.

Figure 11.7 shows possible state machine fragments for implementing the four-cycle handshake with memory. We assume a Moore machine controller implementation. In the read cycle, we enter a state that drives the address bus from the MAR, asserts the Read and Request signals, and latches the data bus into the MBR. This last transfer catches correct data only if memory has unasserted Wait, so we must loop in this state until this is true. On exit to the next state, the Request signal is unasserted and the address bus is no longer driven. The memory signals that it is ready for a new request by asserting Wait. To remain interlocked with memory, we loop in this state until Wait is asserted. The write cycle is similar.

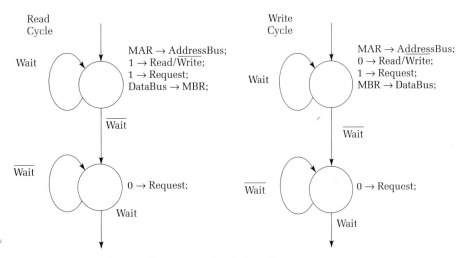

Figure 11.7 Conservative state diagrams for read and write cycles.

Depending on detailed setup and hold time requirements, it may be necessary to insert additional states in the fragments of Figure 11.7. For example, if the memory system requires that the address lines and read/write direction be stable before the request is asserted, this should be done in a state preceding the one that asserts Request.

Remember that only the register transfer operations being asserted in a given state need to be written there. If an operation is not mentioned in a state (or state transition for a Mealy machine), it is implicitly unasserted. Thus, you don't have to explicitly set Request to its unasserted value in the second state of the handshake fragments. However, you should include such register transfer operations to improve the clarity of your state diagram.

11.1.5   Input/Output: The Third Component of Computer Organization

We have dealt with the interconnections between the processor and memory. The organization of the computer has a third component: input/output devices. We cover them only briefly here.

Input/output devices provide the computer's communication with the outside world. They include displays, printers, and massive storage devices, such as magnetic disks and tapes. For the purposes of this discussion, the main attribute of I/O devices is that they are typically much slower than the processor to which they are attached.

Memory-Mapped I/O   I/O devices can be coupled to the processor in two primary ways: via a dedicated I/O bus or by sharing the same bus as the memory system. Almost all modern computers use the second method. One advantage of this method is that there are no special instructions to perform I/O operations. Load and store operations can initiate device reads and writes if they are directed to addresses that are recognized by the I/O device rather than memory. This strategy is called *memory-mapped I/O* because the devices appear to the processor as though they were part of the memory system.

I/O access times are measured in milliseconds, whereas memory access times are usually less than a microsecond. It isn't productive to hold up the processor for thousands of instruction times while the I/O device does it job. Therefore, the control coupling between the processor and I/O devices is somewhat more complex than the memory interface.

Polling Versus Interrupts   Because of the (relatively) long time to execute I/O operations, they are normally performed in parallel with CPU processing. An I/O device often has its own controllers, essentially an independent computer that handles the details of device control. The CPU asks the controller to perform an I/O operation, usually by writing information to memory-mapped control registers. The processor continues to execute a stream of instructions while the I/O controller services its request.

The I/O controller notifies the CPU when its operation is complete. It can do this in two main ways: *polling* and *interrupts*. In polling, the I/O controller places its status in a memory-mapped register that the CPU can access. Every once in a while, the system software running on the CPU issues an instruction to examine the status register to see if the request is complete.

With interrupts, when the I/O operation is complete, the controller asserts a special control input to the CPU called the interrupt line. This forces the processor's state machine into a special interrupt state. The current state of the processor's registers, such as the PC and AC, is saved to special memory locations. The PC is overwritten with a distinguished address, where the system software's code for interrupt handling can be found. The instructions at this location handle the interrupt by copying data from the I/O device to memory where other programs can access it.

Polling is used in some very high performance computers that cannot afford to have their instruction sequencing disturbed by an I/O device's demand for attention. Interrupt-based I/O is used in almost all other computers, such as personal computers and time-sharing systems.

Changes to the Control State Diagram We need only modest changes to add interrupt support to the basic processor state diagram of Figure 11.2. Before fetching a new instruction, the processor checks to see whether an interrupt request is pending. If not, it continues with normal instruction fetch and execution.

If an interrupt has been requested, the processor simply enters its special interrupt state sequence. It saves the state of the machine, particularly the PC, and tells the I/O device through a standard handshake that it has seen the interrupt request. At this point, the machine returns to normal instruction fetch and execution, except that the PC now points to the first instruction of the system software's interrupt handler code.

A machine with interrupts usually provides a Return from Interrupt instruction. The system software executes this instruction at the end of its interrupt handling code, restoring the machine's saved state and returning control to the program that was running when the interrupt took place.

11.2   Busing Strategies

One of the most critical design decisions for the datapath is how to connect together its hardware resources. There are three general strategies: point-to-point connections, a single shared bus interconnection, or multiple special-purpose buses. Each represents a trade-off between datapath and control complexity and the amount of parallelism supported by the hardware. This determines the processor's *efficiency*, defined as the number of control states (or clock cycles) needed to fetch and execute a typical instruction. When a datapath supports many simultaneous transfers among datapath elements, the control unit requires fewer states (and clock cycles) to execute a given instruction.

In this section, we will examine methods for organizing the interconnection of datapath components, using the example of four general-purpose registers. We will consider how the datapath can support the operation of a register-to-register swap—that is, simultaneous exchange of the contents of one register with another. In register transfer notation, we write the instruction's execution sequence as

SWAP (R_i , R_j):

$$R_i \rightarrow R_j;$$

$$R_j \rightarrow R_i;$$

where R_i and R_j are the registers whose contents are to be swapped.

11.2.1   Point-to-Point Connections

In a *point-to-point interconnection scheme*, there is a path from every possible source to every possible destination. Figure 11.8 shows how this can be implemented for the four-register example using 4-to-1 multiplexers.

Each of the four registers receives its parallel load inputs from an associated multiplexer block. R_i is an edge-triggered register, which is loaded when the LD_i input is asserted. We assume the load signal takes effect only on the appropriate clock edge; that is, it is a synchronous control signal. If each register is N bits wide, the multiplexer blocks must contain N 4-to-1 multiplexers, one multiplexer for each bit in the

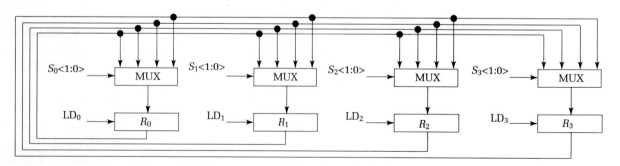

Figure 11.8   Point-to-point register interconnection.

register. These are controlled by the 2-bit-wide selection inputs, S_i<1:0> for register R_i.

Register Transfer Operations and Event Timings To see some of the possible transfers and how they may be implemented, consider the register transfers $R_1 \rightarrow R_0$ (transfer the contents of R_1 to R_0) and $R_2 \rightarrow R_3$ (transfer the contents of R_2 to R_3). The following detailed register transfer operations describe the necessary sequencing of the control signals:

$$01 \rightarrow S_0<1:0>;$$

$$10 \rightarrow S_3<1:0>;$$

$$1 \rightarrow LD_0;$$

$$1 \rightarrow LD_3;$$

The first two register transfer operations connect R_0's input lines to the output of R_1, and similarly for R_3 being driven from R_2. The last two assert the load signals for registers R_0 and R_3, respectively.

Figure 11.9 shows a state diagram fragment to illustrate when the control signals are asserted and when they take effect. We assume a Moore machine implementation (a synchronous Mealy with registered outputs behaves analogously). When entering state X the multiplexer control signals are asserted, gating R_1 and R_2 to the inputs of R_0 and R_3. The state also asserts the R_0 and R_3 load signals. But because these are synchronous, they do not take effect until the next state transition.

Thus, the R_1 and R_2 signals have time to propagate through the multiplexer blocks and become stable for the requisite setup times before the clock edge arrives that advances the finite state machine to state Y. The contents of R_0 and R_3 change on this state transition, not the one that caused the load inputs to become asserted. Since the new values take some time to propagate through the register load circuitry before they emerge at the outputs, the hold time requirements at the register inputs are easily met.

The SWAP Operation To see how the interconnection scheme can implement a SWAP operation, you need to understand the timing relationship between register transfer operations and their effect on the datapath. Consider a SWAP between registers R_1 and R_2. The control signal settings are

$$01 \rightarrow S_2<1:0>;$$

$$10 \rightarrow S_1<1:0>;$$

$$1 \rightarrow LD_2;$$

$$1 \rightarrow LD_1;$$

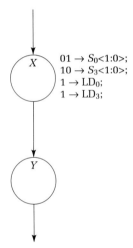

$$\begin{aligned}01 &\rightarrow S_0<1:0>;\\10 &\rightarrow S_3<1:0>;\\1 &\rightarrow LD_0;\\1 &\rightarrow LD_3;\end{aligned}$$

Figure 11.9 Transfer state diagram.

On entering state X, the multiplexer selection signals establish the desired pathways between register outputs and inputs. The load signals are asserted, but the registers have not yet received their new values. This occurs only at the clock edge that causes the transition to state Y. Fortunately, the new values appear at the outputs well after the hold time requirements at the inputs have been met.

Discussion The point-to-point scheme is so flexible that it can transfer new values into the four registers at the same time. But there is a significant hardware cost. A 4-to-1 multiplexer requires at least five gates for its implementation (recall Figure 4.29). Assuming a 32-bit-wide datapath, this means 160 gates per register or 640 gates for the four-register example. For this reason, point-to-point connections can only be used in rare cases in which the flexibility far outweighs the implementation cost.

11.2.2   Single Bus

A *bus* is a set of interconnection pathways that are shared by multiple data sources and destinations. If the point-to-point connection scheme is too hardware intensive, a lower-cost alternative is to use a single interconnection bus. This is shown in Figure 11.10. The block with a multiplexer for each register has been replaced by a block with a single multiplexer that is shared by all registers. The hardware cost is 25% of that of the point-to-point approach. The multiplexer places selected data on a bus that feeds the load inputs of all registers.

This dramatic reduction in hardware cost comes at a price: The shared bus (and its multiplexer) is a *critical resource* because it can be used by only one transfer at a time. However, the single source register can still "broadcast" simultaneously to more than one destination register.

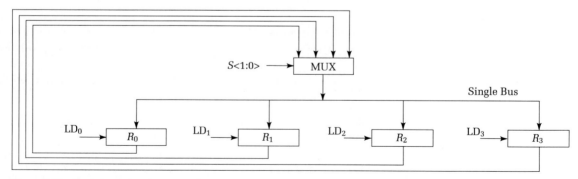

Figure 11.10   Single-bus register interconnection.

The Register Transfers Revisited To see that transfers now require more states, let's again consider the transfer of R_1 to R_0 and R_2 to R_3. These now require two separate states, asserting the following control signals:

State X: $(R_1 \rightarrow R_0)$
$\qquad 01 \rightarrow S<1:0>$;
$\qquad 1 \rightarrow LD_0$;

State Y: $(R_2 \rightarrow R_3)$
$\qquad 10 \rightarrow S<1:0>$;
$\qquad 1 \rightarrow LD_3$;

The SWAP Operation Revisited Since the datapath no longer supports two simultaneous transfers, the register swap operation becomes much more difficult for us to implement. We must stage the data to be swapped through a temporary register that we introduce into the datapath. Let's call the temporary register R_4. This means that we have to expand to a 5-to-1 multiplexer.

Swapping the contents of registers R_1 and R_2 now requires the following register transfer operations:

State X: $(R_1 \rightarrow R_4)$
$\qquad 001 \rightarrow S<2:0>$;
$\qquad 1 \rightarrow LD_4$;

State Y: $(R_2 \rightarrow R_1)$
$\qquad 010 \rightarrow S<2:0>$;
$\qquad 1 \rightarrow LD_1$;

State Z: $(R_4 \rightarrow R_2)$
$\qquad 100 \rightarrow S<2:0>$;
$\qquad 1 \rightarrow LD_2$;

With point-to-point connections, SWAP could be implemented in a single state and just one clock cycle (we assume one clock cycle per state). Using a single bus interconnection, however, SWAP requires an extra register, a larger MUX, and three control states.

Discussion This illustrates a fundamental trade-off in computer hardware: extra complexity in the datapath can reduce the control complexity and vice versa. The correct design decision depends critically on the frequency of operations. If you seldom require multiple simultaneous transfers, your correct choice is the simpler datapath. If you need to SWAP frequently, you should choose the point-to-point method.

A compromise strategy is also possible. It strikes a balance between control and datapath complexity by introducing a small number of additional buses just where they are needed. We will see this in Section 11.2.3.

Multiplexers Versus Tri-State Drivers So far, we have used multiplexers to make connection between sources and destinations. An alternative that dramatically reduces the necessary hardware takes advantage of tri-state or open-collector buffers. Recall that these kinds of circuits allow multiple sources to share the same wire, as long as only one buffer is driving the shared data line at a time.

We show the method, using tri-states, in Figure 11.11. Any of the four registers can be the source for the single bus or be loaded from it. The decoder guarantees that only one of the registers is gated onto the bus through its tri-state buffers. Most packaged logic registers include tri-state devices, so this form of interconnection is convenient.

11.2.3 Multiple Buses

Real datapath designs incorporate the usual engineering trade-offs between control and datapath complexity. Typically, they have more than one bus but less than a full point-to-point scheme. In this subsection, we compare a single-bus scheme to an interconnection arrangement that uses a small number of buses. The metric of comparison we will use is the number of processor states (and clock cycles) it takes to implement a simple instruction.

Single-Bus Register Transfer Diagram Figure 11.12 gives a simple single-bus design for the processor described in Figure 11.4. The registers are MAR, MBR, PC, IR, and AC, and the only functional unit is the ALU. The AC is hardwired to the *A* input of the ALU and the MAR is write-only. We call this figure a *register transfer diagram* because it highlights the way registers and functional units are interconnected.

By examining the datapath, we can quickly determine the register transfer operations it supports:

Bus as destination: PC → BUS, IR → BUS, AC → BUS,
MBR → BUS, ALU Result → BUS;

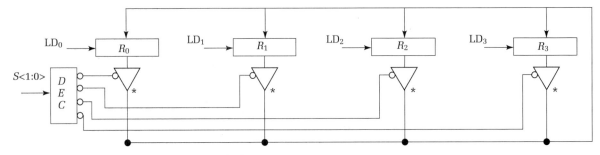

Figure 11.11 Single-bus register interconnection with tri-states.

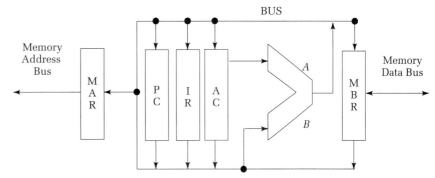

Figure 11.12 Single-bus processor datapath.

Bus as source: BUS → PC, BUS → IR, BUS → AC, BUS → MBR, BUS → ALU B, BUS → MAR;

Hardwired: AC → ALU A;

Single-Bus Cycle-by-Cycle Instruction Execution Consider the simple CPU instruction "ADD Mem[X]" which adds the contents of memory location X to the AC and stores the result back into the AC. With the connection scheme of Figure 11.12, the set of register transfer steps to execute the instruction are the following (we group the operations by state and cycle):

Fetch Operand

> **Cycle 1:**
>> IR <operand address> → BUS;
>>> BUS → MAR;

> **Cycle 2:**
>> Memory Read;
>> Databus → MBR;

Perform ADD

> **Cycle 3:**
>> MBR → BUS;
>> BUS → ALU B;
>> AC → ALU A;
>> ADD;

Write Result

> **Cycle 4:**
>> ALU Result → BUS;
>> BUS → AC;

During cycle 3, the bus connects the operand in the MBR to the ALU input. The bus cannot be used at the same time as a pathway between the ALU result and the AC. Thus, this transfer must be deferred to the next cycle. With this organization, the ALU must have a latch to hold the result until it can be transferred at the next cycle.

Multiple Bus Register Transfer Diagram Figure 11.13 gives an alternative three-bus organization that supports higher parallelism in the datapath. More parallelism means that more transfers can take place in the same state. This should lead us to a reduced state and cycle count for the typical instruction.

We partition the single bus functionally into a Memory Bus (MBUS), Result Bus (RBUS), and Address Bus (ABUS). The first connects the MBR with the ALU and IR, the second establishes a pathway between the ALU result and the AC and MBR, and the last provides connections between the IR, PC, and MAR.

Multiple-Bus Cycle-by-Cycle Instruction Execution The cycle-by-cycle register transfer operations now become

Fetch Operand

Cycle 1:
IR <operand address> → ABUS;
ABUS → MAR;

Cycle 2:
Memory Read;
Databus → MBR;

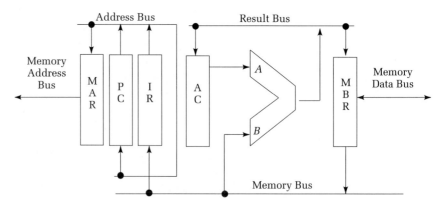

Figure 11.13 Three-bus processor datapath.

Perform ADD

Cycle 3:

MBR → MBUS;
MBUS → ALU *B*;
AC → ALU *A*;
ADD;

Write Result

ALU Result → RBUS;
RBUS → AC;

Since MBUS and RBUS decouple the ALU inputs from the outputs, we can implement operations like ADD in a single cycle. Introducing the extra buses has decreased the execution cycle count from four to three. This doesn't quite represent a savings of 25% on the execution time of a typical program, since this cycle tally does not include the instruction fetch.

11.3   Finite State Machines for Simple CPUs

In this section, we will derive the state diagram and datapath for a simple processor. The machine will have 16-bit words and just four instructions. Although this may be an oversimplified example, it illustrates the process for deriving the state diagram and datapath and the interaction between the state diagram and the datapath's register transfer operations.

11.3.1   Introduction

In general, the design of the processor's control goes hand-in-hand with the design of the datapath interconnect. We can summarize the step-by-step as:

1. Start by developing the state diagram and associated register transfer operations for the processor control unit, assuming that point-to-point connections are supported by the datapath.

2. Next, identify the register interconnections that are not used at the same time in any control state. You can now replace these by bus-structured interconnect.

3. Revise the state diagram to reflect the register transfer operations supported by the modified datapath.

4. Finally, determine how to implement the register transfer operations by detailed control signal sequences. Revise the state diagram to assert these signals in the desired sequences.

Now we are ready to begin the specification of our example machine.

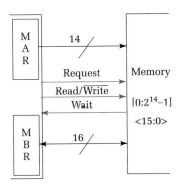

Figure 11.14 Instruction format and encoding.

Processor Specification To a first approximation, a computer is described by its instruction set and programmer-visible registers. Ours is a single accumulator machine. Its instruction format and encoding are shown in Figure 11.14.

Instruction and data words are 16 bits wide. The two high-order bits of the instruction contain an operation code to denote the operation type. The remaining 14 bits are used as the memory address of the operand word.

Figure 11.15 shows the processor-memory interface, based on the scheme introduced in Section 11.1.4. The memory data bus and memory address bus are 16 bits and 14 bits wide, respectively.

The processor's instructions are:

1. *Load from Memory*
   LD XXX: Memory[XXX] → AC;

2. *Store to Memory*
   ST XXX: AC → Memory[XXX];

3. *Add from Memory*
   ADD XXX: AC + Memory[XXX] → AC;

4. *Branch if Accumulator Negative*
   BRN XXX: IF AC<15> = 1 THEN XXX → PC;

Figure 11.16 gives a high-level state diagram for the processor's control. This is the starting point for deriving the detailed state machine in this section. You shouldn't be surprised that its major components are the familiar sequence of instruction fetch, operation decode, and operation execution.

Figure 11.15 Processor to memory interface.

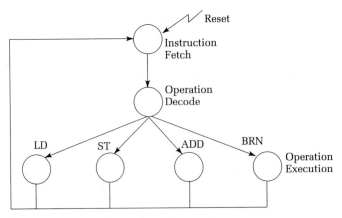

Figure 11.16 High-level state diagram for example processor.

11.3.2   Deriving the State Diagram and Datapath

The state diagram of Figure 11.16 provides only a rough beginning for the detailed state machine. For example, fetching an instruction involves a memory access, and this requires several states. And, as pointed out in the previous section, the details of the datapath interconnections affect the number of cycles required to execute the instruction. The final state diagram will contain several more states than we have shown.

Refining the State Diagram: Overview   We start by decomposing the state diagram into its three major components: instruction fetch, operation decode, and operation execution. Throughout this section, we will refine each of these.

To begin, we must decide between a Moore or Mealy style of implementation. Let's choose the latter and assume that our controller will be a synchronous Mealy machine. Control outputs are now associated with transitions rather than states. Asserted control signals take effect when entering the next state.

Reset State   It is a good idea to make *Reset* (RES) the first state. This starts the machine in a known state when the reset signal is asserted. Also, it provides the place in the state diagram from which a control signal can be asserted to force parts of the datapath to known starting values. Perhaps the most important register to set at Reset is the program counter. In our machine, we will set the PC to 0. The Memory Request line should also be driven to its unasserted value on start-up.

Instruction Fetch   Reset (RES) is followed by a sequence of states to fetch the first instruction from memory (IF_0, IF_1, IF_2). The PC is moved to the MAR, followed by a memory read sequence. Revising the Moore machine state fragment of Figure 11.7, we obtain the four-state Mealy sequence shown in Figure 11.17.

Let's examine the control signals on a transition-by-transition basis. When first detected, the external reset signal forces the state machine into state RES. This state resets the PC and Memory Request signals. It does so by the explicit operation $0 \rightarrow PC$ for resetting the PC on entry to RES; Request is unasserted because it is not otherwise mentioned. We assume that register transfer operations not listed in a transition are implicitly left unasserted.

Once the Reset signal is no longer asserted, the machine advances to state IF_0. On this transition, the control signals to transfer the PC to the MAR are asserted. This is as good a place as any to increment the PC, setting it to point to the next sequential instruction. You should remember that register transfer statements are not like statements in a conventional

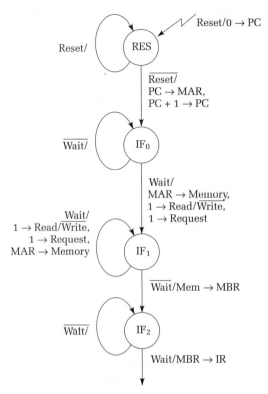

Figure 11.17 Reset and instruction fetch states.

programming language. The PC increment takes place on the same clock edge that causes the MAR to be loaded with the old value of the PC. Assuming edge-triggered devices, the setup/hold times and propagation delays guarantee that the old value of the PC is transferred to the MAR. We will reexamine these timing considerations in the next subsection.

Figure 11.7 showed that the four-cycle handshake with memory can begin only when the memory Wait signal is asserted. So we loop in state IF_0 until this Wait is asserted.

Once memory is ready to accept a request and Wait is asserted, we can begin a read memory sequence to obtain the instruction. On the transition to state IF_1, we set up control signals to gate the MAR to the Memory Address Bus and assert the Read and Request signals.

Once we have entered IF_1, the instruction address has been presented to memory and a memory read request has been made. As long as the Wait signal is asserted, these must remain asserted.

We advance to state IF_2 when memory finally unasserts Wait, signaling that data is available on the Memory Databus. On this transition it is safe to transfer the values on the memory bus into the MBR. This transition also unasserts the Request signal, indicating to memory that the processor is ready to end the memory cycle. The four-cycle handshake keeps us in this state until the Wait signal is again asserted. On this exit transition, the MBR can be transferred to the IR to begin the next major step in the state machine: *operation decode.*

Operation Decode Because of the simplicity of our instruction set, the decode stage is simply a single state that tests the op code bits of the instruction register to determine the next state. This is shown in Figure 11.18. The notation on the transitions from state OD indicates a conditional test on IR bits 15 and 14. For example, if IR<15:14> = 00, the next state is LD_0.

Instruction Execution: LOAD Now we examine the execution sequences for the four instructions, starting with LD. The load execution sequence is given in Figure 11.19. The transition is taken to state LD_0 if the op code bits of the IR are both 0. On this transition, we transfer the address portion of the IR to the MAR. States LD_0, LD_1, and LD_2 are almost identical to the instruction fetch states, except that the destination of the data from memory is the AC rather than the IR. The rationale for the state transitions is also identical: When memory is ready, we assert Read and Request and keep these asserted until Wait is unasserted. At this point, the data is latched into the MBR and then moved to the AC.

Instruction Execution: STORE The store execution sequence is shown in Figure 11.20. In essence, it is a memory write sequence that is similar to the load's read sequence. On the transition from the decode state, the address portion of the current instruction is transferred to the MAR while the AC is moved to the MBR. If memory is ready to accept a new

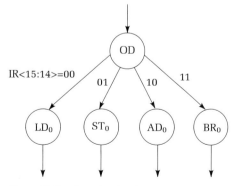

Figure 11.18 Operation decode state.

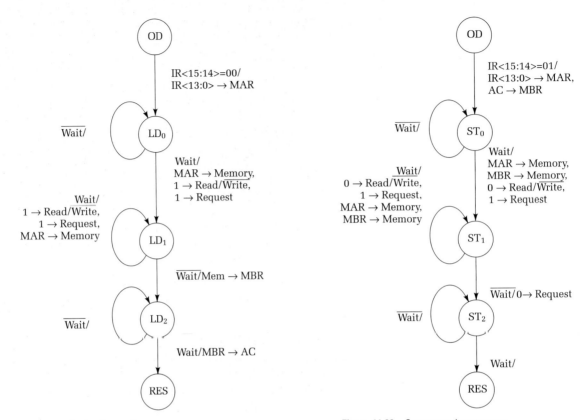

Figure 11.19 Load execution sequence.

Figure 11.20 Store execution sequence.

request, we begin a write cycle by gating MAR and MBR to the appropriate memory buses while asserting $\overline{\text{Write}}$ and Request. These signals remain asserted until Wait is unasserted. At this point, the processor resets the handshake and waits for the memory to do the same.

Instruction Execution: ADD Figure 11.21 shows the execution sequence for the ADD instruction. The basic structure repeats the load sequence. Only the transition from state AD_2 back to the reset state has a slightly different transfer operation.

Instruction Execution: BRANCH NEGATIVE Figure 11.22 gives the final execution sequence, for the Branch if AC Negative instruction. If the high-order bit of AC is 1, the IR's address bits replace the contents of the PC. Otherwise the current contents of the PC, already incremented in the previous RES-to-IF_0 transition, determine the location of the next instruction.

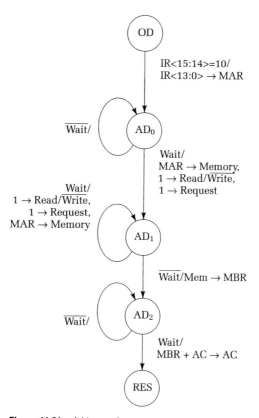

Figure 11.21   Add execution sequence.

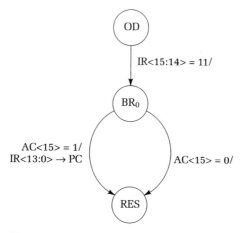

Figure 11.22   Branch execution sequence.

Simplification of the State Diagram Since the instruction fetch sequence already checks whether memory is ready to receive a new request by verifying that Wait is asserted, we can eliminate state ST_2. For the same reason, we can eliminate the $\overline{Wait}$ loop/Wait exit of states LD_2 and AD_2. Similarly, since the IF_2 state completes the processor-memory handshake, we can eliminate the loop back and exit conditions for states LD_0, ST_0, and AD_0. Figure 11.23 gives the complete state diagram, but does not show the detailed register transfer operations.

At this point in our refinement of the state machine, the list of control inputs and outputs is as follows.

Control Signal and Conditional Inputs:

Reset

Wait

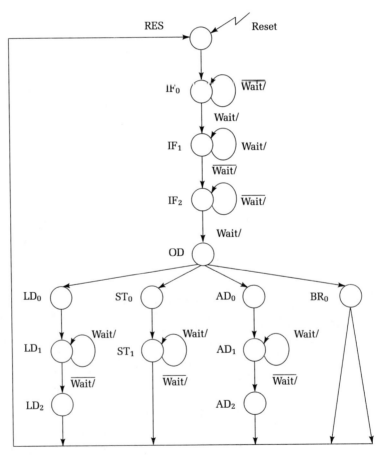

Figure 11.23 Complete state diagram.

IR<15:14>

AC<15>

Control Signal Outputs:

$0 \rightarrow$ PC

PC + 1 $\rightarrow$ PC

PC $\rightarrow$ MAR

MAR $\rightarrow$ Memory Address Bus

Memory Data Bus $\rightarrow$ MBR

MBR $\rightarrow$ Memory Data Bus

MBR $\rightarrow$ IR

MBR $\rightarrow$ AC

AC $\rightarrow$ MBR

AC + MBR $\rightarrow$ AC

IR<13:0> $\rightarrow$ MAR

IR<13:0> $\rightarrow$ PC

$1 \rightarrow$ Read/$\overline{\text{Write}}$

$0 \rightarrow$ Read/$\overline{\text{Write}}$

$1 \rightarrow$ Request

Figure 11.24 gives a revised block diagram showing the flow of signals between the control, datapath, and memory.

11.3.3 Register Transfer Operations and Datapath Control

In deriving the state diagram of the previous subsection, we assumed there was a direct path between any source and destination of a register transfer operation that we needed. Figure 11.25 shows the implications of this assumption for our datapath. We label the connections with the instruction type (Load, Store, Add, Branch) or stage (Fetch, Decode, Execute) that makes use of the path.

We must now determine which of these point-to-point connections can be combined into shared buses. We can combine connections when they are never (or infrequently) used in the same state.

Datapath Interconnections Since instruction fetch and operand fetch take place in different states of the state machine, we can use a single bus to connect the IR, PC, and MAR. Similarly, the connections between the MBR and the IR, ALU B, and AC can be combined in a single bus. The

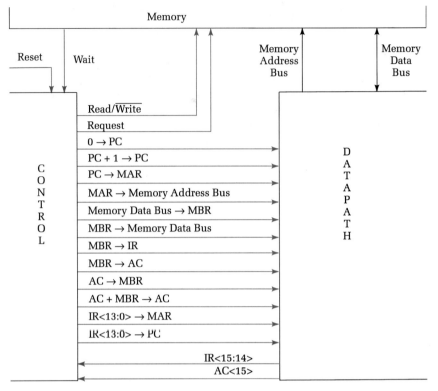

Figure 11.24   Processor signal flow.

Store and Add paths between the ALU, AC, and MBR can be combined as well, yielding the three-bus architecture of Figure 11.26. This is almost identical to the datapath of Figure 11.13.

With this organization we can implement the transfer operation $AC + MBR \rightarrow AC$ in a single state. Otherwise we would need to revise the portion of the state diagram for the ADD execution sequence to reflect the true sequence of transfers needed to implement this operation.

In Figure 11.26 the AC is the only register connected to more than one bus (it can be loaded from the Result Bus or the Memory Bus). This is called a *dual-ported* configuration, and it requires additional hardware. It is useful to try to reuse existing connections whenever possible. By using an ALU component that has the ability to pass its *B* input through to the output, we can implement the load path from the MBR to the AC in the same manner as the add path. We simply instruct the ALU to PASS *B* rather than ADD *A* and *B*. This yields the three-bus architecture introduced in Figure 11.13, eliminating the extra datapath complexity associated with a dual-ported AC. We assume this organization throughout the rest of this subsection.

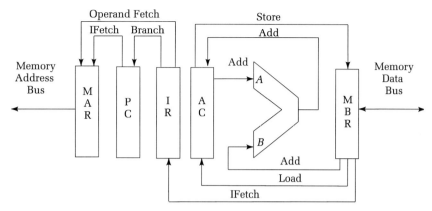

Figure 11.25 Point-to-point connections implied by the state diagram.

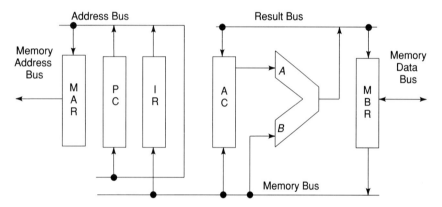

Figure 11.26 Three-bus processor datapath with dual-ported AC.

Implementation of the Register Transfer Operations Now that we have set-
tled on the detailed connections supported by the datapath, we are ready
to examine how register transfer operations are implemented. A datapath *control point* is a signal that causes the datapath to perform some
operation when it is asserted. Some control operations, such as ADD,
PASS B, $0 \rightarrow PC$, $PC + 1 \rightarrow PC$, are implemented directly by the ALU
and PC functional units. For other operations, such as $PC \rightarrow MAR$, we
have to assert more than one control point within the datapath. These
more detailed control signals are often called *microoperations*. Thus, we
can decompose a register transfer operation into one or more microoperations, and there is one microoperation for each control point (for example, a register load or tri-state enable control input) in the datapath.

As an example, let's examine the register transfer operation PC → MAR. To implement this, the PC must be gated to the Address Bus while the MAR is loaded from the same bus. In terms of microoperations, PC → MAR is decomposed into PC → ABUS and ABUS → MAR.

Figure 11.27 shows how these operations manipulate control points in the datapath. The PC is a loadable counter, attached to the ABUS via tri-state buffers. The MAR is a loadable register whose parallel load inputs are driven from the ABUS. Asserting the microoperation PC → ABUS connects the PC to the ABUS. Asserting the ABUS → MAR microoperation loads the MAR from the ABUS.

Timing of Register Transfer Operations   Figure 11.28 shows the timing for these signals. The waveform begins with entering state RES, followed by advancing to state IF_0. In this timing diagram we assume the Reset signal is debounced and synchronized with the system clock and 0 → PC is directly tied to the synchronized Reset. We use positive edge-triggered registers and counters with synchronous control inputs throughout. Although we assume positive logic in this timing diagram, you should realize that most components come with active low control signals.

The Reset signal is captured by a synchronizing flip-flop on the first rising edge in the figure. A propagation delay later, the synchronized version of the reset signal is presented as an input to the control. No matter what state the machine is in, the next state is RES if Reset is asserted. The 0 → PC microoperation is hardwired to the synchronized Reset signal. The synchronous counter CLR input takes effect at the next rising edge. This coincides with the transition into state RES.

Once we are in state RES, we assume that the Reset input becomes unasserted. Otherwise we would loop in the state, continuously setting the PC to 0 until Reset is no longer asserted. With Reset unasserted, IF_0

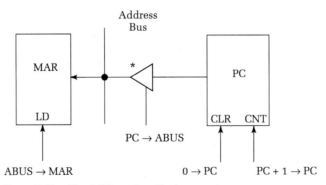

Figure 11.27   PC-to-MAR transfer with microoperations.

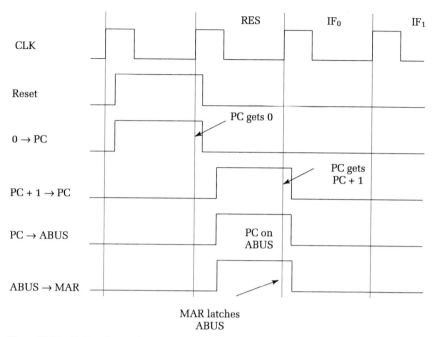

Figure 11.28 Timing of state changes and microoperations.

is the next state and the microoperations $PC + 1 \rightarrow PC$, $PC \rightarrow ABUS$, and $ABUS \rightarrow MAR$ are asserted.

Because of the way they are implemented in the datapath, some of these operations take place immediately while others are delayed until the next clock edge/entry into the next state. For example, asserting $PC \rightarrow ABUS$ turns on a tri-state buffer. This takes place immediately. Microoperations like $PC + 1 \rightarrow PC$ (counter increment) and $ABUS \rightarrow MAR$ (register load) are synchronous and therefore are deferred to the next clock event.

In the waveform, soon after entry into RES with Reset removed, we gate the PC onto the ABUS. Even though the PC count signal is asserted, it will not take effect until the next rising edge, so the ABUS correctly receives 0.

On the next rising edge, the MAR latches the ABUS and the PC is incremented. Because the increment propagation delay exceeds the hold time on the MAR load signal, the 0 value of the PC is still on the ABUS at the time the load is complete. When a bus is a destination, the microoperation usually takes place immediately; if a register is a destination, the microoperation's effect is usually delayed.

Tabulation of Register Transfer Operations and Microoperations   The relationships between register transfer operations and microoperations are:

Register Transfer	Microoperations
$0 \rightarrow PC$	$0 \rightarrow PC$ (delayed);
$PC + 1 \rightarrow PC$	$PC + 1 \rightarrow PC$ (delayed);
$PC \rightarrow MAR$	$PC \rightarrow ABUS$ (immediate), $ABUS \rightarrow MAR$ (delayed);
$MAR \rightarrow$ Address Bus	$MAR \rightarrow$ Address Bus (immediate);
Data Bus $\rightarrow MBR$	Data Bus $\rightarrow MBR$ (delayed);
$MBR \rightarrow$ Data Bus	$MBR \rightarrow$ Data Bus (immediate);
$MBR \rightarrow IR$	$MBR \rightarrow MBUS$ (immediate), $MBUS \rightarrow IR$ (delayed);
$MBR \rightarrow AC$	$MBR \rightarrow MBUS$ (immediate), $MBUS \rightarrow ALU\ B$ (immediate), ALU PASS B (immediate), ALU Result $\rightarrow RBUS$ (immediate), $RBUS \rightarrow AC$ (delayed);
$AC \rightarrow MBR$	$AC \rightarrow ALU\ A$ (immediate, hard-wired), ALU PASS A (immediate), ALU Result $\rightarrow RBUS$ (immediate, hard-wired), $RBUS \rightarrow MBR$ (delayed);
$AC + MBR \rightarrow AC$	$AC \rightarrow ALU\ A$ (immediate, hard-wired), $MBR \rightarrow MBUS$ (immediate), $MBUS \rightarrow ALU\ B$ (immediate), ALU ADD (immediate), ALU Result $\rightarrow RBUS$ (immediate, hard-wired), $RBUS \rightarrow AC$ (delayed);
$IR{<}13{:}0{>} \rightarrow MAR$	$IR \rightarrow ABUS$ (immediate), $ABUS \rightarrow IR$ (delayed);
$IR{<}13{:}0{>} \rightarrow PC$	$IR \rightarrow ABUS$ (immediate), $ABUS \rightarrow PC$ (delayed);
$1 \rightarrow$ Read/$\overline{\text{Write}}$	Read (immediate);
$0 \rightarrow$ Read/$\overline{\text{Write}}$	Write (immediate);
$1 \rightarrow$ Request	Request (immediate);

Some of these operations can be eliminated because a connection is dedicated to a particular function and thus does not have to be controlled explicitly. AC → ALU A and ALU Result → RBUS are examples of this, since the AC is the only register that connects to ALU A and the ALU Result is the only source of the RBUS.

This leads us to the revised microoperation signal flow of Figure 11.29. Two control signals go to memory, Read/Write and Request, and 16 signals go to the datapath. The control has a total of five inputs: the two op code bits, the high-order bit of the AC, the memory Wait signal, and the external Reset signal. It is critical that the latter two be synchronized to the control clock.

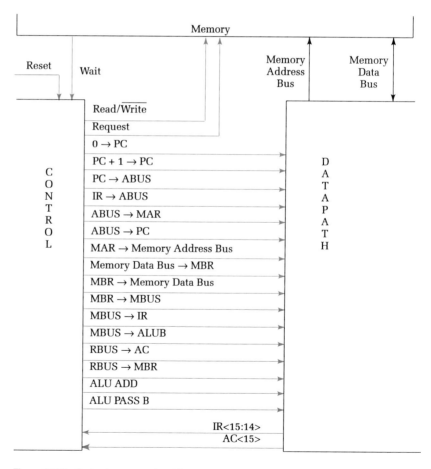

Figure 11.29   Revised processor signal flow.

Chapter Review

In this chapter, we have examined the fundamental structure of computers. A computer, like many digital systems, consists of datapath and control. The datapath contains the storage elements (registers) that hold operands, the functional units (ALUs, shifter registers) that operate on data, and the interconnections (buses) between them.

The computer's control is nothing more than a finite state machine. It cycles through a collection of states that fetch the next instruction from memory, decode this instruction to determine its type, and then execute the instruction. The control executes the instruction by asserting signals to the datapath to cause it to move data from registers to functional units, perform operations, and return the results to the registers.

Register transfer operations provide a notation for describing functional unit operations and the data movements between registers and functional units. The register transfer operations are normally written in a form that is independent of the detailed interconnections supported by the datapath.

Once the datapath interconnections are determined, we replace each register transfer operation by a sequence of microoperations. These correspond to detailed control signals to the datapath that must be asserted to cause a register transfer operation to take place.

Computers are interesting because they are particularly complex digital hardware systems. The datapath is not where this complexity comes from. It comes from the control portion of the machine. In the next chapter, we will look at ways to organize the complex control state machine of a digital computer.

Further Reading

Unfortunately, most textbooks on logic design do not provide much coverage on computer organization. After all, a detailed treatment of computer architectures, instruction sets, and their implementation is a topic for another book. Notable exceptions include Johnson and Karim, *Digital Design: A Pragmatic Approach*, PWS Engineering, Boston, 1987, and Prosser and Winkel, *The Art of Digital Design,* 2nd ed., Prentice-Hall, Englewood Cliffs, NJ, 1987. Both of these have several chapters on computer structures and their implementations in hardware.

For a historical perspective on how computer architectures have developed, a wonderful book is D. Patterson and J. Hennessy, *Computer Architecture: A Quantitative Approach*, Morgan-Kaufmann, Redwood City, CA, 1990.

Exercises

11.1 *(Register Transfer and State Diagrams)*   Assume that you have a bus-connected assembly of a 4-bit subtractor and four registers, as shown in Figure Ex11.1. All registers are positive edge-triggered, and registers R_2 and O have tri-state outputs. All buses are 4 bits wide.

You are to perform the following sequence of register transfer operations: (1) compute R_1–R_0, latching the result into R_2, (2) display the result on the LEDs attached to register O, and (3) replace R_0 with the result.

a. Tabulate all of the register transfer operations and their detailed microoperations that are supported by this datapath organization.

b. Create a timing waveform for the control signals LD (load), S (select), and OE (output enable) to implement this sequence in a minimum number of clock cycles. This diagram should include traces for all of the control signals in the figure: R_0:LD, R_1:LD, A:S, B:S, R_2:LD, R_2:OE, O:LD, O:OE. Recall that the state changes on the positive edge of the clock, and don't forget to incorporate signal propagation delays in your timing waveforms.

c. Show the state diagram, annotated with control signal assertions and their corresponding register transfer operations, that corresponds to the timing waveforms you filled out in part (b).

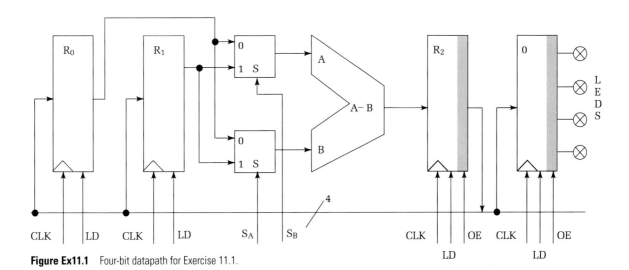

Figure Ex11.1   Four-bit datapath for Exercise 11.1.

11.2 *(Memory Interface)* A read-only memory and a microprocessor need to communicate asynchronously. The processor asserts a signal to indicate READ and sets the ADDRESS signals. The memory asserts COMPLETE when the data is available on the DATA signals. Draw two simple state diagrams that indicate the behavior of the processor and the memory controller for a simple read operation. The READ and COMPLETE signals should follow the four-cycle handshake protocol. Assume that the memory controller cycles in an initial state waiting for a memory READ request.

11.3 *(Memory Interface)* For the memory interface and state diagrams in this chapter, we assumed a Princeton architecture. In this exercise, you will rederive these for a Harvard architecture.

   a. Modify the memory interface of Figure 11.5 for a Harvard architecture. Provide two separate memory interfaces, one for instructions and one for data.

   b. What changes are necessary in the state diagram of Figure 11.23 to reimplement this machine for a Harvard architecture?

   c. What new register transfer operations are needed to support this alternative memory interface? Modify Figure 11.24 to reflect these additions.

11.4 *(Instruction Prefetch)* In Exercise 11.3 you modified the memory interface to provide separate instruction and data memories. Modify the state diagram of Figure 11.23 to allow the next instruction to be fetched while the current instruction is finishing its execution. Tabulate the register transfer operations used in each state.

11.5 *(Control State Diagram)* The state diagram derived in Section 11.3.2 assumed a synchronous Mealy implementation. Rederive the state diagram, but this time assume a Moore machine implementation. Associate the appropriate register transfer operations with the states you derive. Also describe for each state the function, such as instruction fetch, operand fetch, or decode that it is implementing.

11.6 *(Datapath Design)* Consider the following portion of a simple instruction set encoded in 4-bit words. The machine has a single accumulator (R_0), a rotating shifter (R_1), four general-purpose registers (R_0, R_1, R_2, R_3), four accumulator/shifter oriented instructions (COMP, INC, RSR, ASR), and two register-register instructions (ADD, AND). In register transfer–like notation, these instructions are defined as follows:

Op Code (Binary)	Op Code (Symbolic)	Function
00 X_1X_0	ADD	$R[0] := R[0] + R[X_1X_0]$
01 X_1X_0	AND	$R[0] := R[0]$ AND $R[X_1X_0]$
10 00	COMP	$R[0] := \sim R[0]$
10 01	INC	$R[0] := R[0] + 1$
10 10	RSR	$R[1]<0> := R[1]<1>,$
		$R[1]<1> := R[1]<2>,$
		$R[1]<2> := R[1]<3>,$
		$R[1]<3> := R[1]<0>;$
10 11	ASR	$R[1]<0> := R[1]<1>,$
		$R[1]<1> := R[1]<2>,$
		$R[1]<2> := R[1]<3>,$
		$R[1]<3> := R[1]<3>;$

Note that X_1X_0 represents a 2-bit encoding of the operand register. The RSR is a logical shift right: the 4-bit word is shifted from left to right, with the low-order bit replacing the high-order bit. ASR is an arithmetic shift right: the high-order bit fills the bit to its right during the shift while retaining its value. If the register contains signed data, the shift has the effect of dividing by 2 whether the stored number is positive or negative.

a. Design a point-to-point datapath that is appropriate for this instruction set fragment. Assume that you can use an appropriately designed ALU and a shifter as functional units in your datapath. You may use multiplexers wherever you need them. Draw the register transfer diagram associated with your design.

b. Tabulate the register transfer operations and microoperations supported by your datapath.

c. Consider the execution of the ADD instruction. Draw a state diagram fragment that shows the sequencing of control signal assertions to implement the ADD instruction. How many states are required to execute the instruction?

d. Repeat part (c), but this time for the RSR instruction.

11.7 *(Datapath Design)* Repeat Exercise 11.6, but this time design the datapath using a single-bus interconnection scheme.

11.8 *(Datapath Design)* Repeat Exercise 11.6, but this time design a compromise multiple-bus datapath. Your goal should be to reduce the number of states it takes to implement the ADD and RSR instructions, short of using the point-to-point scheme.

11.9 *(Control State Machine)* The instruction set fragment of Exercise 11.6 provides no way to load the registers. We add the following multiple-word instructions to accomplish these functions:

1100 $Y_3Y_2Y_1Y_0$	XFER	$R[Y_3Y_2] := R[Y_1Y_0]$
1101 $Y_7Y_6Y_5Y_4$ $Y_3Y_2Y_1Y_0$	LD	$R[0] := MEM[Y_7Y_6Y_5Y_4\ Y_3Y_2Y_1Y_0]$
1110 $Y_7Y_6Y_5Y_4$ $Y_3Y_2Y_1Y_0$	ST	$MEM[Y_7Y_6Y_5Y_4\ Y_3Y_2Y_1Y_0] := R[0]$

The XFER instruction, encoded in two adjacent words in memory, replaces the register indicated by the high-order 2 bits of the instruction's second word with the register denoted by its 2 low-order bits. The LD (load) and ST (store) instructions are encoded in three adjacent words: the first denotes the instruction, the second and third the memory address (this machine can address up to 256 four-bit words). For completeness, the last instruction is BRN, Branch if R_0 is Negative:

1111 $Y_7Y_6Y_5Y_4$ $Y_3Y_2Y_1Y_0$	BRN	IF R[0]<3> = 1 THEN
		$PC := Y_7Y_6Y_5Y_4\ Y_3Y_2Y_1Y_0$

a. Draw the state diagram fragment for the instruction fetch and operation decode, given that an instruction may be encoded in one, two, or three 4-bit words.

b. Draw the memory interface register transfer diagram and the control's set of registers (PC, IR, possibly others).

c. What new register transfer operations and microoperations are added by these four instructions?

11.10 *(Datapath Design)* How does the register-to-register transfer operation (XFER) affect your datapath designs in Exercises 11.6 (point-to-point), 11.7 (single bus), and 11.8 (multiple buses)?

11.11 *(Datapath Design)* Put together a unified datapath, integrating the control registers (PC, IR, etc.) from Exercise 11.9 with your datapaths from Exercises 11.6, 11.7, and 11.8. How many processor states (total clock cycles) does it take to implement the ADD and RSR instructions in each datapath? Explain how you derived your state/cycle count.

11.12 *(Datapath Design)*   Consider the following change to the instruction set description of Exercise 11.6. The RSR and ASR are eliminated from the instruction set and replaced by the following two instructions:

1010	CLC	CARRY := 0
1011	ADC	R[0] := R[0] + CARRY
		CARRY := Carry out from ALU

The ADD instruction now saves its carryout into a special Carry register. This is cleared by the CLC instruction and can be added to R_0 by the ADC (add with carry) instruction.

a. How should the datapath be modified to support these instructions? Assume the ALU can perform only standard ADD, INCrement, AND, and COMPlement operations.

b. Draw the state diagram fragment implementing the execution sequences for the ADC and CLC instructions.

c. Describe how the execution sequence for ADD is changed by introducing these instructions.

11.13 *(Processor Datapath and Control)*   Consider the instruction format for a 16-bit computer in Figure Ex11.13. The high-order 4 bits specify the operation code. Every instruction contains two operands. The first operand is always one of the processor's general-purpose registers, which is specified by the Reg A field in the instruction (the machine has four general-purpose registers, R_0, R_1, R_2, and R_3). The second operand is always in memory. Its address is formed by the sum of the contents of a register, indicated by the Reg B field, and the offset value within the instruction. The machine's initial datapath is shown in Figure Ex11.13. The ALU implements ADD, SUB, and so forth.

a. Tabulate the microoperations implied by the above datapath. Group the operations by common sources or destinations.

b. Write a sequence of register transfer microoperations to implement the execution of an Add instruction (assume the instruction has already been fetched and decoded), given the following "macrodefinition" of the add:

ADD Ra, (Rb)offset   Ra := Ra + Memory[Rb + Offset]

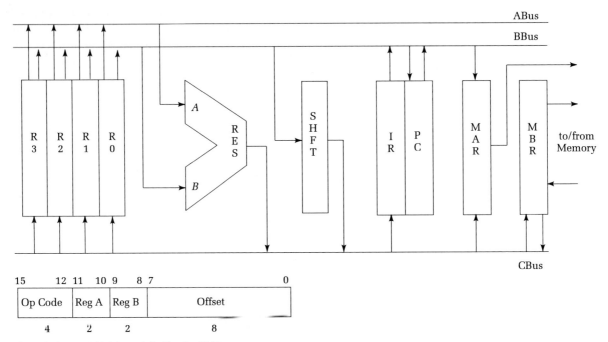

Figure Ex11.13   Initial datapath for Exercise 11.13.

For example, if the instruction is "Add R0, (R1) 10" and R_1 contains 5, then the contents of memory location 15 are added to the contents of R_0, with the result stored back into R_0.

Assume that a memory access requires only a single state. Indicate any changes to or assumptions about the register transfer operations supported by the datapath to implement the instruction's execution sequence (you may need to add additional paths or operations). In your answer, show how register transfer operations should be grouped into states.

c. Write a sequence of register transfer microoperations to implement the execution of a Branch Negative instruction (assume the instruction has already been fetched and decoded), given the following macrodefinition of the branch:

BRN Ra, (Rb)offset   If Ra < 0 then PC := Rb + Offset

d. However, unlike the add instruction, the offset in the branch instruction is a twos complement number. In other words, the offset can be interpreted as a number between +127 and −128.

State any additions to or assumptions about the datapath that must be made to implement the execution sequence of this instruction. As in part (b), group the register transfer instruction into states.

11.14 *(Processor Specification and Datapath Design)* In this exercise, you will describe the architecture of a simple 4-bit computer. The machine is organized around an evaluation stack, an ALU that supports the twos complement operations SUB, ADD, and INCRement and the logical operators AND, OR, and COMPlement, and a rotating shifter supporting both logical rotating shifts and arithmetic shifts. The machine supports 16 different instructions, including those for accessing memory, call/return from subroutine, and conditional/unconditional branches. These instructions are encoded in one to three 4-bit word parcels. The machine can address 256 four-bit words, organized as a Harvard architecture.

A stack is a data structure in which the element last added is the first to be deleted. Hence, stacks are often called last in, first out data structures. Items are PUSHed to the top of the stack and POPed from the top of the stack. Consider the expression $9 - (5 + 2)$. This can be implemented by the following sequence of stack-oriented operations:

PUSHC	9	; Push constant 9 to top of stack
PUSHC	5	; Push constant 5 to top of stack
PUSHC	2	; Push constant 2 to top of stack
ADD		; Top two elements of the stack are added
		; Remove and replace with the number 7
SUB		; Top two elements of the stack are subtracted
		; Remove and replace with the number 2

The sequence and its effects on the stack are shown in Figure Ex11.14(a). The expression can be rewritten without parentheses as $9\ 5\ 2 + -$.

We assume that the Top of Stack pointer is initialized to −1 at processor restart. This represents an empty stack. The TOS pointer is incremented before an item is added to the stack, and is decremented after an item is removed.

Instructions are encoded in one to three four-bit words. Arithmetic, logical, and shift instructions are encoded in a single word: all four bits form the op code. The operands are implicitly the elements on the top of the stack. The arithmetic/logical instructions are: ADD, SUB, AND, OR, COMP, INCR, RSR (rotating shift to the right), and ASR (arithmetic shift to the right), and their encodings are the following:

0000	ADD	Mem[TOS−1] := Mem[TOS−1] + Mem[TOS];
		TOS := TOS − 1;
0001	SUB	Mem[TOS−1] := Mem[TOS−1] − Mem[TOS];
		TOS := TOS − 1;
0010	AND	Mem[TOS−1] := Mem[TOS−1] AND Mem[TOS];
		TOS := TOS − 1;
0011	OR	Mem[TOS−1] := Mem[TOS−1] OR Mem[TOS];
		TOS := TOS − 1;
0100	COMP	Mem[TOS] := ~Mem[TOS];
0101	INCR	Mem[TOS] := Mem[TOS] + 1;
0110	RSR	Mem[TOS]<0> := Mem[TOS]<1>,
		Mem[TOS]<1> := Mem[TOS]<2>,
		Mem[TOS]<2> := Mem[TOS]<3>,
		Mem[TOS]<3> := Mem[TOS]<0>;
0111	ASR	Mem[TOS]<0> := Mem[TOS]<1>,
		Mem[TOS]<1> := Mem[TOS]<2>,
		Mem[TOS]<2> := Mem[TOS]<3>,
		Mem[TOS]<3> := Mem[TOS]<3>;

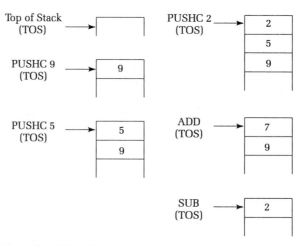

Figure Ex11.14(a)   Stack evaluation of 9 − (5 + 2).

The next instruction group places data into the stack or removes data from the stack. The PUSHC instruction is encoded in two 4-bit words, one that contains the op code and one that contains 4-bit twos complement data to place on the top of the stack. PUSH and POP are three words long: one for the op code and two subsequent 4-bit words that when taken together contain an 8-bit address:

1000 $X_3X_2X_1X_0$	PUSHC data	TOS := TOS + 1; Mem[TOS] := $X_3X_2X_1X_0$;
1001 $A_7A_6A_5A_4\ A_3A_2A_1A_0$	PUSH address	TOS := TOS + 1;
		Mem[TOS] := Mem[$A_7A_6A_5A_4\ A_3A_2A_1A_0$];
1010 $A_7A_6A_5A_4\ A_3A_2A_1A_0$	POP address	Mem[$A_7A_6A_5A_4\ A_3A_2A_1A_0$] := Mem[TOS];
		TOS := TOS − 1;

The remaining instructions are conditional/unconditional branches and subroutine call and return. All but RTS (Return from Subroutine) are encoded in three 4-bit words: one word for the op code and two words for the target address. The conditional branch instructions, BRZ and BRN, test the top of stack element for = 0 or < 0, respectively. If true, the PC is changed to the target address. In either case, the TOS element is left undisturbed.

JSR (Jump to Subroutine) is a special instruction that is used to implement subroutines. The current value of the PC is placed on the stack and then the PC is changed to the target address. Any values placed on the stack by the subroutine must be POPed before it returns. The RTS instruction restores the PC from the value saved on the stack. It is important to organize the processor state machine so that the PC always points to the next instruction to be fetched while executing the current instruction.

1011 $A_7A_6A_5A_4\ A_3A_2A_1A_0$	JSR address	TOS := TOS + 1;
		Mem[TOS] := PC; PC := $A_7A_6A_5A_4\ A_3A_2A_1A_0$;
1100	RTS	PC:= Mem[TOS];
		TOS := TOS − 1;
1101 $A_7A_6A_5A_4\ A_3A_2A_1A_0$	BRZ address	IF Mem[TOS] = 0
		THEN PC := $A_7A_6A_5A_4\ A_3A_2A_1A_0$;
1110 $A_7A_6A_5A_4\ A_3A_2A_1A_0$	BRN address	IF Mem[TOS] < 0
		THEN PC := $A_7A_6A_5A_4\ A_3A_2A_1A_0$;
1111 $A_7A_6A_5A_4\ A_3A_2A_1A_0$	JMP address	PC := $A_7A_6A_5A_4\ A_3A_2A_1A_0$;

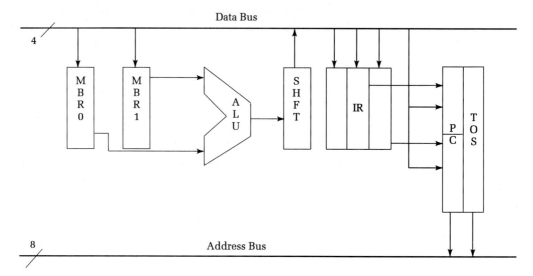

Figure Ex11.14(b)   Starting datapath design for Exercise 11.14.

Figure Ex11.14(b) shows an initial datapath design for this instruction set.

a. Extend this datapath with a Harvard architecture memory interface.

b. What register transfer operations and microoperations are supported by this datapath?

c. How can the microoperations you found in part (b) be used to implement the execution portion for each of the 16 instructions of the instruction set?

11.15 *(Processor Controller Design)*   Design a state diagram for the processor and instruction set described in Exercise 11.14. You can choose a Moore or Mealy design style.

a. Draw the modified state design. Identify in general terms what is happening in each state.

b. What microoperations should be associated with each state?

c. For each of the 16 instructions in the instruction set, describe the number of states required for its fetch and execution. You may assume that the memory system responds in a single processor cycle for the purposes of this calculation.

12 Controller Implementation

Any sufficiently advanced technology is indistinguishable from magic.
—*Arthur C. Clarke*

A man is known by the company he organizes.
—*Ambrose Bierce*

Introduction

In this, our final chapter, we examine alternative ways to implement a processor's control portion. In real machines, the control unit is often the most complex part of the design.

We study four alternative controller organizations. The first is based on *classical finite state machines*, using a Moore or Mealy structure. This approach is sometimes disparagingly called "random logic" control, to contrast it with more structured methods based on ROMs and other forms of programmable logic. The classical method is the only approach we used in Chapter 11.

The second method is called *time state*. It decomposes a single classical finite state machine into several simpler, communicating finite state machines. It is a strategy for partitioning a finite state machine that is well matched to the structure of processor controllers.

The third method makes use of *jump counters*, which we introduced in Chapter 10. This approach extensively uses MSI-level components like counters, multiplexers, and decoders to implement the controller.

The final method, *microprogramming*, uses ROMs to encode next states and control signals directly as bits stored in a memory. We examine three alternative microprogramming methods: *branch sequencers*, *horizontal microprogramming*, and *vertical microprogramming*. A branch sequencer encodes multiple next-state choices within the ROM. Horizontal microprogramming dedicates one ROM bit for each controller output. Vertical microprogramming carefully encodes the controller outputs to reduce the width of the ROM word. Any practical microprogramming approach includes some combination of these methods.

12.1   Random Logic

In this section, we examine classical controller structures based on the standard methods for implementing Moore and Mealy machines. This controller organization is sometimes called *random logic*, because the next-state and output functions are formulated in terms of discrete logic gates. We could just as easily use programmable logic, such as a PAL/PLA, EPLD, FPGA, or ROM, to implement these functions.

In this section, we examine two alternative control implementations for the instruction set and datapath introduced in the last chapter. Since we examined the Mealy implementation in Chapter 11, we concentrate on the Moore approach in the next subsection.

A Mealy machine is often the most economical way to implement the controller state machine, but its asynchronous outputs introduce timing problems. We will look at the differences between synchronous and asynchronous Mealy machines and the timing relationship between signal assertions and their effect in the datapath. You'll see that it doesn't take much to convert an asynchronous Mealy machine into its synchronous cousin.

12.1.1   Moore Machine

Figure 12.1 gives the complete state diagram, including register transfer operations, for a Moore machine implementation of the processor of Section 11.3. It requires more states than the equivalent Mealy diagram, but the difference is small. In particular, we need an extra state in the reset/instruction fetch sequence and another one in the branch negative sequence.

The assignment of register transfer operations to states is reasonably straightforward. Only one combination of register transfer operations in the same state is surprising. This is where the memory read request is used at the same time as latching the memory databus into the MBR (see states IF_2, LD_1, and AD_1). Does this result in latching invalid data?

No, it doesn't. Figure 12.2 shows the detailed timing of events for the state sequence IF_1, IF_2, and IF_3. Each time we loop in such a state, the MBR captures the current value of the memory bus. For the first few times looping in the state, the data captured by the MBR is invalid. However, the Wait signal remains asserted until the memory places

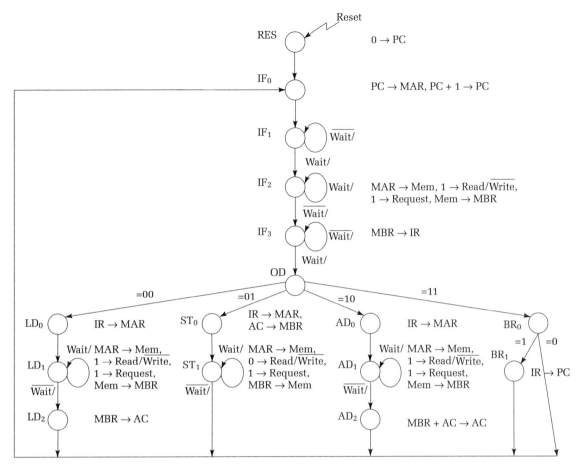

Figure 12.1 Complete Moore state diagram.

valid data on the bus. When Wait is unasserted, the value latched into MBR at the next clock transition is valid. This is the same state transition that advances the state machine to its next state (IF_3, LD_2, or AD_2).

Moore Machine Block Diagram The block diagram of the Moore machine is given in Figure 12.3. It requires 16 states. We encode this densely in a 4-bit state register. The next-state logic has nine inputs (four current-state bits, Reset, Wait, two IR bits, and one AC bit) and four outputs (the next state). Since the datapath control signals are decoded from the state, this block of logic has four inputs and 18 outputs.

Implementation Choices: ROM Versus PAL/PLA We can implement the next-state logic block and the output logic block as either ROMs or PAL/PLAs. Using ROMs, we can implement the next-state logic by a 512 by

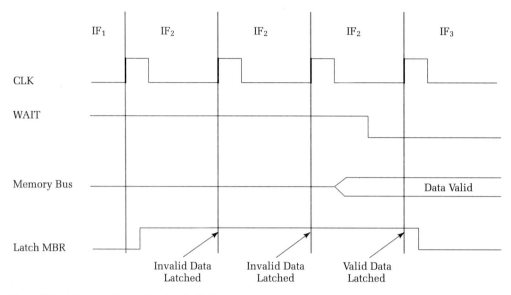

Figure 12.2   Moore machine register transfer timing.

4-bit memory and the output logic by a 16 by 18-bit memory. Since single device ROMs come in widths that are powers of 2, we would implement the latter with several 4-bit- or 8-bit-wide ROMs.

We begin implementing the controller by obtaining the symbolic next-state table. This is shown in Figure 12.4. A couple of things are worth observing about this table. First, we can make extensive use of the don't cares among the inputs/address lines. Notice that a given input signal is examined in very few states. For example, the IR bits are examined in state OD and the AC sign bit is tested only in state BR_0.

Second, the number of register transfer operations asserted in any given state is rather small. In Figure 12.4, no more than four register transfer operations are asserted in any state. Some of the outputs, like those associated with memory references, are always asserted together. We will exploit this in some of the controller implementation strategies later in this chapter.

Of course, a ROM-based implementation cannot take advantage of don't cares. You must program all 512 ROM words for the next-state logic, a rather tedious task. However, one advantage of using a ROM is that you need not worry about a careful state assignment.

If you use a PAL or a PLA, then a good state assignment is essential for reducing the complexity of the next-state logic. For example, the naive state assignment suggested by Figure 12.4 (basically, a depth-first enumeration) yields a 21-product-term implementation. This compares rather unfavorably with the equivalent of 512 product terms in the ROM case (one term for each ROM word).

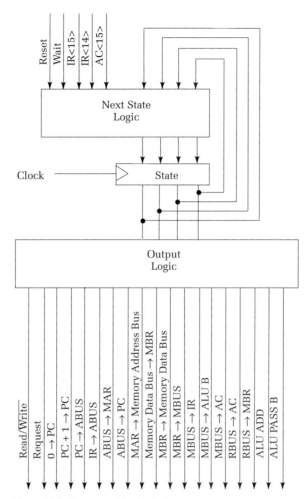

Figure 12.3 Moore machine block diagram.

Figure 12.5 shows the *espresso* inputs and outputs for this particular state assignment. The next-state logic is fairly complex. Each next-state bit requires seven to nine product terms for its implementation. This implies that you should use a PAL component with large OR gate fan-ins, like the P22V10. For a PLA-based implementation, all you need is a PLA that provides 21 unique product terms.

A *nova* state assignment can do even better. It requires only 18 product terms:

```
state IF0: 0000   state ST0: 0101
state IF1: 1011   state ST1: 0110
state IF2: 1111   state AD0: 0111
state IF3: 1101   state AD1: 1000
```

Reset	Wait	IR<15>	IR<14>	AC<15>	Current State	Next State	Register Transfer Ops
1	X	X	X	X	X	RES (0000)	0 →PC
0	X	X	X	X	IF0 (0001)	IF1 (0001)	PC→ MAR, PC + 1 → PC
0	0	X	X	X	IF1 (0010)	IF1 (0010)	
0	1	X	X	X	IF1 (0010)	IF2 (0011)	
0	1	X	X	X	IF2 (0011)	IF2 (0011)	MAR → Mem, Read,
0	0	X	X	X	IF2 (0011)	IF3 (0100)	Request, Mem → MBR
0	0	X	X	X	IF3 (0100)	IF3 (0100)	MBR → IR
0	1	X	X	X	IF3 (0100)	OD (0101)	
0	X	0	0	X	OD (0101)	LD0 (0110)	
0	X	0	1	X	OD (0101)	ST0 (1001)	
0	X	1	0	X	OD (0101)	AD0 (1011)	
0	X	1	1	X	OD (0101)	BR0 (1110)	
0	X	X	X	X	LD0 (0110)	LD1 (0111)	IR → MAR
0	1	X	X	X	LD1 (0111)	LD1 (0111)	MAR → Mem, Read,
0	0	X	X	X	LD1 (0111)	LD2 (1000)	Request, Mem → MBR
0	X	X	X	X	LD2 (1000)	IF0 (0001)	MBR → AC
0	X	X	X	X	ST0 (1001)	ST1 (1010)	IR→ MAR, AC → MBR
0	1	X	X	X	ST1 (1010)	ST1 (1010)	MAR → Mem, Write,
0	0	X	X	X	ST1 (1010)	IF0 (0001)	Request, MBR → Mem
0	X	X	X	X	AD0 (1011)	AD1 (1100)	IR →MAR
0	1	X	X	X	AD1 (1100)	AD1 (1100)	MAR → Mem, Read,
0	0	X	X	X	AD1 (1100)	AD2 (1101)	Request, Mem → MBR
0	X	X	X	X	AD2 (1101)	IF0 (0001)	MBR + AC → AC
0	X	X	X	0	BR0 (1110)	IF0 (0001)	
0	X	X	X	1	DR0 (1110)	BR1 (1111)	
0	X	X	X	X	BR1 (1111)	IF0 (0001)	IR →PC

Figure 12.4 Symbolic state transition table.

```
state OD:   0001   state AD2: 1001
state LD0:  0010   state BR0: 1010
state LD1:  0011   state BR1: 1100
state LD2:  0100   state RES: 1110
```

12.1.2   Synchronous Mealy Machine

The organization of a synchronous Mealy machine is not very different from the Moore machine just described. The key is merging the next-state and output Boolean functions into a single logic block. For the Mealy machine, the logic has nine inputs and 22 outputs (four state outputs and 18 microoperation control outputs).

The combined next-state and output functions have some interesting implications for a ROM-based implementation. The Moore machine required only 2336 ROM bits for its implementation ($512 \times 4 + 16 \times 18$). The Mealy machine needs 11,264 ROM bits (512×22). This shows some of the inherent inefficiency of the ROM-based approach. Many of those ROM bits are really don't cares. Of course, ROMs are very dense and even large ROMs are not too expensive. We will see more efficient methods for using ROMs in our discussion of microprogramming.

```
.i 9
.o 4
.ilb reset wait ir15 ir14 ac15 q3 q2 q1 q0
.ob p3 p2 p1 p0
.p 26
1---- ---- 0000
0---- 0001 0001
00--- 0010 0010
01--- 0010 0011
01--- 0011 0011
00--- 0011 0100
00--- 0100 0100
01--- 0100 0101
0-00- 0101 0110
0-01- 0101 1001
0-10- 0101 1011
0-11- 0101 1110
0---- 0110 0111
01--- 0111 0111
00--- 0111 1000
0---- 1000 0001
0---- 1001 1010
01--- 1010 1010
00--- 1010 0001
0---- 1011 1100
01--- 1100 1100
00--- 1100 1101
0---- 1101 0001
0---0 1110 0001
0---1 1110 1111
0---- 1111 0001
.e
```

(a) *Espresso* input

```
.i 9
.o 4
.ilb reset wait ir15 ir14 ac15 q3 q2 q1 q0
.ob p3 p2 p1 p0
.p 21
0-00-0101 0110
0-01-0101 1001
0-11-0101 1110
0-10-0101 1011
01---1010 1010
00---0111 1000
00----011 0100
0----1000 0001
0---11110 1110
01---011- 0100
0----0001 0001
01---01-0 0001
0----1001 1010
0----1011 1100
00---1--0 0001
0----1100 1100
0----0-10 0010
0-----110 0001
0----11-1 0001
0----01-0 0100
01---0-1- 0011
.e
```

(b) *Espresso* output

Figure 12.5   *Espresso* input and output for the Moore processor control.

Synchronous Versus Asynchronous Mealy Machines A conventional Mealy machine is asynchronous. Input changes lead to output changes, independent of the clock. This can play havoc when the outputs are signals that immediately control the datapath. We must be able to assert control signals in a well-behaved, synchronous manner.

To some extent, we can minimize the danger of asynchronous control signals by selecting datapath components with synchronous controls. These inputs need not stabilize until a setup time before the controlling clock edge.

However, there is still a problem for control signals that take effect immediately. The safest remedy is to make the Mealy machine synchronous. In a synchronous Mealy machine, the outputs change only when the state changes and remain stable throughout the state time. We achieve this by placing registers between the input signals, the combinational logic that computes the outputs, and the output signals. Let's examine the approaches for constructing synchronous Mealy machines next.

Synchronizing a Mealy Machine   Figure 12.6 shows three possible ways to construct a Mealy machine with synchronized outputs: using edge-triggered devices (a) at the input and output, (b) only at the inputs, and (c) only at the outputs. Each affects the timing of control signals in a slightly different way. In the figure, we assume that output f should be asserted whenever input A is asserted.

Let's start with case (a), which synchronizes both the inputs and the outputs. Assuming that A is asserted in cycle 0, the synchronized output f will not be asserted until cycle 2. This delays the calculation of f by two cycles. Thus, if A is asserted in state S_0, the output f is not asserted until state S_2. The timing and state diagrams of Figure 12.7 make this more clear.

You should realize that placing synchronizing registers at both the inputs and outputs is overkill. We can get the desired synchronization

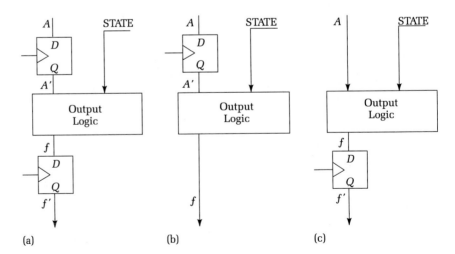

(a)   (b)   (c)

Figure 12.6   Three approaches to building a Mealy machine with synchronous outputs.

by placing flip-flops at one side or the other of the output logic. Let's consider case (b): only the inputs are synchronized. Figure 12.8 shows the effects. If A is asserted in cycle 0, f is asserted in the following cycle. Alternatively, we can label the state transitions in the next state with the synchronized input A' and the output f.

Case (c) places synchronizing logic only on the outputs. The timing diagram is similar to Figure 12.8 and is shown in Figure 12.9. The synchronized output signal f' takes effect in the state after the one in which A is first asserted.

Synchronizing the Simple CPU Mealy State Diagram To make these ideas concrete, let's examine a Mealy implementation of the processor control state machine we derived in Section 11.3. Case (b), which places registers on the inputs, makes the most sense for synchronizing this machine. Of

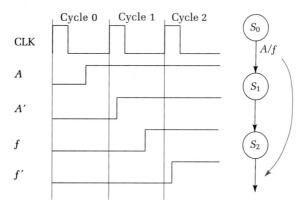

Figure 12.7 Synchronized inputs and outputs: timing and state diagrams.

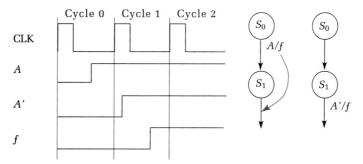

Figure 12.8 Synchronized inputs.

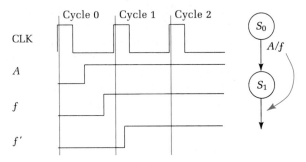

Figure 12.9   Synchronized outputs.

the five inputs, IR<15:14> and AC<15> are already synchronized because they are datapath registers clocked by the same clock as the control state machine. The delayed effect of control signals does not apply here; we are not placing an additional register in the path between the IR and the AC and the control. For example, we can load the IR with a new instruction in one state and compute a multiway branch based on the op code in the very next state.

Reset and Wait are another matter. Because these signals come from outside the processor, it is prudent to pass them through synchronizing flip-flops anyway. This means that the external Reset and Wait signals are delayed by one clock cycle before they can influence the state machine.

Delaying reset by one cycle has little effect because the state of the machine will be reset anyway. However, the one state delay of the Wait signal does affect performance. The processor normally loops in a state until there is a change in Wait. This means that the machine stays in the loop for an extra cycle. Even a memory that responds to a request immediately requires one processor clock cycle before the processor can recognize that the operation is complete.

If we design the memory system to be synchronous with the processor, we can avoid this performance loss. Since the memory system's controller is clocked with the same clock as the processor, the Wait signal no longer needs to be synchronized.

12.2   Time State (Divide and Conquer)

The classical approaches for implementing finite state machines yield a monolithic implementation that is sometimes unwieldy and difficult to change. An alternative approach, based on a divide-and-conquer strategy, partitions the single finite state machine into several simpler communicating state machines.

12.2.1   Partitioning the State Machine

A common partitioning is to divide the controller into three state machines: the time state finite state machine, the instruction state finite state machine, and the condition state finite state machine. The *time state finite state machine* determines the current phase of instruction interpretation. These phases include instruction fetch, instruction decode, and instruction execute.

The *instruction state finite state machine* identifies the current instruction being executed, such as load, store, add, or branch. It handles the process of instruction decoding.

The *condition state finite state machine* represents the state of the current condition of the datapath. In our example processor, the only interesting condition is the high-order bit of the AC. Other possible datapath conditions include whether the last ALU operation resulted in a zero, an overflow, or an underflow.

The partitioning into these three kinds of state machines is advantageous because there are usually only minor differences among the control sequences for different instructions. If these sequences are suitably parameterized, we can avoid a unique sequence for each instruction. Given that the instruction state can be readily decoded from the IR and the condition state from the datapath, we can even reduce the number of states in the overall finite state machine.

12.2.2   Time State Machines for the Example Processor

We start with the Moore state diagram of Figure 12.1. To obtain the time state finite state machine, we must look for the worst-case path through the classical state diagram. In the example processor, the worst-case path is eight states long (ADD or LOAD).

Given this eight-state sequence, the idea is to parameterize the basic sequence by the outputs of the instruction state (LD, ST, ADD, BRN) and the condition state (the high-order bit of the AC: $AC \geq 0$, $AC < 0$) finite state machines. These outputs are associated with the transitions in the time state finite state machine. Under the appropriate conditions, the time state finite state machine will advance to its next state.

The parameterized time state finite state diagram is shown in Figure 12.10. The instruction state and condition state finite state machines are given in Figure 12.11. We handle Reset by another state machine that is not shown. Every instruction, regardless of type, sequences through the first five states, IF_0 through IF_3 and OD. These are assigned to time states T_0 through T_4, respectively.

After this, the instructions follow different execution paths. Fortunately, much of this sequencing is still common. The states LD_0–LD_2,

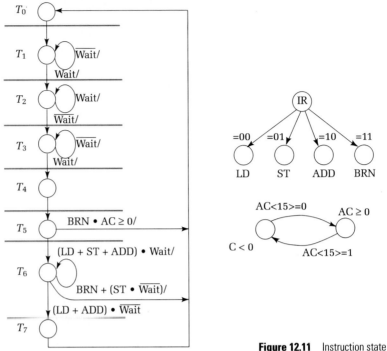

Figure 12.10   Time state finite state machine.

Figure 12.11   Instruction state and condition state FSMs.

ST_0, ST_1, AD_0–AD_2, and BR_0, BR_1 have been collapsed onto the time states T_5, T_6, and T_7. The only output from the time state machine is its current state, T_0 through T_7.

Figure 12.10 also shows how outputs from the instruction state and condition state machines influence the next-state sequencing in the time state finite state machine. For example, in time state T_5, if the instruction is BRN and the AC ≥ 0, the time state machine returns to state T_0. Otherwise, it advances to state T_6. This quick return to the beginning of the time state machine is called a *short-circuit* transition. Although we could force all instructions to sequence through to T_7 before returning, this would be less efficient because every instruction would have to take as many cycles as the longest possible instruction.

As another example, let's consider time state T_6. If the instruction is LD, ST, or ADD and Wait is asserted, the machine stays in T_6. If the instruction is BRN or ST with Wait unasserted, the machine returns to T_0. Otherwise it advances to T_7.

Generation of Microoperations   It is not difficult to generate the microoperation outputs from the time state, condition state, and instruction state. The various register transfer operations are asserted under the following conditions:

$0 \rightarrow$ PC: Reset

PC + 1 $\rightarrow$ PC: T0

PC $\rightarrow$ MAR: T0

MAR $\rightarrow$ Memory Address Bus: T2 + T6 • (LD + ST + ADD)

Memory Data Bus $\rightarrow$ MBR: T2 + T6 • (LD + ADD)

MBR $\rightarrow$ Memory Data Bus: T6 • ST

MBR $\rightarrow$ IR: T4

MBR $\rightarrow$ AC: T7 • LD

AC $\rightarrow$ MBR: T5 • ST

AC + MBR $\rightarrow$ AC: T7 • ADD

IR<13:0> $\rightarrow$ MAR: T5 • (LD + ST + ADD)

IR<13:0> $\rightarrow$ PC: T6 • BRN

$1 \rightarrow$ Read/$\overline{\text{Write}}$: T2 + T6 • (LD + ADD)

$0 \rightarrow$ Read/$\overline{\text{Write}}$: T6 • ST

$1 \rightarrow$ Request: T2 + T6 • (LD + ST + ADD)

The condition state is not explicitly used for generating any of the register transfer operations. Of course, it does influence the next-state transitions in the time state finite state machine.

Discussion In general, the time state approach can reduce states and simplify the next-state logic, at the possible expense of introducing more flip-flops. The short-circuit technique makes the next-state logic somewhat more complex but allows short cycle count instructions to finish early. This has the effect of leading to faster program execution.

12.3 Jump Counter

In Section 10.2 we described methods for implementing finite state machines using a counter as the state register. We called this the *jump counter* method. The approach uses MSI components, such as synchronous counters, multiplexers, and decoders, to implement the finite state machine. In this section we expand the description, showing how jump counters can be used to implement the control unit of a CPU.

Jump counters fall into two classes: *pure* and *hybrid*. A pure jump counter permits only one of four possible next states: the current state (the counter holds), the next sequential state (the counter counts), state 0 (the counter clears), or a single "jump" state (the counter loads). In the pure jump counter, the jump state is strictly a function of the current state. A hybrid counter supports the same kinds of transitions but allows the jump state to be a function of the inputs as well as the current state.

12.3.1 Pure Jump Counter

Figure 12.12 is a block diagram view of a pure jump counter. The jump state is a function of the current state, while the clear, load, and count inputs to the state register depend on the current state and the current inputs. We assume that clear takes precedence over load, which takes precedence over count. The logic blocks in the figure can be implemented with discrete logic gates, PALs/PLAs, or ROMs. We frequently use ROMs for the jump state logic.

The restricted sequencing of states in the pure jump counter is shown in Figure 12.13. To take maximum advantage of the counter state register, we should assign the states in count sequence. The most frequent target of a transition should be assigned state 0.

This usually proves too restrictive for states that require a more general multiway branch, such as the operation decode state in a processor state diagram. For states with multiway branches, a pure jump counter approach must introduce a number of extra states, as shown in Figure 12.14.

Figure 12.14(a) shows the operation decode state diagram fragment from Figures 11.23 and 12.1. To implement this as a pure jump counter, we would need the state diagram fragment of Figure 12.14(b). We must introduce two new decode states and increase the total number of states

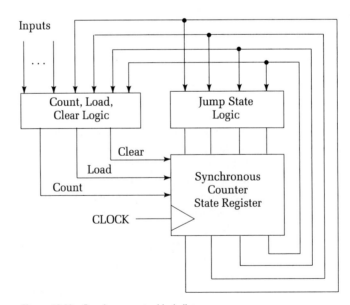

Figure 12.12 Pure jump counter block diagram.

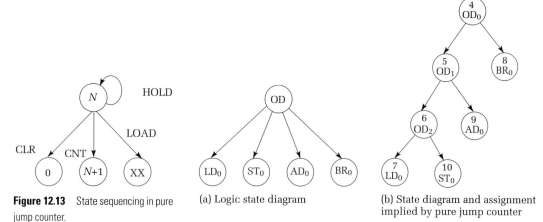

Figure 12.13 State sequencing in pure jump counter.

(a) Logic state diagram

(b) State diagram and assignment implied by pure jump counter

Figure 12.14 Effect on multiway branching in pure jump counter.

needed to execute a load, store, or add instruction. It is not too surprising that some enterprising designer invented the more general hybrid jump counter.

12.3.2 Hybrid Jump Counter

The hybrid jump counter solves the multiway branch problem. It simply makes the jump state a function of the inputs as well as the current state. This is made clear in the block diagram of Figure 12.15. The jump state, clear, load, and count logic are all functions of the input and the current state.

Mealy State Diagram for the Simple CPU Let's see how to implement the Mealy state diagram of Figure 11.23 with a hybrid jump counter. Our first consideration is how to assign encoded states to the state diagram. Most state transitions advance forward or hold in the current state, depending on the value of the Wait signal. Thus, we can use a natural depth-first state assignment. See Figure 12.16.

Next, we find a state to assign as 0. Since the RES state is the most frequent target of a transition, it is the best candidate. Starting with 0, we simply assign the states in sequence as we advance down through the state diagram.

The last consideration is to identify the *branch states*, those whose next-state transitions cannot be described simply in terms of hold (stay in

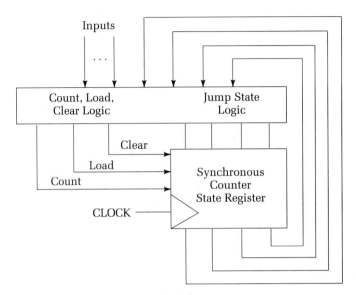

Figure 12.15 Hybrid jump counter block diagram.

the current state), count (advance to the next state in sequence), or reset (go to state 0). The only such state is OD, operation decode. Fortunately, we can describe the next-state transitions as a function of the current state and the IR op code bits. In fact, since this is the only multiway branch in the whole state diagram, the jump state logic is a function solely of the IR op code bits.

The complete state assignment is shown in Figure 12.16. We assume that the states are numbered S_0 through S_{13}. For the transitions to the RES state (S_0), the state counter CLR signal should be asserted in states S_7, S_9 (if $\overline{\text{Wait}}$ is also asserted), S_{12}, and S_{13}.

The counter LD signal is asserted only for states with a multiway branch. For this state diagram, it should be asserted in state S_4, the OD state. The jump state logic, determined by the IR op code bits, generates the new state to be loaded into the state counter.

When to assert the CNT signal is slightly more complicated. The Boolean equations to count or to hold (don't count) are

$$\text{CNT} = (S_0 + S_5 + S_8 + S_{10}) + \text{Wait} \bullet (S_1 + S_3) + \overline{\text{Wait}} \bullet (S_2 + S_6 + S_9 + S_{11})$$

$$\text{HOLD} = \overline{\text{Wait}} \bullet (S_1 + S_3) + \text{Wait} \bullet (S_2 + S_6 + S_9 + S_{11})$$

The HOLD equation ($\overline{\text{CNT}}$) is simpler than the CNT equation. You might save some logic by implementing HOLD and then inverting it to obtain the CNT signal.

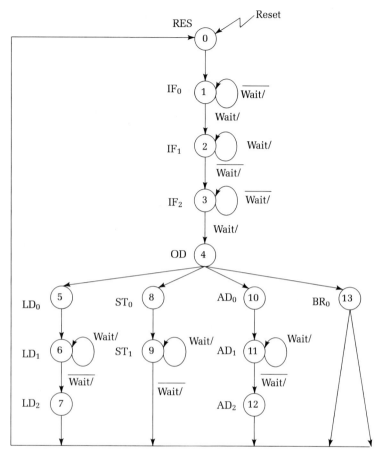

Figure 12.16 Hybrid jump counter state assignment.

The jump state logic for S_4 (OD) is straightforward. It can be implemented by a 4 word by 4-bit ROM whose address inputs are the two IR op code bits.

Schematic Level Implementation of the Jump Counter A schematic description of the jump counter is shown in Figure 12.17. The major components are (1) a synchronous counter (74163) used as the state register; (2) a 4-to-16 decoder (74154) to generate signals to identify the current state; (3) jump state logic implemented as a 4 word by 4-bit ROM, indexed by the IR's two op code bits; (4) a PAL implementing the Boolean logic for the state counter's CNT input; and (5) discrete logic implementing the state counter's CLR input (CLR could also have been implemented as an output of the CNT PAL). Since LD is asserted only

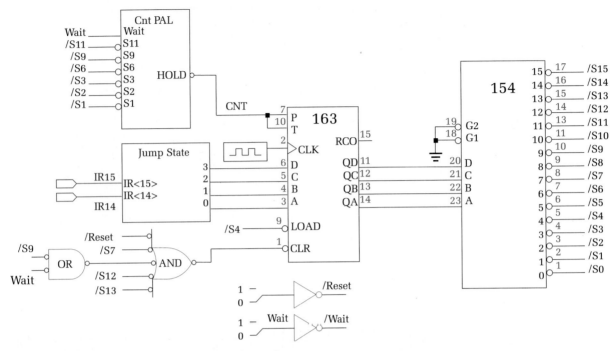

Figure 12.17   Schematic description of jump counter implementation.

in one state, S_4, the decoder output for that state drives the load input directly.

Let's look at the logic for this hybrid jump counter controller in a little more detail, starting with the contents of the jump state ROM. For each op code bit pattern, the appropriate next-state bits are stored in the ROM:

Address	Contents (Symbolic State)
00	0101 (LD$_0$)
01	1000 (ST$_0$)
10	1010 (AD$_0$)
11	1101 (BR$_0$)

The design of the rest of the jump counter implementation is reasonably straightforward, but there is one complication. This is the negative polarity of the 74163 counter's LD and CLR control signals, as well as the 74154 decoder's active low outputs. Let's look at the CLR signal first. In positive logic, it can be expressed as

$$CLR = Reset + S_7 + S_{12} + S_{13} + (S_9 \bullet \overline{Wait})$$

Since the CLR input is active low, the function should be rewritten using DeMorgan's theorem:

$$\overline{CLR} = \overline{Reset} \bullet \bar{S}_7 \bullet \bar{S}_{12} \bullet \bar{S}_{13} \bullet (\bar{S}_9 + Wait)$$

Fortunately, the decoder delivers exactly these active low state signals. A five-input AND gate and a two-input OR gate implement the $\overline{CLR}$ signal.

Sometimes it is more convenient to implement HOLD (DON'T CNT) rather than CNT. In other words, the complement of HOLD is CNT. HOLD can be implemented by using a PAL with programmable output polarity and choosing the output to be negative logic. The PAL function becomes

$$HOLD = S_1 \bullet \overline{Wait} + S_2 \bullet Wait + S_3 \bullet \overline{Wait} + S_6 \bullet Wait + S_9 \bullet Wait + S_{11} \bullet Wait$$

$$(CNT) \quad \overline{HOLD} = \overline{S_1 \bullet \overline{Wait} + S_2 \bullet Wait + S_3 \bullet \overline{Wait} + S_6 \bullet Wait + S_9 \bullet Wait + S_{11} \bullet Wait}$$

Since the decoder gives the current state in negative logic, it is just as easy to specify the HOLD function using the active low versions of the state inputs. The PAL is actually programmed with the following:

$$HOLD = \bar{S}_1 \bullet \overline{Wait} + \bar{S}_2 \bullet Wait + \bar{S}_3 \bullet \overline{Wait} + \bar{S}_6 \bullet Wait + \bar{S}_9 \bullet Wait + \bar{S}_{11} \bullet Wait$$

$$(CNT) \quad \overline{HOLD} = \overline{\bar{S}_1 \bullet \overline{Wait} + \bar{S}_2 \bullet Wait + \bar{S}_3 \bullet \overline{Wait} + \bar{S}_6 \bullet Wait + \bar{S}_9 \bullet Wait + \bar{S}_{11} \bullet Wait}$$

Alternative MSI-Based Implementation of the Jump Counter In the previous subsection, we implemented the CLR, LD, and CNT signals with discrete logic or PALs. We can use another method, based on multiplexers, to compute these signals.

Figure 12.18 shows how to do this for the simple CPU's state diagram. We compute CLR, LD, and CNT by using the current state to select exactly one multiplexer input. For example, the LD signal should be asserted in state S_4 (OD) and no other. When the LD multiplexer's select lines are driven to 0100 (state 4), the E4 input is gated to the EOUT output. E4 is tied high while all the other inputs to the multiplexer are tied low. The multiplexer's output is asserted active low in this case. It is unasserted high in all other cases.

The active low outputs of the multiplexer make this implementation a bit tricky. Since the counter's LD input is also active low, we maintain the correct polarity. An asserted positive logic input of the multiplexer generates an *asserted* negative logic output, which causes the counter to load.

Let's now turn to the CLR and CNT signals. The CLR signal from the multiplexer, CLR_m, must be ORed with Reset to form the counter CLR signal:

$$CLR = CLR_m + Reset$$

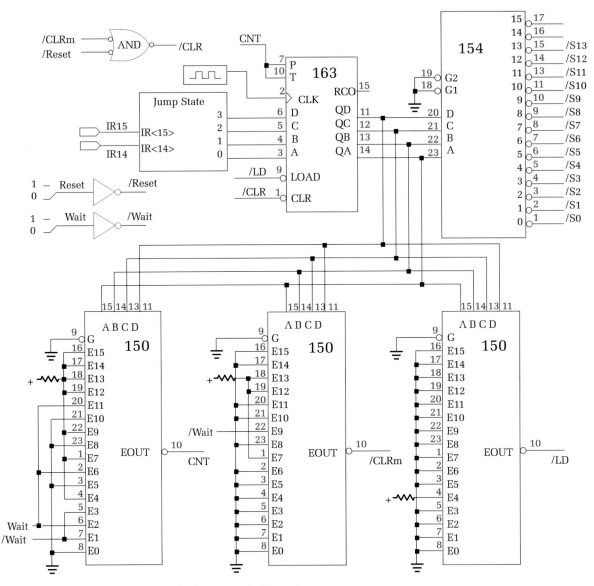

Figure 12.18 Schematic description of another jump counter implementation.

But since the counter's clear signal is active low, we must apply DeMorgan's theorem. Now it becomes a NOR function:

$$\overline{CLR} = \overline{\overline{CLR}_m + Reset} \qquad \overline{CLR} = \overline{\overline{CLR}_m} \bullet \overline{Reset}$$

We use the second implementation in Figure 12.18 (AND is the same as OR with complemented inputs and output). The CLR multiplexer's active low output is now in the correct polarity. Combined with the global Reset signal, it can return the machine to S_0.

Let's return to the inputs to the CLR multiplexer. Once again, they are active high: assert a multiplexer input high if the CLR signal is to take effect in the associated state. Thus E7, E12, and E13 are tied high, since these correspond to states S_7, S_{12}, and S_{13}. We always return to S_0 from these states. On the other hand, the transition from S_9 to S_0 takes place only when Wait is no longer asserted. Thus, the input to E9 is the signal $\overline{\text{Wait}}$, the condition for returning to S_0.

The CNT control is the most complex, since the multiplexer's output is active low but the counter's control signal is active high. The solution is simply to "push the bubble" through to the inputs. In this case, assert a multiplexer input low if you want a count to take place. Since a count takes place unconditionally in states S_0, S_5, S_8, and S_{10}, then E0, E5, E8, and E10 are all tied low.

For the states in which the count is conditional, the multiplexer inputs are tied to the complement of the condition. Thus, S_1 and S_3 advance when Wait is asserted, and E1 and E3 are tied to $\overline{\text{Wait}}$. S_2, S_6, and S_{11} advance when $\overline{\text{Wait}}$ is asserted, so E2, E6, and E11 are tied to Wait.

Generation of Microoperations Microoperations can be generated from the decoded state and the inputs. The logic expressions are shown below. To ensure proper synchronous operation, the Wait and Reset inputs should be synchronized before being used to form these expressions:

$0 \rightarrow$ PC: Reset

PC + 1 $\rightarrow$ PC: S_0

PC $\rightarrow$ MAR: S_0

MAR $\rightarrow$ Memory Address Bus:

    Wait $\bullet$ $(S_1 + S_2 + S_5 + S_6 + S_8 + S_9 + S_{11} + S_{12})$

Memory Data Bus $\rightarrow$ MBR:

    $\overline{\text{Wait}}$ $\bullet$ $(S_2 + S_6 + S_{11})$

MBR $\rightarrow$ Memory Data Bus:

    Wait $\bullet$ $(S_8 + S_9)$

MBR $\rightarrow$ IR: Wait $\bullet$ S_3

MBR $\rightarrow$ AC: Wait $\bullet$ S_7

$$\text{AC} \rightarrow \text{MBR: IR15} \bullet \text{IR14} \bullet S_4$$

$$\text{AC} + \text{MBR} \rightarrow \text{AC: Wait} \bullet S_{12}$$

$$\text{IR<13:0>} \rightarrow \text{MAR:}$$

$$(\overline{\text{IR15}} \bullet \overline{\text{IR14}} + \overline{\text{IR15}} \bullet \text{IR14} + \text{IR15} \bullet \overline{\text{IR14}}) \bullet S_4$$

$$\text{IR<13:0>} \rightarrow \text{PC: AC15} \bullet S_{13}$$

$$1 \rightarrow \text{Read/} \overline{\text{Write}}:$$

$$\text{Wait} \bullet (S_1 + S_2 + S_5 + S_6 + S_{11} + S_{12})$$

$$0 \rightarrow \text{Read/} \overline{\text{Write}}:$$

$$\text{Wait} \bullet (S_8 + S_9)$$

$$1 \rightarrow \text{Request:}$$

$$\text{Wait} \bullet (S_1 + S_2 + S_5 + S_6 + S_8 + S_9 + S_{11} + S_{12})$$

These are most easily implemented with some form of programmable logic.

Discussion We used several multiplexers in the schematic of Figure 12.18, which may not appear to be much of a savings in terms of package count. Nevertheless, this particular implementation approach is extraordinarily flexible. The regularity of the design makes it easier to debug: it is easy to trace the signals causing a state transition. It is just as easy to modify these transitions, simply by changing the inputs to the multiplexers. The jump counter is a reasonable way to organize state machines with a modest number of states, in the range of 16 to 32.

In a general hybrid jump counter, the jump state is a function of the current state and the inputs. But CNT, CLR, and LD are functions of exactly the same signals. Why implement them with discrete logic when they could be stored in the jump state ROM along with the jump states? We could simply extend the width of the ROM with 1 bit for each of the three output signals. Of course, since we have added five new inputs (Wait plus the four current-state bits), taking this approach increases the number of words in the ROM by a factor of 32.

This general strategy of replacing external logic, like gates, multiplexers, and PALs, with ones and zeros in a ROM is called *microprogramming*. We will learn more about this approach in the next two subsections.

12.4 Branch Sequencers

In a classical finite state machine, the next states are explicitly computed as output functions of the machine. One straightforward strategy is to place the bits representing the next state in a ROM addressed by the current state and the inputs. The problem with this approach is that the ROM doubles in size for each additional input.

The jump counter represents a trade-off between ROM size and external circuitry. Only jump states are placed in ROM. In a pure jump counter, the ROM is addressed only by the current state. Even the hybrid approach typically selects a small subset of the inputs to form part of the ROM address. Other machine outputs are formed by logic that combines the decoded state and the processor's inputs.

Our next organization is called a branch sequencer. It stands between the two extremes of a ROM-based classical state machine implementation and the jump counter. The next states are stored in a ROM, but each state is constrained to have only a limited number of next states, which is always a power of 2.

Since it is rarely the case that the finite state machine needs to see all of its inputs to determine the next state in any given state, only a (preferably small) subset of the inputs must be examined. The idea is to use some external logic to select the appropriate input subset, determined by the machine's current state, to use as part of the ROM address. The ROM word at this address will contain the machine's next state. In return for a small amount of external hardware, the size of the ROM can be dramatically reduced.

12.4.1 Organization of a Branch Sequencer

Example **Four-Way Branch Sequencer** Figure 12.19 shows the structure of a 2^2 or *four-way branch sequencer* implementing a Mealy controller. The high-order bits of the ROM address are formed by the current state, the low-order bits by the values of the two inputs α and β. Thus, each state has four possible next states. If a given state has only one next state, the same value is placed in all four of the ROM words dedicated to storing its next state and outputs.

Notice that the address bits α and β are driven by multiplexer outputs. The state selects among the inputs the particular two-input subset that determines the machine's next state.

As an example, consider the Mealy state machine for the simple CPU (Figure 11.23). The inputs to the machine are the Wait signal, the high-order bit of the AC, and the two IR op code bits. In the operation decode state, OD, only the IR bits need to be examined to determine the next state. In the state that executes the BRN instruction, the machine looks only at AC<15>. Many of the other states need only test the Wait signal. No state needs access to more than two of the four possible inputs.

Generalization of the Branch Sequencer It is possible to construct a 2^N-way branch sequencer by simply using N selected input signals to form part of the ROM address. A four-way branch sequencer is an appropriate

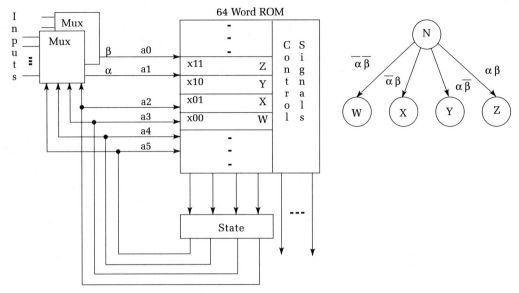

Figure 12.19   Four-way branch sequencer block diagram and state diagram.

structure for our example processor state machine, because no states contain a multiway branch to more than four next states. A different state diagram might require a higher degree of branching.

Of course, there is a trade-off between the degree of the multiway branch the implementation supports, the size of the ROM, and the number of states in the state machine. Consider a machine with a single 16-way branch in its state diagram but many four-way branches. The 16-way branch sequencer requires four input selectors, but the four-way sequencer needs only two. This machine could be implemented more economically by replacing the single 16-way branch with multiple four-way branching states. The ROM for the four-way sequencer is likely to be half the size of that for the 16-way sequencer.

The Simple CPU Implemented with a Branch Sequencer   Figure 12.20 shows the ROM programming for the Mealy processor controller. The address is formed from the Reset signal, the current state (4 bits), and the conditional inputs α and β. Including Reset in the address doubles the size of the ROM, but this is the easiest way to implement the reset function. You can also use methods that explicitly clear the state flip-flops.

The α and β multiplexers are wired so that IR<15> and IR<14> are connected to the inputs selected by state 4 (OD). Wait is wired to both multiplexers for selector inputs 1, 2, 3, 6, 9, and 11, the states in which the signal needs to be examined. AC<15> is connected to both of the muxes' input 13. The multiplexer configurations are shown in Figure 12.21.

	ROM ADDRESS		ROM CONTENTS	
	(Reset, Current State, α, β)		Next State	Register Transfer Operations
RES	0	0000	X X	0001 (IF0)	PC $\rightarrow$ MAR, PC + 1 $\rightarrow$ PC
IF0	0	0001	0 0	0001 (IF0)	
	0	0001	1 1	0010 (IF1)	MAR $\rightarrow$ Mem, Read, Request
IF1	0	0010	0 0	0011 (IF2)	MAR $\rightarrow$ Mem, Read, Request
	0	0010	1 1	0010 (IF1)	Mem $\rightarrow$ MBR
IF2	0	0011	0 0	0011 (IF2)	
	0	0011	1 1	0100 (OD)	MBR $\rightarrow$ IR
OD	0	0100	0 0	0101 (LD0)	IR $\rightarrow$ MAR
	0	0100	0 1	1000 (ST0)	IR $\rightarrow$ MAR, AC $\rightarrow$ MBR
	0	0100	1 0	1001 (AD0)	IR $\rightarrow$ MAR
	0	0100	1 1	1101 (BR0)	IR $\rightarrow$ MAR
LD0	0	0101	X X	0110 (LD1)	MAR $\rightarrow$ Mem, Read, Request
LD1	0	0110	0 0	0111 (LD2)	Mem $\rightarrow$ MBR
	0	0110	1 1	0110 (LD1)	MAR $\rightarrow$ Mem, Read, Request
LD2	0	0111	X X	0000 (RES)	MBR $\rightarrow$ AC
ST0	0	1000	X X	1001 (ST1)	MAR $\rightarrow$ Mem, $\overline{\text{Write}}$, Request, MBR $\rightarrow$ Mem
ST1	0	1001	0 0	0000 (RES)	
	0	1001	1 1	1001 (ST1)	MAR $\rightarrow$ Mem, $\overline{\text{Write}}$, Request, MBR $\rightarrow$ Mem
AD0	0	1010	X X	1011 (AD1)	MAR $\rightarrow$ Mem, Read, Request
AD1	0	1011	0 0	1100 (AD2)	
	0	1011	1 1	1011 (AD1)	MAR $\rightarrow$ Mem, Read, Request
AD2	0	1100	X X	0000 (RES)	MBR + AC $\rightarrow$ AC
BR0	0	1101	0 0	0000 (RES)	
	0	1101	1 1	0000 (RES)	IR $\rightarrow$ PC
	1	XXXX	X X	0000 (RES)	PC $\rightarrow$ 0

Figure 12.20 Branch sequencer ROM encoding.

We can make two immediate observations about the structure of this controller. First, relatively few states use the controller's ability to support four-way next-state branches. This is no surprise, since only the operation decode state is more than two-way. Typically the wide branchiness is needed only at the decode step(s). Since each input bit doubles the size of the ROM, this illustrates how wasteful it is to include all of the inputs in the ROM address.

Second, there are many fewer inputs than states. In this case, we have four inputs but (approximately) 16 states. Since the state machine looks at only three different sets of inputs (IR<15>/IR<14>, AC<15>, and WAIT), it seems like overkill to make use of 16-to-1 multiplexers on the α and β signals. This leads us to the next variation on the branch sequencer.

Horizontal Branch Sequencer Organization   At the expense of some additional multiplexers, we can replace the tall thin ROM of Figure 12.19 with a short fat ROM, as shown in Figure 12.22. There are two fundamental differences. First, the multiplexers are controlled by encoded signals output from the ROM rather than directly by the state. You should notice that these encoded signals are a function solely of the state, since the state bits alone form the ROM address. This also implies that the implementation of Figure 12.22 is a Moore machine.

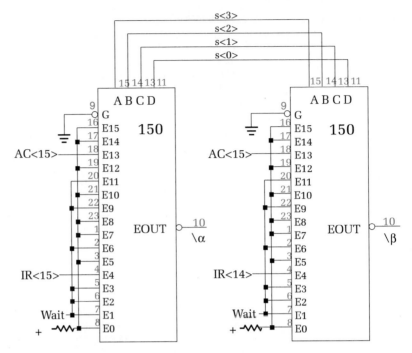

Figure 12.21 Multiplexer setup for example branch sequencer.

Second, the four possible next states are laid out horizontally within the ROM rather than in four sequential ROM words of shorter length. If the state machine has a large number of states but relatively few inputs, the multiplexer control bits embedded in the ROM make it possible to use multiplexers with fewer inputs to control the next-state logic.

Let's look at the simple CPU's state machine as an example of this controller organization. Using this approach, we can replace the vertical 16-to-1 multiplexers with 2-to-1 multiplexers. The α multiplexer has IR<15> and AC<15> as its inputs; the β multiplexer's inputs are IR<14> and Wait. Each of the multiplexers is controlled by a single bit in the ROM word. When the machine is in the OD state, the α and β multiplexer control bits are set to select IR<15> and IR<14>, respectively. The horizontal multiplexers select A_0 if both bits are 0; A_1 if IR<15> = 0, IR<14> = 1; A_2 if IR<15> = 1, IR<14> = 0; and A_3 if both bits are 1.

When the machine is in its execution state for the BRN instruction, the multiplexer control bits are set to select AC<15> from the α multiplexer. The β multiplexer bit is a don't care, so A_0 and A_1 should contain the same next-state bits, as should A_2 and A_3. A_0/A_1 is selected if AC<15> = 0; otherwise A_2/A_3 is selected.

A similar argument explains how the multiplexers work when the state needs to examine the Wait signal. In this case, the α multiplexer is

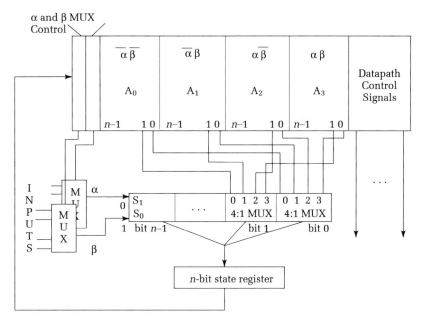

Figure 12.22   Horizontal next-state organization.

the don't care and the β multiplexer is set to select Wait. A_0 and A_2 should contain the same value, as should A_1 and A_3. If Wait is asserted, then A_1/A_3 determines the next state. Otherwise it is set to the state specified by A_0/A_2.

The horizontal next-state scheme is advantageous in large and complex controllers with many-way branches. Adding length to the ROM word usually requires fewer bits than increasing the number of ROM words. Once again, let's consider the simple CPU state machine. Its controller has 14 register transfer outputs. With the four next-state bits, the ROM contains 64 by 18 bits or 1152 ROM bits (we assume that reset is handled by external logic). The horizontal method requires the same 14 control bits, plus four 4-bit next states as well as two additional multiplexer control bits. This yields a total ROM word length of 32 bits. But since the horizontal organization requires only 16 ROM words, the total number of ROM bits is much smaller: just 512 bits. In the next subsection, we will examine the trade-offs between vertical and horizontal ROM organizations more closely.

12.5   Microprogramming

We have concentrated so far on alternative methods for organizing the next-state logic. Now we can discuss various ways to organize the output signals controlling the datapath. We usually think of control signals as implemented by discrete logic, even if the implementation makes use of PALs or PLAs. *Microprogramming*, on the other hand, is an approach for implementing processor control in which the output signals are stored within a ROM.

The two main variations of microprogramming are the horizontal and vertical methods. In the previous section, we already saw some distinction between horizontal and vertical next-state organizations. In *horizontal microprogramming*, there is one ROM output for each control point in the datapath. *Vertical microprogramming* is based on the observation that only a subset of these signals is ever asserted in a given state. Thus, the control outputs can be stored in the ROM in an encoded form, effectively reducing the width of the ROM word at the expense of some external decoding logic.

Encoding the control signals may limit the datapath operations that can take place in parallel. If this is the case, we may need multiple ROM words to encode the same datapath operations that could be performed in a single horizontal ROM word.

For example, consider a microprogrammed control for a machine with four general-purpose accumulators. Most computer instruction formats limit the destination of an operation to a single register. Realizing this, you may choose to encode the destination of a register transfer operation in 2 bits rather than 4. The destination register select line is driven by logic that decodes these 2 bits from the control. Thus, at any given time, only one of the registers is selected as a destination.

The art of engineering a microprogrammed control unit is to strike the correct balance between the parallelism of the horizontal approach and the ROM economy of a vertical encoding. For example, the encoded register enable lines eliminate the possibility of any state loading two registers at the same time, even if this was supported by the processor datapath. If a machine instruction must load two registers, it will require multiple control states (and ROM words) to implement its execution.

We begin our study with the horizontal approach to microprogramming. We will see that the instruction set and the datapath typically do not support the full parallelism implied by horizontal control, so we will examine methods of encoding the ROM word to reduce its size.

12.5.1   Horizontal Microprogramming

The horizontal next-state organization of Figure 12.22 offers the core of a horizontal microprogrammed controller. An extremely horizontal control word format would have 1 bit for each microoperation in the datapath. Let's develop such a format for the simple CPU's control.

Our sample processor supports 14 register transfer operations. We further decompose these into 22 discrete microoperations (ordered by destination):

PC → ABUS
IR → ABUS
MBR → ABUS
RBUS → AC
AC → ALU A
MBUS → ALU B
ALU ADD
ALU PASS B
MAR → Address Bus
MBR → Data Bus
ABUS → IR
ABUS → MAR
Data Bus → MBR
RBUS → MBR
MBR → MBUS
0 → PC
PC + 1 → PC
ABUS → PC
Read/$\overline{\text{Write}}$
Request
AC → RBUS
ALU Result → RBUS

A very long ROM word for a four-way branch sequencer would have α and β multiplexer bits, four 4-bit next states, and 22 microoperation bits. This yields a total ROM word length of 40 bits, as shown in Figure 12.23.

Figure 12.24 gives the ROM contents for the Moore controller of Figure 12.1 (the branch sequencer of Figure 12.22 implements a Moore machine). The α multiplexer inputs are $Sel_0 = Wait$, $Sel_1 = IR<15>$ and the β inputs are $Sel_0 = AC<15>$, $Sel_1 = IR<14>$. We assume the next-state register is reset directly.

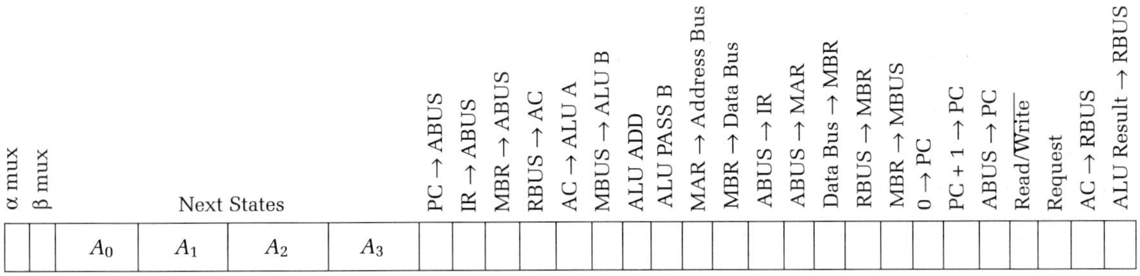

Figure 12.23 Extremely wide horizontal microcode format for four-way branch sequencer.

Current State (Address)	α mux	β mux	A_0	A_1	A_2	A_3	PC → ABUS	IR → ABUS	MBR → ABUS	RBUS → AC	AC → ALU A	MBUS → ALU B	ALU ADD	ALU PASS B	MAR → Address Bus	MBR → Data Bus	ABUS → IR	ABUS → MAR	Data Bus → MBR	RBUS → MBR	MBR → MBUS	0 → PC	PC + 1 → PC	ABUS → PC	Read/Write	Request	AC → RBUS	ALU Result → RBUS
RES (0000)	0	0	0001	0001	0001	0001	0	0	0	0	0	0	0	0	0	0	0	0	0	0	0	1	0	0	0	0	0	0
IF$_0$ (0001)	0	0	0010	0010	0010	0010	1	0	0	0	0	0	0	0	0	0	0	1	0	0	0	0	1	0	0	0	0	0
IF$_1$ (0010)	0	0	0010	0010	0011	0011	0	0	0	0	0	0	0	0	0	0	0	0	0	0	0	0	0	0	0	0	0	0
IF$_2$ (0011)	0	0	0100	0100	0011	0011	0	0	0	0	0	0	0	0	1	0	0	0	1	0	0	0	0	0	1	1	0	0
IF$_3$ (0100)	0	0	0100	0100	0101	0101	0	0	1	0	0	0	0	0	0	0	1	0	0	0	0	0	0	0	0	0	0	0
OD (0101)	1	1	0110	1001	1011	1110	0	0	0	0	0	0	0	0	0	0	0	0	0	0	0	0	0	0	0	0	0	0
LD$_0$ (0110)	0	0	0111	0111	0111	0111	0	1	0	0	0	0	0	0	0	0	0	1	0	0	0	0	0	0	0	0	0	0
LD$_1$ (0111)	0	0	1000	1000	0111	0111	0	0	0	0	0	0	0	0	1	0	0	0	1	0	0	0	0	0	1	1	0	0
LD$_2$ (1000)	0	0	0001	0001	0001	0001	0	0	0	1	0	1	0	1	0	0	0	0	0	0	1	0	0	0	0	0	0	1
ST$_0$ (1001)	0	0	1010	1010	1010	1010	0	1	0	0	0	0	0	0	0	0	0	1	0	1	0	0	0	0	0	0	1	0
ST$_1$ (1010)	0	0	0001	0001	1010	1010	0	0	0	0	0	0	0	0	1	1	0	0	0	0	0	0	0	0	0	0	1	0
AD$_0$ (1011)	0	0	1100	1100	1100	1100	0	1	0	0	0	0	0	0	0	0	0	1	0	0	0	0	0	0	0	0	0	0
AD$_1$ (1100)	0	0	1101	1101	1100	1100	0	0	0	0	0	0	0	0	1	0	0	0	1	0	0	0	0	0	1	1	0	0
AD$_2$ (1101)	0	0	0001	0001	0001	0001	0	0	0	1	1	1	1	0	0	0	0	0	0	0	1	0	0	0	0	0	0	1
BR$_0$ (1110)	0	1	0001	1111	0001	1111	0	0	0	0	0	0	0	0	0	0	0	0	0	0	0	0	0	0	0	0	0	0
BR$_1$ (1111)	0	0	0001	0001	0001	0001	0	1	0	0	0	0	0	0	0	0	0	0	0	0	0	0	0	1	0	0	0	0

Figure 12.24 ROM contents for the Moore processor controller.

The multiplexers on the next state work just as in Figure 12.22. For example, consider state IF$_1$. We stay in this state if Wait is unasserted. If Wait is asserted, we advance to state IF$_2$. The α and β mux controls are set to examine Wait and AC<15>, respectively. Thus, the 0X next-state bits (A_0, A_1) are set to the encoding for IF$_1$, 0010. Similarly, the 1X next states (A_2, A_3) are set to the encoding for IF$_2$, 0011.

Reducing ROM Word Width Through Encoding The horizontal approach offers the most flexibility by providing access to all of the datapath control points at the same time. The disadvantage is the width of the ROM word, which can exceed a few hundred bits in complex controllers.

A good way to reduce the ROM size is by encoding its output. This need not lead to an inherent loss of parallelism. After all, certain control combinations may not make sense logically (for example, 0 → PC and PC + 1 → PC are logically exclusive) or might be ruled out by the datapath busing strategy (for example, PC → ABUS and IR → ABUS cannot take place simultaneously).

Furthermore, the ROM contents of Figure 12.24 are very sparse. In any given state, very few of the control signals are ever asserted. This means we can group the control signals into mutually exclusive sets to encode them. We decode them outside the ROM with additional hardware.

For example, the three PC microoperations, $0 \rightarrow PC$, $PC + 1 \rightarrow PC$, and $ABUS \rightarrow PC$, are never asserted in the same state. For the cost of an external 2-to-4 decoder, a ROM bit can be saved by encoding the signals as follows:

00	No PC control
01	$0 \rightarrow PC$
10	$PC + 1 \rightarrow PC$
11	$ABUS \rightarrow PC$

There are many other plausible encoding strategies for this controller. $MAR \rightarrow$ Address Bus and Request are always asserted together, as are $RBUS \rightarrow AC$, $MBUS \rightarrow ALU$ B, $MBR \rightarrow MBUS$, and $ALU \rightarrow RBUS$. If we have designed the ALU to pass its A input selectively, we can combine $AC \rightarrow ALU$ A in state LD_2 with this list of signals. As another example, we can combine $MBR \rightarrow ABUS$ and $ABUS \rightarrow IR$. Taken together, these encodings save six ROM bits.

We can save additional ROM bits by finding unrelated signals that are never asserted at the same time. These are good candidates for encoding. For example, we can combine $PC \rightarrow ABUS$, $IR \rightarrow ABUS$, and Data Bus $\rightarrow MBR$, encoding them into 2 bits. Applying all of these encodings at the same time yields the encoded control unit in Figure 12.25. The direct ROM outputs have been reduced from 22 to 15.

As more control signals are placed in the ROM in an encoded form, we move from a very horizontal format to one that is ever more vertical. We present a systematic approach to vertical microprogramming next.

12.5.2   Vertical Microprogramming

Vertical microprogramming makes more use of ROM encoding to reduce the length of the control word. To achieve this goal, we commonly use multiple microword formats. For example, many states require no conditional next-state branch; they simply advance to the next state in sequence. Rather than having every microword contain a next state and a list of microoperations, we can shorten the ROM word by separating these two functions into individual microword formats: one for conditional "branch jumps" and another for register transfer operations/microoperations.

Shortening the ROM word does not come free. We may need several ROM words in a sequence to perform the same operations as a single horizontal microword. The combination of extra levels of decoding, multiple ROM accesses to execute a sequence of control operations, and sacrifice of the potential parallelism of the vertical approach leads to slower implementations. The basic machine cycle time increases, and the number of machine cycles to execute an instruction also increases.

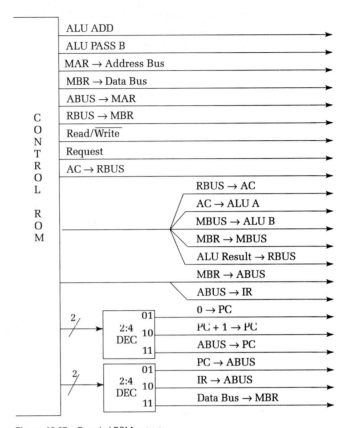

Figure 12.25 Encoded ROM outputs.

Despite this inefficiency, designers prefer vertical microcode because it is much like coding in assembly language. So the trade-off between vertical and horizontal microcode is really a matter of ease of implementation versus performance.

Vertical Microcode Format for the Simple CPU Let's develop a simple vertical microcode format for our simple processor. We will introduce just two formats: a *branch jump* format and a *register transfer/operation* format.

In a branch jump microword, we include a field to select a signal to be tested (Wait, AC<15>, IR<15>, IR<14>) and the value it should be tested against (0 or 1). If the signal matches the specified value, the rest of the microword contains the address of the next ROM word to be fetched. The condition selection field can be 2 bits in length; the condition comparison field can be 1 bit wide.

The register transfer/operation microword contains three fields: a register source, a register destination, and an operation field for instructing functional units like the ALU what to do. To start, let's arrange the microoperations according to these categories:

Sources:

PC → ABUS
IR → ABUS
MBR → MBUS
AC → ALU A
MAR → Mem Address Bus
MBR → Mem Data Bus
MBR → MBUS
AC → RBUS
ALU Result → RBUS

Destinations:

RBUS → AC
MBUS → ALU B
MBUS → IR
ABUS → MAR
Mem Data Bus → MBR
RBUS → MBR
ABUS → PC

Operations:

ALU ADD
ALU PASS B
0 → PC
PC + 1 → PC
Read (Read, Request)
Write ($\overline{\text{Write}}$, Request)

We can encode the nine sources in a 4-bit field, the seven destinations in 3, and the six operations also in 3 (we have combined Read/$\overline{\text{Write}}$ and Request in the operation format).

It would certainly be convenient to encode all the fields in the same number of bits. At the moment, we have several more sources than destinations. A close examination of the datapath of Figure 11.26 indicates that we can do better at encoding the destinations. We can assume that the AC is hardwired to the ALU *A* input, just as the MBUS is wired to the ALU *B* input. Also, the MBR is the only source on the MBUS, so we can eliminate the microoperation MBR → MBUS. This gives us seven sources and six destinations, easily encoded in 3 bits each.

There is still one hitch. On writes to memory, such as during a store, the MAR must drive the memory address lines and the MBR must drive the data lines. But as listed above, these two microoperations are now mutually exclusive.

Fortunately, there is a reasonable solution. We can move the operation MBR → Mem Data Bus from the sources to the destinations, simply by thinking of the memory as a destination rather than the MBR as a source. The encoding of the two formats can fit in a very compact 10 bits, as shown in Figure 12.26.

We show the ROM contents for the Moore controller in Figure 12.27. We handle Reset externally. The symbolic format should be intuitively obvious and bears a striking resemblance to assembly language programs. The two alternative formats are denoted by *BJ* for branch jump and *RT* for register transfer. The former is written as the condition followed by the next address. For example,

BJ Wait = 0, IF0

is a branch jump microinstruction that tests whether the Wait signal is unasserted. If it is, the microinstruction causes the next microinstruction to be fetched from the ROM location with label IF_0.

The RT format is written as SRC → DST followed by any operations that are performed in parallel with the register transfer. For example,

Branch Jump Format

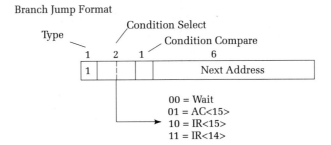

Register Transfer Format

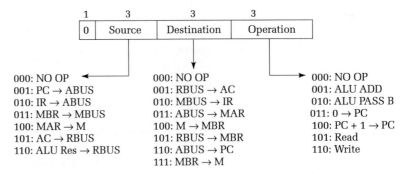

Figure 12.26 Vertical microcode format.

RT PC $\rightarrow$ MAR, PC + 1 $\rightarrow$ PC

is a register transfer operation that maps onto the microoperations PC $\rightarrow$ ABUS, ABUS $\rightarrow$ MAR, and PC + 1 $\rightarrow$ PC.

Discussion   Figure 12.27 leads us to a few observations. First, we have not included an unconditional branch operation in our microcode instruction set. This is handled by two BJ instructions in sequence, testing a condition and its complement, branching to the same place in both cases. Obviously, the microinstruction format could be revised to include such a branch.

Second, it is important that signals to the outside world, such as those that connect the MAR and MBR to external buses and those that drive the Read/$\overline{\text{Write}}$ and Request lines, be latched at the controller output. We need this because RT operations that assert these signals are usually followed by BJ operations testing the Wait signal. To implement

ROM ADDRESS	SYMBOLIC CONTENTS		BINARY CONTENTS
000000	RES	RT PC$\rightarrow$ MAR, PC + 1 $\rightarrow$ PC	0 001 011 100
000001	IF0	RT MAR $\rightarrow$ M, Read	0 100 000 101
000010		BJ Wait=0, IF0	1 000 000 001
000011	IF1	RT MAR $\rightarrow$ M, M $\rightarrow$ MBR, Read	0 100 100 101
000100		BJ Wait=1, IF1	1 001 000 011
000101	IF2	RT MBR $\rightarrow$ IR	0 011 010 000
000110		BJ Wait=0, IF2	1 000 000 101
000111		RT IR $\rightarrow$ MAR	0 010 011 000
001000	OD	BJ IR<15>=1, OD1	1 101 010 101
001001		BJ IR<14>=1, ST0	1 111 010 000
001010	LD0	RT MAR $\rightarrow$ M, Read	0 100 000 101
001011	LD1	RT MAR $\rightarrow$ M, M $\rightarrow$ MBR, Read	0 100 100 101
001100		BJ Wait=1, LD1	1 001 001 011
001101	LD2	RT MBR $\rightarrow$ AC	0 110 001 010
001110		BJ Wait=0, RES	1 000 000 000
001111		BJ Wait=1, RES	1 001 000 000
010000	ST0	RT AC $\rightarrow$ MBR	0 101 101 000
010001		RT MAR $\rightarrow$ M, MBR $\rightarrow$ M, Write	0 100 111 110
010010	ST1	RT MAR $\rightarrow$ M, MBR $\rightarrow$ M, Write	0 100 111 110
010011		BJ Wait=0, RES	1 000 000 000
010100		BJ Wait=1, ST1	1 001 010 010
010101	OD1	BJ IR<14>=1, BR0	1 111 011 101
010110	AD0	RT MAR $\rightarrow$ M, Read	0 100 000 101
010111	AD1	RT MAR $\rightarrow$ M, M $\rightarrow$ MBR, Read	0 100 100 101
011000		BJ Wait=1, AD1	1 001 010 111
011001	AD2	RT AC + MBR $\rightarrow$ AC	0 110 001 001
011010		BJ Wait=0, RES	1 000 000 000
011011		BJ Wait=1, RES	1 000 000 000
011100	BR0	BJ AC <15>=0, RES	1 010 000 000
011101		RT IR $\rightarrow$ PC	0 010 110 000
011110		BJ AC<15>=1, RES	1 011 000 000

Figure 12.27   Vertical microprogramming ROM contents.

the handshake with external devices correctly, we must hold the external signals until we encounter the next RT operation. Simple registers for the control outputs, loaded only when executing an RT microoperation, will do the job.

The microprogram requires 31 words by 10 ROM bits, or a total of 310 bits. The horizontal implementation described previously used 16 × 38 bit ROM words (16 next-state bits plus 22 microoperation bits), yielding 608 ROM bits. The vertical format is highly efficient in terms of the number of ROM bits required to implement this particular controller. A good part of this savings comes from the separate branch jump format. We use it only in cases that loop in a state or jump out of sequence.

Vertical Microcode Controller Implementation Details We show a straightforward implementation of the vertical microprogrammed controller in Figure 12.28. We implement the next-state register as a microprogram counter, with CLR, CNT, and LD. A conditional logic block determines whether to assert CNT or LD based on the microinstruction type and the conditions being tested. External decoders map the encoded register transfer operations onto the microoperations supported by the datapath.

The condition block logic is shown in Figure 12.29. The condition selector bits from the microinstruction select one of four possible signals to be tested. The selected condition is compared with the specified bit. The µPC load signal is asserted if the current microinstruction is a branch jump (type 1) and the condition and the comparator bit are identical. The value to be loaded comes from the low-order 6 bits of the microinstruction. The count signal is asserted if the instruction type is register transfer (type 0) or the condition and the comparator bit are different.

12.5.3   Writable Control Store

Control store need not be fixed in ROM. Some computers map part of the control store addresses onto RAM, the same memory that programmers use for instructions and data. This has the added flexibility that assembly language programmers can write their own microcode, extending the machine's "native" instruction set with special-purpose instructions.

Of course, most programmers are not sophisticated enough to write their own microcode, yet many machines with complex instruction sets still provide a writable control store. The reason is simple. Since the microprogram for a complex state machine is itself rather complex, it is not uncommon for it to be filled with bugs. Having a writable control store makes it easy to revise the machine control and update it in the field. At power-up time, the machine executes a "boot" microprogram sequence from ROM that loads the rest of the microcode into RAM from an external device like a floppy disk.

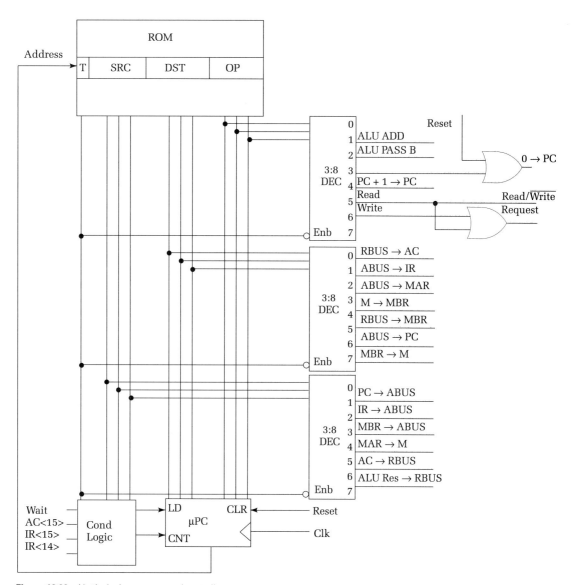

Figure 12.28 Vertical microprogrammed controller.

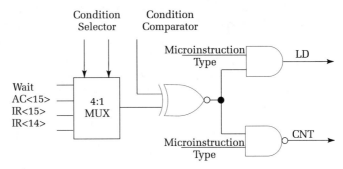

Figure 12.29 Condition logic.

Chapter Review

In this chapter, we have described alternative methods for organizing the control unit of a simple processor. We began by discussing classical Moore and Mealy machine implementations. Although appropriate for simple finite state machines, these monolithic implementations are not much help in structuring a complex state machine.

As an alternative, we examined a divide-and-conquer approach based on decomposing the state machine into time, instruction, and condition state machines—the so-called time state approach. Most instructions follow a similar path through the state machine, and the time state approach captures this sequencing with the time state machine. The microoperations are implemented as Boolean functions of the time state, the instruction state, and the condition state.

Next we looked at *jump counters*, a method of using MSI TTL components such as counters, multiplexers, and decoders to implement the next-state and output functions of the finite state machine. This leads to a clean implementation of the finite state machine that is easy to debug and to modify. However, it is limited to machines with a modest number of states.

The next controller organization was the *branch sequencer*. This is a method for arranging the next-state logic that places potential next states into a ROM. Selector logic uses the machine's inputs to choose conditionally among the candidates for the next state.

Finally, we examined *microprogramming*, including its horizontal and vertical varieties. Microprogramming avoids discrete logic implementations of the next-state and output functions by implementing these as a table of ones and zeros stored in memory. Horizontal microprogramming dedicates a single ROM bit to each control signal, and vertical microcode formats seek to reduce the size of the ROM by extensive encoding. A typical vertical microcode implementation supports multiple microword formats within the ROM.

All these approaches are suitable for implementation with programmable logic devices or ROMs. ROM-based design is perhaps the simplest, but you can construct enormous control ROMs if you are not careful. In its most naive implementation, every possible input signal could become part of the ROM address! In part, the jump counter and branch sequencer techniques were developed as ways to reduce the size of the ROM by moving some of the conditional next-state sequencing to external logic. Similarly, vertical microprogramming reduces the size of the control ROM by separating the choice of the next state from the register transfer operations and by heavily encoding the latter.

It is worthwhile to compare discrete logic "hardwired" controllers to the microprogramming approach. Hardwired control tends to lead to faster implementations, but they are harder to modify. They form the basis of machines with simple or "reduced" instruction sets.

Microprogrammed controllers, on the other hand, take advantage of memory density by implementing complex control functions as ones and zeros stored in a ROM. The architecture of such controllers is more general than that of the hardwired variety, making it possible to change the instruction set without changing the underlying datapath. However, this flexibility comes at some expense in processor cycle time, and an effort is usually made to keep the size of the ROM as small as possible. Compared to the hardwired approach, microprogramming provides a reasonable way to structure the design and implementation of a complex controller. This is the implementation approach of choice for machines with complex instruction sets, and therefore processor controllers, like Digital Equipment Corporation's VAX, the Intel 80x86, or the Motorola 68x00.

Further Reading

Although the controller implementation techniques described in this chapter are a natural application of digital design methods, few books on digital design spend much time on them. Exceptions include Johnson and Karim's book *Digital Design: A Pragmatic Approach*, PWS Engineering, Boston, 1987 (see Chapter 13), and Prosser and Winkel, *The Art of Digital Design,* 2nd ed., Prentice-Hall, Englewood Cliffs, NJ, 1987 (see Chapter 10).

Several good books focus on microprogramming as an implementation technique. For example, see M. Andrew's book *Principles of Firmware Engineering in Microprogram Control*, Computer Science Press, Woodland Hills, CA, 1980.

Exercises

12.1 *(Moore Machine)* Figure 12.1 gives a Moore state diagram for implementing the simple CPU. Figure 12.2 showed the waveforms for the memory interface, to demonstrate the correct execution of a memory read operation in the instruction fetch states. Repeat this analysis for the state sequence OD, ST_0, ST_1, IF_0 to verify that the interface signals correctly handle a memory write operation. Draw a timing diagram similar to Figure 12.2 labeled by the current state and including the waveforms for the memory address bus, memory databus, request, and read/write signals. Annotate the waveform with comments about the arrival of the appropriate data in the MAR and MBR registers.

12.2 *(Synchronous Mealy Machine)* Section 12.1.2 described a strategy for constructing a synchronous Mealy machine by placing flip-flops between the inputs and the next-state logic. Assume that the state diagram of Figure 11.23 has been implemented as a synchronous Mealy machine in which the memory Wait signal is delayed by a synchronizing flip-flop. Verify that the memory interface operates correctly by drawing timing diagrams for all control signals asserted by the instruction fetch states. Include in your diagram the Wait signal as it leaves the memory subsystem and Wait' as it is delayed by the synchronizing flip-flop.

12.3 *(Horizontal Branch Sequencer)* Figure 12.22 gave a block diagram for a horizontal branch sequencer. Draw a complete schematic showing how this organization can be used to implement a four-way branch sequencer with a 4-bit state register. Show the data connections between the ROM outputs and the horizontal multiplexer inputs and the control connections between the α and β multiplexers and the horizontal multiplexers' select inputs.

12.4 *(Classical FSM Implementation)* Write the truth table for a pure ROM and state register implementation of the state diagram in Figure Ex12.4.

12.5 *(Hybrid Jump Counter)* Draw a schematic diagram for the state diagram of Figure Ex12.4 using a hybrid jump counter. Use a 74163 counter as the state register and multiplexers to implement the CNT, $\overline{\text{CLR}}$, and $\overline{\text{LD}}$ signals. Show the contents of any ROMs you use in your implementation.

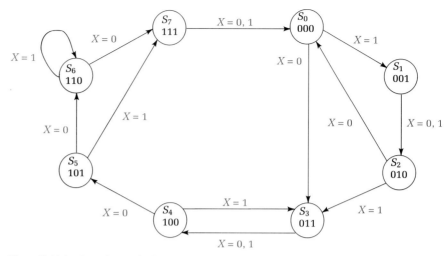

Figure Ex12.4 State diagram for Exercises 12.4, 12.5, and 12.11.

12.6 *(Jump Counter)* Given the state diagram in Figure Ex12.6, draw a circuit schematic that implements the state diagram as a hybrid jump counter. Note that any input combinations not shown on transitions in the state diagram imply that the machine remains in its current state. Also, assume that the state register is implemented by a 74163 counter and that CLEAR dominates LOAD, which dominates COUNT. The finite state machine has two inputs, A and B. Show the contents of the next-state ROM and use 16-to-1 multiplexers to compute the CLR, CNT, and LD signals.

12.7 *(Jump Counter)* Given the schematic of a jump counter in Figure Ex12.7 for a controller with input signals labeled U, V, W, X, Y, Z and output signals labeled A, B, C, derive the associated state diagram. The contents of the jump state ROM are as follows:

Address	Contents	Address	Contents
0000	0101	1000	0000
0001	0100	1001	0000
0010	0000	1010	0000
0011	0000	1011	0000
0100	0111	1100	0000
0101	0000	1101	0000
0110	1000	1110	0000
0111	0000	1111	0000

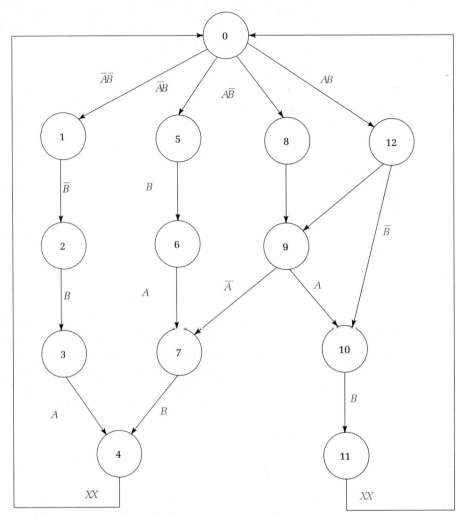

Figure Ex12.6   State diagram for Exercise 12.6.

12.8   *(Jump Counter)*   Given the schematic of a jump counter in
Figure Ex12.8 for a controller with input signals *A*, *B*, *C*, derive
the associated state diagram. The contents of the jump state ROM
are as follows:

Address	Contents		Address	Contents
0000	1011		1000	1111
0001	1110		1001	1001
0010	0101		1010	1101
0011	1000		1011	0011

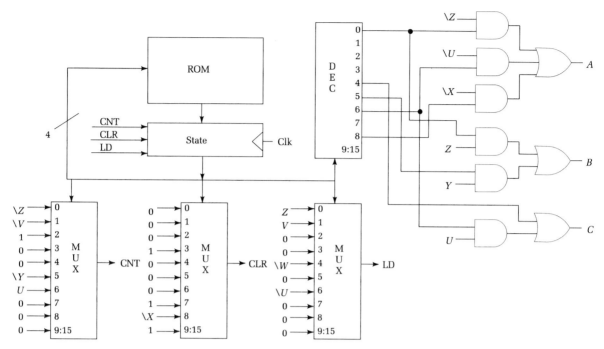

Figure Ex12.7 Circuit schematic for Exercise 12.7.

Address	Contents	Address	Contents
0100	0000	1100	1010
0101	1001	1101	0011
0110	0010	1110	0000
0111	1111	1111	0011

Recall that the counter's CLR input dominates the LD, which in turn dominates the CNT.

12.9 *(Branch Sequencers)* Figure Ex12.9(a) gives a block diagram of a four-way branch sequencer implementation of a finite state machine. The machine has four inputs (*A, B, C, D*) and four outputs (*W, X, Y, Z*), and the contents of the ROM are shown in Figure Ex12.9(b). Draw the state diagram corresponding to this finite state machine implementation.

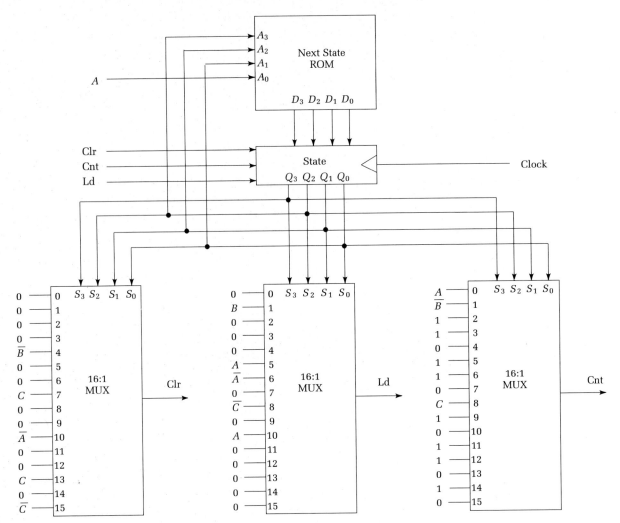

Figure Ex12.8 Schematic for the jump counter of Exercise 12.8.

12.10 *(Branch Sequencers)* The block diagram of Figure Ex12.10(a) shows a four-way branch sequencer implementation of a finite state machine. The machine has eight inputs: *A, B, C, D, E, F, G, H.* Implement the state diagram of Figure Ex12.10(b), by creating a table for the control ROM's contents.

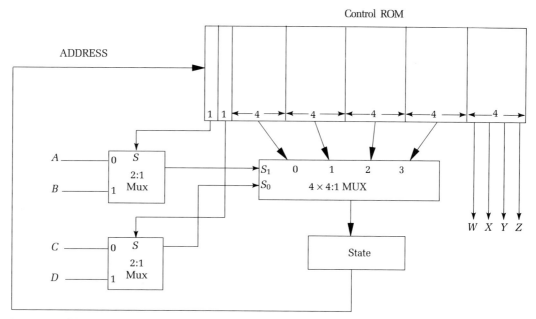

Figure Ex12.9(a)   Block diagram for Exercise 12.9.

A_3	A_2	A_1	A_0			ROM Contents				
0	0	0	0	0	0	0001	1000	1110	1110	0100
0	0	0	1	0	0	0010	0010	0010	0010	0110
0	0	1	0	0	0	0011	0011	0011	0011	1100
0	0	1	1	0	0	0100	0100	0100	0100	1001
0	1	0	0	0	0	0101	0101	0101	0101	1001
0	1	0	1	1	1	0110	0111	1100	1101	0001
0	1	1	0	1	0	0000	0000	0000	0000	0010
0	1	1	1	0	1	0000	0000	0000	0000	0100
1	0	0	0	0	0	1001	1001	1001	1001	0001
1	0	0	1	0	0	1010	1010	1010	1010	1010
1	0	1	0	0	1	0100	1011	0100	1011	0011
1	0	1	1	1	0	1101	1100	1101	1100	0110
1	1	0	0	1	1	0000	0000	0000	0000	1000
1	1	0	1	0	0	0000	0000	0000	0000	0000
1	1	1	0	0	0	1111	1111	1111	1111	1111
1	1	1	1	0	0	1010	1010	1010	1010	0000

Figure Ex12.9(b)   ROM contents for Exercise 12.9.

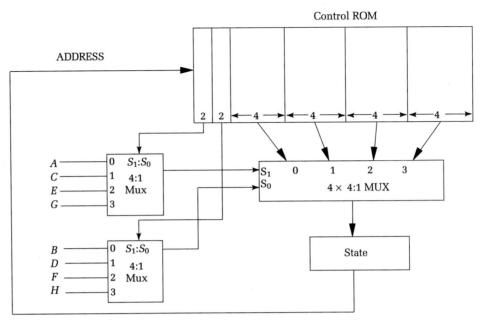

Figure Ex12.10(a) Four-way branch sequencer block diagram for Exercise 12.10.

12.11 *(Horizontal Microprogramming)* Reimplement the controller of Figure Ex12.4 using a horizontal microprogramming approach for the next-state logic. You are restricted to an eight-word ROM, but you choose the ROM width and the external hardware needed to select the correct next state. Describe your ROM layout and its contents, and draw a schematic of your controller.

12.12 *(Controller State Diagram)* In the previous chapter, Exercises 11.6 through 11.9 stepped you through the design of a datapath for a simple processor with 10 instructions (ADD, AND, COMP, INC, RSR, ASR, XFER, LD, ST, BRN). Using your multiple-bus solution to Exercise 11.8, do the following:

a. Develop the Mealy state diagram for this processor. Assign register transfer operations appropriate for your datapath to the state transition arcs.

b. Develop the Moore state diagram for this processor. Assign register transfer operations appropriate for your datapath to each state in the diagram.

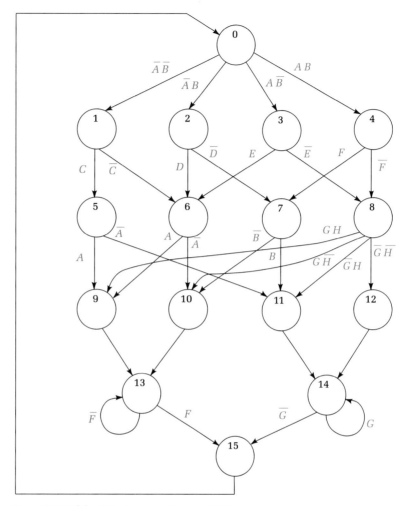

Figure Ex12.10(b)   State diagram for Exercise 12.10.

12.13 *(Classical State Machine Implementation)*   For the state diagrams derived in Exercise 12.12, tabulate the ROM contents necessary to implement the machine.

12.14 *(Time State Implementation)*   Using your Mealy state diagram from Exercise 12.12, show how to implement the machine using the time state approach. Note that the time state FSM may be somewhat more complicated because of the multiple-step instruction fetch process for this instruction set.

12.15 *(Jump Counter Implementation)*   Using your Mealy state diagram from Exercise 12.12, show how to implement the machine using the hybrid jump counter approach. You may assume that multiplexers with very large numbers of inputs and decoders with very large numbers of outputs are available as single components. Describe the jump state ROM contents, the multiplexer inputs, and the Boolean logic equations for your microoperations.

12.16 *(Branch Sequencer)*   Using your Moore state diagram from Exercise 12.12, show how to implement the machine using a horizontal branch sequencer approach. Modify the state diagram to reflect your limitation on state fan-out. How are the input conditions organized? Show your ROM organization and tabulate its contents.

12.17 *(Horizontal Microcode)*   Using your solution to Exercise 12.16 as a starting point, describe how you can encode the microoperation outputs to reduce the width of the control ROM.

12.18 *(Vertical Microcode)*   Starting with the microcode format presented in Section 12.5.2, describe how to modify it for your datapath and the processor state machine from Exercise 12.12. Tabulate the vertical microcode to implement the instruction set.

12.19 *(Controller Implementation)*   In the last chapter, Exercise 11.14 described a 16-operation instruction set for a stack-based computer.

   a. Develop the Mealy state diagram for this processor. Assign register transfer operations appropriate for your datapath to the state transition arcs.

   b. Develop the Moore state diagram for this processor. Assign register transfer operations appropriate for your datapath to each state in the diagram.

   Exercise 11.15 let you choose between a Mealy and a Moore state diagram for this processor controller. In this exercise and the ones to follow, we will need both methods.

12.20 *(Classical State Machine Implementation)*   For the state diagrams derived in Exercise 12.19, tabulate the ROM contents necessary to implement the machine.

12.21 *(Time State Implementation)*   Using your Mealy state diagram from Exercise 12.19, show how to implement the machine using the time state approach.

12.22 *(Jump Counter Implementation)*   Using your Mealy state diagram from Exercise 12.19, show how to implement the machine using the hybrid jump counter approach. Assume that you can use multiplexers with very large numbers of inputs and decoders with very large numbers of outputs as single components. Describe the jump state ROM contents, the multiplexer inputs, and the Boolean logic equations for your microoperations.

12.23 *(Branch Sequencer)*   Using your Moore state diagram from Exercise 12.19, show how to implement the machine using a horizontal branch sequencer. Modify the state diagram to reflect your limitation on state fan-out. How are the input conditions organized? Show your ROM organization and tabulate its contents.

12.24 *(Horizontal Microcode)*   Using your solution to Exercise 12.23 as a starting point, describe how you can encode the microoperation outputs to reduce the width of the control ROM.

12.25 *(Vertical Microcode)*   Starting with the microcode format presented in Section 12.5.2, describe how to modify it for your datapath and the processor state machine from Exercise 12.19. Tabulate the vertical microcode to implement the instruction set.

A Number Systems

Introduction

In this appendix, we briefly review the concept of positional number systems, the methods for conversion between alternative number systems, and the basic elements of binary addition and subtraction. If you are not familiar with these concepts, it is probably a good idea to read this appendix before starting out with Chapter 1.

Throughout much of our lives, we have been exposed to the base 10 number system. The preference for 10-digit number systems is no surprise: we have 10 fingers! However, this is not natural for digital hardware systems, where arithmetic is based on the binary digits 0 and 1. We will also discuss number systems that are variations on the binary system: octal (the digits 0 through 7) and hexadecimal. The latter is a base 16 system, with 0 through 9 extended by the additional digits A (10), B (11), C (12), D (13), E (14), and F (15).

A.1 Positional Number Notation

In this section, we cover the main positional number systems used in digital hardware: decimal, binary, octal, and hexadecimal.

A.1.1   Decimal Numbers

The decimal number system represents quantities using the digits 0 through 9, arranged in a positional notation. For example, in base 10, the number 154 can be represented as

$$154_{10} = 1 \times 100 + 5 \times 10 + 4$$
$$= 1 \times 10^2 + 5 \times 10^1 + 4 \times 10^0$$

This is called *positional* because a digit's "place" in the sequence determines its weight. The least significant digit, in the rightmost position, has a weight of 1. The next digit to the left has a weight of 10. The most significant digit, in the leftmost position, has a weight of 100.

Each additional position to the left has a weight 10 times as much as the position to its immediate right. This is why the decimal number system is called a base 10 system. You should also notice that numbers are represented by sequences consisting of the ten digits 0 through 9.

A.1.2   Binary, Octal, and Hexadecimal Numbers

Digital hardware systems almost universally use the binary number system rather than base 10. However the basic concepts of positional number systems still apply. A number is written from the most significant digit at the left to the least significant digit at the right.

Binary Numbers   A binary number can be represented only by using the two digits 0 and 1. These are called *binary digits*, or simply *bits*. As the number is written down, each bit has twice the weight of its neighbor to its immediate right.

For example, consider the 8-bit binary number 10011010_2. The subscripted 2 reminds us that the number is in base 2. When a number is represented without a subscript, it usually means that it is a base 10 number.

What is the value of 10011010_2? Let's rewrite it in positional notation:

$$10011010_2 = 1 \times 2^7 + 0 \times 2^6 + 0 \times 2^5 + 1 \times 2^4 + 1 \times 2^3$$
$$+ 0 \times 2^2 + 1 \times 2^1 + 0 \times 2^0$$
$$= 1 \times 128 + 0 \times 64 + 0 \times 32 + 1 \times 16 + 1 \times 8$$
$$+ 0 \times 4 + 1 \times 2 + 0 \times 1$$
$$= 128 + 16 + 8 + 2 = 154_{10}$$

The binary number 10011010_2 denotes the same quantity as the decimal number 154_{10}. We can always place a binary number into base 10 by expanding it using positional notation.

Octal and Hexadecimal Numbers   Writing down even relatively small quantities in base 2 requires a large number of bits. To simplify the chore, designers have introduced alternative octal and hexadecimal number systems, based on 8 and 16 digits, respectively. It is easy to convert between binary and these systems, because the base in each case is a power of 2.

An octal number is represented by a sequence of digits drawn from 0 through 7. For example, the number 232_8 denotes the same quantity as 154_{10}. We can verify this by expanding the positional notation:

$$232_8 = 2 \times 8^2 + 3 \times 8^1 + 2 \times 8^0$$
$$= 128 + 24 + 2 = 154_{10}$$

Converting from base 16 is very similar. Remember that the 16 digits used in the hexadecimal system are 0 through 9 and A through F. Thus, the hexadecimal number $9A_{16}$ can be expanded as follows:

$$9A_{16} = 9 \times 16^1 + 10 \times 16^0$$
$$= 144 + 10 = 154_{10}$$

Once again, the hexadecimal represents the same quantity as 154_{10}.

A.2   Conversion Between Binary, Octal, and Hexadecimal Systems

We cover the methods for converting between the various binary-based systems in this subsection.

A.2.1   Conversion from Binary to Octal or Hexadecimal

It is always easy to rewrite a binary number in the octal or hexadecimal system. All we have to do is group the binary digits into 3-bit groupings (octal) or 4-bit groupings (hexadecimal), starting at the right of the number. For example, starting with the binary number 10011010_2, we derive its octal and hexadecimal equivalents as follows:

$$\underbrace{10}\underbrace{011}\underbrace{010}_{\ \ 2 \quad\ \ 3 \quad\ \ 2_8} \qquad \underbrace{1001}\underbrace{1010}_{\ \ 9 \quad\ \ A_{16}}$$

To see why this grouping strategy is correct, let's look at a generalized representation of a binary number and how we convert it to a hexadecimal number. We assume that the binary number always has a multiple of 4 bits. Of course, for any binary number, we can prepend additional zeros to the most significant bits to make this assumption true.

The generalized representation is shown below. The binary number starts out with n bits and will be converted to a hexadecimal number with $k = n/4$ hex digits:

$$a_{n-1}2^{n-1} + a_{n-2}2^{n-2} + a_{n-3}2^{n-3} + a_{n-4}2^{n-4} + \dots +$$

$$a_{4i+3}2^{4i+3} + a_{4i+2}2^{4i+2} + a_{4i+1}2^{4i+1} + a_{4i}2^{4i} + \dots +$$

$$a_3 2^3 + a_2 2^2 + a_1 2^1 + a_0 2^0$$

The process of putting the bits into groups of four is equivalent to factoring powers of 16 within the expression. By doing the grouping, we can rewrite the generalized expression as follows:

$$(a_{n-1}2^3 + a_{n-2}2^2 + a_{n-3}2^1 + a_{n-4}2^0)\, 2^{4(k-1)} + \dots +$$

$$(a_{4i+3}2^3 + a_{4i+2}2^2 + a_{4i+1}2^1 + a_{4i}2^0)\, 2^{4(i)} + \dots +$$

$$(a_3 2^3 + a_2 2^2 + a_1 2^1 + a_0 2^0)\, 2^{4(0)}$$

We can now rewrite each of the 4-bit numbers in the parentheses as a single hexadecimal digit, raised to an appropriate power of 2^4. We could apply a similar method to demonstrate why grouping by threes performs the conversion from binary to octal.

A.2.2   Conversion from Octal to Hexadecimal and Vice Versa

To convert between octal and hexadecimal, you should first convert the number into binary. By appropriate grouping of bits, you then form the number in the target base. Let's see how this works for the conversion between 232_8 and $9A_{16}$:

232_8 maps into the binary number $010\ 011\ 010_2$, which can be regrouped to form the number $9A_{16}$. The mapping from hex to octal works analogously.

A.2.3   Conversion from Base 10 to Base 2: Successive Division

So far, you have seen how to map binary, octal, and hexadecimal numbers into base 10, by expanding the positional notation. You have also seen how to map between the binary system and the octal and hex systems. The missing link is how to get from base 10 to base 2.

The method we use is called *successive division*. It works by successively dividing the base 10 number by the base to which it is to be converted. For example, we successively divide by 2 if the target is base 2. We collect the remainders to form the number in the target base. The first division yields the least significant bit as its remainder. The process continues until the quotient is 0.

Let's look at an example: the conversion of 154_{10} to base 2. The process is as follows:

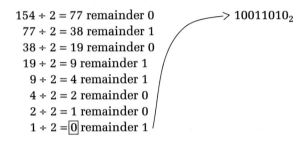

$$154 \div 2 = 77 \text{ remainder } 0$$
$$77 \div 2 = 38 \text{ remainder } 1$$
$$38 \div 2 = 19 \text{ remainder } 0$$
$$19 \div 2 = 9 \text{ remainder } 1$$
$$9 \div 2 = 4 \text{ remainder } 1$$
$$4 \div 2 = 2 \text{ remainder } 0$$
$$2 \div 2 = 1 \text{ remainder } 0$$
$$1 \div 2 = \boxed{0} \text{ remainder } 1$$

$\longrightarrow 10011010_2$

The same method works for conversion from base 10 to other bases. For example, to convert 154_{10} to base 8, we proceed as follows:

$$154 \div 8 = 19 \text{ remainder } 2$$
$$19 \div 8 = 2 \text{ remainder } 3$$
$$2 \div 8 = \boxed{0} \text{ remainder } 2$$

$\longrightarrow 232_8$

The conversion to base 16 works like this:

$$154 \div 16 = 9 \text{ remainder } 10$$
$$9 \div 16 = \boxed{0} \text{ remainder } 9$$

$\longrightarrow 9A_{16}$

The Theory Behind Successive Division   Given that the number N in base 10 is equivalent to an n-digit number in a different base R, we should be able to rewrite N in base R as $(a_{n-1} \, a_{n-2} \, \ldots \, a_0)_R$. As we successively divide by R, each subsequent division liberates the next lower-order digit a_i from the base R representation.

To see this, consider the following description of successive division. Since N is represented as an n-digit number in base R, the first division yields the quotient Q_0 and the remainder a_0. The latter is exactly the value of the lowest-order digit in base R. Dividing R into Q_0 results in a new quotient Q_1 and a new remainder a_1, the next lowest-order digit. If we repeat the process n times, we obtain a quotient of zero and a remainder that is equal to the highest-order digit in base R. The process of successive division is shown below:

$$N = (a_{n-1}a_{n-2}\ldots\; a_0)_R$$
$$= a_{n-1}R^{n-1} + a_{n-2}R^{n-2} + \ldots + a_1R^1 + a_0R^0$$

$$Q_0 = \frac{N}{R} = a_{n-1}R^{n-2} + a_{n-2}R^{n-3} + \ldots + a_1R^0 \qquad \text{remainder } a_0$$

$$Q_1 = \frac{Q_0}{R} = a_{n-1}R^{n-3} + a_{n-2}R^{n-4} + \ldots + a_2R^0 \qquad \text{remainder } a_1$$

$$\vdots$$

$$Q_{n-1} = \frac{Q_{n-2}}{R} = 0 \qquad\qquad\qquad\qquad\qquad\qquad \text{remainder } a_{n-1}$$

To summarize, Figure A.1 shows the various conversion methods that we have covered. We use successive division to convert from base 10 to any other base. By expanding the positional notation, we can convert from any base to base 10. We perform conversions between base 2 and other bases that are powers of two, such as base 8 and base 16, through the process of bit grouping.

A.3   Binary Arithmetic Operations

We examine the arithmetic operations in the binary number system next.

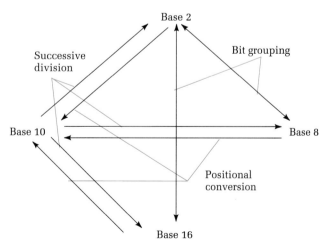

Figure A.1   Conversion methods.

A.3.1   Addition in Positional Notation

Let's begin by reviewing how addition works in the base 10 positional number system. Consider the addition of 95 and 16 to yield 111:

$$95_{10}$$
$$+\ 16_{10}$$

$$\downarrow$$

$$111_{10}$$

$$9\times10^1 +\ 5\times10^0$$
$$+\ \ 1\times10^1 +\ 6\times10^0$$
$$\overline{10\times10^1 + 11\times10^0}$$

$$\downarrow$$

$$1\times10^2 + (0+1)\times10^1 +\ 1\times10^0$$

The numbers are added column by column, one position at a time. Should the column sum exceed 9, the largest digit that can be represented in base 10, we must generate a carry-out to the next higher-order position.

You are familiar with a shorthand method for addition in positional notation. You proceed column by column, from right to left. $5+6=11$, which is written as a sum of 1 with a carry of 1 to the next column. The *carry* represents an excess quantity that is too big to be represented in a single column. It is then added to the column sum of the next higher position. In the example, $1+9+1=11$, which again is represented as a column sum of 1 with a carry of 1. Since there are no additional column sums to be formed, the final carry-out is written as part of the sum. This process, as illustrated by the example, is summarized below:

$$1\ 1\quad \longleftarrow \text{Column carries}$$
$$9\ 5_{10}$$
$$1\ 6_{10}$$
$$\overline{1\ 1\ 1_{10}}$$

The same process applies to addition in any base. Next, we will see how addition is applied to base 2.

Addition in Base 2   In the binary number system, we have the following addition table:

$$0+0=0$$
$$0+1=1$$
$$1+0=1$$
$$1+1=0 \text{ with a carry of } 1$$

Let's illustrate addition in binary with an example. Consider the addition of 101_2 and 11_2 to yield 1000_2 ($5_{10}+3_{10}=8_{10}$):

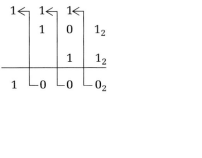

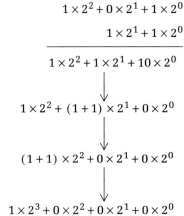

The step-by-step process is shown at the right, the shorthand method at the left. In longhand, the columns are added up individually. If the column quantity cannot be represented, it must "carry out" a power of two to the next higher column.

Since 10_2 in the sum's ones column cannot be represented directly, we must add 1×2^1 to the next higher column, leaving the 0 behind. The twos column undergoes a similar carry-out: $1 + 1$ yields 0 with a carry of 1 to the fours column. This, in turn, cascades to the eights column: $1 + 1$ again yields 0 with a carry-out of 1.

It is much easier to work with the shorthand method, of course. We proceed from right to left, adding one column at a time. Beginning with the ones column, $1 + 1 = 0$ with a carry of 1 to the twos column. In the twos column, we add the carry of $1 + 0 + 1 = 0$ with a carry of 1 to the fours column. Continuing with the fours column, the carry-in of 1 plus 1 is 0 with a carry-out of 1 to the eights column. This results in the final sum, 1000_2.

As another example, let us look at the addition of 95_{10} and 16_{10}, but this time in binary:

$$
\begin{array}{r}
& & & 1 \leftarrow & & & & \\
95_{10} = & 1 & 0 & 1 & 1 & 1 & 1 & 1 \\
+\ 16_{10} = & 0 & 0 & 1 & 0 & 0 & 0 & 0 \\
\hline
& 1 & 1 & 0 & 1 & 1 & 1 & 1 = 111_{10}
\end{array}
$$

95_{10} maps into 1011111_2, while 16_{10} is equivalent to 10000_2. In adding, we work from the rightmost column to the left. In the first column, the sum is 1, as it is in columns two, three, and four. In the fifth column, two 1's are being summed, yielding 0 with a carry of 1. This leads to a sum in the sixth column of 1. The final column also sums to 1. You should verify that $1101111_2 = 111_{10}$.

A.3.2   Subtraction in Positional Notation

Let's review the process of subtraction in base 10. Then we will show how the process applies in base 2.

To illustrate, consider the subtraction of 16_{10} from 95_{10} to yield 79_{10}:

$$
\begin{array}{c}
95 = 9{\times}10^1 + 5{\times}10^0 = 8{\times}10^1 + 15{\times}10^0 \\
-16 = 1{\times}10^1 + 6{\times}10^0 = 1{\times}10^1 + 6{\times}10^0 \\
\hline
7{\times}10^1 + 9{\times}10^0
\end{array}
$$

The longhand method is shown at the right, the shorthand at the left. At the right, the numbers are rearranged into the positional notation. If the digit to be subtracted is larger than the digit it is being subtracted from, we must *borrow* from the next higher position to the left. A 10 is subtracted from this column and added back to the original column. This borrowing guarantees that the subtraction can now proceed in the ones column.

Let's start by looking at the example in its long form at the right. Starting with the ones column, 5 is smaller than 6, so we must move 10 units from the tens position to the ones position. Now we can subtract 6 from the resulting 15 to yield 9. For the next column, we subtract 1 from the remaining 8 to obtain 7 in the tens position.

Looking at the shorthand form, since 5 is less than 6, we borrow from the tens column to form 15. $15 - 6 = 9$. For the tens column, we subtract 1 from 8 to get 7. So the result is 79. Obviously, the process of borrowing can cascade from right to left in much the same way that carries can propagate.

Subtraction in Base 2   Subtraction in base 2 is much like subtraction in base 10, except that the borrowing process moves two from a higher-order column to a lower-order column. If a column subtraction cannot proceed without yielding a negative result, borrowing causes 1×2^1 to be subtracted from the adjacent column to the left, which is then added back as 10_2 to the original column.

To see how subtraction proceeds in base 2, we begin with the example of subtracting 11_2 from 101_2 to get 10_2 ($5_{10} - 3_{10} = 2_{10}$):

$$
\begin{array}{rcl}
101_2 = 1 \times 2^2 + 0 \times 2^1 + 1 \times 2^0 & = & 0 \times 2^2 + 10 \times 2^1 + 1 \times 2^0 \\
-11_2 = 1 \times 2^1 + 1 \times 2^0 & = & 1 \times 2^1 + 1 \times 2^0 \\
\hline
10_2 & & 1 \times 2^1 + 0 \times 2^0
\end{array}
$$

Starting with the ones column, we subtract 1 from 1 to obtain 0. In the twos column, 0 is smaller than 1, so we must borrow from the fours column. In essence, we borrow one from the fours column to add two to the twos column. $2 - 1 = 1$, which is the result in the middle column. The high-order column is left with a 0.

As another example of borrowing, consider the subtraction of 111_2 from 10001_2 to yield 1010_2. To see borrowing in the longhand form, let's look at the step-by-step process:

(i) $$1 \times 2^4 + 0 \times 2^3 + 0 \times 2^2 + 0 \times 2^1 + 1 \times 2^0$$

(ii) $$1 \times 2^4 + 0 \times 2^3 + (0 - 1) \times 2^2 + (0 + 10) \times 2^1 + 1 \times 2^0$$

(iii) $$1 \times 2^4 + (0 - 1) \times 2^3 + (0 - 1 + 10) \times 2^2 + (0 + 10) \times 2^1 + 1 \times 2^0$$

(iv) $$(1 - 1) \times 2^4 + (0 - 1 + 10) \times 2^3 + (0 - 1 + 10) \times 2^2 + (0 + 10) \times 2^1 + 1 \times 2^0$$

(v) $$1 \times 2^3 + 1 \times 2^2 + 10 \times 2^1 + 1 \times 2^0$$

$$- \qquad\qquad 1 \times 2^2 + 1 \times 2^1 + 1 \times 2^0$$

$$\overline{\qquad\qquad 1 \times 2^3 + 0 \times 2^2 + 1 \times 2^1 + 0 \times 2^0}$$

Steps (i) through (v) show the transformations to the positional notation to get a form suitable for subtraction of 111_2. (i) is 10001_2 in the standard form. Since the twos position is smaller than the digit being subtracted from it, we must borrow from the fours position. This is shown in (ii). Now the fours column is negative, so the borrowing process must cascade. The result is shown in (iii). Now the eights column is negative, so the process continues, as (iv) shows. The final form, suitable for subtraction, is shown in (v). Now we can perform the subtraction column by column to obtain the final result of 1010_2.

In general, the strategy for subtraction is summarized by

$0 - 0 = 0$
$0 - 1 = 1$ with a borrow of 1
$1 - 0 = 1$
$1 - 1 = 0$

Using this table, let's subtract 10000_2 from 1011111_2 ($95_{10} - 16_{10}$):

$95_{10} =$		1	0	1	1	1	1	1	
$-16_{10} =$	$-$	0	0	1	0	0	0	0	
		1	0	0	1	1	1	1	$= 79_{10}$

In this example, there is no need to borrow. You should verify that $1001111_2 = 79_{10}$.

As a final example, let's consider the subtraction of 1 from 10000_2 to yield 1111_2:

$$
\begin{array}{r}
16_{10} = \quad 1 \quad 0 \quad 0 \quad 0 \quad 0 \\
- \; 1_{10} = \quad 0 \quad 0 \quad 0 \quad 0 \quad 1 \\
-1 \quad -1 \quad -1 \quad -1 \\
\hline
0 \quad 1 \quad 1 \quad 1 \quad 1 \; = 15_{10}
\end{array}
$$

This example exhibits cascaded borrows. We begin with the rightmost column. 0 is smaller than 1, so the result is 1 with a borrow of 1 from the column to the left.

Let's look at the second column. It has a deficit of 1, because it has lent a 1 to the column to its right. This is equivalent to subtracting 1 from this column. We must borrow from the next column to the left to make good on this deficit. Thus the column computation is the same as $10_2 - 1 = 1$ with another borrow from the left.

The process repeats for the third column. The deficit of 1 used as the borrow into the second column must be made good. Since the current column has 0 in it, we must borrow from the fourth column. After the borrow, the calculation becomes $10_2 - 1 = 1$ with yet another borrow from the left.

The reasoning for the fourth column is the same as for the third. The borrow comes from the fifth column to make good on the deficit for the fourth column. $10_2 - 1 = 1$. In the fifth column, the calculation becomes $1 - 1$, based on the borrow deficit. The final result is 01111_2.

Appendix Review

In this appendix, we have examined the methods for representing numbers in positional notation. We use positional notation to represent numbers in a variety of different bases, including base 10 (decimal), base 2 (binary), base 8 (octal), and base 16 (hexadecimal). Of course, it is also possible to represent numbers in bases other than these four.

We then presented the methods for converting numbers in one base to the other. A number can be converted to base 10 simply by expanding the positional notation. Base 10 can be converted to another base by successive division. Since 8 and 16 are powers of 2, there is a simple method for mapping between these bases. All we need do is group the binary representation into adjacent groups of three bits for base 8 and four bits for base 16.

Finally, we looked at the mechanics of binary addition and subtraction, using our intuition about how these operations work for base 10. For the addition operation, when the column sum exceeds the quantity that can be represented by a single digit, the "overflow" amount is carried over to the next higher-order column. Similarly for subtraction, when the column difference is negative, we must borrow an amount equal to the underlying base from the adjacent higher-order column. This guarantees that the column difference yields a nonnegative result. Both carries and borrows can cascade from the rightmost columns toward the left columns.

In this appendix, we concentrated on the representation of nonnegative numbers in a variety of alternative number bases. We will study number representations in more detail in Chapter 5. In particular, we will examine alternative methods for representing negative numbers in binary, as well as the detailed circuitry for implementing binary addition and subtraction.

Exercises

A.1   *(Conversion to Base 10)*   Convert each of the following numbers into its equivalent form in base 10:

   a. 757_8

   b. 1101100_2

   c. FFA_{16}

   d. 1000_2

   e. 1000_8

   f. 1000_{16}

A.2   *(Conversion to Target Base)*   Convert each of the following base 10 numbers into its equivalent form in the indicated base:

   a. 53 to base 2

   b. 127 to base 8

   c. 1023 to base 16

   d. 500 to base 2

   e. 798 to base 8

   f.   4000 to base 16

A.3 *(Conversion Between Base 2 and Base 8 or Base 16)* Convert each of the following binary numbers to the indicated base:

a. 1110011_2 to base 8

b. 10011100_2 to base 16

c. 1011011_2 to base 8

d. 11110011_2 to base 16

e. 1001000111000101_2 to base 8

f. 1110001100110001000_2 to base 16

A.4 *(Convert Between Base 8 or Base 16 and Binary)* Convert each of the numbers in the indicated base to binary:

a. 252_8

b. $AFE0_{16}$

c. 4077_8

d. 4077_{16}

e. 101_8

f. $0FC_{16}$

A.5 *(Convert Between Base 8 and Base 16)* Using the same numbers as in Exercise A.4, convert the numbers in base 8 to base 16 (a, c, e) and the numbers in base 16 to base 8 (b, d, f).

A.6 *(Alternative Number Systems)* People on the planet Mars use a quarternary number system, consisting of the digits 0, 1, 2, and 3 (that is, base 4). Perform the following conversions to and from base 4:

a. Convert 597 to base 4

b. Convert 32021_4 to base 10

c. Convert 223_4 to base 2

d. Convert 32210_4 to base 8

e. Convert 1230322_4 to base 16

f. Convert $AB0_{16}$ to base 4

g. Convert 771_8 to base 4

h. Convert 110010011_2 to base 4

A.7 *(Binary Addition)* Perform the following additions in binary:

    a. $100110_2 + 111_2$

    b. $110111_2 + 101_2$

    c. $111110_2 + 10111_2$

    d. $111001_2 + 10001_2$

    e. $11011100110_2 + 10011001_2$

    f. $10101010_2 + 1111111_2$

A.8 *(Binary Subtraction)* Perform the following subtractions in binary:

    a. $100110_2 - 111_2$

    b. $110111_2 - 101_2$

    c. $111110_2 - 10111_2$

    d. $111001_2 - 10001_2$

    e. $11011100110_2 - 10011001_2$

    f. $10101010_2 - 1111111_2$

A.9 *(Base Conversions)* Perform the following base conversions. Use successive division where necessary.

    a. 200_{10} to base 7

    b. 200_{16} to base 3

    c. 356_7 to base 2

    d. $A9DE_{16}$ to base 3

    e. 591_{10} to base 5

    f. 1001011_2 to base 4

A.10 *(Addition/Subtraction in Different Bases)* Perform the indicated arithmetic operations:

    a. $200_3 + 22_3$ in base 3

    b. $43_5 - 24_5$ in base 5

    c. $10A_{16} + 201_8$ in base 16

    d. $77_8 - 25_{10}$ in base 8

    e. $95_{10} + 211_3$ in base 3

    f. $71_8 - 32_4$ in base 8

B Basic Electronic Components

Introduction

Digital hardware systems can be viewed from many alternative perspectives, including Boolean logic, logic gates, and behavioral specifications. For most of this book, the most primitive abstraction we use is the logic gate. In this appendix, we peek beneath the sheets to get some idea of how logic gates are actually implemented by more primitive electrical components.

We begin by reviewing briefly the concepts of electricity that influence the fundamental operation of logic gates. We will also examine the basic implementation technologies from which logic gates are constructed, such as diodes, capacitors, resistors, bipolar transistors, and MOS transistors.

B.1 Basic Electricity

In this subsection we introduce the basic terminology, fundamental quantities, and laws of electricity.

B.1.1   Terminology

Electricity is energy that can be transported. An *electric circuit* consists of an energy source, such as a battery or power supply, and interconnected electrical components implementing a useful function. The connections are formed by wires, also known as *conductors*, which are made of materials such as copper or some other metal that can conduct electricity. Electrical charge transported across a conductor is called electric *current*. Charge is carried by *electrons*, which are negatively charged, or by positively charged *ions* in the conductor. Current is the intensity of the flow of charge. Between two points in a circuit, electrons flow from the more negatively charged point toward the one that is more positively charged. Positive charges, sometimes called *holes*, move in the opposite direction. By convention, current flows in the direction of holes, which is opposite to the direction of electron flow.

Voltage is associated with any two points in the circuit, and represents the difference in electrical potential between those points. Stated differently, voltage is the electric force that causes electrons to flow in a circuit. Voltage is defined as a relative quantity. In a typical digital circuit, the lowest possible voltage is called *ground* and is arbitrarily assigned 0 volts. In most existing digital circuits, the highest possible voltage value is defined not to exceed 5.5 volts (industry is starting to move toward a 3.3-volt power supply). In digital systems, we assign logic 1 to "high" voltages and 0 to "low" voltages, but these assignments are somewhat arbitrary. For TTL technology of the kinds described in this book, a voltage in the range of 0 to 0.4 volts is interpreted as logic 0, while 2.5 to 5.5 volts is interpreted as a logic 1. Voltages outside these ranges are not guaranteed to be interpreted as either a 0 or a 1.

The fundamental concepts of electricity can often be described by analogy with water. The greater the electrical potential, the larger the voltage, and the greater the force on the flow of the charge-carrying electrons. Think of a waterfall. A large voltage corresponds to a waterfall of great height. As a water molecule flows "downhill," a good deal of pressure is exerted on it by gravity and the force of water behind it. By analogy, water molecules correspond to electrons and electrical current corresponds to the speed of the water flow.

Suppose that the voltage difference is 0, so that both points in the circuit are at the same potential. In this case, the water is a stagnant pool, with no water flow, and there is no current. Given a waterfall of only modest height, the water trickles slowly downhill. This is analogous to a small current. But if the waterfall is of a great height, the flow of water will be forceful and the current is large.

Whereas conductors transport electricity, other materials, called *insulators*, are impervious to electricity. An important class of materials is the *semiconductors*, materials that can change from being conductors at one moment to being insulators at the next. This makes it possible to form electrically controlled switches, which are at the heart of all digital logic circuits.

B.1.2   Fundamental Quantities and Laws

Quantity	Symbol	Units
Charge	Q	Coulomb
Voltage	V	Volt
Current	I	Ampere
Resistance	R	Ohm
Capacitance	C	Farad

Figure B.1   Electrical quantities and their units.

The key electrical quantities and their units are shown in Figure B.1. Charge measures the number of positive or negative charges at a given point in the circuit and is described in units of coulombs. One coulomb is equivalent to the charge on 6.24×10^{18} electrons. Voltage is the difference in electrical potential between two points in a circuit and is measured in volts. At a given point in a circuit, current is the change in charge as a function of time. Thus, one ampere is defined to be one coulomb per second.

Resistance   Figure B.1 introduces two important new quantities: resistance and capacitance. *Resistance* is the "friction" that limits current. Doubling resistance cuts the current in half. When two resistors are connected in series, one immediately following the other, their resistances add. Placing two resistors in parallel results in a resistance that is less than the component resistances. To be more precise, if the resistances, measured in ohms, are R_1 and R_2, the parallel resistance will be $(R_1 \times R_2) / (R_1 + R_2)$.

A *short circuit* is a path of conductors with no (or very low) resistance. An *open circuit* is a conductive path with infinite resistance. Semiconductor materials make it possible to construct connections between two points that can be varied between low and high resistance.

One of the most important expressions for analyzing electrical circuits is Ohm's law (for the German scientist Georg Simon Ohm). It describes the relationship between voltage (V), current (I), and resistance (R) as follows:

$$V = I \times R$$

To understand this relationship, let's consider the water analogy again. V is the height of the waterfall. We can think of R as inversely proportional to the diameter of a water pipe: a high resistance corresponds to a narrow pipe, a low resistance to a wide pipe. A narrow pipe restricts the flow more than a wide pipe. With a high resistance, current is reduced, because fewer electrons can move through the conductor per unit time. By reducing the resistance (that is, increasing the cross section of the pipe), we increase the flow of electrons.

An alternative formulation of Ohm's law allows us to describe resistance as a function of voltage and current: $R = V/I$. Thus, if a power supply provides voltage V and the current is measured as I, then the resistance of the circuit being driven by the power supply is R.

Capacitance   Capacitance is the ability to store charge and is measured in units of farads (named for the great 19th-century British scientist Michael Faraday). A capacitor is a device with two parallel conducting plates separated by a nonconducting material. Placing negative charges on one plate will attract positive charges to the other plate. A capacitor uses current to charge the plates up slowly to a new voltage. Once charge is stored, the capacitor can also provide a "discharge" current to the rest of the circuit. Thus, capacitors are often used to smooth out variations in the current provided by the circuit's power supply.

Continuing with our water analogy, a capacitor behaves much like a water holding tank. A hole at the bottom of the tank provides a steady "outflow" of current, even though the inflow may be sporadic.

Charge, voltage, and capacitance are related by

$$Q = C \times V$$

Charge is equal to capacitance times voltage. By placing a voltage V across a capacitor of C farads, we can store a charge of Q coulombs.

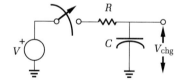

Figure B.2   Charging a capacitor through a resistor.

RC Delay   There is an interesting relationship between time, resistance, and capacitance. Consider how long it takes to charge up a discharged capacitor. Figure B.2 shows a possible setup. In the schematic, the voltage source is labeled V, the resistor R, and the capacitor C.

We assume that the capacitor is completely discharged and the switch is in the open position. When the switch is closed, the power supply begins to charge up the capacitor toward the voltage V_{chg}. If you measure the voltage across the capacitor with a voltmeter, initially the voltage changes very quickly, but then it slows down.

There is a precise relationship between the resistance and capacity of the circuit and the time it takes to charge the capacitor. It is directly related to $R \times C$, also known as the *RC time constant* (it may seem strange that ohms times farads is seconds, but this is the case). After one *RC* delay, the capacitor is charged up to slightly more than 60% of its final value. After two *RC* delays, it reaches almost 90% of its final value. It takes five *RC* delays before the capacitor reaches 99% of its final value. This is shown in Figure B.3.

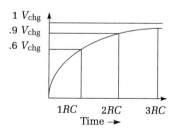

Figure B.3   *RC* time constant and time to charge a capacitor.

RC delays play an important role in determining the true performance of digital circuits. Even though wires are excellent conductors, they do present some resistance to the current flow. But even more important, wires introduce capacitance: a wire forms one plate of a capacitor whose second plate is the circuit board itself. Changes in voltages on wires require this capacitance to be either charged or discharged, and this translates into a significant source of delay in real circuits.

B.2 Logic Gates from Resistors, Diodes, and Transistors

In this subsection, we investigate how to construct logic functions from fundamental electrical objects like resistors, diodes, and transistors.

B.2.1 Voltage Dividers

When a voltage spans two resistors in series, the voltage measured at the point between the resistors is divided in proportion to the ratio of the individual resistors and the sum of the resistances. As an example, see Figure B.4(a). The voltage across R_1 is given by $V \times R_1 / (R_1 + R_2)$, where V is the voltage across the series resistors, R_1 is the resistance between the power supply and the output node, and R_2 is the resistance between the ground and the power supply. R_1 is often called the *load* or *pull-up* resistor, while R_2 is the *pull-down* resistor.

In the example, R_1 – 900 ohms, $R_2 = 100$ ohms, and $V = 5$ volts. The voltage drop across R_1 is

$$\frac{R_1}{R_1 + R_2} \times V = \frac{900}{1000} \times 5 = 4.5 \ V$$

Thus, the voltage measured between the output node and ground would be 0.5 V. Alternatively, we could have arrived at this directly by calculating the voltage across R_2, namely $V \times R_2 / (R_1 + R_2)$. By appropriately sizing the relative resistances, we can choose any desired output voltage.

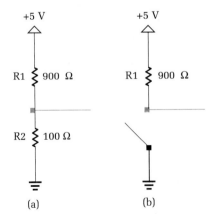

(a)   (b)

Figure B.4   Voltage divider view of a logical inversion.

Now suppose that R_2 is a variable resistor with two basic settings: low resistance or very high resistance. When the pull-down resistor has a sufficiently high resistance, it behaves like an open circuit, as shown in Figure B.4(b). The output node reaches 5 V.

An electrical device that can switch between low resistance and very high resistance is called a transistor, as we will see in Sections B.3 and B.4. A *transistor* is a three-terminal device that establishes a low-resistance path between two terminals when a high voltage is placed on the third terminal. When a low voltage is placed on this control terminal, the remaining two terminals are separated by a high resistance. If R_2 is replaced by a transistor, it's easy to see that we obtain an inverter. When the input voltage is high, the output voltage is low. When it is low, the output voltage is high.

But before we can examine transistors in more detail, we need to take a look at a simpler, two-terminal device: the diode.

B.2.2   Diode Logic

A *diode* is a two-terminal electrical device that allows current to flow in one direction but not the other. It is like a pipe with an internal valve that allows water to flow freely in one direction but shuts down if the water tries to flow backward. The schematic diagram for a diode is shown in Figure B.5. The diode's two terminals are called the *anode* and *cathode*. In the diode symbol, the arrow points from the anode (flat part of triangle) toward the cathode (point of the triangle).

The device operates by allowing current to flow from anode to cathode, basically in the direction of the triangle. Recall that current is defined to flow from the more positive voltage toward the more negative voltage (electrons flow in the opposite direction). If the diode's anode is at a higher voltage than the cathode, the diode is said to be *forward biased*, its resistance is very low, and current flows. The diode is not a perfect conductor, so there is a small voltage drop, approximately 0.7 V,

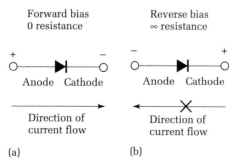

Figure B.5   Diode operation.

across it. If the anode is at a lower voltage than the cathode, the diode is *reverse biased*, its resistance is very high, and no current flows.

We can construct simple gates with nothing more than two or more diodes and a resistor. See Figure B.6. At the left of the figure is a diode AND gate, and at the right a diode OR gate. Let's examine the AND gate first. If one of the inputs A or B is grounded, current flows through the diode and the output node X is at a low voltage. The only way to get a high output is by having both inputs high. This is clearly a logical AND function.

Now we turn to the OR gate. Whenever one or the other of the inputs A and B are high, current flows through the associated diode. This brings the output node Y to a high voltage. This circuit clearly implements a logical OR.

Unfortunately, it is difficult to cascade circuits of this kind into multiple levels of logic gates. The voltage drops across the diodes add up as they are cascaded in series, leading to significantly degraded voltage levels.

For example, suppose we wire up five diode-resistor AND gates in series. If a string of inputs are logic 0 and the series diodes are conducting, then the output from the final stage should be recognized as a logic 0 as well. But because each diode adds a 0.7-V drop, the measured output would actually be at 3.5 V. This is pretty far from any voltage that would be recognized as logic 0.

One solution is to increase the power supply voltage, redefining the range that is recognized as a logic 0 and logic 1. Of course, the higher the voltage, the higher the power consumed and the more heat the circuit generates. And no matter what you set the power supply to, there is still a limit to the number of logic levels that can be cascaded. This is hardly an adequate solution.

Also note that it is not possible to construct an inverter with only diodes and resistors. AND and OR functions by themselves are not a complete logic without NOT. Thus, there are some logic functions that cannot be implemented in diode-resistor logic. Fortunately, transistors solve all of these problems.

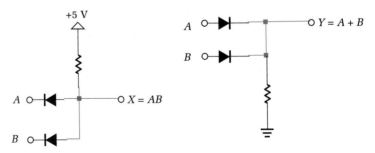

Figure B.6   Simple gates from diodes and resistors.

B.3 Bipolar Transistor Logic

In this subsection, we examine how to build logic gates from bipolar transistors, the dominant technology of the 1970s and early 1980s.

B.3.1 Basic Bipolar Transistor Logic

A *bipolar transistor* is a three-terminal semiconductor device. Under the control of one of the terminals, called the *base*, current can flow selectively from the *collector* terminal to the *emitter* terminal. Using transistors as electronically controlled switches is critical for building modern digital logic.

Using our water analogy, a transistor is like a water spigot. The base is like a screw. When it is tightened down, no water (current) flows through the spigot. The transistor is in its "off" region of operation. As the screw is turned, the flow of water begins to trickle and then increases. This is the so-called linear operating region. The current increases linearly as the voltage across the transistor is increased. Eventually, the flow reaches a point where opening the screw further does not increase the flow, it being limited by the diameter of the pipe. This is called the saturation region. Despite changes in voltage across the transistors, there is no change in current. Transistors in digital logic pass quickly from the off region to the saturation region.

The basic inverter constructed from transistors and resistors is shown in Figure B.7 (for those in the know, the transistor shown is an NPN transistor). A high voltage at the base turns on the transistor. The output F is discharged to ground, getting close to 0 V but never quite reaching it (it reaches a voltage drop away from 0 V).

When a low voltage is placed on the base, the transistor is turned off. The output node F is charged up toward the power supply voltage through the pull-up/load resistor R1.

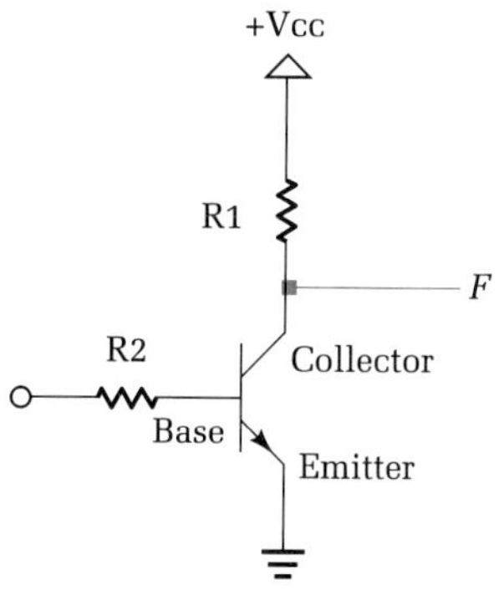

Figure B.7 Transistor-resistor inverter.

B.3.2 Diode-Transistor Logic

Diodes, transistors, and resistors can be used to implemented a wide variety of gates. Basically, we combine the diode logic of Figure B.6 with the transistor inverter of Figure B.7 to form NAND (not AND) and NOR (not OR) functions.

A two-input DTL (diode-transistor logic) NAND gate is shown in Figure B.8. It works like this. The diodes marked D1 and D2, together with resistor R1, form a two-input AND function. At the input to D3, a logic 0 is represented by approximately 0.7 V, while a logic 1 is in the range 4 to 5 V. D3 increases the voltage required to turn on the transistor. This gives a better separation between the voltage levels recognized as a logic 0 and logic 1.

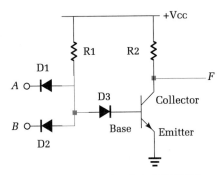

Figure B.8 Diode-transistor logic (DTL) NAND gate.

For the transistor to conduct, D3 must be turned on. This happens when the anode voltage reaches 1.4 V. If the voltage at the anode is much higher than this, the base will be driven to a high voltage. The transistor will be strongly turned on, with low resistance, and thus F will be discharged toward 0 V. If the anode is at a low voltage, the base will also be low. This keeps the transistor off (essentially infinite resistance), allowing the output node to reach a logic 1 voltage level.

Gates constructed as in Figure B.8 have a limit to the number of gate inputs to which their output can be connected. This is called *fan-out*. The pull-up resistor R2 is what limits the fan-out. The output F is at Vcc as long as no current is being drawn from the power supply to charge electrical nodes to which F is connected. However, if F is connected to the A or B input of a similar gate, current is drawn through R2. The voltage at F is reduced according to Ohm's law. If there are too many connections drawing current, the voltage at F may be so reduced that it can no longer be recognized as a logic 1. Thus, the number of fan-outs must be carefully limited in this kind of logic.

DTL has several advantages. NAND and NOR functions, which are easy to build in DTL, are *logically complete*. This means that any logical function can be expressed as a collection of only NAND gates or only NOR gates. NAND and NOR gates form the heart of all logic designs. In addition, this logic family uses lower voltages, less power, and operates at higher speeds, since only small currents are needed to turn on the transistors.

Another feature of DTL is its ability to implement a "wired AND" function. For example, if we wired several DTL NAND gates together, we would observe the following behavior. If any one of the NAND gates had a logic 0 as its output, the whole output function would also be at a logic 0 voltage. All the output functions would have to be at logic 1 for the output to be 1. See Figure B.9, which shows the internal wiring and the equivalent logic schematic for the wired AND function. The AND gate does not actually exist. The notation is used simply to represent that the interconnection forms the AND function.

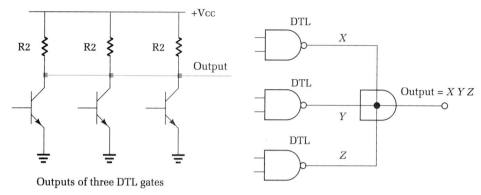

Figure B.9   Wired-AND DTL gates.

B.3.3   Transistor-Transistor Logic

We can think of a bipolar transistor as two diodes placed very close together, with the point between the diodes being the transistor base. Thus, we can use transistors in place of diodes to obtain logic gates that can be implemented with transistors and resistors only. This is called *transistor-transistor logic* (TTL), and it is the most widely used family of components available today.

A smart designer realized that the DTL NAND gate of Figure B.8 could be constructed from a two-emitter transistor connected to a transistor inverter. The multi-emitter transistor is the critical piece of technology that makes TTL logic gates possible.

A *two-input* TTL NAND gate is shown in Figure B.10 (some of the details have been eliminated). This circuit replaces the three diodes of Figure B.8 with a dual emitter transistor. This configuration has one significant advantage over the diode implementation. Besides being voltage-controlled switches, transistors also act as amplifiers. When the transistor

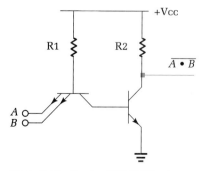

Figure B.10   Two-input TTL NAND gate.

base is undergoing a change in voltage, the transistor can amplify this change, thus speeding up the rate at which the transistor turns on or off. The result is faster gate switching.

In simplified terms, the circuit of Figure B.10 works as follows. When one of the inputs A or B is low, the current available through R1 at the transistor base is diverted to ground. No current flows from the base to the collector, and therefore no current reaches the base of the output transistor. Thus, the output transistor is off. The pull-up resistor R2 charges the output node to the high-voltage state. Only when both inputs are high can the current flow through R1 from base to collector to turn on the output transistor. In this case, the output path discharges to ground.

A more realistic circuit for a NAND logic gate, such as that found in the TTL 7400 component, is shown in Figure B.11. The output configuration with transistor Q4 in the pull-up path and transistor Q3 in the pull-down path is called a *totem pole output*. Q4 makes it possible to pull up the output faster, using lower power than is possible with just a resistor. In principle, this circuit behaves much like the simplified schematic of Figure B.10.

In Section 4.2.4, we introduce the concept of *open-collector gates*. These are gates with internal organizations that allow them to participate in a wired-AND configuration, similar to the DTL gates in Figure B.9. The pull-up path, namely the R3 resistor, Q4 transistor, and the diode of the output stage of Figure B.11, is eliminated in an open-collector gate. Thus, an open-collector gate only has the ability to pull down its output node. We need a resistor external to the gate. This pulls up the wired-AND output if none of the attached gates have an input combination that provides a pull-down path to ground.

Section 4.2.4 also introduces the concept of *tri-state gates*. These are gates with three possible interpretations of their outputs: logic 0, logic 1, and no connection. The latter is called the *high-impedance state* and is

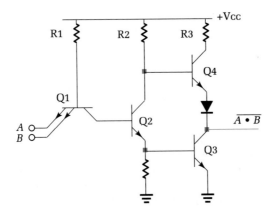

Figure B.11   Two-input TTL NAND gate with totem pole output.

denoted by the "value" Z. In Figure B.11, the totem pole output transistors Q3 and Q4 are not designed to be on simultaneously. Q4 is on when the output is 1, and Q3 is on when the output is 0. In a tri-state gate, both of these transistors can be off at the same time when a special *enable* input is left unasserted. The output node is disconnected from +Vcc or ground, making it appear to other logic as an open circuit.

B.3.4   TTL Circuits and Noise Margin

A major achievement of TTL logic is the ease with which different circuits can be interfaced and cascaded to form more complex logic functions. In part, this is due to the concepts of guaranteed voltage levels and noise margins. A *guaranteed voltage* is one at which circuits always detect the correct voltage level, within a specified temperature range (0–70°C), voltage range (5 V ± 5%), loading, and the parametric variance of the semiconductor devices themselves.

TTL circuits are characterized by four voltage specifications: V_{oh}, V_{ol}, V_{ih}, and V_{il}. V_{oh} (output high voltage) is the minimum voltage at which the circuit delivers a logic 1. V_{ol} (output low voltage) is the maximum voltage at which the circuit can produce a logic 0.

Similarly, V_{ih} (input high voltage) is the minimum voltage at which a circuit detects a logic 1. V_{il} (input low voltage) is the maximum voltage at which it recognizes a logic 0.

For TTL circuits, $V_{oh} = 2.4$ V, $V_{ol} = 0.4$ V, $V_{ih} = 2$ V, and $V_{il} = 0.8$ V. The input and output voltages differ by 0.4 V. This permits the output signals to be degraded by the wires between circuits but still be recognized as good logic values. The difference between V_{oh} and V_{ih} is called the *high-state DC noise margin*. The difference between V_{ol} and V_{oh} is called the *low-state DC noise margin*.

B.4   MOS Transistors

We now turn our attention to logic functions constructed from MOS transistors, the dominant technology of today.

B.4.1   Voltage-Controlled Switches

The operation of an MOS transistor is considerably easier to explain than that of a bipolar transistor. The voltage-controlled switches introduced in Section 1.3.1 correspond directly to MOS transistors. In this section, we describe the operation of MOS transistors and how they can be used to implement logic gates.

An MOS transistor is nothing more than a voltage-controlled switch. It has three connection points: a *source*, a *drain*, and a *gate* (a transistor gate bears no resemblance to a logic gate, an unfortunately ambiguous use of the term).

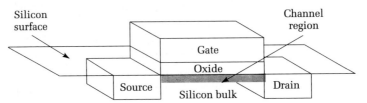

Figure B.12   Cross section of a MOS transistor.

A cross section of the metal-oxide-silicon sandwich that forms the transistor is shown in Figure B.12. The bottommost material layer is made of silicon, an insulating oxide layer sits on top of it, and the topmost layer is the metal gate. (More modern integrated circuit processes have replaced the metal layer with a material called polycrystalline silicon, but the older "metal gate" terminology still holds.) The source and drain regions contain silicon material with a large excess of electrons separated by the slightly positively charged bulk silicon. The source and drain are called *diffusion regions* because of the chemical process used to create them. Negatively charged ions (atoms with extra valence electrons) are placed onto the silicon surface and are diffused into the surface by heating the silicon material. The materials of the source and drain are identical. By convention, the source is the electrical node with the lower of the two voltage potentials at either end of the channel.

The electrical behavior of the transistor is generally as follows. When a positive voltage is placed on the gate, electrons from the silicon bulk are attracted to the transistor *channel*, an initially nonconducting region between the source and drain very close to the silicon surface. When the gate voltage becomes sufficiently positively charged, enough electrons are pulled into the channel from the bulk to establish a charged path between the source and the drain. Electrons flow across the transistor channel, and the voltage-controlled switch is conducting. If a 0 or very small voltage is placed on the gate, no electrons (or at least very few) are attracted to the channel. The source and drain are disconnected, no current flows across the channel, and the switch is not conducting.

There are two fundamentally different kinds of MOS transistors, called *n-channel* and *p-channel* transistors, or *nMOS* and *pMOS* for short. Their schematic symbols are shown in Figure B.13. Because they are made from materials with different affinities for electrons, the two transistor types behave quite differently. The transistor operation described above is actually for the nMOS transistor. The bulk is positively charged, while the diffusion is negatively charged. The transistor switch is "closed" (conducting) when a logic 1 is placed on its gate and "open" (nonconducting) when the gate is connected to a logic 0. The pMOS transistor is complementary. The diffusion regions are positively

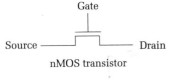

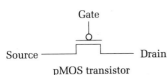

Figure B.13   nMOS and pMOS transistor symbols.

charged and the silicon bulk is negatively charged. A pMOS transistor behaves in a complementary way: It is "closed" (conducting) when a logic 0 is placed on the gate and is "open" (nonconducting) when a logic 1 is placed there.

The symbols for the two different kinds of transistors make it easy to remember how they operate. An nMOS transistor conducts when the gate voltage is asserted in positive logic. The pMOS transistor conducts when the gate is asserted in negative logic. This is why there is a polarity bubble on the gate of the pMOS transistor's symbol.

B.4.2   Logic Gates from MOS Switches

Any logic gate can be constructed from a combination of nMOS and pMOS transistors. Figure B.14 shows transistor networks for (a) an inverter, (b) a two-input NAND gate, and (c) a two-input NOR gate. The power supply (+5 V) and ground (0 V) represent logic 1 and logic 0, respectively. The inverter is constructed from an nMOS and a pMOS transistor connected in series between power and ground. It operates as follows (see Figure B.15). When A is a logic 1, the nMOS transistor is conducting and the pMOS transistor is not. The only unbroken connection path is from ground to the output node. Thus, a logic 1 at the input yields a logic 0 at the output.

Now let's look at the case in which A is a logic 0. Now the pMOS transistor conducts while the nMOS transistor does not. The output node is connected to a logic 1. A 0 at the input yielded a 1 at the output. The series transistors implement an inverter.

The transistor-level implementations of the NAND and NOR gate work similarly. Let's start with the NAND logic gate, constructed from two nMOS transistors in series between the output node and ground and two pMOS transistors in parallel between the output node and the power supply. A path between the output node and ground can be established only when both of the nMOS transistors are conducting.

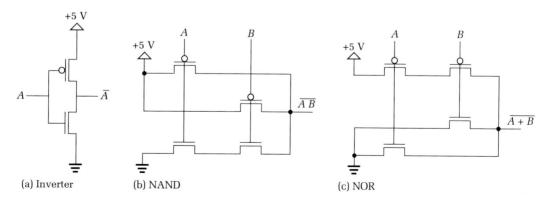

(a) Inverter   (b) NAND   (c) NOR

Figure B.14 Gates implemented from MOS transistors.

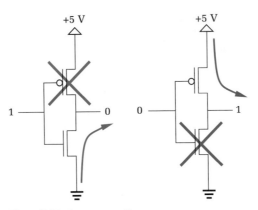

Figure B.15 Inverter operation.

This happens only if A and B are both at a logic 1. In this case, the two pMOS transistors are not conducting, breaking all paths between the output node and the logic 1 at the power supply. This is the case $A = B = 1$, output $= 0$,

Now what happens if one or both of A and B are at a logic 0? Let's take the case $A = 0$ and $B = 1$ (see Figure B.16). The nMOS transistor controlled by A is not conducting, breaking the path from the output to ground. The pMOS transistor it controls is conducting, establishing the path from the power supply to the output. The other path, controlled by B, is broken, but this has no effect on the output node as long as some path exists between it and some voltage source.

The case $A = 1$ and $B = 0$ is symmetric. If both inputs are 0, there are now two paths between the power supply's logic 1 and the output node. Of course, this doesn't change the logic signal at the output: it is still a logic 1. From this discussion it should be obvious that the circuit configuration performs the function of a NAND gate.

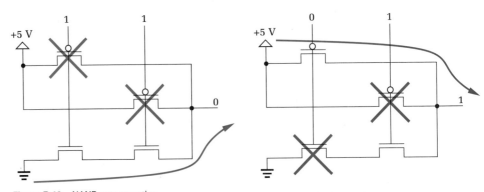

Figure B.16 NAND gate operation.

The *pull-down network* switches between the output and the ground signal. We define the *pull-up network* similarly between the output and the power supply. The pull-down network is $A \bullet B$, since the transistors are two nMOS transistors in series. The pull-up network consists of two pMOS devices in parallel. This logic function is $\overline{A} + \overline{B}$. Another way to say this is that the function is 0 when $A \bullet B$ is true and is 1 when $\overline{A} + \overline{B}$ is true. Of course, by DeMorgan's theorem, $\overline{A} + \overline{B}$ is the same function as $\overline{A \bullet B}$.

We can apply the same kind of analysis to the NOR gate implemented as transistors. Using the observation we just made, the pull-up network is $\overline{A} \bullet \overline{B}$, the pull-down network is $A + B$, and the function is 0 when $A + B$ is true and is 1 when $\overline{A} \bullet \overline{B}$ $(\overline{A + B})$ is true. Analyzing the transistor network directly (see Figure B.17), the output node can be 1 only if both transistors between it and the power supply are conducting. Thus the output is 1 if both inputs are 0. If either or both inputs are 1, then the path to the power supply is broken while at least one path from the output to ground is established. The network does indeed implement the NOR function.

B.4.3 CMOS Transmission Gate

Any gate logic function can be implemented as a pull-up network of pMOS transistors and a pull-down network of nMOS transistors. In fact, this is the standard way to construct digital logic from CMOS transistors. Yet there is an even richer set of things you can do with switching networks. The key to constructing these networks is a special circuit structure called the transmission gate. We examine it next.

For electrical reasons that are beyond the scope of this discussion, it turns out that pMOS transistors are great at transmitting a logic 1 voltage without signal loss, but the same cannot be said about logic 0 voltages. Having 0 V at one side of a conducting pMOS transistor yields a voltage at the other side somewhat higher than 0 V. NMOS transistors have a

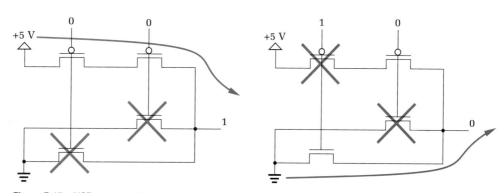

Figure B.17 NOR gate operation.

complementary problem: they are great at passing logic 0 but awful at passing logic 1. In the circuits we have looked at so far, pMOS transistors in the pull-up network passed only ones while the nMOS transistors in the pull-down network passed only zeros. So everything works out fine.

As you may guess, the best possible transmission behavior can be obtained by combining both kinds of transistors. This yields the *CMOS transmission gate*, which is shown in Figure B.18. The pMOS and nMOS transistors are connected in parallel and are controlled by complementary control signals in the figure. When signal A is asserted, the transmission gate conducts a logic 0 or 1 equally well. Signal A at a logic 1 makes the nMOS transistor conduct, while $\overline{A}$ at a logic 0 makes the parallel pMOS transistor conduct as well. When A is unasserted, the gate no longer conducts. A at logic 0 breaks the connection through the nMOS transistor, while $\overline{A}$ at 1 has the same effect on the pMOS transistor. In circuit diagrams, the transmission gate is often denoted by a "butterfly" or "bow tie" symbol, as shown in the figure.

Section 4.2 covers how to use CMOS transmission gates to implement digital subsystems with many fewer transistors than would be the case if traditional gates were used.

Appendix Review

In this appendix, we have examined the basic electrical building blocks of digital logic: resistors, capacitors, diodes, and transistors.

We began with the basic concepts of electricity: voltage, current, resistance, and capacitance. Voltage is electrical force, current is the intensity of the flow of electrical charge, resistance restricts current flow, and capacitance represents an ability to store electrical charge. Ohm's law $(V = IR)$ and the charge-capacitance-voltage equation $(Q = CV)$ describe the relationships among these electrical quantities.

Next we examined how to build useful logic functions from the primitive electrical components at our disposal: resistors, diodes, and transistors. We started with primitive diode-resistor logic. This has the

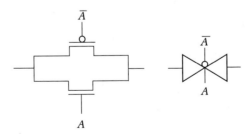

Figure B.18   CMOS transmission gate.

serious drawbacks that it is not easy to cascade and an inverter cannot be built in the logic. The introduction of the transistor changed all this, and the resulting diode-transistor logic was a popular implementation technology in the 1950s and 1960s. More recently, it has been replaced by the more efficient transistor-transistor logic.

We also covered an important class of transistor structures, the *field effect MOS (metal-oxide-silicon) transistors*. Logic gates constructed from such transistors are much simpler to analyze than bipolar transistors. MOS switching structures are covered in more detail in Chapter 4.

Other forms of high-speed bipolar logic gates, such as current mode logic (CML) and emitter-coupled logic (ECL), are beyond the scope of our presentation here. See the reference to Wakerly's book in the next section if you are interested in learning more about these.

Some of the more detailed aspects of TTL logic are described in Sections 2.5.2, 3.5.1, and 3.5.2. Section 2.5.2 discusses the packaging of TTL gates into convenient building blocks called *integrated circuits*. Sections 3.5.1 and 3.5.2 cover the detailed technical specification of the electrical performance of TTL logic gates, as well as methods for correctly computing the gate fan-outs and power consumption.

Further Reading

Our review of the electronics is necessarily brief. A number of good books cover material similar to the topics of this appendix but in more detail. For example, T. M. Frederiksen's *Intuitive Digital Computer Basics*, McGraw-Hill, New York, 1988, is a book-length tutorial on basic electronics. G. G. Langdon's book *Computer Design*, Computeach Press, San Jose, CA, 1982, concentrates on computer design rather than digital logic design, but it contains an excellent appendix on the underlying technology. See Appendix B, "Electronic Devices and Useful Interface Circuits." Finally, J. F. Wakerly's textbook *Digital Design Principles and Practices*, Prentice Hall, Englewood Cliffs, NJ, 1990, dedicates a whole chapter to the details of electrical devices. See Chapter 2, "Digital Circuits."

Index